AS Level

PSYCHOLOGY

AS Level PSYCHOLOGY

FOURTH EDITION

Michael W. Eysenck

Psychology Press
Taylor & Francis Group

HOVE AND NEW YORK

Published 2008 by Psychology Press Ltd
27 Church Road, Hove, East Sussex, BN3 2FA

www.psypress.com
www.a-levelpsychology.co.uk

Simultaneously published in the USA and Canada
by Psychology Press Inc
270 Madison Avenue, New York, NY 10016

*Psychology Press is an imprint of the Taylor & Francis Group,
an informa business*

© 2008 by Psychology Press Ltd
Reprinted 2009

British Library Cataloguing in Publication Data
A catalogue record for this book is available from the British Library

ISBN 978–1–84169–711–6

Cover design by Richard Massing
Typeset in India by Newgen Imaging Systems (P) Ltd
Printed and bound in China by 1010 Printing International Ltd.

To Maria, with love

CONTENTS

ABOUT THE AUTHOR

Michael W. Eysenck is one of the best-known psychologists in Europe. He is Professor of Psychology in the psychology department at Royal Holloway University of London, where he was Head of Department between 1987 and 2005. He is especially interested in cognitive psychology (about which he has written several books) and most of his research focuses on the role of cognitive factors in anxiety within normal and clinical populations.

He has published 36 books. His previous textbooks published by Psychology Press include *Psychology for AS Level (3rd ed.)* (2005), *Psychology for A2 Level* (2001), *A2 Psychology: Key Topics (2nd ed.)* (2006), *Psychology: An International Perspective* (2004), *Psychology: A Student's Handbook (5th ed.)* (with Mark Keane) (2005), *Simply Psychology (3rd ed.)* (2007), *Fundamentals of Cognition* (2006), *Psychology: A Student's Handbook* (2000), *Perspectives on Psychology* (1994), and *Individual Differences: Normal and Abnormal* (1994). He has also written two research books for Psychology Press based on his research on anxiety: *Anxiety: The Cognitive Perspective* (1992) and *Anxiety and Cognition: A Unified Theory* (1997), as well as the popular title *Happiness: Facts and Myths* (1990). He is also a keen supporter of Crystal Palace football club and lives in hope that one day they will return to the Premiership.

The study skills you need to be successful in the AS exam are based on psychological principles involving learning and memory. So psychology students should already be well placed to gain maximum advantage in the exam room! This chapter is divided into two sections that address your own study skills and the ways in which the exam will be assessed and marked.

SECTION 1
How can I study effectively? p. 3
How to develop your study skills, including increasing your motivation and improving reading skills using the SQ3R approach. Managing your time to get the best results from your work.

SECTION 2
How can I do well in the exam? p. 7
Discover your own personal learning style, and how your performance in the exam will benefit from this knowledge. What the examiners will be looking for, and how they award marks.

NOTE: At the start of each chapter there is a list of specification content. Check this list to see what you could be examined on.

PREPARING FOR THE AS EXAM
By Roz Brody (Senior tutor, Brighton, Hove, and Sussex Sixth Form College)

Studying psychology is both enjoyable and useful. Students of psychology not only gain knowledge that helps them understand themselves and others, they can also apply this knowledge to everyday life. So psychology can enable you to improve your memory, give you strategies for effective studying, and help you manage your stress and do well in your exams.

This chapter is designed to take some of the stress out of the exam by giving you hints on how to study, and letting you know what the exam involves and what the examiners look for. You will probably return to this chapter as you work through the rest of the book.

SECTION 1
HOW CAN I STUDY EFFECTIVELY?

Students of psychology should find it easy to develop good study skills because they are based on psychological principles. For example, study skills are designed to promote effective learning and remembering, and learning and memory are key areas within psychology. Study skills are also concerned with motivation and developing good work habits, and these also fall very much within psychology, although they are not part of your AS-level course. Most of what is involved in study skills is fairly obvious, so we will focus on detailed pieces of advice rather than on vague generalities (e.g. "work hard", "get focused").

Motivation

Most people find it hard to maintain a high level of motivation over long periods of time. We all know what happens. You start out with high ideals and work hard for the first few weeks. Then you have a bad week and/or lose your drive, and everything slips. What can you do to make yourself as motivated as possible? One psychological theory of motivation (Locke, 1968) suggested the following seven ways to set appropriate goals and maintain motivation:

1. You must set yourself a goal that is hard but achievable.
2. Once you have your goal, you need to commit yourself to it. Telling others about it can keep you motivated.
3. You should focus on goals that can be achieved within a reasonable period of time (e.g. no more than a few weeks). Long-term goals like "I will get a grade A in my psychology exam" need to be broken down into a series of short-term goals (e.g. I'll read and summarise the key points of Chapter 3 by Friday", "I'll do two timed answers on this chapter in the next week").

Set a realistic goal.

Commit to achieving the goal.   Enjoy your achievement!

4. Set clear goals, and avoid vague goals.
5. Obtain feedback on your progress.
6. Once you have achieved your goal, move on to slightly harder goals.
7. Be honest about any setbacks and try to work out what went wrong, rather than simply saying it was bad luck. We can and do learn from our mistakes.

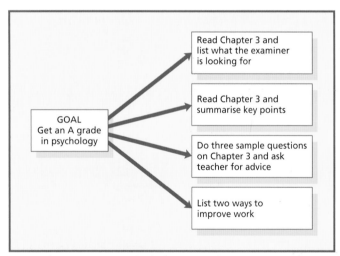

A major goal broken down into smaller goals.

Your attempts to motivate yourself are only likely to be successful if you make use of all seven points. If you set yourself a very clear, medium-term goal, and obtain feedback, but the goal is impossible to achieve, then you are more likely to *reduce* rather than *increase* your level of motivation.

Reading Skills

If you have ever turned over a few pages in a book and had no idea what you have just read, then this next section is for you. Studying psychology involves effective reading and being able to remember and use the information you have read. Morris (1979) described the **SQ3R** approach—Survey, Question, Read, Recite, Review, representing the five stages in effective reading—which has proved to be very useful. We will consider these five stages with respect to the task of reading a chapter.

Survey
The Survey stage involves getting an overall view of the way in which the information in the chapter is organised. If there is a chapter summary, this will probably be the easiest way to achieve that goal. Otherwise, you could look through the chapter to find out what topics are discussed and how they are linked to each other.

Question
The question stage should be applied to fairly short parts of the chapter of no more than six pages. The essence of this stage is to get you to think about the

KEY TERM

SQ3R: five strategies for effective reading: Survey, Question, Read, Recite, Review.

questions you want answered by reading the text, such as "What does the S and Q in SQ3R stand for?"

Read

While the read stage obviously involves reading the text to answer your questions, it is also very important to integrate any new information with your pre-existing knowledge of the topic.

You might also want to use a highlighter pen to emphasise key points.

Recite

The recite stage involves trying to remember all the key ideas that were contained in the part of the chapter you have been reading. Try explaining what you have just read to someone else. If you cannot remember some of the ideas, go back to the Read stage.

Review

When you have read the entire chapter, you should review the key ideas from the text and be able to combine the information from different parts of the chapter into a coherent structure. Producing a mind map of the key ideas can often help. If your mind seems a total blank you need to go back to the earlier stages in the reading process.

Time Management

Studying effectively involves managing your time well. Often you may have good intentions at the start of the week, but as the time flies by you realise that the two or three essential pieces of work you were going to do haven't been tackled. And yet, when you know you will be extremely busy you often manage your time more effectively because you know that if you don't do the work now, there will be no time at the end of the week.

So what do you do with the 100 hours or more at your disposal each week? You probably only have some vague idea where most of the time goes. As time is such a valuable commodity, it is a good idea to make the most efficient use of it, as you will probably be surprised at how much time you tend to waste. Here are some suggestions on how to manage your time:

- Create a timetable of the times that are available and unavailable over a week. Now indicate which subjects you can study on different days, and how much time within each day you are going to spend on any subject.
- Decide what is, for you, a reasonable span of attention (possibly 30–40 minutes). Set aside a number of periods of time during the week for study. Make a commitment to yourself to use these periods for study.
- Note that the more of a habit studying becomes, the less effortful it will be, and the less resistant you will be to making a start.

 Have you got any questions? Always question everything you read by saying, for example, "Does this explain my own knowledge of the world?" or "Do I understand all the words?"

> **EXAM HINT**
>
> In order to succeed in exams, you must be able to recall the information you need. The Recite and Review stages of the SQ3R approach are designed to achieve precisely that.

One motivational strategy is to reward yourself at regular intervals. For example, after you have read 10 pages or worked for an hour, have a cup of tea, go for a brief walk, or phone or text a friend. Make sure your rewards are for easily achievable goals—but not too easy!

? Why do many people fail to achieve work targets, despite the fact that they really should know better?

KEY TERM

Planning fallacy: the false belief that a plan will succeed even though past experience suggests it won't.

- No one has limitless concentration. After initially high levels of concentration, the level decreases until the end is in sight. So make sure that the time you commit to studying is realistic. You can probably improve your level of concentration by including short (10-minute) rest periods. Remember to avoid distractions like the television in your study area (don't kid yourself that you can watch TV *and* study—reward yourself later with an hour slumped in front of the TV).
- During these study times, there will be a tendency to find other things to do (e.g. phoning a friend). This is where the hard part begins. You must try to be firm and say to yourself that this is time you have committed to studying, and that is what you are going to do. However, you will have time available later for other things. It is hard to do to start with, but it gets easier.

Planning fallacy

Although you might have never heard of the **planning fallacy**, there is a good chance that you may have experienced it. Kahneman and Tversky (1979) defined the planning fallacy as "a tendency to hold a confident belief that one's own project will proceed as planned, even while knowing that the vast majority of similar projects have run late". In other words, we all kid ourselves that it will be easy despite knowing that, on previous occasions, we and other people have not managed to fulfil our planned intentions.

As we are psychologists, we might be interested to know if there is evidence to support this planning fallacy, and indeed there is. Buehler, Griffin, and Ross (1994) found that, on average, students submitted a major piece of work 22 days later than they had predicted, even when they were specifically told that the purpose of the study was to examine the accuracy of people's predictions. Buehler et al. found that students were much better at predicting completion times for other students than for themselves. The reason for this is that they were more likely to use what is called "distributional" information (which comes from knowledge about similar tasks completed in the past) when making predictions about other students, whereas with themselves they tended to use "singular" information (related to the current task).

The testing effect

When students are revising for an exam, they often skim through their notes, discovering to their delight (or even surprise) that most of the material seems familiar. What this means is that they have reasonable recognition memory for the material. However, there is a large difference between *recognising* information as familiar and being able to produce it at will during an anxiety-inducing exam. To succeed in written exams, you must *recall* the information you need. As generations of students have discovered to their cost, good recognition memory for the information relevant to an exam is no guarantee at all that recall will be equally good.

This leads us neatly into the *testing effect*. This is the finding that long-term retention for information is better when memory for that information is tested during the time of learning than when it is not. Roediger and Karpicke (2006) reported convincing evidence that the testing effect is strong. Students read a prose passage covering a general scientific topic and tried to memorise it in one of three conditions:

1. Repeated study: the passage was read four times and there was no test.
2. Single test: the passage was read three times and then students recalled as much as possible from it.
3. Repeated test: the passage was read once and then students recalled as much as possible on three occasions.

Finally, memory for the passage was tested again after 5 minutes or 1 week.

The findings are shown in the figure on the right. Repeated study was the most effective strategy when the final test was given 5 minutes after learning, and the repeated test was the least effective. However, there was a dramatic reversal of the conditions when the final test occurred 1 week after learning (this is the testing effect). The size of the testing effect is striking—average recall was 50% higher in the repeated test condition than in the repeated study condition! This happened even though students in the repeated study condition predicted they would recall more of the prose passage after 1 week than did those in the repeated test condition.

How can we explain the testing effect? Bjork and Bjork (1992) argued that an excellent way to improve long-term memory is via effortful retrieval, as happened in the repeated test condition. The take-home message is that if you make the effort to recall information several times as you study it, this will make the information in question much more memorable in the long term.

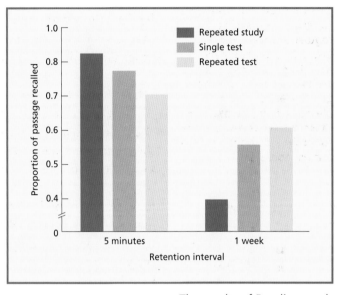

The results of Roediger and Karpicke's (2006) study on the testing effect.

SECTION 2
HOW CAN I DO WELL IN THE EXAM?

Very few students like exams, but there are a lot of strategies that you can use to make them less stressful, so that on the day of the exams you will be very keen to let the examiner know what you have learned about psychology.

Four key factors will help you do well in an exam:

1. Knowing how you learn.
2. Knowing what you will be examined on *(how the specification is divided into units)*.
3. Knowing how you will be assessed and what form the questions will take.
4. Knowing how to prepare for the exam and what to do in the examination room.

If you know what to expect in an exam it removes the element of surprise and allows you to be prepared. This preparation will involve:

- organising your information;
- learning the information;
- understanding how the information can be used to answer questions in the exam.

But studying psychology also helps. Chapter 6 looks at stress management, so reading that before the exam will give you some ideas about how to lessen stress.

Coping with stress in exams

In chapter 6 you will be studying stress and how to manage it. Here is some advice from that chapter:

- THINK POSITIVELY: This will increase your sense of control: "I can only do my best."
- AVOID DEFENCE MECHANISMS SUCH AS DENIAL: Recognise the feeling of stress and intellectualise your problem.
- RELAX: At intervals during the exam have a break and think positive thoughts unrelated to the exam.
- SOCIAL SUPPORT: Think about comforting people or things.
- PHYSICAL EXERCISE AND EMOTIONAL DISCHARGE: Go for a run before the exam, stretch your legs, find some means of discharging tension during the exam (that doesn't disturb anyone else).

Knowing How You Learn

Think about the strategies that work for you. Some students like summarising their notes onto cards. Others devise posters or put "post-its" around their room. Others find it much easier to learn information by discussing their ideas with a friend.

Try the quiz below to help you think about how you learn.

Look at the following questions and answer yes or no	YES	NO
1. I often see my notes in my head when I sit an exam.		
2. I can never seem to start my work.		
3. When I explain my ideas to someone else, they often become clearer to me.		
4. I find it easy to remember conversations word for word.		
5. If a friend phones me I'll stop working and chat for hours.		
6. I often say what I am writing down to myself.		
7. I find it easier to remember my notes when I highlight key points.		
8. I can remember my notes by repeating them over and over again to myself.		
9. I often look at my book, but nothing ever goes in.		
10. I like it when people ask me questions about psychology and I can explain things to them.		

11. I like using different coloured pens when making revision notes.		
12. I find it hard to work on my own.		
13. I can always find something else to do when I am meant to be studying.		
14. I can remember where things are on a page.		
15. I enjoy talking about psychology to my friends.		
16. I often hear my teacher's voice when I read through my notes.		

- If you answered yes to questions 1, 7, 11, and 14, you enjoy learning using a visual approach. Making posters, using "post-its" and coloured pens and highlighters will help you for the exam.
- If you answered yes to questions 2, 5, 9, and 13, you are easily distracted and find it hard to start work. You need to remove all distractions (e.g. mobile phone) and realise that it might take you 5–10 minutes to settle into doing the work. Focus on the task you have set yourself for a certain amount of time (e.g. 30 minutes) and then take a break.
- If you answered yes to 3, 10, 12, and 15, you enjoy learning in a social way. Working with a friend as you revise and discussing ideas will help you for the exam.
- If you answered yes to questions 4, 6, 8, and 16, you enjoy learning information using sound. Some students make tape recordings of the key points they need to remember, and then listen to them before they go to sleep.
- If you answered yes to a range of questions, you don't have a preferred method of learning information and may use a range of strategies to help you.

Throughout the book the red boxes, like this one, give cross-references to *Revise AS Level Psychology* by Roz Brody and Diana Dwyer (the revision guide).

See Chapter 1 of the revision guide for a summary of revision techniques.

Knowing What You Will be Examined on

The AS psychology exam is divided into *two* units but it is essential to know which topics are assessed in each unit.

- UNIT 1: Explores cognitive psychology, developmental psychology, and research methods.
- UNIT 2: Explores biological psychology, social psychology, and individual differences.

Each exam paper lasts 1 hour 30 minutes and consists of three compulsory/structured questions, *one* on each of the three areas studied from each unit.

These questions may include short answer questions, questions about stimulus material, and one or more 12-mark questions requiring a more extended answer. (Paper one will contain one 12-mark question, paper 2 will contain one or more.)

Each topic in the unit is broken down into subsections, shown overleaf. Make sure you are clear about what topics are covered in each section.

EXAM HINT

Read the specification—this will help you reduce the amount you need to revise!

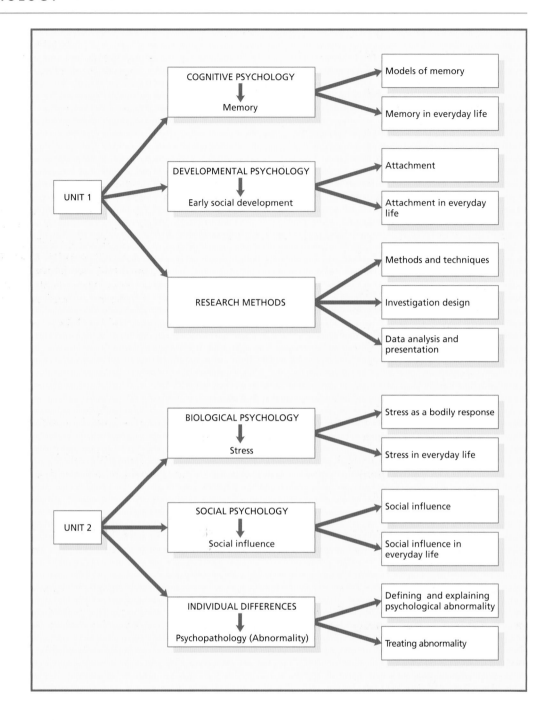

Knowing How You Will be Assessed

There are two exams in AS Psychology and each lasts for 1 hour and 30 minutes. Each exam is worth 50% of the AS result (but 25% of the overall A level).

There are three main assessment objectives in the exams. These are:

- **AO1 Knowledge and understanding of science and how science works**
  Where the examiners will be looking to see whether students can:
  a) recognise, recall, and show understanding of scientific knowledge;

b) select, organise, and communicate relevant information in a variety of forms.

- **AO2 Application of knowledge and understanding of science and how science works**
  Where candidates should be able to:
  a) analyse and evaluate scientific knowledge and processes;
  b) apply scientific knowledge and processes to unfamiliar situations including those related to issues;
  c) assess the validity, reliability, and credibility of scientific information.

- **AO3 How science works—psychology**
  Where candidates should be able to:
  a) describe ethical, safe, and skilful practical techniques and processes, selecting appropriate qualitative and quantitative methods;
  b) know how to make, record, and communicate reliable and valid observations and measurement with appropriate precision and accuracy, through using primary and secondary sources;
  c) analyse, interpret, explain and evaluate the methodology, results, and impact of their own and others' experimental and investigative activities in a variety of ways.

> ■ **Activity:** To see if you have got the idea of the differences, see if you can identify whether the following questions are measuring AO1, AO2, or AO3 skills.
>
> (a) Outline research into the effects of privation.
> (b) Outline and evaluate two or more attempts to define abnormality.
> (c) To what extent does psychological research support the view that eyewitness testimony will always be unreliable?
> (d) How could researchers have obtained less biased samples in Type A behaviour research?
> (e) Describe the key features of one psychological approach to abnormality.
> (f) Discuss ethical issues raised by conformity/obedience research.
> (g) Explain why cross-cultural studies on attachment have been criticised as lacking in validity.
>
> See overleaf for the answers.

You might want to return to this page as you read through the book so you get a better understanding of what the examiner is looking for as you progress through the course.

Because the assessment objectives are different, the questions designed to see whether you have achieved these objectives are also different. Thus, AO1 focuses on *knowledge and understanding*, AO2 focuses on *application* of that knowledge and understanding, and AO3 focuses on *psychological research and methodology*.

Typical AO1 questions might include:

- *Outline two behaviours that are characteristic of a securely attached infant.*
- *Using your knowledge of the factors affecting obedience, explain one reason why you obey.*
- *Using the multi-store model of memory, outline how information is transferred from short-term memory to long-term memory.*

Typical AO2 questions might include:

- *Kate is revising for her driving test. She needs to remember a variety of information such as rules relating to speed limits and stopping distances.*

> **EXAM HINT**
>
> Avoid "common-sense" answers: you must convince the examiner that your answer is drawn from what you have learned, not from everyday knowledge.

EXAM HINT

If there is a question asking for a comparison (e.g. give two differences between . . .) make sure you draw the comparison, rather than describing each separately and expecting the examiner to identify the comparison, as this would receive no marks! So make sure you've used WHEREAS or IN COMPARISON.

Outline two strategies Kate might use to improve her recall and explain why each of the strategies you suggest should improve recall.

- *James is afraid of flying. Just thinking of flying causes him distress and even going to the airport is a problem. In order to overcome this fear he consults a behavioural psychologist who feels that he may benefit from systematic desensitisation.*

Describe how this therapy might be carried out to overcome James's fear of flying.

Typical AO3 questions might include:

- *A psychologist wishes to investigate early child development. She decides to interview some mothers and ask them questions about their infant's social behaviour.*
  a) *Explain one disadvantage of using an interview to collect data.*
  b) *Write one question the psychologist could ask about social behaviour that would generate* ***quantitative*** *data.*
  c) *Write one question that the psychologist could ask that would generate* ***qualitative*** *data.*

How the Exams are Marked

Examiners are given mark schemes to enable them to work out how many marks to award to an answer. Some mark schemes are based on skill cluster AO1 and others are based on skill cluster AO2 and AO3, as can be seen below.

However, the good news for people taking the new specification is that the questions are mainly short-answer types, and that the skills required, AO1 or AO2 or AO3, are implicit in these short questions. For example, if the question asks you to *explain an advantage of doing research using interviews* your answer won't be a description—you will write that your chosen point is an advantage *because* . . . and that will automatically make it an AO3 point. If the question had asked you to *describe an advantage of doing research using interviews* then a plain description would gain the AO1 marks.

This shows how vital it is to read the questions very carefully, and perhaps even to underline or highlight the examiner's commands—"describe", "explain", "comment on", and so on.

The one question that is different is the 12-mark question, where there will be 6 marks for AO1 and 6 marks for AO2. The commands here could be things like *describe and evaluate*, or *outline and comment on* some topic or theory. You will need to think carefully about exactly what you are describing or outlining (AO1) and then how you are going to evaluate or comment on this (AO2). You may well find that for the latter the "description" words and phrases that link comments together to form a flowing whole are really useful. These words and phrases include "whereas", "however", "this is because", "on the other hand", "this supports", "this challenges".

■ Activity answers

(a) AO1
(b) AO1/AO2
(c) AO1/AO2
(d) AO3
(e) AO1
(f) AO3
(g) AO3

Mark scheme for AS-level examination

Assessment objective 1 (AO1)

These marks are for clear and accurate and relevant descriptions.

6 marks	The description is *accurate* and *detailed* and shows both a very good knowledge *and* understanding of the carefully selected material, presented in a clear and coherent way.
5–4 marks	The description is *limited*. It is generally *accurate* but *less detailed*, showing knowledge and understanding and some appropriate selection of material.
3–2 marks	The description is *basic*, *lacking detail*, and may be *muddled* and/or *flawed* though showing some relevant knowledge. There is little evidence of selection of material to fit the question, and the information is not presented in an appropriate form.
1 mark	Very brief or faulty description that shows very little knowledge or understanding of the research. Selection and presentation of information is mainly or completely inappropriate.
0 marks	The description is *inappropriate* or the description is *incorrect*.

Where an answer is marked out of a different total, then the marks are changed accordingly.

Assessment objective 2 (AO2)

These marks are for clear, accurate, and relevant discussions.

6 marks	There is an *informed commentary* and *reasonably thorough analysis* of the relevant psychological research. Material has been used in an *effective* manner, within the time constraints of answering this part of the question, and the commentary is informed with an effective evaluation of research. Either a broad range of evidence and/or issues in reasonable detail or a narrow range in greater depth is present. Expression of ideas is clear, using a good range of specialist terms with few grammatical, punctuation, or spelling errors.
5–4 marks	There is a *reasonable commentary* and *slightly limited analysis* of the relevant psychological studies/methods, with either a range of issues/evidence in limited depth or a narrow choice in greater depth. Expression of ideas is reasonable, using a range of specialist terms with some grammatical, punctuation, and spelling errors.
3–2 marks	There is a *basic commentary* and *limited analysis* of the relevant psychological studies/methods. Material has been used in a superficial manner with a restricted range of issues/evidence. Expression of ideas is unclear/muddled, with a restricted range of specialist terms used. The grammatical, punctuation, and spelling errors contribute to the lack of clarity.
1 mark	There is *rudimentary commentary* and evaluation. Evaluation of research is minimal or absent. Expression is poor, few specialist terms are used, and there are major grammatical, punctuation, and spelling errors that often hide the meaning.

Where the question is out of a different total the mark scheme would be adjusted to match.

Assessment objective 3 (AO3)

4 marks	Comments and evaluations show sound analysis and understanding; ideas are well structured and expressed showing coherent elaboration, with effective use of psychological terminology.
3 marks	Comments and evaluations show reasonable analysis and understanding with generally appropriate structure and reasonable expression, elaboration, and use of psychological terminology.
2 marks	Comments and evaluations are basic and understanding is superficial. There is some evidence of elaboration but expression of ideas lacks clarity and there is only limited use of psychological terminology.
1 mark	Commentary and evaluation are rudimentary showing very limited understanding, and ideas are muddled, confused, and/or ambiguous, with poor structure.
0 marks	There is no creditworthy material present.

As before, where the question is out of a different total the mark scheme would be adjusted to match.

EXAM HINT

The number of marks for AO1 is variable but you can judge how much to write by writing approximately 1 minute per mark on these short-answer questions. Be careful not to write too much or too little. Your answers may be correct but just lacking in detail. Use research evidence and examples to increase the content.

See Chapter 1 of the revision guide for a summary of the exam format.

Some idea of how examiners use this mark scheme can be shown by looking at the following questions:

Question: Describe **one** *study of duration of short-term memory. (6 marks)*

Candidate's answer: Peterson and Peterson did a study on the capacity of short-term memory. Participants were shown three-letter consonants, such as RTG. Then they were asked to recall them either after 3, 12, 15, or 18 seconds. The longer the interval, the worse their recall was.

Examiner's comment: The candidate has included some information, such as who did the study and what they did, but there is minimal detail. The findings have been treated rather briefly and certain other details were omitted (such as what the participants did while they were waiting to recall the digits). Therefore this answer would be described as "limited", close to "basic", and would get 3 out of 6 marks.

Remember that your answer needs to be *accurate and detailed* to gain full marks.

Question: "People who witness a crime want to be able to provide useful information to the police to help them catch the criminal." Outline and evaluate psychological research into the accuracy of eyewitness testimony. (12 marks)

Candidate's answer: Psychological research has investigated many areas of memory that are relevant to eyewitness testimony.

The first area I will consider is Loftus's research on the way the language used in questioning the eyewitness will affect recall. In her experiment it was found that, if people were asked "About how fast were the cars going when they smashed into each other?", they estimated the cars' speed as being faster than if the word "hit" was used in the question. This shows that the accuracy of their recall is very much influenced by the way they are asked questions, and questions that suggest a particular answer are known as leading questions. The use of specific words, e.g. "smashed" or "hit", can cause a memory to be altered or reconstructed, without the person being aware that this is happening. So they are not deliberately lying when they give a wrong answer as they are relying on their reconstructed memory, which is in fact inaccurate. So Loftus's work suggests we should be cautious in accepting eyewitness testimony as a factually correct account. Bartlett's research on schemas explains how the reconstruction happens. This is because we alter things in our memory to fit in with pre-existing knowledge.

Another line of evidence has looked at the age of the witnesses. Bronfenbrenner showed that younger children's memories were very easily reconstructed. Perhaps this is because they may be yielding to social pressure to agree with adults, as children are often taught that "good" behaviour is to comply with adults. Furthermore the children may be affected by a lack of social support, meaning no-one else agreeing with them and challenging the adults. Research also suggests that it is not that the children are only complying, or agreeing in public with the adults. It seems their memories actually do reconstruct as shown by Bruck et al. There is also the issue of children's lack of worldly experience affecting their testimony and recall. They are too young to realise how difficult it is to be certain about what we see, their interpretations will be immature and possibly mistaken. An example of this is Keast et al.'s study, which suggests that children assume that in a line-up (an identity parade) the culprit will be there, whereas in some cases this isn't so. This can lead to more issues. Adults such as jurors seem to readily accept children's testimony as they are seen as having no reason to lie, and also they seem confident. However, because of the reasons discussed above it is clear that children's testimony is as likely to be as, or more, flawed and inaccurate compared to adults'.

EXAM HINT

Remember: There are no right answers, only answers that are well-informed, well-constructed, well-argued, and in which the material used is well-selected.

This is not to say that adults' memories are always correct. Several research studies, e.g. Brewer et al., have shown that older adults are as likely to have reconstructed memories as children, much more so than younger adults. Older adults also seem very suggestible, which makes their testimony less accurate. This could be explained by the young and the old being concerned to please the questioners and not wanting to cause trouble.

There are other factors which might reduce accuracy of eyewitness memory. Loftus showed that anxiety, especially when there was a physical threat such as a gun or knife at the incident, focused the eyewitness's attention on the weapon and not the culprit, and so their memory of the culprit was poor. They called this weapon focus. On the other hand, these studies were laboratory experiments and so we cannot be sure the findings would be generalisable to everyday behaviour. This criticism is supported by other studies, such as Valentine et al., which found no weapon effect on accuracy of eyewitnesses.

This research on flashbulb memories suggests that eyewitness recall may be less accurate than people like to think it is.

Another kind of evidence is that people often don't remember things until they have their memory jogged. Psychologists have shown that a lot of forgetting can be explained in terms of not having the right cues (Tulving & Psotka, 1971), which act as keys to unlock a particular memory. These cues can be context dependent, and this is why it is good for police to stage reconstructions of a crime scene to help witnesses recall what happened. The similar context or environment will help them recall more details.

Finally we should consider face recognition. It is very hard to recognise an unfamiliar face and one that is still rather than moving.

> *Examiner's comment: The candidate has presented a well-structured answer to the question. It is all relevant and there has been good use of evidence—the candidate has not just presented evidence but has also explained what it demonstrates ("effective use of material"). Some of the points have been backed up by specific references and they continue to demonstrate that the candidate is reasonably well "informed". The AO1 material (description of psychological research) is accurate and detailed but limited (5 out of 6 marks). The AO2 material (commentary on the research) is reasonable but perhaps slightly limited (5 out of 6 marks). This gives a total of 10 marks, which would be equivalent to a Grade A.*

See Chapter 1 of the revision guide for more detail on how you will be assessed and how to evaluate psychological studies.

Strategies You Can Use to Improve Your AO2 Marks

One way to think about how you can improve your marks for AO2 questions is to consider how you can evaluate the research and theories you have studied. Focus on:

- *Application.* Can the research or theories be applied to everyday life? Does the research benefit humanity?
- *Methodology.* How was the research done? Can you comment on the validity, reliability, or credibility of the research or information? What sampling technique was used, and can we generalise from this sample? Did the participants simply do what they thought the researcher wanted them to do? Could the researcher have been biased?
- *Culture/gender.* How universal are the findings? Do the findings have any relevance for non-Western societies and are the findings gender specific?
- *Commentary/constructing a coherent answer.* Use evidence to support your answer. Consider the strengths and weaknesses of the evidence. Explore how psychologists have challenged different theories. Discuss how effective these challenges have been.

EXAM HINT

When in doubt, try writing a sentence that starts "This suggests that . . ." or "Therefore, one can conclude . . .".

See Chapter 1 of the revision guide for guidance on what not to say in the exam!

Don't expect the examiner to read your mind. Unless it is written down, they cannot know what you intended to say. Spell out the points to the examiners. Use phrases like:

- "This research on eyewitness testimony clearly has applications to everyday life where mistaken identity has led to the wrong person being imprisoned . . ."
- "One major problem with this research was that the sample was male and hence it is unclear whether these findings can be generalised to females . . ."
- "It is important to recognise the limitations of this definition in that what may be seen as normal in one culture (e.g. having three wives) might be seen as abnormal in other cultures."

Constructing coherent arguments takes practice. One way to construct your argument is by thinking about your conclusion, and then working backwards. For example if you were given the question:

To what extent does day care affect the social development of the child?

You might want your conclusion to make the following point:

- Day care can have a beneficial effect on social development.

Working backwards your answer would need to include:

- The evidence that might support your view.
- The strengths and weaknesses of this evidence.
- Other factors that need to be taken into consideration such as:
  ○ The type of day care being offered.
  ○ Individual differences.
  ○ The alternative care provided at home.

Some examiners suggest that answers to 12-mark questions can be broken down into two paragraphs. Using the knowledge that you can only get 6 marks for AO1 and that 6 marks are given for AO2, the first paragraph can be predominantly an AO1 response while the second paragraph would be AO2. For example if you were given the question:

To what extent have studies of obedience been shown to lack validity?

- *Paragraph 1* might describe the concerns that psychologists have about internal and external validity in the context of research into obedience, e.g. the highly unusual task and environment means we cannot be sure that people would obey in the same way in everyday life.
- *Paragraph 2* might weigh up the evidence for and against the view that studies on obedience lack internal validity, e.g. social norms affect levels of obedience; for example in the 1950s and 1960s challenging authority was not seen as good behaviour, possibly as a legacy of the USA and UK having been at war in Europe and the East so recently, whereas nowadays civil disobedience is often seen as a valid way to change opinion. This means that levels of obedience are not set in stone, but vary.

EXAM HINT
The list of possible 12-mark questions may seem long but is not infinite. Prepare model answers as you work your way through a topic so you will have a complete set of all questions to revise from. Practising writing perfect answers in timed conditions can be much more effective as revision than just reading or writing notes. You can then compare your answers with the sample answers on the website.

Strategies You Can Use to Improve Your AO3 Marks

Focus on developing AO2 comments, plus consider:

- *Ethics.* Did the research cause physical or psychological harm? Do you consider the research treated the participants with respect? How have psychologists used the information they have gained? For example, "Although it is clear that Milgram's research caused his participants stress, there has been some debate as to whether the means justified the ends . . ."
- *Methodology.* Can you explain or evaluate in more than one way? Can you suggest appropriate qualitative and quantitative methods and explain

Proper preparation for the exam, and an understanding of how to gain marks, will increase your chances of getting a good grade.

when and why each would be good to use? For example, for a question that asks you to explain one research method used by the biological approach to abnormality you could choose twin studies and explain how these are done, what the rationale behind these studies is, and assess the strengths and weaknesses of this method of research, i.e. what they can and cannot tell us.

AO3 marks are research methods marks, which are spread throughout the units. These marks are for demonstrating that you have a real understanding of psychological theory and practice.

You will need to know research methods for all the units, so you can use this knowledge to answer questions like

Outline what this scattergraph of STM scores and age seems to show about STM as we grow older, and explain difficulties in drawing conclusions from this data.

or

Discuss one ethical issue raised by research into conformity.

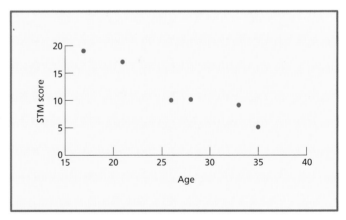

Each of these questions is worth 4 AO3 marks. In the first example there would be 2 marks for outlining what the graph seems to show; the other 2 marks would be for drawing conclusions such as:

Even a strong correlation does not infer causation, i.e. cannot show cause and effect. This means that we can't say that growing older has a direct effect on STM. Also, we would need details about the sampling method and sample size to be able to say if the sample was representative of the population, so that we could generalise the findings to that population. One measurement of STM is unlikely to be a good estimate of STM as a whole.

For the second example there would be 2 marks for identifying one relevant ethical issue and explaining why it is an issue, and the other 2 marks would be for brief discussion of that issue. For example, if you chose the ethical issue of informed consent, explaining that today we believe it is important to respect participants and avoid deceiving them and that is why our guidelines say that informed consent before the research starts is important, then you could go on to say that in Asch's time there were no official ethical guidelines so researchers did what they felt was right. Also, it would be really difficult to test conformity if participants knew that was what you were doing—researchers would not know if they were measuring natural behaviour or not, and most people would find it impossible to act naturally if they knew what was being investigated, so the findings would very likely not be valid.

So now you know what each unit is about and how you will be assessed. The last aspect of doing well in exams is to focus on exam technique.

Knowing How to Prepare for the Exam

Revise the topics you know you will be tested on:

- Make a glossary of key terms or concepts for each topic.
- Make sure you can discuss theories, models, and evidence to support or challenge these theories.
- Make sure you can apply your knowledge to real-life examples.
- Make sure you can evaluate psychological theories and research in terms of:
  - APPLICATION
  - METHODOLOGY
  - ETHICS
  - GENDER AND CULTURAL FACTORS
- Make sure you know how you will be assessed.
- Make sure you know the difference between AO1, AO2, and AO3.
- Make sure you know how many marks are assigned to each question.

Methodology

Whenever you read about research ask yourself the following questions:

- What research method did they use?
- How did they select the sample?
- Was the sample biased in any way?
- Were there any other biases in the study?
- How were the data collected?
- How were the data analysed?
- What did they conclude from the study?
- What other conclusions could they have drawn?
- How ethical was the study?

EXAM HINT

Remember that quantity doesn't equal quality. Stick to the point and organise your answer clearly so that the examiner can follow your argument.

In the Examination Room

- Read all the questions carefully BEFORE YOU START WRITING. Remember you have to answer all questions, so you need to plan your time wisely.
- Underline the key words in the question, so that if you are asked to describe the *weakness* of a certain method you don't describe its *strength*.
- Before you start writing, quickly jot down the key points you want to include in your answer, so you don't forget your points as you start answering the question.
- Keep focused on the question set so that you don't fall into the trap of:
  - writing down everything you know about the topic, whether it is relevant or not;
  - repeating the same point over and over again;
  - drifting away from the question.

- Make sure each paragraph relates back to the question.
- Use the marks by the side of the question to help you plan your time. You should aim to spend approximately just over a minute per mark. If the question is worth 12 marks you need to spend three times as long answering this question as a 4-mark question.
- Be careful about how you express yourself:
  - Avoid making sweeping, inaccurate, ill-informed, or judgemental statements.
  - Avoid expressing personal opinions such as "I really don't like this study." Instead use phrases like "This study has been criticised for causing the participants stress."
  - Always back up your views with evidence.
  - Avoid one-word criticisms like "this study was unethical". Instead expand on your answer by stating why the study was unethical.
- And above all else, DON'T PANIC. Even if the examination questions aren't the ones you wanted, if you have prepared for the exam and understand how you can gain marks, you will be able to write an answer.

Throughout the book we provide hints and tips on exam technique. We also provide references to the revision guide (*Revise AS Level Psychology* by Roz Brody and Diana Dwyer) where the content is summarised to make exam preparation easier. This will help you if you choose to read the revision guide in conjunction with the textbook from the start of the course. Alternatively, you may prefer to read the revision guide when the exams are around the corner. Further exam advice as well as structured guidance on studying the course can be found in our *AS Level Psychology Workbook* by Clare Charles.

> See Chapter 1 of the revision guide for more advice on exam technique before, during, and after the exams.

REVISION QUESTIONS

At the end of each chapter you will find sample exam-style questions. These will give you an idea of the type of question you might be asked in the exam. You could also use them to practise writing answers under timed conditions and can then check your work against the sample answers we provide online. See http://www.a-levelpsychology.co.uk

It is very important to read this chapter of the book because it sets the scene for all that follows. You might be asking some of the following questions:

"What is psychology?"
"Is psychology just common sense?"
"What is research?"
"What do psychologists do?"
"How do psychologists explain behaviour?"

This chapter of the book is divided into two sections to look at these questions.

SECTION 3
Introducing psychology p. 21
A brief look at what psychology is, and how it is more than just common sense. In addition, there is an explanation of what psychological research involves and what is involved in taking a scientific approach to psychological research. We also take a look at what psychologists do, considering the core areas of psychology.

SECTION 4
Psychological explanations p. 27
A look at the psychologists' "toolkit" containing a set of explanations and theoretical approaches (tools) they use to explain behaviour.

The content of this chapter is not included in the exam syllabus so there will be no direct exam questions on it, but we hope it will help foster an interest in psychology and explain the later concepts.

STARTING PSYCHOLOGY

2

Welcome to psychology. Presumably you are reading this book because you have elected to study AS-level psychology, and what a good choice! The AS-level course should give you some fundamental and lasting insights into human behaviour to help you to cope better with your own life and with the people around you. Besides learning about human behaviour, you should also learn how to express yourself coherently, how to challenge information, how to be confident about yourself, and to be a better friend, employee, and member of society! The previous chapter, "Preparing for the AS Exam", has been written to provide guidance on exam strategy and help you gain the maximum marks, but this chapter is designed to introduce you to the general issues that make psychology so fascinating.

SECTION 3
INTRODUCING PSYCHOLOGY

What is Psychology?

Psychology is the science of mind, behaviour, and experience.

The term "science" refers to the objective study of something. Psychologists study *behaviour*—what people (and other animals) *do*. "Behaviour" includes being aggressive or kind, thinking and seeing, breathing and walking, growing up and getting old, being a friend or a parent, and so on. These are all examples of "behaviour".

Psychologists are also interested in "experience". If we want to understand behaviour we also need to consider what the experience is like for the individual doing the behaving. For example, if we want to study aggression, it matters what the person who is behaving aggressively *feels like*.

Psychology is concerned with the study of all human and non-human animals. In this book, however, we will focus on the study of human behaviour.

Is Psychology Just Common Sense?

Many people say "Well, psychology is only common sense!" Everyone is an "armchair psychologist". We all have views about why people behave as they do and, in a sense, these are "theories of psychology". For example, your friend might say "Those football fans act like that because they're hooligans". By saying "They're hooligans" your friend is presumably offering an explanation for the fans' behaviour, such as "They have no care for the feelings of others". But how do we *know* this explanation is correct? That's the starting point for psychological research.

KEY TERM

Research: the process of gaining knowledge and understanding via either theory or empirical data collection.

Common sense can be contradictory: "Look before you leap" vs. "He who hesitates is lost".

Psychologists observe behaviour, put forward an explanation or theory to account for the behaviour, and then conduct a test to see if their theory is correct. Consider the following example:

Several years ago, a young woman was stabbed to death in the middle of a street in a residential section of New York City. Although such murders are not entirely routine, the incident received little public attention until several weeks later when the New York Times disclosed another side to the case: at least 38 witnesses had observed the attack—and none had even attempted to intervene. Although the attacker took more than half an hour to kill Kitty Genovese, not one of the 38 people who watched from the safety of their own apartments came out to assist her. Not one even lifted the telephone to call the police. (From A.M. Rosenthal, 1964, Thirty-eight witnesses. New York: McGraw-Hill.)

? Have you ever been in a situation where someone was in trouble and you did nothing? Can you explain why you did not help?

Two psychologists John Darley and Bibb Latané (1968) read this report. It made them wonder, "Why *do* bystanders in an emergency fail to offer assistance?" The *common-sense* answer, given by the *New York Times*, was that city dwellers were a callous and uncaring lot of people. Darley and Latané thought that perhaps the reason was related to the number of bystanders—in this case there were 38 "silent witnesses". Could it be that each individual witness assumed someone else was taking action to end the emergency situation and therefore they personally didn't need to do anything?

Up to this point you might say that Darley and Latané's thinking was not necessarily more than common sense (although it *was* an unusual explanation). But what they did next is what distinguishes psychology from common sense. They set up an experiment to test their opinions—they arranged for students to discuss personal problems with each other over an intercom. Except that there was only one actual student involved: the other participants were confederates of the experimenter pretending to be participants. During the conversation, one of the "students" appeared to have an epileptic fit. If the real student was under the impression that five people were listening to the conversation it took them three times longer before they offered help than if they thought there were only two people.

We expect bystanders to help in emergency situations, but sometimes they don't. Why is this? Psychological research has tried to find clear answers to this so-called "bystander behaviour".

This study appears to demonstrate that it is the number of people present that affects how likely one is to offer help in an emergency situation. This is psychology—the attempt to explain why people behave in the way they do, and to support these explanations with objective evidence.

Hindsight bias

You still might think "I knew it all along", but this is called **hindsight bias**—the tendency to be wise after the event. Two psychologists, Fischhoff and Beyth, conducted a study to demonstrate hindsight bias in action. Fischhoff and Beyth (1975) asked American students to estimate the probability of various possible outcomes on the eve of President Nixon's trips to China and Russia. After the

KEY TERM

Hindsight bias: the tendency to be wise after the event, using the benefit of hindsight.

trips were over, the students were asked to do the same task, but without taking into account their knowledge of what had actually happened. In spite of these instructions, participants did use the benefit of hindsight and couldn't remember how uncertain things had looked before the trips, thus demonstrating hindsight bias.

Hindsight bias seems to be very strong, and is hard to eliminate. In another study, Fischhoff (1977) told the participants about hindsight bias, and encouraged them to avoid it. However, this had little or no effect on the size of the hindsight bias. Hindsight bias poses a problem for teachers of psychology, because it produces students who are unimpressed by almost everything in psychology!

 Can you think of any ways in which we could try to eliminate hindsight bias?

What is Research?

Darley and Latané's bystander study, described earlier, is an example of one kind of psychological research. It is an **experiment**. Psychologists use other methods of research besides the experiment, and we will look at them in Chapter 5 of this book. Some of the methods are rather less "artificial" and more like real life. For example, in another study of bystander behaviour, that took place in 1969, Piliavin, Rodin, and Piliavin (or Piliavin et al., 1969) arranged for someone to "collapse" on an underground train, in one instance appearing sober but carrying a black cane and in the other appearing to be drunk, and timed how long it took for people on the train to offer help.

If research is like "real life" we say it has greater **external validity**—therefore perhaps it will tell us more about "real" behaviour. The problem is that the more the research is like real life, the less easy it is to control other factors that might influence the particular behaviour we want to study (called the "target behaviour")—in our example the extent of helping behaviour. The case of Kitty Genovese was in fact real life, but just observing what happened did *not* allow us to know for sure why the witnesses didn't respond. We have to narrow down the possibilities to determine if the number of people was the cause. There may be other explanations as well, and to find them out we would need to conduct other research. In each research study, we have to control irrelevant factors to demonstrate the effect of the one we think is important. We will consider external validity again, later in the book.

> When there are more than two authors of a research paper we use "et al.", which means "and others", to refer to all the other researchers.

What Do Psychologists Do?

If you don't quite understand what psychology is, then maybe another way to approach it is to ask, "What do psychologists do?" Some psychologists conduct research into different branches of psychology, such as the core areas of cognitive, developmental, biological, individual differences, and social psychology. Other psychologists apply this research in areas such as health, business, crime, and education, and many work as clinical psychologists helping people with mental disorders.

Cognitive psychology

Cognitive psychologists look at topics such as memory, perception, thought, language, attention, and so on. In other words they are interested in mental processes and seek to explain behaviour in terms of these mental processes.

There are many applications of cognitive psychology, ranging from suggestions about how to improve your memory (useful for examination candidates!) to how

KEY TERMS

Experiment: a procedure undertaken to make a discovery about causal relationships. The experimenter manipulates one variable to see its effect on another variable.
External validity: the validity of an experiment outside the research situation itself; the extent to which the findings of a research study are applicable to other situations, especially "everyday" situations.

to improve performance in situations requiring close attention (such as air traffic control).

Developmental psychology

Developmental psychologists study the changes occurring over a person's lifetime, starting from conception and infancy through adolescence, adulthood, and finally old age. This approach has also been called lifespan psychology. Developmental psychologists focus on how particular behaviours change as individuals grow older, for instance, they look at the changes in the way children think. They also look at how children acquire language; at moral, social, and gender development; and at changes such as coping with retirement or with memory loss.

The experiences we have during childhood have a great impact on our adult lives.

Biological psychology

Biological psychologists are interested in how to explain behaviour in terms of bodily processes. They look at topics such as how the nerves function, how hormones affect behaviour, and how the different areas of the brain are specialised and related to different behaviours.

Biological and psychological explanations

Neurology and biochemistry underlie all behaviour. What happens when a person sees a sunset? The biological explanation would be that light reflected from the landscape forms an image on the retina, which is converted into a neural signal and transmitted to the brain, and so on. No one disputes that this is true, and the process is absolutely essential, but does it give a full and adequate explanation of what is going on? A psychological explanation would probably include the personal and social relevance of the experience, which many would argue are of equal value.

See *AS Level Psychology Online* to download a podcast containing an interview with Michael Eysenck on psychology.

KEY TERM

Abnormal or atypical psychology: the study of individuals who differ from the norm, such as those with mental disorders.

Individual differences

The study of "individual differences" is literally the study of the ways that individuals differ in terms of their *psychological* characteristics, for example, intelligence, aggressiveness, willingness to conform, masculinity and femininity, and just about every behaviour you can think of.

An important individual difference can be found in the degree to which a person is mentally healthy. This is specifically referred to as the study of abnormal behaviour and forms the basis of **abnormal or atypical psychology**, which studies childhood and adult disorders such as dyslexia, autism, schizophrenia, and depression, seeking to find explanations and valid methods of treatment.

Social psychology

Social psychologists are interested in the way people affect each other. They look at, for example, interpersonal relationships, group behaviour, leadership, majority and minority influence, obedience to those in authority, and the influence of the media. Social psychology differs from sociology in placing greater emphasis on the individual as a separate entity; sociologists are interested in the structure and functioning of groups, whereas social psychologists look at how these processes influence the individual members of a social group.

Other branches of psychology

The five core areas just described form the basis of this book, but there are other areas of psychology as well. For example, **comparative psychology** is the study of non-human animals—comparisons are made between animals of different species to find out more about human behaviour. The study of **animal behaviour** is a field of study in its own right and straddles psychology and biology.

Psychology and Science

Studying psychology not only introduces you to what psychologists study and what they do, it also gives you a broader understanding of how science works. It is hoped that by studying psychology you will be able to explore the place and contribution of science in the wider world.

Like many other sciences, psychology developed from philosophy, and questions about human behaviour, morality, and thought are not new. The debate as to whether psychology is a science has also been around for some time and hopefully will get you thinking about what is involved in something being a science.

Does being a science depend on the theoretical underpinning of the research, the questions being asked, or the nature of the hypotheses that are tested? Does it depend on the methodology used and the way in which the information is presented and interpreted? Does it depend on where the research is published or how the research is used? Does it depend on whether you can disprove your ideas?

The following box is designed to get you thinking about what is involved in undertaking research into humans.

Comparative psychologists study non-human animals and make comparisons between them and humans.

Research into humans

Say you read a magazine article that said:

Blondes have more fun than brunettes.

How would you find out if there was any support for the statement? At first sight this might seem a simple area to research. Find some blondes, find some brunettes, and ask them who has more fun. But even a moment's thought about this question clearly raises problems.

Who will be our sample?
Men? Women? Under tens? Over seventies?

Which culture?
Sweden? Egypt?

How will we define blonde/brunette?
Is the hair style more important than the colour?
Will we only use natural blondes and brunettes or should we also look at people who change their hair colour? Would we make sure that everyone has the same hair style?

How will we define fun?
Should the participant or the experimenter define "fun"?

What research method should we use?
If we use a **questionnaire**, participants may realise the purpose of the questions and give biased answers (**demand characteristics**).

KEY TERMS

Interview: a verbal research method in which the participant answers a series of questions.

Experimenter bias: the effect that the experimenter's expectations have on the participants and therefore the results of the study.

Experiment: a procedure undertaken to make a discovery about causal relationships. The experimenter manipulates one variable to see its effect on another variable.

Individual differences: the characteristics that vary from one individual to another.

Quantitative data: data in the form of scores or numbers (e.g. on a scale running from 1 to 7).

Qualitative data: data in the form of categories (e.g. has fun watching movies; has fun watching TV).

If we **interview** the participants, the experimenter may be biased and subconsciously get the answers expected (**experimenter bias**).

How about running an **experiment** and getting someone to change their hair colour, so that in condition A their hair colour is brunette and in condition B their hair colour is blonde. But once again how do we define having fun? One person's idea of fun might differ from someone else's and so we need to take **individual differences** into account.

What data are we trying to collect and how would we present it?
This is an important question. Are we looking to collect **quantitative data** (e.g. mark on a scale how much fun you think you have, with 1 being "very little" and 5 being "a great deal") or are we looking for **qualitative data** where people describe what type of fun they have, and how often?

Having collected the data we need to know what to do with them. Should we describe our findings using averages and graphs, or should we use inferential statistics to analyse the probability of these results occurring by chance?

Who would publish our research?
Having undertaken the research we might need to explore who would publish it. It would need to be reviewed by our peers who might decide that the methodology was flawed or the data were biased.

Have we taken ethical considerations into account?
Did we deceive any of the participants about the nature of our study? Might it encourage inappropriate stereotyping of blondes?

How might wider society use this information?
Has the information gained been used inappropriately? For example, a hair dye company might decide to use these data to boost their sales.

What underlying theories might we use to explain our findings?
Is the link between hair colour and genetics a possible basis for a theory?

Could hair colour influence other people's perception of us and so influence how we act?

Does hair colour have any survival value?

Disproving scientific theories
According to Popper all scientific theories should be able to be falsified. How would you go about falsifying a theory that suggests that the gene for blonde hair is intrinsically linked to having fun?

Hopefully these questions will help you realise that a scientific approach may sometimes lead to more questions rather than answers.

SECTION SUMMARY

What is psychology?

❖ Psychology is the science of behaviour and experience.

❖ It is more than common sense because psychologists conduct and apply research and use research-based evidence to support their theories.

❖ This research aims to achieve a balance between external validity and a good control of irrelevant factors.

What are the core areas of psychology?

❖ The core areas of psychology include:
  – Cognitive psychology: examines mental processes.
  – Developmental psychology: explores the physical and psychological changes that occur in relation to age.
  – Biological psychology: looks at bodily processes.

– Individual differences: looks at how we differ from each other, for example in terms of differing degrees of mental health.
– Social psychology: considers the way in which individuals of the same species affect each other.

❖ The nature of science is complex, and both theory and methodology are essential to broadening our scientific understanding of ourselves and others.
❖ As a science, psychology needs to explore not only which questions to ask but also how information is gained and what use might be made of it within our society.

Psychology and science

SECTION 4
PSYCHOLOGICAL EXPLANATIONS

How Do Psychologists Explain Behaviour?

In discussing the issue of what psychologists do, we have touched on the question of *how* they explain behaviour. For example, biological psychologists clearly explain behaviour in terms of bodily processes, and social psychologists explain behaviour in terms of the interactions between people. The ways that psychologists explain behaviour are explored in later sections of the book.

Some kinds of explanation are more general to all areas of psychology, such as learning theory, social learning theory, psychodynamic theory, cognitive or information-processing theory, and evolutionary theory. We will now consider all these more general kinds of explanation.

> A theory is basically an organised collection of related statements that seem to explain observed phenomena.

Ivan Pavlov (1849–1936), a Russian physiologist.

Learning Theory

One way to explain behaviour is in terms of **learning**. This form of explanation is called **learning theory** and is based on the principles of **conditioning**.

Classical conditioning

The origins of behaviourism lie in Ivan Pavlov's (1849–1936) work as a physiologist. He was conducting research into the digestive system and accidentally discovered a new form of learning by association. This is how it happened. When his experimental dogs were offered food, saliva production increased. But he also noticed something particularly interesting—salivation started to increase as soon as a researcher opened the door to bring them the food. The dogs had learned that "opening door" signalled "food coming soon". It was in their nature to salivate when they smelled food—a reflex response—but the dogs had now *learned* a link between "door" and their reflex response (salivation). What Pavlov had demonstrated is **classical conditioning**, which is learning by association.

> **KEY TERMS**
> **Learning**: a relatively permanent change in behaviour, which is not due to maturation.
> **Learning theory**: the explanation of behaviour using the principles of classical and operant conditioning; the view that all behaviour is learned.
> **Conditioning**: simple forms of learning in which certain responses become more or less likely to occur in a given situation.
> **Classical conditioning**: learning through association; a neutral stimulus becomes associated with a known stimulus–reflex response.

Diagram of the apparatus used by Pavlov for his study of conditioning with dogs (adapted from Yerkes & Morgulis, 1909)

■ **Activity:** Consider the following situations and, for each, try to identify the US, UR, NS, CS, CR:

A puff of air is directed at your eye. Your reflex response is to blink. At the same time as the air is blown, a bell is sounded. In time, the bell produces a blink response.

As you walk into the examination room you are filled with a sense of dread. There is a smell of roses from outside the window. A few weeks later you smell the same perfume of roses and are filled, inexplicably, with a sense of fear.

Just to make the basic idea clear, here is another example of classical conditioning. Imagine you have to go to the dentist. As you lie down on the reclining chair, you may feel frightened. Why are you frightened *before* the dentist has caused you any pain? The sights and sounds of the dentist's surgery lead you to expect or predict that you are shortly going to be in pain. Thus, you have formed an *association* between the neutral stimuli of the surgery and the painful stimuli involved in drilling.

Drilling is an unconditioned stimulus (US) and fear is an unconditioned response (UR). No learning is required for this stimulus–response (S–R) link, which is why both stimulus and response are described as "unconditioned".

The sights and sounds of the dentist's surgery form a neutral stimulus (NS). There is no inborn reflex response to being in the surgery.

If an NS and a US occur together repeatedly they become associated, until eventually the NS also causes the UR. Now the NS is called a conditioned stimulus (CS) and the UR becomes a conditioned response (CR) to this—the CS will produce the CR. A new **S–R link** has been learned, and you start to experience fear before the dentist has set to work on you.

Have you ever noticed how a cat comes running as soon as it hears the cupboard door opening? Classical conditioning can explain this.

KEY TERM

S–R link: an abbreviation for stimulus–response link.

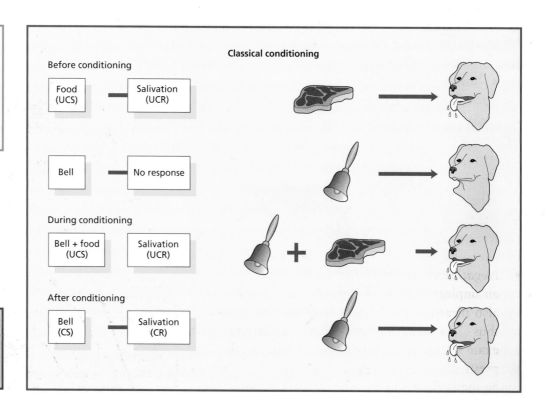

Classical conditioning

Before conditioning

| Food (UCS) | — | Salivation (UCR) |

| Bell | — | No response |

During conditioning

| Bell + food (UCS) | — | Salivation (UCR) |

After conditioning

| Bell (CS) | — | Salivation (CR) |

Operant conditioning

Classical conditioning may be important, but it doesn't explain *all* learning. Another important form of learning was studied by Edward Thorndike (1874–1949). He suggested that learning could take place through *trial and error*, rather than just by association as in classical conditioning. He demonstrated this by placing a hungry cat in a "puzzle box" with a fish hanging nearby. The cat scratched and clawed and miaowed to try to get out of the box, and eventually, by accident, tripped the catch and could jump out. The next time the cat was placed in the box, it went through the same sequence of somewhat random behaviours but took less time

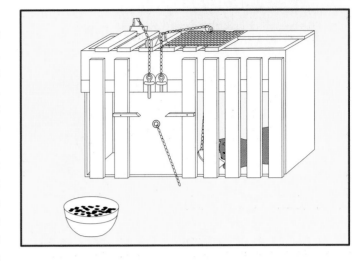

to escape. After a few more trials the cat had learned what to do and, each time it was imprisoned, would release the catch immediately. This led Thorndike to state his "Law of Effect":

- Positive effects (rewards) lead to the *stamping in* of a behaviour.
- Negative effects (punishments) lead to the *stamping out* of a behaviour.

This theory was further developed by B.F. Skinner (1904–1990) into **operant conditioning**, which is learning that is controlled by its consequences (i.e. rewards or punishments). Thorndike's and Skinner's approaches were similar in that they concentrated on the *effects* of behaviour, in contrast with Pavlov's focus on the behaviours themselves.

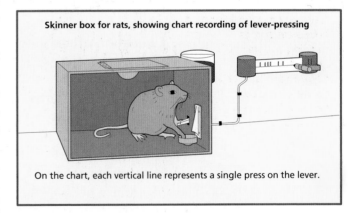

B.F. Skinner, 1904–1990.

The essence of operant conditioning can be seen in Skinner's (1938) experiments with rats. A rat was placed in a cage with a lever sticking out on one side. If the lever was pressed, a pellet of food would be delivered. At first the rat accidentally pressed the lever but soon learned that there was a link between lever pressing and food appearing. Skinner stated that the rat *operated* on the environment. When there was a reward (food) this **reinforced** the likelihood of the behaviour occurring again. When an animal performs a behaviour (or operates on the environment) there are four possible consequences:

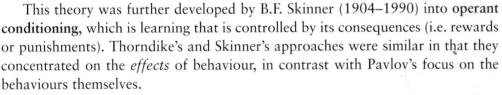

Skinner box for rats, showing chart recording of lever-pressing

On the chart, each vertical line represents a single press on the lever.

- *Positive reinforcement* is pleasurable (e.g. receiving food) and therefore increases the likelihood of a behaviour occurring again.
- *Negative reinforcement* refers to the avoidance of an unpleasant stimulus, but the result is that it is also pleasurable (like positive reinforcement) and thus increases the likelihood of a behaviour. For example, if the floor of the cage was electrified and pressing the lever stopped this, then the rat would be more likely to press the lever.

KEY TERMS

Operant conditioning: learning through reinforcement; a behaviour becomes more likely because the outcome is reinforced. Learning that is contingent on the response.
Reinforced: a behaviour is more likely to re-occur because the response was agreeable.

Note that reinforcement always makes behaviour more likely.

- *Positive punishment* such as receiving an electric shock decreases the likelihood of a behaviour, e.g. if the rat received a shock every time it pressed the lever it would stop doing it.
- *Negative punishment* such as removing a pleasant stimulus decreases the likelihood of a behaviour, e.g. a teenager being grounded for staying out late. The removal of a desirable option (going out) reduces the likelihood of staying out late.

John Watson and behaviourism

John Watson was very impressed with the principles of conditioning and felt they offered psychology a way to become a more objective science. This led him to found behaviourism, based on the principles of learning outlined by Pavlov and Thorndike. The behaviourists argued that a scientific approach to psychology involves focusing on things that can be *observed* and *measured*, especially behaviour. It is easy to measure the amount of salivation produced by a dog, the time taken by a cat escape from a puzzle box, or the number of lever presses of a rat in 5 minutes.

"Well, I simply trained them to give me fish by pressing this over and over again."

The concepts of classical and operant conditioning are important elements in the psychologist's toolkit. It is important that you try to learn the terminology that is used.

We can perhaps see the appeal of behaviourism when we think of what came before it. Up until the end of the 19th century, psychology was still quite close to philosophy and most research relied on **introspection**, studying human behaviour by asking well-trained participants to report what was going on in their mind. Watson argued that this approach was vague and subjective. He and other behaviourists felt there was no need to explain what went on in the mind, or as they called it, the "**black box**"; it was sufficient to talk in terms of a stimulus and a response.

Evaluation of learning theory

The greatest strength of the behaviourist approach was that it was a systematic attempt to turn psychology into a proper science via the careful observation and measurement of behaviour. All psychologists accept that the learning theory put forward by the behaviourists explains *some* aspects of behaviour, and so it is an important part of our toolkit. The evidence of Pavlov, Thorndike, Skinner, and others shows clearly that classical conditioning and operant conditioning both exist. However, no psychologists today claim that we can explain *all* behaviour in terms of learning theory. As you may have noticed, learning theory was originally developed through work with non-human animals such as dogs, cats, and rats. Many experts argue that learning theory is more relevant to the learning shown by these species than it is to human learning. We are more complex than other species, and possess language, and much of our learning seems to go beyond classical and operant conditioning.

There are ethical concerns about behaviourist explanations. A central aim of the behaviourists is the prediction and control of behaviour. Both Watson and Skinner wanted to use their principles of learning to produce a better society. Behaviourist approaches have been used in this way. For example, people in some prisons, schools, and psychiatric institutions are trained to behave in "desirable" ways. Some people regard this as a good thing, but many others feel it may be unethical. The issue of ethics will be considered later in this book.

 How do classical and operant conditioning differ?

Assumptions of the behaviourist approach

- Behaviourists think that behaviour is all that matters: the stimulus and the response.
- It doesn't matter what goes on inside the "black box".
- All behaviour is learned.
- The same laws apply to all animal behaviour, including humans. Attempts have been made to justify this in terms of the **theory of evolution**, which shows that we have evolved from non-human animals. However, we are quite different from other species in having language.

What is "evaluation"?

- At the start of this chapter, you found out that psychology would help you to learn how to challenge information. The skill of "evaluation" is the key to this. To evaluate means to determine the value of something.
- Is it good? Positive criticism considers what is right with a theory. We might consider to what extent a theory has been useful. Or to what extent it has been supported by research studies.
- As an example of positive criticism, there is the point that behaviourism changed psychology by making it more scientific and objective through its emphasis on observable behaviour.
- Another example of positive criticism is the point that there is much research support for both classical and operant conditioning.
- Is it bad? Negative criticism considers what is wrong with a theory. It might not be supported by all studies. It might apply only in some situations. It might lead to undesirable applications.
- As an example of negative criticism, there is the point that the behaviourist approach is more relevant to non-human species than to the human species.
- Another example of negative criticism is that the behaviourist approach raises some ethical issues concerning attempts to control human behaviour.

Social Learning Theory

Albert Bandura was one of the first psychologists to propose an alternative to learning theory that incorporated mental processes. In **social learning theory**, Bandura suggested that behaviour is learned *but* not always through direct conditioning. We often learn by watching what other people do. If they appear to be rewarded for their actions then we are likely to imitate them. This is called **vicarious conditioning**.

A key difference between *social* learning theory and learning theory is the introduction of mental states. In order to imitate someone's behaviour there must be an intervening cognitive state (i.e. we perceive and interpret their behaviour). Whereas behaviourists rejected the concept of mind, saying there was no need for it, social learning theorists introduced a role for cognition (internal mental processes) as well as the influence of social factors.

KEY TERMS

Theory of evolution: an explanation for the diversity of living species. Darwin's theory was based on the principle of natural selection.

Social learning theory: the view that behaviour can be explained in terms of direct and indirect reinforcement, through imitation, identification, and modelling.

Vicarious conditioning: receiving reinforcement by observing someone else being rewarded.

The social learning of aggression

A classic study used to support Bandura's theory deals with the social learning of aggression in children. According to Bandura's theory, **observational learning** or **modelling** is of great importance in producing aggressive behaviour. Observational learning is a form of learning in which the behaviour of others is copied. Bandura, Ross, and Ross (1961) carried out a study in which young children watched as an adult (the model) behaved aggressively towards a Bobo doll, punching the doll and hitting it with a hammer. After 10 minutes the children were moved to another room where there were some toys, including a hammer and a Bobo doll. They were watched through a one-way mirror and rated for their aggression. The children who had watched the model behaving aggressively were more violent and imitated exactly some of the behaviours they had observed, as compared with children who had either seen no model or watched a model behaving in a non-aggressive manner.

Bandura (1965) carried out another study on aggressive behaviour towards the Bobo doll. One group of children simply saw a film of an adult model kicking and punching the Bobo doll. A second group saw the same aggressive behaviour performed, but this time the model was rewarded by another adult for his aggressive behaviour by being given sweets and a drink. A third group saw the same aggressive behaviour, but the model was punished by another adult, who warned him not to be aggressive in future.

Those children who had seen the model rewarded, and those who had seen the model neither rewarded nor punished, behaved much more aggressively towards the Bobo doll than did those who had seen the model punished. The children in all these groups showed comparable levels of memory for the aggressive behaviour they had seen, and thus had the same amount of observational learning. However, those who had seen the model punished were least likely to apply this learning to their own behaviour.

There are reasons for arguing that Bandura exaggerated the meaning of his findings, as it is unlikely that those children would so readily imitate aggressive

? Does this study have external validity? In other words, to what extent can we generalise the findings obtained in this study to real life?

Children watched adults behaving aggressively with a "Bobo" doll. Afterwards they were filmed imitating this behaviour.

behaviour towards another child. Bandura consistently failed to distinguish between real aggression and playfighting, and it is likely that much of the behaviour observed by Bandura was playfighting (Durkin, 1995). Also, as a novelty item, the Bobo doll provided interest to young children. Cumberbatch (1990) reported that children unfamiliar with the doll were *five* times more likely to imitate aggressive behaviour against it than those children who had played with it before. Finally, it could be argued that the whole set-up of the experiment indicated to the children that they should behave aggressively towards the Bobo doll. In other words, the Bobo doll experiment provided cues that "invited" the children to behave in certain predictable ways.

? What are some of the limitations of Bandura's research?

Evaluation of social learning theory

The social learning explanation is found throughout psychology and is an important one. It is a neo-behaviourist account because it still emphasises the role of learning as a way of explaining why people behave as they do, but with the additional involvement of cognitive (mental) and social factors. Children learn many of their behaviours by observing others and modelling their own behaviour on what they have seen. Likely role models include parents, friends, TV characters, pop stars, footballers, and fashion models.

A limitation is that behaviour doesn't depend only on observational learning; people's internal emotional state, their interpretation of the current situation, and their personality are other important factors that need to be taken into account.

? How important do you think observational learning is with respect to producing aggressive behaviour?

Psychodynamic Theory

In the 19th century another form of psychological explanation grew out of Sigmund Freud's (1856–1939) theory of personality development. Freud practised as a psychiatrist in Vienna and collected a lot of information from his patients about their feelings and experiences, especially those related to early childhood. He developed his ideas into a theory (**psychodynamic theory**) and a form of therapy (**psychoanalysis**).

Psychodynamic theory tries to explain human development in terms of an interaction between **innate** drives (such as the desire for pleasure) and early experience (the extent to which early desires were gratified). The idea is that individual personality differences can be traced back to early conflicts between desire and experience. For example, a child may want to behave badly (e.g. steal sweets) but be in conflict because of the guilt experienced afterwards. Some of these conflicts remain with the adult and are likely to influence his/her behaviour. In order to understand this we need to look briefly at Freud's description of development.

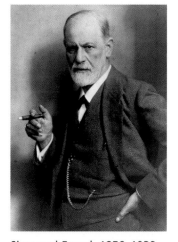

Sigmund Freud, 1856–1939.

The structure of the personality

You probably imagine that most (or even all) of the mind exists at the conscious level. The fact that you are generally consciously aware of why you have the emotions you do, and why you behave as you do, suggests that our conscious mind has full access to all relevant information about ourselves. However, Freud's views were very different. He argued that the conscious mind was like the tip of an iceberg, with

KEY TERMS

Psychodynamic theory: this is an approach to understanding human behaviour and development pioneered by Freud and then developed by others; it forms part of the basis for psychoanalysis and other forms of psychodynamic therapy.
Psychoanalysis: the form of therapy derived from psychoanalytic theory.
Innate: inborn, a product of genetic factors.

A "Freudian slip" is a mistake that betrays the concerns of the unconscious mind. Think of a time when you might have called someone by the wrong name. In what way might this have been a Freudian slip?

Note that the term "sexual" is roughly equivalent to "physical pleasure".

most of the mind (like most of the iceberg) out of sight. More specifically, Freud assumed there were *three* levels of the mind:

- The conscious—those thoughts that are currently the focus of attention; in other words, what we are thinking about at any moment.
- The preconscious—information and ideas that can be retrieved easily from memory and brought into consciousness.
- The unconscious—this is the largest part of the mind, containing information that is almost impossible to bring into conscious awareness. Much of the information in the unconscious mind relates to very emotional experiences from our past (e.g. being bullied at school; being rejected by someone of great importance in our lives).

We have just seen that Freud assumed that the mind exists at three different levels. He also assumed that the mind is divided into *three* parts. In broad terms, Freud argued that the mind contains basic motivational forces (the id), the cognitive system used to perceive the world and for thinking and problem solving (the ego), and a conscience based on the values of family and of society generally (the superego). Let's now consider each of these parts of the mind in more detail.

1. *Id.* This contains basic motivational forces, especially innate sexual and aggressive instincts. The id follows the **pleasure principle**, with the emphasis being on *immediate* satisfaction. It is located in the unconscious mind. The sexual instinct is known as libido.
2. *Ego.* This is the conscious, rational mind, and it develops during the first two years of life. It works on the **reality principle**, taking account of what is going on in the environment.
3. *Superego.* This develops at about the age of 5 and embodies the child's conscience and sense of right and wrong. It is formed when the child adopts many of the values of the same-sexed parent (the process of identification).

Defence mechanisms

An important part of Freud's theory was the notion that there are frequent *conflicts* among the id, ego, and superego, which cause the individual to experience anxiety. More specifically, what generally happens is that there are conflicts between the id (which wants immediate satisfaction) and the superego (which wants the person to behave in line with society's rules). These conflicts force the ego to devote much time to trying to resolve them. The ego protects itself by using a number of **defence mechanisms** (strategies designed to reduce anxiety), some of which are as follows:

1. *Repression.* Keeping threatening thoughts out of consciousness, e.g. not remembering a potentially painful dental appointment.
2. *Displacement.* Unconsciously moving impulses away from a threatening object and towards a less threatening object, e.g. someone who has been made angry by their teacher may shout at their brother.
3. *Projection.* An individual may attribute their undesirable characteristics to others, e.g. someone who is unfriendly may accuse other people of being unfriendly.

KEY TERMS

Pleasure principle: the drive to do things that produce pleasure or gratification.
Reality principle: the drive to accommodate to the demands of the environment.
Defence mechanisms: strategies used by the ego to defend itself against anxiety.

4. *Denial*. Refusing to accept the existence or reality of a threatening event, e.g. patients suffering from life-threatening diseases often deny that their lives are affected.
5. *Intellectualisation*. Thinking about threatening events in ways that remove the emotion from them, e.g. responding to a car ferry disaster by thinking about ways of improving the design of ferries.

Psychosexual development

One of Freud's key assumptions was that adult personality depends very much on childhood experiences. In his theory of **psychosexual development**, Freud assumed that all children go through *five* stages:

1. *Oral stage* (occurs during the first 18 months of life). During this stage, the infant obtains satisfaction from eating, sucking, and other activities using the mouth.
2. *Anal stage* (between about 18 and 36 months of age). Toilet training takes place during this stage, which helps to explain why the anal region becomes so important.
3. *Phallic stage* (between 3 and 6 years of age). The genitals become a key source of satisfaction during this stage. At about the age of 5, boys acquire the **Oedipus complex**, in which they have sexual desires for their mother and therefore want to get rid of their father, who is a rival. They then also fear their father, who might realise what they are thinking. This complex is resolved by identification with their father, involving adopting many of their father's attitudes and developing a superego. So far as girls are concerned, Freud argued that girls come to recognise that they don't have a penis and blame their mother for this. The girl's father now becomes her love-object and she substitutes her "penis envy" with a wish to have a child. This leads to a kind of resolution and ultimate identification with her same-sex parent. If you think Freud's ideas of what goes on in the phallic stage are very fanciful, you're absolutely right!
4. *Latency stage* (from 6 years of age until the onset of puberty). During this stage, boys and girls spend very little time together.
5. *Genital stage* (from the onset of puberty and throughout adult life). During this stage, the main source of sexual pleasure is in the genitals.

> **Useful mnemonic**
>
> To help you remember Freud's stages of psychosexual development, the following mnemonic is made from the initial letter of each stage: Old Age Pensioners Love Greens!

> Freud developed his Oedipus complex at a time when lone-parent families were very rare. What bearing do you think this had on his theorising?

Personality theory

Freud coupled the theory of psychosexual development with a theory of personality. If a child experiences severe problems or excessive pleasure at any stage of development, this leads to **fixation**, in which basic energy or libido becomes attached to that stage for many years. Later in life, adults who experience very stressful conditions are likely to show **regression**, in which their behaviour becomes less mature, and more like that displayed during a psychosexual stage at which they fixated as children. According to Freud, these processes of fixation and regression play important roles in determining adult personality. Some personality types are shown in the box overleaf, along with descriptions and a link to the stage of psychosexual development at which fixation may have occurred.

> **KEY TERMS**
>
> **Psychosexual development**: Freud's stages in personality development based on the child's changing focus on different parts of the body (e.g. the mouth and the anal region). "Sexual" is roughly equivalent to "physical pleasure".
> **Oedipus complex**: Freud's explanation of how a boy resolves his love for his mother and feelings of rivalry towards his father by identifying with his father.
> **Fixation**: in Freudian terms, spending a long time at a given stage of development because of over- or under-gratification.
> **Regression**: in Freudian terms, returning to an earlier stage of development as a means of coping with anxiety.

Freud suggested that adult personality types could be linked with fixations during each stage of development.

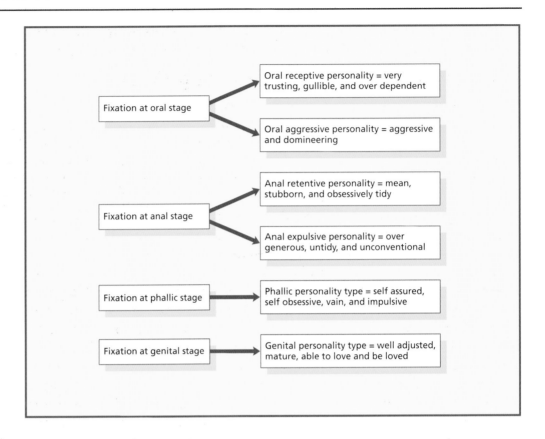

Freud's work was largely with middle-class women in Vienna in the 1890s and 1900s. How relevant do you think his ideas are to other cultures, particularly given the social changes during the 20th century?

? Considering that Freud was working in a strict Victorian society, why was sexual behaviour so strongly emphasised in his theory of development?

Evaluation of psychodynamic theory

- Freud and his psychodynamic theory have had an enormous impact on psychology. Indeed, he is the most influential psychologist of all time.
- As Freud argued, adult personality depends in part on the experiences of early childhood.
- There is increasing evidence that our conscious minds are less powerful than we like to think, and that Freud was right to emphasise the importance of the unconscious mind.
- It is to Freud's credit that he put forward what was probably the first systematic theory of personality.
- Freud's method of investigation was to focus on the individual, observing particular "cases" in fine detail. Many people see this approach as a drawback, mainly because Freud's observations were largely based on a rather narrow sample of people: white, middle-class Victorian Viennese women.
- Freud over-emphasised sex because he developed his theory at a time of great sexual repression, which may have caused sex to be something that was repressed in many minds (Banyard & Hayes, 1994).
- Freud's stage-based theory suggests that personality development occurs in a neater and tidier way than is actually the case.

Assumptions of the psychoanalytic approach

- Development is the result of an interaction between innate drives and early experience.
- Childhood experiences are of fundamental importance.
- Early conflicts result in unconscious forces that drive many aspects of adult behaviour.

- It is very hard to prove that early childhood experiences have actually determined adult personality many years later, and so the theory is hard to test properly.

Cognitive or Information-Processing Theory

Cognitive psychology developed in the 1950s because of a growing dissatisfaction with the behaviourist approach. It is very hard to understand cognitive abilities, such as language or problem solving, from the behaviourist perspective, with its emphasis on observable behaviour. For example, what someone is thinking is generally not obvious from their behaviour. What is also needed is a focus on internal processes, and this is what cognitive psychologists tried to do.

> **Assumptions of the cognitive approach**
> - Whereas the behaviourists reduced psychology to stimulus and response (S–R), cognitive psychologists have added another dimension.
> - Cognitive psychologists focus on a central, internal stage (stimulus–information processing–response).
> - The internal cognitive processes and the issue of how the stimulus provokes the response are not dismissed.

The arrival of the computer revolution provided an ideal analogy and a good basis for understanding human cognition, with cognitive psychologists explaining human cognition in terms of an information-processing system. There is input in the form of data or information to the brain and to the computer. This is followed by various kinds of information processing in the brain and the computer. Finally, there is some kind of output. Suppose you are given an input in the form of a problem in mathematics (e.g. $13 \times 12 = ?$). You engage in information processing, and then finally you output the answer by saying (hopefully!) 156. In similar fashion, computers can be programmed to work out the answer when given the same problem, printing it out or displaying it on the screen.

Evaluation of the cognitive theory

Cognitive explanations tend to be as machine-like as behaviourist ones, often ignoring the role of emotion or the influence of other people—not surprising when they are based on the behaviour of a machine. Also, the research on which they are based is often rather artificial, lacking external validity, because most experiments are carried out under highly controlled laboratory conditions.

Charles Darwin, 1809–1882.

Evolutionary Theory

Charles Darwin presented the most influential theory of evolution. Darwin composed a theory to account for the fact that animal species have evolved and continue to evolve (i.e. change their characteristics). The essential principles of this theory are:

- Environments are always changing, or animals move to new environments.
- Living things are constantly changing, partly because of sexual reproduction where two parents create a new individual by combining their **genes**, and also through chance **mutations** of the genes. In both cases new **traits** are produced.
- Those individuals who possess traits best adapted to the environment are more likely to survive to reproduce (it is reproduction rather than survival that matters); or, to put it another way, those individuals who best "fit" their environment survive (survival of the fittest); or, to put it still another way, the *genes* of the individuals with these traits are naturally selected.

In order to understand the concept of **natural selection** consider this example. A farmer chooses which males and females have the best characteristics for milk production or for increased reproduction (giving birth to lots of twins), and mates

> **KEY TERMS**
> **Gene**: a unit of inheritance that forms part of a chromosome. Some characteristics are determined by one gene whereas for others many genes are involved.
> **Mutation**: a genetic change that can then be inherited by any offspring.
> **Trait**: a characteristic distinguishing a particular individual.
> **Natural selection**: the process by which individuals are selected because they are best adapted to their environment.

All dogs have the same distant ancestors, but selective breeding (artificial selection) has resulted in major variations.

these individuals. This is selective breeding or artificial selection. In nature, no-one does the selecting, it is natural pressures that do it—it is called "natural selection".

The end result is that the genes carrying physical characteristics and behaviours that are **adaptive**, i.e. help the individual to better fit its environment, are the ones that survive to the next generation. Those traits that are non-adaptive tend to disappear. However, it should be emphasised it is not the individual but his/her genes that disappear.

The adaptive role of genes

A classic example of the adaptive role of the genes can be seen in the tendency for parents to risk their lives to save their offspring. This is described as altruism. Darwin could not explain this behaviour because, according to his theory, it is only the *individuals* who survive that count. If a parent dies saving their offspring this would appear to be a non-adaptive behaviour. However, altruism is adaptive at the level of the genes. A parent who dies in order to save his or her offspring is ensuring that their genetic line survives. Therefore altruism can be seen to be adaptive behaviour.

Assumptions of the evolutionary approach

- Animal species have evolved and continue to evolve.
- Physical characteristics and behaviours that are adaptive are kept, whilst the genes for non-adaptive characteristics and behaviours disappear.
- It is the genes, not the individuals, that are either selected or disappear with natural selection.

Evaluation of evolutionary theory

The theory of natural selection offers a good account of the facts. However, we can only point to fossil records and the evidence from a few species who have changed before our eyes, seemingly in response to environmental demands. A good example of this is the peppered moth, which is described in the **Case study** given below.

Two colours of peppered moth on the bark of a tree.

CASE STUDY: THE PEPPERED MOTH

What has often been regarded as fairly direct support for some of the assumptions of Darwin's theory was obtained by Kettlewell (1955). He studied two variants of the peppered moth, one of which was darker than the other. The difference in colour is inherited, with the offspring of the darker type being on average darker than those of the lighter type. Both types of peppered moth are eaten by birds such as robins and redstarts that rely on sight to detect them. Kettlewell observed the moths when they were on relatively light lichen-covered trees and when they were on dark, lichen-less trees in industrially polluted areas. The lighter-coloured moths survived better on the lighter trees and the darker-coloured moths survived better on the darker trees.

According to Darwin's theory, the number of darker moths should increase if there is an increase in the proportion of dark trees. Precisely this happened in England due to the industrial revolution, when pollution killed the lichen and coated the trees with sooty deposits. The proportion of peppered moths that were dark apparently went from almost nil to over half the resident population in a period of about 50 years. However, the baseline evidence that there were few dark peppered moths before the industrial revolution comes from moth collections. As Hailman (1992, p.126) pointed out, "Those collections were not scientific samples but were made by amateurs . . . Perhaps they did not like ugly black moths." ■

One criticism is that the theory of evolution offers mainly *post-hoc* (after the fact) evidence. It is hard to know whether a behaviour is actually beneficial, and that's why it remained, or whether it was simply neutral, and was never selected against.

■ Activity: Divide the class into five groups and give each group one of the approaches covered: behaviourist, psychoanalytic, cognitive, social learning, evolutionary. They should draw up a list of the advantages and disadvantages of their approach. Each group should give a brief presentation of their approach and, at the end of the lesson, let everyone decide which approach gets their vote for being the most valuable.

SECTION SUMMARY

❖ Psychologists use a range of different explanations, or "tools" to explain behaviour. For instance:
  – Biological explanations explore our behaviour in terms of our bodily processes.
  – Social psychological explanations look at our behaviour in terms of our interactions with each other.
❖ There are general explanations that are used more or less throughout psychology, which are each described below.

The range of explanations

❖ One key explanation of behaviour is learning theory. This theory suggests that all our behaviour is learned, and was largely developed from studies on animal behaviour.

Learning theory

❖ Learning theory is based on two types of conditioning:
  – Classical conditioning: occurs when a neutral stimulus is paired with an unconditioned stimulus, eventually producing a conditioned stimulus and response.
  – Operant conditioning: the result of reinforcement or punishment, which either increases or decreases the likelihood of a behaviour being repeated.
❖ Learning theory has been criticised:
  – first, for being based on animal research;
  – second, in its application to humans, where the emphasis on controlling behaviour has led to ethical concerns.

❖ Social learning theory adds to the learning theory explanations by explaining learning in terms of conditioning *and* observation.
❖ This theory suggests that we also learn via vicarious reinforcement and identification or modelling.
❖ Some of the findings apparently supporting social learning are open to other interpretations.

Social learning theory

❖ Another important psychological theory is psychodynamic theory. This theory is both an account of personality development and a therapy.
❖ This theory focuses on the unconscious mind, and suggests that our early experiences may result in unconscious conflicts that motivate adult behaviour.

Psychodynamic theory

❖ Freud described the mind in terms of three levels (conscious, preconscious, and unconscious) and three structures:
  - The ID: is made up of our innate sexual and aggressive instincts and follows the pleasure principle.
  - The EGO: describes our conscious rational mind and follows the reality principle.
  - The SUPEREGO: embodies the child's conscience.
❖ These structures are likely to come into conflict because they are motivated by different principles.
❖ Conflicts create anxieties that are dealt with by defence mechanisms.
❖ These defence mechanisms include:
  - repression,
  - displacement,
  - projection,
  - denial,
  - intellectualisation.
❖ Freud also suggested that there were five stages in development:
  1. oral,
  2. anal,
  3. phallic,
  4. latency,
  5. genital.
❖ Children may fixate at any one of these stages, and this fixation can be linked to their adult personality.
❖ Freudian theory has been criticised in terms of bias, but there is no doubt that his theories have had an enormous influence on 20th-century thought.

Cognitive explanations

❖ Cognitive explanations of behaviour focus on mental processes and use the analogy of information-processing systems.
❖ This comparison of human thought and behaviour to computer systems has resulted in the accusation of offering mechanistic explanations of behaviour.

Evolutionary explanations

❖ Evolutionary explanations of behaviour describe behaviour in terms of adaptiveness.
❖ They suggest that any characteristic that enhances reproduction is more likely to be perpetuated than those that do not. Natural selection chooses those genes that are desirable. Altruism is a good example.
❖ One major problem with evolutionary explanations centres on the evidence used to support the theory.

Which explanation is right?

❖ It is important to stress that no one explanation or approach is right.
❖ They are all used as part of the psychologist's "toolkit" for studying behaviour.

FURTHER READING

Two useful books on perspectives are C. Tavris and C. Wade (1997) *Psychology in perspective* (New York: Longman), and W.E. Glassman (1995) *Approaches to psychology* (Milton Keynes, UK: Open University Press). Books written more specifically for AS and A-level include M.W. Eysenck (1994) *Perspectives on psychology* (Hove, UK: Psychology Press), and A.E. Wadeley, A. Birch, and A. Malim (1997) *Perspectives in psychology (2nd edn.)* (Basingstoke, UK: Macmillan). For a general introduction to psychology you could try M.W. Eysenck (2002) *Simply psychology (2nd edn.)* (Hove, UK: Psychology Press). A readable account of the major approaches within psychology is provided by Matt Jarvis (2000) *Theoretical approaches in psychology* (London: Routledge).

Cognitive psychology is an approach or perspective in psychology. Cognitive psychologists are interested in internal mental (cognitive) processes such as those of perceiving, thinking, talking, and attention. Behaviour and experience are explained in terms of these internal processes rather than in terms of external influences. The emphasis is on how we perceive and interpret a stimulus rather than the stimulus itself. Here is an example to clarify the point. Consider the stimulus, "I would like to go to the cinema with you." That stimulus would have a very different effect on someone who understands English than on someone who knows no English at all. Thus, what is important is how a stimulus is interpreted. Essentially, cognitive psychology is the study of how the mind works and how it influences our behaviour and experience.

SECTION 5
Models of memory p. 43

Short-term memory (STM) is the part of the memory system in which information is initially stored. Information that we remember is held in long-term memory (LTM). What causes information to be moved from STM to LTM? Some answers to that question are considered. There is also consideration of the nature of short-term memory and whether it is best regarded as a system consisting of various components. The working memory model is an example of a theoretical approach based on the assumption that short-term memory is complex and consists of several components.

Specification content: The multi-store model including the concepts of encoding, capacity, and duration. Strengths and weaknesses of the model. The working memory model, including its strengths and weaknesses.

SECTION 6
Memory in everyday life p. 63

This section looks at practical applications of memory research. Eyewitness reports involve identifying suspects or describing what happened when a crime was committed. How reliable are eyewitnesses when they try to recall what happened? In our everyday lives we often find it frustrating or embarrassing when we simply forget something that is really important (e.g. a close friend's birthday). Ways in which we can all improve our memories are discussed.

Specification content: Eyewitness testimony (EWT) and factors affecting the accuracy of EWT, including anxiety, and the age of the witness. Misleading information and the use of the cognitive interview. Strategies for memory improvement.

COGNITIVE PSYCHOLOGY
Memory

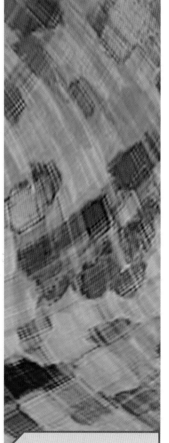

You may think that in an ideal world we would remember every detail of things that happen, especially when they are important. However, if we did remember everything our memories would be very full, and we would find it hard to think because of the enormous wealth of detail we would always be remembering. In fact, of course, we actually forget lots of things, many of them (alas!) things we didn't want to forget. What makes some things memorable and others forgettable?

This chapter explores one topic in cognitive psychology—human memory. How important is memory? Imagine if we were without it. We would not recognise anyone or anything as familiar. We would not be able to talk, read, or write, because we would remember nothing about language. In many ways we would be like newborn babies.

We use memory for numerous purposes—to keep track of conversations, to remember telephone numbers while we dial them, to write essays in exams, to make sense of what we read, and to recognise people's faces. There are many different kinds of memory, suggesting that we have a number of memory systems. This chapter explores in detail some of the sub-divisions of human memory, the accuracy of eyewitness testimony, and ways in which you can improve your memory.

SECTION 5
MODELS OF MEMORY

The Multi-Store Model

Memory is the process of retaining information for some time after it was learned. Thus, there are close links between *learning* and **memory**. Something that is learned is lodged in memory, and we can only remember things that were learned in the past.

Memory and learning can most clearly be demonstrated by good performance on a memory test. For example, we could give someone a list of words for a specified period of time and then some time later ask them to recall the list. When learning and memorising the words in the list, there are three stages:

1. **Encoding:** When the person is given the list, they encode the words. They place the words in memory. "Encoding" means to put something into a code, in this case the code used to store it in memory—some kind of memory trace. For example, if you hear the word "chair", you might encode it in terms of

? Are learning and memory different? If so, what is the difference?

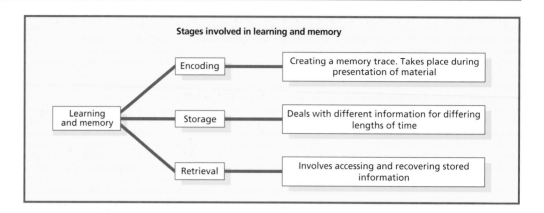

your favourite chair that you normally sit in at home. In other words, your encoding of the word "chair" involves converting or changing the word you hear into a meaningful form.

2.   **Storage**: As a result of encoding, the information is stored within the memory system. As we will see, some information remains stored in memory for decades or even an entire lifetime.

3.   **Retrieval**: Recovering stored information from the memory system. This is known as "recall" or "remembering".

Psychologists who are interested in learning focus on encoding and storage. In contrast, those interested in memory concentrate most on retrieval. However, it is important to note that all these processes depend on each other.

Short-term and long-term memory

Most psychologists agree that there is an important distinction between two kinds of memory: short-term and long-term memory. Information in short-term memory lasts for only a short time (a few seconds), whereas information in long-term memory can theoretically last forever or at least for a very long time.

Trying to remember a telephone number for a few seconds is sometimes used as an example of the use of **short-term memory**. The example illustrates two of the key features of short-term memory: a very limited capacity and a very limited duration. **Long-term memory**, on the other hand, has unlimited capacity and lasts (potentially) forever. As an example, you might think of some of your most vivid childhood memories.

The model of memory put forward by Atkinson and Shiffrin (1968) is the most important theoretical approach based on the notion that there are separate short-term and long-term memory stores. In fact,

---

Testing memory

Psychologists use various methods to test recall or learning.

• Free recall. Give participants some words to learn and then ask them to recall the words in any order.
• Cued recall. After presenting the material to be learned, provide cues to help recall. For example, saying that some of the items are minerals.
• Recognition. Giving a list of words which includes some of those in the initial presentation. Participants are asked to identify those in the original list.
• Paired-associate learning. Participants are given word pairs to learn and then tested by presenting the first word in each pair and asking them to recall the second word.
• Nonsense syllables. Participants are asked to memorise meaningless sets of letters. These may be trigrams (three letters).

KEY TERMS

Storage: storing a memory for a period of time so that it can be used later.
Retrieval: the process of recovering information stored in long-term memory. If retrieval is successful, the individual remembers the information in question.
Short-term memory: a temporary place for storing information during which it receives limited processing (e.g. verbal rehearsal). Short-term memory has a very limited capacity and short duration, unless the information in it is maintained through rehearsal.
Long-term memory: a relatively permanent memory store with an unlimited capacity and duration, containing different components such as episodic (personal events), semantic (facts and information), and procedural (actions and skills) memory.

they actually argued that there are three kinds of memory stores. This explains why their approach is known as the **multi-store model** of memory. Here are the crucial assumptions built into this model:

1. Human memory consists of three kinds of memory stores.
2. Information from the environment is initially received by the sensory stores. There is one sensory store for each sense modality—a store for what we see, one for what we hear, and so on. Information lasts for a very short period of time (fractions of a second, or a second or two) in these sensory stores.
3. Some of the information in the sensory stores is attended to (and processed further) within the short-term store. The main feature of the short-term store is that it has limited capacity—we can't keep more than about *seven* items in this store at any one time.
4. Some of the information processed in the short-term store is transferred to the long-term store. How does information get into the long-term store? We need to rehearse or repeat verbally information in the short-term store to put it into the long-term store. The more something is rehearsed, the stronger the memory trace in long-term memory.
5. The key feature of the long-term store is that information in it can often last for a long time. As I have already mentioned, in some cases information in the long-term store remains there for our entire lifetime.
6. There are important differences between short-term and long-term memory in forgetting. When information is forgotten from the short-term store, it has simply disappeared from the memory system. In contrast, most information that is forgotten from the long-term store is still in the memory system but can't be accessed (e.g. because of interference from other information).

We all know that certain kinds of information disappear rapidly from memory whereas others last for years and years. Accordingly, you may think it is obvious that there are separate short-term and long-term stores. However, if we are going to prove the point (or get as close to proof as we can), we need to start by listing all the likely differences between the short-term and long-term memory stores. When we have done that, we can have a look at the relevant research evidence. Finally, we will evaluate the evidence and decide how accurately the multi-store

Even if we don't pay attention when we're spoken to, we are often able to repeat the last few things said. This is because that information is held for a few seconds in a sensory memory store, before entering short-term memory.

See *As Level Psychology Online* for interactive exercises on memory.

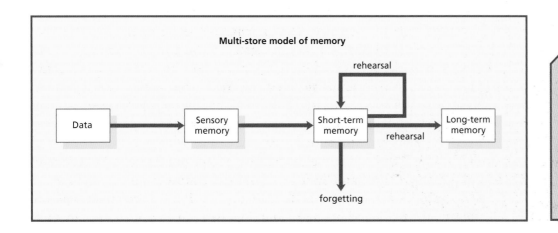

KEY TERM

Multi-store model: a model in which memory is divided into three stores; sensory, short-term, and long-term memory. This model is no longer favoured, as research has shown that memory is much more complex than this.

model actually accounts for human memory. Here is a list of possible differences between the short-term and long-term memory stores:

1. *Encoding*: Remember that encoding involves changing the information presented into a different form. Since words or other items in the short-term store are rehearsed or repeated in the short-term store, we might assume they are encoded in terms of their sound (this is known as acoustic coding). In contrast, the information we have stored in long-term memory nearly always seems to be stored in terms of its meaning (this is known as semantic coding).

2. *Capacity*: The short-term store has very limited capacity. As mentioned already, its capacity is about seven items. In contrast, the capacity of the long-term store is so large that we are in no danger at all of filling it.

3. *Duration*: It is obvious from the names short-term memory store and long-term memory store that information has greater duration (i.e. it lasts longer) in the long-term store than in the short-term store! As we will see, information in the short-term store, if not rehearsed, disappears within about 18–20 seconds. In contrast, we will see that elderly people can recognise the names of fellow students from 48 years previously (Bahrick, Bahrick, & Wittinger, 1975). Thus, we have proof that long-term memory can last virtually 50 years at least.

Now we will have a look at the evidence relating to these various assumptions about the short-term and long-term memory stores. After that, we will evaluate the multi-store model, trying to identify its main strengths and weaknesses.

Short-term memory: Capacity

It is harder than you might imagine to estimate the capacity of short-term memory. Psychologists have devised two main strategies: span measures and the recency effect in free recall.

Span measures

In 1887, Joseph Jacobs used memory span as a measure of how much can be stored in short-term memory at any one time. Jacobs presented his participants with a random sequence of digits or letters, and then asked them to repeat the items back in the same order. **Memory span** was the longest sequence of items recalled accurately at least 50% of the time. Jacobs found that the average number of items recalled was between five and nine, and that digits were recalled better (9.3 items) than letters (7.3 items), with both spans increasing with age. These findings suggested that short-term memory has a limited storage capacity of between about five and nine items, a conclusion that was confirmed by subsequent research.

Jacobs' approach was limited. First, his research lacked **mundane realism**, because his span tasks were not representative of everyday memory demands.

Second, if we could only remember a few letters, we would be unable to remember the following sequence of 10 letters: P S Y C H O L O G Y! In fact, of course, we can remember that sequence because it's easy to organise the information in memory. Miller (1956) took account of that point, and argued that the span of immediate memory is "seven, plus or minus two", whether the units are numbers, letters, or words. He claimed that we should focus on **chunks** (integrated pieces or units of information). About seven chunks of information can be held in short-term memory at any time. The question of what constitutes a "chunk" depends on your personal experience. For example, "IBM" would be one chunk if you know about International Business Machines, but it would be three if you didn't know what IBM stood for.

Herb Simon (1974) carried out a thorough study of Miller's ideas about the importance of **chunking**. Simon argued that the size of a chunk corresponds to the highest-level integration of the stimulus material available to the individual. In his research, he studied memory span for words, two-word phrases, and eight-word phrases. When he focused on the number of words in the span, he found this increased from seven words to nine with two-word phrases and 22 with eight-word phrases. At the level of chunks, Simon argued that an entire phrase should be regarded as a single chunk. When he did this, the number of chunks fell from six or seven with unrelated words to four with two-word phrases and three with eight-word phrases.

Simon confirmed that it makes sense to measure memory span in terms of chunks. However, the number of chunks in the memory span varied across different types of material more than expected on Miller's hypothesis. Such research has useful applications. For example phone numbers are easier to remember if you chunk them, although this skill is much less useful now that most people store numerous phone numbers in their mobile phones! As with Jacobs' earlier research, the study by Simon (1974) lacks mundane realism in that the demands on the participants were very different from those of our everyday lives.

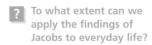 To what extent can we apply the findings of Jacobs to everyday life?

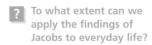 Are there any problems with using letter or digit span as a measure of the capacity of short-term memory?

 HOW SCIENCE WORKS: CHUNKING

Scientific method involves observing what occurs and seeing if there is a pattern. For example, you know that Miller found most people have an STM capacity of 7 plus or minus 2, which we call Miller's magic number. But you can test the idea that we can store far more than 9 items in STM by chunking them. This means we group similar things together in one category, for example: mug+spoon+teabag+sugar+milk. Ask whoever does the main shopping at home how they remember what's needed—do they chunk their list?

From such observations you could construct a prediction, called a hypothesis, and then you could test it. You could predict that people will recall more things, or recall them faster, if they chunk items rather than trying to remember them randomly.

You could try compiling and printing out a random shopping list for the supermarket, mixing up about 25 items from all round the store. Then make a second list of 25 different items but this time chunk them, i.e. group together similar items (like fresh vegetables; tinned goods; but don't use headings!). Test someone—not the main shopper—on the first list: give them 1 minute to read and learn, then 2 minutes to recall by writing items down. Then do the same for the second list. They will probably do better or faster on the second list, and you can explain why to them.

In science it is important to test the hypothesis, and find out whether it is correct or wrong. This is the way we increase scientific knowledge.

KEY TERMS

Chunks: integrated units of information.
Chunking: the process of combining individual items (e.g. letters; numbers) into larger, meaningful units.

■ **Activity:** Read quickly through the following list of digits once. Cover the list and try to write the digits down in the correct order.

73515698274

How many did you remember in the correct order? This is one way of measuring your memory span. Now try the following digits:

1939106618051215

More digits, but if you recognised the "chunks" you should have remembered them all:

1939 Start of Second World War
1066 Battle of Hastings
1805 Battle of Trafalgar
1215 Signing of the Magna Carta

Did you find any recency effects when you tried to recall the list of digits? Try the test again (with different data) with this in mind.

? If you were shown these ten words: cat, butter, car, house, carpet, tomato, beer, river, pool, tennis; and then asked to recall them immediately in any order, what words are likely to be best remembered?

KEY TERM

Recency effect: better free recall of the last few items in a list, where higher performance is due to the information being in short-term store.
Rehearsal: the verbal repetition of information (often words), which typically has the effect of increasing our long-term memory for the rehearsed information.

The recency effect

A familiar example of the **recency effect** is the observation that a pop group is only as good as their last hit song. People generally have a good memory for most-recent things (e.g. the movie they saw last). In relation to short-term memory, the recency effect can be measured using free recall—participants are shown a list of words or syllables, and immediately asked to recall them in any order. The recency effect is demonstrated by the fact that the last two or three items in a list are usually much better remembered than items from the middle of the list. As we will see, it has been argued that these last few items (which are often recalled before the other list items) are well remembered because they are in the short-term store when the list presentation comes to an end.

Glanzer and Cunitz (1966) investigated the effect of introducing an interference task involving counting backwards by threes for 10 seconds between the end of the list and the start of recall. This eliminated the recency effect but otherwise had no effect on recall of the rest of the list. The two or three words at the end of the list were in a fragile state (not well encoded) in short-term memory, and so were easily wiped out by the task of counting backwards. In contrast, the other list items were in the long-term store and so were unaffected.

If you compare findings from measures of memory span and of the recency effect, you'll see what appears to be a problem. The recency effect suggests the capacity of the short-term store is about two or three items. However, span measures indicate a capacity of about seven items. Why do these two techniques produce such different results? One reason relates to different patterns of **rehearsal**. Participants carrying out a span task rehearse as many items as possible, whereas those asked to learn a list for free recall rehearse only a few items at a time (Rundus, 1971). Both measures indicate that the capacity of short-term memory is strictly limited. In contrast, no effective limits on the capacity of long-term memory have been discovered.

Duration in short-term memory

We have seen that the capacity of short-term memory is very limited. However, this leaves open another important issue—how long does information last in short-term memory? This is a crucial question. If information is lost rapidly from short-term memory, this must limit our ability to think about several things at once.

The classic study to work out the duration of short-term memory was carried out by Peterson and Peterson (1959), using what became known as the Brown–Peterson technique. They aimed to test the hypothesis that information that is not rehearsed is lost rapidly from short-term memory. On each trial, participants were presented with a trigram consisting of three consonants (e.g. BVM, CTG), which they knew they would be asked to recall in the correct order. Recall was required after a delay of 3, 6, 9, 12, 15, or 18 seconds. The participants had to count backwards in threes from a random three-digit number (e.g. 866, 863, 860, and so on) between the initial presentation of the trigram and the time when they were asked to recall it. This was done to prevent rehearsal of the trigram, because rehearsal would have improved performance by keeping information in short-term memory. Recall had to be 100% accurate and in the correct order (serial recall) to be regarded as correct. The participants were tested repeatedly with the same time delays. The experimenters varied the time delay, and the effect of time delay on memory was assessed in terms of the number of trigrams recalled.

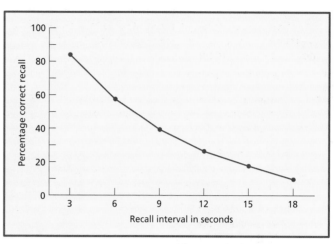

Peterson and Peterson (1959) found that there was a rapid increase in forgetting from short-term memory as the time delay increased (see Figure). After 3 seconds, 80% of the trigrams were recalled, after 6 seconds 50% were recalled, and after 18 seconds fewer than 10% were recalled. Thus, very little information remained in short-term memory for more than 18 seconds or so. One conclusion is that information in short-term memory is fragile and easily forgotten. Another conclusion is that short-term memory is distinct from long-term memory in that forgetting is enormously faster from short-term memory than from long-term memory.

We could make some criticisms of this study. First, Peterson and Peterson (1959) used very artificial stimuli (i.e. trigrams) that are essentially lacking in meaning. Thus, the study lacks mundane realism and external validity. For example, short-term memory is likely to be better in everyday life than for the stimuli used in this study.

Second, the findings depended in part on the fact that the participants were given many trials with different trigrams and may have become confused. Keppel and Underwood (1962) used the same task as Peterson and Peterson (1959) but observed *no* forgetting over time on the very first trial. Why was this? Forgetting is caused in part by proactive interference (disruption of current learning and memory by previous learning), and only the first trigram presented is free from proactive interference.

Third, Peterson and Peterson (1959) only considered short-term memory duration for one type of stimulus. Their study did not provide information about the duration of short-term memory for other kinds of stimuli (e.g. pictures; melodies; smells).

Duration in long-term memory

How can one assess how long a memory lasts? This is difficult. Even if you can't remember something at this moment, it is hard to prove that it's not in memory somewhere but you simply can't bring it into your conscious mind. If you can remember something, it might be an inaccurate memory that you have constructed.

In spite of the problems, psychologists have successfully conducted research into "very-long-term memory" (VLTM). It is said that the elderly don't lose their childhood memories, and many skills (e.g. riding a bicycle) are never forgotten. Bahrick et al. (1975) produced a clever demonstration of very-long-term memory using photographs from high-school yearbooks (an annual publication in American High School where everyone's picture is shown with their name and

The graph shows a steady decline in short-term memory recall after longer retention intervals (from Peterson & Peterson, 1959).

? Why was information in short-term memory forgotten so quickly?

? Was the approach taken by Peterson and Peterson (1959) too artificial to tell us much about short-term forgetting in everyday life?

See *As Level Psychology Online* for stimulus material suggesting how to replicate Peterson and Peterson's (1959) and Bahrick's (1975) classic studies.

Some memories never fade. Can you remember the names of your primary school classmates?

other details). Bahrick et al. asked ex-high-school students of various ages to free recall the names of any of their classmates. They also showed them a set of appropriate photographs and asked them to identify individuals.

What did Bahrick et al. (1975) find? There was 90% accuracy in face and name recognition even for those participants who had left high school 34 years previously. After 48 years, this declined to 80% for name recognition and 40% for face recognition. These findings support the view that people do have genuine very-long-term memories. Compared to the vast majority of research, which is based entirely in the laboratory, Bahrick et al.'s research has high mundane realism. Asking participants to recall their classmates tests real-life memory. Thus, the research is more representative of natural behaviour and so has high external validity.

Encoding in short-term vs long-term memory

When psychologists talk about encoding, they are referring to the way in which information is stored in memory. For example, encoding can be in terms of acoustic (sound) or semantic (meaning) coding. The words "cap" and "can" are acoustically similar; "cap" and "hat" are semantically similar. We can remember words by the way they sound or by their meaning.

It seems that short-term and long-term memory differ in the way information is coded. If you have to remember something for a short while (e.g. a phone number), you probably repeat it to yourself (rehearsal). People do this whether they heard the number or saw it, suggesting that short-term memory may encode information acoustically. Baddeley (1966) reported evidence that short-term memory depends mainly on **acoustic coding**. If participants recalled words from short-term memory, they didn't confuse words having the same meaning (e.g. "big" and "large"). However, they often confused words that sounded similar (e.g. remembering "cat" instead of "cap"). The opposite was true for long-term memory. This suggests that short-term memory largely uses an acoustic code, and that long-term memory depends on mostly on **semantic coding** based on the meaning of words. These findings convinced many psychologists that the distinction between short-term and long-term memory is both genuine and important.

Baddeley's (1966) approach was limited in that he didn't consider the possibility of *visual* codes existing in short-term memory. Posner (1969) found evidence that visual codes are used. For example, when "A" was followed by "A", people were faster to decide that it was the same letter than when "A" was followed by "a". The visual code for the second letter differed from that of the first letter when "A" was followed by "a", and that slowed people down.

KEY TERM

Acoustic coding: encoding words in terms of their sound using information stored in long-term memory.
Semantic coding: encoding or processing words in terms of their meaning based on information stored in long-term memory.

Comparing STM and LTM	Short-term memory	Long-term memory
Duration (how long it lasts)	Short (seconds)	Long, potentially forever
Capacity (how much it holds)	Limited by duration	Unlimited
Encoding differences	Acoustic	Semantic

■ **Activity:** You could test the effects of semantic and acoustic recall by using Baddeley's word lists and asking for immediate or delayed recall. Construct four word lists:

Acoustically similar: man, cap, can, cab, mad, mat, map
Acoustically dissimilar: pit, few, cow, pen, sup, bar, day
Semantically similar: great, large, big, huge, broad, fat, high
Semantically dissimilar: good, safe, thin, deep, strong, foul, hot

Divide participants into two groups—immediate recall (short-term memory) and longer-term recall. Participants should be randomly allocated to conditions to ensure that both groups of participants are equivalent.

For each group, which lists are they best at recalling and which lists do they perform least well on?

Is there more than one long-term memory store?

According to Atkinson and Shiffrin's (1968) multi-store model, there is only one long-term memory store. As soon as you start thinking about it, that seems unlikely. We have an enormous variety of information stored in long-term memory, including such things as the knowledge that Keira Knightley is a film star, how to ride a bicycle, that we had fish and chips for lunch yesterday, and the meaning of the word "bling". It seems improbable that all of this knowledge is stored within a *single* long-term memory store.

Cohen and Squire (1980) argued that long-term memory is divided into two memory systems: **declarative knowledge** and **procedural knowledge**. Declarative knowledge is concerned with "knowing that". For example, we know that we had roast pork for Sunday lunch and we know that Paris is the capital of France. In contrast, procedural knowledge is concerned with "knowing how". For example, we know how to play various sports, play the piano, and so on.

How can we show that there is a genuine difference between these two memory systems? If declarative knowledge and procedural knowledge belong to separate systems in different regions of the brain, then some brain-damaged patients might suffer problems with only one of the two systems. This is exactly

? Which type of memory (procedural or declarative) is likely to be tested in a memory experiment?

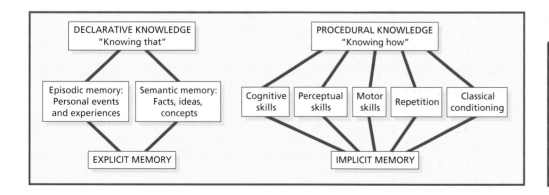

CASE STUDY: THE MAN WHO NEVER GOT OLDER

In the 1950s a man known as "HM" sought medical help for his epileptic seizures. He had been forced to give up his job because the seizures had become so frequent and severe, and it was not possible to control them with drugs. In desperation the doctors decided to remove a structure called the hippocampus from both hemispheres of his brain because this was the seat of his seizures. No-one quite knew what the outcome would be. The operation did reduce his epilepsy but it also had a dramatic effect on his memory.

His personality and intellect remained the same, but his memory was severely affected. Some aspects of his memory were fairly intact: he could still talk and recall the skills he knew previously (semantic memory), he continued to be able to form short-term memories, but was unable to form any new long-term ones. For example, given the task of memorising a number he could recall it 15 minutes later but, after being distracted, he had no recollection. He could read the same magazine over and over again without realising that he had read it before.

HM moved house after his operation and had great difficulty learning his new route home. After 6 years he was finally able to at least find his way around the house. This shows that he did have some memory capacity and, intellectually, he was quite "intact" so he did have some awareness of his predicament.

For many years he reported that the year was 1953 and he was 27 years old. As time went on he clearly realised this could not be true and he started to guess a more appropriate answer. In other words he tried to reconstruct his memories, although not very successfully. ■

■ **Activity:** State whether the following involve procedural or declarative knowledge.

- Your name
- Driving a car
- The capital city of Japan
- The value of m^2 when $m = 6$
- Balancing on one leg

Think of some other examples of procedural and declarative knowledge.

what has been found. There was a famous case study (detailed investigation of a single individual) involving a man known as HM. He suffered from frequent epileptic seizures, and so it was decided to carry out brain surgery. After the operation, his memory for declarative knowledge was very poor—he couldn't remember most of the events and experiences he had after the operation. However, he was still able to acquire and remember procedural knowledge. For example, he learned mirror drawing (tracing a figure seen only in mirror image) almost as rapidly as non-brain-damaged individuals.

Spiers et al. (2001) reviewed 147 cases of amnesia (severe problems with long-term memory). Every one of them had poor declarative knowledge, but *none* of them had any problems with procedural knowledge. The procedural skills the amnesic patients had acquired included learning to play the piano and mirror drawing. This is convincing evidence that declarative knowledge and procedural knowledge are separate forms of long-term memory.

Evaluation of the multi-store model

We have considered the evidence concerned with short-term and long-term memory, and it is now time to draw up a balance sheet of the strengths and weaknesses of the multi-store model. We start with the strengths and follow with the weaknesses.

- Strength: There is strong support for the basic distinction between short-term and long-term memory stores from studies on brain-damaged patients. Patients with amnesia have severe problems with long-term memory but not with short-term memory. In addition, some patients have problems with short-term memory but not with long-term memory (Shallice & Warrington, 1970).
- Strength: There is reasonable support for the notion that encoding is different in short-term and long-term memory. For example, Baddeley (1966) found evidence for acoustic or sound encoding in short-term memory and semantic or meaning encoding in long-term memory.
- Strength: The capacity of the two stores is radically different. The capacity of the short-term store is about seven items (Jacobs, 1887; Simon, 1974). In contrast, there are no known limits on the capacity of the long-term store.

For example, Standing et al. (1970) found that 90% of 2560 pictures presented once were remembered on a test of long-term memory.

- Strength: There are huge differences in the duration of information in short-term and long-term memory. Unrehearsed information in short-term memory vanishes within about 20 seconds (Peterson & Peterson, 1959). In contrast, some information in long-term memory is still there 48 years after learning (Bahrick et al., 1975).
- Weakness: The model argues that the transfer of information from short-term to long-term memory is through rehearsal. However, in daily life most people devote very little time to rehearsal, although they are constantly storing away new information in long-term memory. Rehearsal may describe what happens when psychologists conduct experiments on word lists in laboratories but this isn't true to life.
- Weakness: It is assumed that information in the short-term store is encoded in terms of its sound (acoustic coding) whereas information in the long-term store is encoded in terms of its meaning (semantic coding). I don't want to seem frivolous, but it seems to me like magic for information to change from sound to meaning as it proceeds along an arrow from the short-term to the long-term store!
- Weakness: Atkinson and Shiffrin (1968) argued that information is processed in short-term memory *before* proceeding to long-term memory. Matters can't be that simple. Suppose you use short-term memory to rehearse "IBM" as a single chunk. This is only possible after you have contacted long-term memory to work out the meaning of IBM! Most information in short-term memory must have made contact with information in long-term memory before being rehearsed.
- Weakness: The model is oversimplified in its assumption that there is a *single* long-term memory store. In fact, there are a number of long-term memory stores. Atkinson and Shiffrin (1968) focused almost exclusively on declarative knowledge and had practically nothing to say about procedural knowledge (e.g. the learning of skills).
- Weakness: The model is oversimplified in its assumption that there is a *single* short-term store. Evidence from brain-damaged patients suggests there are a number of short-term stores (Warrington & Shallice, 1972). Additional convincing evidence that there is more than one short-term store comes from work on the working memory model, to which we now turn.

EXAM HINT

If you have a question asking you to outline the main features of the multi-store model, you might find it useful to include a diagram in your answer IN ADDITION TO the written description.

The Working Memory Model

What is the point of short-term memory in everyday life? Textbook writers sometimes answer the question by pointing out that it allows us to remember a telephone number for the few seconds it takes to dial it. However, even that use of short-term memory is rapidly disappearing now that nearly everyone has a mobile phone that stores all the phone numbers they use regularly.

In 1974, two British psychologists, Alan Baddeley and Graham Hitch, came up with a convincing answer to the above question. They pointed out that we use short-term memory when we are working on a complex problem (e.g. in arithmetic) and need to keep track of where we have got to in the problem. Suppose you were given the addition problem 13 + 18 + 24.

See *AS Level Psychology Online* to download a podcast containing an interview with Alan Baddeley on his memory research.

You would add 13 and 18 and keep the answer (31) in short-term memory. You would then add 24 to 31 and produce the correct answer of 55. Baddeley and Hitch used the term working memory to refer to a system involving processing and short-term memory in combination, and theirs was a **working memory model**.

Baddeley and Hitch's (1974) working memory model differed from previous ideas about short-term memory not only in emphasising its general usefulness in everyday life but also by arguing (very reasonably) that rehearsal is only one of the possible processes occurring in short-term memory.

It is now time to consider in more detail the **working memory system** put forward by Baddeley and Hitch (1974). It consisted of three components, each of which has limited capacity:

- **Central executive**: This is a modality-free component, meaning that it can process information from any sensory modality (e.g. visual, auditory). It is like attention.
- **Phonological loop** (originally called the articulatory loop): This is a temporary storage system holding verbal information in a phonological (speech-based) form. It is involved in verbal rehearsal and in speech perception.
- **Visuo-spatial sketchpad** (sometimes called a scratch pad): This is specialised for the rehearsal and temporary storage of visual and spatial information.

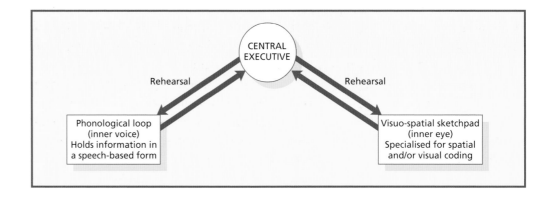

KEY TERMS

Working memory model: the model of short-term memory proposed to replace the multi-store model. It consists of a central executive plus slave systems that deal with different sensory modalities.
Working memory system: the concept that short-term (or working) memory can be subdivided into other stores that handle different modalities (sound and visual data).
Central executive: the key component of working memory. It is a modality-free system (i.e. not visual or auditory) of limited capacity and is similar to "paying attention" to something.
Phonological loop: a component of the working memory system concerned with speech perception and production.
Visuo-spatial sketchpad: a component within the working memory system designed for spatial and/or visual coding.

How can we tell which component or components of the working memory system are being used when people perform a given task? According to the model, every component has limited capacity and is relatively independent of the other components in its functioning. Two predictions follow:

1. If two tasks make use of the *same* component, they cannot be performed together successfully.
2. If two tasks make use of *different* components, it should be possible to perform them as well together as separately.

Here is a simple example showing the correctness of the second prediction. Your ability to make sense of the material in this book mainly involves focusing on visual information (using the visuo-spatial sketchpad) and attending to it (using the central executive). If you said "the" over and over again (using the phonological loop) while reading this book, it would have little effect on your comprehension. At any rate, that is what I would predict!

Robbins et al. (1996) carried out an experiment to show in more detail how the working memory model works in practice. Chess players selected moves from various chess positions while performing a second task at the same time. This second task involved the central executive, the visuo-spatial sketchpad, or the phonological loop. The quality of the chess moves selected was reduced when the second task involved the central executive or the visuo-spatial sketchpad, but not when it involved the phonological loop. That means that selecting good chess moves requires use of the central executive and the visuo-spatial sketchpad but not the phonological loop. This study demonstrates that the working memory model can be used to clarify which processes people use when performing complex tasks such as selecting chess moves.

According to Robbins et al. (1996), selecting good chess moves requires use of the central executive and the visuo-spatial sketchpad but not the phonological loop.

Here is another example of how the working memory system operates. Hitch and Baddeley (1976) asked participants to carry out a verbal reasoning task to decide whether each in a set of sentences provided a true or false description of the letter pair that followed it (e.g. A is followed by B: BA). At the same time, the participants had to do either a task where little thought or attention was involved (only using the phonological loop by saying 1 2 3 4 5 6 rapidly) or a task that involved the central executive as well as the phonological or articulatory loop (remembering six random digits). As predicted, reasoning performance was slowed down by the additional task when it involved using the central executive but not when it involved only the phonological loop.

■ **Activity:** You can investigate some of the processes involved in comprehension by using an approach similar to the one used by Hitch and Baddeley (1976). Start by selecting a fairly short text (250–300 words) that could be taken from a book or newspaper. There are three groups of participants who are assigned at random to the conditions. In the first condition, participants read the text and at the same time count backwards by threes, a task that involves the central executive and the phonological loop. In the second condition, participants read the text and at the same time say the numbers 1 2 3 4 5 6 rapidly over and over again, a task that involves only the phonological loop. In the third condition, participants only read the text and do not perform a second task at the same time. A few seconds after the text has been read, participants in all three conditions are given the same comprehension test to assess how much information they have extracted from it. You should find that participants in the first condition have the lowest level of comprehension and that there is little difference between the second and third conditions. These findings would indicate that the central executive (including attention) is important for comprehension, whereas the phonological loop is not. This experiment shows how the working memory approach can be used to assess the processes involved in comprehension.

? If you add up two items in your head—real life mental arithmetic!—when out shopping, which parts of your working memory are you using?

These findings are easy to explain within the working memory model. The reasoning task and saying 1–6 rapidly made use of different components of working memory, and so the two tasks didn't interfere with each other. It is less clear how the findings could be accounted for within the multi-store model. According to that model, even saying 1–6 rapidly should have used up the capacity of the short-term memory store, and this would have meant that it would be hard to carry out the reasoning task at the same time.

Phonological loop

There is much evidence that verbal rehearsal (saying words over and over to oneself) is of central importance in the functioning of the phonological loop. Baddeley, Thomson, and Buchanan (1975) studied the phonological loop. They asked participants to recall sets of five words immediately in the correct order. Participants' ability to do this was better with short words than with long ones. Further investigation of this word-length effect showed that participants could recall as many words as they could read out loud in 2 seconds. This suggests that the capacity of the phonological or articulatory loop is determined by how long it takes to rehearse verbal information.

Baddeley and Hitch (1974) assumed that the phonological loop is generally used when people are trying to remember visually presented words in the correct order. It follows from that assumption that it should be harder to remember words having similar sounds than words having dissimilar sounds—there would be much confusion and interference among the words having similar sounds. This prediction was tested by Larsen, Baddeley, and Andrade (2000). Here is one of their lists of words with similar sounds: FEE, HE, KNEE, LEE, ME, and SHE, and here is a list with dissimilar sounds: BAY, HOE, IT, ODD, SHY, and UP. As predicted, the ability to recall the words in order was 25% worse with the words having similar sounds. This indicates that speech-based rehearsal processes within the phonological loop were used in remembering these visually presented lists.

What is the value of the phonological loop in everyday life? Children with a deficient phonological loop generally have problems with reading. For example, Gathercole and Baddeley (1990) found that children with reading problems had an impaired memory span and found it difficult to decide whether words rhymed, suggesting they had a phonological loop deficit. The phonological loop is also useful when learning *new* words. In a study by Papagno, Valentine, and Baddeley (1991), native Italian speakers learned pairs of Italian words and pairs of Italian–Russian words. In one condition, participants had to perform an articulatory suppression task (saying something meaningless over and over again) during the learning task. Articulatory suppression (which prevented use of the phonological loop on the learning task) greatly slowed down the learning of foreign vocabulary.

More is known about the phonological loop than either of the other two components of the working memory system. It is the component that most closely resembles the short-term store in the multi-store model. However, the big difference is that the phonological loop is merely one component out of three in the working memory model, whereas the role of rehearsal is much more central within the multi-store model.

Visuo-spatial sketchpad

The visuo-spatial sketchpad is used for the temporary storage and manipulation of visual patterns and spatial movement. It is important to note that there are significant differences between visual and spatial processing. For example, consider individuals who have been blind since birth. They can generally find their way around a familiar environment (e.g. their own living room) without knocking into the furniture—this is achieved by using spatial processing since they are unable to use visual processing.

The visuo-spatial sketchpad is used in many situations in everyday life, such as finding the route when walking, or playing computer games. Logie et al. (1989) used a complex computer game called Space Fortress, which involves manoeuvring a spaceship around a computer screen. Performance on Space Fortress (especially early in training) was much worse when participants had to perform an additional visuo-spatial task at the same time. This indicates that the visuo-spatial sketchpad was needed for effective performance on the computer game.

What is the visuo-spatial sketchpad like? One possibility is that it consists of a *single* system combining visual and spatial processing. Another possibility is that there are partially or completely separate visual and spatial systems. The issue of whether there are separate visual and spatial systems was studied by Klauer and Zhao (2004). They used two main tasks: (1) a spatial task involving memory for dot locations; and (2) a visual task involving memory for Chinese ideographs (symbols). Participants sometimes had to perform a second task at the same time as the main task. This second task involved spatial interference or visual interference.

What would we predict if there are separate spatial and visual components? First, the spatial interference task should disrupt performance more on the spatial main task than on the visual main task. Second, the visual main task should disrupt performance more on the visual main task than on the spatial main task. As shown in the Figure, both predictions were confirmed. If the visuo-spatial sketchpad consisted of a single system, this pattern of results would not be expected.

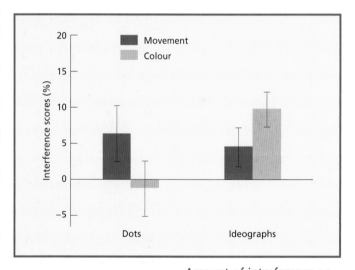

Amount of interference on a spatial task (dots) and a visual task (symbols) as a function of secondary task (spatial: movement distribution vs visual: colour discrimination).

Additional evidence supporting the notion of separate visual and spatial systems within the visuo-spatial sketchpad was reported by Smith and Jonides (1997) in an ingenious study. Two visual stimuli were presented together, followed by a probe stimulus. Participants either decided whether the probe was in the same location as one of the initial stimuli (spatial task) or they decided whether it had the same form or shape (visual task).

Even though the stimuli were identical in the two tasks, there were clear differences in patterns of brain activation. There was more activity in the *right* hemisphere during the spatial task than the visual task. However, there was more activity in the *left* hemisphere during the visual task than the spatial one. These findings suggest that there is a visual processing system based mainly in the left hemisphere and a spatial processing system based mostly in the right hemisphere.

There has been interest over the years in whether there are gender differences in terms of the functioning of the visuo-spatial sketchpad. More specifically, it has been argued that males are slightly better on average than females at spatial processing and navigation. This has been studied using tasks involving **mental rotation**. There are many such tasks, but what they have in common is that

KEY TERM

Mental rotation: a type of task in which participants imagine rotating two- or three-dimensional objects in order to perform some task.

you have to imagine rotating a shape or object to perform a task. In one of the best-known mental rotation tasks, participants are presented with a letter in its normal form or in reversed mirror-image form and have to decide which form it is in. The further from its upright form the letter is presented, the longer it takes participants to make the decision (Cooper & Shepard, 1973) because mental rotation to the upright position takes longer.

Richardson (1994) found in two experiments that male students outperformed female students on mental rotation. However, the gender difference was smaller than had been found 20 years previously using comparable students. Collins and Kimura (1997) pointed out that especially large gender differences in mental rotation have been found when complex, three-dimensional tasks have been used, but it wasn't clear whether the complexity or the three-dimensionality was more important. They used a complex two-dimensional mental rotation task, and found a large superiority of males over females, suggesting that it is complexity that is important.

Montello et al. (1999) found evidence that males outperform females on spatial processing but not visual processing. Males acquired more spatial information from a campus walk than did females. However, there was no gender difference on tasks depending more on visual processing—such as geographical knowledge at local, national, and international levels.

In sum, the visuo-spatial sketchpad is of major importance to us in our everyday lives. Nearly all the time we are engaging in visual and/or spatial processing and such processing necessarily involves the visuo-spatial sketchpad. Research has shown that the systems involved in visual and spatial processing are at least somewhat different from each other. It has been found that there are interesting gender differences in spatial processing within the visuo-spatial sketchpad.

In spite of these achievements, much remains to be done. First, we don't know much about the interconnections between visual and spatial processing—for example, how we combine visual and spatial information when walking. Second, it is clear that there are limits on the amount of visual or spatial processing that can be done at any moment, but precisely what those limits are is not known. Third, if we are engaged in complex visual or spatial processing, then the central executive will be involved as well as the visuo-spatial sketchpad. However, it is hard to predict how much complexity is needed before the visuo-spatial sketchpad is unable to cope on its own.

The central executive

The central executive, which resembles an attentional system, is the most important and versatile component of the working memory system. Indeed, it is so important that it is almost always used when we perform any kind of complex task (e.g. understanding a psychology textbook; listening to a talk). In the original working memory model (Baddeley & Hitch, 1974), it was suggested that the central executive was unitary, meaning that it functioned as a single unit. In recent years, however, theorists have increasingly argued that the central executive is more complex than that.

Various suggestions have been made concerning exactly what the central executive is used for, and there is by no means total agreement. One of the most influential suggestions stems from the research of Miyake et al. (2000), who gave their participants several tasks requiring the central executive. They found that these tasks varied in terms of which of the following three functions they used:

1. *Inhibition function*: this is used when you need to prevent yourself from attending to task-irrelevant stimuli or responses. In other words, it is used to reduce distraction effects. For example, consider the **Stroop task**, on which participants have to name the colours in which words are printed. In the most difficult condition, the words are conflicting colour words (e.g. the word BLUE printed in red). In this condition, performance is slowed down and there are often many errors. The inhibition function is needed to minimise the distraction effect created by the conflicting colour word.

2. *Shifting function*: this is used when you need to shift attention from one task to another. Suppose, for example, that you are presented with a series of trials, on each of which two numbers are presented. In one condition there is task switching: on some trials you have to multiply the two numbers and on other trials you have to divide one by the other. In the other condition there are long blocks of trials on which you always have to multiply the two numbers and there are other long blocks of trials on which you always have to divide one number by the other. Performance is slower in the task-switching condition, because attention has to be switched backwards and forwards between the two tasks. Task switching involves the shifting function, which is used to allow us to shift attention rapidly from one task to another.

3. *Updating function*: this is used when you need to update the information you remember to take account of changes in the world. For example, motorists need to update their stored information when the speed limit changes from 30 mph to 20 mph or vice versa. In the laboratory, the updating function is required when participants are presented with members of various categories and have to keep track of the most recently presented member of each category.

One important way of trying to understand the importance of the central executive in our everyday functioning is to study brain-damaged individuals whose central executive is impaired. Such individuals are said to suffer from **dysexecutive syndrome**, which involves problems with planning, organising, monitoring behaviour, and initiating behaviour. They typically have damage within the frontal lobes of the brain. Brain-damaged patients are often tested with the Behavioural Assessment of the Dysexecutive Syndrome (BADS) (Wilson et al., 1996). This consists of various tests designed to assess the ability to shift rules, to devise and implement a solution to a practical problem, to divide time effectively among various tasks, and so on. As you might imagine, individuals with dysexecutive syndrome as assessed by the BADS typically have great problems in holding down a job and functioning adequately in everyday life (Chamberlain, 2003).

The notion of a dysexecutive syndrome implies that brain damage to the frontal lobes typically damages *all* the functions of the central executive. However, this is an oversimplification. Stuss and Alexander (2007) identified *three* different functions based in different parts of the frontal lobes: task setting (planning); monitoring (checking one's own performance, or "quality control"); and energisation (sustained attention or concentration). Many patients had major problems with only *one* of these central executive functions rather than all of them.

The Stroop task

RED

BLUE

RED

BLUE

KEY TERMS

Stroop task: a task that involves naming the colours in which words are printed. Performance is slowed when the words are conflicting colour words (e.g. the word RED printed in green).
Dysexecutive syndrome: a condition caused by brain damage (typically in the frontal lobes) in which there is severe impairment of the functioning of the central executive component of working memory.

Thus, rather than thinking in terms of a *single* global dysexecutive syndrome, it is more accurate to identify *three* more specific dysexecutive syndromes, each based on one of the functions proposed by Stuss and Alexander. However, Stuss and Alexander also found that patients with widespread damage to the frontal lobes DID have a global dysexecutive syndrome.

In sum, the central executive is the most important component of working memory. In approximate terms, whenever we are engaged in tasks that involve attentional processes and/or planning, task shifting, organising, and monitoring, then we make use of the central executive. As we saw earlier, there is experimental evidence that it is involved in selecting chess moves (Robbins et al., 1996) and in verbal reasoning (Hitch & Baddeley, 1976). Brain-damaged patients with dysexecutive syndrome show the problems encountered by anyone whose central executive is impaired.

A major issue is to work out the number and nature of functions carried out by the central executive. Miyake et al. (2000) and Stuss and Alexander (2007) argued that there are three major functions, but unfortunately their two lists of functions only overlap in part. That means that further research is needed to establish more clearly what happens within the central executive.

How important is working memory?

There is much evidence that working memory is of fundamental importance in information processing and thinking. This has been shown in research stemming from the work of Daneman and Carpenter (1980), who argued that the essence of a working memory system is that it is used for storage and processing at the same time. They used a task in which participants read several sentences for comprehension (a processing task) and then recalled the final word of each sentence (storage task). The largest number of sentences from which a participant could recall all the final words more than 50% of the time was his/her **reading span**. This reading span was taken as a measure of working memory capacity. It was assumed that the processes involved in comprehending the sentences require a smaller proportion of the available working memory capacity of those with a large capacity. As a result, they have more capacity available for retaining the last words of the sentences.

It has been shown that working memory capacity as measured by reading span is fairly closely associated with intelligence. For example, Conway, Kane, and Engle (2003) reviewed research on working memory capacity and general intelligence. They found that the typical correlation was about +0.6, indicating that the two constructs, while by no means identical, are nevertheless similar.

Evaluation of the working memory model

- Strength: The working memory model is an advance on the account of short-term memory provided by the short-term store, in part because it is concerned with both active processing and the brief storage of information. As a result, it is relevant to activities such as mental arithmetic, verbal reasoning, and comprehension, as well as to traditional short-term memory tasks. In other words, it is much more than just a theory of memory.
- Strength: The working memory model views verbal rehearsal as an *optional* process occurring within the phonological or articulatory loop, which doesn't

KEY TERM

Reading span: the largest number of sentences read for comprehension from which an individual can recall all the final words more than 50% of the time; it is used as a measure of working memory capacity.

have to be used to remember things. Information in working memory can be processed without involving rehearsal. This view is more realistic than the central importance of verbal rehearsal in the multi-store model.

- Strength: Performance on almost any task of any complexity depends on some combination of the three major components of the working memory model, indicating that they are particularly important parts of the human cognitive processing system. For example, we saw that choosing moves at chess depends very much on the central executive and visuo-spatial sketchpad (Robbins et al., 1996).

- Strength: There is convincing evidence that all of the components of the working memory model are important in everyday life. This is especially true of the central executive—brain-damaged individuals with dysexecutive syndrome have enormous difficulties in coping with other people and with the environment. It is also noteworthy that working memory capacity correlates moderately highly with intelligence.

- Strength: Knowledge of the functioning of the working memory system can be used for the benefit of brain-damaged individuals. They can be taught how to make the best use of those components of the working memory system that are still functioning reasonably well.

- Weakness: Relatively little is known about the central executive. It has limited capacity, but this capacity has not been measured with precision. It is argued that the central executive is "modality-free" (i.e. it does not rely on any specific way of receiving information, such as sound or vision) and is used in many different processing operations. However, the details of its functioning remain unclear.

- Weakness: It was originally proposed that the central executive was unitary in the sense that it "spoke with one voice". However, it now appears that it fulfils at least three functions (Miyake et al., 2000; Stuss & Alexander, 2007). As yet, the number and nature of its functions are unclear.

- Weakness: The three main components of the working memory model undoubtedly interact with each other in the performance of many tasks. However, it is not very clear *how* this happens in practice.

- Weakness: The model is concerned with memory. However, it tells us very little about long-term memory and the ways in which processing in the working memory system relate to the long-term storage of information. In this respect, the working memory model is less informative than the multi-store model.

SECTION SUMMARY

❖ Learning and memory involve the retention of information, but the study of memory focuses on cognitive processes and retrieval.

❖ Memory tests assess learning.

❖ Psychologists distinguish between short-term and long-term memory in terms of:
  – capacity,
  – duration,
  – encoding.

What is memory?

Nature of short-term memory	❖ The short-term store is described as:
	  – having limited capacity of 7 plus or minus 2 chunks;
	  – having limited duration;
	  – using mainly acoustic coding.
	❖ Capacity: Span measures indicate an STM capacity of about 7 items but this can be increased by chunking. Capacity for STM can also be seen in the recency effect (higher recall for the last few items in a list).
	❖ Duration: The Brown–Peterson technique is a means of showing STM duration. If rehearsal is prevented, there is little recall beyond 18 seconds.
	❖ Encoding: This differs from long-term memory, which is more semantically coded.
	❖ Evidence about different kinds of short-term memory comes from the study of brain-damaged individuals, which also supports a distinction between short-term and long-term memory. However, it is hard to generalise from case studies.

Nature of long-term memory	❖ The long-term memory store is described as:
	  – having an unlimited capacity;
	  – lasting forever;
	  – using mainly semantic coding.
	❖ Capacity: Unlike in STM, we never reach the upper limit of the LTM store capacity.
	❖ Duration: Its duration has been shown in studies of VLTMs (very-long-term memories).
	❖ Encoding: This differs from long-term memory which is more acoustically coded.
	❖ Long-term memory can be divided into:
	  – Declarative knowledge: knowing that certain things are the case;
	  – Procedural knowledge: knowing how to do certain things (e.g. play the piano).

Multi-store model	❖ The multi-store model of memory supports the distinction between three separate stores and proposes that information is transferred from the short-term memory store to the long-term memory store by rehearsal.
	❖ This model has been criticised in that:
	  – Rehearsal is much less important in forming long-term memories than is assumed within the model.
	  – It is not correct that information always goes into short-term memory before long-term memory.
	  – The model is oversimplified in assuming there is only one short-term store and one long-term store.

Working memory model	❖ The working memory model consists of a central executive, a phonological loop, and a visuo-spatial sketchpad. ❖ Two tasks can be performed together without disruption if they use different components of working memory, but not if they use the same ones. ❖ The phonological loop is used when learning new words, the visuo-spatial sketchpad when finding a route or playing computer games, and the central executive for complex thinking and reasoning.

- ❖ Three of the functions of the central executive are as follows:
  - – inhibition function: this is used to reduce distraction effects;
  - – shifting function: this is used to shift attention from one task to another;
  - – updating function: this is used to update the information in working memory.
- ❖ Working memory is of fundamental importance in information processing and thinking, and working memory capacity is closely associated with intelligence.
- ❖ The working memory model has been criticised in that:
  - – The number and nature of the functions of the central executive remain unclear.
  - – We don't know in detail how the components of working memory interact with each other.
  - – The model is concerned with memory but tells us very little about long-term memory.

Eyewitness Testimony

In this section, our focus will be on a major practical application of our knowledge of human memory—**eyewitness testimony**. As Brown (1986, p. 258) pointed out, "Judges, defence attorneys and psychologists believe it to be just about the least trustworthy kind of evidence of guilt, whereas jurors have always found it *more* persuasive than any other sort of evidence." Brown's concerns were supported in a study by Wells, Liepe, and Ostrom (1979). Participants were told to wait in a cubicle before the start of the experiment. There was a calculator in the cubicle, and a *confederate* of the experimenter appeared and popped it into her purse while each participant waited. Only 58% of the participants correctly identified the "thief" from a set of six photographs. However, when the same participants were asked to "testify" at a mock trial, 80% of them were believed by the jury.

Eyewitness testimony has been found by psychologists to be extremely unreliable, yet jurors tend to find such testimony highly believable. This is very worrying. What can we do about it?

DNA tests can establish with virtual certainty who was responsible (or not responsible) for certain crimes. In the United States, about 200 people have been shown to be innocent by means of DNA tests, and more than 75% of them were found guilty on the basis of mistaken eyewitness identification. The 100th innocent American freed following DNA testing was Larry Mayes of Indiana. He was convicted of raping a cashier at a filling station after she identified him in court, and spent 21 years in prison for a crime he didn't commit (Loftus, 2004).

As you can imagine, the accuracy of eyewitness testimony depends on various factors. It seems reasonable to assume that children and older adults would tend to have less accurate memories than young adults. It also seems reasonable to assume that eyewitnesses who are very anxious might find it more difficult to

> **KEY TERM**
>
> **Eyewitness testimony**: an account or evidence provided by people who witnessed an event such as a crime, reporting from their memory. Research suggests that this evidence may not be factually accurate.

EXAM HINT

With regard to eyewitness testimony be ready to discuss two issues in essay questions:

- The reliability of eyewitness testimony.
- How research has helped to improve the reliability of eyewitness testimony.

KEY TERMS

Meta-analysis: a form of analysis in which the data from several related studies are combined to obtain an overall estimate.
Misleading information: incorrect information that may be given in good faith or deliberately (also known as misinformation).

remember what they have witnessed. We will consider these (and other) factors in our subsequent discussion.

Age of witness

Do you think the age of an eyewitness is relevant when deciding whether his/her memory for an event is likely to be accurate? I would guess that your answer is "Yes", and that you believe that young children and older people have greater memory problems than young and middle-aged adults. As we will see, most of the evidence supports those beliefs.

Children vs adults

Pozzulo and Lindsay (1998) carried out a **meta-analysis** combining the data from numerous studies on children and adults. They reported three main findings. First, young children up to the age of 5 were less likely than older children and adults to make correct identifications when the culprit was present in the line-up. Second, children over the age of 5 performed as well as adults at correct identifications when the culprit was present. Third, children up to the age of 13 were much more likely than adults to make a choice when the culprit was *not* present in the line-up. One reason for this is that children are more sensitive than adults to the social demands to make a choice.

There is much evidence that younger children are more suggestible than older ones. For example, Bronfenbrenner (1988) compared memory in young children (3 or 4 years old), older children (10, 11, or 12 years old), and adults, some of whom were provided with **misleading information** about an incident they had heard about previously. Two days after hearing about the incident, all the participants were tested for their memory of it. Memory performance was only slightly affected by age when no misleading information had been presented. In contrast, memory accuracy was much lower in younger than in older children when misleading information had been given.

Why are young children so inclined to produce systematically distorted reports of events when exposed to suggestive influences? There are two main possibilities (Bruck & Melnyk, 2004). First, young children may yield to social pressure and a lack of social support even when their own recollection is accurate. This is especially likely when they are being interviewed by someone much older than themselves. Second, there is cognitive incompetence. Young children may come to believe their own distorted memory reports because of limitations in processing, attention, or language. Evidence for this comes from the findings of several studies (Bruck & Melnyk, 2004). In these studies, children continued to produce false memories even after having been warned that the interviewer may have been mistaken in his/her suggestions.

Keast, Brewer, and Wells (2007) confirmed that children are much more likely than adults to choose someone when shown a line-up not containing the culprit. In addition, children were much more overconfident than adults in their ability to make correct memory decisions. This overconfidence could lead jurors to accept too readily what children claim to remember.

According to Keast, Brewer, and Wells (2007), children are much more likely than adults to choose someone from a line-up that does not actually contain a culprit.

HOW SCIENCE WORKS: MEMORY AND AGE

Do your parents remember what you tell them? Do your friends remember what you tell them? Is memory an age thing?

You could do a correlational analysis of memory and age, starting by constructing a simple STM memory game—perhaps a picture that could be looked at for 1 minute and then replaced by 20 questions about it. Careful planning of research is really important. For example, you need to write standardised instructions (and either read them out yourself or give them to each participant to read) so that every participant receives exactly the same information, in order to minimise investigator effects and extraneous variables. Ethical issues are also important, as outlined in the BPS Guidelines. You should test only participants aged over 16, as you would need written informed consent from parents if you used younger participants, an important ethical consideration in the UK. Another practical and ethical point is that you could state at the beginning of your instructions that you will need to know the participant's age in years—then if anyone doesn't want to tell you this personal information they can withdraw from your study and not waste their or your time, or feel obliged or stressed. If you have about 10 participants spread through four or five decades in age you could then present, analyse, and interpret the data by plotting a scattergram, with age in years on the horizontal axis and STM game score on the vertical axis. Then you could draw a line of best fit and see what correlation you get.

You will also recall that even a strong correlation does not infer a causal link—it might be a causal relationship between your two co-variables, or it might not. You could present your scattergram and conclusion to your class or group, and ask for non-causal explanations of your findings.

What can be done to enhance the memory accuracy of very young eyewitnesses? Some of the information that young children store away in memory after witnessing an event is likely to be in visual form rather than in the form of language. Accordingly, Gross and Hayne (1999) argued that it might be possible to improve matters by asking children to draw what they could remember about an event before asking them to provide a verbal report. Children aged 5 and 6 visited Cadbury's chocolate factory and were taken there by a woman wearing a purple suit who called herself "Charlie Chocolate". Memory for the event was tested 1 day and 6 months later. Children who had produced drawings recalled about 30% more information in their verbal reports than did children who hadn't produced a drawing.

Older vs younger adults

Brewer, Weber, and Semmler (2005) reviewed research on eyewitness identification in older people (in the 60- to 80-year-old range). Older people are more likely than younger adults to choose someone from a line-up even when the culprit is not present. In addition, older people are strongly influenced by misleading suggestions. In one study (Mueller-Johnson & Ceci, 2004), older adults with an average age of 76 and young adults (average age 20) underwent relaxation techniques including body massage and aromatherapy. Several weeks later, the participants were given misleading information (e.g. that they had been massaged on parts of their body that had not been touched). The misleading information distorted the memories of the older adults much more than those of the young adults.

Dodson and Krueger (2006) showed a video to younger and older adults, who later completed a questionnaire that misleadingly referred to events not shown on the video. The older adults were more likely than the younger ones to produce false memories triggered by the misleading suggestions. Worryingly, the older adults tended to be very confident about the correctness of their false memories. In contrast, the younger adults were generally rather uncertain about the accuracy of their false memories.

? Do you remember saying what you thought adults wanted to hear when you were young? Did this happen often? Do you think you would be able, now, to speak out your real opinion even if it was going to disappoint the other person?

"Well I know he was wearing tights."

Wright and Stroud (2002) considered differences between younger and older adults who tried to identify the culprits after being presented with crime videos. They found an "own age bias", with both groups being more accurate at identification when the culprit was of a similar age to themselves. Thus, older adults' generally poorer eyewitness memory is less noticeable when the culprit is an older person, perhaps because they pay more attention to the facial and other features of culprits the same age as themselves.

What can be done to enhance the memory of older adults? One of the central memory problems that older adults have is that their memories are very easily distorted by misleading or interfering information. For example, Jacoby et al. (2005) presented misleading information to younger and older adults. On a subsequent test of recall, older adults had a 43% chance of producing false memories based on the misleading information compared to only 4% for the younger adults. Two recommendations follow from the findings of this and other studies. First, it is even more important with older adults than with younger ones to ensure that they are not exposed to any misleading information that might distort their memory. Second, older adults often produce memories that are genuine in the sense that they are based on information or events to which they have been exposed. The problem specifically is that older adults often misremember the context or circumstances in which the information was encountered. Thus, it is essential to engage in detailed questioning with older adults to decide whether remembered events actually occurred at the time of the crime or other incident.

> **EXAM HINT**
>
> Age has an important effect on EWT. When revising make sure you know the following:
>
> (a) How young children and younger adults differ in terms of:
>   - likelihood of choosing the wrong person from a line-up;
>   - suggestibility;
>   - confidence that their false memory is correct.
> (b) How younger adults and older adults differ in terms of:
>   - likelihood of identifying the wrong person from a line-up;
>   - effect of misleading suggestions;
>   - confidence that their false memory is correct.
>
> Also ensure that you know how the memory of young people and older adults can be enhanced.

Anxiety

Eyewitnesses (especially if they are also victims) are often very anxious and stressed during the witnessing of a crime because of the potential danger to themselves. Before discussing the effects of anxiety on eyewitness memory, we need to consider two points. First, eyewitnesses remember attended aspects of the crime situation much better than non-attended aspects. Since the precise details of the crime situation determine what an eyewitness is likely to attend to, we must be beware of simple generalisations. Second, while the threat or danger in which the eyewitness is placed is the main factor determining his/her level of anxiety, it is not the only one. Eyewitnesses who have an anxious personality are likely to experience more anxiety in a given crime situation than those who do not.

It seems reasonable to assume that eyewitnesses exposed to a violent crime will attend mainly to those aspects of the situation most directly posing a threat. This assumption lies behind research on **weapon focus**—high levels of attention to (and good memory for) the criminal's weapon but not other information in the situation. Loftus (1979) discussed a study in which some participants overheard a hostile and aggressive argument between two people followed by one of them emerging holding a letter opener covered with blood. Other participants overheard a harmless conversation between two people followed by one of them emerging holding a pen. When participants tried to identify the culprit from a set of photographs, only 33% of those in the weapon condition did so compared to 49% in the other condition. This shows weapon focus.

Loftus, Loftus, and Messo (1987) asked participants to watch one of two sequences:

1. A person pointing a gun at a cashier and receiving some cash.
2. A person passing a cheque to the cashier and receiving some cash.

Eyewitnesses looked more at the gun than they did at the cheque (weapon focus). As a result, memory for details unrelated to the gun/cheque was poorer in the weapon condition.

We need to be somewhat cautious about accepting findings on weapon focus at face value for two reasons. First, it is possible that a weapon attracts attention because it is unusual (or unexpected) in most of the contexts in which it is seen by eyewitnesses as well as because it poses a threat. Pickel (1999) found no evidence of weapon focus when eyewitnesses saw someone pointing a gun in a situation (a shooting range) in which guns are expected. Second, most of the research has been laboratory based. Valentine, Pickering, and Darling (2003) considered the evidence from over 300 line-ups and found the presence of a weapon had no effect on the probability of an eyewitness identifying the suspect.

Deffenbacher et al. (2004) carried out meta-analyses combining findings from numerous studies on the effects of anxiety and stress on eyewitness memory. In the first meta-analysis, they considered the effects of anxiety and stress on accuracy of face identification. Average correct identifications were 54% for low anxiety or stress conditions compared to 42% for high anxiety or stress conditions. Thus, heightened anxiety and stress have a definite negative impact on

KEY TERM

Weapon focus: the finding that eyewitnesses pay so much attention to a weapon that they ignore other details and so can't remember them.

Eyewitness memory can be impaired by misleading post-event information. However, important information, such as the weapon used in a crime, is less likely to be distorted than trivial information.

? Why might very anxious people not remember so much about the inoculating nurse?

eyewitness identification accuracy. In the second meta-analysis, Deffenbacher et al. considered the effects of anxiety and stress on eyewitness recall of culprit details, crime scene details, and actions of central characters. The average percentage of details correctly recalled was 64% in low anxiety or stress conditions compared to 52% in high anxiety or stress conditions. This difference indicates that high anxiety or stress reduces the ability of eyewitnesses to remember details of a crime.

The importance of considering individual differences in anxiety was shown by Bothwell et al. (1987) and by Peters (1988). Bothwell et al. compared groups low and high in the personality dimension of neuroticism (high scorers tend to be very anxious). When the stress level was low, 68% of those high in neuroticism and 50% of those low in neuroticism correctly identified the culprit. In contrast, when the stress level was high, only 32% of those high in neuroticism identified the culprit, much lower than the figure of 75% for those low in neuroticism. Thus, individuals who were extremely anxious (high neuroticism + high stress condition) had much worse memory than any other group.

In the study by Peters (1988), students received an inoculation and had their pulse taken 2 minutes later. Two groups were formed: (1) those whose heart rate was much higher during inoculation than 2 minutes later (high reactive); and (2) those whose heart rate was similar on both occasions (low reactive). Identification accuracy for the inoculating nurse was 31% for the high-reactive group and 59% for the low-reactive group. Thus, participants who regarded the inoculation as a stressful and anxiety-provoking procedure showed much worse memory than those who regarded it as innocuous.

In sum, anxiety and stress have mostly negative effects on eyewitness memory. That is the case for both identification of the culprit and for memory of details of the crime and the culprit. However, it is important to note that anxiety affects what eyewitnesses attend to as well as how much they can remember. Eyewitnesses who are terrified by the criminal's gun or knife are likely to attend closely to it. As a result, they will have excellent memory for the weapon but not for other details (the weapon effect).

Relevance of laboratory findings

How well do laboratory findings on eyewitness testimony apply to the real world? Doubts have been raised because there are several important differences between eyewitnesses' typical experiences in the laboratory and when observing a real-life crime. First, in the overwhelming majority of laboratory studies, the event in question is observed by eyewitnesses rather than by the victim or victims. This is very different from real-life crimes, where evidence is much more likely to be provided by the victim than by eyewitnesses. Second, it is obviously less stressful and anxiety-provoking to watch a video of a violent crime than to experience a real-life violent crime (especially from the perspective of the victim). Third, in laboratory experiments on face memory, participants typically have only a few seconds to study each face. In contrast, with real-life crimes, eyewitnesses and victims have on average between 5 and 10 minutes' exposure to the criminal (Moore, Ebbesen, & Konecni, 1994). Fourth, in laboratory research the consequences of an eyewitness making a mistaken identification are trivial (e.g. disappointment at his/her poor memory). In contrast, they can literally be a matter of life or death in an American court of law.

We have seen that there are several differences between observers' experiences in the laboratory and in real life. However, what is of crucial importance is whether these differences have large effects on the accuracy of eyewitness memory. Evidence that they may not was reported by Ihlebaek et al. (2003). They made use of a staged robbery involving two robbers armed with handguns. In the live condition, the eyewitnesses were ordered repeatedly to "Stay down!". A video taken during the live condition was presented to eyewitnesses in the video condition. Participants in both conditions exaggerated the duration of the event. In addition, the patterns of memory performance (i.e. what was well and poorly remembered) were similar in both conditions. However, eyewitnesses in the video condition estimated the age, height, and weight of each robber more closely, and also identified the robbers' weapons more accurately. These findings suggest that witnesses to real-life events are more inaccurate in their memories of those events than those observing the same events in the laboratory. If confirmed, it means that the inaccuracies and distortions in eyewitness memory obtained under laboratory conditions *underestimate* eyewitnesses' memory deficiencies for real-life events and are not simply artificial errors.

Tollestrup, Turtle, and Yuille (1994) analysed police records on identifications by eyewitnesses to crimes involving fraud and robbery. They discovered that factors shown to be important in laboratory studies (e.g. weapon focus; poorer memory at longer time intervals) were also important in real-life crimes.

Misleading Information and the Use of the Cognitive Interview

Misleading information

One obvious reason why eyewitness testimony is so unreliable is because the events witnessed are typically unexpected. As a result, eyewitnesses may not be paying close attention to what is going on. A less obvious reason is that the memories eyewitnesses have of an event are fragile, so can easily be distorted and made inaccurate by the questions asked of an eyewitness. The most celebrated study in the whole history of research on eyewitness testimony was by Elizabeth Loftus and John Palmer (1974), and it was on precisely this issue. Participants were shown a film of a multiple-car accident. After viewing the film, they described what had happened and then answered some specific questions. Some were asked, "About how fast were the cars going when they hit each other?" whereas for other participants the word "hit" was replaced by "smashed into". Control

Loftus and Palmer (1974) found that assessment of the speed of a videotaped car crash and recollection of whether there was broken glass present were affected by the verb used to ask the question. Use of the verbs "hit" and "smash" have different connotations as shown in (a) and (b).

participants weren't asked a question about car speed. The estimated speed was affected by the verb used in the question, averaging 41 mph when the verb "smashed" was used versus 34 mph when "hit" was used. Thus, the information contained in the question influenced how the accident was remembered.

One week later, all of the participants were asked, "Did you see any glass?" There wasn't actually any glass in the film of the accident. However, 32% of those who had previously been asked about speed using the verb "smashed" said they had seen broken glass (see Figure overleaf). In contrast, only 14% of the participants

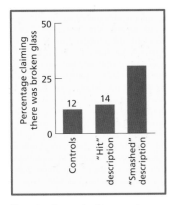

Results from Loftus and Palmer's (1974) study showing how the verb used in the initial description of a car accident affected recall of the incident after 1 week.

See *AS Level Psychology Online* for stimulus material suggesting how to do a variation of Loftus and Palmer's (1974) classic study.

previously questioned with the verb "hit" said they had seen broken glass, and the figure was 12% for the control participants. Thus, our memory for events is so fragile that it can be distorted by changing *one* word in *one* question!

Further evidence that apparently trivial differences in the way in which a question is asked can have a clear effect on the answers produced was reported by Loftus and Zanni (1975). They showed people a short film of a car accident, and then asked them various questions. Some eyewitnesses were asked, "Did you see a broken headlight?", whereas others were asked, "Did you see the broken headlight?" In fact, there was no broken headlight, but the latter question implied that there was. Only 7% of those asked about *a* broken headlight said they had seen it compared to 17% asked about *the* broken headlight.

The tendency for eyewitness memory to be influenced by misleading information provided after the event is very strong. Eakin, Schreiber, and Sergent-Marshall (2003) showed participants slides of a maintenance man repairing a chair in an office and stealing some money and a calculator. Eyewitness memory was impaired by misleading post-event information in the form of a narrative about the event that participants read after watching the slides. More surprisingly, memory was impaired even when the eyewitnesses were warned immediately about the presence of misleading information and told to disregard any details they remembered reading in the narrative.

We have just seen that eyewitness memory can be distorted by misleading information presented *after* an event or incident. There is also evidence that eyewitness memory can be distorted by misleading information presented *before* the event. Lindsay et al. (2004) showed eyewitnesses a video of a museum burglary. On the previous day, they had listened to a narrative that was either thematically similar (a palace burglary) or thematically dissimilar (a school trip to a palace) to the video. Eyewitnesses made many more errors when recalling information from the video when the narrative was thematically similar than when it was thematically dissimilar. This is potentially an important finding. In the real world, eyewitnesses often have some experiences of relevance to the questions they are asked about the event or crime, and these experiences may distort their answers.

Why does misleading information distort what eyewitnesses report? One possibility is that eyewitnesses in experiments are simply responding to social pressures (e.g. to please the experimenter). However, that seems unlikely. If that were the main reason, then eyewitnesses would presumably be less influenced by misleading information if they were offered money for being accurate in their recollections of an incident. In fact, Loftus (1979) found that participants offered $25 for accurate memory were just as influenced by misleading information as those offered no reward. What seems more likely is that there is misinformation acceptance (Loftus, 1992). Eyewitnesses "accept" misleading information presented to them after an event and subsequently regard it as forming part of their memory for that event.

Although the majority of studies show that eyewitness memory can be unreliable and can be distorted, some studies show that real-life recall can be very accurate. One such study is by Yuille and Cutshall (1986). They interviewed people who had witnessed a crime where one person was shot dead and another person seriously injured. These interviews (given some months later), along with interviews given to the police immediately after the incident, were analysed.

? Why do people still believe eyewitnesses when we know memory is faulty?

The eyewitness accounts were found to be very accurate, and the accuracy and amount of information recalled didn't diminish over time. The eyewitnesses' accounts were also not distorted by leading questions. Yuille and Cutshall concluded that laboratory studies such as those outlined above are not always generalisable to real life (i.e. Yuille and Cutshall's study has more external validity) and that more field research is needed.

There is another limitation with research on the effects of post-event information on eyewitness memory. What has typically been found is that such information can distort memory of relatively minor details (e.g. broken glass). Heath and Erickson (1998) found that there was less memory distortion for central or important details than for trivial ones. This may limit the practical importance of this line of research.

Reconstructive nature of memory

One of the most influential ways of understanding the unreliability of eyewitness memory is based on the ideas of Sir Frederic Bartlett (1932). One of his central ideas was the notion of **schema**, which is an organised package of information containing certain knowledge about the world. Schemas are stored in long-term memory and help us to make sense of the world. Your schemas tell you that if you were wearing a short-sleeved shirt it was likely to be summer. Bower, Black, and Turner (1979) showed that most people share similar schemas. Several people listed the most important events associated with having a restaurant meal. Most included the following events: sitting down, looking at the menu, ordering, eating, paying the bill, and leaving the restaurant.

According to Bartlett (1932), memory does *not* simply involve remembering the information presented to us. He claimed that our prior knowledge in the form of schemas influences what we remember and how we remember it. More specifically, Bartlett believed in reconstructive memory, with memory being an active process in which what we remember depends on the information we were exposed to at the time of learning *and* our relevant schematic knowledge. The impact of schematic knowledge means that what we recall is sometimes in error—it is consistent with one of our schemas but does not correspond precisely to what we learned. In other words, we sometimes fill in the gaps in our memory on the basis of what we *think* might have happened. What we think might have happened often depends on schemas known as stereotypes (oversimplified generalisations about certain groups). For example, your stereotypical knowledge might lead you not to expect that a little old woman wearing a suit would commit a crime. As a result, you might "recall" that it was a man rather than a woman.

Tuckey and Brewer (2003a, 2003b) obtained evidence showing how Bartlett's views could account for some of the memory errors made by eyewitnesses. Tuckey and Brewer (2003a) obtained information about people's bank robbery schema, which typically included the following aspects: robbers are male; they wear disguises; they wear dark clothes; they make demands for money; and they have a getaway car with a driver in it. Tuckey and Brewer (2003b) made use of this information in their study. Eyewitnesses tried to recall the details of a simulated crime they had observed. What was of interest was how they remembered ambiguous information. As predicted, eyewitnesses tended to interpret the ambiguous information as being consistent with their crime schema. This led

Can you imagine elderly ladies like these committing a robbery? Our stereotypical schemas may influence expectations of what a person is likely to wear, say, do, and so on.

KEY TERM

Schema: an "organised" packet of information about the world, events, or people that is stored in long-term memory. For example, most people have a schema containing information about the normal sequence of events when having a meal in a restaura

In a study by Allport and Postman (1947) participants were shown this picture. Later they were more likely to recall that the black man was holding the razor, presumably because this fitted in with the stereotype at the time.

them to make memory errors based on information that was contained in the crime schema but not in the crime they had observed.

There is no doubt that people's memory can be distorted by schemas. We sometimes "remember" information that is consistent with our schematic knowledge but didn't actually happen. However, schema theory often fails to make clear predictions. We often don't know what schemas someone is using to understand or to recall information. This limits our ability to predict *what* they will remember and *how* they will remember it.

Use of the cognitive interview

Many innocent people have been put in prison purely on the basis of eyewitness testimony. Mistakes by eyewitnesses may occur because of what happens at the time of the crime or incident, or because of what happens afterwards. It follows from what we discussed in the previous section on misleading information that the questions asked during a police interview may distort an eyewitness's memory, and thus reduce its reliability. What happened at one time in the United Kingdom was that an eyewitness's account of what happened was often repeatedly interrupted. The interruptions made it hard for the eyewitness to concentrate fully on the process of recalling the event, and thus reduced recall. As a result of psychological research, the Home Office issued guidelines recommending that police interviews should proceed from free recall (i.e. spontaneous reporting of what was remembered) to general open-ended questions, concluding with more specific questions. That has the advantage of reducing the chances of eyewitness memory being distorted by misleading information, but psychologists have gone further and developed even more effective interview techniques.

Geiselman et al. (1985) argued that interview techniques should take account of some basic characteristics of human memory:

- Memory traces are complex, and contain various features and/or kinds of information.
- The effectiveness of a retrieval cue depends on the extent to which the information it contains is *similar* to information stored in the memory trace. For example, if you wanted to remember the events of your early childhood, visiting the area in which you lived at that time would probably provide good retrieval cues.
- Various retrieval cues may permit access to any given memory trace. For example, an eyewitness may remember additional information if they imagine themselves viewing the crime or incident from the perspective of another eyewitness who was also present.

Geiselman et al. (1985) used the above considerations to develop the basic **cognitive interview**. The eyewitness tries to recreate mentally the context that existed at the time of the crime, including environmental and internal (e.g. mood state) information. The eyewitness then simply reports everything he/she can think of relating to the incident, even if the information is fragmented. In addition, the eyewitness reports the details of the incident in various orders and from various perspectives (e.g. that of another eyewitness).

Geiselman et al. (1985) compared the effectiveness of the basic cognitive interview with that of the standard police interview. The average number of correct statements produced by eyewitnesses was 41.1 using the basic cognitive interview compared to only 29.4 using the standard police interview. Fisher et al. (1987) devised the enhanced cognitive interview. This makes use of the following recommendations (Roy, 1991, p. 399):

Investigations should minimise distractions, induce the eyewitness to speak slowly, allow a pause between the response and next question, tailor language to suit the individual eyewitness, follow up with interpretive comment, try to reduce eyewitness anxiety, avoid judgmental and personal comments, and always review the eyewitness's description of events or people under investigation.

Fisher et al. (1987) found that the enhanced cognitive interview was more effective than the basic cognitive interview. Eyewitnesses produced an average of 57.5 correct statements when given the enhanced interview compared to 39.6 with the basic cognitive interview. However, there were 28% more incorrect statements with the enhanced interview. Fisher et al.'s findings were obtained under artificial laboratory conditions. Fisher, Geiselman, and Amador (1990) trained detectives in the Robbery Division of Metro-Dade Police Department in Miami in the techniques of the enhanced cognitive interview. Training produced an average increase of 46% in the number of pieces of information elicited from eyewitnesses at interview. Where confirmation was possible, over 90% of these pieces of information were shown to be accurate.

Evidence that the enhanced cognitive interview is generally very effective was reported by Kohnken et al. (1999) in a meta-analysis combining data from over 50 studies. The enhanced cognitive interview consistently elicited more correct information than standard police interviews. Indeed, the average eyewitness given an enhanced cognitive interview produced more correct items of information than 81% of eyewitnesses given a standard interview. However, there was a small cost in terms of reduced accuracy. The average eyewitness given an enhanced cognitive interview produced more errors than 61% of those given a standard interview.

How should we evaluate the cognitive interview? It has clearly proved to be very successful in increasing the amount of information about crimes that can be obtained from eyewitnesses. However, three points need to be made. First, it is somewhat worrying that there is a small increase in the amount of incorrect information provided by witnesses when the cognitive interview is used. Second, the cognitive interview is generally less effective at enhancing recall when used at longer intervals of time after the crime or incident (Geiselman & Fisher, 1997). That means that eyewitnesses should be interviewed as soon as possible after the

> **?** Have you had the experience of not being able to remember something until you found a clue to cue that memory, like running upstairs to get something and then being unable to remember what it was until you were back in the kitchen again? What was the memory cue in your own example?

crime or incident. Third, the cognitive interview contains several components, and it is not very clear whether all of them contribute to the success of the technique. However, Milne and Bull (2002) found that four components (context reinstatement; change perspective; change order; and report everything) all had roughly equal beneficial effects on eyewitness recall by children and young adults.

Memory Improvement

Nearly everyone complains about their memory. In spite of the power and elegance of the human memory system, it is not infallible and we have to learn to live with that fallibility. However, we can improve our memory, and some of the main ways are discussed here. Hopefully, you will find the material to be discussed of interest not only as a topic in psychology but also as the source of practical tips about improving your memory to cope more effectively with exams!

Organisation

The single most important principle if you want to improve your memory is to make full use of your pre-existing knowledge when learning something new. This is important because using pre-existing knowledge makes it much easier to organise the information you are trying to learn. "Organisation" is a somewhat vague notion, but here is Mandler's (1967, p. 330) definition of it: "A set of objects or events are said to be organised when a consistent relation among the members of the set can be specified and, specifically, when membership of the objects or events in subsets (groups, concepts, categories, chunks) is stable and identifiable."

It is very important to realise that organisation is *not* the only factor that is important in improving memory. Relating what you want to learn to what you already know is also very important. In addition, as we say in Chapter 1 (page 7) with the findings of Roediger and Karpicke (2006), simply practising recall of to-be-remembered material can improve memory by up to about 50%.

As we will see, there are many different ways in which psychologists have studied the role of organisation in memory. We will start by considering studies in which the material itself is arranged so that it is generally fairly easy for the learner to organise it. We then move on to studies that have focused on our ability to organise information during learning even when the learning material consists of random words. Such studies show how powerful the tendency is for us to *impose* organisation on what we are learning. Finally, we discuss studies on organisation in memory in which learners are provided with special strategies or methods allowing them to organise even random information very efficiently.

Organisation in the learning material

We can see clearly the importance of organisation and knowledge in studies carried out using categorised word lists (see Activity). For example, a categorised word list might consist of four words belonging to each of six categories (e.g. four-footed animals; articles of furniture; girls' names; birds; sports; and cities).

One group is presented with the words neatly organised into their categories, whereas another group is presented with the words in random order. After the list has been presented, all participants recall as many words as possible in any order (this is free recall). There are three key findings (Shuell, 1969). First, recall is much higher when the words are presented in an organised way than when they are not. Second, participants given the organised list typically recall the words category by category (this is known as **categorical clustering**), and those given the random list also show evidence of categorical clustering. Third, those participants who show the greatest categorical clustering recall more words than those who show the least categorical clustering whether they received the list in an organised or random order. Thus, how much you can remember depends very much on the extent to which you can use your knowledge (e.g. of categories) to organise that information during learning and retrieval.

How do people make use of their knowledge of categories to enhance their recall of categorised word lists? One possibility is that organisation is used at the time of learning or storage. Another possibility is that organisation is used at the time of retrieval and recall (e.g. with category names being used to generate recall of the members of each category). As we will see, organisation benefits learning *and* retrieval. Very direct evidence that organisational processes occur during learning was obtained by Weist (1972). He presented a categorised word list in a random order followed by a test of free recall. In addition, he introduced the novel twist of asking participants to rehearse out loud during learning, and he took a tape recording of their rehearsal. Rehearsal showed clear evidence that organisation into categories occurs during learning. The more organised the rehearsal was, the better the participant's recall tended to be.

Tulving and Pearlstone (1966) found that categorical information can increase retrieval. They presented lists of categorised word lists followed by free recall. After free recall, the participants were presented with the category names as retrieval cues and told to try again to recall the list words. Recall was much higher on the second attempt, especially when the list contained many categories. Thus, our knowledge of categories and the members of categories can be used to improve retrieval and recall.

Bower et al. (1969) provided a very clear illustration of the importance of organisation in memory. All participants were given four trials to learn and remember 112 words belonging to four hierarchies each of which had four levels. For one group, the words were presented in an organised way reflecting participants' knowledge (see Figure overleaf). In the other condition, the same 112 words were presented in an entirely random order. Memory performance was strikingly different in the two conditions (see Figure overleaf) being three and a half times greater in the organised condition than the random one on the first trial. Indeed, participants in the random condition recalled fewer words after four trials than those in the organised condition did after just one trial!

■ **Activity:** You can demonstrate that organisation aids memory by constructing two lists of the same words. List 1 will be a categorised word list containing a number of words belonging to each of several categories (e.g. four-footed animals; sports; flowers; articles of furniture). List 2 will consist of the same words but presented in a random order (e.g. golf, rose, cat, tennis, carnation, and so on). To avoid bias, you should allocate participants to conditions (list 1 or list 2) on a random basis. Give them a set time to study the list. After an interval (during which they should count backwards in threes to prevent rehearsal and to prevent recall from short-term memory), give them a test of free recall. You should find that participants given list 1 recall more words than those given list 2, and that they are much more likely to recall the words category by category. The conclusion is that organisation benefits memory.

KEY TERM

Categorical clustering: the tendency for categorised word lists (even with the words presented in random order) to be recalled category by category.

Bower et al. (1969) obtained strong evidence that the participants given the list of words in an organised way used the hierarchical structure in their recall. First, a higher-level category was almost always recalled *before* the members of that category. Second, participants who failed to recall a higher-level category typically had poor (or no) recall of the members of that category.

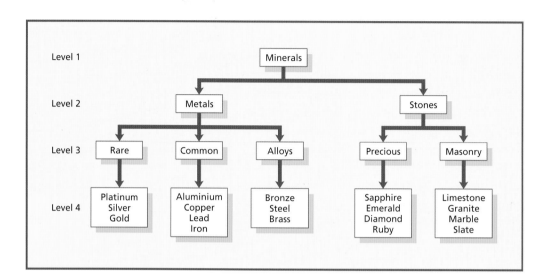

One of the hierarchies used by Bower et al. (1969).

Organising random words

So far we have seen that people are generally very good at organising categorised or hierarchical lists of words. What happens if we ask people to learn a list of *random* words that can't readily be organised into categories? Tulving (1962) answered this question in a study in which a random list of words was presented repeatedly for free recall with the words being presented in a different order on each trial. Any given participant tended increasingly to recall the words in roughly the same order, but this order varied across participants. The term **subjective organisation** was used to describe this phenomenon, which suggested that participants were imposing their own organisational structure on the random words. However, it wasn't clear how the participants went about the task of organising the random words.

Mandler (1967) showed in a different way how effectively people can organise a list of randomly selected words. Participants were given a pack of 52 cards, each of which had a word on it. Participants sorted the cards into piles having been told to use between two and seven categories according to any system they wanted. They were instructed to continue with the sorting task until they had assigned all the words to the same category on two different attempts at sorting. If anyone was still trying to achieve this after 1¼ hours they were excluded from the experiment! Most participants took about six sorts to gain 95% consistency. At this point, they were given an unexpected test of free recall. This memory test was unexpected because the participants hadn't been told to learn the words.

Mandler (1967) found that recall was poorest for those who had decided to use only two categories and best for those who used seven categories. There was an average increase of 3.9 words recalled per additional category used in sorting. According to Mandler, those participants using several categories in sorting imposed more organisation on the list than those who used only a few. This led Mandler (1967, p. 328) to conclude that "Memory and organisation are not only correlated, but organisation is a necessary condition for memory." There was clear evidence in recall that the words had been organised—the words tended to be recalled category by category.

You may be wondering why Mandler (1967) used a maximum of seven categories. When he allowed participants to use more than seven categories, he found they often completely forgot some of the categories in their recall. Thus, it is very hard to remember more than about seven categories, and the association between number of categories and recall breaks down. Earlier in the chapter, we discussed Miller's (1956) claim that the span of immediate memory is "seven, plus or minus two", and this seems to apply to memory for categories in long-term memory as well. The practical application of this is that when trying to remember a lot of information you should organise it into manageable-size chunks.

Can you spot any problems with the experiment we have just discussed? Bear in mind that the best way of carrying out an experiment is generally to assign participants *randomly* to the various conditions to ensure there are no systematic differences in the participants in each condition. However, Mandler (1967) allowed participants to *choose* which group to belong to. Perhaps those who used a larger number of categories simply had better memories than those who used a smaller number. In fact, that didn't turn out to be a real problem. Mandler (1967) carried out other experiments in which participants were randomly assigned to use two, three, four, five, six, or seven categories. Thankfully, the findings were very much the same—free recall went up progressively as the number of categories increased.

There are three other potential problems with Mandler's (1967) experimental approach. First, across various experiments, 21% of participants failed to sort the words consistently and so their data were excluded from analysis. We don't know whether these participants would have had the same relationship between number of categories and recall shown by the other participants. Second, across the experiments 26% of participants used categories that were essentially irrelevant to learning and memory. For example, some organised on the basis of the alphabet (e.g. one category might consist of all the words starting with A–D). These participants were excluded from analysis, but would probably have failed to show much relationship between number of categories and recall. Third, participants who used several categories might have taken more trials to sort the words consistently than those who used only a few categories, and this extra time might have allowed them to learn more about the list. In fact, however, there was only a modest association between number of trials and recall, so this problem had little effect on the findings.

There is another issue with Mandler's (1967) research and that concerns the interpretation of his findings. At a general level, learners who used several categories imposed more organisation and structure on the list to be learned than did those who only used a few categories. However, we don't know *precisely* what kinds of organisation and structure were involved.

Does organisation always enhance memory?

By now you may be convinced that organisation *always* improves memory. However, that is NOT the case, as we will see by considering the ideas of

■ **Activity:** In small groups, write your own schemas for the following:

• Catching a train
• Buying a newspaper
• Starting school

How easy was it to agree on a uniform pattern of events? Were any of the themes easier to agree on than the others? Why might this be?

See *AS Level Psychology Online* for stimulus material suggesting how to replicate Bartlett's (1932) classic study.

In Sulin and Dooling's (1974) study, participants used their schematic knowledge of Hitler to incorrectly organise the information about the story they had been told. The study revealed how schematic organisation can lead to errors in long-term memory and recall.

Bartlett (1932; discussed at more length on page 71). He focused on the notion of schema, which is an organised collection of knowledge about certain aspects of the world. For example, most students have an examination schema—they know that examinations involve written tests of their knowledge, that they will be given paper to write on, that the starting and finishing times will be announced, and that their papers will be collected up at the end. According to Bartlett, what we remember is influenced by our relevant schematic knowledge. This schematic knowledge provides a retrieval plan that assists us in thinking of the information we are trying to remember. However, we may "remember" information that fits our schematic knowledge but wasn't actually present at the time of learning.

Sulin and Dooling (1974) obtained evidence that schematic organisation can produce errors in memory. They presented participants with a story about an evil dictator. One group was told the story was about Adolf Hitler, whereas the other group was told it was about Gerald Martin. One week later, all the participants were given a recognition test on which they were presented with several sentences. They had to decide whether each sentence had been presented in the story. The crucial sentence was as follows: "He hated the Jews particularly and so persecuted them." Participants in the group told the story was about Adolf Hitler were much more likely to indicate (mistakenly) that the sentence had been in the story. This happened because those participants used their schematic knowledge of Hitler to organise the information in long-term memory, and this schematic knowledge led them into error.

There is a related phenomenon first shown by Deese (1959). He presented participants with lists of associated words such as the following: thread, pin, eye, sewing, sharp, point, pricked, thimble, haystack, pain, hurt, and injection. After each list, the participants were given a free recall test. The key finding was that a non-presented word closely associated with all of the list words (e.g. needle) was mistakenly recalled by a large proportion of the participants. Using recognition memory, McDermott and Roediger (1998) found that 57% of participants were sure they recognised a non-presented high associate compared to only 4% for a low associate of the presented words. It is generally assumed that this false memory effect occurs because participants' schematic knowledge leads them to believe the high associate had been presented. That assumption allows us to make a counterintuitive prediction. Young children have much less schematic knowledge than older ones, and so their memory should be *better* in the sense of being less susceptible to the false memory effect. Precisely that has been found in several studies (Brainerd & Reyna, 2004).

Mnemonic techniques

The world is full of books promising to improve your memory dramatically. As you might imagine, the authors of these books are inclined to exaggerate the effectiveness of the techniques they describe. However, many memory techniques *are* extremely effective. The term **mnemonic techniques** is used to refer to methods or systems devised to improve people's memory. There are more of these techniques than you could shake a stick at, but we will focus on the most important ones. We will divide them up into those that rely mainly on visual imagery and those that are mostly word based. It is important to note that while these techniques typically increase the organisation of the material to be learned, they depend mainly on using previous knowledge to facilitate the learning process. As you may have discovered to your cost, it can be very time consuming to learn and remember something totally new (e.g. how to use brand-new computer software).

Visual imagery mnemonic: Method of loci

Suppose you have to remember a list of 10 unrelated words such as the following: shirt; eagle; paperclip; rose; camera; mushroom; crocodile; handkerchief; sausage; and mayor. You would probably find the task reasonably difficult. However, you could probably do it easily if you organised the to-be-learned words using the **method of loci**. This involves associating the words with a series of locations well known to you. You could think of 10 locations in your home, choosing them so that the sequence of moving from one to the next is obvious—for example, front door to entrance hall to kitchen to bedroom, and so on. Check that you can imagine moving through your 10 locations in a consistent order without difficulty. Now think of the above 10 words in order and imagine them in those locations. You could imagine a shirt hanging on the knob of the door, an eagle perched on the lampshade in the entrance hall, and so on.

The method of loci is very effective. Bower (1973) compared recall of five lists of 20 nouns each for groups using or not using the method of loci. The former group recalled 72% of the nouns on average against only 28% for the latter group. Even more impressively, Ross and Lawrence (1968) found that people using the method of loci could recall more than 95% of a list of 40 or 50 items after a single study trial! The method of loci is so effective because it provides a way of organising random material in a way that makes use of pre-existing knowledge about sequences of locations. More specifically, it makes it much easier to *recall* the information, because you have a convenient cue (i.e. given location) for every word you are trying to remember.

The method of loci is clearly very useful if you are trying to remember a list of random words in order. However, it has often been argued that it is of little use when you are learning complex material in the real world. This issue was studied by De Beni, Moè,

KEY TERMS

Mnemonic techniques: artificial systems or methods that are used to enhance people's memory. The techniques all involve providing a structure so that even random material can be organised effectively at the time of learning, and they provide a retrieval structure (typically through the use of cues) that makes it easy to recall learned material.

Method of loci: a mnemonic technique in which various items of information are remembered by associating them with successive locations (e.g. along a favourite walk).

and Cornoldi (1997). They presented a 2000-word text orally or in written form to students, who used either the method of loci or rehearsal to remember the text. Memory was tested shortly after presentation and 1 week later. With oral presentation of the material, the method of loci led to greatly increased recall at both retention intervals, indicating that it was very effective with a lecture-style presentation. However, there was no effect of the learning method when the text was presented in written form. Presumably the method of loci was ineffective with written presentation because the visual nature of the presentation interfered with the use of visual imagery within the method of loci.

Evaluation

The method of loci provides a way of using previous knowledge and organising information that can be very effective in improving memory. It has mainly been used to facilitate the learning of lists of unrelated words. However, we have seen that it is also effective when people are trying to learn and remember an extended text presented orally (De Beni et al., 1997). It might be thought there would be interference and confusion if people used the method of loci with several different lists of words, but Bower's (1973) findings suggested that that is not the case. Note that a crucial reason why the method of loci is so effective is because it provides a very detailed set of retrieval cues (i.e. the locations) to assist the rememberer.

Here are the weaknesses of the method of loci:

- It is harder to use the method when the material to be remembered is abstract rather than concrete because abstract material doesn't lend itself to visual imagery.
- If the to-be-learned material is presented visually, there is a danger that it will interfere with the use of visual imagery that is needed with the method of loci (De Beni et al., 1997). Why doesn't visual presentation seem to cause a problem when learners use the method of loci with word lists? The reason is that learners don't have to engage in continuous visual processing of the words, thus permitting visual imagery to be used. In contrast, reading an extended text as in the De Beni et al. study requires almost constant visual processing.
- The method of loci involves treating each item to be learned (e.g. words; facts) separately from the others. This is fine if you want to learn a list of unrelated words, but would probably be less effective if you wanted to *integrate* the to-be-learned information in some way.
- You need reasonable visual imagery ability to use the method of loci, it is hard to recall any given item without working through the list, and it is hard to use if the information to be learned is presented rapidly. Finally, while the same locations can be used repeatedly with the method of loci, it becomes hard to recall anything other than the most recent list.

Visual imagery mnemonic: Pegword method

The **pegword method** resembles the method of loci in that it relies on visual imagery and allows you to remember sequences of 10 unrelated items in the

> **KEY TERM**
>
> **Pegword method**: a mnemonic technique in which each word on a to-be-learned list is associated with those from a previously memorised list; an interactive image is formed of each pair of words.

correct order—the method can be extended for longer sequences. As with the method of loci, it works largely because it makes use of your pre-existing knowledge.

Here's what is involved in the pegword method. First of all, you have to memorise 10 pegwords. Since each pegword rhymes with a number from one to ten, this is fairly easy. Try it for yourself.

One = *bun*   Two = *shoe*   Three = *tree*   Four = *door*
Five = *hive*   Six = *sticks*   Seven = *heaven*   Eight = *gate*
Nine = *wine*   Ten = *hen*

Having mastered this, you are ready to memorise 10 unrelated words. Suppose these are as follows: *battleship, pig, chair, sheep, castle, rug, grass, beach, milkmaid, binoculars*. Take the first pegword, bun (rhyming with one), and form an image of a *bun* interacting with *battleship*. You might, for example, imagine a battleship sailing into an enormous floating bun. Now take the second pegword, *shoe*, and imagine it interacting with *pig*, perhaps a large shoe with a pig sitting in it. Pegword three is *tree*, and the third word on the list is *chair*—you might imagine a chair wedged in the branches of a tree. Work through the rest of the items, forming an appropriate interactive image in each case. I am confident that when you have completed the task, you will be able to recall all 10 items in the correct order.

There is experimental evidence showing that the pegword method is very effective. For example, Morris and Reid (1970) found that twice as many words were recalled when the system was used than when it was not. It is effective because strong visual images are formed and because the pegwords themselves provide powerful retrieval cues when people are trying to remember the list.

There are various limitations with the pegword method. First, it requires fairly extensive training for it to be effective, especially if the words to be learned are presented rapidly. Second, the method is easier to use with concrete than with abstract material, because it can be very hard to form interactive images with abstract words. Third, the method can be very useful if you want to remember 10 random words in the correct order, but that is not necessarily a very useful skill in everyday life! Fourth, interference has sometimes been found when people use the pegword method to learn a list of words and are asked to re-learn the same list with the words re-assigned to different pegwords (Bellezza, 1982).

■ **Activity:** You can show that the pegword method is effective by comparing two groups of participants with *random* allocation to the two groups. One group receives training in the pegword method and the other group does not. Everyone is then presented with the same list of 10 unrelated concrete nouns [nouns referring to things you can see]. The list needs to be presented fairly slowly so that those in the pegword method group have time to form interactive images. When the list is finished, you could ask everyone to count backwards by threes for 10 seconds to prevent recall from short-term memory. Finally, everyone writes down as many words as possible IN THE CORRECT ORDER. You should find that the pegword method group does much better at this serial recall task. The conclusion is that the pegword method enhances memory because it provides an effective way of organising the material at learning and it also facilitates retrieval.

Verbal mnemonic: Story method

The **story method** is one of the most effective verbal mnemonics. It is used to remember a series of unrelated words in the correct order by linking them together within the context of a story. One of the main reasons why it is effective is that it imposes *meaning* on the material—a series of unrelated words doesn't

KEY TERM

Story method: a mnemonic technique in which a list of words is learned by linking them together within the context of a story.

naturally convey much meaning! I will show this method at work with the 10 words I used to illustrate use of the pegword method:

> *In the kitchen of the BATTLESHIP, there was a PIG that sat in a CHAIR. There was also a SHEEP that had previously lived in a CASTLE. In port, the sailors took a RUG and sat on the GRASS close to the BEACH. While there, they saw a MILKMAID watching them through her BINOCULARS.*

Bower and Clark (1969) showed that the story method can be extremely effective. They gave their participants the task of recalling 12 lists of 10 nouns each in the correct order when given the first word of each list as cues. Those who had constructed narrative stories recalled 93% of the words compared to only 13% for those who didn't do so. This is one of the largest differences in long-term memory between groups I have ever come across—learners using the story method recalled *seven* times as many words as the controls!

The story method has some limitations. First, it requires fairly extensive training—it took me as a novice a few minutes to construct the story given above! Second, it is hard to use if the information is presented rapidly. Third, you generally have to work your way through the list if you want to find a given item (e.g. the seventh one). Fourth, the ability to recall unrelated words in the correct order is of little general value.

Why do mnemonic techniques work?

Why are mnemonic techniques so effective? An important part of the answer is that they allow us to make use of our knowledge of the world around us. However, the full story is more complicated. Suppose we asked taxi drivers and students to recall lists of streets in the city in which they lived. We would expect that the taxi drivers (with their superb knowledge of the spatial layout of the city's streets) would always outperform the students. In fact, that is *not* the case. Kalakoski and Saariluoma (2001) asked Helsinki taxi drivers and students to recall lists of 15 Helsinki street names in the order presented. In one condition, the streets were connected and were presented in the order forming a spatially continuous route through the city. In this condition, the taxi drivers recalled 87% of the street names correctly against only 45% by the students. In another condition, non-adjacent street names taken from all over Helsinki were presented in a random order. This time there was no difference in recall between the taxi drivers and the students.

What can we conclude from the above findings? It is obvious that the taxi drivers knew considerably more than the students about the spatial structure of Helsinki's streets. This knowledge could be used effectively to facilitate learning and retrieval when all the streets were close together in that spatial structure. However, the taxi drivers couldn't use their special knowledge effectively to organise the to-be-remembered information when the street names were distributed randomly around the city.

Why are techniques such as the method of loci, the pegword method, and the story method so effective? Ericsson (1988) argued that there are three requirements if we are to achieve very high memory skills:

1. *Meaningful encoding*: the information should be processed meaningfully, relating it to pre-existing knowledge. This is clearly the case when you use

In Kalakoski and Saariluoma's (2001) study, taxi drivers exhibited a superior recall ability for a list of street names only when the street names were presented as a spatially continuous route through the city.

known locations (the method of loci) or the number sequence (pegword method), or when taxi drivers use their knowledge of their own town or city. This is the encoding principle.

2. *Retrieval structure*: cues should be stored with the information to aid subsequent retrieval. The connected series of locations or the number sequence both provide an immediately available retrieval structure, as does the knowledge of spatial layout possessed by taxi drivers. This is the retrieval structure principle.

3. *Speed-up*: extensive practice allows the processes involved in encoding and retrieval to function faster and faster. The importance of extensive practice can be seen in the generally superior memory for street names shown by taxi drivers compared to students in the study by Kalakoski and Saariluoma (2001). This is the speed-up principle.

Overview and evaluation of organisation, knowledge, and memory

We have discussed several ways in which the effects of organisation and pre-existing knowledge on learning and long-term memory have been studied. In spite of the diversity of the experimental approaches adopted, there are important common themes (see Figure). First, in every case, people use pre-existing knowledge to organise the to-be-learned material at the time of learning. This knowledge can take many different forms—it may be knowledge that nearly everyone possesses, it may be idiosyncratic knowledge, or it may be knowledge that has been specifically acquired to enhance memory (e.g. pegword method).

Organisation at learning	Organisational cues at retrieval
• Knowledge of categories: catagorised word lists	Category names: general
• Knowledge of hierarchies: hierarchical word lists	Levels within hierarchy: general
• Schematic knowledge	Schema-relevant cues: general
• Idiosyncratic knowledge: subjective organisation, Mandler's (1967) approach	Idiosyncratic cues: general
• Knowledge of locations	Location cues: specific
• Specially acquired knowledge, pegword method	Pegword cues: specific

Different approaches to studying organisation and memory. General cues are ones that cue several words, whereas specific cues are ones that cue only a single word.

Second, organisation provides a systematic retrieval plan that assists in the recall of the relevant information. The retrieval cues associated with the retrieval plan can be general or specific. General retrieval cues are relevant for several possible words. For example, the cue "four-footed animals" may lead us to think of dozens of four-footed animals. In contrast, specific retrieval cues are relevant for only one word. For example, using the pegword method, you may have formed an association between "bun" and "battleship". The cue "bun" *only* cues "battleship".

Here are the strengths of research on organisation and on the use of pre-existing knowledge in memory:

- All of the methods and techniques we have discussed are effective or very effective in improving memory in part because they capitalise on our previous knowledge.
- The effects that are observed occur in part because organisation enhances learning (meaningful encoding). That is perhaps especially the case with the story method.
- Use of mnemonic techniques such as the method of loci and the pegword method has the advantage that we can identify precisely the pre-existing knowledge that learners are using to enhance memory.

- The effects also occur because organisation provides a retrieval plan to assist recall.
- One of the key reasons why organisation benefits memory is because we have a limited ability to chunk information into more than about seven chunks (Mandler, 1967).
- Some of the techniques have fairly broad applicability in the real world. For example, the method of loci has been found to enhance memory for a 2000-word text presented orally (De Beni et al., 1997).

Here are the limitations of research on organisation and on the use of pre-existing knowledge in memory:

- The notion of "organisation" is somewhat vague. For example, it is not very clear whether the same organisational principles explain all of the findings we have discussed.
- We assume that learners use their pre-existing knowledge to organise lists of random words, but we really don't know *what* knowledge they are using or *why* they selected that particular knowledge.
- Some of the mnemonic techniques (e.g. method of loci; pegword method) are limited in that they can only readily be used with concrete material and when information at retrieval is accessed in a rigid order.
- Many of the methods are of limited applicability. For example, they typically don't allow for much integration of the to-be-learned material, and they are hard to apply to complex learning (e.g. mastering AS Psychology).
- We know that people are good at organising random words (e.g. subjective organisation; Mandler's approach), but we don't really know in detail how this is achieved.
- Organisation generally enhances memory. However, when the retrieval cues are general, there is a danger of an increase in the number of errors (e.g. Sulin & Dooling, 1974; McDermott & Roediger, 1998).

Mind maps

In recent years, there has been a substantial increase in the use of mind maps (Buzan & Buzan, 1993). A **mind map** can be defined as "a diagram used to represent words, ideas, tasks or other items linked to and arranged radially around a central key word or idea" (Wikipedia). A concrete example of a mind map is shown in the Figure. As you can see, information is presented in a very flexible way. However, the most important concepts and words are typically written in large letters fairly close to the central concept and the less important ones are written in smaller letters farther away from the central concept.

As we will see, several factors help to determine the effectiveness of mind maps. However, one of the main factors is undoubtedly that mind maps serve to organise and integrate the information that needs to be learned.

The available evidence suggests that mind maps are effective. Farrand, Hussain, and Hennessey (2002) presented medical students with a 600-word text that they were told to learn. Half had been trained in the mind-map technique and the others were simply instructed to use study techniques they had learned previously. One week after learning, students in the mind-map

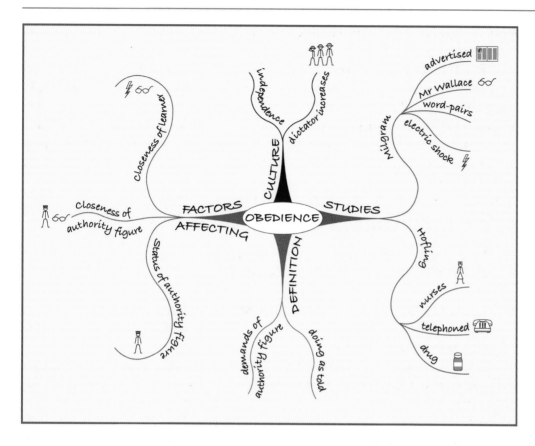

The beginnings of a mind map for obedience.

group recalled 10% more factual knowledge from the text than those using ordinary study techniques. Nesbit and Adescope (2006) carried out a meta-analysis combining the findings from 55 studies. The use of mind maps was consistently associated with increased knowledge retention among students of all ages studying a wide range of subjects including psychology, science, statistics, and nursing.

Hardy and Stadelhofer (2006) compared learning of science texts in students who were given expert-produced mind maps and those who constructed their own. Those given the expert-produced maps showed better learning. However, when both groups had to construct their own mind maps when learning new material, those who had previously developed expertise in constructing mind maps performed better.

Budd (2004) pointed out that many students don't seem to be very motivated when using mind maps. He found that those favouring a "doing" learning style felt they learned a lot from using mind maps, and rated the use of mind maps as highly as lectures. In contrast, students preferring a "thinking" learning style were less sure about the value of mind maps, and rated lectures much more favourably than the use of mind maps.

Mind maps seem to possess various advantages compared to the traditional approach based on note taking. First, students need to be actively involved in the learning process to produce satisfactory mind maps, whereas note taking often mainly involves writing down word for word phrases or sentences read in a textbook or spoken by the teacher. Second, the concepts contained within mind maps are shown as having several links or associations to each other. This makes it easier for the learner to organise the material effectively, and is

? Try making a mind map of the multi-store model, and then another of eyewitness testimony research and look to see where you have used categories more realistic and useful than the linear presentation of information in texts or conventional notes. It is interesting that a study on nursing students found that their initial mind maps consisted of a linear sequence of concepts but their later ones involved more complex patterns (Hsu & Hsieh, 2005). Third, each concept is typically reduced to one or two words within mind maps, thus reducing ideas to their essence. Note takers often include lots of trivial details. Fourth, mind maps provide striking visual images that may be easier to remember than conventional notes.

SECTION SUMMARY

Reliability of eyewitness testimony

❖ Eyewitness testimony is often inaccurate but is generally believed by jurors.

Factors affecting the accuracy of influencing eyewitness accuracy

❖ Age is an important factor influencing the accuracy of eyewitness testimony—young children and older adults are generally less accurate than young adults.
❖ High anxiety or stress lead to reduced ability of eyewitnesses to make accurate face identifications and to remember details of a crime.

Relevance of laboratory findings

❖ Doubts have been expressed about the value of laboratory findings for eyewitness testimony in the real world. However, most factors found to be important in the laboratory are also important in the real world.
❖ If anything, eyewitness inaccuracies and distortions observed in the laboratory underestimate the memory problems experienced by eyewitnesses to real crimes.

Misleading information and the use of the cognitive interview

❖ Eyewitness testimony can be distorted by misleading information presented before or after an incident.
❖ There is some evidence that misleading information has less of a negative impact with real-life crimes, and that memory distortions occur mainly to minor details rather than to information of central importance.
❖ Schema theory describes memory retrieval as a process of active reconstruction based on schemas. This can lead people to "remember" events that didn't happen but which are consistent with their schemas.
❖ The cognitive interview is used to enhance eyewitness memory. It involves mental recreation of the context at the time of the crime, reporting of all details, and recall in various orders and from different perspectives.
❖ The cognitive interview is an effective technique, but the enhanced cognitive interview (including minimising of distractions, avoidance of personal comments, and review of what the eyewitness says) is even more effective.
❖ There are some limitations with the cognitive interview:
  – it produces an increase in the amount of incorrect information recalled compared to standard techniques;
  – it is less effective when used at long intervals after a crime;
  – it is not very clear which components of the cognitive interview contribute most to its success.

❖ It is very important for learners to make full use of their pre-existing knowledge when learning something new, because this makes it much easier to organise the information.

❖ There are various forms of organisation, including organisation by categories and hierarchical organisation.

❖ Organisation is often used at the time of learning AND at the time of retrieval.

❖ Even lists of unrelated words can be organised—this is known as subjective organisation.

❖ Mandler (1967) found that learners who sorted a list of words into several categories recalled much more than those who used only a few. However, there are some problems with his approach:
  – the data from many participants had to be excluded because they didn't use meaningful categories or didn't sort the words consistently into categories;
  – Mandler generally didn't assign participants at random conditions varying in the number of categories;
  – it wasn't clear how participants were organising the list words.

❖ Organisation is not always effective—it can sometimes lead to an increase in the number of memory errors.

❖ The method of loci is one of the best known visual imagery techniques. It is very effective when the to-be-learned information is presented orally but not always when it is presented visually. It capitalises on the learner's pre-existing knowledge.

❖ There are some limitations with the method of loci:
  – it is hard to use with abstract material;
  – it doesn't produce integration of the to-be-learned material;
  – it is hard to recall any given item without working through the list.

❖ The pegword method is another visual imagery mnemonic that provides learners with the knowledge needed to memorise successfully. It is also very effective but suffers from similar limitations to the method of loci.

❖ The various mnemonic techniques work because they involve:
  – meaningful encoding;
  – retrieval structure;
  – speed-up.

❖ Mind maps can be very effective at enhancing memory, in part because they help to organise and integrate the information that needs to be learned. In addition, the learner is actively involved in the learning process.

Strategies for memory improvement

You have reached the end of the chapter on cognitive psychology. Cognitive psychology is an approach or perspective in psychology. The material in this chapter has exemplified the way that cognitive psychologists explain behaviour. They look at behaviour in terms of the way that it can be explained by reference to mental (cognitive) processes. This is sometimes regarded as a rather "mechanistic" approach to the study of behaviour because it focuses on machine-like processes and tends to exclude the influence of social or emotional factors.

See Chapter 2 of the revision guide for guidance on revising this chapter for the exam.

FURTHER READING

Most of the topics discussed in this chapter are dealt with in detail in M.W. Eysenck (2006) *Fundamentals of cognition* (Hove, UK: Psychology Press). There is a good account of the main factors influencing the accuracy of eyewitness testimony in G.L. Wells & E.A. Olson (2003) Eyewitness testimony (*Annual Review of Psychology, 54,* 277–295). Some of the reasons why eyewitness testimony is fallible are discussed by E.F. Loftus (2004) Memories of things unseen (*Current Directions in Psychological Science, 13,* 145–147). Several key topics in memory are discussed in an accessible way in J.A. Groeger (1997) *Memory and remembering: Everyday memory in context* (Harlow, UK: Addison Wesley Longman). Useful memory techniques are discussed by P.E. Morris & C.O. Fritz (2006) How to . . . improve your memory (*The Psychologist, 19,* 608–611). There is a thorough discussion of the strengths and limitations of numerous techniques and strategies designed to improve memory in F. McPherson (2004) *The memory key: Unlock the secrets to remembering* (New York: Barnes & Noble Books). K.A. Ericsson (2003) Exceptional memorisers: Made not born (*Trends in Cognitive Sciences, 7,* 233–235) focuses on the major processes involved in developing an exceptional memory.

WEBSITES

http://www.apa.org/releases/testing06.html
> Tests help improve memory: It seems those dreaded classroom tests are actually good for us!

http://www.apa.org/releases/mental_exercise.html
> Exercise age, play and memory: In mice, at any rate, exercise and play can improve memory.

http://www.sciencedaily.com/releases/2007/10/071025112103.htm
> Recognition and memory.

http://www.bbc.co.uk/science/humanbody/mind/articles/psychology/psychology_10.shtml
> A modern view on memory: ties sensory memory and working memory model.

http://www.bbc.co.uk/science/humanbody/mind/interactives/intelligenceandmemory/memorytest/
> Test and train your memory.

http://www.bbc.co.uk/radio4/memory/improve/
> More memory tips from the BBC Radio 4 site.

REVISION QUESTIONS

The examination questions aim to sample the material in this whole chapter. For advice on how to answer such questions refer to Chapter 1, Section 2.

When you are provided with a stimulus question do not panic if you have not seen that specific question before. Stimulus questions require you to apply your knowledge to a specific scenario. Whilst you may not have seen such a scenario before, if you have revised everything you *will* have the knowledge needed to answer the question.

Question 1
a. Outline key features of the multi-store model of memory.   (6 marks)
b. Explain **one** weakness of the multi-store model of memory.   (4 marks)

Question 2
a. Outline research into eyewitness testimony.   (6 marks)
b. Explain why studies of eyewitness testimony have been criticised as
    lacking validity.   (5 marks)

Question 3
a. Explain what is meant by encoding, capacity, and duration.   (6 marks)
b. Explain why studies into the above processes lack validity.   (5 marks)

Developmental psychology is an approach or perspective in psychology. It is concerned with the way people change as they get older. Some of these changes are innate—for example, puberty occurs as a result of a hormonal surge that is biologically driven. However, many of the changes that occur during development are a result of experience—for example, a girl learns many aspects of feminine behaviour by modelling herself on women around her. Therefore, developmental changes occur as a result of an interaction between innate factors (nature) and experience (nurture). Developmental psychologists aim to describe how children and adults develop and also to explain why they develop as they do.

SECTION 7
Attachment p. 91

When do infants first become attached? What is the sequence of attachment development, and are there individual differences and cultural variations? Are there theories that can account for why children form attachments, and why they become attached to one person rather than another? What happens when children are separated from their caregivers? In the short term, infants become anxious. We will consider how this subsequently influences the child's development. We will also explore the important distinction between deprivation (separation from caregivers) and privation (a lack of attachment).

Specification content: Explanations of attachment, including learning theory and evolutionary perspective, including Bowlby. Types of attachment, including insecure and secure attachment and studies by Ainsworth. Cultural variations in attachment. Disruption of attachment, failure to form attachment (privation) and the effects of institutionalisation.

SECTION 8
Attachment in everyday life p. 127

What are the effects (beneficial and adverse) of day care on children? Does the type of day care matter? We will focus on day care's effects on social development. We will also consider what should be done in terms of practices to ensure that day care has a positive impact on as many children as possible.

Specification content: The impact of different forms of day care on children's social development, including the effects on aggression and peer relations. Implications of research into attachment and day care for child-care practices.

DEVELOPMENTAL PSYCHOLOGY
Early Social Development

People develop attachments to all sorts of things—footwear, favourite restaurants, friends, lovers, and parents. You form attachments throughout your life, but among the most important ones are those that are formed early in development.

Attachment is like a piece of invisible string that binds individuals in a way that allows healthy development. The tie is reciprocal—parents are as attached to their children as the children are to their parents. Attachment is a central topic in developmental psychology. In this chapter we will consider how attachment develops and why it happens at all, as well as other related issues. One of these other issues is disruption of attachment, which happens when children are separated from their parent or caregiver. Such separation can involve deprivation, privation, and institutionalisation.

Finally, we move on the issue of day care and its effects on social development. This is an important issue because literally millions of young children in the United Kingdom and numerous other countries are placed into day care several days a week. The research carried out by psychologists on day care has important implications for child care practices, and these are considered in detail.

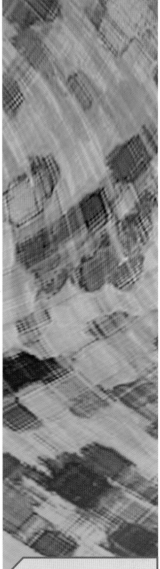

SECTION 7
ATTACHMENT

What is Attachment?

According to Shaffer (1993), an attachment is "a close emotional relationship between two persons, characterised by mutual affection and a desire to maintain proximity [closeness]". It is an emotional relationship experienced throughout the lifespan. When you are attached to someone, it makes you feel good to be in that person's company and also makes you feel anxious when they aren't there. You may also experience a longing to be reunited. This is the "desire to maintain proximity".

Maccoby (1980) identified four key behaviours of attachment:

- *Seeking proximity to primary caregiver.* The infant tries to stay close to its "attachment figure".
- *Distress on separation.* When caregiver and infant are separated, *both* experience feelings of distress.
- *Pleasure when reunited.* Obvious pleasure is shown when the child is reunited with his/her caregiver.

KEY TERM

Attachment: a strong, emotional bond between an infant and his or her caregiver(s) that is characterised by a desire to maintain proximity. Such bonds may be secure or insecure.

There are certain behaviours that characterise attachment: distress on separation, pleasure when reunited, seeking out the attachment figure, and general orientation to each other.

? In what way might the sample used by Schaffer and Emerson make it difficult to generalise from these data?

- *General orientation of behaviour towards primary caregiver*. The infant is aware of his/her caregiver at all times and may frequently make contact for reassurance.

The earliest attachment (that between an infant and his/her caregiver) has a special role to play in development, as we will see.

When Do Attachments Begin?

The stage approach is a popular way to describe how children develop—to identify the ages at which certain typical changes occur for the first time (e.g. crawling; walking; talking). Schaffer and Emerson (1964) argued that infants go through *three* stages in the early development of attachments to others (see box below). This theory was based on findings from their classic large-scale **longitudinal** study in which they followed 60 infants from a mainly working-class area of Glasgow over a period of 2 years. The infants were observed every 4 weeks until they were 1 year old and then again at 18 months. Attachment was measured in two ways:

- Using **separation protest** in seven everyday situations. The infant was left alone in a room, left with other people, left in his/her pram outside the house, left in his/her pram outside the shops, left in his/her cot at night, put down after being held by an adult, or passed by while sitting in his/her cot or chair.
- Using **stranger anxiety**. Every visit started with the researcher approaching the infant and noting the point at which the infant started to whimper, thus displaying anxiety.

Separation protest and stranger anxiety are signs that an attachment has been formed. Before this stage of specific attachments, infants show neither of these types of behaviour.

KEY TERMS

Longitudinal: over an extended period of time, especially with reference to studies.
Separation protest: the infant's behaviour when separated—crying or holding out their arms. Some insecurely attached infants show no protest when left by their attachment figure, whereas securely attached children do.
Stranger anxiety: the distress experienced by a child when approached by a stranger.

Stages of attachment

Asocial stage 0–6 weeks	Indiscriminate attachment 6 weeks–7 months	Specific attachments 7–11 months
Smiling and crying, not directed at any special individuals	Attention sought from different individuals	Strong attachment to one individual. Good attachments to others often follow

Schaffer and Emerson (1964) found that half of the children showed their first specific attachment between 25 and 32 weeks (6–8 months). Fear of strangers occurred about a month later in all of the children. In addition, the intensity of attachment peaked in the first month after attachment behaviour first appeared as assessed by the strength of separation protest. However, there were large individual differences. Intensely attached infants had mothers who responded quickly to their demands (high responsiveness) and who offered the child the most interaction, whereas infants who were weakly attached had mothers who failed to interact.

Soon after one main attachment was formed, the infants also became attached to other people. By 18 months very few (13%) were attached to only one person and 31% had five or more attachments such as the father, grandparent, or older sibling. In 65% of the children the first specific attachment was to the mother, and in a further 30% the mother was the first joint object of attachment. Finally, Schaffer and Emerson (1964) found that in 39% of cases the person who usually fed, bathed, and changed the infant was *not* his/her primary attachment object. Thus, many of the mothers (and some of the fathers) were not the person who performed these tasks yet they were the main attachment object.

Infants distrust strangers and cling to familiar people.

Some criticisms can be made of this study. The data were collected *either* by direct observation *or* from the record kept by the mothers, and both methods are prone to bias and inaccuracy. Mothers recorded situations in which separation protest was shown and indicated the person to whom these protests were shown. Busy mothers may have produced these records some days after the events in question. However, such data would have been more accurate than the much longer time periods over which participants tried to remember in other studies. They would have had more external validity than data collected under laboratory conditions (e.g. the Strange Situation, which is described shortly).

[?] Compare the method of measuring attachment behaviour used by Schaffer and Emerson with the methods used in the Strange Situation (see page 98).

Evaluation of Schaffer and Emerson's theory

Schaffer and Emerson's stage theory is generally correct. Most infants are easily comforted by almost anyone. As they get older, they are less willing to be separated from their caregiver and show **separation anxiety**. This is the main characteristic of being attached. We know when an infant is attached because he/she recognises the *absence* of an attachment figure and becomes anxious. Before an attachment has been formed, absence causes little concern. In addition, infants also start to show stranger anxiety—when a strange person comes close and tries to interact, the infant may withdraw and show signs of distress. Both of these forms of anxiety show that the infant has now formed schemas for known and unknown people, and has reached an emotional stage of development during which the unknown creates a fear response.

The asocial stage (the stage at which infants' emotional reactions aren't directed at specific individuals) may be less asocial than Schaffer and Emerson (1964) assumed. Even very young infants typically do respond to one special person in a unique way. Carpenter (1975) showed that 2-week-old babies could recognise their mother's face and voice. He set up a situation in which infants looked at a face while hearing a voice. Sometimes the face and the voice belonged to the same person, and sometimes they didn't. The infants looked at the face for the longest time when it was the mother's face, and when it was accompanied by her voice. More convincing evidence that the infants recognised their mother's face and voice were obtained when they were presented with their mother's face but an unfamiliar voice or vice versa. Most of the infants found this distressing, and rapidly looked away from the face.

KEY TERM

Separation anxiety: the sense of concern felt by a child when separated from their attachment figure.

One problem with Carpenter's (1975) study is that those rating the behaviour of the infants knew which condition was being used at any given time, and this may have biased their ratings. However, the findings have been supported using improved versions of Carpenter's design. Bushnell, Sai, and Mullin (1989) presented 2-day-old babies with the faces of their mother and a female stranger until they had spent a total of 20 seconds fixating on one of the faces. Almost two-thirds of them showed a preference for their mother over the stranger, indicating some ability to recognise their own mother within a few days of birth.

? How else could the problems of interpretation of Carpenter's study have been overcome?

Types of Attachment, Including Insecure and Secure Attachment

Many psychological theories seem to assume that everyone is the same. However, as I am sure you will agree, each one of us is different. For example, Schaffer and Emerson (1964) found that some babies like cuddling whereas others prefer not to be touched. They also found that some infants are attached to only one person, whereas others have multiple attachments. Indeed, at the age of 18 months, only 18% of the children they studied were attached to only one person. What is true of nearly all infants is that they are attached to at least one caregiver, even those children who have been neglected or abused (see box on abuse and attachment). The main individual differences lie in the type of attachment, with the main difference being between children showing secure attachment and those showing insecure attachment.

In this section we will focus on describing secure and insecure attachment and on indicating reasons *why* the type of attachment an infant has with its mother or other caregiver is so important. This includes considering some of the major consequences of an infant (human or monkey) being securely or insecurely

KEY TERMS

Secure attachment: the result of a strong positive bond between infant and caregiver, so that although the child shows distress at separation, he or she is easily comforted by the caregiver's return.
Insecure attachment: a weak emotional bond between child and caregiver(s) leading to an anxious and insecure relationship, which can have a negative effect on development.

Abuse and attachment

Harris (1998) notes that it is a "sad and paradoxical fact that abuse may actually increase a child's clinginess." A number of studies have investigated the consequences of neglect or abuse on the bonds that form between caregiver and infant. In one of Harlow's studies of rhesus monkeys, the cloth "mother" blasted the infant monkey with a strong current of compressed air (Rosenblum & Harlow, 1963). The findings were that these abused monkeys appeared to be *more* strongly attached to their "mother" than the other monkeys. This is confirmed by a report from a researcher studying imprinting in ducklings. He found that when he accidentally stepped on the foot of one of the ducklings who had already imprinted on him, then the duckling followed him more closely than ever (Harris, 1998).

However, this link between abuse and attachment may not extend to humans. Lynch and Roberts (1982) suggested that abuse leads to bonding failure rather than stronger attachment. One example is seen in mothers described as "primary rejectors" (Jones et al., 1987). These tend to be middle-class women who have had an unwanted child, a difficult pregnancy, and/or experienced early separation from their infant due to problems at the time of birth. The mothers may have good relationships with other children. Rejection starts from the time of birth and the mother–infant relationship never recovers. It is possible that children who experience this "primary rejection" go on to suffer from reactive attachment disorder, which is described on page 122. These children do not appear to be attached to their rejecting caregiver, and in fact are unable to form any attachments. Therefore, this suggests that abuse does not create a stronger bond in humans.

attached. In the following section, we will extend our coverage of attachment types in various ways. First, we will consider the notion that there are *three* types of insecure attachment: avoidant; resistant; and disorganised. Second, we will discuss ways of assessing attachment type in the laboratory. Third, we will consider ways of explaining why children differ so much in attachment type.

Secure and insecure attachment

Nearly all child psychologists claim that the nature of the attachment between an infant and a caregiver (e.g. mother) is of great importance to its emotional development. However, it is rarely possible for researchers to observe infants and their caregivers over long periods of time in the home setting, which makes it hard to assess infant–caregiver attachments. When we describe a child as "being attached", this seems to imply a secure attachment. Alas, not all children are securely attached. The evidence suggests that about 70% of young children in most countries are securely attached. In a cross-cultural study discussed more fully later, van IJzendoorn and Kroonenberg (1988) found that the majority of infants in eight different countries were securely attached. However, it is a matter of great concern that about 30% of infants are insecurely attached.

Most psychologists agree that the nature of the attachment between infant and caregiver is crucial to its emotional development.

Why are some children insecurely attached?

There are several reasons why some children (but not others) are insecurely attached. Two explanations discussed in detail later are as follows:

1. There are great differences in maternal sensitivity, and infants whose mother lacks sensitivity are more likely than others to be insecurely attached.
2. The temperament with which a child is born may help to determine whether or not he/she becomes insecurely attached.

A third explanation was discussed by Baer and Martinez (2006). They argued that children who are maltreated are more likely than children who aren't maltreated to be insecurely attached. They tested this argument by carrying out a meta-analysis of studies investigating the effects of maltreatment (e.g. malnutrition; physical abuse) on attachment type. Insecure attachment was more common among maltreated children, and this was especially the case with the more serious forms of maltreatment.

Does secure attachment last?

There have been numerous studies designed to establish whether infants are securely or insecurely attached. To what extent do infants who are securely attached remain so some years later? If there is consistency in type of attachment over time, then that is likely to be of great significance in each child's development. Conversely, if early attachment type doesn't predict later attachment type, then early attachment type is unlikely to predict subsequent development.

Wartner et al. (1994) assessed infants' attachment patterns to their mother at the age of 12 months using the category of secure attachment plus three insecure attachment categories. They then re-assessed the children's attachment at the age of 6. Strikingly, 82% of the children remained in the same category over the 5-year period—this indicates great consistency of attachment type over time.

Similar findings have been reported in most other research. However, consistency of attachment type hasn't been found in all groups of children. For example, Weinfield, Whaley, and Egeland (2004) carried out a longitudinal study on children considered to be at high risk at birth because of poverty. Attachment type was assessed at 12 and 18 months, and again at the age of 19. Weinfield et al. (2004, p. 73) concluded as follows: "Contrary to findings from low-risk samples, analyses demonstrated no significant overall continuity in attachment security." Some of the reasons why there was little or no continuity of attachment types were changes in maternal life stress, changes in family functioning during childhood, and changes in child maltreatment.

Mothers who remember their attachment experience with their own mother as being secure are more likely to have securely attached children (reviewed by Thompson, 2000). Young children also start to form an **internal working model** based on their expectations about important attachments in their lives. When changes occur in the lives of mothers and/or their children that alter their internal working models, the result is often changes in the child's attachment type (Thompson, 2000).

How valuable is secure attachment?

There are many advantages for infants to be securely rather than insecurely attached. For example, Wartner et al. (1994) observed the preschool behaviour of securely and insecurely attached children. The securely attached ones showed more competence in their play, were better at conflict resolution, and had fewer behaviour problems. Szewczyk-Sokolowski, Bost, and Wainwright (2005) found that securely attached preschool children were more accepted by their peers. Pauli-Pott et al. (2007) assessed attachment type in 18-month-old children and then used a structured clinical interview at the age of 30 months to measure behaviour problems. Securely attached children had fewer behaviour problems.

One of the most thorough studies on the relationship between child attachment type and subsequent development was reported by Belsky and Fearon (2002). Attachment type was assessed at the age of 15 months and then five developmental outcomes were recorded at the age of 3. Infants categorised as securely attached generally had greater social competence, school readiness, expressive language (speaking), and receptive language (language comprehension) than insecurely attached ones, and also had fewer behaviour problems. However, the mother's sensitivity was also very important: "In the case of all outcomes, insecurely attached children who subsequently experienced high-sensitive mothering significantly outperformed secure children who subsequently experienced low-sensitive mothering" (Belsky & Fearon, 2002, p. 361). Thus, the mother's sensitivity was even more important than whether the children were securely or insecurely attached at 15 months.

Nearly all the findings discussed in this section are basically correlational—there are associations between security of attachment and various measures such as peer acceptance, fewer behaviour problems, and higher social competence. Since there wasn't **random allocation** of children to secure and insecure attachment groups, we can't be confident that these desirable outcomes were *caused* by secure attachment. For example, children who have a temperament that makes them sociable and non-anxious may find it easier to be securely attached, to gain peer acceptance, and to become socially competent.

Attachment in monkeys

Secure attachment is not only important in humans but also in numerous other species. Compelling evidence of what can happen to monkeys lacking any secure attachment (indeed, lacking any kind of attachment) was reported by Harlow and Harlow (1962). They raised monkeys for long periods of time in total isolation. When the monkeys were placed with other monkeys, they remained withdrawn and extremely fearful. In comparison, monkeys raised with a cloth "mother" were much more able to engage in social activity. This shows that the cloth mother (even though not providing secure attachment) was better than nothing.

In another experiment, four young monkeys were raised on their own without even a cloth or wire "mother". These monkeys spent the first few months huddled together, but gradually developed more independence and finally seemed to have suffered no ill effects. These findings suggest that secure attachment based on the infant–infant affectional bond can be just as effective as secure attachment based on the mother–infant bond. (See Freud and Dann's study on page 121 for more effects of infant–infant bonding.)

The monkeys in Harlow's study appeared to be more attached to a cloth-covered artificial "mother" than to a wire version.

? Why should one be cautious in using results from animal studies to explain human behaviour?

Attachment in Humans: Ainsworth

Mary Ainsworth devised the **Strange Situation** as a short but effective way of assessing the quality of an infant's attachment to its caregiver. Here we discuss the important study by Ainsworth and Bell (1970) on infants' attachments based on the Strange Situation. They aimed to investigate individual variation in infant attachments, especially differences between secure and insecure attachments. They hoped that their method of assessing attachments (the Strange Situation test) would prove to be a reliable and valid measure of attachments.

The Strange Situation test lasts for just over 20 minutes and was used on American infants aged between 12 and 18 months. It takes place in the laboratory and the method used is controlled observation. The Strange Situation consists of *eight* stages or episodes as follows:

Stage	People in the room	Procedure
1 (30 seconds)	Mother or caregiver and infant plus researcher	Researcher brings the others into the room and rapidly leaves
2 (3 minutes)	Mother or caregiver and infant	Mother or caregiver sits; infant is free to explore
3 (3 minutes)	Stranger plus mother or caregiver and infant	Stranger comes in and after a while talks to mother or caregiver and then to the infant. Mother or caregiver leaves the room

(continued)

> **KEY TERM**
>
> **Strange Situation**: an experimental procedure used to test the security of a child's attachment to a caregiver. The key features are what the child does when it is left by the caregiver, and the child's behaviour at reunion, as well as responses to a stranger.

Stage	People in the room	Procedure
4 (3 minutes)	Stranger and infant	Stranger keeps trying to talk to and play with the infant
5 (3 minutes)	Mother or caregiver and infant	Stranger leaves as mother or caregiver returns to the infant. At the end of this stage, the mother or caregiver leaves
6 (3 minutes)	Infant	Infant is alone in the room
7 (3 minutes)	Stranger and infant	Stranger returns and tries to interact with the infant
8 (3 minutes)	Mother or caregiver and infant	Mother or caregiver returns and interacts with the infant, and the stranger leaves

? **What are the strengths of the experimental approach used by Ainsworth and Bell?**

Several important findings were reported by Ainsworth and Bell (1970). There were considerable individual differences in behaviour and emotional response in the Strange Situation. Most infants displayed behaviour categorised as typical or secure attachment (70%), while 10% were resistant and 20% avoidant. The securely attached infants were distressed when separated from the caregiver and sought contact and soothing on reunion. Resistant attachment was characterised by ambivalence (conflicting emotions) and inconsistency as the infants were very distressed at separation but resisted the caregiver on reunion. Avoidant attachment was characterised by detachment as the infants didn't seek contact with the caregiver and showed little distress at separation.

Ainsworth et al. (1978) reported the findings from several studies using the Strange Situation in the United States. They confirmed the notion that there are three main attachment types and provided a detailed account of them:

? **What factors determine infants' attachment style?**

- *Secure attachment*: the infant is distressed by the caregiver's absence. However, he/she rapidly returns to a state of contentment after the caregiver's return, immediately seeking contact with the caregiver. There is a clear difference in the infant's reaction to the caregiver and to the stranger. Ainsworth et al. reported that 70% of American infants show secure attachment.
- *Resistant attachment*: the infant is insecure in the presence of the caregiver, and becomes very distressed when the caregiver leaves. He/she resists contact with the caregiver upon return, and is wary of the stranger. About 10% of American infants were found to be resistant.
- *Avoidant attachment*: the infant doesn't seek contact with the caregiver, and shows little distress when separated. The infant avoids contact with the caregiver upon return. The infant treats the stranger in a similar way to the caregiver, often avoiding him/her. About 20% of American infants were avoidant.

EXAM HINT

If you are asked to outline individual differences in attachment, you could use Ainsworth's research and identify:
- secure attachment—the characteristics of this type of attachment;
- insecure attachments—the characteristics of avoidant, resistant, and disorganised attachment.

What conclusions can we draw from the approach adopted by Ainsworth and Bell (1970)? First, the Strange Situation provides a good measure

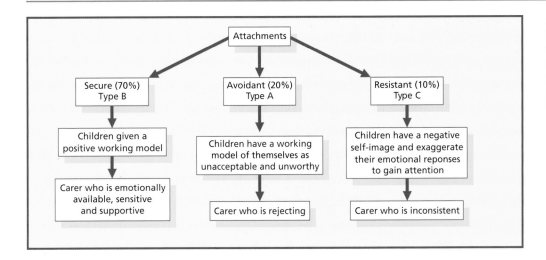

Ainsworth and Bell proposed three attachment types (A, B, and C). Main and Solomon proposed a fourth category, Type D, which they described as "Insecure: Disorganised".

of attachment because it allows us to discriminate between attachment types. Second, secure attachment is the preferred type of attachment, and is linked to healthy emotional and social development. For example, Wartner et al. (1994) found that attachment classifications at 6 years were very similar to those at 12 months. Stams, Juffer, and van IJzendoorn (2002) found that children who were securely attached to their mother at 12 months had superior social and cognitive development at the age of 7. Third, as we will see, the Strange Situation has been used successfully to explore cultural variations in infants' attachments.

Evaluation: Weaknesses

There are various weaknesses of the approach adopted by Ainsworth and Bell (1970). First, the validity of the classification was questioned and a fourth attachment type suggested by Main and Solomon (1986). They found that a small number of infants displayed disorganised attachment, in which the infants showed no consistent pattern of behaviour and fitted none of the three main attachment types. However, Main and Solomon accepted the validity of the three attachment types identified by Ainsworth.

Second, the Strange Situation was developed in the United States and so may be culturally biased. In other words, attachment behaviour regarded as healthy in the United States may not be so regarded elsewhere in the world, and the same may be true of attachment behaviour regarded as unhealthy in the United States. This issue is discussed in detail later in the section on cultural variations in attachment.

Third, the Strange Situation is artificial in ways that may well distort behaviour. For example, some mothers or caregivers are likely to behave differently towards their child when they know they are being observed than they would do at home when alone with their child.

Fourth, Ainsworth and Bell (1970) and Ainsworth et al. (1978) put infants into three categories. This is neat and tidy. However, it oversimplifies matters because infants *within* any given category differ from each other in their attachment behaviour. For example, two children might both be classified as showing avoidant attachment, but one might display much more avoidant behaviour than the other. We can take account of such individual differences by using dimensions

? Are there problems with using the Strange Situation in very different cultures?

See *AS Level Psychology Online* for stimulus material relating to this classic study.

A two-dimensional model of individual differences in attachment. Group A has avoidant attachment, Group B has secure attachment, and Group C has resistant attachment. From Fraley and Spieker (2003).

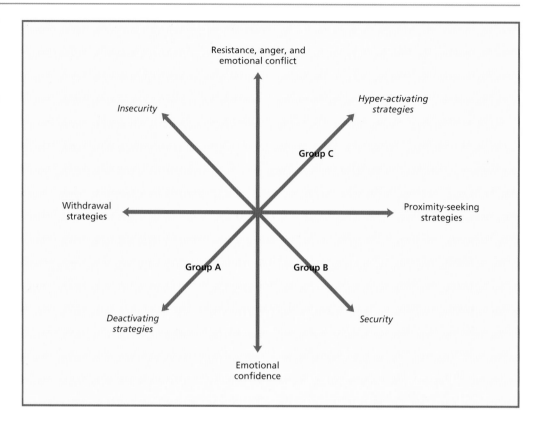

(going from very low to very high) instead of categories. Fraley and Spieker (2003) identified two attachment dimensions:

1. *Avoidant/withdrawal vs proximity-seeking strategies*: This is concerned with the extent to which the child tries to maintain physical closeness to his/her mother.
2. *Angry and resistant strategies vs emotional confidence*: This is concerned with the child's emotional reactions to the attachment figure's behaviour.

As can be seen in the Figure, secure, resistant, and avoidant attachment all fit neatly into this two-dimensional framework. The dimensional approach is preferable to the categorical one of Ainsworth because it takes much more account of small individual differences in attachment behaviour.

Why are there individual differences in attachment?

Why do some infants have a secure attachment to their mother, whereas others don't? Several answers to that question have been proposed. In essence, however, what is likely to be most important is either aspects of the mother's or caregiver's behaviour (e.g. their sensitivity) or aspects of the infant's temperament or personality. We will consider these two possibilities in turn.

Maternal sensitivity hypothesis

Ainsworth et al. (1978, p. 152) tried to explain individual differences in infant attachment in their **maternal sensitivity hypothesis**: "The most important aspect of maternal behaviour commonly associated with the security-anxiety dimension of infant attachment is . . . sensitive responsiveness to infant signals and communications". Ainsworth et al. reported that most of the caregivers of

KEY TERM

Maternal sensitivity hypothesis: the notion that individual differences in infant attachment are due mainly to the sensitivity (or otherwise) of the mother.

securely attached infants were very sensitive to their needs, and responded to their infants in an emotionally expressive way. In contrast, the caregivers of resistant infants were interested in them but often misunderstood their infants' behaviour. Of particular importance, these caregivers varied in the way they treated their infants, and so the infant couldn't rely on the caregiver's emotional support.

Finally, there were the caregivers of avoidant infants. Ainsworth et al. (1978) reported that many of these caregivers were uninterested in their infants. The caregivers often rejected their infants and tended to be self-centred and rigid in their behaviour. However, some caregivers of avoidant infants behaved rather differently. These caregivers acted in a suffocating way, always interacting with their infants even when the infants didn't want any interaction. What these types of caregivers had in common was that they weren't very sensitive to the needs of their infants.

The maternal sensitivity hypothesis has received much support. De Wolff and van IJzendoorn (1997) carried out a meta-analysis across many studies and obtained a correlation of +0.24 between maternal sensitivity and security of infant attachment. This indicates a positive (but fairly weak) association. De Wolff and van IJzendoorn also found that aspects of mothers' behaviour only partly related to sensitivity were also important. These aspects included stimulation (any action of the mother directed at her baby) and attitude (mother's expression of positive emotion to her baby).

Most research on the maternal sensitivity hypothesis is correlational. As a result, it doesn't prove that differences in maternal sensitivity *cause* differences in security of attachment. Clearer evidence can be obtained by looking at the effects on infant attachment of interventions designed to increase maternal sensitivity. A meta-analysis of relevant studies indicated that such interventions made infants more securely attached (Bakermans-Kranenburg, van IJzendoorn, & Juffer, 2003).

The maternal sensitivity hypothesis exaggerates the role of the mother. De Wolff and van IJzendoorn (1997) carried out a meta-analysis of studies in which *paternal* sensitivity had been assessed. There was a correlation of +0.13 between the father's sensitivity and infant–father attachment. Thus, paternal sensitivity is modestly associated with the infant's security of attachment to the father. However, the association is smaller than that between maternal sensitivity and security of infant–mother attachment. Another weakness with the maternal sensitivity hypothesis is that it ignores the role played by the infant himself/herself. This issue is discussed next.

Temperament hypothesis

We could try to account for individual differences in infant attachment by using the **temperament hypothesis**. According to this hypothesis (initially proposed by Kagan, 1984), an infant's relationships with primary caregivers (and those later in life) can be explained in terms of the infant's innate temperament (the character it inherits through its genes). Some infants' temperaments are better suited at forming attachments than those of others.

There is some support for the temperament hypothesis. For example, Belsky and Rovine (1987) reported that newborns showing signs of behavioural instability (e.g. tremors or shaking) were less likely than others to become securely attached to their mother. This finding suggests that their innate personality was of importance in attachment formation.

> Remember that the term "maternal" means mothering, which could be done by anyone, not just the infant's mother.

> **KEY TERM**
>
> **Temperament hypothesis**: the view that a child's temperament is responsible for the quality of attachment between the child and its caregiver, as opposed to the view that experience is more important.

The most effective way of testing the temperament hypothesis is to study pairs of identical twins (sharing 100% of their genes) and fraternal twins (sharing 50% of their genes). If the infant's temperamental characteristics influence his/her attachment style, then identical twins should show more agreement than fraternal twins with respect to attachment style. O'Connor and Croft (2001) found modest support for this hypothesis, suggesting that genetic factors probably influence young children's attachment type to a small extent. However, more negative findings were reported by Bokhorst et al. (2003) in a study on identical and fraternal twins. First, the role of genetic factors in accounting for individual differences in infant attachment type was negligible. Second the **concordance rate** (extent of agreement on attachment type) between twins within a pair was not influenced by similarities or differences in temperamental reactivity.

There are various reasons why we must be careful not to exaggerate the role played by the infant's genetic make-up and personality in determining its attachment style. First, infants' temperament as assessed by their parents is not usually associated with their attachment type as determined by the Strange Situation assessment (Durkin, 1995). Second, there is only a modest tendency for infants' attachment type with their father to be the same as their attachment type with their mother (de Wolff & IJzendoorn, 1997). This suggests that an infant's attachment to his/her mother depends mainly on the parents' characteristics.

Overall summary

Neither caregiver characteristics (e.g. sensitivity) nor infant temperament is wholly responsible for the development of attachment. Instead, there is an *interaction* between these two factors (Belsky & Rovine, 1987), meaning that *both* factors make a contribution in combination. Supporting evidence was reported by Spangler (1990) in a study of German mothers. Their responsiveness to their infants was influenced by their perceptions of the infants' temperament.

Explanations of Attachment: Learning Theory and the Evolutionary Perspective, Including Bowlby

We have seen that the great majority of infants form secure attachments with their mother or principal caregiver. We have also seen that forming secure attachments is of great value in ensuring the happiness and healthy social development of infants. Now we turn to a consideration of some of the major theories that have been proposed to provide an explanation of why attachments are formed and maintained.

Learning theory

The most basic principle of learning theory is that all behaviour has been learned. That means that behaviour isn't innate and doesn't depend on genetic factors. Learning theorists (also called "behaviourists") argued that learning is the result of conditioning, which is a form of learning. According to learning theorists or behaviourists, there are two main forms of conditioning—classical conditioning and operant conditioning (see Chapter 2, Section 4). A reminder of these processes is shown in the box.

We will start by considering how infant attachment behaviour can be explained in terms of classical conditioning before turning to explanations based on operant conditioning. An infant is born with reflex responses. The stimulus of food (an unconditioned stimulus) produces a sense of pleasure (an unconditioned response). The person providing the food (usually the mother) becomes associated with this pleasure. As a result, the provider of food becomes a conditioned stimulus that independently produces the unconditioned stimulus (pleasure). The food-giver thus becomes a source of pleasure independent of whether or not food is supplied by him/her. According to classical conditioning theory, this is the basis of the attachment bond.

According to the approach based on operant conditioning (e.g. Skinner, 1938), any response followed by **positive reinforcement** (some kind of reward such as food or praise) will be strengthened. All such responses are more likely to be produced in the future when the individual is in the same situation. Dollard and Miller (1950) provided a more detailed explanation for the development of attachments based on operant conditioning. Their focus was on motivation, i.e. the forces driving behaviour:

- All humans possess various primary motives or drives, such as those of hunger, thirst, and sex. Stimuli that satisfy these primary drives are known as **primary reinforcers**.
- A person will be "driven" to seek food to satisfy his/her hunger.
- Eating food results in drive reduction and is positively reinforcing or rewarding.
- According to the principles of operant conditioning, anything that is rewarded is likely to be repeated and so this behaviour is repeated (learned).
- The mother or other caregiver provides the food that reduces the drive, and so becomes a **secondary reinforcer**—he/she becomes a reinforcer by association with a primary reinforcer.
- From then on, the infant seeks to be with the person who has become a secondary reinforcer, because he/she is now a source of reward in themselves. The infant has become attached.

Mothers can also learn to be attached to their infants because of positive reinforcement. For example, mothers are rewarded when they make their child smile or stop crying.

We always need to be careful when assuming that the findings obtained from other species are applicable to humans. However, Harlow carried out a series of important studies on infant monkeys that seem to have real relevance to human infants and that cast doubt on the learning theory approach. To test whether monkeys prefer the activity of feeding to that of bodily comfort, Harlow (1959)

Classical conditioning

- Unconditioned stimulus (US) e.g. food → causes → reflex response e.g. salivation.
- Neutral stimulus (NS) e.g. bell → causes → no response.
- NS and US are paired in time (they co-occur).
- NS (e.g. bell) is now a conditioned stimulus (CS) → which produces → a conditioned response (CR) [a new stimulus–response link is learned, the bell causes salivation].

Operant conditioning

- A behaviour that has a positive effect is more likely to be repeated.
- Negative reinforcement (escape from aversive stimulus) is agreeable.
- Punishment is disagreeable.

See *AS Level Psychology Online* for an interactive exercise on this topic.

KEY TERMS

Positive reinforcement: a reward (e.g. food; money) that serves to increase the probability of any response produced shortly before it is presented.

Primary reinforcer: something that provides positive reinforcement because it serves to satisfy some basic drive; for example, food and drink are primary reinforcers because they satisfy our hunger and thirst drives, respectively.

Secondary reinforcer: a reinforcer that has no natural properties of reinforcement but, through association with a primary reinforcer, becomes a reinforcer, i.e. it is learned.

Although the wire mother on the left is where the baby monkey receives his food, he runs to the cloth mother for comfort when he is frightened by the teddy bear drummer (Harlow, 1959).

arranged for very young rhesus monkeys to be taken from their mothers and placed in cages with two surrogate [substitute] mothers as shown in the picture. One of the "mothers" was made of wire and the other was covered in soft cloth. Milk was provided by the wire mother for some of the monkeys, whereas it was provided by the cloth mother for the others. The monkeys spent most of their time clinging to the cloth mother even when she didn't supply milk—this is NOT as predicted by learning theory. The reason was that the cloth mother provided "contact comfort", which they clearly regarded as more important than food. If the monkeys were frightened by a teddy-bear drummer, they ran to their cloth mother.

Unfortunately, the monkeys didn't develop into normal adults. Later in life they were either indifferent or abusive to other monkeys, and had difficulty with mating and parenting. The findings show that contact comfort is preferable (but not sufficient) for healthy development.

Social learning theory

Social learning theory is a more sophisticated version of the learning theory approaches we have discussed so far. Learning theory claims that learning takes place *directly* with no intervening mental process or processes. In other words, direct associations are formed between stimuli and responses. For example, a rat sees a lever and presses it to receive food reward. Within social learning, on the other hand, it is argued that we also learn in a more indirect way. As you would probably agree, much of what we learn is based on observing the behaviour of others. This is known as observational learning. Of most relevance here is vicarious reinforcement—we learn to produce a new form of behaviour by seeing someone else perform that behaviour and being reinforced or rewarded for performing it. According to social learning theorists, the kind of imitation involved in vicarious reinforcement is very important.

Hay and Vespo (1988) used social learning theory to explain attachment. They suggested that attachment occurs because parents "deliberately teach their children to love them and to understand human relationships" (p. 82). Some of the techniques involved are:

Some psychologists think of attachment behaviour as something that is learned because it is reinforced. Young children may learn about human relationships by imitating the affectionate behaviours of their parents.

- *Modelling*: Learning based on observing and imitating a model's behaviour.
- *Direct instruction*: Providing reward or reinforcement when the child behaves in the required way.
- *Social facilitation*: Using the presence of others to encourage the child to understand positive relationships between people.

Evaluation

The learning theory approach has various strengths. First, there is some experimental support (e.g. Hay & Vespo, 1988) for the view that one way in which children acquire attachment behaviour is via social learning. Second, social learning theory has led to a detailed consideration of the interactional processes occurring between parents and children. Third, it seems likely that young children start to imitate aspects of the loving behaviour of their caregiver or caregivers as a result of observational learning. Fourth, research on social learning theory has practical applications. Parents or other caregivers need to be aware that their children use observation and imitation when developing attachments. That means that it is very important for parents to act as positive role models.

Here are the main weaknesses with the learning theory approach to attachment:

- Harlow's evidence indicates that young monkeys preferred a cloth mother that didn't provide milk to a wire mother that did. This is the *opposite* of the prediction from learning theory, which claims that infants form attachments to the person who feeds them. However, it could be argued that research on monkeys doesn't apply to humans. Against that, human infants often become attached to adults who are *not* involved in feeding or in basic caregiving (Schaffer & Emerson, 1964).
- Learning theory is generally criticised for being **reductionist**, "reducing" the complexities of human behaviour to over-simple ideas such as stimulus, response, and reinforcement. These ideas are then used to build blocks to explain complex behaviours such as attachment. It is probable that these ideas are too simple to explain attachment.
- Social learning theory provides a description of some of the processes involved in parent–child attachments. However, as Durkin (1995) pointed out, the strong emotional intensity of many parent–child attachments is not really *explained* by social learning theorists.

Evolutionary perspective: Bowlby

John Bowlby (1907–1990) was a child psychoanalyst whose main interest was in the relationship between caregiver and child. He realised that Freud's views of the importance of maternal care could be combined with key ideas of the ethologists to produce a major new theory based on an evolutionary perspective. What does that mean? **Ethologists** study animals in their natural surroundings. **Imprinting** is the tendency for the young of some species of birds to follow the first moving object they see and to continue to follow it after that. The idea was that infants would show imprinting to their own mother, and this would explain the strong attachment most infants have for their mother. This theory has had a profound effect on the way psychologists think about attachment and infant development.

The fundamental principle of Bowlby's theory is that attachment is an innate and adaptive process for both infant and parent. As such, it provides an evolutionary perspective. Attachment behaviour has evolved and endured because it promotes survival, as proposed by Darwin's **theory of evolution**. Attachment promotes survival in several ways:

1. *Safety*: Attachment results in a desire to maintain proximity and thus ensure safety. Both infant and caregiver experience feelings of anxiety when separated and this creates a proximity-seeking drive (striving to be close to the other person).

? Do you think that there are problems with generalising from the behaviour of one species to another?

EXAM HINT

You need to know two explanations of attachment BUT it is best to make sure one of these is BOWLBY's explanation as this provides the most content and so would be the most suitable for the question: "Outline ONE explanation of attachment" for six marks.

KEY TERMS

Reductionist: an argument or theory that reduces complex factors to a set of simple principles.

Ethologists: individuals who study animal behaviour in its natural environment, focusing on the importance of innate capacities and the functions of behaviours.

Imprinting: a restricted form of learning that takes place rapidly and has both short-term effects (e.g. a following response) and long-lasting effects (e.g. choice of reproductive partner).

Theory of evolution: an explanation for the diversity of living species. Darwin's theory was based on the principle of natural selection.

The attachment between a child and his or her caregiver serves many important functions. According to Bowlby, it maintains proximity for safety, the caregiver acts as a secure base for exploration, and the attachment relationship acts as a template for all future relationships.

? How should you respond when you hear a baby cry?

See *AS Level Psychology Online* for an interactive exercise on this topic.

KEY TERMS

Social releasers: a social behaviour or characteristic that elicits a caregiving reaction. Bowlby suggested that these were innate and critical in the process of forming attachments.

Critical period: a biologically determined period of time during which an animal is exclusively receptive to certain changes.

2. *Emotional relationships*: Attachment enables the infant to learn how to form and conduct healthy emotional relationships. Bowlby used the concept of the internal working model—a set of conscious and/or unconscious rules and expectations regarding our relationships with others—to explain how this happens. This model develops out of the primary attachment relationship and is a model or schema used as a template or pattern for future relationships.

3. *A secure base for exploration*: Attachment also provides a safe base for exploration, a process of fundamental importance for cognitive and social development. The child often returns periodically to "touch base" with its attachment figure. An insecurely attached child is less willing to wander. Exploration is very important for cognitive development, as was shown by Bus and van IJzendoorn (1988). They assessed the attachment types of children aged 2 years old using the Strange Situation. Three years later the children were assessed for their reading interests and skills. In addition, their pre-school teachers completed a questionnaire about preparatory reading and intelligence. The securely attached children showed more interest in written material than did the insecurely attached children regardless of their intelligence and the amount of preparatory reading instruction.

Role of social releasers

According to Bowlby, attachment must be innate or the infant and parent might *not* show it. The infant and the mother/caregiver must both take an active part for the attachment to be secure and lasting. Bowlby argued that the infant innately elicits caregiving from its mother-figure by means of social releasers. **Social releasers** are behaviours such as smiling or crying that encourage a response—humans are innately programmed to respond to these social releasers.

Most people feel uncomfortable when they hear an infant or adult crying, which helps to ensure that someone will respond. It is a mechanism that has evolved to maximise the chances of survival by keeping the caregiver close. These innate behaviours and innate responses are a fundamental part of the process of forming an attachment.

Bowlby's theoretical approach also provides an explanation for the notion (discussed later) that children separated from their parent or caregiver show three successive stages of reaction (Robertson & Bowlby, 1952): protest; despair; and detachment. The protest stage increases the probability that the mother will find the infant. The following despair stage conserves energy and allows the defenceless infant to survive as long as possible in a dangerous environment.

Critical period

I mentioned earlier that Bowlby was influenced in his thinking by the work of the ethologists, who study various species in their natural environment. The ethologists emphasise the concept of a **critical period**. In the case of biological characteristics, development

Bowlby's proposed phases in the development of attachment

Bowlby proposed that an infant is born with a set of behavioural systems that are ready to be activated, for example crying, sucking, and clinging (all called "social releasers"), and an ability to respond to the "stimuli that commonly emanate from a human being"—sounds, faces, and touch. Shortly thereafter other behaviours appear which are equally innate though not present at birth, such as smiling and crawling. From these small beginnings, sophisticated systems soon develop.

In the table below, four phases in the development of attachments are described, with very approximate ages.

Phase 1 Birth–8 weeks	Orientation and signals towards people without discrimination of one special person	Infants behave in characteristic and friendly ways towards other people but their ability to discriminate between them is very limited, e.g. they may just recognise familiar voices
Phase 2 About 8/10 weeks–6 months	Orientation and signals directed towards one or more special people	Infants continue to be generally friendly but there is beginning to be a marked difference of behaviour towards one mother-figure or primary caregiver
Phase 3 6 months through to 1–2 years old	Maintenance of proximity to a special person by means of locomotion as well as signals to that person	The infant starts to follow his or her mother-figure, greet her (him) when she (he) returns, and use her (him) as a base from which to explore. The infant selects other people as subsidiary attachment figures. At the same time the infant's friendly responses to other people decrease and the infant treats strangers with increasing caution
Phase 4 Starts around the age of 2	Formation of a goal-corrected partnership	The child develops insight into the mother-figure's behaviour and this opens up a whole new relationship where the infant can consciously influence what she (or he) does. This is the beginning of a real partnership

Adapted from J. Bowlby (1969), *Attachment and love, Vol. 1: Attachment.* London: Hogarth.

The features of a baby face are very appealing. They act as a "social releaser", a social stimulus that "releases" a desire to offer caregiving.

has to take place during a set period, otherwise it won't take place at all. Ethologists suggested that this principle of a critical period might also apply to attachment. The ethologist Konrad Lorenz found that the young of some species of birds tended to follow the first moving object they saw on hatching, and they continued to follow it from then on. This is imprinting, the main characteristics of which are:

1. It occurs during a short critical period. If the infant isn't exposed to a "mother" within a critical time window, then imprinting won't take place.

See *AS Level Psychology Online* for an interactive exercise on this topic.

Lorenz hatched some goslings and arranged it so that he would be the first thing that they saw. From then on they followed him everywhere and showed no recognition of their actual mother. The goslings formed a picture (imprint) of the object they were to follow.

2. It is irreversible—once imprinting to an object has occurred, it can't be changed.

3. It has lasting consequences. It results in the formation of a bond between the caregiver and its young and so has consequences in the short-term for safety and food. It also affects the individual in the long-term because it acts as a template or pattern for reproductive partners. For example, Immelmann (1972) arranged for zebra finches to be raised by Bengalese finches and vice versa. In later years, when the finches were given a free choice, they preferred to mate with the species on which they had been imprinted.

Like attachment, this **bonding** process is desirable. It means that the offspring are more likely to survive and so the parents' genes are passed on to the next generation.

Evaluation of imprinting

While reading the last few paragraphs, you may have found yourself thinking (totally understandably!) that human infants are much more complex than young birds, and so the findings of ethologists may have limited application in the human case. That is absolutely right. In addition, however, there has been some controversy concerning notions such as imprinting and critical periods even in birds. For example, Guiton (1966) found that he could reverse imprinting in chickens. Guiton's chickens were initially imprinted on some yellow rubber gloves. When the chickens matured, this early imprint acted as a mate template or pattern and the chickens tried to mate with the rubber gloves. This appears to support the claims made for imprinting. However, after the chickens had spent some time with their own species, they engaged in normal sexual behaviour with their own kind.

> **Imprinting**
>
> The BBC television series *Supernature* used imprinting as a means of obtaining spectacular close-up film of geese in flight. A member of the production company made sure he was the first thing a group of goslings saw when they hatched, and from then on the birds followed him everywhere, even into the office! When the geese were young adults, their adopted "parent" took to the skies as a passenger in a microlight aircraft. The geese followed and flew alongside, allowing him to film their flight to produce a truly breathtaking sequence for the television series.

The idea of a critical period is of some value but is too strong. It would be more appropriate to describe it as a *sensitive period*. Thus, although imprinting is *less* likely to occur outside a given time window, it does still occur at other times. The notion of a sensitive period is that imprinting takes place most easily at a certain time but may still happen at any time during development.

Bowlby (1969) claimed that something like imprinting occurs in infants. He proposed that infants have an innate tendency to orient towards one individual. This attachment is innate, and like all biological mechanisms should have a critical period for its development. Bowlby argued that this critical period ends at some point between 1 and 3 years of age, after which it would no longer be possible to establish a powerful attachment to the caregiver.

Klaus and Kennell (1976) were in general agreement with Bowlby (1958) that early contact between infant and mother is of great importance. In fact, they

CASE STUDY: AMOROUS TURKEYS

Some psychologists were conducting research on the effects of hormones on turkeys. In one room there were 35 full-grown male turkeys. If you walked into the room, the turkeys fled to the furthest corner and if you walked towards them, the turkeys slid along the wall to maintain a maximum distance between you and them. This is fairly normal behaviour for wild turkeys. However, in another room, there was a group of turkeys who behaved in a very different manner. These turkeys greeted you by stopping dead in their tracks, fixing their eyes on you, spreading their tail into a full courtship fan, putting their heads down and ponderously walking towards you, all at the same time. Their intention was clearly one of mating. (Fortunately turkeys in mid-courtship are famously slow so it is easy to avoid their advances.)

What was the difference between these two groups? The first set were raised away from humans, whereas the second group had received an injection of the male hormone, testosterone, when they were younger. The hormone created an artificial sensitive period during which the turkeys imprinted on their companion at the time—a male experimenter. Subsequently, these turkeys showed little interest in female turkeys, however they were aroused whenever they saw a male human—displaying their tail feathers and strutting their stuff.

It has been suggested that the reason this learning was so strong and apparently irreversible was because it took place at a time of high arousal—when hormones were administered. In real life, hormones may be involved as well. Perhaps, for these birds, a moving object creates a sense of pleasure and this pleasure triggers the production of endorphins, opiate-like biochemicals produced by the body, which in turn create a state of arousal that is optimal for learning.

(From Howard S. Hoffman, 1996, *Amorous turkeys and addicted ducklings: A search for the causes of social attachment*. Boston, MA: Author's Cooperative.) ■

argued there is a *sensitive period* immediately after birth in which bonding (an initial part of the attachment process) can occur through skin-to-skin contact. Klaus and Kennell compared the progress of two groups of infants. One group had much more contact with their mother during the first three days of life. One month later, more bonding had occurred in the extended-contact group than in the routine contact group. During feeding, the extended-contact mothers cuddled and comforted their babies more, and also maintained more eye contact with them.

Later research failed to repeat the findings of Klaus and Kennell (1976). Durkin (1995) pointed out that most of the mothers in the original study were unmarried teenagers from disadvantaged backgrounds. As a result, it may not be reasonable to generalise from this rather atypical sample. The extended-contact mothers may have become more involved with their babies because of the special attention they received than because of the hours of skin-to-skin contact.

Cross-cultural evidence supports the above conclusions. Lozoff (1983) reported that mothers were no more affectionate towards their babies in cultures encouraging early bodily contact between mother and baby. However, there is some support for the skin-to-skin hypothesis. De Chateau and Wiberg (1977) found that mothers who had skin-to-skin contact with their unwashed babies immediately after birth (and also immediately put the baby to their breast to suckle) engaged in significantly more kissing and embracing with their infants, and breastfed on average for 2½ months longer than "traditional contact" mothers.

Klaus and Kennell suggested that prolonged skin-to-skin contact between baby and mother gave rise to greater bonding. However, recent research, including cross-cultural studies, indicates that other forms of attention also promote bonding.

The general view nowadays is that the relationship between mother and baby develops and changes over time rather than being fixed shortly after birth. However, early bonding experiences may well be helpful.

Monotropy or multiple attachments?

There has been much debate about whether infants become attached to only one person or to many people. Attachment to one person is called "monotropy", which means "leaning towards one thing". Bowlby (1953) claimed that infants have a hierarchy of attachments, at the top of which is one central caregiver—this is the **monotropy hypothesis**. This one person is generally (but not invariably) the mother. Thus, the terms "maternal" and "mothering" don't have to refer to a woman. Bowlby (1969) said, "It is because of this marked tendency to monotropy that we are capable of deep feelings."

The special significance of monotropy is that it alone provides the experience of an intense emotional relationship that forms the basis of the internal working model—the schema the child has for forming future relationships. However, Bowlby's notion that young children typically only have one very close attachment is exaggerated. Think back to the research of Schaffer and Emerson (1964; see page 92). They found that 31% of infants had five or more attachments and only 13% were attached to only one person.

Parenting is one of the most important relationships in adult life. A person's attachment to their own parents will influence their subsequent relationship with their own child.

Do early attachments affect future relationships?

According to Bowlby, infants construct an internal working model consisting of rules and expectations concerning their relationships and attachments with other people. This model influences the individual's subsequent relationships including those formed in adulthood. Supporting evidence was reported by Hazan and Shaver (1987). They devised a "love quiz" consisting of a simple adjective checklist of childhood relationships with parents, and parents' relationships with each other, to measure attachment style, and a questionnaire that assessed individuals' beliefs about romantic love. Hazan and Shaver used the responses from 620 adults to classify them (1) as secure, ambivalent, or avoidant "types" based on their description of their childhood experiences, and (2) on their adult style of romantic love. Secure types described their love experiences as happy, friendly, and trusting, and accepted their partners regardless of any faults. Ambivalent types experienced love as involving obsession, desire for reciprocation, intensity, and jealousy, and worry that their partners might abandon them. Avoidant lovers typically feared intimacy, emotional highs and lows, and jealousy. They believed that they didn't need to be loved to be happy. These attachment types are based on research discussed earlier in the chapter using the Strange Situation.

A major problem with the study by Hazan and Shaver (1987) is that some of the data concerning childhood relationships were collected several years after childhood. As a result, what was recalled may not have been very accurate. A second problem is that the data were collected through self-report questionnaires,

KEY TERM

Monotropy hypothesis: the notion that infants have an innate tendency to form strong bonds with one caregiver, usually their mother.

and people don't always give honest answers. A third issue is that Hazan and Shaver (1987) assumed that attachment type is consistent and determines the style of love. However, reality is more complex than that. In subsequent research, Shaver and Hazan (1993) found that 22% of their adult sample changed their attachment style over a 12-month period. These changes often occurred as a result of relationship experiences. Thus, attachment style can influence style of love, but actual experiences of love can also influence attachment style.

Evaluation of Bowlby's theory

Bowlby's theory of attachment has deservedly been one of the most influential theories in the history of psychology. There are several reasons for this. First, Bowlby rightly emphasised the importance of attachment in infants and children. Indeed, it could be argued that nothing matters more for healthy infant development than to have one or more secure attachments. Second, Bowlby put forward the first ever systematic and comprehensive theory of attachment, and most subsequent theorists have made at least some use of his main ideas. Third, the fundamental notion that attachment has great value in maximising the infant's chances of survival helps us to understand why attachment is so important. Fourth, Bowlby's theorising strongly influenced the development of the Strange Situation (discussed earlier), which is easily the most popular way of studying attachment behaviour in infants. Fifth, Bowlby's theory is on the right general lines even if several predictions from his theory have only limited support.

As with any ambitious theory, Bowlby's possesses several weaknesses. First, most of the assumptions of the theory are expressed in terms that are too strong and dogmatic. In other words, many of Bowlby's views are exaggerations.

Second, the evidence generally fails to provide much support for the monotropy hypothesis with its emphasis on a single main attachment. As we saw earlier, Schaffer and Emerson (1964) found that 31% of 18-month-old infants had five or more attachments. Most infants form two or more strong attachments at a relatively early age.

Third, healthy psychological development is not always served by having only one primary attachment. Thomas (1998) suggested that it may be better to have a network of close attachments to sustain the needs of a growing infant. This is certainly true in some cultures such as Caribbean countries. Even in European countries, infants probably benefit from the differences among their attachments. For example, fathers' style of play is more often physically stimulating and unpredictable whereas mothers are more likely to hold their infants, soothe them, attend to their needs, and read them stories (Parke, 1981). In Bowlby's defence, it could be argued that there is nearly always a hierarchy among an infant's attachments. For example, an African tribe, the Efe, from Zaire live in extended family groups. The infants are looked after and even breastfed by different women but usually sleep with their own mother at night. By the age of 6 months, the infants still show a preference for their mothers (Tronick, Morelli, & Ivey, 1992).

Fourth, Bowlby's view of attachment as a template (pattern) for future relationships leads us to expect any given child to form similar relationships with others. However, the similarities among a child's various relationships are actually quite low (Main & Weston, 1981). Evidence links attachment style to later relationships (e.g. Hazan & Shaver, 1987, discussed earlier), but this is not a universal finding. For example, Howes, Matheson, and Hamilton (1994) found that parent–child relationships were not always positively correlated with child–peer relationships. Even when there are positive correlations between the main attachment relationship and later relationships, there are other possible explanations. Perhaps some infants are simply better than others at forming relationships. Children who are appealing to their parents tend to be appealing to other people. As a result, a child who does well in one relationship is likely to do well in others (Jacobson & Wille, 1986).

Fifth, the notions that attachment in infants resembles imprinting in birds and that there is a critical period for strong attachments to be formed are at best only partially true. There is very little direct evidence that infant attachment involves processes resembling imprinting, and it is preferable to focus on sensitive periods rather than critical periods. As we will see later, some children who have been kept in isolation or severely deprived circumstances for the first several years of their lives nevertheless manage to form strong attachments following adoption. Thus, it is NOT absolutely essential for children to form a strong attachment when very young.

> ■ **Activity:** List all the theories of attachment covered in this section. For each of them, suggest how the following questions would be answered: Why do attachments form? With whom are attachments formed? What is the major drawback of this explanation?

Sixth, not everyone accepts Bowlby's evolutionary argument. Bowlby looked back into our evolutionary past and argued that attachment behaviour must be adaptive because it has persisted. However, we can't test this argument. The fact that attachment behaviour has probably persisted throughout human history doesn't prove it is adaptive.

Cultural Variations in Attachment

If attachment is an innate behaviour, then we would expect attachment behaviours to be very similar around the world. Reality is actually more complex than that. Cultural variations in attachment have mostly been studied using the Strange Situation test. One of the most important studies on cultural variations was carried out by van IJzendoorn and Kroonenberg (1988), and is considered in detail below.

Van IJzendoorn and Kroonenberg (1988) aimed to study cultural variations in attachment types through a meta-analysis of research (combining findings from many studies) in which attachments in other cultures had been considered. They compared only the findings of studies using the Strange Situation, to draw inferences about the external validity of this as a measure of attachment in other populations and other settings.

Van IJzendoorn and Kroonenberg (1988) compared the findings from 32 studies that had used the Strange Situation to measure attachment and to classify the attachment relationship between mother and infant. None of the children in the various studies was older than 24 months of age. Research from eight different countries was compared, including Western cultures (USA, Great Britain, Germany, Sweden, and the Netherlands) and non-Western cultures (Japan, China, Israel). Van IJzendoorn and Kroonenberg researched various databases for studies on attachment.

Considerable consistency in the overall distribution of attachment types was found across all the cultures studied. Secure attachment was the most common type of attachment in all eight countries. However, significant differences were found in the distributions of insecure attachments. For example, in Western

See *AS Level Psychology Online* for stimulus material relating to this classic study.

cultures the dominant insecure type is avoidant. In contrast, the dominant insecure type in non-Western cultures is resistant, with China being the only exception (avoidant and resistant were equally common there). A key finding was that the variation in attachment type *within* cultures was one and a half times as great as variation *between* cultures.

What conclusions can we draw from this study? First, the overall consistency in attachment types suggests that there may be universal characteristics that underpin infant and caregiver interactions. Second, the significant variations show that there are greater variations in attachment types among different cultures than had previously been assumed. These differences presumably reflect at least in part cultural differences in child-rearing practices. Third, the greater variation found within cultures than between cultures indicates that focusing at the cultural level may blind us to the substantial differences in patterns of attachment in sub-cultural groups. Thus, it may be more useful to focus on comparisons between sub-cultural groups (e.g. defined by social class or ethnicity) within cultures rather than on cultural comparisons. Fourth, all of the above conclusions are based on findings involving young children under 24 months of age. It is entirely possible that the patterns of attachment shown during the first 2 years of life in any given country will differ somewhat after that.

Why are van IJzendoorn and Kroonenberg's findings important? First, they were the first researchers to carry out a thorough meta-analysis to consider *all* findings on cultural variations using the Strange Situation. Second, their findings indicate strongly that it is wrong to think of any given culture as consisting of the same practices. The notion that there is a *single* British or American culture is a gross oversimplification. In fact, there are several sub-cultures within most large countries which probably differ very much in their child-rearing practices. Third, and related to the second point, the findings of van IJzendoorn and Kroonenberg suggest that the idea of focusing on cultural variations in attachment lacks validity.

There are various weaknesses of the study by van IJzendoorn and Kroonenberg (1988). First, the study is limited in that it doesn't tell us *why* patterns of attachment vary so much within any given culture. We can speculate that variations in child-rearing practices are important, but the study didn't provide any concrete evidence to support this speculation. Some progress on this issue was reported by Sagi, van IJzendoorn, and Koren-Karie (1991) in research discussed shortly.

Second, the greater variation found within than between cultures shows that it is wrong to think of any culture as a whole—most countries have many sub-cultures differing in the nature of attachment types. Thus, the findings may not be representative of the culture they are assumed to represent, and will generalise only to the sub-cultures that were sampled.

Third, the Strange Situation was created and tested in the United States, which means that it may be culturally biased (ethnocentric). In other words, the Strange Situation reflects the norms and values of American culture. More generally, as Rothbaum et al.

Thinking of your own area, your town or village, what sub-cultures are you aware of? Could any of these have different ideas on child-rearing?

EXAM HINT

If you are asked to outline two cultural variations in attachment, you could use the Van IJzendoorn and Kroonenberg (1988) study to discuss:

- The higher number of avoidant infants in individualistic cultures.
- The higher number of resistant infants in collectivistic cultures.

If you are asked to outline two factors that influence cross-cultural attachment, you could discuss:

- Childrearing practices.
- The different cultural norms of individualistic vs collectivistic cultures.

If you are asked to outline two effects of cross-cultural variation in attachment, you could discuss:

- The higher incidence of avoidant attachment in individualistic cultures.
- The higher incidence of resistant attachment in collectivistic cultures.

KEY TERMS

Amae: a Japanese word referring to a positive form of attachment that involves emotional dependence, clinging, and attention-seeking behaviour. Such behaviour is regarded more negatively in Western countries.
Imposed etic: the use of a technique developed in one culture to study another culture.

How similar is attachment behaviour in different cultures?

(2000, p. 1101) pointed out, "Assumptions . . . such as that children are the logical focus of attention and that behaviour in reunions best captures the dynamics of close relationships, are based in Western thought." For example, the Japanese have a word *amae*, which means emotional dependence (literally "indulgent dependence"). Infants showing amae exhibit much clinging behaviour and need for attention. These forms of behaviour are regarded as indicating insecure attachment by Western psychologists but indicate good adjustment in Japan. Thus, the Strange Situation lacks external validity, which means that the findings and insights based on it may be less meaningful than used to be thought. We can summarise by saying that the research discussed by van IJzendoorn and Kroonenberg (1988) involves an imposed etic—this is the use of a technique developed in one culture to study another culture.

Fourth, the various findings were based exclusively on children aged no more than 24 months. In other words, the study by van IJzendoorn and Kroonenberg (1988) doesn't tell us anything directly about children's attachments from the third year of life onwards. There is no reason to suppose that what is true during the second year of life is also true at later stages of development.

Sagi et al. (1991) reported a detailed study on cultural variations in the Strange Situation test in the United States, Israel, Japan, and Germany. The findings for the American infants were very similar to those reported by Ainsworth et al. (1978): 71% of them showed secure attachment, 12% showed resistant attachment, and 17% were avoidant.

The Israeli infants behaved rather differently. Secure attachment was shown by 62% of the Israeli infants, 33% were resistant, and only 5% were avoidant. These infants lived on a kibbutz, which is a communal settlement in which children are looked after much of the time by adults who are not part of their family. However, since they mostly had a close relationship with their mothers, they tended not to be avoidant.

Japanese mothers practically never leave their infants alone with a stranger. However, in spite of the differences in child-rearing practices in Japan and in Israel, the Japanese infants showed similar attachment styles to the Israeli ones. Two-thirds of them (68%) had a secure attachment, 32% were resistant, and

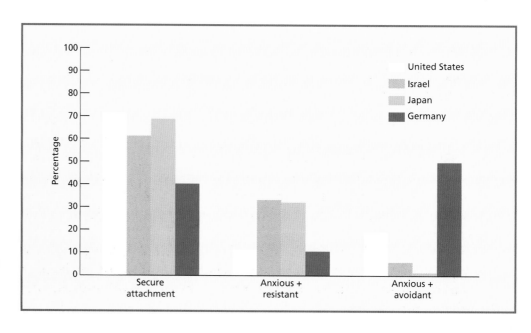

Children from different countries vary in their attachment types. The graph summarises research from Sagi et al. (1991) and Ainsworth and Bell (1970).

none was avoidant. It is not surprising that none of the Japanese infants treated a stranger similarly to their mother given that most of them have rarely if ever been on their own with a stranger. Durrett et al. (1984) studied Japanese families in which the mothers were pursuing careers and so had to leave their children in the care of others. Their children showed a similar pattern of attachment styles to those in the United States.

Finally, the German infants showed a different pattern of attachment from the other three groups of infants. Only 40% of them were securely attached, 49% were avoidant, and 11% were resistant. Why was that? Part of the answer is that German parents regard some aspects of securely attached behaviour as indicating that infants are spoiled (Sagi & Lewkowicz, 1987). In addition, Grossmann et al. (1985, p. 253) argued that German culture requires distance between parents and children: "The ideal is an independent, non-clinging infant who does not make demands on the parents but rather unquestioningly obeys their commands."

? Do you think we all tend to judge other social groups or cultures from our own point of view? Do you ever comment on another type of behaviour, different from your own? How do you do this? Could it be a type of cultural relativism?

Cross-cultural research

There are several reasons for conducting cross-cultural research; that is, research that looks at the customs and practices of different countries and makes comparisons with our own cultural norms. First of all, such research can tell us about what might be universal in human behaviour. If the same behaviours are observed in many different cultures, all of which have different ways of socialising children, then the behaviour may be due to innate (universal) factors rather than learning. The second reason for conducting cross-cultural research is that it offers us insights into our own behaviour. Insights that we may not otherwise be aware of. Perhaps that is the appeal of watching programmes on the television that show foreign lands and different people.

There are some major weaknesses to cross-cultural research. First of all, any sample of a group of people may well be biased and therefore we may be mistaken in thinking that the observations made of one group of people are representative of that culture. Second, where the observations are made by an outsider, that person's own culture will bias how they interpret the data they observe. Finally, the psychological tools that are used to measure people, such as IQ tests and the Strange Situation, are designed in one particular culture and based on assumptions of that culture. They may not have any meaning in another culture.

Therefore cross-cultural research has the potential to be highly informative about human behaviour but also has many important weaknesses.

Disruption of Attachment, Failure to Form Attachment (Privation), and Effects of Institutionalisation

In the real world, circumstances such as divorce between parents or the death of a parent can disrupt the child's attachments or even prevent them from being formed at all. If attachment is critical to healthy psychological development, then Bowlby's theory would predict that any disruption to this process should result in the opposite effect—unhealthy psychological development. One way of determining the validity of Bowlby's theory is to consider the effects of such disruption.

In this section, we discuss the effects on the young child of being separated from one or more of the most important adults in his/her life. Most studies have focused on the long-term effects of deprivation. However, we will first consider some of the short-term effects.

Separation from the mother can have severe emotional effects on a child. The first stage of the child's response to the separation is known as protest: an intense period during which the child cries for much of the time.

Short-term effects of separation

Even fairly brief separation from a primary caregiver can have severe emotional effects on the child. Separation can be distinguished from deprivation. **Separation** involves distress when separated from a person to whom there is an attachment bond for a relatively short period of time. In contrast, **deprivation** occurs when a bond has been formed and is then broken for what are generally fairly long periods of time. Thus, separation is a mild form of deprivation.

One of the main predictions from Bowlby's theory is that young children might suffer severe emotional effects as a result of even short-term separation from their primary caregiver. At the start of the 1950s this view was somewhat controversial, and the necessary evidence wasn't available. However, as we will see, relevant evidence was published in 1952.

Robertson and Bowlby (1952) studied young children separated from their mother for some time, often because she had gone into hospital. They observed three stages in the child's response to separation, which led them to produce the protest–despair–detachment (PDD) model:

1. Protest, which is often very intense. The child cries much of the time, and sometimes seems panic-stricken. Anger and fear are present.
2. Despair, involving a total loss of hope. The child is often apathetic, and shows little interest in its surroundings. The child often engages in self-comforting behaviour such as thumb-sucking or rocking.
3. Detachment, during which the child seems to behave in a less distressed way. If the mother of caregiver re-appears during this stage, she is not responded to with any great interest.

It used to be thought that children in the third stage of detachment had adjusted fairly well to separation from their mother. However, the calm behaviour shown by the child when its mother re-appears is probably a disguise for true feelings. Fortunately, most children do re-establish an attachment to the mother over time.

The research of Robertson and Bowlby (1952) is important for various reasons. First, they were among the first researchers to study in detail the effects of short-term separation on young children. Second, they identified clearly the main stages in children's response to separation. Third, their research highlighted the importance of minimising the adverse effects of separation on young children.

Evaluation of the PDD model

Is it inevitable that short-term separation produces the various negative effects predicted by the PDD model? Robertson and Robertson (1971) suggested that it isn't. They looked after several young children separated from their mothers in their own home. They ensured that the children became familiar with their new surroundings beforehand to minimise any distress they might experience. They also tried to provide the children with a similar daily routine and discussed the children's mothers with them. This approach proved successful, with the children showing much less distress than most separated children.

The Robertsons also studied other children who were separated from their mothers but who spent their time in a residential nursery. These children's didn't cope well—they received good physical care but lacked emotional care. The Robertsons said that the nursery children experienced **bond disruption**, whereas the others didn't because they were offered substitute mothering. Therefore, we might conclude that separation need not lead to deprivation, but it may do so if accompanied by bond disruption.

Barrett (1997) was much more critical of the PDD model. Barrett pointed out that there is no strong evidence for the proposed sequence of protest, despair, and detachment. Of importance, the model doesn't take individual differences into account. For example, a securely attached child may show little initial protest and cope relatively well, whereas an avoidant child would be plunged more immediately into protest and despair and become very disoriented. Barrett also argued that the PDD model is flawed because it assumes that very young children are much less socially competent than is actually the case. Thus, many young children have a greater ability to cope with separation than was assumed by Robertson and Bowlby (1952).

Long-term effects of separation: Maternal deprivation

Prior to the development of his theory of attachment, John Bowlby proposed the **maternal deprivation hypothesis** (1953), which focused more on the effects of deprivation. According to this hypothesis, breaking the maternal bond with the child during the early years of its life is likely to have serious effects on its intellectual, social, and emotional development. Bowlby also claimed that many of these negative effects could be permanent and irreversible. However, contrary to popular belief, Bowlby argued that about 25% (rather than 100%) of children suffer long-term damage from maternal deprivation (Di Dwyer, personal communication). Finally, Bowlby endorsed monotropy. This is the notion (discussed earlier) that human infants have an innate tendency to form strong bonds with one particular individual (typically the mother).

When Bowlby put forward his maternal deprivation hypothesis in the early 1950s, it was regarded as revolutionary. Most professionals at that time felt that adequate physical provision was most important for healthy development. In addition, however, it was accepted by the early 1940s that children could suffer to some extent if separated from their mother for a long period of time. However, the full extent of such suffering hadn't been clearly established.

Findings

In the context of the time, Bowlby's (1944) classic study of juvenile thieves had a major impact. He carried out his well-known study on clients from the child guidance clinic where he worked. He interviewed the children and their families, and gradually built up a record of their early life experiences. He found that some children had experienced "early and prolonged separation from their mothers", and some of them were emotionally maladjusted. In particular, he diagnosed the condition of affectionless psychopathy in some of the children, a disorder involving a lack of guilt and remorse. Could there be a link between this form of emotional maladjustment and early separation?

Bowlby focused on a group of children referred to the clinic because of stealing (these were the juvenile thieves). He compared them with a control group of children referred to the clinic because of emotional problems but who hadn't committed any crimes. He found that 32% of the thieves were affectionless psychopaths lacking a social conscience, whereas none of the control children was an affectionless psychopath. Of the thieves diagnosed as affectionless psychopaths, 86% had experienced early separation (even if only for a week

How might the findings from the Robertson and Robertson study be applied to helping children in institutional care?

KEY TERM

Maternal deprivation hypothesis: Bowlby's view that separation from the primary caregiver leads to disruption and perhaps breaking of the attachment bond, with long-term adverse and possibly permanent effects on emotional development.

before the age of 5). In contrast, only 17% of the thieves without affectionless psychopathy had been maternally deprived.

This study by Bowlby is important for various reasons. First, the findings seemed to show that maternal deprivation can have very severe effects, including producing a lack of emotional development (affectionless psychopathy). Second, Bowlby's results suggested that early maternal deprivation could have negative effects still present several years later. Third, the findings of this study led many other researchers to examine the relationship between children's early experience and their subsequent emotional development.

Some of the main evidence used by Bowlby (1951, 1953) to support his hypothesis was the research of Spitz (1945) and Goldfarb (1947). Spitz visited several very poor orphanages and other institutions in South America. Children in those orphanages received very little warmth or attention from the staff and had become apathetic. Many of these children seemed to suffer from **anaclitic depression**, a state involving resigned helplessness and loss of appetite. This was attributed to their lack of emotional care and separation from their mothers. Spitz and Wolf (1946) studied 100 apparently normal children who became seriously depressed after staying in hospital—the children generally recovered well only if the separation lasted less than 3 months.

Goldfarb (1947) compared two groups of infants who before fostering spent either only the first few months or 3 years at a poor and inadequately staffed orphanage. Both groups were tested at various times up to the age of 12. Those children who had spent 3 years at the orphanage did less well than the others on intelligence tests, were less socially mature, and more likely to be aggressive.

In the 1950s, orphanages in the UK gradually began to disappear and so research into the negative effects of living in such institutions was limited. More recently, however, there has been a new opportunity to study orphans—children from Romania. The findings on these children are discussed shortly.

Evaluation

Bowlby was correct in emphasising the importance of the relationship between mother or other caregiver and the child. However, his approach was oversimplified in various ways. First, the emotional problems shown by children in orphanages and other institutions may be due to the poor quality of those institutions rather than to maternal deprivation itself. Second, as we will see, many of the adverse effects of maternal deprivation are more reversible than was assumed by Bowlby. Third, Bowly didn't distinguish clearly between deprivation (in which the child is separated from a major attachment) and privation (in which the child has never had a close attachment with anyone).

Distinguishing deprivation, privation, and institutionalisation

Rutter (1972) pointed out that Bowlby had assumed that *all* experiences of deprivation were the same, whereas there are some very important differences. Children may experience short-term separation, as in the Robertsons' studies, or they may have repeated and prolonged separations. Children may experience separation without bond disruption, as with Bowlby's sanatorium study, or they may have no adequate substitute care. Finally, children may experience deprivation as a result of never having formed any close attachments.

Rutter argued that there is a crucial difference between deprivation and privation, a distinction *not* made by Bowlby. Deprivation occurs when a child has formed an important attachment from which it is then separated. In contrast, **privation** occurs when a child has never formed a close relationship with anyone.

Many of Bowlby's juvenile delinquents had experienced several changes of home/principal caregiver during their early childhood. This indicated to Rutter (1981) that their later problems were due to privation rather than to deprivation. Rutter argued convincingly that the effects of privation are much more severe and long-lasting than those of deprivation. Research directly focusing on privation is discussed next.

As was discussed earlier, there are issues of interpretation with the research of Spitz (1945) and Goldfarb (1947) based on children in orphanages and other institutions. The reason is that the experiences of these children differed in two important ways from those of most other children. First, as emphasised by Bowlby, these children had experienced deprivation (and others had experienced privation). Second, these children had experienced spending long periods of time in an institution, and the quality of most of these institutions was generally very poor. As a result, it is hard to know the relative importance of these factors. However, in recent decades there has been an increasing interest in studying the effects on children of living in an institution. Researchers in this area focus on **institutionalisation**—the negative effects on speed of social and/or cognitive development that occurs when children are placed in institutions (e.g. hospitals; orphanages) for short or long periods of time. We will discuss studies on institutionalisation shortly.

Long-term effects of privation

Hodges and Tizard (1989) carried out an important study into the effects of privation but one that also tells us something about the effects of institutionalisation. They investigated the permanence (or otherwise) of the effects of privation (the state of a child who has never formed a close relationship with anyone) considering both emotional and social effects in adolescence. Sixty-five children taken into care before the age of 4 months formed an opportunity sample. This was a natural experiment using a matched pairs design, because the institutionalised children were compared with a control group raised at home. It was a longitudinal study (age on entering care to 16 years). Each child had been looked after on average by 24 different caregivers by the age of 2. By the age of 4 years, 24 had been adopted, 15 restored to their natural home, and the rest remained in the institution. The children were assessed at the ages 4, 8, and 16 on emotional and social competence through interview and self-report questionnaires.

What did Hodges and Tizard (1989) find? At the age of 4, the children hadn't formed attachments. By the age of 8, significant differences existed between the adopted and restored children. At the age of 8 and 16, most of the adopted children had formed close relationships with their caregiver. This was less true of the children who had returned to their own families, because their parents were often unsure they wanted their children back. However, negative social effects were evident in both the adopted and restored children at school—they were attention seeking and had difficulty in forming peer relationships.

At the age of 16, the family relationships of the adopted children were as good as those of families in which none of the children had been removed from the family home. However, children who had returned to their families showed little

See *AS Level Psychology Online* for stimulus material relating to Hodges and Tizard's (1989) classic study.

 How does a natural experiment differ from a laboratory experiment?

KEY TERMS

Privation: an absence of attachments, as opposed to the loss of attachments, due to the lack of an appropriate attachment figure. Privation is likely to lead to permanent emotional damage.

Institutionalisation: the adverse effects on children of being placed in an institution; these effects can influence cognitive and social development.

? How might we account for the different patterns of behaviour shown by adopted children and children who returned to their families?

? How has the research of Hodges and Tizard added to our knowledge of the effects of deprivation?

affection for their parents, and their parents weren't very affectionate towards them. Both groups of adolescents were less likely than adolescents in ordinary families to have a special friend or to regard other adolescents as sources of emotional support. Overall, however, the adopted children were better adjusted than would have been predicted by Bowlby.

What conclusions can we draw? The above findings show that some of the effects of privation can be reversed, because the children were able to form attachments in spite of their privation (and experience of institutionalisation). However, some privation effects are long-lasting, as shown by the difficulties the institutionalised children faced at school. What seems to be especially important is for children who have been institutionalised to move to a loving environment. That was more likely to be the case for children who were adopted than those who returned to their own families.

Extreme privation

A few researchers have considered the effects of very extreme privation and isolation on children. The really surprising finding is how resilient many of these children seem to be. Koluchová (1976) studied identical twins in Czechoslovakia who had spent most of the first 7 years of their lives locked in a cellar. They had been treated very badly and were often beaten. They were barely able to talk and relied mainly on gestures rather than speech. The twins were fostered at about the age of 9 by a pair of loving sisters. By the time they were 14, their behaviour was essentially normal. By the age of 20, they were of above average intelligence and had excellent relationships with the members of their foster family (Koluchová, 1991).

Curtiss (1989) and Rymer (1993) reported a case study (detailed investigation of a single individual) concerned with Genie (not her real name). She spent most of her childhood locked on her own in a room at her home in Temple City, Los Angeles. She was found on 4 November 1970 when 13½ years old. She hadn't been fed properly, couldn't stand erect, and had no social skills. At that time, she didn't understand language and couldn't speak. One reason why she didn't speak was that she had been beaten many times for making a noise.

After she was found, Genie was put in the Children's Hospital in Los Angeles and received help from a team of scientists (the Genie Team). Within a few months, Genie could understand more than 100 words even though she was still practically silent. Her "talking" at that time was limited to short high-pitched squeaks. A few months later, Genie was placed in a foster home. She showed a

Case studies

Some of the studies of privation described in this chapter are case studies. The advantage of such research is that it produces rich data that can be used by a researcher to develop new theoretical ideas. Case studies can provide information about exceptional types of behaviour or performance that had been thought to be impossible.

However, we need to be very careful when interpreting the evidence from a case study. The greatest limitation is the typically low reliability. The findings that are obtained from one unusual or exceptional individual are unlikely to be repeated in detail when another individual is studied. Thus, it is often very hard to generalise from a single case study. Second, many case studies involve the use of lengthy, fairly unstructured interviews that may produce subjective information. Third, researchers generally only report some of the data they obtained from their interviews with the participant. They may be unduly selective in terms of what they choose to report or to omit.

great interest in learning and her vocabulary increased dramatically. However, she had very little ability to put words together to form meaningful sentences. This inability was *not* due to low intelligence—Genie showed very good spatial ability and an ability to see patterns. Strikingly, the use of brain imaging revealed that Genie had practically no left-brain activity—the side of the brain typically dominant in language processing.

Later on, Genie's story became tragic again. She went back to live with her mother, who proved unable to look after her. As a result, she was sent to several foster homes. In one of these homes, she was abused. She began to deteriorate physically and mentally, and she was sent to live in a home for retarded adults.

Much more encouraging findings were reported in a study on Tom (Soutter, 1995). Up to the age of 10 he was kept by his parents in a bare room. At that age he was terrified of other children and had a totally expressionless face. There was a transformation in Tom during 8 years of treatment. At the age of 18 he was studying at university and had some friends. In addition, his face registered a range of emotions, and his general behaviour was appropriate to someone of that age.

As we have seen, not all children who experience privation experience permanent emotional damage. Freud and Dann (1951) provided evidence that young children who form strong attachments with other young children can avoid the severe damage resulting from privation. They studied six war orphans whose parents had been murdered in a concentration camp when the children were only a few months old. The infants lived together in a deportation camp for about 2 years until the age of 3, and had very distressing experiences such as watching people being hanged. In this camp, they were put in the Ward for Motherless Children, and had very limited contact with anyone other than each other. After the camp was liberated at the end of the Second World War, the children were flown to England. When freed from the camp, the children hadn't yet developed speech properly, they were underweight, and they expressed hostility towards adults. However, they were greatly attached to each other. According to Freud and Dann (1951, p. 131), "The children's positive feelings were centred exclusively in

? What ethical issues might be involved in the case study of Genie? Do these outweigh any understandings gained from this study?

Children in concentration camps experienced terrible early privation. The children in this picture are awaiting release from Auschwitz in January 1945. Freud and Dann studied six such children who only had each other for companions throughout their early lives.

their own group . . . They had no other wish than to be together and became upset when they were separated from each other, even for short moments."

As time went by, the six children became attached to their adult carers. In addition, they developed rapidly at a social level and in their use of language. It is hard to say whether their early experiences had any lasting adverse effects. One of them (Leah) received psychiatric assistance and another (Jack) sometimes felt very alone and isolated (Moskovitz, 1983). However, it wouldn't be exceptional to find similar problems in six adults selected at random.

Evaluation of studies of privation

The evidence indicates that most adverse effects of maternal deprivation or privation can be reversed, and that children are more resilient than Bowlby believed. Much of the available evidence doesn't support Bowlby's (1951) argument that the negative effects of maternal deprivation couldn't be reversed or undone. Instead, the evidence indicates that even privation doesn't always have permanent effects. Clarke and Clarke (1998) noted that early experience represents "no more than an initial step on the ongoing path of life". In other words, for most people early experience is very much related to what happens later on. Bad experiences are often likely to be followed by more of the same. However, where severely bad experiences are followed by much better ones, the outcome may well be good, as happened to the Czech twins who went to a loving home. Unfortunately, as we have seen, Genie found herself in a foster home in which she was once again abused.

In spite of the positive findings from most of the research, there is one set of children for whom the outcome is typically very discouraging. These are children with reactive attachment disorder, which is described in the box below.

Reactive attachment disorder

Consider a child in the early months of life. The child is hungry, or wet. What does the child do? He or she screams out for attention, and in the rage expressed, the mother comes to the child's aid and feeds or changes the child. Day after day, week after week, the closeness of eye contact, touch, movements, and smiles creates a bond of trust between the child and its mother.

But what happens if this cycle is broken? What if the mother doesn't want to respond to the demanding needs of the child? What if there is an undiagnosed condition in the child that is never appropriately responded to and so the child is never comforted? In these instances, the child does not learn to trust, does not learn to bond, and proceeds on with the next lesson to learn in life.

This leads to a condition called "reactive detachment disorder". Children with attachment disorders have trouble trusting others. Trusting means to love, and loving hurts. They attempt to control everyone and everything in their world. Lack of a conscience appears to be caused by their lacking trust in anyone. They become so dependent on themselves that they ignore the needs of others to the point that they will steal, damage, and destroy anything that they feel hinders their control. In short, they do not trust any caregiver or person in authority.

As a relatively new diagnosis to the DSM-IV manual, reactive attachment disorder is often misunderstood, and relatively unknown. All too often these individuals grow up untreated and become sociopaths without conscience and without concern for anyone but themselves. This condition was made popular by the academy award-winning movie Good Will Hunting. But unlike the movie, the hero or heroine rarely drives off into the sunset to have a happy-ever-after life. More realistically, parental dreams are lost, and the children grow up uncaring and without social conscience.

(Adapted from http://members.tripod.com/~radclass/index.html)

It is important to study the details of many of the studies on privation. They involve very small samples and this makes it hard to generalise from them. In some cases, it is possible that the children were abnormal from birth—we can only look back at their experiences and abilities. The fact that Genie had very little activity in the left half of her brain could possibly indicate some inborn problem. However, it is probably more likely to reflect her almost total lack of language experience for the first several years of her life.

News reports in the 1980s highlighted deprivation in Romanian orphanages, with many children demonstrating anaclitic depression, having received basic sustenance but little human warmth or contact.

Clearer evidence comes from Hodges and Tizard's (1989) longitudinal research. At one level, this study seems to support our conclusion that deprivation and privation can both be recovered from given good subsequent care. However, Hodges and Tizard's research also suggests a rather different conclusion, which is that recovery is only possible within the context of a loving relationship. Hodges and Tizard found that those children who went on to have good relationships at home coped well at home but found relationships outside the home difficult. In some way, they lacked an adequate model for future relationships. This would seem to support Bowlby's attachment theory.

Long-term effects of institutionalisation

As was mentioned earlier, much research in recent years has focused on Romanian children who spent some of their early lives in orphanages. The study of such children provides information about the effects of institutionalisation. Rutter and the ERA Study Team (1998) followed 111 Romanian orphans adopted in the UK before the age of 2. When the orphans first arrived in the UK they were physically and mentally underdeveloped. By the age of 4, however, all of them had improved, presumably as a result of improved care. Those who were adopted latest showed the slowest improvements educationally and in emotional development. However, reasonable recovery occurred given good subsequent care.

CASE STUDY: THE RILEY FAMILY

Jean Riley (54) and her husband Peter (58) adopted two children from Romania who are now aged 17 and 9. Cezarina, when they first saw her, was cross-eyed, filthy, and about four years behind in her physical development. First Cezarina's physical problems had to be sorted out, but from then on she made good progress. However, Cezarina is "laid back" about things that seem important to Jean and Peter. Jean understands this attitude, though, because clearly examinations seem less important when a child has had to struggle to survive.

According to Jean, Cezarina is bright, but needs to have information reinforced over and over again. She has also struggled to understand jokes and sarcasm, although this may be due to difficulties with learning the language. Jean sees Cezarina as naive and emotionally immature. Cezarina says herself that initially she was frustrated because she couldn't communicate. She does see herself as being different from other girls, although she likes the same things, such as fashion and pop music. Jean runs The Parent Network for the Institutionalised Child, a group for people who have adopted such children. Cezarina has partly recovered from her poor early experiences.

(Account based on an article in Woman, 21 September 1998.) ■

O'Connor et al. (2000) studied Romanian children exposed to very severe deprivation and neglect in Romania before being adopted by caring British families. They compared those children adopted between 24 and 42 months (late-placed adoptees) and those adopted between 6 and 24 months (early-placed adoptees). Both groups showed significant recovery from their ordeal in Romania. However, the late-placed adoptees had greater difficulty in achieving good cognitive and social development than early-placed adoptees.

Gunnar and van Dulmen (2007) reported similar findings in a study on children institutionalised in various countries around the world before being adopted by an American family. Compared to children being brought up by their parents, the previously institutionalised children had increased rates of attention and social problems. In addition, those who were adopted after the age of 24 months had more behaviour problems than those adopted at a younger age.

Smyke et al. (2007) carried out a thorough study in which they studied young children being raised in institutions in Romania. Compared to young children of the same age being raised at home by their parents, the institutionalised children showed severe delays in cognitive development, had poorer physical growth, and had much inferior social competence. Smyke et al. addressed the issue of the factors responsible for the low levels of cognitive development and social competence in the institutionalised children. They argued that two factors seemed likely to be important: (1) the percentage of their lives these children had spent in an institution; and (2) the quality of caregiving the children received (assessed by analysing videotapes of child–caregiver interaction). What they found was that the institutionalised children's cognitive development and social competence depended far more on the quality of caregiving they received than on the percentage of their lives they had spent in an institution. This is very important—it indicates

HOW SCIENCE WORKS: PRIVATION

Attachments and the issue of day care are personal subjects and scientists have to be sensitive when investigating them, as researchers are obliged to consider possible psychological (as well as physical) risks to participants such as becoming upset, anxious, or stressed about their personal behaviour and/or history. This means that questionnaires and surveys must be constructed sensitively and participants told that they do not have to take part if they would prefer not to.

You could use ICT to find and print out a short piece about the Romanian orphans studied by Rutter and others, or one of the case studies of privated children. Survey a few participants by asking then to read this and then say what they think were the four most important factors missing in these children's early lives. You could then look at your findings and see if there is much agreement, and get a snapshot of our cultural beliefs.

http://news.bbc.co.uk/1/hi/world/europe/4630855.stm is a short article about the orphanages.

EXAM HINT

If the answer is on privation you can still use Bowlby's "44 juvenile thieves" study as evidence. Remember that Rutter (1972) made the criticism that Bowlby didn't distinguish between deprivation and privation, and in fact some of the juveniles did suffer from privation. You can then use other studies to further weigh up the effects of privation. These could include Hodges and Tizard (1989), as well as case studies such as Genie (Curtiss, 1989) and Tom (Soutter, 1995), remembering to discuss the limitations of such case studies.

that being brought up in an institution doesn't inevitably cause major problems provided that caregiver quality is high.

Are there any very long-term effects of institutionalisation? Sigal et al. (2003) addressed this issue in a study of middle-aged adults (mean age = 59 years) who had been placed in an institution at birth or early childhood. These adults were far more likely never to have married than a randomly selected control group (45% vs 17%), they reported fewer social contacts, and more psychological distress including depression. In addition, the adults who had been institutionalised were much more likely than the controls to suffer from a range of physical illnesses (e.g. migraine; stomach ulcers; and arthritis). Thus, adults who were institutionalised several decades earlier seem to suffer very long-term consequences psychologically and physically.

SECTION SUMMARY

❖ There is an important distinction between secure and insecure attachment. Maltreated children are more likely than other children to be insecurely attached.

❖ Most children show consistency of attachment style over time.

❖ Secure attachment is associated with greater social competence and language skills.

❖ Studies on monkeys show that infant–infant affectional bonds can be as effective as mother–infant bonds.

Types of attachment, including insecure and secure attachment

❖ Ainsworth found using the Strange Situation that about 70% of infants show secure attachment, 20% avoidant attachment, and 10% resistant attachment.

❖ Research based on the Strange Situation has the following weaknesses:
  – it is culturally biased;
  – it is artificial because caregivers know they are being observed;
  – it is oversimplified because of the reliance on a small number of categories. It is preferable to think in terms of two attachment dimensions: avoidant-withdrawal vs proximity-seeking and angry and resistant strategies vs emotional confidence.

❖ Maternal sensitivity is positively associated with secure infant attachment, and there is a small positive association between paternal sensitivity and secure attachment.

❖ According to the temperament hypothesis, infants' attachment style depends on their innate temperament. This hypothesis doesn't explain why there is only a modest tendency for infants' attachment type with their father to be the same as that with their mother.

Attachment in humans

❖ According to learning theorists, infant attachment behaviour can be explained in terms of classical and/or operant conditioning. The basic assumption is that the mother is rewarding for the infant because she provides a source of food.

❖ According to social learning theorists, infant attachment to the caregiver occurs through modelling, direct instruction, and social facilitation.

❖ The learning theory approach exaggerates the importance of food in infant attachment, and it is reductionist and oversimplified.

Explanations of attachment: Learning theory and evolutionary perspective, including Bowlby

❖ According to Bowlby, attachment is an innate and adaptive process for both infant and parent. There is a critical period early in life during which bonding or attachment needs to take place. This resembles imprinting in some species of birds. In fact, it is preferable to think in terms of sensitive periods rather than critical periods.

❖ According to Bowlby's monotropy hypothesis, infants have a hierarchy of attachments at the top of which is one caregiver (typically the mother). In fact, many secure infants have strong attachments to two or more adults.

Cultural variations in attachment

❖ Van IJzendoorn and Kroonenberg (1988) found that secure attachment was the most common type of infant attachment in eight different countries. The dominant insecure attachment type was avoidant in Western cultures but resistant in non-Western cultures.

❖ In spite of cultural differences in attachment, van IJzendoorn and Kroonenberg (1988) found that the variation in attachment types within cultures was greater than the variation between cultures.

❖ There are various weaknesses with the research of van IJzendoorn and Kroonenberg (1988):
  – It doesn't tell us why patterns of attachment vary so much within any given culture.
  – It is misleading to focus on cultures rather than sub-cultures. The research involved the Strange Situation test, which was created and tested in the United States and so may be culturally biased.
  – It considered only children aged no more than 24 months, and so tells us nothing about children's attachments at older ages.

Disruption of attachment, failure to form attachment (privation), and effects of institutionalisation

❖ According to Robertson and Bowlby (1952), young children separated from their mother go through three stages: protest; despair, and detachment. There is no strong evidence for this sequence of stages, and this approach doesn't take account of individual differences among children.

❖ According to Bowlby's maternal deprivation hypothesis, breaking the maternal bond with a young child often causes serious effects to its social, intellectual, and emotional development.

❖ Studies by Bowlby and others seem to indicate that maternal deprivation can produce negative effects that are still evident several years later.

❖ There are various weaknesses with the maternal deprivation hypothesis:
  – Bowlby failed to distinguish clearly between deprivation and privation, in which the child has never formed a close relationship.
  – It is often unclear whether the adverse effects observed in children who have been maternally deprived are due to the deprivation or due to poor quality care they receive afterwards.
  – The effects of maternal deprivation are often more reversible than was assumed by Bowlby.

❖ It is important to distinguish among deprivation (separation from a close attachment), privation (never having had a close attachment), and institutionalisation (adverse effects of living in an institution).

❖ Hodges and Tizard (1989) found that some of the negative effects of privation can be reversed, with the children concerned forming strong attachments. What was most important was for children who had been institutionalised to move to a loving environment.

❖ Some children have shown reasonable recovery from extreme privation. This is especially likely when such children form strong attachments with other children.

❖ Many of the studies on extreme privation are limited because they involve very small samples and so it is hard to generalise the findings.

❖ Children brought up in institutions in Romania generally have poor social and cognitive skills. However, those who received a high quality of caregiving did much better than other institutionalised children.

❖ Middle-aged adults who had been institutionalised in early childhood were found to have long-term negative psychological and physical effects.

SECTION 8
ATTACHMENT IN EVERYDAY LIFE

Some people interpreted Bowlby's maternal deprivation hypothesis as meaning that **day care** was a bad thing. Separation would harm the child's emotional development if he/she spent time away from a primary caregiver. However, this is only an interpretation put on Bowlby's views. Bowlby himself didn't specifically suggest that women should stay at home to look after their children. However, it seems logical that if absent mothers create unhappy children, then mothers need to be present full-time. It is even possible that Bowlby's views were popularised by post-war governments to encourage women to stay at home—a cheaper alternative than having to provide universal child-care facilities.

On the other side of the coin, there were those who argued for the *benefits* of day care, at least for certain children. In America in the 1960s there was a move towards providing pre-school care for disadvantaged children to enable them to start school on a par with their middle-class peers. The best-known project of this kind was called Headstart, which involved half a million children in its first year. Kagan, Kearsley, and Zelazo (1980) asked whether there wasn't some kind of dual standard: lower-class children might benefit from day care as a source of intellectual enrichment, whereas middle-class children would be harmed because of maternal deprivation.

Many parents have to work for economic reasons, and others want to because they enjoy their work or would otherwise feel trapped at home. In several countries, very large numbers of young children are put into day care for several days a week while their mothers are at work. In the United States, for example, 80% of children under the age of 6 spend an average of 40 hours a week in non-parental care every week. Until the 1960s, this happened only rarely.

It is important to note that there are many different forms of day care. For example, young children can be looked after at home by a relative, they can go to a day nursery, they can be looked after at a home by a childminder, and so on. As we will see, the precise effects of day care often vary depending on what kind of day care a child experiences.

In view of the millions of children affected, the question of the effects of day care is of great practical concern. We have seen that there are arguments for and against it. We will now consider how much day care affects the social development of children. After that, we consider the implications of research into

KEY TERM

Day care: care that is provided by people other than the parent or relatives of the infant, for example, nurseries, childminders, play groups, etc. A temporary alternative to the caregiver, day care is distinct from institutionalised care, which provides permanent substitute care.

? Did you or one of your siblings have day care? What can be recalled about that experience?

attachment and day care for child-care policy and practices, including the availability of quality day care.

Impact of Different Forms of Day Care on Children's Social Development, Including Effects on Aggression and Peer Relations

We will very shortly start to discuss research concerned with the effects of day care on children's social development, focusing especially on peer relations and aggression. Before we do that, however, it is important to emphasise that much of the early research in this area was limited in various ways. For example, we should distinguish between the effects on children of the quantity of day care (e.g. number of hours per week) and of the quality of day care (e.g. does it provide for children's needs?). We should also distinguish between different types of day care—there is no reason to assume that day care provided by grandparents will have precisely the same effects as day care provided in a group setting (e.g. preschool nursery). However, these (and other) distinctions have very often been ignored.

Childminding

Some parents prefer childminding (including what are called child-care home and in-home care in the National Institute of Child Health and Human Development (NICHD) research) because it appears more similar to the care that a child might get in its own home. Mayall and Petrie (1983) studied a group of London children aged under 2 and their mothers and childminders. The quality of care offered to these children varied considerably. Some childminders were excellent, but others provided a rather unstimulating environment and the children in their care didn't thrive.

Bryant, Harris, and Newton (1980) also studied childminding. They found that some of the children were actually disturbed. Many minders felt they didn't have to form emotional bonds with the children or to stimulate them. They often rewarded quiet behaviour and so encouraged the children to be passive and under-stimulated.

? Why do you think that it might be significant that the staff at the Boston school had responsibility for a small number of children, and maintained close emotional contact with them?

Day nurseries

Kagan et al. (1980) studied nursery care by setting up their own nursery school in Boston. The school had a fairly mixed intake from middle- and lower-class families and from various ethnic groups. The staff at the school each had special responsibility for a small group of children, thus ensuring close emotional contact. The study focused on 33 infants who attended the nursery full-time from the age of 3½ months who were compared with a matched home control group. Kagan et al. assessed the children throughout the 2 years they were at the nursery school. The researchers measured attachment, cognitive achievements, and general sociability, finding no consistently large differences between the nursery and home children.

There are some studies in which day nurseries were found to have adverse effects on children. For example, consider a study by Vandell and Corasaniti (1990) in Texas. Children with extensive child-care experiences from infancy were rated by parents and teachers as having poorer peer relationships and emotional health. This probably happened because Texas at that time had very low official requirements for child-care facilities. As a result, most of the carers weren't highly trained and the child-to-caregiver ratios were high. This emphasises the point that it is quality of care that should concern us rather than the issue of whether or not day care is a good thing.

? How might you use this evidence to advise parents on which form of child care to use?

National Institute of Child Health and Human Development (NICHD)

Much of the research investigating the effects of day care is limited and hard to interpret. However, the excellent news is that large-scale, high-quality research has been carried out by the National Institute of Child Health and Human Development (NICHD) since the early 1990s. Details of the research findings will be provided in what follows. First of all I want to indicate some of the reasons why the NICHD research on day care is generally regarded as outstanding. That will prove useful when it comes to identifying limitations in other research.

What are the strengths of the NICHD approach? First, it is important to distinguish among effects due to the quality of care, the quantity or amount of care, and the type of care. Before the NICHD research it was almost unheard of for research to examine all three features.

Second, if we are to have a fairly complete picture of the effects of day care on children's social and cognitive development, it is essential to carry out a *longitudinal* study in which the children are followed up over a long period of time. In the NICHD research, information on the children was collected at frequent intervals from early infancy through to the age of 54 months. Subsequent research funded by the NICHD considered possible long-term consequences of day care through to the age of 12 (Belsky et al., 2007).

Third, children's development depends very much on the quality of parenting they receive as well as possible effects of day care. However, children are not randomly assigned to receive or not to receive day care—the decision is influenced very much by the particular circumstances in which each family finds itself. Thus, a major issue in research designed to compare development in children exposed and not exposed to day care is that of selection bias. **Selection bias** occurs when two groups (e.g. children receiving vs not receiving day care) consist of different types of individuals. For example, Borge et al. (2004) found major selection bias—50% of children in their study looked after full-time by their mothers had very socially disadvantaged backgrounds compared to only 25% in the day-care group. In the NICHD research, detailed information about family backgrounds was obtained, and this information was taken fully into account when working out the effects of day care on children's development.

Fourth, as mentioned earlier, most early researchers didn't think it was important to distinguish clearly among different types of day care. In contrast, the NICHD research involved comparing the effects of five different types of day care. These were as follows: (1) father care; (2) grandparent care; (3) child-care home: home-based care outside the child's home excluding care by grandparents; (4) in-home care: any caregiver in the child's home except the father or grandparent; (5) centre care: group care (e.g. at a day nursery).

Social development: Effects on attachment

The effects of day care on **social development** can be significant. Bowlby said there could be irrevocable harm if infants are separated from a primary caregiver, and there is limited support for this. For example, Belsky and Rovine (1988) found that there was an increased risk of an infant developing insecure attachments if they were in day care for at least 4 months and if this had begun before their first birthday. Sroufe (1990) also believed that the first year of life was vital for mother–child attachment and so day care should be delayed until the second year.

KEY TERMS

Selection bias: when different types of individuals are assigned to groups that are to be compared, differences in behaviour between the two groups may be due to this bias rather than to differences in the ways in which the groups are treated.

Social development: the development of a child's social skills, such as the ability to relate to and empathise with others, which is the result of interaction between the child's genes and their environment.

? What special ethical
considerations should be
taken into account when
conducting work with
young children?

In fact, however, there is much evidence that day care typically doesn't affect emotional development. Clarke-Stewart et al. (1994) studied the relationship between time spent in day care and quality of attachment in over 500 children. They found that 15-month-old children who experienced "high-intensity" child care (30 hours or more a week from 3 months of age) were no more distressed when separated from their mothers in the Strange Situation than "low-intensity" children (less than 10 hours a week). This suggests that attachment was not affected by the experiences of separation. Roggman et al. (1994) also found no ill-effects from early day care when they looked at behaviour in the Strange Situation. They compared infants cared for at home with those who attended day care before the age of 1. Both groups were equally securely attached to their mothers.

One of the most thorough attempts to assess the effects of day care on social development was reported by Erel, Oberman, and Yirmiya (2000). They carried out several meta-analyses in which they related day care to six measures of child social development:

1. Secure vs insecure attachment to the mother.
2. Attachment behaviours: avoidance and resistance (reflecting insecure attachment) and exploration (reflecting secure attachment).
3. Mother–child interaction: responsiveness to the mother, smiling at mother, obeying mother, and so on.
4. Adjustment: self-esteem, lack of behaviour problems, and so on.
5. Social interaction with peers.
6. Social interaction with non-parental adults.

Erel et al. (2000) found that day care had non-significant effects on all six measures described above for both girls and boys. The effects remained non-significant even for children who had spent a long time in day care and went there several days a week. In addition, Erel et al. also found that day care did not have any effects on cognitive development in terms of school performance, IQ, and so on.

Social development: Effects on peer relations

It might be thought that the effects of group day care on young children would be variable. It is certainly possible that there are some negative consequences of children being away from their mothers for many hours a week, and we might expect this to be especially the case with very young children. However, there might well be positive consequences. For example, spending many hours a week with other children (as in centre care) might help children to develop social skills and to interact happily with other children of the same age (their peers).

Various studies of social development have found that children who go more often to a day nursery become more active, outgoing, and playful. For example, Shea (1981) videotaped 3- and 4-year-old children in the playground during their first 10 weeks at nursery school. **Sociability** (involving seeking out and enjoying the company of others) increased over time. There was a decrease in the distance from the nearest child and an increase in frequency of peer interaction (interaction with children of the same age). These increases in sociability were greater in those children attending the nursery school for 5 days a week than in those attending for only 2 days. This finding suggests that it was the experience of nursery school rather than maturation or some other factor that produced most of the changes.

KEY TERM
Sociability: the tendency to seek and enjoy the company of others.

Clarke-Stewart et al. (1994) also found that peer relationships were more advanced in day-care children. This study looked at 150 children from Chicago aged between 2 and 3 and from various social backgrounds. The children in day care had more advanced peer relationships probably due to their extensive experience coping with peers in the day-care setting. They learned earlier how to cope in social situations and how to negotiate with peers. This is useful experience for later years at school.

However, it would not be true to say that day care has beneficial effects on the peer relations of all children. When children are shy and unsociable, the nursery experience can be threatening. This in turn can have a negative effect on their school career (Pennebaker et al., 1981).

Children attending nursery school are more likely to develop proper social behaviour in relation to other infants.

Earlier we discussed the work of Erel et al. (2000) in which they carried out various meta-analyses to assess the effects of day care. Of greatest relevance here is their finding that day care had no effect overall on children's social interactions with peers. This was the case regardless of the amount of day care per week, the number of months the child had had in day care, and the child's gender.

Finding an association between day-care quality and children's social development (e.g. on peer relations) is insufficient to show that it has a causal effect on children's social development. The reason is that children experiencing high-quality day care tend to have parents who are better educated and more responsive than those experiencing low-quality care (Marshall, 2004). Thus, it is difficult to determine whether it is the parenting or the day care that is responsible for the association between day-care quality and children's development.

The above issue was addressed in a large National Institute of Child Health and Human Development Study (NICHD study) in which over 1000 children were studied from birth onwards. When the effects of family environment were controlled, the influence of day-care quality during the first 4½ years of life on social development including peer relations was modest (NICHD, 2003a). However, higher-quality child care was associated with higher levels of cognitive skills and language performance.

The NICHD study (2003b) focused on the effects of amount of time spent in child care on children's development. When the effects of family environment were controlled, increased time in non-maternal care during the first 4½ years of life was associated with less social competence reported by mothers and caregivers at 54 months of age. However, the effect was fairly small.

Effects on aggression

In recent years there has been an increasing interest in the possibility that group day care may affect children's levels of aggression. There are two main reasons for this. First, children in group day care spend much of their time with their peers, and this potentially provides many more opportunities for physical aggression than would be the case with home care. We could also look at this in a more positive way—perhaps children in group day care have more opportunities to learn effective ways of resolving interpersonal conflict without resorting to physical aggression. Second, physical aggression reaches a peak in the preschool years (the years during which the great majority of day care takes place) and such behaviour is an important risk factor for subsequent anti-social behaviour.

Much research in this area has focused on **externalising problems**, which are problem behaviours including aggression, disobedience, and some kinds of assertiveness. Different externalising problems tend to be found together. However, when researchers find that day care is associated with externalising problems it isn't always clear whether the level of aggression increased.

It seems likely that any negative effects of day care on aggression would be more obvious over fairly long periods of time. Accordingly, Vandell and Corasaniti (1990) studied 8-year-olds. Children who received full-time day care starting in their first year of life and continuing until they started school were rated by mothers and by teachers as being more non-compliant than other children. Bates et al. (1994) found that children who spent more time receiving any type of day care during their first 5 years of life had more behaviour problems, peer-rated aggression, and observed aggression than those receiving less day care. Belsky (1999) found that more time in day care over the first 5 years of life was associated with more aggression and other behaviour problems.

It seems likely that adverse effects of day care on children's aggression would be greatest when the children spend their days in large groups. Support for this prediction was reported by Haskins (1985) and Schwarz et al. (1974). They studied children in high-quality day-care centres, and found that behaviour problems were greatest among those children spending the most time there.

Borge et al. (2004) compared physical aggression in large numbers of 2- and 3-year-old Canadian children attending group day care or being looked after full-time by their own mothers. In contrast to much previous research, more children looked after by their own mothers showed high levels of physical aggression (7.4% vs 5.2%). Much of that difference occurred because the families of children being looked after by their own mothers were twice as likely as those of children in day care to be very socially disadvantaged. When the focus was only on children from very socially disadvantaged families, children receiving day care were still significantly *less* likely to show high levels of physical aggression than those being looked after full-time by their own mothers. However, the two groups of children didn't differ in physical aggression when the focus was on children who didn't come from very disadvantaged families.

Clarke-Stewart (1989) raised an important point. He argued that researchers often fail to distinguish between aggressive and disobedient behaviour on the one hand and assertive behaviour on the other hand. Day care may be associated with assertive behaviour (often regarded as positive) rather than with aggressive behaviour (typically regarded as negative). Precisely this issue was addressed in the NICHD research on day care (NICHD, 2003a, 2003b). Answers to a questionnaire were assigned to separate subscales for aggression (e.g. cruelty to others; gets in many fights) and assertiveness (e.g. bragging or boasting; demands or wants attention). The key finding was that levels of aggression *and* of assertiveness at 54 months were higher in children who had spent more time in day care.

Bates et al. (1994) found that children who spent more time receiving day care during their first 5 years of life exhibited more behavioural problems such as peer-directed aggression.

Van IJzendoorn et al. (2004) re-analysed the above data from the NICHD research programme and reported some additional important findings. First, the effects of spending a long time in day care on externalising problems mainly occurred when day care involved non-relatives (i.e. nannies, babysitters, day-care homes, and centres) than when it did not. Second, and more specifically, it was especially centre-based care (involving much time in groups) that was associated with externalising problems.

Belsky et al. (2007) considered the long-term effects of day care on the children in the NICHD programme through to the age of 12 years. The amount of time spent in day care in early childhood predicted externalising problems less well at the age of 12 than at the age of 54 months. There was also some evidence that problem behaviours at the age of 12 years were associated with large amounts of time in centres involving large groups of peers but were NOT associated with amount of day care in other settings.

Evaluation. On the face of it, it looks as if young children who spend large amounts of time in group day care have an increased risk of displaying physical aggression. However, we need to be careful before accepting that that is the case. The issue in essence is that children are not assigned *randomly* to receive group day care or to be looked after continuously by their mothers. As a result, children receiving group day care may show more physical aggression because of factors (e.g. problems within the family) that have nothing to do with the group day care itself. In principle, it would be useful to compare children's physical aggression *before* they receive group day care and *during* the period when they receive such day care. However that is generally not feasible, because children mostly start to receive group day care at a very early age.

It is also important to distinguish between aggression and assertiveness. The finding that day care can increase assertiveness would be generally be regarded as a positive outcome.

> **EXAM HINT**
>
> When answering questions that involve the effect of day care on aggression, ensure that you:
>
> - understand what is meant by the term "externalising problems";
> - use a selection of research with differing results and consider the reasons why findings are so variable;
> - understand the differences between assertive and aggressive behaviour.

Implications of Research into Attachment and Day Care for Child-Care Practices

What are the implications of the research we have discussed (and research on attachment) for child-care practices? The starting point is the major conclusion that most adverse effects of day care on children occur because of the poor *quality* of care rather than simply because of separation. That is basically an optimistic conclusion, because it strongly implies that nearly all children would suffer few or no adverse effects provided that they received day care of sufficient quality. That conclusion fits with the views of many authorities. Bowlby's arguments, as we have mentioned, could be interpreted as favouring *improved* child care. He suggested that separation could be compensated for by adequate bond substitution in

> **HOW SCIENCE WORKS: DAY CARE**
>
> Our government has promoted day care for as many preschool children as possible, but opinions about day care are varied and strongly held. In this sort of case, scientific research is particularly important as it is evidence-based and not anecdote-based. You could produce a short questionnaire asking participants to rate various factors (which have been identified in real research) as important in determining the quality of day care on a scale of 1 to 5, with 1 = not important and 5 = very important. In this way you could compare a sample of people's opinions with actual research, and see whether or not the two match. You could then interpret what your comparison means, and decide what conclusion you would draw from your findings.

which the children's emotional needs are emphasised. For many parents, there is little choice about day care—it is simply an economic necessity.

There is one important issue that needs to be addressed before we discuss those factors associated with day care that have beneficial or adverse effects on children. Suppose that researchers compare young children receiving day care in two different kinds of settings: in one the child–staff ratio is low and in the other it is high. Suppose also that we find that the social development of children in the former setting is greater than that of children in the latter setting. Could we conclude that the difference in child–staff ratio is responsible for the findings? The short answer is "No". All we have here is basically correlational evidence—there is an association between child–staff ratio and social development. It is possible that the child–staff ratio does actually make a difference. However, there are other possibilities. If it costs more for parents to place their children in day care with a favourable child–staff ratio, it may simply be that children in day care with a high child–staff ratio come from more socially disadvantaged homes than those in day care with a low child–staff ratio.

Features of high-quality day care

We have discussed much research on day care, and we will be discussing more such research shortly. Before considering implications for child-care practices, it will be useful simply to list the features of high-quality day care. This then provides the goal towards which practices should be aimed.

- The caregiver or caregivers should provide sensitive emotional care and should not be emotionally detached.
- Caregivers should have numerous interactions with the children in their care, and should ensure that the children are actively engaged with their environment.
- Consistency of care (minimal change of caregivers) is associated with high-quality day care.
- Day care provided by relatives is associated with less aggression by children than is day care provided by non-relatives.
- Day care provision in which there is a low child-to-caregiver ratio tends to be of higher quality than where there is a high ratio.
- Day care provided by well-trained caregivers is typically of higher quality than day care provided by poorly trained or untrained caregivers.
- Research on attachment indicates that insecurely attached children tend to have poorer peer relations and more behaviour problems, so it is especially important that they receive high-quality care.

Implications for child-care practices

The research on day care carried out by psychologists has several implications for child-care practices. In this section we will discuss some of the major implications that seem justified in the light of the evidence.

Consistency of care

Several studies point to the importance of consistency of care. For example, in Hodges and Tizard's study of institutional care (1989; see page 119), one of the reasons the children didn't form attachments was because they had an average of 50 different caregivers before the age of 4. In contrast, in Kagan et al.'s (1980) study of day care, one of the key criteria was that the children received consistent emotional support. The NICHD study (1997) reported that the highest infant-to-caregiver ratio should be 1:3 in order to ensure that infants had sensitive and positive interactions. In order to improve consistency, a day-care facility needs to find some way of ensuring minimal turnover of staff, and to arrange that each child is assigned to *one* specific individual who is more or less constantly available and feels responsible for the child. It may also be important to establish consistent routines and physical environments.

Quality of care

There is nearly universal agreement that high-quality care is of fundamental importance if children in day care are to show good social development. Schaffer notes that it is very hard to define "quality of care" although

Quality of day care can be dramatically improved with the provision of sufficient toys and books to stimulate learning and development.

we can identify some features of day care that contribute to it. One important characteristic of high-quality day care is the amount of verbal interaction between caregiver and child. Related to that, Ridley, McWilliam, and Oates (2000) found that in child-care classrooms observed engagement (the extent to which children actively interacted with each other or with a task) was positively related to the quality of the day care. Tizard (1979) found that mothers had more complex conversations with their children than teachers did, because teachers have to divide their attention.

A second way to improve the quality of day care is by increasing the availability of suitable toys, books, and other playthings. Sufficient stimulation is clearly important for development.

Third, and perhaps most important, is the issue of providing sensitive emotional care. The NICHD study found that just over a quarter of the infant care providers gave highly sensitive infant care, and half of them provided moderately sensitive care. Worryingly, one-fifth of the caregivers were "emotionally detached" from the infants under their care. As we have seen, infant development will suffer when day care lacks emotional involvement.

It may be possible to improve the quality of care offered by day-care providers. Howes, Galinsky, and Kontos (1998) found that a modest intervention programme (providing caregivers with in-service training to increase their sensitivity) improved the attachment security of children within child care. Six months after training, Howes et al. found that the children (aged around 2 years) had become more secure and the caregivers were rated as more sensitive. There was a control group of caregivers who received no training. The attachment of the children in their care and their own sensitivity remained unchanged.

Other ways of improving the quality of day care were investigated by Howes, Smith, and Galinsky (1995). State legislation in Florida required child-care providers to adopt higher caregiver-to-child ratios and to ensure that teachers/caregivers were more highly qualified. The manipulation of these two variables had several beneficial effects:

1. There was an improvement in the children's emotional and intellectual development.
2. Teachers became more responsive than before.
3. Negative management techniques were used less often.

Note that this study is particular important because it involves a manipulation of key variables rather than simply relying on correlational evidence. This makes a causal explanation more likely (e.g. higher caregiver-to-child ratios cause improved day care).

Similar findings were reported by Phillips et al. (2000), who considered centre-based child care and children's development in three American states. They found that the quality of what was provided to children was higher in states with more stringent child-care regulations and lower in those with less stringent regulations.

Why are caregiver-to-child ratios and caregiver training important? NICHD Early Child Care Research Network (2002, p. 206) came up with an interesting answer: "More caregiver training may lead to better interactions between children and adults, while lower ratios may lead to more interactions."

What are the implications of research on attachment (discussed earlier in the chapter)? The importance of high-quality care is even greater for children who are insecurely attached than for those who are securely attached for two main reasons. First, securely attached children are more accepted by their peers (Szewczyk-Sokolowski et al., 2005), and so find it easier to cope successfully with day care. Belsky and Fearon (2002) found that children securely attached at 15 months showed more social competence than those insecurely attached at 15 months. The implication is that insecurely attached children are less likely than securely attached ones to form good peer relations during day care, and so they are more in need of high-quality day care to enhance their social skills.

Second, securely attached children have fewer behaviour problems (Belsky & Fearon, 2002; Wartner et al., 1994) and they are also better at conflict resolution (Wartner et al., 1994). The implication is that insecurely attached children are more likely than securely attached ones to be disruptive and aggressive in day care, and so excellent quality day care is needed to reduce or eliminate these problems.

There is another important implication of research into attachment for quality of care. Wartner et al. (1994) found that the type of attachment that young children showed at the age of 12 months predicted reasonably well their type of attachment at the age of 6 years. The finding that early attachments have long-lasting effects on children makes it all the more important that those providing day care provide high-quality and sensitive care.

There is a final important implication stemming from attachment research. It has been found that it is possible to make infants more securely attached by interventions designed to increase maternal sensitivity (Bakermans-Kranenburg et al., 2003). This suggests that similar training designed to enhance the sensitivity of care givers would have beneficial effects in enhancing children's attachment security and ability to cope successfully in day-care situations.

Child–environment fit

Parents often have little or no option but to place their child in day care for several days every week, and financial issues may limit their options in terms of the type of day care. However, wherever it is feasible, it would make sense for parents or other caregivers to try to relate their decisions with respect to day care to the needs and personality of their child. Here are three examples. First, there is the evidence that externalising problems including aggression are greater in centre-based care than when the child is in a child-care home or receives in-home care. If a child is displaying aggressive tendencies, it may be advantageous for him/her to be in a child-care home or to receive in-home care rather than to receive centre-based care.

Second, Borge et al. (2004) found that only very socially disadvantaged children were less aggressive in group day care than when looked after full-time by their

According to Howes et al. (1995) one way of improving the quality of day care is to adopt a higher caregiver-to-child ratio.

mother. The implication is that group day care may be more beneficial than being looked after all the time by their mother for children from very socially disadvantaged backgrounds but not for those from less disadvantaged backgrounds.

Third, we have seen that there is evidence that children who attend group day care tend to have more advanced peer relationships (Clarke-Stewart et al., 1994) than those who do not. It would seem likely that the beneficial effects on peer relationships would depend on other aspects of the child's background. For example, young children who have no siblings and very limited opportunities otherwise to play with their peers might be expected to gain more from attending group day care than other young children.

Effects of separation on parents

As Clarke-Stewart (1989, p. 270) pointed out, the reason for any adverse effects of day care on children's development may not be "that 40 hours of day care is hard on infants but that 40 hours of work is hard on mothers." Harrison and Ungerer (2002) considered the mother's position in families in which she had returned to paid employment during the first year of her infant's life. Infants were less likely to be securely attached to their mother if she wasn't committed to work and had anxieties about making use of child care. To reduce mothers' feelings of anxiety or guilt, it may be helpful to provide more interlinking between home and day care, for example by providing workplace nurseries.

According to Clarke-Stewart (1989) the adverse effects of day care on a child's development may not be "that 40 hours of day care is hard on infants but that 40 hours of work is hard on mothers."

It might also help to relieve some of the guilt experienced by mothers to recognise that day care is *not* necessarily associated with negative effects. For some children there are actually benefits of having parents who work. For example, Brown and Harris (1978) found that women who didn't work and who had several young children to care for were more likely to become seriously depressed. Shaffer (1993) reported that children of working mothers tend to be more confident in social settings. It might be that going out to work enables some women to be *better* mothers.

SECTION SUMMARY

❖ Some childminders don't feel the need to form emotional bonds with the child they are looking after.

❖ Day nurseries in areas in which the official requirements for child-care facilities are low often have adverse effects on children.

Different forms of day care

❖ Erel et al. (2000) found in a meta-analysis that day care on average had no effects on attachment to the mother, adjustment, and social interaction.

❖ Children in day care often show more advanced peer relationships than other children. However, the effects tend to be very small or even negative when the effects of family environment are controlled.

Social development

❖ Much research shows that levels of aggression and assertiveness are higher in children who have been in day care. These effects are greater in children who have spent the most time in day care. However, increased aggression and other externalising problems occur mainly when children are in centres with large groups of peers rather than being looked after by relatives.

Implications of research into attachment and day care for child-care practices

❖ High-quality day care possesses various features:
 – sensitive emotional care by caregivers;
 – numerous interactions between caregivers and children;
 – consistency of care and minimal change of caregivers;
 – day care provided by relatives is associated with less aggression by children;
 – a low child-to-caregiver ratio;
 – well-trained caregivers;
 – special attention to the needs of insecurely attached children.

Implications for practices

❖ It is important that each child is assigned to one specific individual rather than to different individuals at different times.
❖ Of great importance is the provision of sensitive emotional care and the avoidance of emotional detachment.
❖ Insecurely attached children are in special need of high-quality day care. They tend to have poorer peer relations and behave more disruptively than securely attached children, and so caregiver sensitivity and emotional engagement are of particular importance.
❖ Another reason why it is important to focus on insecurely attached young children in day care is that type of attachment tends to be consistent over a period of years. Accordingly, it is important for children to become securely attached at the youngest age possible.
❖ Account needs to be taken of child–environment fit. For example, children with aggressive tendencies should probably not receive centre-based care, which may encourage those tendencies.
❖ Mothers' feelings of anxiety or guilt can be reduced by providing more interlinking between home and day care (e.g. workplace nurseries).

You have reached the end of the chapter on developmental psychology. Developmental psychology is an approach or perspective in psychology. The material in this chapter has exemplified the way that developmental psychologists explain behaviour. They look at behaviour in terms of the way that people change as they grow older, and the forces that create this change. Many of the changes, as we have seen, are due to inherited factors (nature). However, a major contribution also comes from the influence of other people and the physical environment (nurture). Development doesn't stop when you leave childhood, it continues through the lifespan. If you go on to study psychology further, you will consider this wider area of developmental, or lifespan, psychology.

FURTHER READING

Chapter 6 in M. Harris and G. Butterworth (2002) *Developmental psychology: A student's handbook* (Hove, UK: Psychology Press) contains a good account of the development of attachment behaviour. An accessible account of early development is provided by J.C. Berryman, D. Hargreaves, M. Herbert, and A. Taylor (1991) *Developmental psychology and you* (Leicester, UK: BPS Books). There is accessible and up-to-date coverage of the topics discussed in this chapter in L.E. Berk (2006) *Child development (7th Edn.)* (New York: Pearson). Various chapters in P.K. Smith, H. Cowie, and M. Blades (2003). *Understanding children's development (4th Edn.)* (Oxford: Blackwell) give good accounts of research on early social development.

See Chapter 3 of the revision guide for guidance on revising this chapter for the exam.

WEBSITES

http://www.apa.org/releases/relationships.html
Attachment and romance: The link between early attachment and adult romantic relationships.

http://www.bbc.co.uk/parenting/childcare/available_index.shtml
What daycare is there?: Different kinds of daycare which may be available.

http://www.apa.org/monitor/sep07/teaching.html
Can we learn from primate studies?: A clinical psychologist's idea that we can learn from our close relatives.

http://abc.net.au/news/stories/2007/10/24/2068400.htm?section=australia
Quality of childcare: Staff to children ratios.

http://www.news.com.au/heraldsun/story/0,21985,22697119-663,00.html
Separated at birth: The tale of identical twins reunited as adults.

REVISION QUESTIONS

The examination questions aim to sample the material in this whole chapter. For advice on how to answer such questions refer to Chapter 1, Section 2.
See the note on page 89 regarding stimulus questions.

Question 1
a. Outline **two** behaviours that are characteristic of a securely attached child. (2 marks)
b. Outline **two** behaviours that are characteristic of an insecurely attached child. (2 marks)
c. Explain why the validity of Ainsworth's research into types of attachment has been criticised. (5 marks)

Question 2
a. Outline the behavioural explanation of attachment formation. (4 marks)
b. Outline Bowlby's explanation of attachment formation. (6 marks)
c. Explain how the behavioural explanation of attachment differs from the evolutionary explanation of attachment. (4 marks)

Question 3
a. Consider the effects of day care on social development. (12 marks)

The difference between "common sense" ideas about what causes behaviour and theories in psychology is that psychological theories are tested to see if they are true (or false!). In order to test theories systematically, psychologists conduct research.

SECTION 9
Methods and techniques p. 141

Psychologists use a wide range of research methods and techniques to shed light on human behaviour. What are the advantages and weaknesses of these methods and techniques? How are they used?

Specification content: Knowledge and understanding of the following research methods, their advantages and weaknesses: experimental method including laboratory, field and natural experiments, studies using a correlational analysis, observational techniques, self-report techniques including questionnaire and interview, case studies.

SECTION 10
Investigation design p. 167

There are numerous aspects of investigation design that need to be adhered to to ensure that the findings obtained are valid and can be replicated. The main aspects (including a consideration of ethical issues) are discussed.

Specification content: The following features of investigation design: aims, hypotheses including directional and non-directional, experimental design (independent groups, repeated measures, and matched pairs, design of naturalistic observations including the development and use of behavioural categories, operationalisation of variables including independent and dependent variables, pilot studies, control of extraneous variables, reliability and validity, awareness of the BPS Code of Ethics, ethical issues and the ways in which psychologists deal with them, selection of participants and sampling techniques, selection of participants and sampling techniques including random, opportunity, and volunteer sampling, demand characteristics and investigator effects.

SECTION 11
Data analysis and presentation p. 197

A key aspect of the research process is the final interpretation of the results. What statistical methods enable us to interpret research findings and draw conclusions?

Specification content: The following features of data analysis, presentation, and interpretation: presentation and interpretation of quantitative data including graphs, scattergrams, and tables, analysis and interpretation of quantitative data, measures of central tendency including ranges and standard deviations, analysis and interpretation of correlational data, positive and negative correlations and the interpretation of correlation coefficients, presentation of qualitative data, processes involved in content analysis.

RESEARCH METHODS

In a sense, we are all "armchair psychologists"—everyone has opinions about human behaviour. Psychologists don't just present theories about why people behave as they do, but they also seek to support or challenge these theories with research—systematic study of a problem—including experiments, interviews, and case studies. Throughout this book we rely on such evidence as a means of analysing theories. In this chapter we will consider the different methods used to conduct research, as well as other important features of the research process.

SECTION 9
METHODS AND TECHNIQUES

The Scientific Approach

In common with other sciences, psychology is concerned with theories and with data. All sciences share one fundamental feature: they aim to discover facts about the world by using systematic and objective methods of investigation. The research process starts with casual observations about one feature of the world, for example, that people imitate the violence they see on television or that there are concerns about how the Nazis so easily made ordinary people obey them (see page 282). These observations collectively form a theory (a general explanation or account of certain findings or data). For example, someone might put forward a theory in which it is assumed that genetic factors play a role in all mental disorders.

Theories invariably produce a number of further expectations, which can be stated as a research hypothesis—a formal and unambiguous statement about what you believe to be true. Here is an example of a hypothesis: Schizophrenia is a condition that depends in part on genetic factors (see page 324). A hypothesis is stated with the purpose of attempting to prove or disprove it. And that is what scientists conduct research to do—prove or disprove their hypotheses. If it is disproved, then the theory has to be adjusted, and a new hypothesis produced, and tested, and so on. This process is shown in the diagram overleaf.

Psychologists spend a lot of their time collecting data in order to test various hypotheses. In addition to laboratory experiments, they make use of many different methods of investigation, each of which can provide useful information about human behaviour.

KEY TERMS

Science: a branch of knowledge conducted on objective principles. It is both an activity and an organised body of knowledge.

Theory: a general explanation of a set of findings. It is used to produce an experimental hypothesis.

Research hypothesis: a statement put forward at the beginning of a study stating what you expect to happen, generated by a theory.

Laboratory experiment: an experiment conducted in a laboratory setting or other contrived setting away from the participants' normal environments. The experimenter is able to manipulate the IV and accurately measure the DV, and considerable control can be exercised over confounding variables.

EXAM HINT
Research methods are not tested in any one section of the exam paper. Instead, questions on research methods will appear on both exam papers. In paper one there are twice as many AO3 marks as there are on paper two so expect more research methods questions on paper one.

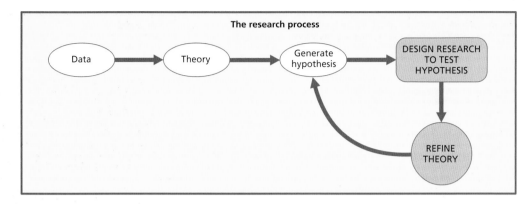

The research process

A variable is something that varies! How long you sleep each night is a variable, whereas the number of days in a week is a fixed quantity.

The experimental process can be summarised thus:

• Experimenter acts on IV
• Changes in IV lead to changes in DV
• Changes in DV measured by experimenter

Apply this by referring to one of the experiments into short-term memory processing (e.g. Baddeley, 1966; Jacobs, 1887; Peterson & Peterson, 1959) and operationalise the IV and DV.

KEY TERMS

Variables: things that vary or change.
Independent variable (IV): some aspect of the research situation that is manipulated by the researcher in order to observe whether a change occurs in another variable.
Dependent variable (DV): an aspect of the participant's behaviour that is measured in the study.

The Experimental Method

The most-used method of investigation is the experimental method. Use of this method can involve experiments that are conducted in a laboratory or other contrived setting that is not the participants' natural environment. This method is not the *only* scientific method, but it is perhaps the *most* scientific because it is highly objective and systematic.

Dependent and independent variables

In order to understand what is involved in the experimental method, we will consider a concrete example. Put yourself in the position of the British psychologist Alan Baddeley (1966), who thought that acoustic coding was important in short-term memory, with people tending to confuse similar-sounding words when they tried to recall them in the right order. This led him to test the following hypothesis: More errors will be made in recalling acoustically similar word lists in the correct order than in recalling acoustically dissimilar word lists (see page 50).

In order to test this hypothesis, Baddeley compared the numbers of errors in short-term memory with lists of words that were acoustically similar and others that were acoustically dissimilar. This hypothesis refers to two **variables**—whether the list words were acoustically similar or dissimilar and the performance of the people learning the lists (errors made). The variable directly manipulated by the experimenter is called the **independent variable** (IV), i.e. acoustic similarity vs dissimilarity. The other variable, the one affected by the IV, is called the **dependent variable** (DV), i.e. how many errors are made on each type of list. (It is called *dependent* because it depends on something the experimenter controls.) The DV is some aspect of behaviour that is going to be measured or assessed, to decide whether or not the IV caused a change in behaviour.

Experimental control

We come now to the most important principle of the experimental method: control. The IV is manipulated and the DV is free to vary. However, all other variables *must* be *controlled*, i.e. kept constant, so we can assume that the only variable causing any subsequent change in the DV *must* be the IV. In our example, we would control all aspects of the situation (extraneous variables) other than acoustic similarity by trying to make sure that both types of word lists had words of the same length, frequency of occurrence in the language, and so on. Other factors we may need to control when using the experimental method are always using the same room for the experiment, keeping the temperature the same, and having the same lighting.

Confounding variables

The variables that are *not* controlled may become **confounding variables**. Confounding variables are not of interest to the researcher, but may get in the way of the link between the independent and dependent variable. For example, suppose the words used in the acoustically similar lists were much longer words than those used in the acoustically

The type of experimenter could act as a confounding variable. Some participants may feel more comfortable than others in the study situation...

dissimilar lists. We wouldn't know whether the higher number of errors with acoustically similar lists than with acoustically dissimilar lists was due to the independent variable (acoustic similarity vs dissimilarity) or to the confounding variable of word length. The presence of any confounding variables is really serious, because it prevents us from being able to interpret our findings.

You might think that it would be easy to ensure that there were no confounding variables in an experiment. However, there are many well-known experiments containing confounding variables. Consider, for example, the study by Jenkins and Dallenbach (1924). They gave a learning task to a group of participants in the morning, and then tested their memory for the material later in the day. The same learning task was given to a second group of participants in the evening, and their memory was tested the following morning after a night's sleep.

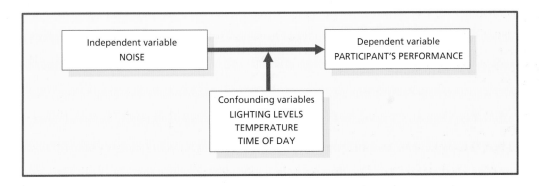

See *AS Level Psychology Online* for interactive exercises on this chapter.

What did Jenkins and Dallenbach find? Memory performance was much higher for the second group than for the first. They argued that this was due to there being less interference with memory when people are asleep than when they are awake. Can you see the flaw in this argument? The two groups learned the material at different times of day, and so time of day was a confounding variable. Hockey et al. (1972) discovered many years later that the time of day at which learning occurs is much more important than whether or not the participants sleep between learning and the memory test.

Participants and settings

Proper use of the experimental method requires careful consideration of the ways in which the participants are allocated to the various conditions. The main way

KEY TERM

Confounding variables: variables that are mistakenly manipulated or allowed to vary along with the **independent variable** and therefore affect the **dependent variable**.

Participants in psychological experiment should be tested under constant controlled conditions (e.g. consistent lighting, temperature, and sound levels).

? What are the main obstacles to replication in research using human participants?

of guarding against this possibility is by means of **randomisation**, in which participants are allocated at random.

Numerous studies are carried out using students as participants, raising the issue of whether students are representative of society as a whole. For example, students tend to be more intelligent and much younger than most members of society. However, they are representative in the sense that about half of all students are male and half are female.

Advantages of the experimental method

What is generally regarded as the greatest advantage of the experimental method is that it can allow us to establish causal (or cause and effect) relationships. In the terms we have been using, the independent variable in an experiment is often regarded as a cause, and the dependent variable is the effect. We assume that, if y (e.g. many errors in recall) follows x (e.g. acoustically similar word list), then it is reasonable to infer that x caused y.

But findings from studies based on the experimental method do *not* necessarily establish causality. For example, consider the following imaginary study. An experiment is carried out in a hot country. Half of the participants sleep in bedrooms with the windows open, and the other half sleep in bedrooms with the windows closed. Those sleeping in bedrooms with the windows open are found to be more likely to catch malaria. Having the window open or closed is *relevant* to catching the disease, but it tells us nothing direct about the major causal factor in malaria (infected mosquitoes).

The other major advantage of the experimental method concerns what is known as **replication**. If an experiment has been conducted in a carefully controlled way, other researchers should be able to repeat or replicate the findings. That would help to establish internal validity.

Replication is important in order to confirm an experimental result. If the result is "real", then it should be possible to obtain the same result when you repeat the experiment, but if it was a fluke, then it is not likely to be repeatable. Therefore, it is highly desirable in research to be able to replicate a study using precisely the same techniques and conditions. If the conditions aren't the same, that may explain why the results are not the same. This may allow us to make sense of the inconsistent findings from studies following up on Hofling et al.'s (1966) study on nurses obeying doctors when they shouldn't (see page 287).

Then there is the issue of objectivity. The experimental method is a more objective method than others. However, total objectivity is impossible since the experimenter's interests, values, and judgements will always have some influence, and the control of all confounding variables is impossible. Nevertheless, the experimental method offers the best chance of objectivity.

Weaknesses of the experimental method

It would appear that one weakness of most uses of the experimental method is that of artificiality. In fact, however, there are different views on this issue. Heather (1976) declared that the only thing learned from laboratory experiments is how people behave in laboratory experiments. But Coolican (1998) pointed out that, "In scientific investigation, it is often *necessary* to create artificial circumstances in order to *isolate* a hypothesised effect." If we are interested in studying basic cognitive processes, such as those involved in perception or attention, then the artificiality of the laboratory is unlikely to affect the results. On the other hand, if we are interested in studying social behaviour, then the issue of artificiality *does* matter.

Carlsmith et al. (1976) drew a distinction between **mundane realism** and **experimental realism** (see Chapter 7). Experimental realism (where participants are fooled that an artificial set-up is real) may be more important than mundane realism (where an artificial situation closely resembles a real-life situation) in producing findings that generalise to real-life situations.

An important reason why laboratory experiments are more artificial than other research methods is because the participants in laboratory experiments are aware that their behaviour is being observed. As Silverman (1977) pointed out, "Virtually the only condition in which a [participant] in a psychological study will not behave as a [participant] is if he does not know he is in one." One consequence of being observed is that the participants try to work out the experimenter's hypothesis, and then act accordingly. In this connection, Orne (1962) emphasised the importance of **demand characteristics**—the features of an experiment that "invite" participants to behave in certain predictable ways. Demand characteristics may help us to explain why Milgram (1963, 1974) found higher levels of obedience in his experiments at Yale University than in a run-down office building (65% vs 48%, respectively). Demand characteristics were also probably involved in Zimbardo's Stanford Prison Experiment, where the prison-like environment suggests that certain forms of behaviour were expected.

Another consequence of the participants in laboratory experiments knowing they are being observed is **evaluation apprehension**, a term used by Rosenberg (1965). The basic idea is that most people are anxious about being observed by the experimenter, and want him/her to evaluate them favourably. This may lead them to behave in ways they normally wouldn't.

Sigall, Aronson, and Van Hoose (1970) contrasted the effects of demand characteristics and evaluation apprehension on the task of copying telephone numbers. The experimenter told participants doing the task for the second time that he expected them to perform it at a rate *slower* than their previous performance. Adherence to demand characteristics would have led to slow performance, whereas evaluation apprehension and the need to be evaluated positively by the experimenter would have produced *fast* times. The participants actually performed more quickly than they had done before, indicating the greater importance of evaluation apprehension.

This conclusion was strengthened by the findings from a second condition, in which the experimenter not only said that he expected the participants to perform at a slower rate, but also told them that those

■ **Activity:** Experimental method
Asch's famous line-matching experiment had experimental realism (see p. 265). Discuss with a partner or in a small group how you could adapt the experiment to increase its mundane realism, and produce a list of your recommendations.

Participants in psychological experiments usually try to perform the task set by the experimenter as well as they can, in order to gain his or her approval.

? In what way have you altered your own natural behaviour when you were aware of being observed? Was this because of evaluation apprehension or some other reason?

KEY TERMS

Mundane realism: the use of an artificial situation that closely resembles a natural situation.
Experimental realism: the use of an artificial situation in which participants become so involved that they are fooled into thinking the set-up is real rather than artificial.
Demand characteristics: features of an experiment that help participants to work out what is expected of them, and lead them to behave in certain predictable ways.
Evaluation apprehension: concern felt by research participants that their performance is being judged.

who rush are probably obsessive compulsive. The participants in this condition performed the task slowly, because they wanted to be evaluated positively.

> **A LABORATORY EXPERIMENT: EYEWITNESS TESTIMONY**
> Loftus has run a large number of laboratory experiments looking at the factual accuracy of eyewitnesses' memory. Several of these involved participants looking at slides or film of car crashes. In one such experiment there were two conditions. Some of the participants were asked if they had seen any broken glass after the accident whereas others were asked if they had seen the broken glass. The only difference between the two groups was the wording, "any" or "the", with the latter suggesting the glass was there, thus being a leading question.
> This type of experiment has been criticised as having low external/ecological validity and low mundane realism. Can you explain why this was a *laboratory* experiment, and exactly why it has those criticisms?

Laboratory experiments

Advantages:

- Establishes cause and effect relationships
- Allows for replication
- Good control of confounding variables

Limitations:

- Artificial
- Participants know they are being observed (demand characteristics and evaluation apprehension)
- Low in external validity
- Ethical concerns, such as the right to withdraw

To apply this, find a study to illustrate each of the above points (e.g. Asch's 1951, 1956 experiment has been replicated many times, thus showing it is reliable).

Experiments and ethical issues

Ethical issues in psychological research are discussed in detail later in Section 10. Here are a few ethical issues of special relevance to laboratory experiments. In an experiment, there is a danger that the participants will be willing to behave in a laboratory in ways they would not behave elsewhere. Milgram (1974) found in his work on obedience to authority that 65% of his participants were prepared to give very intense electric shocks to someone else when the experiment took place in a laboratory at Yale University. In contrast, the figure was only 48% when the same study was carried out in a run-down office building.

Another ethical issue that applies especially to laboratory experiments concerns the participant's **right to withdraw** from the experiment at any time. It is general practice to inform participants of this right at the start of the experiment. However, participants may feel reluctant to exercise this right if they think it will cause serious disruption to the experimenter's research.

There can be ethical issues with experiments that initially seem totally acceptable. For example, consider the study by Bahrick et al. (1975; see page 46) on very long-term memory for the faces and names of fellow students. It is possible that this experiment may have caused unhappy or stressful memories to resurface for some of the participants.

Field Experiments

Field experiments are carried out in natural settings such as in the street, in a school, or at work. Some of the advantages of the experimental method are shared by both laboratory and field experiments. Field experiments, like laboratory experiments, involve direct control of the independent variable by the experimenter and also direct allocation of participants to conditions. This means that causal relationships can be determined (provided the experiment is carried out carefully and confounding variables are avoided!). Field experiments are also reasonably well controlled, which means that they can be replicated.

KEY TERMS

Right to withdraw: the basic right of participants in a research study to stop their involvement at any point, and to withdraw their results if they wish to do so.

Field experiment: a study in which the experimental method is used in a more naturalistic situation.

As an example of a field experiment, let us consider a study by Shotland and Straw (1976). They arranged for a man and a woman to stage an argument and a fight fairly close to a number of bystanders. In one condition, the woman screamed, "I don't know you!" In a second condition, she screamed, "I don't know why I ever married you!" When the bystanders thought the fight involved strangers, 65% of them intervened, against only 19% when they thought it involved a married couple. Thus, the experiment showed that people were less likely to lend a helping hand when it was a "lovers' quarrel" than when it was not. The bystanders were convinced that the fight was genuine, as was shown by the fact that 30% of the women were so alarmed that they shut the doors of their rooms, turned off the lights, and locked their doors.

Laboratory vs field experiments

The greatest advantage of laboratory experiments over field experiments is that it is generally easier to eliminate confounding variables in the laboratory than in the field. The experimenter is unlikely to be able to control every aspect of a natural situation. Another clear advantage of laboratory experiments over field experiments is that it is much easier to obtain large amounts of very detailed information from participants in the laboratory. Field experiments are limited in this way because (1) it is not generally possible to introduce bulky equipment into a natural setting, and (2) the participants in a field experiment are likely to realise they are taking part in an experiment if attempts are made to obtain a lot of information from them, and then the study loses its "naturalness".

One of the advantages of field experiments over laboratory experiments is that the behaviour of the participants is often more *typical* of their normal behaviour and therefore less artificial, i.e. field experiments tend to have greater external validity.

The respective strengths and weaknesses of laboratory experiments and field experiments can be summed up with reference to the two different kinds of validity:

> ### Field experiments
> *Advantages*:
>
> - Establishes cause and effect relationships
> - Allows for replication
> - Behaviour of participants more typical than in a laboratory experiment, high external validity
>
> *Limitations*:
>
> - Ethical issues, such as a lack of voluntary informed consent
> - Low in internal validity, poor control
>
> To apply this, describe a field study and clearly identify its advantages and disadvantages (e.g. Bickman, 1974).

- Internal validity—the validity of an experiment within the confines of the context in which it is carried out.
- External validity—the validity of an experiment outside the research situation itself.

> ### A FIELD EXPERIMENT: **PREJUDICE**
> A study in 2001 found that people were less likely to help gays and lesbians compared to heterosexuals. How was this done? Researchers telephoned over 200 British men and women at home and said it was a wrong number, but asked if the participant would make a call on to the caller's partner. This partner was of course a confederate, and was either same-sex or opposite-sex, to give the impression of a gay/lesbian or heterosexual partnership. The apparently heterosexual callers were most likely to receive the requested help, and the apparently gay men the least likely, with the apparently lesbian women in between.
> Can you think what extraneous or confounding variables might have had an effect here in producing these findings?

> ### KEY TERMS
> **Internal validity**: the validity of an experiment in terms of the context in which it is carried out. Concerns events within the experiment as distinct from **external validity**.
> **External validity**: the validity of an experiment outside the research situation itself; the extent to which the findings of a research study are applicable to other situations, especially "everyday" situations.

■ Activity: Field experiments and ethics find a partner and toss a coin to see who is going to support doing field experiments and who is going to oppose them on ethical grounds. Then give yourselves 5 minutes to write an argument supporting your view of why these experiments are, or are not, ethically all right. Exchange your written comments, and discuss what each of you has said.

KEY TERMS

Debriefing: attempts by the experimenter at the end of a study to provide detailed information for the participants about the study and to reduce any distress they might have felt.
True experiment: research where an independent variable is manipulated to observe its effects on a dependent variable and so determine a cause-and-effect relationship.
Quasi-experiment: research that is similar to an experiment but certain key features are lacking, such as the direct manipulation of the independent variable by the experimenter and random allocation of participants to conditions.

? A true experiment involves manipulation of the IV by the experimenter. How is a quasi-experiment different?

Quasi-experiments

Advantages	Limitations
• Participants behave naturally • Investigates the effects of independent variables that it would be unethical to manipulate	• IV not directly manipulated • Participants not allocated at random to conditions • Difficult to identify what aspects of the independent variable have caused the effects on behaviour • Requires ethical sensitivity

Laboratory experiments tend to be high in internal validity but low in external validity. In contrast, field experiments are high in external validity but low in internal validity.

Field experiments and ethical issues

So far as field experiments are concerned, the main ethical issue relates to the principle of voluntary informed consent, which is regarded as central to ethical human research (see Section 10). By their very nature, most field experiments don't lend themselves to obtaining informed consent from the participants. For example, the study by Shotland and Straw (1976) would have been rendered almost meaningless if the participants had been asked beforehand to give their consent to witnessing a staged quarrel! In addition, the participants in that study could reasonably have complained about being exposed to a violent quarrel.

Another ethical issue is that it is impossible to offer the right to withdraw or debriefing. Obviously participants who don't even know they are taking part in an experiment can't be given the right to withdraw from it!

Quasi-experiments

"True" experiments based on the experimental method provide the best way of being able to draw causal inferences with confidence. However, there are often practical or ethical reasons why it is simply not possible to carry out a **true experiment**. So investigators often carry out what is known as a **quasi-experiment**—these "resemble experiments but are weak on some of the characteristics" (Raulin & Graziano, 1994). The two main differences between true and quasi-experiments are as follows:

1. The manipulation of the independent variable is often not under the control of the experimenter in quasi-experiments.
2. It is usually not possible to allocate the participants randomly to groups in quasi-experiments.

There are numerous hypotheses in psychology that can only be studied by means of quasi-experiments rather than true experiments. For example, if we are interested in studying the effects of divorce on young children we could do this by comparing children of divorced and married parents—but random allocation would not be possible! Studies in which pre-existing groups are compared often qualify as quasi-experiments, e.g. comparing the learning performance of males and females (gender is the IV).

A good example of a quasi-experiment is the famous study on personality and coronary heart disease (CHD) carried out by Friedman and Rosenman (1974; see page 242). They found that men with Type A personality (competitive; stressed; hostile) were much more likely to suffer from CHD than those with

Type B personality (more relaxed and laid-back). This is a quasi-experiment because the researchers didn't allocate individuals at random to the Type A and Type B groups—these groups were pre-existing.

Natural experiments

In the studies just described, use is made of pre-existing groups of people. We might also make use of a naturally occurring event for research purposes. Such **natural experiments** are a kind of quasi-experiment. Such studies don't qualify as genuine experiments. Use of the experimental method requires that the independent variable is *manipulated* by the experimenter, but clearly the experimenter cannot decide whether a given person is going to be male or female for the purposes of the study!

The issue of whether or not there is a correlation between violence on television and aggressive behaviour is frequently debated in the media.

An example of a natural experiment is a study reported by Charlton (1998) and Charlton et al. (2000). There has been much controversy as to whether watching television increases violence among young people, but it has proved hard to obtain convincing findings. The natural experiment was based on the introduction of television to the island of St. Helena, which is best known for the fact that Napoleon spent the last few years of his life there. Its inhabitants received television for the first time in 1995 (the naturally occurring event), but there was no evidence of any negative effects on the children. According to Charlton (1998):

> *The argument that watching television turns youngsters to violence is not borne out, and this study on St. Helena is the clearest proof yet. The children have watched the same amounts of violence, and in many cases the same programmes as British children. But they have not gone out and copied what they have seen on TV.*

? What might be the practical uses of results such as those from the Mount St Helens study?

Charlton et al. (2000) compared the children's playground behaviour 4 months before and 5 years after television broadcasting began. There was no increase at all in anti-social behaviour (e.g. fighting), and hardly any changes in helping and cooperative behaviour.

Another example of a natural experiment is the study by Hodges and Tizard (1989; see page 119) on the long-term effects of privation in children who had been taken into care when very young. Some of the children were adopted whereas others returned to their natural home. The decision about whether each child should be adopted or should be restored to his/her home was the naturally

---

A NATURAL EXPERIMENT: EXAM STRESS
So do you think exams are stressful? How would we test this? A natural experiment could ask for student volunteers to give blood samples 8 weeks before exams and again after the first exam. Analysis would give levels of the stress hormones adrenaline, noradrenaline, and cortisol.

What would you expect to see happen? Can you write this as a hypothesis?

Can you identify the IV, the variable that was changing naturally (because this would be a natural experiment)?

And what would be the DV, the variable that the research team measured?

KEY TERM

Natural experiment: a type of experiment where use is made of some naturally occurring variable(s).

occurring event outside the control of the researchers. Contrary to what might have been expected, the adopted children on average showed better emotional adjustment than the restored children.

Advantages of natural experiments

The main advantage is that the participants in natural experiments are often not aware they are taking part in an experiment, even though they are likely to know that their behaviour is being observed, so they behave more naturally. Also, natural experiments allow us to study the effects on behaviour of independent variables that it would be unethical for the experimenter to manipulate. For example, consider the study by Hodges and Tizard (1989). No ethical committee would have allowed children to be taken into care and then either adopted or restored to their natural home to satisfy the requirements of the researchers. The obvious risks to the well-being of the children concerned mean that studies on the effects of adoption can only possibly be carried out as a natural experiment rather than as a true experiment.

Studies on the effects of natural disasters on stress reactions and physical health provide another example (see Kario, McEwen, & Pickering, 2003). It would be totally unethical to expose participants deliberately to extremely stressful situations. However, it is acceptable to study those who have become highly stressed as a result of being exposed to a natural disaster such as the Kobe earthquake (see page 223).

There is another advantage to studying those exposed to natural disasters. It is reasonable to assume that those closest to the natural disaster don't differ in any important way (e.g. susceptibility to stress) from those further away. This approximates to the ideal of random allocation of participants to conditions.

Weaknesses of natural experiments

? Natural experiments are such a good way of doing research, so why are there so few actually done?

The greatest weakness occurs because the participants have not been assigned at random to conditions, so observed differences in behaviour between groups may be due to differences in the types of participants in the groups rather than to the effects of the independent variable. For example, in the study by Hodges and Tizard (1989), there was evidence that the children who were adopted were *initially* better adjusted than the children who were restored to their natural home. Thus, the finding that the adopted children subsequently showed better emotional adjustment than the restored children may be due to their personality or early experiences rather than to the fact that they were adopted.

It is usually possible to check whether the participants in the various conditions are comparable, with respect to variables such as age, sex, socioeconomic status, and so on. If the groups do differ significantly in some respects irrelevant to the independent variable, then this greatly complicates the task of interpreting the findings of a natural experiment.

The other major weakness of natural experiments involves the independent variable. In some natural experiments it is hard to know exactly what aspects of the independent variable have caused any effects on behaviour. For example, consider research on the effects on stress and physical health of natural disasters such as the Kobe earthquake. The most obvious explanation of the finding that those closest to the Kobe earthquake had more heart attacks than those further away (Kario et al., 2003) is that they were in greatest physical danger. However, it may also be that those closest to the earthquake became highly stressed because of the distressed reactions of their friends and neighbours (see page 223).

Natural experiments and ethical issues

It can be argued that there are fewer ethical issues with natural experiments than with many other kinds of research—after all, the experimenter is not responsible for the fact that the participants have been exposed to the independent variable. However, there can be issues about voluntary informed consent, since participants are often unaware they are taking part in an experiment. In addition, experimenters need to be sensitive to the situation in which the participants find themselves. For example, researchers studying the effects of natural disasters need to be aware of the sensitivities of some of the participants, who may have lost relatives or friends in the disaster.

> ■ **Activity:** In groups of three, design a summary table to illustrate the ethical issues involved in laboratory, field, and natural experiments, with each group member taking one type of experiment then reporting back to the group.

Studies Using Correlational Analysis

If we were interested in the hypothesis that watching violence on television leads to aggressive behaviour, we could test this hypothesis by obtaining information from a number of people about: (1) the amount of violent television they watched, and (2) the extent to which they behaved aggressively in various situations. If the hypothesis is correct, we would expect that those who have seen the most violence on television would tend to be the most aggressive, i.e. this study would be looking for a **correlation**, or association, between watching violent programmes and being aggressive. The closer the link between them, the greater would be the correlation or association.

One of the best-known uses of the correlational approach is in the study of life events and stress-related illnesses. For example, Rahe et al. (1970; see page 234) found that there was a significant positive correlation between the stress of recent life events (taking account of the number and severity of these events) and physical illness. These findings support those of many other researchers.

See *AS Level Psychology Online* for an interactive exercise on this topic.

? When would one have to use a correlational design?

A CORRELATIONAL ANALYSIS: TELEVISION VIOLENCE AND AGGRESSIVE BEHAVIOUR

Positive correlations between hours of television violence watched and actual aggressive behaviour for children and adolescents are shown by the majority of correlational analyses on this topic. Such research has been done in many countries including Poland, the UK, Finland, Australia, and the USA. But does this mean that watching violence on TV actually causes people to become more hostile in their behaviour? One important point is that correlations cannot infer cause and effect, because they merely show a link that may, or may not, be causal. For example, it is possible that people who are naturally more aggressive prefer to watch violent programmes, as they find them more enjoyable, more exciting. And another point in this research area is that although studying in a wide range of countries seems to have allowed for cultural relativism, in fact these are all Western industrialised types of culture and so there may be cross-cultural differences that have not been demonstrated.

Weaknesses of correlational studies

Correlational designs are generally regarded as inferior to experimental designs, because it is hard (or impossible) to establish cause and effect. In our first example, the existence of an association between the amount of television violence watched and aggressive behaviour would certainly be consistent with the hypothesis that watching violent programmes can *cause* aggressive behaviour. However, it could

> **KEY TERM**
>
> **Correlation:** an association that is found between two variables.

Correlation or causation?

equally be that aggressive individuals may choose to watch more violent programmes than those who are less aggressive, in other words the causality operates in the other direction. Or there is a third variable accounting for the association between watching violent programmes and aggressive behaviour, e.g. people in disadvantaged families may watch more television and their deprived circumstances may also cause them to behave aggressively. If that were the case, then the number of violent television programmes watched might have no direct effect at all on aggressive behaviour.

In our second example (Rahe et al., 1970), it is possible that stressful life events play a role in causing physical illness. However, it is also possible that illness increases the chance of experiencing life events. Alternatively, it may be that there is a third variable at work which accounts for the correlation between stressful life events and physical illness. Perhaps some people are naturally rather weak physically and psychologically, and this makes them tend to experience negative life events and to suffer from physical illness.

Advantages of correlational studies

In spite of the interpretive problems posed by the findings of correlational studies, there are several reasons why psychologists continue to use this method. First, many hypotheses cannot be examined directly by means of experimental designs. For example, the hypothesis that life events cause various physical diseases cannot be tested by forcing some people to experience lots of negative events! All that can be done is to examine correlations or associations between the number and severity of negative life events and the probability of suffering from various diseases. Such a study might start with the hypothesis that "life events are related to ill health", and a correlational study would obtain data for each individual about, for example, the number and types of life events (negative and positive) they have experienced over a period of time and the types of physical illness from which they have suffered.

Second, it is often possible to obtain large amounts of data on a number of variables in a correlational study much more rapidly and efficiently than would be possible using experimental designs. Use of a questionnaire, for example, would permit a researcher to investigate the associations between aggressive behaviour and a wide range of activities (such as watching violent films in the cinema, reading violent books, being frustrated at work or at home).

Third, correlational research *can* produce reasonably definite information about causal relationships if there is *no* association between the two **co-variables**. For example, if it were found that there was no association at all between stressful life events and physical illness, this would provide fairly strong evidence that physical illnesses are *not* caused by stressful life events.

Finally, the greatest use of **correlational analysis** is in prediction, because if you find that two variables are correlated, you can predict one from another. It is also a useful method when manipulation of variables is impossible.

KEY TERMS

Co-variables: the variables involved in a correlational study that may vary together (co-vary).
Correlational analysis: testing a hypothesis using an association that is found between two variables.

Correlational studies

Advantages	Limitations
• Allows study of hypotheses that cannot be examined directly	• Interpretation of results is difficult
• More data on more variables can be collected more quickly than in an experimental set-up	• Cause and effect cannot be established
	• Direction of causality is uncertain
• Problems of interpretation are reduced when no association is found	• Variables other than the one of interest may be operating

To apply this, consider a correlational study that looks at the relationship between stress and the immune system, or stress and personality. With reference to this study identify the advantages and disadvantages as outlined above.

Correlational studies and ethical issues

There is the possibility that the public at large will misinterpret the findings from correlational studies. For example, the finding that there is a correlation between the amount of television violence watched by children and their level of aggression led many influential people to argue that television violence was having a damaging effect. In other words, they mistakenly supposed that correlational evidence can demonstrate a causal relation. Television companies may have suffered from such over-interpretation of findings. In similar fashion, the findings on Type A and coronary heart disease reported by Friedman and Rosenman (1974) may have unduly alarmed many people who feared that their Type A personality meant they were almost certain to have a heart attack.

Correlational analyses are often used in research that raises political and/or social issues. For example, consider the correlational evidence suggesting that individual differences in intelligence depend in part on genetic factors. Some people have argued, mistakenly, that this implies that *race* differences in intelligence also depend on genetic factors. The key ethical issue here (and in many other correlational studies) is for the researcher to be fully aware of the social sensitivity of the findings that he/she has obtained, and the lack of causal evidence.

Observational Techniques

Behaviour is observed in virtually every psychological study. For example, in Milgram's (1963; see Chapter 7) research on obedience to authority, a film record was made of the participants' behaviour so that their emotional states could be observed. However, we will consider studies in which **observational techniques** are of central importance.

There are several types of observational techniques (Coolican, 2004). However, the three most important techniques are as follows: controlled observations; naturalistic observations, and participant observations. **Controlled observations** involve the researcher exercising control over the environment in which

Naturalistic observation, for example, observing children's behaviour in a playground, can provide more extensive information than a laboratory study. However, the participants' behaviour may alter if they are aware that they are being observed.

When conducting observational studies researchers need to decide whether participants will be aware that they are being observed, as this may affect the participants' behaviour.

the observations are made. **Naturalistic observations** involve observations of participants in natural situations without any direct intervention from the observers. **Participant observations** involve natural situations in which the observer is directly involved in the interactions of the participants, who are typically group members.

We will consider each of these types of observational study shortly. However, there are some general issues that apply to all of them. For example, how can observers avoid being overloaded in their attempts to record their observations of others' behaviour? One approach is **event sampling**, focusing only on actions or events that are of particular interest to the researcher. Another approach is **time sampling**, where observations are made only during specified time periods (e.g. the first 10 minutes of each hour). Yet another approach is **point sampling**, where one individual is observed in order to categorise their current behaviour, after which a second individual is observed, and so on.

Another general issue relates to the information recorded by the observer or observers. In the past, observers typically made immediate ratings of participants' behaviour using pre-determined categories. More recently, however, there has been increased use of video or film recording, which means that ratings can be made in a more leisurely way and re-checked if necessary. There is a more detailed discussion of the development and use of behavioural categories in observational studies later in the chapter. Here we note that it is important for researchers to develop precise and unambiguous categories. After that, they need to make sure that observers are trained in the use of the categories being used to produce high reliability or consistency of measurement. Reliability can be assessed by correlating the observational records of two or more observers, producing a measure of inter-observer reliability.

There is a final general issue. Researchers setting up an observational study have to decide whether participants will or will not be aware that they are being observed. The disadvantage with the participants knowing they are being observed is that this knowledge may very well influence their behaviour. For example, Zegoib, Arnold, and Forehand (1975) found that mothers who knew they were observed interacted more with their children and behaved more warmly towards them than did mothers who didn't know they were observed. The main disadvantage with participants not knowing they are being observed is that it is regarded as unethical for participants not to give full informed consent to their involvement in a study.

Controlled observations

There are many studies (perhaps especially in developmental psychology) that have involved the use of controlled observations using situations subject to at least some experimental control. For example, Ainsworth and Bell (1970; see Chapter 4) carried out a laboratory study in which infants were observed as

---

KEY TERMS

Naturalistic observation: an unobtrusive observational study conducted in a natural setting.
Participant observations: observations in natural situations where the observer interacts directly with the participants.
Event sampling: a technique for collecting data in an observational study. The observer focuses only on actions or events that are of particular interest to the study.
Time sampling: a technique used in observational studies. Observations are only made during specified time periods (e.g. the first 10 minutes of each hour).
Point sampling: a technique used in an observational study. One individual is observed in order to categorise their current behaviour, after which a second individual is observed.

they responded to a carefully organised sequence of events involving the mother/caregiver leaving the infant and returning. These observations were used to categorise the infants' behaviour in terms of attachment style. In the years since then there have been numerous similar studies on children's attachment behaviour.

Advantages of controlled observations

- Controlled observations are often used in the context of a laboratory experiment. In principle, this can provide the positive features of the experimental method (e.g. possibility to infer cause-and-effect relationships) together with detailed observational information.
- If the situation is well controlled, there is less risk of unwanted extraneous variables influencing participants' behaviour than is the case with naturalistic or controlled observations.
- Richer and more complete information is often obtained from studies using controlled observations than from conventional experimental studies in which participants are only required to produce limited responses.

Weaknesses of controlled observations

- Carrying out studies in artificial situations (e.g. laboratories) can influence the participants' behaviour. This may be especially the case with young children who can become anxious in a strange environment.
- The artificiality of the situation may make it hard to generalise the findings to more natural situations.
- Problems such as investigator effects (due to experimenter expectations) and demand characteristics (due to participant expectations) may arise in studies using controlled observations.

> **A CONTROLLED OBSERVATION: ATTACHMENT AND CUDDLY TOYS**
> Toddlers' attachment to their cuddly toys was investigated in an observational study. Their mothers were asked about each child's favourite toys. Then with their mothers nearby the toddlers were assessed with varying levels of stress, and the preferred toys in each situation were noted. As expected, the children's preference for familiar toys increased as the stress of their situation increased.
>
> What do you think of the ethics of such experiments? What precautions would you take to make sure the participants were always well looked after?

Naturalistic observations

Naturalistic observations involve methods designed to examine behaviour in natural situations *without* the experimenter interfering with it in any way. This approach was originally developed by the ethologists such as Lorenz (see Chapter 4) who studied non-human species in their natural habitat and discovered much about the animals' behaviour. An example of the use of naturalistic observations in human research is the attachment study by Anderson (1972). He observed children in a London park and noticed that it was very unusual to see a child under the age of 3 who wandered further than 200 feet from his/her mother before returning, perhaps just to touch her knee or come close.

Naturalistic observations were also used by Schaffer and Emerson (1964), who carried out a longitudinal observational study on children. They obtained clear evidence that children differ considerably from each other in their attachment behaviour. However, most children develop fairly strong attachments to one or more adults during early childhood.

> ■ **Activity:** Observations
> This could be done in small groups. People often assume that boys' play is more rough than girls' play. This is a casual observation, but you could devise a hypothesis from it, then operationalise this. How would you do your observations, and how would you ensure inter-observer reliability? What behavioural categories would you use? What might be problems in doing this naturalistic observation? One person should act as the recorder and make a list of what the group says, and this could then be shared with other groups.

? What advantages might be gained by observing children in a naturalistic environment rather than in a laboratory?

Advantages of natural observations

Here are the main advantages of natural observations:

- If the participants are unaware that they are being observed, this method provides a way of observing people behaving naturally. That means there are no problems from demand characteristics (guessing what the experiment is about) or evaluation apprehension (seeking the approval of the researcher).
- Many studies based on naturalistic observations provide richer and fuller information than typical laboratory experiments. For example, Schaffer and Emerson's (1964) naturalistic observations on attachment behaviour in children can be compared with Ainsworth and Bell's (1970) structural observation research (see Chapter 4). Schaffer and Emerson's approach allowed them to show very clearly that young children often form multiple important attachments, an important finding not considered by Ainsworth and Bell.
- It is sometimes possible to use naturalistic observations when other methods can't be used (e.g. with unwilling participants; when participants can't be disrupted at work). Naturalistic observations may work better than other methods with children and non-human animals.

? How can an experiment tell us more about "why" a behaviour has occurred than an observational study can?

Weaknesses of naturalistic observations

Here are the most important weaknesses of naturalistic observations:

- The experimenter has essentially no control over the situation. This makes it very hard (or impossible) to decide what caused the participants to behave as they did.
- The participants are often aware they are being observed and so their behaviour isn't natural. Note, however, that this is also true of most other kinds of research.
- Many researchers haven't taken the time to develop precise categories of behaviour and to train their observers thoroughly, leading to unreliable data.
- There can be problems of replication with studies of naturalistic observations. For example, consider naturalistic observations carried out in schools. There are enormous differences in character among schools, and this is likely to produce large differences in observational data from one school to the next.
- Naturalistic observations pose ethical issues if the participants don't realise their behaviour is being observed (**undisclosed observation**). This can happen if one-way mirrors are used or participants are observed in public places and voluntary informed consent isn't obtained.

See *AS Level Psychology Online* for an interactive exercise on this topic.

KEY TERM

Undisclosed observation: an observational study where the participants have not been informed that it is taking place.

A NATURALISTIC OBSERVATION: SOCIAL BEHAVIOUR

A lot of research puts people into unusual settings or situations where we cannot be sure we are seeing real-life behaviours. This is a justification for doing naturalistic observations, seeing natural everyday behaviour. It is also a strategy for some very sensitive research areas. For example, social behaviours of pre-school children who have a history of abuse can be observed and compared with those of children with no such history. The results of these observations of children at play have shown that the abused children made fewer social interactions, were more withdrawn, and when they did interact they used more negative behaviours such as aggression, compared to the other group.

How would you decide what counted as negative behaviours, as aggression? How would you set up your behavioural categories so that you could use several observers yet have reliable data?

What factors or issues might cause difficulties in observing people like this?

Participant observations

The extent of the observer's participation in the activities of the participants can vary enormously. At one extreme, the observer may not disclose his/her research role in order to be accepted as a fully-fledged member of the group. At the other extreme, the observer may fully disclose his/her role and act primarily as an observer in his/her dealing with the group.

Try to fit in as a member of the group and remain detached as an observer.

We will discuss very briefly two well-known studies involving participant observations. Whyte (1943) joined an Italian street gang in Chicago, and became a participant observer. He didn't indicate that he was involved in research, but simply said he was writing a book about the area. The problem he encountered in interpreting his observations was that his presence in the gang influenced their behaviour. One gang member expressed this point as follows: "You've slowed me down plenty since you've been down here. Now, when I do something, I have to think what Bill Whyte would want me to know about it and how I can explain it."

Festinger, Riecken, and Schachter (1956) became participant observers by joining a religious sect that believed that the world was about to come to an end. When the world didn't end on the day the sect members thought it would, their leader argued that they had saved the world through their faith. The participants didn't reveal to the sect members that they were engaged in research.

Advantages of participant observations

Here are some of the main advantages of participant observations:

- As Coolican (2004) pointed out, the observer in studies involving participant observations typically has a reasonable amount of flexibility in terms of the extent of his/her involvement in the group being observed.
- Some studies using participant observations (e.g. Whyte's, 1943, study of an Italian street gang) are long-lasting and this helps to ensure that detailed and rich information is obtained.
- In studies such as those of Whyte (1943) and Festinger et al. (1956), it would have been extremely difficult for useful research to have been carried out by researchers who didn't join the street gang or the religious sect, respectively.

Weaknesses of participant observations

There are various weaknesses with the use of participant observations:

? What ethical issues would you flag up for participant observation research? And what issue of validity could there be?

- There are ethical problems about researchers deceiving the members of groups in order to join them. There is an obvious failure to obtain fully informed consent from group members.
- The presence of a participant observer can change and distort the behaviour of group members. This is shown in the quotation above from a member of the street gang observed by Whyte (1943).

? Sometimes it is not possible to write field notes as events are happening. What does memory research tell us about the usefulness and accuracy of notes written after the event?

- There can be real problems concerning the accuracy and objectivity of the reports produced by participant observers. Participant observers who have not disclosed their research role generally write down what happened some time after any given event so as not to arouse suspicion. In addition, if participant observers become involved with the group they are observing, this may bias their reports.

> **A PARTICIPANT OBSERVATION: FOOTBALL**
> Football fans—are they supporters or are they hooligans? Much of what is reported in the media might suggest the latter, but when Marsh (1996) joined supporters' clubs and attended games to do his participant observations he found that there was a clear social order among the fans, and an understood set of social norms about what behaviours were and were not acceptable. For example, aggressive chants and gestures were acceptable, but actual violent contact was not. These findings did not apply to a minority who attended games not for the actual football but for opportunities to fight, but Marsh focused on the vast majority of genuine supporters.
>
> Do you think it is ethically acceptable to join an organisation in order to observe people without their consent? Why do some researchers do this, and what problems might arise if consent was sought?

Self-Report Techniques Including Interview and Questionnaire

Non-psychologists often think that the best way to understand the behaviour of other people is by asking them about it. This can be done in various ways including the use of interview and questionnaire techniques. It is indisputable that much of value can be learned in this way. However, there are at least two major problems with **self-report techniques**. First, most people want to create a favourable opinion of themselves and this may lead them to distort their answers to personal questions. Second, many people don't understand themselves very well, and so their self-reports may not be very informative. In spite of these problems, there is much of value with interview and questionnaire techniques.

Interview techniques

Interviews come in many different shapes and sizes. More specifically, they differ in terms of the amount of structure built into the interview and in terms of the types of questions that are asked. Coolican (2004) identified several types of interview of which the following are the most important:

- *Non-directive interviews*: These possess the least structure, with the person being interviewed (the interviewee) being free to discuss almost anything he/she wants. The interviewer guides the discussion and encourages the interviewee to be more forthcoming. Such interviews are used in the treatment of mental disorders but are of less relevance to research.
- *Semi-structured or guided interviews*: These possess a moderate amount of structure. The interviewer identifies the issues to be addressed beforehand. During the interview, further decisions are made about how and when to raise these issues. All interviewees are asked similar questions, but the precise questions vary from interviewee to interviewee.
- *Clinical interviews*: These resemble guided interviews. All the interviewees are asked the same initial questions, but the choice of follow-up questions depends on the answers given. The researcher can be given the flexibility to ask questions

See *AS Level Psychology Online* for an interactive exercise on this topic.

KEY TERMS
Self-report techniques: participants provide their own account of themselves, usually by means of questionnaires, surveys, or interviews.
Interview: a verbal research method in which the participant answers a series of questions.

in various ways. Such interviews are often used by clinical psychologists to assess patients with mental disorders. Clinical interviews give interviewers the flexibility to explore interesting or unexpected answers as they see fit.

- *Fully structured interviews*: In this type of interview, a standard set of questions is asked in the same fixed order to all interviewees. The interviewees are only allowed to choose their answers from a restricted set of possibilities (e.g. "Yes", "No", "Don't know"). As Coolican (2004, p. 153) pointed out, "This approach is hardly an interview worth the name at all. It is a face-to-face data-gathering technique, but could be conducted by telephone or by post."

> ■ **Activity:** Divide the class into small groups and ask each group to prepare one kind of interview technique. They should present a short demonstration to the class. Which ones worked best? What problems arose? Which would be the best ways to collect data?

> **?** Have you ever been interviewed while out shopping? How would you classify this interview style?

Advantages of interviews

As might be expected, the precise advantages of interviews depend on the type of interview. Unstructured or non-directive interviews can produce very rich and personal information from the person being interviewed. It could be argued that this is often the case when therapists interview clients in order to assess their experiences and emotions. Most experimental studies focus on a very narrow aspect of behaviour, but non-directive interviews can range over a large number of topics within a manageable period of time.

Structured interviews can compare the responses of different interviewees, all of whom have been asked the same questions. Another advantage is good reliability, in that two different interviewers are likely to obtain similar responses from an interviewee when they ask exactly the same questions in the same order. In addition, there is a reasonable chance of being able to replicate the findings in another study. Finally, it is usually fairly easy to analyse the data obtained from structured interviews because the data tend to be in numerical form.

Weaknesses of interviews

Non-directive or unstructured interviews have a problem with the unsystematic variation of information obtained from different interviewees, making the data hard to analyse. Another weakness is that what the interviewee says is determined in a complex way by the interaction between him/her and the interviewer. For example, the gender, age, and personality of the interviewer may influence the course of the interview, making it hard to work out which of the interviewee's contributions are or are not affected by the interviewer. Such influences are known as **interviewer bias**. Finally, the fact that the information obtained from interviewees is influenced by the interviewer means that the data obtained can be regarded as unreliable.

> **?** How would research results be affected by the possibility that people might decide to give the socially acceptable response to statements such as "Smacking children is an appropriate form of punishment"?

In structured interviews, what the interviewee says may be somewhat constrained and artificial because of the high level of structure built into the interview. Interviewees may find this off-putting, and it may lead them to give short, formal answers. In addition, there is none of the flexibility associated with unstructured interviews.

Three weaknesses are common to all the types of interview (with the first two also being common to most questionnaires). First, there is the issue of social desirability bias due to the fact that most people want to convey a positive impression of themselves. For example, people are much more willing to admit they are unhappy when filling in a questionnaire anonymously

> **KEY TERM**
>
> **Interviewer bias**: the effects of an interviewer's expectations on the responses made by an interviewee.

People adjust what they say to fit the circumstances.

AN INTERVIEW: **GENDER STEREOTYPES**

We are all familiar with gender stereotypes, but when do we start learning this type of social norm? One study showed that 5-year-old children in the USA already have well-established gender stereotypes. These children were read short stories in which the main character was described by "masculine" adjectives (e.g. tough, forceful) or "female" ones (e.g. emotional, excitable). Then each child was interviewed and asked about whether the characters were male or female. Almost all of the children were clear which sex the character belonged to.

If you were going to replicate this study what would you do as a pilot study, and why would you be doing one?

than when being interviewed (Eysenck, 1990). Second, we can only extract information of which the interviewee is consciously aware. This is a significant weakness, because people are often unaware of the reasons why they behave in certain ways (Nisbett & Wilson, 1977). Third, many interviewers lack some of the skills necessary to conduct interviews successfully. Good interviewers can make an interview seem natural, are sensitive to non-verbal cues, and have well-developed listening skills (Coolican, 2004).

Questionnaire techniques

What happens with use of questionnaire techniques is that participants are given a set of questions together with instructions about how to record their answers. In principle, questionnaires can be used to explore an almost endless range of issues. In practice, however, most questionnaires focus on an individual's personality or his/her attitudes and beliefs.

The types of items found in questionnaires can vary considerably. At one extreme, there are fixed-choice items, which require respondents to select from a small number of choices (e.g. Yes or No). At the other extreme, there are open-ended items, which give respondents great flexibility in their responses. Most questionnaires use fixed-choice items. Such items are easier to score and tend to produce more reliable or consistent data. However, open-ended items have their own advantages. For example, they are more realistic, in that in everyday life we generally have much scope to answer questions in our own way, and they produce richer information than fixed-choice questions.

As is discussed later in the chapter, it is harder to produce good questionnaires than might be imagined. Coolican (2004) identifies the following common mistakes that plague questionnaire construction:

- Complexity: the item is difficult to understand.
- Ambiguity: the item can be interpreted in more than one way.

See *AS Level Psychology Online* for an interactive exercise on this topic.

- Double-barrelled items: the item effectively contains two questions but the respondent must give an overall "Yes" or "No" response. For example, "Global warming is definitely happening and huge resources should be put into doing something about it."
- Leading questions: the item contains within it the implication that a certain response is expected. For example, "Don't you think that this government is discredited?"

Advantages of questionnaires

One of the main advantages of questionnaires is that large amounts of data can be collected rapidly at relatively little cost. Second, we can explore almost any aspect of personality and any attitudes or beliefs using questionnaires. That means that questionnaire techniques are very versatile. Third, many questionnaires have high reliability or consistency and reasonable validity. For example, there is a fairly strong relationship between people's attitudes towards major political parties and their actual voting behaviour (Franzoi, 1996). There are also reasonable relationships between questionnaire measures of coping strategies and how individuals respond to stressors (see Chapter 6).

Weaknesses of questionnaires

Some of the weaknesses of questionnaire techniques have already been mentioned. First, people may be inclined to pretend that their personalities and their attitudes are more desirable than they actually are—social desirability bias. Second, people may lack conscious awareness of their true personality and attitudes. Third, many questionnaires are poorly constructed and so lack reliability or consistency and validity. Fourth, questionnaire techniques are often used within correlational studies. For example, a questionnaire assessing prejudice may be correlated with actual evidence of prejudice or discrimination. In such research, it isn't clear that the prejudiced attitudes are actually causing prejudice and discrimination. Fifth, participants may need to have high literacy skills to understand the precise meaning of the items on a questionnaire.

Interviews and questionnaires

Advantages:
- Unstructured interviews can be more revealing
- Structured interviews permit comparison between interviewees and facilitate replication
- Questionnaires allow for collection of large amounts of data

Limitations:
- Interviewer bias
- Social desirability bias
- People don't always know what they think
- Good interviewing requires skill

To apply this, consider a study that has used the interview technique to obtain data (e.g. Friedman & Rosenman, 1959). Either obtain a copy of the original journal article to see what sort of questions were asked or try to design your own questions that might have been asked.

Think back to what you learned about eyewitness testimony (see p. 63). How might Loftus' work relate to researching by asking questions? What would researchers have to be very careful about in forming questions for the interview?

A QUESTIONNAIRE: DIFFERENT SMELLS

We know that even though our sense of smell isn't good scents still are important, especially when they trigger memories. One research study looked at memories of a visit to the Jorvik Viking Centre in York where different smells, e.g. of a fish market, are part of the experience. Participants had visited the centre some years before, and were given the questionnaire about that experience either with or without a selection of bottled smells from the centre. The findings showed much better recall with the smells than without them, supporting the idea that these smells acted as memory cues.

How do you think you would find participants for this sort of investigation? What are the advantages and disadvantages of this sort of sampling method?

Case Studies

Case studies differ from the methods and techniques we have discussed so far because they involve the detailed investigation of a single individual or a small number of individuals. There are sometimes good reasons why it isn't feasible to use large numbers of participants in a study. For example, a busy clinician or therapist may find the behaviour of a given patient very revealing, but he/she may have no possibility of collecting data from other patients with the same disorder. Most of the best-known case studies involve patients with mental disorders and the information obtained is mostly based on interviews. However, case studies come in all shapes and sizes. For example, consider HM, a patient who had very severe memory problems (discussed in Chapter 3). Some of the data collected on him came from laboratory tasks using the experimental method.

Several case studies are discussed in various chapters of this book. In Chapter 4, for example, there is detailed information on Genie, a girl who was kept locked up in isolation for the first 13 years of her life. After being rescued, she developed very good spatial ability, but struggled to learn language. Sadly, she was subsequently sent to various foster homes, and was abused. Thus, the case study of Genie suggested that extreme privation for the first several years of life can have severe and permanent adverse effects.

In Chapter 8 I discuss the case of an 11-month-old infant called Albert (Watson & Rayner, 1920). Little Albert was brought up in a hospital, and learned to associate playing with a white rat with hearing a loud noise. This created a fear of the white rat through a process of classical conditioning, and this fear extended to any creatures that were white and furry. However, it has proved somewhat difficult to replicate this finding (Davison, Neale, & Kring, 2004).

One of the most famous case studies of all time is that of Anna O (see Chapter 8), who was investigated by Sigmund Freud. Anna had various physical symptoms (e.g. paralysis of her right hand and leg). According to Freud, the actual problems were psychological in nature and dated back to events connected with the death of her father years earlier. This case study convinced Freud of the power of mental causes to produce psychological and physical symptoms, as well as of the key role played by early life experiences in producing mental disorder.

Advantages of case studies

Here are the main advantages of case studies:

? Case studies are often used as a way of understanding unusual behaviours. What are the advantages and limitations of using this method of research?

- They can provide far more information about a specific individual than is usually obtained from studies involving groups of individuals. For example, very detailed information about Genie's intellectual and social development was obtained over a period of several years.
- Some case studies have been very influential because they have indicated that there are serious problems with some prominent theory.

  There is a good example of this in Chapter 3. According to Atkinson and Shiffrin's (1968) multi-store model, there is only a single long-term memory system. This model was shown to be oversimplified by a case study on HM, an epileptic who received surgery. After the surgery he had very limited ability to acquire new declarative knowledge (e.g. knowing that he had muesli for breakfast; knowing that he went to a local town last week). However, he was able to learn and remember new procedural knowledge (e.g. knowing how to trace a figure in a mirror). These findings suggested that we have somewhat separate declarative and procedural knowledge systems.

- Case studies (even limited ones) can nevertheless provide useful insights that influence future theoretical developments. For example, there is the case study on Little Albert (Watson & Rayner, 1920). This case study influenced the development of behaviour therapy—it showed that fears can be classically conditioned and suggested to behaviour therapists that fears can perhaps be eliminated through conditioning as well.

Weaknesses of case studies

Here are the main weaknesses of case studies:

- Their greatest weakness is that what is true of a given individual may well not be true of other individuals. For example, the case study of Genie suggested that extreme privation causes severe long-term effects and greatly inhibits the development of language. However, other case studies suggest different conclusions. For example, Soutter (1995) studied Tom, who was kept in a bare room for the first 10 years of his life. After being rescued, he became more emotionally expressive, he went to university, he made friends, and his general behaviour was normal. Clearly, extreme privation doesn't always have dire consequences.
- Of direct relevance to the above point is the issue of generalisation and drawing general conclusions from case studies. There are two kinds of problem with respect to generalisation. First, the individual may not be *representative* of individuals of the same age and gender. For example, there was evidence that Genie had very limited brain activity in the left hemisphere, which is very unusual. This can make the findings unreliable and invalid. Little Albert was not representative in that his personality was "on the whole stolid [passive] and unemotional" (Watson & Rayner, 1920, p. 1). Second, even if the individual studied is representative, it is still likely that other individuals of the opposite gender and/or a different age would behave differently. For example, strictly speaking, the case study of Little Albert only tells us about fear conditioning in a boy of 11 months—it is perfectly possible that younger or older boys or girls would show different effects.
- Case studies based on individuals with mental disorders often involve lengthy and intimate interviews between patient and therapist. This can provide rich and informative data, but carries with it the potential weakness of bias on the therapist's part. For example, consider the case of Anna O, who was treated by Sigmund Freud (see Chapter 8). It is entirely possible that the questions that Freud asked her and the way he interpreted her answers were influenced by his own theoretical ideas.
- Another weakness with case studies is that of subjective selection (Coolican, 1994). The therapist or experimenter often only reports a small fraction of the information obtained from the individual being studied, and what is selected may be influenced by his/her preconceptions.

■ **Activity:** List all the research methods covered in this section and, for each of them, say how they might produce qualitative and quantitative data.

A CASE STUDY: A PROFESSIONAL MUSICIAN

Case studies can be fascinating as they contain in-depth information about an individual participant or very small group, and great detail is possible. In one such study, a well-known professional musician known as CW who had suffered brain damage as a result of a rare infection in his hippocampus was monitored. The brain damage had affected his memory. Post-accident his LTM was still fine for knowledge acquired before the infection, such as speech, reading and writing, and playing music, but his STM was badly affected. Its duration was negligible and he had lost the ability to move information from his STM, his immediate awareness, into LTM. This meant that he had no knowledge of what had happened in the years since his accident, and at every moment he thought he had just become conscious for the first time.

While case studies are interesting, their problem is that we cannot generalise from one or two people to the population at large, and so cannot assume we have learned something that is true for each of us. Can you think of four specific reasons or individual differences that show why we should avoid such generalisations?

SECTION SUMMARY

The scientific approach

❖ Much research is scientific. The scientific method involves:
  – making observations;
  – formulating theories that generate hypotheses;
  – testing the hypotheses by designing research, then collecting data, and finally revising the theory in line with the new data.

The experimental method

❖ The key principle of the experimental method is that an independent variable is manipulated (with all confounding variables controlled) in order to observe its effect on a dependent variable.

❖ Participants should be randomly allocated to conditions to further rule out confounding variables.

❖ Use of the experimental method often (but by no means always) allows us to infer causality, and it aims to be replicable.

❖ The experimental method is used in laboratory and field experiments.

Laboratory experiments

❖ Advantages of laboratory experiments:
  – Laboratory experiments permit greater removal of confounding variables.
  – They also allow more detailed data collection than field experiments.

❖ However, they tend to be artificial (lacking external validity and mundane realism).

❖ This artificiality can be compensated for by increased experimental realism (internal validity).

❖ Other concerns include:
  – The problems arising from knowing you are being observed (demand characteristics and evaluation apprehension).
  – Ethical issues such as being obedient to authority and the right to withdraw.

Field experiments

❖ Advantages of field experiments:
  – Field experiments are less artificial (higher external validity) than laboratory experiments.
  – They suffer less from factors such as demand characteristics and evaluation apprehension.

❖ Weaknesses of field experiments:
  – They are less controlled (lower internal validity).
  – They create ethical problems in terms of lack of informed consent.

❖ Quasi-experiments fall short of true experiments because: *Quasi-experiments*
  – The experimenter has not manipulated the independent variable.
  – The participants are not allocated at random to conditions.
❖ Natural experiments are quasi-experiments involving some naturally occurring independent variable.
❖ Advantages of natural experiments:
  – One advantage of natural experiments is that the participants are unaware they are taking part in an experiment, which prevents demand characteristics.
  – Natural experiments also permit the study of variables that couldn't ethically be manipulated by an experimenter.
❖ Weaknesses of natural experiments:
  – These include problems of interpreting the findings due to a lack of randomisation.
  – There is also an ethical concern about taking advantage of people at a time of possible high stress.

❖ Advantages of correlational analysis: *Investigations using*
  – Many issues can only be studied by assessing correlations or associations   *correlational analysis*
    between variables.
  – Correlational studies determine the extent that co-variables vary together, and offer the possibility of obtaining large amounts of data very rapidly.
❖ Weaknesses of correlational analysis:
  – Investigations using correlational analysis are less useful than experimental designs, because they don't permit inferences about causality.
  – In terms of ethical concerns, we should be wary of misinterpretations of correlational evidence.

❖ It is important in observational studies to use unambiguous behavioural   *Observational*
  categories for recording participants' behaviour.   *techniques*
❖ Participants' behaviour is more natural if they are unaware of being observed, but this raises ethical issues due to lack of informed consent.
❖ Controlled observations occur in studies under experimental control. They have the following advantages and weaknesses:
  + Use of the experimental method permits inferences about cause and effect.
  + There is a reduced risk of extraneous variables compared to other types of observational study.
  – Use of artificial situations can reduce generalisability.
  – There can be investigator effects and demand characteristics.
❖ Naturalistic observations occur in natural situations without any interference from the researcher. They have the following advantages and weaknesses:
  + They provide a way of observing people behaving naturally.
  + They provide rich and full information about behaviour.
  – The researcher has no control over the situation.
  – There can be problems of replication.

❖ Participant observations occur in natural situations with the observer being more or less actively involved. They have the following advantages and weaknesses:
+ There is flexibility in terms of the observer's involvement.
+ Participant observation is the most effective way of studying the behaviour of certain groups (e.g. street gangs).
− The presence of the participant observer distorts the behaviour of the group members.
− The reports produced by participant observers are sometimes inaccurate and lacking in objectivity.

Self-report techniques

❖ There are several types of interview ranging from the unstructured to the fully structured.
❖ Unstructured interviews:
− These are responsive to the personality, interests, and motivations of the interviewee and so tend to produce full information.
− However, the data obtained tend to be unreliable.
❖ Structured interviews:
− Structured interviews permit comparisons among interviewees, and they tend to be fairly reliable.
− However, what the interviewee says can be constrained and artificial, and the data tend to be more quantitative.
❖ Questionnaire techniques involve presenting respondents with a set of fixed-choice or open-ended items.
❖ Fixed-choice items are more reliable but open-ended ones are more realistic.
❖ Questionnaires have various advantages and weaknesses:
+ They are inexpensive and involve the rapid collection of much data.
+ Many questionnaires have good reliability and reasonable validity.
− Questionnaires can produce problems due to social desirability bias, and those completing questionnaires can only provide information of which they are consciously aware.
❖ Questionnaire techniques are mostly used in correlational studies, and so causal inferences cannot be drawn.

Case studies

❖ Case studies involve the collection of detailed information from a single individual or from a small number of individuals. They often (but by no means always) involve the use of interviews.
❖ Advantages of case studies:
− They permit the collection of unusually detailed information about a given individual.
− Some case studies have reported findings that are inconsistent with an influential theory.
− Case studies can provide suggestive evidence that leads to the development of new theoretical approaches.
❖ Weaknesses of case studies:
− They typically do not permit generalisation to any larger group or population
− Many individuals studied in case studies are not representative of any population. Even if they are representative in some ways, someone of different age or the opposite sex might well behave differently.

- The experimenter may exhibit bias in the way he/she collects information, especially when interview techniques are used.
- There is a danger that the fraction of the collected information reported by the experimenter will be based on subjective (and biased) selection.

SECTION 10
INVESTIGATION DESIGN

In order to carry out a study successfully, care and attention must be devoted to each stage in its design and implementation. This section is concerned with these issues. We will focus on *experimental designs*, although many of the same issues also apply to non-experimental designs. As we will see, several decisions need to be made when designing an experimental study.

In what way are research aims and hypotheses different?

Aims and Hypotheses

The first step when designing a study is to decide on the aims and hypotheses of the study. The aims are usually more general than the hypotheses, and they help to explain the reasons for the investigator deciding to test some specific hypothesis or hypotheses. In other words, the aims tell us *why* a given study is being carried out, whereas the hypotheses tell us *what* the study is designed to test.

As an example, suppose we decide to test the general theoretical notion that to-be-learned information that is easy to organise will be better remembered than information that is hard to organise. We might present all of our participants with the same list of nouns (24 words with 4 words belonging to each of six categories) either category by category or in random order (see Chapter 3). The main aim of this experiment would be to investigate the theory that organisation enhances memory. The *hypothesis* is more specific: "Free recall from long-term memory is higher when a categorised word list is presented category-by-category than when it is presented in random order."

Common sense recommends a quiet rather than a noisy place for study—but to test the hypothesis that noise interferes with learning requires an experimental design.

Hypotheses

Experimental/alternative hypothesis

Most experimental research using the experimental method starts with someone thinking of an **experimental hypothesis** so that they are clear about what they aim to prove or disprove. The experimental hypothesis is a prediction (or forecast) of what the researcher thinks will happen to the dependent variable when the independent variable changes. For example, "Loud noise will have an effect on people's ability to learn the information in a chapter of an introductory psychology textbook".

We have just seen that we talk about an experimental hypothesis in the context of a proper experiment. However, there is a more general term

A happy dog will eat more

YES / NO

One-tailed hypothesis

Mood affects the appetite of dogs

EAT MORE / EAT LESS

Two-tailed hypothesis

See *AS Level Psychology Online* for an interactive exercise on this topic.

■ Activity: Devising hypotheses

Devise suitable null and experimental hypotheses for the following:

- An investigator considers the effect of noise on students' ability to concentrate and complete a word-grid. One group only is subjected to the noise in the form of a distractor, i.e. a television programme.
- An investigator explores the view that there might be a link between the amount of television children watch and their behaviour at school.

KEY TERMS

Alternative hypothesis: another term for the experimental hypothesis. The experimental hypothesis is the alternative to the null hypothesis.
Directional (one-tailed) hypothesis: a prediction that there will be a difference or correlation between two variables and a statement of the direction of this difference.
Null hypothesis: a hypothesis which states that any findings are due to chance factors and do not reflect a true difference, effect, or relationship.

(alternative hypothesis) that can be used to refer to all hypotheses that aren't null hypotheses (see below). Thus, every experimental hypothesis is also an alternative hypothesis, but *not* every alternative hypothesis is also an experimental hypothesis. For example, we might carry out a correlational study, and form the hypothesis that Type A behaviour will be associated with coronary heart disease (see Chapter 6). That is an alternative hypothesis but *not* an experimental hypothesis.

There are two types of experimental or alternative hypothesis: directional and non-directional. A **directional (one-tailed) hypothesis** predicts the *nature* of the effect of the independent variable on the dependent variable, e.g. "Loud noise will reduce people's ability to learn the information contained in the chapter of a textbook". In contrast, a non-directional (two-tailed) hypothesis predicts that the independent variable will have an effect on the dependent variable, but the *direction* of the effect is not specified, e.g. "Loud noise will have an effect on people's ability to learn the information contained in the chapter of a textbook". This latter hypothesis allows for the possibility that loud noise might actually improve learning, perhaps by making people more alert. So, a one-tailed hypothesis states that the independent variable will lead to either an increase or a decrease in the dependent variable, wheres a two-tailed hypothesis just predicts a change—but not its direction.

Null hypothesis

The **null hypothesis** can simply state that the independent variable will have no effect on the dependent variable. For example, "Loud noise will have no effect on people's ability to learn the information contained in the chapter of the textbook". Sometimes it is easier to state the null hypothesis in relation to group differences. For example, "There will be no significant difference between groups a and b, and any observed differences will be due to chance factors". The purpose of most studies using the experimental method is to decide between the merits of the experimental hypothesis and the null hypothesis. Why do we need a null hypothesis when what we are interested in is the experimental hypothesis? The answer is *precision* and *proof*.

Consider the null hypothesis that loud noise will have no effect on people's learning ability. This is precise, because it leads to a prediction that the single most likely outcome is that performance will be equal in the loud noise and no noise conditions. Failing that, there will probably only be a small difference between the two conditions, with the difference being equally likely to go in either direction. In contrast, consider the experimental hypothesis that loud noise will reduce people's learning ability. This hypothesis is very *imprecise*, because it doesn't indicate how much learning will be impaired. This lack of precision makes it impossible to decide the exact extent to which the findings support (or fail to support) the experimental hypothesis.

If every time I toss a coin it comes down heads, we might form the hypothesis that there are heads on both sides of the coin. However, we can't prove this. The more heads we see, the more likely it would appear that the hypothesis is correct. However, if on one occasion we see tails, we have disproved the hypothesis. It is possible to disprove something but not to prove it. Therefore, we propose a null hypothesis that can be disproved (or rejected) and this implies that we can accept the alternative hypothesis.

> ■ **Activity:** Generating a hypothesis
> 1. Generate a hypothesis for each of these questions:
>   - What are "football hooligans" really like?
>   - Do children play differently at different ages?
>   - What are the effects of caffeine on attention and concentration?
> 2. Identify the independent variable (IV) and dependent variable (DV) from each hypothesis.
> 3. Identify whether your hypotheses are one-tailed or two-tailed (remember, a one-tailed hypothesis predicts the direction of the effect of the IV on the DV, whereas a two-tailed hypothesis does not).
> 4. Write a null hypothesis for each of the experimental hypotheses.

Variables

Experimental hypotheses predict that some aspect of the situation (e.g. the presence of loud noise) will have an effect on the participants' behaviour (e.g. their learning of the information in the chapter). The experimental hypothesis refers to an **independent variable (IV)** (the aspect of the experimental situation manipulated by the experimenter), for example, the presence versus absence of loud noise. The hypothesis also refers to a **dependent variable (DV)** (an aspect of the participants' behaviour measured or assessed by the experiment), for example, measuring learning.

In a nutshell, experimental hypotheses predict that a given independent variable will have some specified effect on a given dependent variable. However, some alternative hypotheses do *not* do this. For example, consider the longitudinal study by Friedman and Rosenman (1974; see Chapter 6) on Type A and coronary heart disease. Their null hypothesis could have expressed as follows: "There is no relation between personality (Type A vs Type B) and coronary heart disease."

> **KEY TERMS**
>
> **Independent variable (IV)**: some aspect of the research situation that is manipulated by the researcher in order to observe whether a change occurs in another variable.
>
> **Dependent variable (DV)**: an aspect of the participant's behaviour that is measured in the study.

> ■ **Activity:** In order to confirm that you do understand what independent (IV) and dependent (DV) variables are, try identifying them in the following examples. Remember:
>
> - The DV depends on the IV.
> - The IV is manipulated by the experimenter or varies naturally.
> - The DV is the one we measure.
>
> 1. Long-term separation affects emotional development more than short-term separation. (The two variables are length of separation and emotional development.)
> 2. Participants conform more when the model is someone they respect. (The two variables are extent of conformity and degree of respect for the model.)
> 3. Participants remember more words before lunch than after lunch. (The two variables are number of words remembered and whether the test is before or after lunch.)
> 4. Boys are better than girls at throwing a ball. (The two variables are gender and ability to throw a ball.)
> 5. Physical attractiveness makes a person more likeable. (The two variables are the attractiveness of a person's photograph and whether they are rated as more or less likeable.)
>
> See overleaf for the answers.

Experimental Design

The second step in the research process is to identify an appropriate design. We will consider experimental design in this section. If we wish to compare two groups with respect to a given independent variable, they must not differ in any other important way. This general rule is important when it comes to selecting participants. For example, if all the least able participants received the loud noise, and all the most able ones received no noise, we wouldn't know whether it was the loud noise or the low ability level that was more responsible for poor learning performance. How should we select our participants so as to avoid this problem? There are three main methods.

1. *Independent groups design.* Each participant is selected for only one group (e.g. no noise or loud noise), most commonly by randomisation. This could involve using a random process such as tossing a coin to allocate one of two conditions for all participants, or you could let all participants draw slips of paper numbered 1 and 2 from a hat. This **random allocation** means that in most cases the participants in the two groups end up equivalent in ability, age, and so on. An example of a study using an independent groups design is the study by Loftus and Palmer (1974, see page 69) on eyewitness testimony. Each group was asked a different question concerning the speed of the cars involved in the accident.

2. *Matched pairs design.* Each participant is selected for only one group, but the participants in the two groups are matched for some relevant factor or factors (e.g. ability, sex, age). In our example, using information about the participants' ability would ensure that the two groups were matched in terms of range of ability. For instance, a study by Kiecolt-Glaser et al. (1995) on slowing of wound healing by psychological stress involved a matched pairs design. The group of women caring for a relative with Alzheimer's disease were matched with the control women in terms of age and family income. This helped to ensure that differences between the groups in time for wound healing could be attributed to the stress of caregiving rather than some other factor.

3. *Repeated measures design.* Each participant appears in both groups, so that there are exactly the same participants in each group. In our example, this would mean that each participant learns the chapter in the loud noise condition and also in the no noise condition. We don't need to worry about the participants in one group being cleverer than those in the other group because the same people appear in both groups! An example of a study using a repeated measures design is the one by Peterson and Peterson (1959; see page 48) on short-term forgetting at various retention intervals, in which all participants were tested at all retention intervals.

Counterbalancing

The main problem with using the repeated measures design is there may be order effects. Participants may perform better when they appear in the second group because they have gained useful information about the experiment or about the task, or less well because of tiredness or boredom. It would be hard to use the repeated measures design in our earlier example—participants are almost certain to show better learning of the chapter the second time they read it regardless of whether they are exposed to loud noise. However, there is a way around this based on **counterbalancing**. Half the participants learn the chapter first in loud noise and then in no noise, whereas the other half learn the chapter first in no noise and then in loud noise. In that way, any order effects should be balanced out.

Experimental and control groups

In some experiments, one of the groups is used to provide baseline information. In our example, one group receives the **experimental treatment** (noise) whereas the other receives nothing (no noise). This latter group serves as the **control group**. Their behaviour informs us about how people behave when they aren't exposed to the experimental treatment so we can make comparisons. The group who have the noise are called the **experimental group**.

If a repeated measures design is used, then we have two different conditions: a control condition and an experimental condition.

Counterbalancing

Group A → Learn words + loud noise → Learn words + no noise

Group B → Learn words + no noise → Learn words + loud noise

> **KEY TERMS**
>
> **Counterbalancing**: used with repeated measures design to overcome the problems of practice and order effects, and involves ensuring that each condition is equally likely to be used first and second by participants.
> **Experimental treatment**: the alteration of the independent variable.
> **Control group**: the group of participants who receive no treatment and act as a comparison to the experimental group to study any effects of the treatment.
> **Experimental group**: the group receiving the experimental treatment.

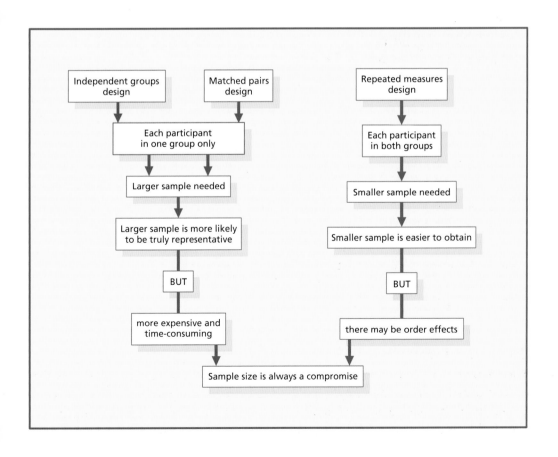

■ **Activity:** Research designs. For each of the three designs mentioned (independent design, matched pairs design, and repeated measures), find at least one study that illustrates the design. With the study you have chosen for repeated measures design, identify the measures that were taken to prevent order effects and explain how counterbalancing was achieved.

Advantages and weaknesses of different research designs

Advantages of the **independent groups design** are that there are no order effects, no participants are lost between trials, and it can be used when a repeated measures design is inappropriate (e.g. when looking at gender differences). Weaknesses include the fact that there may be important individual differences between participants to start with (to minimise this there should be randomisation) and you need more participants than with a repeated measures design.

The **matched pairs design** controls for some individual differences between participants and can be used when a repeated measures design is inappropriate. However, it is fairly difficult to match participants in pairs, and you need a large pool of participants from whom to select (more than with a repeated measures design).

Advantages of the repeated measures design are that it controls for *all* individual differences and it requires fewer participants than the other designs. The weaknesses are that it can't be used in studies in which participation in one condition has large effects on responses in the other, or in which participants are likely to guess the purpose of the study, thus introducing problems with demand characteristics. There are also general problems with order effects.

Design of Naturalistic Observations, Including Development and Use of Behavioural Categories

? Imagine that you are going to conduct an observation of children in a playgroup with two other researchers. To what extent do you think that you will all record the same behaviours? How might you cope with any disagreements?

Earlier in the chapter we discussed various observational techniques used in psychological research. An issue of central importance in observational research is the following: How can observers reduce the bewildering richness and variety of human behaviour to a manageable amount of information? The most common answer is that observers should make use of a set of behavioural categories (e.g. smiles; raises a fist; walks away), recording the frequency with which each of these types of behaviour is exhibited by each of the participants.

There are various stages involved in the development and use of behavioural categories. First, the researchers need to define the behavioural categories that are going to be used in the study. Decisions about which behavioural categories to use depend in part on the specific hypotheses that the researcher wants to test. For example, if the researcher wants to test the hypothesis that boys are more aggressive than girls, it obviously makes sense to focus on behavioural categories relevant to verbal and non-verbal forms of aggression. The development of appropriate categories can be facilitated if the researcher spends some time observing boys and girls to see the various forms of aggressive behaviour they display.

Second, the researcher needs to decide whether the behavioural categories should be based on simple recording or on interpretation. For example, an observer may record that the participant has moved forwards or may interpret that movement as an aggressive action. In either case, what is important is that every behavioural category is unambiguously defined.

In practice, most of the behavioural categories used in research contain at least some interpretation. For example, Bales (1950) developed the interaction process

KEY TERMS

Independent groups design: a research design in which each participant is in one condition only. Each separate group of participants experiences different levels of the IV. Sometimes referred to as an unrelated or between subjects design.

Matched pairs design: a research design that matches participants on a one-to-one basis rather than as a whole group.

analysis, which allows observers to categorise the interactions of members of a group. The observers record inferred meanings for the forms of behaviour shown by members of a group (e.g. "offers suggestion" or "gives information"). Categories based on simple recording are sometimes easier to use (e.g. it is not difficult to decide whether someone is moving forwards) than those based on interpretation. However, behavioural categories based on interpretation are more meaningful and tend to be of more theoretical interest.

Third, when the behavioural categories have been decided on, the next step is to ensure that the observers are properly trained in their use. It is of real importance to show that different observers use the behavioural categories in the same way. The issue here is that of reliability or consistency of measurement. Reliability can be assessed by asking two or more observers to produce observational records at the same time. When these records are correlated, we have a measure of inter-observer reliability (sometimes known as *inter-rater* or *inter-judge reliability*).

Reliability of measurement is very important. However, even if a system of behavioural categories is reliable, that doesn't prove that it is valid in the sense of assessing what we want to assess. Validity can be shown by relating observers' records to other kinds of evidence. For example, Pepler and Craig (1995) had observers rate the aggressiveness of children's interactions using various behavioural categories. The children identified by observers as the most aggressive tended to be those rated as most aggressive by teachers, thus showing evidence for validity in the observers' records.

Design of Interviews and Questionnaires

In this section we focus on appropriate ways of designing questionnaires and interviews. We start by considering interview design and then move on to questionnaire design.

Interview design

As we saw earlier in the chapter, interviews vary in terms of the amount of structure they possess. At one extreme, there are non-directive interviews, in which the interviewer allows the person being interviewed to discuss almost anything he/she wants. At the other extreme, there is the fully structured interview. In this type of interview, a standard set of questions is asked in the same fixed order to all interviewees, who are constrained in their possible answers to each question. There is not much difference between a fully structured interview and a questionnaire. There are also many kinds of interviews between these two extremes—they possess some structure but lack the inflexibility of fully structured interviews.

There are various types of interviews used for psychological experimentation, from nondirective interviews to fully structured designs that have a standard set of questions with restricted-choice answers.

Another difference between types of interviews concerns the nature of the questions that are asked. We can distinguish between closed and open questions. Closed questions require one of a small number of possible answers; example: "Do you approve of the government?" In contrast, open questions allow the interviewee considerable scope as to his/her answer; example: "What do you think about the government?" In general, open questions tend to be associated with non-directive interviews and closed questions with structured interviews.

How should a researcher designing an interview decide which type of interview and question type to choose? Non-directive interviews and open questions would be suitable in the following circumstances:

- The researcher wants to obtain a lot of rich and personal information from each interviewee.
- The researcher wants to maximise the chances that the interviewees will feel involved in the interview.
- The researcher wants to obtain a general impression of the interviewees' views rather than very specific and detailed information.
- It is not of central importance to compare the responses of different interviewees.
- The interviewer or interviewers are well trained to cope with the requirements of conducting non-directive interviews.

Structured interviews and closed questions would be suitable in the following circumstances:

- The researcher wants to obtain information that is easy to analyse.
- The researcher wants to obtain reliable data and to compare directly the answers given by different interviewees.
- The researcher has clear ideas concerning the questions he/she wants interviewees to answer.
- The interviewer(s) have limited training but can cope with the requirements of asking closed questions in a standard order.

Another issue that is important in designing an interview is to consider various characteristics of the interviewer or interviewers. Their gender, ethnicity, age, and personal qualities can all affect the interviewees' answers. For example, Wilson et al. (2002) found that Californian Latino men interviewed by women reported fewer sexual partners than men interviewed by men. In addition, men were more likely to report sex with prostitutes to an older interviewer. There is also the possibility that the views or expectations of the interviewer will bias the responses given by interviewees—this is known as interviewer bias. Interviewer bias can be minimised by instructing interviewers to remain non-evaluative and fairly neutral regardless of whether they personally agree or disagree with what an interviewee is saying.

Questionnaire design

Questionnaires are used for many purposes (e.g. to assess personality; to assess attitudes), and the way in which a questionnaire is designed needs to reflect fully the purpose for which it is being designed. However, some of the general considerations underlying questionnaire design are discussed in the box.

CASE STUDY: QUESTIONNAIRE CONSTRUCTION

The first step is to generate as many ideas as possible that might be relevant to the questionnaire. Then discard those ideas that seem of little relevance, working on the basis (Dyer, 1995, p.114) that: "It is better to ask carefully designed and quite detailed questions about a few precisely defined issues than the same number on a very wide range of topics."

Closed and open questions

There is an important distinction between closed and open questions. Closed questions invite the respondent to select from various possible answers (e.g. yes or no; yes, unsure, or no; putting different answers in rank order), whereas open questions allow respondents to answer in whatever way they prefer. Most questionnaires use closed questions, because the answers are easy to score and to analyse. Open questions have the disadvantage of being much harder to analyse, but they can be more informative than closed questions.

Ambiguity and bias

Questions that are ambiguous or are likely to be interpreted in various ways should be avoided. Questions that are very long or complicated should also be avoided, because they are likely to be misunderstood. Emotive questions should be avoided because they make people defensive and result in answers that are not true. Finally, questions that are biased should be avoided. Here is an example of a biased question: "In view of the superiority of Britain, why should we consider further political integration with the rest of Europe?"

Attitude scale construction

One of the most common ways to construct an attitude scale is to use the Likert procedure. Initially various statements are collected together, and the participants' task is to indicate their level of agreement on a 5-point scale running from "strongly disagree" at one end to "strongly agree" at the other end. For positive statements (e.g. "Most Hollywood stars are outstanding actors"), strongly disagree is scored as 1 and strongly agree as 5, with intermediate points being scored 2, 3, or 4.

For negative statements (e.g. "Most Hollywood stars are not outstanding actors"), the scoring is reversed so that strongly disagree is scored as 5 and strongly agree as 1.

■ Activity: Construct your own questionnaire

1. Select an area of study from the work you are doing in class.
2. Research the topic to gain ideas about the possible questions to ask.
3. Develop sub-topics to investigate. It may be best to generate questions with a group of people because more varied ideas are produced (brainstorming). Each group member should put forward ideas that are received uncritically by the group. Later, the group can select the best questions.
4. Write the questions. It may help to include some irrelevant "filler" questions to mislead the respondent as to the main purpose of the survey.
5. Decide on a sequence for the questions. It is best to start with easy ones.
6. Write standardised instructions, which must include guidance regarding respondents' ethical rights.
7. Conduct a pilot run and redraft your questionnaire in response to areas of confusion or difficulty.
8. After you have conducted your questionnaire, analyse the results using descriptive data (see next section, "Data Analysis and Presentation").
9. Debrief participants and advise them of your findings. ■

Question styles: A survey on chocolate

Closed question: Do you like chocolate? (tick one)
　　　　YES　NO　NOT SURE

Open question: Why do you like or dislike chocolate?
Ambiguous question: Is chocolate likely to do you more harm than a diet that consists mainly of junk food?
Biased question: Plain chocolate is a more sophisticated taste than milk chocolate. Which type do you prefer?

How can you decide how good any given questionnaire is? Three of the key characteristics of a good questionnaire are standardisation, reliability, and validity. **Standardised tests** are ones that have been administered to a large representative sample so that an individual's score can be compared against that of others. For example, a score of 26 out of 60 on an attitude scale measuring prejudice doesn't mean much on its own—it only becomes meaningful when we know what percentage of people score more and less than 26 on that scale.

Reliability refers to the extent to which a given questionnaire provides consistent findings. For example, if individuals who appear prejudiced on a questionnaire on one day don't appear prejudiced when re-tested on the same questionnaire the following day, the questionnaire is unreliable and of little use.

KEY TERMS

Standardised tests: tests on which an individual's score can be evaluated against those of a large representative sample.
Reliability: the extent to which a method of measurement or test produces consistent findings.

The most common way of assessing reliability is the **test–retest** technique—numerous people are given the same questionnaire on two occasions and the scores are then correlated. If the correlation is high, it means that the questionnaire is reliable.

Validity refers to the extent to which a questionnaire is measuring what it is supposed to be measuring. This can be assessed by comparing scores on the questionnaire with some external criterion. For example, suppose we devise a questionnaire to assess aggression in children. This questionnaire would be valid if we showed that children obtaining high scores were rated as more aggressive by their teachers and were more likely to have been disciplined by the school.

Operationalisation of Variables Including Independent and Dependent Variables

Psychologists carry out studies to test hypotheses such as "Organisation benefits memory" or "Social pressure produces majority influence". However, there is no agreement on the best way to measure psychological concepts or variables such as "organisation", "memory", "social pressure", or "majority influence". The most common approach to this problem is to make use of **operationalisation**—defining each variable of interest in terms of the operations taken to measure it. Such a definition is termed an operational definition.

Operational definitions can be used to operationalise independent variables (e.g. organisation; social pressure) and dependent variables (e.g. memory; majority influence). Consider the experiments by Bower et al. (1969; see Chapter 3) and by Asch (1951; see Chapter 7). Bower et al. (1969) operationalised the independent variable of organisation by comparing groups in which words belonging to conceptual hierarchies were presented in an organised or random fashion. They operationalised the dependent variable of memory by measuring the number of words free recalled orally on an immediate test in about 9½ minutes.

Asch (1951) operationalised the independent variable of social pressure by having all or none of the other group members (confederates of the experimenter, unknown to the participants) produce the same wrong answers on a line-judging task. He operationalised the dependent variable of majority influence by the number of incorrect answers produced corresponding to those given by the confederates.

We can see some of the weaknesses in operational definitions by focusing on the ones used by Bower et al. (1969) and by Asch (1951). Manipulating the extent to which words are presented in terms of hierarchies is one way of operationalising organisation but it is clearly not the only way. Memory can be assessed by means of an immediate test of free recall. However, it could also be assessed by means of a delayed recognition test, and the findings wouldn't necessarily be the same. Social pressure can be manipulated by varying the number of group members unknown to the participants producing wrong answers, but it could be manipulated more strongly by using group members known to participants. Finally, the tendency to produce the same wrong answers as other group members is only one possible way of assessing majority influence. For example, participants might have shown majority influence by having reduced self-esteem even if they didn't produce wrong answers on the line-judging task.

Operationalisation is often used when researchers want to assess the effects of intelligence or personality on certain aspects of behaviour. For example, intelligence is generally operationalised by assuming that a given intelligence test

? What might be an operational definition of fatigue, or hunger?

KEY TERMS

Test–retest: a technique used to establish reliability, by giving the same test to participants on two separate occasions to see if their scores remain relatively similar.

Validity: the soundness of the measurement tool; the extent to which it is measuring something that is real or valid.

Operationalisation: defining all variables in such a way that it is easy to measure them.

provides an adequate measure of intelligence. In fact, however, it seems improbable that any single test can capture all the richness of intelligence.

Evaluation

Operationalisation generally provides a clear and fairly objective definition of most variables. For example, it is possible to provide operational definitions for a complex independent variable such as organisation or a complex dependent variable such as majority influence. In the absence of operationalisation, it would simply be impossible to carry out research on most topics in psychology.

There are various weaknesses associated with the use of operational definitions. First, operational definitions are circular and arbitrary. For example, memory can be defined in many ways other than immediate free recall (Bower et al., 1969).

Second, an operational definition typically only covers part of the meaning of the variable or concept. For example, majority influence can reveal itself in terms of how participants feel about themselves as well as in terms of their responses on a task.

Third, as Stretch (1994) pointed out, we need to worry when the findings using one operational definition are very different from those using a different operational definition of the same variable. Such a difference indicates that something is wrong, but it may be hard to discover exactly *what* is wrong.

Pilot Studies

An important consideration in designing good studies is to try out your planned procedures in a small-scale trial run called a **pilot study**. Such a preliminary study can be regarded as a "dress rehearsal" ahead of the experiment itself. There are various advantages associated with carrying out a pilot study:

- At the most general level, pilot studies make it possible to check out standardised procedures and general design before investing time and money in the major study.
- Pilot studies provide a way of checking that the details of the experiment are appropriate. For example, suppose you want your participants to learn a list of 15 words presented in categories or randomly. If you present the words very rapidly, participants may not have enough time to learn the words. However, if you present the words very slowly, the participants may learn nearly all the words even in the condition with random presentation. A pilot study should allow you to select a presentation time that produces an effect of presenting the words in categories or randomly.
- A pilot study may indicate that participants simply don't understand precisely what they are expected to do. For example, there may be ambiguity about some of the instructions they receive or about some of the items on a questionnaire they have to fill in. Carrying out a pilot study provides an opportunity to eliminate such ambiguities.
- Pilot studies can be very useful when researchers want to decide between two possible ways of carrying out their study. For example, Wilson, Roe, and Wright (1998) were not sure whether to use telephone or face-to-face interviews in a study on health care. The pilot study suggested that they would obtain a more representative sample (and that more people would agree to participate) if they used telephone interviews in the main study.

? It might be said that the operational definition of "intelligence" is "that which is measured by intelligence tests". What is the main weakness of this definition?

? If an experimenter used different wording in the instructions to different participants, how might this affect the results of the study?

KEY TERM

Pilot study: a smaller, preliminary study that makes it possible to check out standardised procedures and general design before investing time and money in the major study.

178 AS LEVEL PSYCHOLOGY

You may be asked to explain what a pilot study is and why it should be conducted. Remember:

- A pilot study is carried out to trial-run the materials and procedure.
- It identifies any flaws or areas for improvement that can then be corrected before the main study such as clarity of instructions, ambiguity of questions, or timing.

- When carrying out research, it is important to have enough participants to obtain significant findings. However, it is wasteful of time and resources to use far more participants than is needed to achieve the purposes of the study. A pilot study can often shed light on the appropriate number of participants to include in the main study.

Control of Extraneous Variables

An extraneous variable is "anything other than the independent variable that could affect the dependent variable" (Coolican, 2004, p. 112). Extraneous variables sometimes (but not always) cause problems. We saw an example of an extraneous variable causing problems earlier in the chapter. Jenkins and Dallenbach (1924) claimed to have found that people who sleep during the time interval between learning and a memory test perform better on the test than those who remain awake. However, those who slept learned in the evening, whereas those who remained awake learned in the morning. Thus, we can't tell whether participants who slept performed better because they slept during the retention or because they learned in the evening. In fact, Hockey et al. (1972) subsequently found out that the time of day at which learning occurs is more important than whether or not participants sleep between learning and test.

In the above example, time of learning is an extraneous variable—it was not of any real interest to the researchers. It was also a confounding variable—confounding variables are those that vary along with the independent variable and may influence the dependent variable. If they do so, then it isn't possible to interpret the findings—we don't know whether the independent variable or the confounding variable is having more impact on the dependent variable.

It is of crucial importance in research to avoid the inclusion of extraneous variables that are also confounding variables. Researchers need to examine very closely what they are doing. Consider the following simple study from the 1970s discussed by Coolican (2004). Coca-cola drinkers were asked to drink two glasses of cola, one of which contained Coke and the other of which contained Pepsi. The glass containing Coke was marked 'Q' and the one containing Pepsi was marked 'M'. The participants, who weren't told which product was in each glass, showed a preference for Pepsi. You might think that the extraneous variable (the letter marked on each glass) wouldn't have had any effect, but subsequent testing indicated that people seemed to prefer the letter 'M' to the letter 'Q'! This problem could have been avoided by having no extraneous variables (not marking either glass). Alternatively, 'M' could have been associated with Pepsi on 50% of trials and with Coke on the other 50% of trials, with the same being true of 'Q'.

Reliability and Validity

A central goal of any experiment or other form of study is to provide us with useful knowledge about human behaviour. If that goal is to be achieved, it is necessary for the study to possess reliability (i.e. consistent findings) and validity (i.e. the findings must be genuine or valid). Reliability and validity are both considered in this section.

See *AS Level Psychology Online* for an interactive exercise on this topic.

Reliability

Reliability refers to the extent to which a given method or test provides consistent findings when repeated. Reliability can be considered in terms of internal reliability and external reliability. Internal reliability is how consistently a method measures within itself, whereas external reliability is how consistently a method measures over time, population, and location when repeated.

Problems relating to reliability are likely to arise when a researcher is trying to code the complex behaviour of participants using a manageable number of categories. For example, a study might require a record to be made of the number of aggressive acts performed by an individual. If only one person observes the behaviour, this would produce a rather subjective judgement, and so usually two (or more) judges provide ratings of behaviour. The ratings can then be compared to provide a measure of inter-judge/inter-rater or inter-observer reliability (see discussion in the section on naturalistic observations).

Reliability is established on psychological tests by using the test–retest method where the same test is given to participants on two separate occasions to see if their scores remain similar. The interval between testings must be long enough to prevent a **practice effect** occurring.

A second method of establishing reliability is the **split-half technique**. Items from a test are randomly assigned to two sub-tests and then scores compared on both tests in the same way as on the test–retest method. The same person does both sub-tests during the same experimental session.

Validity

One of the key requirements of research is that any findings obtained are valid. **Validity** refers to the extent to which a study satisfies important standards in the sense that they are genuine and provide us with useful information about the phenomenon being studied. For example, if we carried out an experiment, it wouldn't be valid if we had failed to control various extraneous variables.

Campbell and Stanley (1966) drew a distinction between internal validity and external validity. Internal validity refers to the issue of whether the effects observed are genuine and are caused by the independent variable. In contrast, external validity

---

Internal and external reliability

Internal reliability = consistency within the method of measurement.
For instance, a ruler should be measuring the same distance between 0 and 5 centimetres as between 5 and 10 centimetres.
External reliability = consistency between uses of the method of measurement. For instance, the ruler should measure the same on a Monday as it does on a Friday.

- Reliability = consistent and stable.
- Validity = measuring what is intended.
- Standardisation = comparisons can be made between studies and samples.
- Reliability = consistent and stable. For example, Milgram's study (1963, 1974; see page 282) on obedience to authority produced findings that have been repeated numerous times in many countries, and are thus reliable.
- Validity = measuring what is intended. For example, Rahe et al.'s study (1970; see page 234) showed that scores on the Social Readjustment Rating Scale were associated with physical illness. The findings suggest (but don't prove) that the Social Readjustment Rating Scale is a valid measure of the stress created by life events.

EXAM HINT

Remember the difference between reliability and validity.

- Reliability = CONSISTENCY
- Internal validity = TRUTH
- External validity = GENERALISABILITY

If you are assessing research in a long-answer question do try to improve the quality of your evaluation by assessing reliability and validity.

KEY TERMS

Reliability: the extent to which a method of measurement or test produces consistent findings.
Practice effect: an improvement in performance as a result of having done the task before.
Split-half technique: a technique used to establish reliability by assigning items from one test randomly to two sub-tests (split-halves). The same person does both sub-tests simultaneously and their scores are compared to see if they are similar, which would suggest that the test items are reliable.
Validity: the soundness of the measurement tool; the extent to which it is measuring something that is real or valid.

Many laboratory-based experiments in psychology (like the 1950s' sensory deprivation experiment shown here) show low external validity—that is, their findings do not translate reliably to behaviour outside the laboratory.

refers to the extent to which the findings of a study can be generalised to situations and samples other than those used in the study. This distinction is important—many experiments possess internal validity but lack external validity.

The distinction between internal and external validity is especially relevant to experiments and quasi-experiments because of their potential artificiality. Accordingly, we will focus on experimental research.

Internal validity

Coolican (2004) pointed out that there are many threats to the internal validity of an experiment, most of which are discussed elsewhere in this chapter. These include the existence of any confounding factors; the use of unreliable or inconsistent measures; lack of standardisation and randomisation; investigator effects (those due to the investigator's expectations); and demand characteristics (effects due to participants' expectations).

In a nutshell, virtually all of the principles of experimental design are intended to increase internal validity. Failure to apply these principles threatens internal validity. If internal validity is high, replication of the findings is likely. If internal validity is low, replication may be hard or impossible.

■ **Activity:** Construct a brief outline for each of the following:

- An experiment that should show high internal validity.
- An experiment that will be unlikely to show high internal validity.
- An experiment that is unlikely to show high external validity.

External validity and generalisability

What about external validity? There are close links between external validity and **generalisability**, because both are concerned with the issue of whether the findings of an experiment or study are applicable to other situations. More specifically, there are four main aspects to external validity or generalisability:

1. *Populations*: Do the findings obtained from a given sample of individuals generalise to a larger population from which the sample was selected?
2. *Locations*: Do the findings of the study generalise to other settings or situations? If they do, the study is said to possess external validity. Much cross-cultural research has shown that findings obtained in one country or culture often differ from those obtained in another country or culture.
3. *Measures or constructs*: Do the findings of the experiment or study generalise to other measures of the variables used? For example, suppose we find using one method of assessing Type A that it is associated with an increased risk of coronary heart disease. Would we obtain the same findings if Type A were assessed by a different questionnaire?
4. *Times*: Do the findings generalise to the past and to the future? For example, it could be argued that sweeping changes in many cultures in recent decades have affected majority influence as studied by Asch and obedience to authority as studied by Milgram (see Chapter 7).

KEY TERM

Generalisability: the extent to which the findings of a study can be applied to other settings, populations, times, and measures.

How can we maximise the external validity of an experiment? There is no easy answer to that question. The external validity of an experiment usually only becomes clear when other researchers try to generalise the findings to other samples or populations, locations, measures, and times. It might be thought that the findings of field experiments are more likely than those of laboratory experiments to generalise to other real-life locations or settings, but that isn't necessarily so.

Meta-analyses

One way of trying to determine whether certain findings generalise is to carry out a meta-analysis. In a meta-analysis, *all* the findings from many studies testing a given hypothesis are combined into a single analysis. If the meta-analysis indicates that some finding has been obtained consistently, this suggests that it generalises across populations, locations, measures, and times. For example, Smith and Bond (1993) carried out a meta-analysis on 133 Asch-type studies drawn from 17 countries. Majority influence in the Asch situation was found in every country, but it was greater in collectivistic cultures (e.g. China) in which there is an emphasis on co-operating with others.

The greatest limitation of meta-analyses is that differences in the quality of individual studies are often ignored. This can lead to a situation in which a finding is accepted as genuine when it has been obtained in several poorly-designed studies but not in a smaller number of well-designed studies. It is often hard to know which studies to include and which to exclude. For example, the studies reviewed by Bond and Smith didn't use identical procedures and so they aren't directly comparable.

Our culture today is different from the culture of the 1950s. This means that research conducted then, for example surveying women's attitudes towards domestic work, may not generalise to women's attitudes today.

Awareness of the BPS Code of Ethics

The need for ethical control leads to the establishment of a set of rules or **ethical guidelines** to judge the acceptability of behaviour. During the Second World War the Nazis conducted many horrific experiments on their concentration camp prisoners. At the end of the war those responsible were tried in Nuremberg, and it became apparent that a code of ethics was needed as a reference point for what is acceptable in scientific research. The 10-point "Nuremberg code" was drawn up, which introduced important concepts such as that of informed consent.

This code has been adapted by professional bodies all over the world. Within Britain, the British Psychological Society (BPS) has issued a Code of Ethics and Conduct (2006) that should be followed by anyone involved in psychological research (see page 183). What happens increasingly is that use of the BPS Code of Ethics is combined with the setting up of **ethical committees**. Most institutions (e.g. universities; research units; hospitals) in which research is carried out now have their own ethical committee, which considers all research proposals from the perspective of the rights and dignity of the participants. The existence of such committees helps to correct the power imbalance between experimenter and participant. In order to avoid bias, it is desirable for every ethical committee to include some non-psychologists and at least one non-expert member of the public.

KEY TERMS

Ethical guidelines: written codes of conduct and practice to guide and aid psychologists in planning and running research studies to an approved standard, and dealing with any issues that may arise.

Ethical committees: committees of psychologists and lay individuals who consider all research proposals from the perspective of the rights and dignity of the participants.

This flow chart shows ethical decisions to be taken by researchers designing a psychological study.

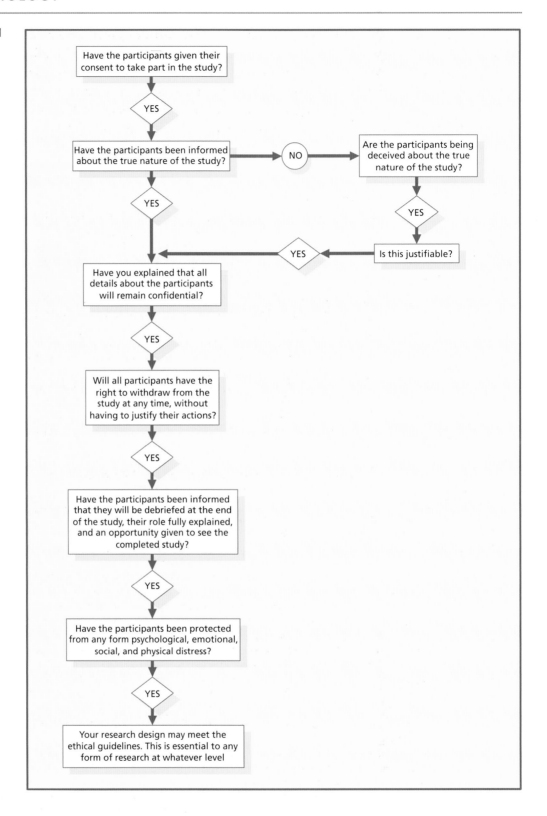

Have the participants given their consent to take part in the study?

YES

Have the participants been informed about the true nature of the study? → NO → Are the participants being deceived about the true nature of the study?

YES

YES

Is this justifiable?

YES ←

Have you explained that all details about the participants will remain confidential?

YES

Will all participants have the right to withdraw from the study at any time, without having to justify their actions?

YES

Have the participants been informed that they will be debriefed at the end of the study, their role fully explained, and an opportunity given to see the completed study?

YES

Have the participants been protected from any form psychological, emotional, social, and physical distress?

YES

Your research design may meet the ethical guidelines. This is essential to any form of research at whatever level

? Why do you think that views about the kinds of research that are ethically acceptable have changed over the years?

Most ethical guidelines have only limited force. Someone who infringes the BPS Code of Ethics isn't committing a crime, although they may be barred from the British Psychological Society. There are other drawbacks. The establishment of a set of ethical guidelines enshrines its principles and may close off discussions regarding more appropriate solutions to a given ethical dilemma. The Code makes it seem that the guidelines are ethical "truths". In fact, however, such guidelines are constantly reviewed, in part because of changing social attitudes. Finally, ethical codes may take personal responsibility away from the individual researcher, and may invite individuals to find loopholes and "play the system" (Homan, 1991). Key issues relating to ethical issues are discussed in the next section. In that section, ways in which psychologists should deal with such issues are also considered.

? Without ethical guidelines, how difficult would it be to express misgivings about questionable research methods?

BPS Code of Ethics and Conduct (2006)

The BPS Code of Ethics and Conduct (2006) applies to all psychologists and not simply those involved in research, and so is also relevant to clinical psychologists and occupational psychologists. The Code contains numerous standards and guidelines, and we will consider only the main ones here. The BPS Code of Ethics is based on four major ethical principles:

- **Respect**: Psychologists should respect individual, cultural, and role differences. They should also avoid practices that are unfair or prejudiced, and be willing to explain the reasons for their ethical decision making.

  Standard of privacy and confidentiality: Confidential information should be stored so as to avoid inadvertent disclosure and the consent of clients/participants should be obtained for disclosure of confidential information.

  Standard of informed consent: "Ensure that clients, particularly children and vulnerable adults, are given ample opportunity to understand the nature, purpose, and anticipated consequences of any professional services or research participation, so that they may give informed consent to the extent that their capabilities allow" (p. 12).

- **Competence**:

  Standard of ethical decision making: Psychologists should accept their responsibility to resolve ethical dilemmas with reflection, supervision, and consultation.

- **Responsibility**:

  Standard of protection of research participants:
  (i)   Consider all research from the standpoints of research participants.
  (ii) Undertake such consideration with due concern for the potential effects of factors such as age, disability, ethnicity, race, and religion.
  (iii) Ask research participants about individual factors that might reasonably lead to risk of harm.
  (iv) Refrain from using financial compensation or other inducements for research participants to risk harm beyond that which they face in their normal lifestyles.
  (v)   When concluding that harm, unusual discomfort, or other negative consequences may follow from research, obtain supplemental informed consent from research participants specific to such issues.
  (vi) Inform research participants from the outset that their right to withdraw at any time is not affected by the receipt or offer of any financial compensation or other inducements for participation.
  (vii) Inform research participants from the outset that they may decline to answer any questions put to them.
  (viii) Exercise particular caution when responding to requests for advice from research participants concerning psychological or other issues.

  Standard of debriefing of research participants:
  (i)   "Debrief research participants at the conclusion of their participation, in order to inform them of the outcomes and nature of the research, to identify any unforeseen harm, discomfort of misconceptions, and in order to arrange for assistance as needed" (p. 19).
  (ii) "Take particular care when discussing outcomes with research participants, as seemingly evaluative statements may carry unintended weight" (p. 19).

- **Integrity**:

  Standard of honesty and accuracy: Psychologists should "be honest and accurate in representing their professional affiliations and qualifications" (p. 20).

Ethical Issues and the Ways in Which Psychologists Deal With Them

The issue of ethics is critical to psychological research. As has often been pointed out, the experimenter in most psychological research is in a more powerful position than the participants, and it is essential to make sure that the participants are not exploited or persuaded to behave in ways they don't want to. In addition, a professional group of people is one that "polices" itself and therefore these ethical standards are a key feature of the professionalism of psychology.

? Which do you think are more important, the interests of the individual or the interests of society as a whole?

Ethics in psychology

Ethics are a set of moral principles used to guide human behaviour. There are few if any absolutes in ethics, but any society or group of people develops ethics as a means of determining what is right or wrong for that group. The term "ethics" tends to be used when considering moral behaviour among professionals such as doctors or lawyers. The term "morals" is used to refer to everyday standards of right and wrong, such as honesty and kindness. Ethics are determined by a balance between means and ends, or a **cost–benefit analysis**. Certain things may be less acceptable than others. However, if the ultimate end is for the good of humankind, then we may feel that it is ethically justified to cause suffering to animals in order to find a cure for some serious human illness than it is merely to develop a new cosmetic.

Diener and Crandall (1978) argued that there are various drawbacks with the cost–benefit approach. First, it is hard (if not impossible) to predict both costs and benefits prior to conducting a study. Second, even after the study has been completed, it is hard to assess them accurately, partly because it can depend on who is making the judgements. A participant may judge the costs differently from the researcher, and benefits may be judged differently in years to come. Third, cost–benefit analyses tend to ignore the important rights of individuals in favour of practical considerations of possible usefulness of the findings. Fourth, as Baumrind (1975) pointed out, cost–benefit analyses inevitably lead to moral dilemmas. This is unfortunate, because the function of ethical guidelines is precisely to avoid such dilemmas!

KEY TERMS

Ethics: a set of moral principles used to guide human behaviour.
Cost–benefit analysis: a comparison between the costs of something and the related benefits, in order to decide on a course of action.

CASE STUDY: SUBJECTS OR PARTICIPANTS?

Until recently members of the public who took part in psychology experiments were called "subjects". This reflected the view that they were only passively involved in the research process (they did what the researcher told them) and it emphasised the power of the researcher (as the person in authority). The subject in a psychological experiment was in a rather vulnerable and exploitable position. Kelman (1972, p. 993) pointed out, "most ethical problems arising in social research can be traced to the subject's power deficiency." It follows that steps need to be taken to ensure that the participant is not placed in a powerless and vulnerable position. This is the task of an ethical code.

As a consequence of this insight it has become the practice to refer to such individuals as participants rather than subjects. Perhaps this process is analogous to the historical shift from having a political regime with "rulers and subjects" to the more modern conception of "leaders and followers". Both participants and followers have an active role to play and it would be foolish to think otherwise. The change in terminology allows for a more humane respect for individuals who participate in psychology experiments. ■

There are probably more major ethical issues associated with research in psychology than in any other scientific discipline. There are various reasons for this. First, all psychological experiments involve the study of living creatures (whether human or the members of some other species). The rights of these participants to be treated in a caring and respectful way can easily be infringed by an unprincipled or careless experimenter.

Second, the findings of psychological research may reveal what seem to be unpleasant or unacceptable facts about human nature, or about certain groups within society. No matter how morally upright the experimenter may be, there is always the danger that extreme political organisations will use research findings to further their political aims. Such research is often described as "socially sensitive", and psychologists have a responsibility to consider very carefully the uses to which their findings may be put.

Third, these political aims may include social control. There is the danger that the techniques discovered in psychological research may be exploited by dictators or others seeking to exert unjustifiable influence on society or to inflame people's prejudices.

The key ethical issues to consider are: the use of deception, informed consent, and the protection of participants from harm.

Use of deception

Honesty is a fundamental moral and ethical principle, and anyone who agrees to take part in psychological research naturally expects to be given full information beforehand. However, **deception** is sometimes necessary. A well-known example of research that had to involve deception is the work of Asch (1951, 1956; see Chapter 7) on group pressure. If the participants had been told the experiment was designed to study conformity to group pressure, and that all the other participants were confederates of the experimenter, then this important research would have been pointless.

Deception is certainly widespread. Menges (1973) considered about 1000 experimental studies that had been carried out in the United States. Full information about what was going to happen was provided in only 3% of cases. However, the substantial increase in concern about ethical issues means that full informed consent is far more common nowadays than it was over 30 years ago.

When is deception justified? Various factors need to be taken into account. First, the less potentially damaging the consequences of the deception, the more likely it is to be acceptable. Second, it is easier to justify the use of deception in studies that are important in scientific terms. Third, deception is more justifiable when there are no alternative, deception-free ways of studying an issue.

How can we deal with the deception issue?

One way of avoiding the ethical problems associated with deception is the use of **role-playing experiments**. Zimbardo's (1973) Stanford prison experiment (see Chapter 7) is an example of such an experiment—the participants played the role of prison guards and prisoners over a period of several days. In role-playing experiments, the participants are not deceived (e.g. they know it isn't a real prison), but they have to try to behave as if they didn't know the true state of affairs. This approach eliminates many of the ethical problems of deception studies, but there is a danger that the behaviour displayed by role-playing

? How would you feel if you found out you were deliberately deceived as a participant in a research study? Would you be willing to take part in another study after knowing this?

KEY TERMS

Deception: in research ethics, deception refers to deliberately misleading participants, which was accepted in the past. Currently the view is that deception should be avoided wherever possible, as it could lead to psychological harm or a negative view of psychological research.

Role-playing experiments: studies in which participants are asked to imagine how they would behave in certain situations.

participants may not correspond to that which would be displayed by participants who didn't know about the deception.

Debriefing is an important method for dealing with deception and other ethical issues. At the end of the study, participants should be told the actual nature and purpose of the research, and asked not to tell any future participants. In addition, debriefing typically involves providing information about the experimental findings and offering participants the opportunity to have their results excluded from the study if they wish.

Debriefing can also be used to reduce any distress that may have been caused by the experimenter. According to Aronson (1988), participants should leave the research situation in "a frame of mind that is at least as sound as it was when they entered". This is *not* necessarily the case after debriefing. For example, suppose you had been fully obedient in a Milgram-type experiment on obedience to authority (see Chapter 7). You might feel somewhat guilty afterwards that you had allowed yourself to give what might have been fatal electric shocks to someone with a heart condition.

Informed consent

It is considered the right of participants (wherever possible) to provide voluntary **informed consent**. This means several things: being informed about what will be required; being informed about the purpose of the research; being informed of your rights (e.g. the right to confidentiality, the right to leave the research at any time); and finally giving your consent. There are many situations in which this is not possible:

- When children or participants who have impairments that limit their understanding and/or communication are involved. In this case, the informed consent of an adult is sought, although some critics might feel that this is insufficient.
- When deception is a necessary part of the research design as in Asch's or Milgram's research. We have seen that role-playing experiments can be used to provide informed consent, but such experiments have serious limitations.
- In field experiments when participants aren't even aware they are taking part in a piece of psychological research. An example is the study by Bickman (1974; see Chapter 7), in which New York pedestrians were ordered to do various things (e.g. picking up a bag).
- There is an issue as to whether truly informed consent is actually possible. How easy is it for a non-psychologist to understand the aims of psychological research and fully comprehend what is expected of him/her? Prior to participation, would the "teacher" in Milgram's research have anticipated how he/she would feel when giving shocks? The evidence of Milgram's pre-experiment surveys suggests that people wouldn't have anticipated their own behaviour, let alone how they would *feel*.

Other ways to obtain consent

One way of obtaining consent is to ascertain the acceptability of a given experiment by asking the opinion of members of the population from which the participants in the research are to be drawn. This is what Milgram did, and it is called seeking **presumptive consent**.

An alternative approach is to gain **prior general consent** (also known as *partially informed consent*). This is what was done by Gamson, Fireman, and Rytina (1982) in a study in which participants were manipulated to produce evidence supporting the unreasonable position of an oil company (see Chapter 7). Gamson et al. advertised for participants. When potential participants phoned, they were asked whether they were willing to take part in any or all of the following kinds of research:

1. Research on brand recognition of commercial products.
2. Research on product safety.
3. Research in which you will be misled about the purpose until afterwards.
4. Research involving group standards.

Most people said, "Yes", to all four and were then told that only the last kind of research was in progress. However, they had agreed to the third kind of research and thus consented to be deceived. An obvious limitation is that what the participants had consented to was very vague—"research in which you will be misled about its purpose". That means they couldn't really give informed consent because they lacked detailed information.

> **?** Could the approach adopted by Gamson et al. be adapted to handle the deception issue in most kinds of research?

Right to withhold data

Another means of offering informed consent is to do it afterwards. When the experiment is over, during debriefing, participants should be offered the chance to withhold their data. In essence, this gives them the same power as if they had refused to take part in the first place. If they withhold their data, it is as if they had been informed at the start and not consented to take part. However, participants who exercise their right to withhold data may nevertheless have had experiences during the experiment that they would not have agreed to if they had realised beforehand what was going to happen to them.

Protection from harm

"Harm" can mean various things. It includes both physical and psychological damage. The key test of whether or not a participant has been harmed is to ask whether the risk of harm was greater than in everyday life.

> **?** If you recall, Watson and Rayner claimed that their experiment with Little Albert was ethical because the psychological harm inflicted was no greater than what he might experience in real life. Is this acceptable?

Physical harm

We might include excessive anxiety as physical harm because the results can be physically evident. For example, if you consider the description of some of Milgram's participants (see Chapter 7), it is clear that they experienced physical as well as psychological harm—some of them had seizures, and many perspired and bit their lips. Stress is a psychological state but it has a physical basis (see Chapter 6).

Psychological harm

Psychological harm is harder to measure, and there is no doubt that many studies infringe what might be called psychological "safety". Many of Milgram's participants would have felt disappointed with their own apparent willingness to

> **KEY TERM**
>
> **Prior general consent**: obtaining apparent consent from research participants by arranging for them to agree in general to taking part in certain kinds of research before enlisting their involvement in an experiment.

When setting up observational research it is important to consider whether the participants would normally expect to be observed by strangers in the situation. For example, making observations of the people in this picture would be acceptable, but observing them in a changing room would not.

obey unjust authority, which may have led to psychological harm in the form of reduced self-esteem.

We can also consider the issues of **confidentiality** and the **right to privacy** as forms of **protection of participants from psychological harm**. Confidentiality means that no information (especially sensitive information) about any given participant should be revealed by the experimenter to anyone else. Right to privacy is a matter of concern when conducting observational research. It wouldn't be appropriate, for example, to observe a person's behaviour in their bedroom without their permission. However, it would be acceptable to observe people in a public place (e.g. a park) where public scrutiny is expected.

Selection of Participants and Sampling Techniques

Studies in psychology rarely involve more than about 100 participants. However, researchers generally want their findings to apply to a much larger group of people than those acting as participants. In technical terms, the participants selected for a study form a **sample** taken from some larger **population** (called the target or sample population), which consists of all the members of the group from which the sample has been drawn. For example, we might select a sample of 20 children aged 5 for a study. The target population would consist of all the 5-year-olds living in England or the population might be the 5-year-olds in a particular primary school, depending on where we selected our sample.

When we carry out a study, we want the findings obtained from our sample to be true of the population from which they were drawn. In order to achieve this, we must use a **representative sample**, i.e. participants who are representative or typical of the population in question. Only if we have a representative sample can we generalise from the behaviour of our sample to the target population in general. In other words, as in the example, we can only make statements about all 5-year-olds in the population studied, i.e. those in England or in the school, not those in the rest of the world. Many studies actually have non-representative samples. For example, the participants in many published studies in psychology are undergraduate university students, who are clearly not representative of society as a whole in terms of age or intelligence. Such studies are said to have a **sampling bias**. Coolican (1994, p. 36) was pessimistic about the chances of truly selecting a representative sample, calling it an "abstract ideal" and stressing the importance of removing "as much sampling bias as possible".

KEY TERMS

Confidentiality: the requirement for ethical research that information provided by participants in research is not made available to other people.

Right to privacy: the requirement for ethical research that no participants are observed in situations that would be considered private.

Protection of participants from psychological harm: an ethical guideline saying that participants should be protected from psychological harm, such as distress, ridicule, or loss of self-esteem. Any risks involved in the research should be no greater than those in the participants' own lives. Debriefing can be used to counter any concern over psychological harm.

Sample: a part of a population selected such that it is considered to be representative of the population as a whole.

Population: the total number of cases about which a specific statement can be made. This in itself may be unrepresentative.

Representative sample: the notion that the sample is representative of the whole population from which it is drawn.

Sampling bias: some people have a greater or lesser chance of being selected than they should be, given their frequency in the population.

Random sampling

The best way of obtaining a representative sample from a population (e.g. students) would be to use **random sampling**. This could be done by picking students' names out of a hat, or by assigning a number to everyone in the population from which the sample is to be selected. After that, a computer or random number tables could be used to generate a series of random numbers to select the sample.

If we wanted to have a representative sample of the entire adult population, we could apply one of the methods of random selection just described to the electoral roll. However, even that would be an imperfect procedure because several groups of people including children and young people, homeless people, illegal immigrants, and prisoners are not listed.

An alternative to random sampling is what is known as **systematic sampling**. This involves selecting participants in a systematic way from a population (e.g. by selecting every 10th or every 100th person). This is a quasi-random procedure that is less effective than random sampling, because it can't be claimed that every member of the population is equally likely to be selected.

> ■ **Activity:** Target populations
> Identify an appropriate target population for each project below. You would select your research sample from this population.
>
> - To discover whether there are enough youth facilities in your community.
> - To discover whether cats like dried or tinned cat food.
> - To discover whether children aged between 5 and 11 watch too much violent television.
> - To discover the causes of anxiety experienced by participants in research studies.

> Systematic sampling is not as effective as random sampling but it does help to overcome the biases of the researcher. If we select every hundredth name on the list, we avoid missing names that we cannot pronounce, or do not like the look of, for whatever reason.

Evaluation of random sampling

It is actually very hard for an experimenter to obtain a random sample. This method typically fails to produce a truly representative sample for various reasons:

1. It may not be possible to identify all of the members of the larger population from which the sample is to be selected.
2. It may not be possible to contact all of those who have been selected randomly to appear in the sample—they may have moved house, or be away on holiday. You would end up with a sample that is definitely not random.
3. Some of those who are selected to be in the sample are likely to refuse to take part in the study. This might not matter if those who agree to take part in research are very similar to those who don't. However, as is discussed below, volunteers typically differ in various ways from non-volunteers.

Ideally, psychological experiments should select a random sample of the population, although true randomness can be hard to achieve.

In sum it is worth bearing in mind what Coolican (1998, p. 720) had to say about random samples: "Many students write that their sample was 'randomly selected'. In fact, research samples are very rarely selected at random." Students usually actually use opportunity sampling, and the same is certainly true of many studies by psychologists.

> **KEY TERMS**
>
> **Random sampling**: selecting participants on some random basis (e.g. picking numbers out of a hat). Every member of the population has an equal chance of being selected.
> **Systematic sampling**: a modified version of random sampling in which the participants are selected in a quasi-random way (e.g. every 100th name from a population list).

Opportunity sampling

Random sampling is often expensive and time-consuming. As a result, many researchers use **opportunity sampling**. This involves selecting participants on the basis of their availability rather than by any other method. Opportunity sampling is often used by students carrying out experiments, and it is also very common in natural experiments.

Evaluation of opportunity sampling

Opportunity sampling is the easiest method to use. However, it has the severe weakness that the participants may be nothing like a representative sample. For example, students who are friends of the student carrying out a study may be more likely to take part than students who are not. It is often hard to know whether the use of an opportunity sample has distorted the results.

Opportunity sampling gives the illusion of being drawn from a large population whereas it is generally drawn from a very small sample, such as people who shop in the centre of town on a weekday. Thus, the sample really depends on who is available at the time. This type of group mostly constitutes a *biased sample*.

Volunteer sampling

In practice, research in psychology typically involves **volunteer sampling**. That is, the participants in a study (whether initially selected via random or opportunity sampling) nearly always consist of volunteers who have agreed to take part. It would obviously be unethical to try to force anyone to become a participant in any given study, and so researchers have to accept that many of those invited to participate in a study will decline the invitation.

Volunteer sampling raises the important issue of whether a volunteer sample differs in important ways from a random sample. If this is the case, we have **volunteer bias**. Manstead and Semin (1996, p. 93) discussed some of the evidence, and concluded, "There *are* systematic personality differences between volunteers and non-volunteers." Volunteers tend to be more sensitive to demand characteristics (cues used by participants to work out what a study is about), and they are also more likely to comply with those demand characteristics. Marcus and Schutz (2005) found that the personalities of volunteers were more agreeable and open to experience than those of non-volunteers, and showed a tendency to be more extraverted.

Volunteer bias is probably especially likely when researchers are trying to recruit participants for a study on a sensitive topic. For example, Strassberg and Lowe (1995) found several differences between volunteers and non-volunteers for several studies on human sexuality. The volunteers had had more sexual experience, had less sexual guilt, and reported a more positive attitude towards sexuality.

[?] Psychology students often use other psychology students as the participants in their research. What problems are likely to arise, for example, in terms of evaluation apprehension and demand characteristics?

[?] Why do you think volunteers are more likely than non-volunteers to be sensitive to the demand characteristics of a study?

■ Activity: Sampling. Find a study to illustrate volunteer sampling and another one to illustrate opportunity sampling. (Clue: most of the studies you have covered used a volunteer sample, whereas some of the studies have used opportunity samples.)

KEY TERMS

Opportunity sampling: participants are selected because they are available, not because they are representative of a population.
Volunteer sampling: choosing research participants who have volunteered, e.g. by replying to an advertisement. Volunteer samples may not be representative of the general population, which means the research may not be generalisable.
Volunteer bias: the systematic difference between volunteers and non-volunteers.

Sample size

One of the important issues relating to sampling that researchers need to consider is the total number of participants to be included in the sample. What is the ideal number of participants in each condition? That is a bit like asking how long is a piece of string (i.e. there is no definite answer). However, here are some of the relevant factors:

- It is generally expensive and time consuming to make use of large samples running into hundreds of participants.
- If we use very small samples (fewer than 10 participants in each condition), this reduces the chances of obtaining a significant effect.
- In general terms, sampling bias is likely to be greater with small samples than with large ones.
- We need to remember that the size of the sample population matters. If a relatively small sample is drawn from a large and diverse population (e.g. the entire population of the UK), it is very likely to be biased.

Consider the total number of participants to be included...

If there is a golden rule that applies to deciding on sample size, this is it:

The smaller the likely effect being studied, the larger the sample size needed to demonstrate it.

For most purposes, however, having about 15 participants in each condition is a reasonable number.

Demand Characteristics and Investigator Effects

The findings that are obtained from any given study can be distorted for several reasons. As Coolican (2004, p. 93) pointed out, "The necessary social interaction that must occur between experimenter and participant makes the psychological experiment different in kind from those in the natural sciences." Distorted findings can occur because participants have mistaken views concerning what is expected of them or because the investigator's or experimenter's expectations influence participants' behaviour. We will consider both of these possibilities in turn.

Demand characteristics

One of the problems that can occur in many kinds of studies is that the participants' behaviour is influenced by demand characteristics. **Demand characteristics** are those aspects of a study that are used by participants to try to work out what is expected of them. These characteristics can then lead participants to behave in certain ways. According to Orne (1962), participants are influenced by demand characteristics because they do their best to comply with what they perceive to be the demands of the situation. This leads them to guess what is expected of them using any available cues and these then become demand characteristics. Of course, their perceptions may often be inaccurate, and this will then distort the findings obtained.

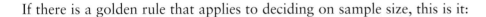

KEY TERM

Demand characteristics: features of an experiment that help participants to work out what is expected of them, and lead them to behave in certain predictable ways.

■ **Activity:** The researcher and participant relationship

This section offers several ways in which the relationship between the researcher and participant can affect the outcome of the research.

To investigate this, select suitable studies to illustrate the following issues: demand characteristics, evaluation apprehension, and investigator effects. For example, in Bowlby's (1944) study of juvenile thieves, he diagnosed the affectionless psychopaths himself and it might have been his own expectations that influenced his decisions.

Claxton (1980) provided an amusing example of how demand characteristics can influence behaviour. He considered an actual laboratory task in which participants have to decide as rapidly as possible whether sentences such as "Can canaries fly?" are true or false. Under laboratory conditions, people perform this task uncomplainingly, perhaps because they think they will impress the experimenter if they reply very quickly and accurately. However, as Claxton pointed out, "If someone asks me 'Can canaries fly?' in the pub I will suspect either that he is an idiot or that he is about to tell me a joke."

Young, Adelstein, and Ellis (2007) obtained evidence of strong demand characteristics in a study on the experience of motion sickness in a virtual environment. They assessed motion sickness by using a questionnaire. In one condition, this questionnaire was given only after the participants had been in the virtual environment. In another condition, the questionnaire was given before and after exposure to the virtual environment. The key finding was that reports of motion sickness after being in the virtual environment were much greater when the questionnaire had also been administered beforehand. Participants given the questionnaire beforehand were alerted to the demand characteristic that the focus of the study was on the experience of motion sickness—it was almost as if taking the questionnaire beforehand made the participants sick!

There is another problem with demand characteristics that applies to participants who have previously taken part in a study in which they were deceived about the experimental purpose. Remember that psychological research often relies on psychology students as participants, and they take part in a number of studies. As a result of being deceived, some participants tend thereafter to respond in an opposite direction to the one suggested by an experiment's demand characteristics. Why should this be so? Silverman et al. (1970) explained this effect:

> Deceived [participants] may have become so alerted to possible further deceptions that they tend to respond counter to any cues regarding the experimenter's hypothesis. An element of gamesmanship may enter the experimental situation in that [participants] become wary of "tricks" underlying the obvious, and do not want to be caught in them.

Reducing demand characteristics

Information about the demand characteristics in any given experimental setting can be obtained by asking participants afterwards to describe in detail what they felt the experiment was about. The experimenter can then take steps to make sure that the results of future experiments aren't adversely affected by demand characteristics.

? Is honesty the best policy? Would demand characteristics be reduced if both participants and experimenters knew the true aims of the experiment?

Some (but not all) of the problems of demand characteristics can be reduced by the **single blind** procedure, in which the participants aren't informed of the condition in which they have been placed. Instead, they are usually given a false account of the purpose of the experiment so they won't seek cues about the nature of the research. The problem with this is that it raises ethical issues, because full informed consent can't be obtained in such circumstances.

Investigator effects

We can draw a distinction between the investigator (the person who designs any given study) and the experimenter (the person who actually carries it out). In practice, however, the investigator and the experimenter are often one and the same person. The ideal investigator/experimenter is someone who behaves in exactly the same mildly positive way with every participant, and who doesn't allow his/her expectations and experimental hypotheses to influence the conduct of a study. In reality, however, the expectations and personality characteristics of the investigator/experimenter often have an effect on the participants' behaviour. These are known as **investigator effects**.

The way in which experimenters behave and talk may influence the behaviour of the participant.

One of the most important investigator effects is **experimenter expectancy**, in which the expectations of the investigator/experimenter have a systematic effect on the performance of the participants. Rosenthal (1966) showed the effects of experimenter expectancy in a study of flatworms. Participants recruited as experimenters recorded twice as many movements in the flatworms they had been told would be "highly active" than the ones they had been told would be "inactive".

The most famous example of an investigator/experimenter effect was reported by Rosenthal and Jacobson (1968). They carried out a study in which they arranged for teachers to "overhear" that certain randomly selected children were expected to make late gains in academic development. What happened was that these children did actually make greater gains than non-selected children. This was described as the **Pygmalion effect**, in which individuals can perform surprisingly well because others expect them to. More specifically, what happened was that the investigator implanted ideas into the minds of the experimenters that then influenced participants' behaviour. Subsequent research produced mixed findings.

As Coolican (2004) pointed out, it proved hard to replicate the Pygmalion effects for several years after the original study. However, Kierein and Gold (2000) reported a meta-analysis of 13 Pygmalion studies

> **KEY TERMS**
>
> **Single blind**: a procedure in which the participants are not informed of the condition in which they have been placed.
> **Investigator effects**: the effects of an investigator's expectations on the response of a participant. Sometimes referred to as experimenter expectancy effect.
> **Experimenter expectancy**: the systematic effects that an experimenter's expectations have on the performance of the participants.
> **Pygmalion effect**: an effect in which individuals perform surprisingly well because others expect them to; it is a kind of self-fulfilling effect in which others' expectations turn into reality.

> **EXAM HINT**
>
> You may be asked to describe one way that investigator effects might threaten the validity of your study. Consider one of the following:
>
> - Researcher bias when setting the research question (formulation).
> - In the carrying out of research (e.g. giving away the demand characteristics and the research expectancy effect).
> - In the analysis of the results (manipulation of data).
> - In the interpretation of results.

carried out in work organisations, and found that there was a moderately strong overall Pygmalion effect. How does the Pygmalion effect occur? Rosenthal (2003) argued that four factors are involved:

1. *Climate*: teachers behave more warmly towards students for whom they have high expectations.
2. *Input*: teachers teach more material to students of whom they expect much.
3. *Output*: teachers ask their "special" students for answers more often than other students.
4. *Feedback*: teachers give more detailed feedback to "special" students.

Reducing investigator effects

What steps can be taken to minimise investigator effects? One approach is to use a **double blind** procedure, in which neither the investigator working with the participants nor the participants know the research hypothesis (or hypotheses) being tested. The double blind procedure reduces the possibility of investigator bias, but it is often too expensive and impractical to use. As more and more studies involve participants interacting with computers rather than with human investigators/experimenters, the incidence of investigator effects is probably less than it used to be. In addition, data are increasingly stored directly in computers, making it harder to misrecord the information obtained from participants.

SECTION SUMMARY

Aims and hypotheses

❖ The first stage in designing a study is to decide on its aims and hypotheses.
❖ Aims tell us *why* and hypotheses tell us *what*.
❖ The null hypothesis:
  – is a statement of no effect.
  – increases precision. One can prove (accept) the experimental/alternative hypothesis by rejecting the null hypothesis.
❖ The experimental/alternative hypothesis:
  – may be directional or one-tailed, or non-directional or two-tailed.
❖ Non-experimental research may also have aims and hypotheses.

Experimental design

❖ There are three main types of experimental design:
  1. Independent groups design, in which there may be an experimental and a control group.
  2. Repeated measures design, in which there may an experimental and a control condition.
  3. Matched pairs design.
❖ With an independent groups design, random allocation is generally used to assign participants to groups. The aim is to ensure that both groups are equivalent.

❖ Repeated measures compensate for any participant variation because the participants in both conditions are the same. However, there is the problem of order effects, which may be overcome by using counterbalancing.

❖ Matched pairs design uses independent groups of participants who are similar. Control groups/conditions provide a baseline measure.

❖ There are several stages in developing behavioural categories for studies using naturalistic observations:

1. Relevant categories need to be identified.
2. Categories based on recording or interpretation need to be produced.
3. Observers need training in use of the categories.
4. Behavioural categories must produce reliable measurement.

Naturalistic observations

❖ Interviews vary in terms of structure and type of question (closed vs open).

❖ Non-directive interviews and open questions are suitable when:
  – the researcher wants rich, personal information;
  – the researcher doesn't intend to compare responses across interviewees;
  – the interviewers have been fully trained.

❖ Structured interviews and closed questions are suitable when:
  – the researcher wants data that are easy to analyse;
  – the researcher wants reliable data;
  – the researcher knows what information he/she wants from interviewees.

❖ Interviewer characteristics such as age, gender, and ethnicity can all influence interviewees' responses. There is also the issue of interviewer bias.

❖ Questionnaire design requires choosing between open and closed questions and avoiding ambiguity and bias.

❖ Questionnaires should be standardised on large representative groups so that any individual's score can be interpreted.

❖ Questionnaires should be reliable in the sense of providing consistent measurement.

❖ Questionnaires should be valid in that they measure what they are supposed to be measuring.

Interviews and questionnaires

❖ Operationalisation can be used to provide operational definitions of independent and dependent variables. This is almost essential for most research in psychology.

❖ Operational definitions tend to be rather narrow in scope.

❖ Different operational definitions of a given variable sometimes produce different findings, which makes it hard to interpret those findings.

Operationalisation of variables

❖ Pilot studies allow researchers to check out standardised procedures and general design with relatively little effort.

❖ Pilot studies help to ensure that participants understand clearly what is expected of them.

❖ Pilot studies can assist researchers to decide between various ways of carrying out a study.

❖ Pilot studies can help researchers to decide how many participants will be needed in the study itself.

Pilot studies

Extraneous variables	❖ Extraneous variables that vary systematically with the independent variable become confounding variables that can bias results. ❖ When there is a confounding variable, we don't know whether the findings are due to it or to the independent variable. ❖ It is essential to good research to avoid allowing any confounding variables to distort the findings.
Reliability and validity	❖ Any given method or test should be reliable or consistent. ❖ Internal reliability is how consistently a method measures within itself. ❖ External reliability is how consistently a method measures over time, population, and location. ❖ Research needs to be valid, producing genuine findings and useful information. ❖ Internal validity is concerned with whether the effects are due to the independent variable. External validity is concerned with generalisability.
BPS Code of Ethics	❖ The BPS issued a Code of Ethics in 2006. ❖ It is based on four principles: respect; competence; responsibility; and integrity. ❖ Researchers need to maintain confidentiality, obtain informed consent, protect participants from harm, and avoid deception. ❖ Researchers should inform participants that they can withdraw from the study at any point and may decline to answer any questions. ❖ Participants should be debriefed at the end of their participation.
Ethical issues	❖ Researchers often use a cost–benefit analysis when deciding whether a study is ethical. However, it is often hard to predict costs and benefits in advance. ❖ Researchers should strive to avoid deception, but this isn't always possible. Debriefing can reduce the negative effects of deception. ❖ It is very important for researchers to have participants' voluntary informed consent. When this isn't feasible, it is possible to use presumptive consent or prior general consent and participants can be offered the right to withhold their data ❖ Researchers must protect participants from physical and psychological harm.
Sampling techniques	❖ The participants selected for a study represent a sample from some target population. They should form a representative sample and be selected to avoid sampling bias. ❖ Random sampling: This is the best approach but is hard to achieve in practice because of problems in identifying whole populations, finding all participants, and obtaining responses from them. ❖ Opportunity sampling: This is the easiest (but least satisfactory) method. The problem is that the sample is likely to be very unrepresentative. ❖ Volunteer sampling: In practice, researchers nearly always have to rely on volunteers. Volunteers often differ in important ways from non-volunteers. They tend to be more likely to comply with demand characteristics and to be more open and agreeable. ❖ The number of participants in each condition or group should depend on the likely size of the effect(s) being studied.
Demand characteristics and investigator effects	❖ Demand characteristics involve the participants responding on the basis of their beliefs about the research hypothesis or hypotheses.

❖ Demand characteristics can be minimised by using a single blind experimental design.

❖ Investigator effects include experimenter expectancy, as in the study by Rosenthal and Jacobson (1968) on teachers' expectations about children's ability. The Pygmalion effect they observed seems to depend on climate, input, output, and feedback.

❖ One way of overcoming investigator effects is to use a double blind procedure.

SECTION 11
DATA ANALYSIS AND PRESENTATION

The data obtained from a study may or may or may not be in numerical or quantitative form, i.e. in the form of numbers. Even if the data aren't in quantitative form, we can still carry out *qualitative* analyses based on the experiences of the individual participants. If the data are in numerical form, then we typically start by working out some descriptive statistics to summarise the pattern of findings. These descriptive statistics include measures of central tendency within a sample (e.g. mean) and measures of the spread of scores within a sample (e.g. range). Another useful way of summarising the findings is through the use of graphs.

We start by considering ways of dealing with quantitative data. After that, we turn our attention to qualitative data, in which the information obtained from participants isn't in the form of numbers. The emphasis in qualitative research is on the stated experiences of the participants and on the stated meanings they attach to themselves, to other people, and to the environment.

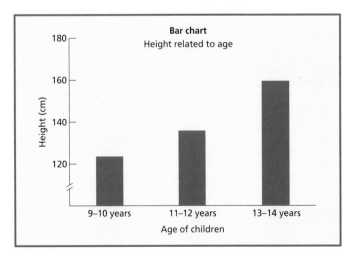

The mean height of these children is 113cm. Stating the mean is one way of describing the data (in this case height).

Analysis and Interpretation of Quantitative Data

Suppose we have carried out an experiment on the effects of noise on learning with three groups of nine participants each. One group was exposed to very loud noise, another to moderately loud noise, and the third was not exposed to any noise. What they had learned from a book chapter was assessed by giving them a set of questions, producing a score between 0 and 20.

What is to be done with the **raw scores**? There are two key types of measures that can be taken whenever we have a set of scores from participants in a given condition: **measures of central tendency**, and **measures of dispersion**.

Bar chart
Height related to age

(Bar chart with y-axis "Height (cm)" showing values 120, 140, 160, 180; x-axis "Age of children" with categories 9–10 years, 11–12 years, 13–14 years)

KEY TERMS
Raw scores: the data before they have been summarised in some way.
Measures of central tendency: any means of representing the mid-point of a set of data, such as the mean, median, and mode.
Measures of dispersion: any means of expressing the spread of the data, such as range or standard deviation.

Mean		
Scores	Number of scores	
1	1	
2	2	
4	3	
5	4	
7	5	
9	6	
9	7	
9	8	
17	9	
63	9	Total
63	÷ 9	= 7

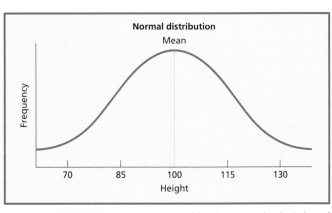

This is a normal distribution. It could represent the height of people in your class or the x-axis could be the "life-time" of a light bulb, given in weeks. Most of the scores will be clustered around the mean. The further away from the mean you get, the fewer cases there are.

Example of a misleading mean		
Scores		
25		
27		
28		
29		
34		
39		
42		
288		
512	÷ 8	= **64**

Measures of central tendency

Measures of central tendency describe how the data cluster together around a central point. They provide some indication of the size of average or typical scores. There are three main measures of central tendency: the mean, the median, and the mode.

Mean

The **mean** in each group or condition is calculated by adding up all the scores in a given condition, and then dividing by the number of participants in that condition. Suppose that the scores of the nine participants in the no-noise condition are as follows: 1, 2, 4, 5, 7, 9, 9, 9, 17. The mean is given by the total (63), divided by the number of participants (9) giving 7 (see the box on the left).

The mean takes all the scores into account, making it a **sensitive** measure of central tendency, especially if the scores resemble the **normal distribution**, which is a bell-shaped distribution in which most scores cluster fairly close to the mean.

However, the mean can be very misleading if the distribution differs markedly from normal and there are one or two extreme scores in one direction. Suppose that eight people complete one lap of a track in go-karts. For seven of them, the times taken (in seconds) are as follows: 25, 27, 28, 29, 34, 39, and 42. The eighth person's go-kart breaks down, and so the driver has to push it around the track, taking 288 seconds to complete the lap. The resulting overall mean of 64 seconds (see the box on the left) is clearly misleading, because no-one took even close to 64 seconds to complete one lap.

Median

Another way of describing the general level of performance in each condition is known as the **median**. If there is an odd number of scores, then the median is simply the middle score, having an equal number of scores higher and lower than it. In the example with nine scores in the no-noise condition, the median is 7 (see the box overleaf). Matters are slightly more complex if there is an even number of scores. In that case, we take the two central values and work out their mean. For example, suppose that we have the following scores in size order: 2, 5, 5, 7, 8, 9. The two central values are 5 and 7, and so the median is (5 + 7)/2 = 6.

The main advantage of the median is that it is unaffected by a few extreme scores, because it focuses only on scores in the middle of the distribution. In the case of our go-kart data the median would be 31.5, a more accurate "average" in this case than the mean. The median also has the advantage that it tends to be easier to work out than the mean.

The main limitation of the median is that it ignores most of the scores, and so it is often less

KEY TERMS
Mean: an average worked out by dividing the total of participants' scores by the number of participants.
Sensitive: in the context of statistics, "sensitive" means more precise, able to reflect small differences or changes.
Normal distribution: a bell-shaped distribution in which most of the scores are close to the mean. This characteristic shape is produced when measuring many psychological and biological variables, such as IQ and height.
Median: the middle score out of all the participants' scores.

An unexpected breakdown would cause the mean lap time to be very misleading.

sensitive than the mean. It is also not always representative of the scores obtained, especially if there are only a few scores.

Mode

The final measure of central tendency is the **mode**. This is simply the most frequently occurring score. In the no-noise condition example, this is 9 (see the box, bottom right).

The mode is unaffected by one or two extreme scores, and is the easiest measure of central tendency to work out. It can be worked out even when some of the extreme scores are not known.

However, its limitations generally outweigh these advantages. The greatest limitation is that the mode tends to be unreliable. For example, suppose we have the following scores: 4, 4, 6, 7, 8, 8, 12, 12, 12. The mode of these scores is 12. If just one score changed (a 12 becoming a 4), the mode would change to 4! Also, information about the exact values of the scores obtained is ignored in working out the mode. This makes it a less sensitive measure than the mean.

A final consideration is that it is possible for there to be more than one mode. In the case of the following scores 4, 4, 4, 4, 5, 6, 6, 8, 8, 8, 8 there are two modes (4 and 8) and the scores are therefore called **bimodal**. And some sets of data have no mode, as in our go-kart data.

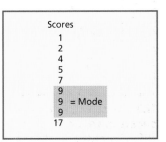

Scores
1
2
4
5
7 = Median
9
9
9
17

Scores
1
2
4
5
7
9
9 = Mode
9
17

The mode is useful where other measures of central tendency are meaningless, for example when calculating the number of children in the average family. It would be unusual to have 0.4 or 0.6 of a child!

Summary

The mean is the most generally useful measure of central tendency, whereas the mode is the least useful. However, there are circumstances in which the mean is less useful, such as when the distribution of scores is very unusual or there are a few extreme scores in the data.

Measures of dispersion

In addition to having an estimate of central tendency, it is also useful to work out what are known as measures of dispersion, such as the range and standard deviation. These measures indicate the extent to which the scores cluster around the average or are spread out.

The range

The simplest of these measures is the **range**, which can be defined as the difference between the highest and the lowest score in any condition. In the case of the following numbers: 4, 5, 5, 7, 9, 9, 9, 17, the range is calculated as follows: highest number − lowest number, or 17 − 4 = 13.

 The term "average" is rather vague. The mean, median, and mode are all averages.

KEY TERMS

Mode: the most frequently occurring score among participants' scores in a given condition.
Bimodal: a distribution with two modes.
Range: the difference between the highest and lowest score in any condition.

See *AS Level Psychology Online* for an interactive exercise on this topic.

In fact, it is preferable to calculate the range in a slightly different way (Coolican, 1994). The revised formula (when we are dealing with whole numbers) is as follows: (highest score − lowest score) + 1, i.e. (17 − 4) + 1 = 14. This formula is preferable because it takes account of the fact that the scores were rounded to whole numbers. In our sample data, a score of 17 stands for all values between 16.5 and 17.5, and a score of 4 represents a value between 3.5 and 4.5. If we take the range as the interval between the highest possible value (17.5) and the lowest possible value (3.5), this gives us a range of 14, which is precisely the figure produced by the formula.

								9								
				5				9								
Scores:	1	2		4	5		7		9							17
Range:	1	2	3	4	5	6	7	8	9	10	11	12	13	14	15	16	17

What has been said so far about the range applies only to whole numbers. Suppose that we measure the time taken to perform a task to the nearest tenth of a second, with the fastest time being 21.3 seconds and the slowest time being 36.8 seconds. The figure of 21.3 represents a value between 21.25 and 21.35, and 36.8 represents a value between 36.75 and 36.85. As a result, the range is 36.85−21.25, which is 15.6 seconds, whereas 36.8 − 21.3 = 15.5.

The range is easy to calculate and takes full account of extreme values. However, it can be greatly influenced by one score that is very different from all of the others. In the example above, the inclusion of the participant scoring 17 increases the range from 9 to 17. Also, it ignores all but two of the scores, and so is likely to provide an inadequate measure of the general spread or dispersion of the scores around the mean or median.

The interquartile range

The **interquartile range** is defined as the spread of the middle 50% of scores. For example, suppose we have the following scores: 4, 5, 6, 6, 7, 8, 8, 9, 11, 11, 14, 15, 17, 18, 18, 19. There are 16 scores, which can be divided into the bottom 25% (4), the middle 50% (8), and the top 25% (4). The middle 50% of scores starts with 7 and runs through to 15. The upper boundary of the interquartile range lies between 15 and 17, and is given by the mean of those two values, i.e. 16. The lower boundary of the interquartile range lies between 6 and 7, and is the mean, i.e. 6.5. The interquartile range is the difference between the upper and lower boundaries, i.e. 16 − 6.5 = 9.5.

The interquartile range has the advantage over the range that it is not influenced by a single extreme score. Thus, it is more likely to provide an accurate

KEY TERM

Interquartile range: the spread of the middle 50% of an ordered or ranked set of scores.

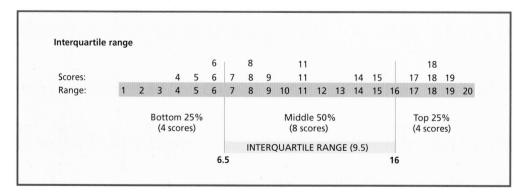

reflection of the spread or dispersion of the scores. It has the disadvantage that it ignores information from the top and bottom 25% of scores.

Standard deviation

The most generally useful measure of dispersion is the **standard deviation**. It is harder to calculate than the range, but generally provides a more accurate measure of the spread of scores. However, many calculators allow the standard deviation to be worked out rapidly and effortlessly. To calculate the standard deviation manually, follow these steps (also illustrated in the worked example in the box on the right):

1. Work out the mean of the sample. This is given by the total of all of the participants' scores $\Sigma x = 130$ (the symbol Σ means "the sum of") divided by the number of participants (N = 13). Thus, the mean ($\bar{x}$) is 10.
2. Subtract the mean in turn from each score $(x - \bar{x})$. The calculations are shown in the fourth column.
3. Square each of the scores in the fourth column $(x - \bar{x})^2$.
4. Work out the total of all the squared scores, $\Sigma (x - \bar{x})^2$. This comes to 136.
5. Divide by one less than the number of participants, N − 1 = 12. This gives us 136 divided by 12, which equals 11.33. This is known as the **variance** (s^2), which is in squared units.
6. Use a calculator to take the square root of the variance. This produces a figure of 3.37. This is the standard deviation (*SD*).

This method is used when we want to estimate the standard deviation of the population. If we want merely to describe the spread of scores in our sample, then the fifth step is to divide the result of the fourth step by N. Where data are normally distributed, about two-thirds of the scores in a sample should lie within one standard deviation of the mean. This is shown in the graph on the right.

In our example, the mean of the sample is 10.0, one standard deviation above the mean will be 13.366 and one standard deviation below the mean will be 6.634. Eight out of the thirteen scores lie between these two values, which is 61.5%, which is only slightly below the expected percentage.

The standard deviation takes account of all of the scores and provides a sensitive measure of dispersion.

Standard deviation: A worked example

Participant	Score (x)	Mean ($\bar{x}$)	Deviation ($x - \bar{x}$)	Deviation^2 ($x - \bar{x}$)^2
1	13	10	3	9
2	6	10	−4	16
3	10	10	0	0
4	15	10	5	25
5	10	10	0	0
6	15	10	5	25
7	5	10	−5	25
8	9	10	−1	1
9	10	10	0	0
10	13	10	3	9
11	6	10	−4	16
12	11	10	1	1
13	7	10	−3	9
13	130	10		$\Sigma(x - \bar{x})^2 = 136$

Total of scores (Σx) = 130

Number of participants (N) = 13

Mean ($\bar{x}$) = $\dfrac{\Sigma x}{N} = \dfrac{130}{13} = 10$

Variance (s^2) = $\dfrac{136}{13-1} = 11.33$

Standard deviation (SD) = $\sqrt{11.3} = 3.37$

Σ means "the sum of"

$\bar{x}$ is the symbol for the mean

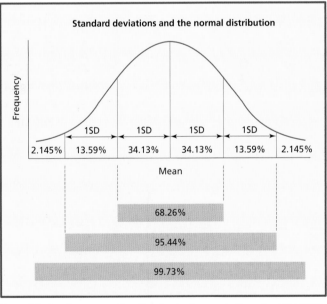

Standard deviations and the normal distribution

Two-thirds of a normally distributed population (or 68.26%) are located within one standard deviation of the mean, 95.44% fall within two standard deviations, and 99.73% fall within three standard deviations.

KEY TERMS

Standard deviation: a measure of the spread of the scores around the mean. It is the square root of the variance and takes account of every measurement.
Variance: the extent of variation of the scores around the mean.

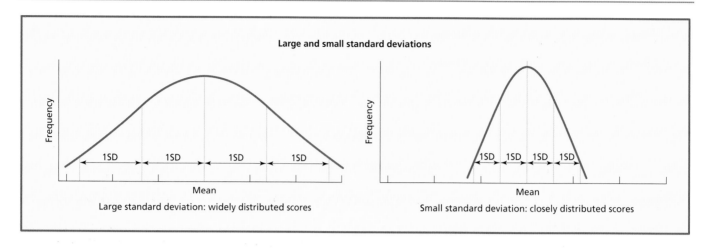

Large and small standard deviations

Large standard deviation: widely distributed scores

Small standard deviation: closely distributed scores

As we have seen, it also has the advantage that it describes the spread of scores in a normal distribution with great precision. The most obvious disadvantage of the standard deviation is that it is much harder to work out than the other measures of dispersion.

Presentation and Interpretation of Quantitative Data

Measures of central tendency and of range are ways of summarising data. Perhaps it is even more helpful to use visual displays to summarise information and get a feel for what it means. Note that I said summarise—there is no advantage in producing a visual display that simply shows the data for each participant! If information is presented in a graph, this may make it easier for people to understand what has been found, compared to simply presenting information about the central tendency and dispersion.

Suppose that we ask 25 male athletes to run 400 metres as rapidly as possible, and record their times (in seconds). Having worked out a table of frequencies (see the boxed example below), there are several ways to present these data.

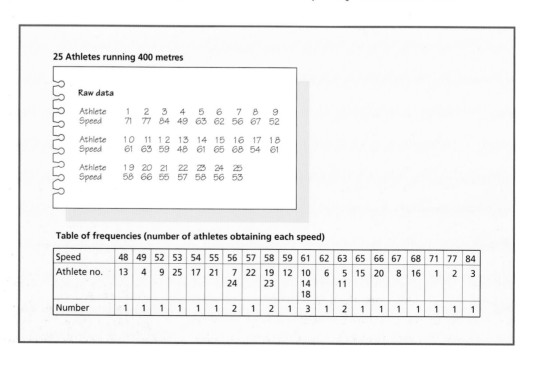

25 Athletes running 400 metres

Raw data

Athlete	1	2	3	4	5	6	7	8	9
Speed	71	77	84	49	63	62	56	67	52

Athlete	10	11	12	13	14	15	16	17	18
Speed	61	63	59	48	61	65	68	54	61

Athlete	19	20	21	22	23	24	25
Speed	58	66	55	57	58	56	53

Table of frequencies (number of athletes obtaining each speed)

Speed	48	49	52	53	54	55	56	57	58	59	61	62	63	65	66	67	68	71	77	84
Athlete no.	13	4	9	25	17	21	7 24	22	19 23	12	10 14 18	6	5 11	15	20	8	16	1	2	3
Number	1	1	1	1	1	1	2	1	2	1	3	1	2	1	1	1	1	1	1	1

Histogram

In a **histogram** (see right), the scores are indicated on the horizontal axis and the frequencies are shown on the vertical axis. The frequencies are indicated by rectangular columns all the same width but varying in height in accordance with the corresponding frequencies. It is important to make sure that the class intervals are not too broad or too narrow. All class intervals are represented, even if there are no scores in some of them. Class intervals are indicated by their mid-point at the centre of the columns. In the present example (see right), the histogram indicates that most of the athletes ran 400 metres fairly quickly. Only a few had extreme times that were below 55 seconds or greater than 70 seconds.

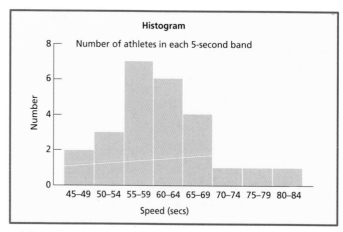

A histogram provides a means of summarising the data.

Bar charts

Bar charts are often used when the data are in categories. The categories are shown along the horizontal axis, and the frequencies are indicated on the vertical axis, as in a histogram. The categories in bar charts cannot be ordered numerically in a meaningful way, but in ascending (or descending) order of popularity. The rectangles in a **bar chart** don't usually touch each other.

The scale on the vertical axis of a bar chart normally starts at zero, although it is sometimes convenient for presentational purposes to have it start at some higher value. If so, it should be made clear in the bar chart that the lower part of the vertical scale is missing. The columns in a bar chart often represent frequencies, but they can also represent means or percentages for different groups (Coolican, 1994).

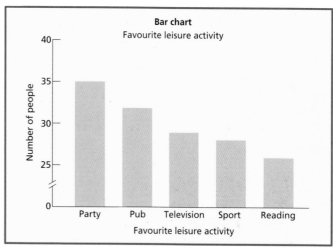

A bar chart makes it easy to compare the popularity of different leisure activities. We can see at a glance that going to a party was the most popular leisure activity, whereas reading a good book was the least popular. The data in this chart are in nominal categories.

Scattergrams

In the case of correlational studies the data, in the form of two measures of behaviour from each member of a single group of participants (called co-variables), can be presented in the form of a **scattergram** (or **scattergraph**), with a dot for each participant indicating where he or she falls on the two dimensions. If there is a positive relationship the dots should form a pattern going from the bottom left of the scattergraph to the top right (see examples overleaf). If there is no relationship between the two variables, then the dots should be distributed in a fairly random way within the scattergraph. If there is a negative relationship between the two variables,

Graphs and charts should be clearly labelled and presented so that the reader can rapidly make sense of the information contained in them. It is also helpful to use squared paper when recording numbers and drawing graphs.

KEY TERMS

Histogram: a graph in which the frequencies of scores in each category are represented by a vertical column; data on the y-axis must be continuous with a true zero.
Bar chart: like a histogram, a representation of frequency data, but the categories do not have to be continuous; used for nominal data.
Scattergram/scattergraph: two-dimensional representation of all the participants' scores in a correlational study.

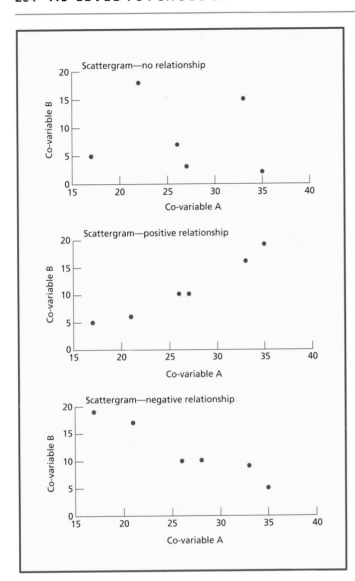

The findings from a study to investigate the effects of loud noise on learning of material in a textbook chapter assessed by performance on a comprehension test (maximum score = 50).

	Group 1: Loud noise	Group 2: No noise (control)
No. of participants	15	15
Mean correct items	23.5	29.5
Standard deviation	4.7	4.9

We can see from the table that comprehension performance was higher in the control group than in the group receiving loud noise based on differences in the means. This suggests that loud noise interferes with learning. We can also see that there was a reasonable number of participants in each group, and that the dispersion of scores (assessed by standard deviation) is similar in both groups.

then the dots will form a pattern going from the top left to the bottom right. The scattergraph gives you a rough idea of the association between two variables. To be more precise you need to calculate a "correlation coefficient", but these statistics are not covered at AS level.

Tables

If we want to provide a summary of our findings from a study, we don't have to produce a graph or visual display. What we can do instead is to produce a table summarising what has happened. Tables have the advantage that a lot of different kinds of summary information can be included in a single table. They also have the advantage that precise figures (e.g. for group means) are provided, whereas it is often only possible to work out approximate figures when looking at graphs. However, tables have the disadvantage that they can be a little harder to interpret than a graph, and it can be more difficult to visualise what has been found.

Tables can also be used instead of a histogram or bar chart. For example, a table could list the eight speed categories shown in our histogram with the number of athletes falling into each category shown next to each category. Our bar chart could be replaced with a table listing the five leisure activities with the number of people having each one as their favourite leisure activity indicated beside each one.

Analysis and Interpretation of Correlational Data

In Section 9 we considered studies using correlational analysis. Strictly speaking, correlation is not a research method but a method of analysing data. Therefore, it is appropriate to consider correlation further in this section on data analysis.

Positive and negative correlations

We can use correlations in numerous situations. In essence, we need to have information concerning the same two variables from each of our participants. In a study on children, for example, we might have information about how much violent television they have watched (variable 1) and how aggressive they are (variable 2). We could use a correlation to see whether children who watch the most violent television tend to be the most aggressive. Here we would expect a **positive correlation**—this happens when two variables (sometimes known as co-variables) increase together.

Alternatively, we could correlate amount of concern about global warming (variable 1) with frequency of flying (variable 2). Here we would expect a **negative correlation**. This happens when there is an inverse relationship between two variables (co-variables)—as one increases, so the other decreases. Illustrations of positive and negative correlations are shown in scattergrams in the box on the left page—note that each dot represents an individual. At the top, there is a scattergram showing no relationship (positive or negative) between two variables.

Correlation coefficients

We can assess the extent to which the co-variables are correlated using the **correlation coefficient**. A coefficient is a number expressing the degree to which two things are related. If two variables are perfectly correlated, then the coefficient is 1.0. Perfect positive correlation is $+1.0$, and perfect negative correlation is -1.0. Of course, perfect correlation is rare. A correlation coefficient of -0.75 would reflect a close inverse or negative relationship between two variables. A correlation coefficient of -0.85 would suggest an even closer inverse relationship. A correlation coefficient of -0.25 or $+0.25$ would suggest a weak relationship between the two variables. A zero correlation coefficient (0.0) indicates a complete lack of relationship. It is possible to calculate the correlation coefficient between co-variables using a statistical test, but this is not covered at AS level.

How can we interpret correlational data? The key point to remember is that a correlation coefficient (even a very strong one) only indicates an association between two variables, it does NOT show that one variable causes the other. For example, suppose we find that children who watch much violent television are more aggressive. This may be because watching violent television causes aggressive behaviour, or it might be that naturally aggressive children choose to watch violent television programmes. We simply don't know which interpretation is preferable on the basis of correlational data alone. In similar fashion, finding that concern about global warming correlates negatively with amount of flying only indicates a negative association between those two variables. It may be that those most concerned about global warming deliberately avoid flying. However, there are many other possibilities. Perhaps relatively poor people are the ones most concerned about global warming, and they don't fly much because they can't afford it. We can't choose between these interpretations purely on the basis of one negative correlation.

Presentation of Qualitative Data

One of the strengths of the qualitative approach is its flexibility. As a result, there are many different kinds of qualitative data. For example, there is

■ **Activity:** Investigating conformity quantitatively and qualitatively

One way to investigate conformity is to stand near a traffic light and observe how many cars go through the red light, i.e. the drivers do not conform to our traffic regulations. The results of such a study would involve a frequency count of the number of people who did this. You could distinguish between male and female drivers, and people who are on their own or with passengers.

A qualitative approach would be to interview individuals about their driving habits and consider the reasons given as to why people do not always conform to traffic signals.

Which approach would provide "better" or more useful information?

KEY TERMS

Positive correlation: when two co-variables increase at the same time.
Negative correlation: as one co-variable increases the other decreases. They still vary in a constant relationship.
Correlation coefficient: a number that expresses the extent to which two variables are related or vary together.

? The term "average" is rather vague. The mean, median, and mode are *all* averages.

discourse analysis, which focuses on language and "assumes people use language to construct the world as they see it, and according to context and interests" (Coolican, 2004, p. 240). Its main emphasis is on meaning (i.e. what is the speaker or writer trying to say), and the key underlying assumption is that the ways we use language are greatly affected by the social context. Gilbert and Mulkay (1984) presented accounts of scientists' research in their writings and when they were being interviewed. It was clear that they appeared much more confident about the meaning of their findings when being interviewed.

Qualitative data are very often used when researchers report a case study in which a single individual is investigated in great detail. The data are often presented in the form of direct quotations from the participant. For example, Griffiths (1993) chronicled one teenage boy's descent into pathological gambling and his subsequent recovery. Most of the data were collected in separate interviews with "David" and his mother. Here is part of what David had to say:

? Many of the data in Griffiths' (1993) study were retrospective. How do you feel this may have affected the results?

> *I always got the feeling of being 'high' or 'stoned' . . . Although winning money was the first thing that attracted me to playing fruit machines, this gradually converted to light, sounds and excitement . . . I was always very upset about losing all my money and I returned many times to try to win back my losses . . . The only time I found it possible to think about giving up was after leaving the arcade at closing time and [vowing] never to return . . . Whenever I felt depressed (which was practically all the time) or rejected, the urge to play machines became even bigger.*

We will use a study by Abrahamsson et al. (2002; reprinted in Coolican, 2004) to illustrate the presentation of qualitative data in more detail. They focused on patients with dental phobia attending a dental fear clinic. The patients were given a semi-structured interview lasting about 1 hour dealing with their dental phobia. The interview was audio-taped and then transcribed. Abrahamsson et al. didn't set out to test any hypotheses; rather, they analysed the interview data very thoroughly to identify underlying themes. They presented their data in the following way:

1. They identified four main categories: threat to self-respect and well-being; avoidance; readiness to act; and ambivalence in coping.
2. They sub-divided the categories into smaller categories. For example, threat to self-respect and well-being was sub-divided into threat to own health and threat to social life, and avoidance was sub-divided into factors preventing problem solving and avoidance and suppression.
3. In their article, Abrahamsson et al. gave numerous concrete examples of statements falling into the various categories and sub-categories. For example, "I'm terribly afraid that my teeth will get in a bad state if I don't go" falls into the threat to own health sub-category and "I have repressed everything . . . just don't think about it" illustrates the sub-category of avoidance and suppression.

In sum, Abrahamsson et al.'s presentation of their qualitative data revolves mainly around the categories and sub-categories they identified from exhaustive analyses of their interview data. These data presentations are strengthened and

KEY TERM

Discourse analysis: a qualitative method involving the analysis of meanings expressed in various forms of language (e.g. speeches; writings). The emphasis is often on effects of social context on language use.

made more convincing by including many examples of patients' statements that fit neatly into this category-based framework.

Qualitative data can be used to test pre-existing hypotheses. For example, Lau and Russell (1980) tested the hypothesis that players and coaches would explain wins and defeats in very different ways. More specifically, they assumed that wins would be explained in terms of internal factors (e.g. "Our players were better than theirs"), whereas defeats would be explained in terms of external factors (e.g. "The pitch was in terrible shape"; "We had no luck with the referee"). The qualitative data were obtained by searching through newspaper articles reporting on 33 major sporting events and categorising the comments of players and coaches. The findings supported the hypothesis.

> An investigator might study attitudes towards A-level psychology by carrying out interviews with several A-level students. One of the categories into which their statements are then placed might be "negative attitudes towards statistics". A consideration of the various statements in this category might reveal numerous reasons why A-level psychology students dislike statistics!

Content Analysis

Content analysis is one of the most important techniques used in qualitative research. What exactly is content analysis? According to Colman (2001, p. 162), content analysis can be defined as techniques "for the systematic and objective description and classification of . . . written or spoken verbal communications". These communications can include articles published in newspapers, speeches made by politicians on radio and television, books, and popular music.

Cumberbatch (1990) used content analysis in a study of advertisements on British television and found that only about 25% of the women in these advertisements seemed to be over 30 years old, compared to about 75% of men. On the face of it (perhaps literally!), this appears to reflect sexist bias. In these advertisements there were twice as many men as women, but 89% of voice-overs (especially those communicating expert/official information) involved men. Note that in this qualitative study (as in many studies using content analysis), some numbers creep into the analysis!

Bruno and Kelso (1980) studied graffiti in men's and women's toilets. They found that women's graffiti were much more interpersonal and interactive, with an emphasis on love and commitment. In contrast, men's graffiti focused more than women's on sexual conquests and sexual prowess. Thus, women explored themes of cooperation and relationships, whereas men explored themes of dominance and power. Kutakoff, Levin, and Arluke (1984) found similar differences in toilet graffiti between men and women, and also found that these differences changed very little over a 12-year period.

There are several stages involved in the effective use of content analysis. First, the researcher puts forward one or more general hypotheses. For example, Cumberbatch (1990) hypothesised that there would be evidence of sexism in television advertisements. In the study by Lau and Russell (1980) discussed above, it was predicted that those on the winning side in sporting events would explain their success in terms of internal factors whereas those on the losing side would favour external factors.

Second, the researcher generally identifies categories of theoretical relevance into which the information from some written or spoken communications will be placed. For example, Cumberbatch used categories of "below 30" and

Content analysis of advertising can tell us a great deal about society's attitudes to men and women.

KEY TERM

Content analysis: A qualitative research method involving the analysis of behaviours or the written or spoken word into pre-set categories, a process known as coding, to produce an overview of the research area.

"above 30", predicting that a sexist approach would lead to far more women than men being young. There can be difficulties here—for example, do you agree that the appropriate definition of young is "under the age of 30"?

Third, the researcher needs to decide which sources of information to use as his/her sample. This is an important step because the findings that are obtained often depend to some extent on the specific context in which the data are obtained. In the research of Cumberbatch (1990), for example, the extent of sexism in television advertisements will depend on whether there is a regulatory body that monitors television advertisements and on the powers possessed by such a body. It is also likely that sexist advertisements are less likely to be shown on programmes that appeal mainly to women than on programmes that appeal mainly to men (e.g. most sports programmes). In similar fashion, nearly all of the newspaper articles used by Lau and Russell (1980) were written by journalists from one of the cities involved in each sporting event. Perhaps players and coaches would have responded differently if explaining wins and losses to journalists from a neutral city.

Fourth, it is desirable to have two or more judges or coders assign the information into categories to ensure that this is being done in a reliable or consistent way. For example, Lau and Russell (1980) had two coders decide whether each statement reflected internal or external factors. There was an 88% agreement, and nearly all the discrepancies were resolved by discussion. Ideally, the coders or judges should not know the researcher's hypotheses or the identities of those providing the material in order to minimise the chances of distortion in the coding.

Fifth, the results of the content analysis need to be related to the hypotheses that motivated the study. For example, Cumberbatch et al. found that there was much evidence to support the hypothesis that television advertisements are sexist.

Evaluation of qualitative techniques

Qualitative techniques have several advantages. First, they offer the prospect of understanding people as rounded individuals in a social context, and the approach can be broader than the quantitative one. Second, qualitative techniques can suggest interesting hypotheses that could be tested in subsequent research. For example, Griffiths' (1993) study on the teenage gambler David suggested that depression was responsible in part for him starting to gamble and then continuing to do so. Third, qualitative research such as the study by Ainsworth and Bell (1970) on children's attachment (see pages 97–99) can successfully reduce very complex forms of behaviour to a manageable number of meaningful categories. Fourth, content analysis and discourse analysis have shown convincingly that the ways in which we talk or write are strongly influenced by the immediate social context.

What are the main weaknesses of the qualitative approach? First, there is social desirability bias—the tendency for people to present themselves in the best possible light, so they say things that are not strictly true. Second, the qualitative data may come from a very unrepresentative sample. For example, consider the study by Bruner and Kelso (1980). Presumably only a tiny fraction of men or women produce graffiti in toilets, and so it is hard to generalise the findings. Third, if the researcher accumulates a huge amount of

> ■ **Activity:** Qualitative and quantitative analysis
> Ask each of the class or another group of people to answer two questions:
> a. Does having a tan make a person look more attractive? Yes/no
> b. Is it healthy and safe to stay out in the sun for as long as possible in the summer? Yes/no
> Then count your answers and make two bar charts. Is this qualitative or quantitative analysis?
> Do the two bar charts match or not? Why? Is this now qualitative or quantitative analysis?

material (e.g. in a case study), he/she can easily show bias by emphasising only those bits of the material fitting his/her favoured hypothesis. Fourth, qualitative analysis isn't very useful in several areas of psychology (e.g. memory). For example, it wouldn't have made much sense if Peterson and Peterson (1959; see page 48) in their study of short-term memory had described their findings in qualitative terms!

> You have reached the end of the chapter on research methods in psychology. Research is fundamental to the status of psychology as a scientific subject. It enables us to be more than "armchair psychologists". We should be able to provide systematic, reliable, and valid evidence for our views.

SECTION SUMMARY

❖ When we have obtained scores from a group of participants, we can summarise our data by working out:
  – a measure of central tendency (average);
  – a measure of dispersion of spread of scores around the central tendency.
❖ The mean is the most generally useful measure of central tendency because it takes all the scores into account.
❖ However, other measures of central tendency include the median and mode.
❖ The median is less affected than the mean by extreme values.
❖ The standard deviation is the most useful and precise measure of dispersion. However, the range is much simpler to calculate, although it is affected by extreme scores.

Analysis and interpretation of quantitative data

❖ Summary data from a study can be presented in the form of a graph or table of frequencies so that it is easy to observe general trends.
❖ Among the possible ways of using graphs to present the data are the following:
  – Histogram: used when scores can be ordered from low to high.
  – Bar chart: used when the scores are in the form of categories.
  – Scattergram: the data from correlational studies can be presented in a scattergram where the scores on the two co-variables are recorded from every participant as a dot.
❖ Tables can be used to summarise the data. This can be done for groups or to summarise categorical data.

Presentation and interpretation of quantitative data

❖ The correlations between two variables can be positive (variables increase together) or negative (variables change in an inverse fashion; as one increases, the other decreases).
❖ The extent to which the co-variables are related is expressed by a correlation coefficient.
❖ Perfect correlation is +1.0 or −1.0 for positive or negative correlations, respectively.
❖ Correlations only indicate an association between two variables, and can't be used to establish causality.

Correlational data

❖ Qualitative data are often collected for use in discourse analysis (based on language) and in case studies of individuals studied in detail.
❖ Qualitative data have various advantages and weaknesses:
  + The data are often rich and informative.
  + The data often suggest testable hypotheses.

Presentation of qualitative data

  – The data can be distorted by social desirability bias.

  – There can be problems with generalisability.

Processes involved in content analysis

❖ Content analysis involves the following processes:

  – Hypotheses are formed.

  – Categories are devised that are relevant to the hypotheses being tested.

  – An appropriate sample of data is located. Biased sampling will produce findings of limited interest.

  – The reliability of assignment of data to categories is checked using judges or coders who don't know the hypotheses being tested.

  – The results of the content analysis are related to the hypotheses.

EXAM HINT

- There are so many different types of research methods question that it really is a good idea to prepare for the different types of question as you work your way through the topic.
- PRACTISE, PRACTISE, PRACTISE—it's more important than with any of the other topics because unlike the other topics where you can know all the possible questions without looking at an exam paper, with this question you need to be familiar with the research summary that is part of the question.
- Contextualise—research methods questions often include the phrase ". . . in the context of this investigation", which means you must relate your answer to the study described in the question. For example, if you are asked to give a criticism don't generalise, but instead pick up on something specific from the summary in the question.

FURTHER READING

A book that covers most research methods in a very accessible way is H. Coolican (2004) *Research methods and statistics in psychology (4th Edn.)* (London: Hodder & Stoughton). A good reasonably priced student book is by A. Searle (1999) *Introducing research and data in psychology* (London: Routledge). Another useful textbook is J.J. Foster and J. Parker (1995) *Carrying out investigations in psychology: Methods and statistics* (Leicester, UK: BPS Books). The various forms of non-experimental study are described in C. Dyer (1995) *Beginning research in psychology* (Oxford, UK: Blackwell).

WEBSITES

http://www.mcli.dist.maricopa.edu/proj/res_meth/login.html
 The five main research methods: An easy to use, interactive site, with optional self-tests.

http://www.bath.ac.uk/e-learning/gold/glossary.html#indexOfEntries
 An index of research methodology terms.

http://psychology.about.com/od/researchmethods/a/simpexperiment.htm
 Basic experimental method: A simple and straightforward guide.

http://psychology.about.com/od/researchmethods/f/reliabilitydef.htm
 What is reliability?: This site gives clear explanations.

http://psychology.about.com/od/researchmethods/f/validity.htm
 What is validity?: More clear explanations.

See Chapter 4 of the revision guide for guidance on revising this chapter for the exam.

REVISION QUESTIONS

Research methods are not tested in a separate section of the exam paper. Instead, questions on research methods will appear on both exam papers. In paper one there are twice as many A03 marks as there are on paper two, so expect more research methods questions on paper one (the Cognitive and Developmental sections). Here are two sample questions on research methods that are based on those you might expect to find in the Cognitive section and the Developmental section of paper one.

Question 1
Research into privation such as Genie, children of the Holocaust, and the Czech twins has involved the case study method.

a. Explain what the case study method is. (2 marks)
b. Why does the case study method generate qualitative data? (3 marks)
c. Give strengths and/or weaknesses of the qualitative approach. (5 marks)

Question 2
Research such as the Peterson and Peterson (1959) study takes place in a laboratory setting and has enabled conclusions to be drawn as to the duration of short-term memory. In this study Peterson and Peterson provided participants with a series of trigrams. They then tested the participants to see if they could recall the trigrams after various time intervals. All participants experienced the different time intervals.

a. What were the IV and the DV in this experiment? (1 + 1 marks)
b. Which experimental design was used? Explain your answer. (1 + 2 marks)
c. Explain why memory research, such as this study, is criticised in terms
   of external validity (4 marks)

Biological psychology is an approach or perspective in psychology. It is concerned with explanations of behaviour that refer to the body system's cells, muscles, blood, hormones, and the nervous system—as well as to genetic factors. There is no doubt that much human behaviour can be explained in biological terms. However, it may not be possible to explain higher cognitive processes such as problem solving in this way. Even something as relatively "basic" as emotion might seem rather simplistic when described in terms of the flow of hormones and heart rate. For this reason, psychologists increasingly combine biological explanations with psychological or social ones—this is called the biopsychological approach.

SECTION 12
Stress as a bodily response p. 213

We may dislike feeling stressed, but stress is a healthy and adaptive response to many situations. How exactly does the body react to stress? What are the effects of prolonged stress on the body?

Specification content: The body's response to stress, including the pituitary–adrenal system and the sympathomedullary pathway in outline. Stress-related illness and the immune system.

SECTION 13
Stress in everyday life p. 232

What are the main sources of stress in modern life? Why do different people respond so differently to stressful situations? How do we try to reduce stress in our everyday lives? How effective are the major coping strategies? How effective are approaches based on psychological techniques and drugs?

Specification content: Life changes and daily hassles. Workplace stress. Personality factors including Type A behaviour. Distinction between emotion-focused and problem-focused approaches to coping with stress. Psychological and physiological methods of stress management, including Cognitive Behavioural Therapy and drugs.

BIOLOGICAL PSYCHOLOGY
Stress

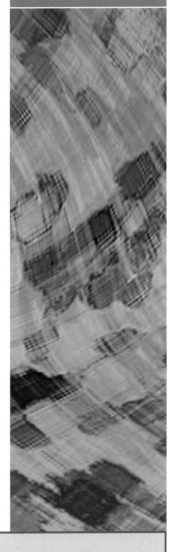

6

Stress is an example of a behaviour and experience that can be explained in physiological and psychological terms. It is something with which most of us are all too familiar. If the media are to be believed, the pressures of everyday life are so great that most of us are highly stressed much of the time. No-one denies that millions of people suffer from stress, but we may be too concerned about it. Indeed, we may be in danger of becoming stressed because we can't stop thinking about stress! In this chapter we consider the processes involved in stress and the management of stress.

SECTION 12
STRESS AS A BODILY RESPONSE

We will make a start by considering the meaning of the term **stress**. Selye (1950) defined it as "the nonspecific response of the body to any demand". In other words, stress is a generalised reaction to a demand placed on the body. Interestingly, the term "stress" had not been used in relation to behaviour until Selye (1936) suggested using it to describe what happened when an organism was exposed to a noxious (unpleasant) stimulus. Thus, stress refers to our reactions (e.g. behavioural; physiological) when exposed to a stressful situation. It is *really* important to note that the way psychologists use the term "stress" is *not* exactly the way we often use it in everyday life. For example, we say, "I'm under so much stress!"—here "stress" refers to the excessive demands we face and *not* to our response to those demands. In psychology-speak, we should say, "I'm exposed to too many stressors", as we will see in the next paragraph.

"Demands" are called **stressors**—events that throw the body out of balance and force it to respond, such as cold, pain, or viruses. The stress response is useful in situations in which an animal needs to react quickly—for example, when a mouse sees a cat. Stress results in arousal, which makes the animal ready to respond in situations that threaten survival. A stress response is an innate, defensive, and adaptive reaction that promotes survival.

There are other situations in which stressors require a less immediate response. One example is when you know you have to get an assignment done by the following day and feel psychologically stressed (or even distressed!) as a result. This stress response is important because it makes you feel

KEY TERMS

Stress: a state of psychological and physical tension produced, according to the transactional model, when there is a mismatch between the perceived demands of a situation (the stressor[s]) and the individual's perceived ability to cope. The consequent state of tension can be adaptive (eustress) or maladaptive (distress).

Stressor: any factor that can trigger the stress response. Stressors are examples of individual differences, as different people respond differently to different stressors, such as exam revision. Stressors may be major life changes or daily hassles, and may be environmental or in the workplace.

The stress response is important for survival. An animal that does not feel stress when being pursued by a predator is not likely to survive because it does not become mobilised to respond.

physiologically aroused, and this should increase your motivation and concentration. However, as we will see, there are times when the stress response has the opposite effect.

Role of the Autonomic Nervous System

In order to understand stress as a bodily response, we first need to understand the physiology of arousal (the response to stress). This basically involves the **autonomic nervous system (ANS)**. Your nervous system is divided into two main sub-systems:

- The **central nervous system (CNS)**: the brain and the spinal cord.
- The **peripheral nervous system (PNS)**: all the other cells in the body.

The PNS is further subdivided into:

- The somatic nervous system concerned with voluntary movements of skeletal muscles (those attached to our bones).
- The autonomic nervous system concerned with involuntary movements of non-skeletal muscles (e.g. those of the heart).

The ANS is a largely *automatic* or self-regulating system, which means it responds with little or no conscious thought on your part. It is concerned with many vital functions such as breathing and digestion.

Sympathetic and parasympathetic systems

The ANS has two general functions: to activate internal organs and to save energy. These two functions are represented by what are called "branches" of the ANS:

- The **sympathetic branch** activates internal organs in situations needing energy and arousal, such as for "fight or flight". The sympathetic nervous system produces increased heart rate, reduced activity within the stomach, pupil dilation or expansion, and relaxation of the bronchi of the lungs.
- The **parasympathetic branch** is involved when the body is trying to conserve and store resources. It monitors the relaxed state, and promotes digestion and **metabolism**. The parasympathetic nervous system produces *opposite* effects to the sympathetic nervous system. Thus, it produces decreased heart rate, increased activity within the stomach, pupil contraction, and constriction of the bronchi of the lungs.

The sympathetic and parasympathetic nervous systems often operate in opposition (antagonistically) to each other. For example, heart rate will tend to be high if there is more sympathetic nervous activity but low if parasympathetic activity is greater. Sometimes, however, the two systems need to work cooperatively to achieve a goal. For example, consider sex in the male. Parasympathetic activity is need to obtain an erection, whereas sympathetic activity is needed for ejaculation.

Endocrine system

The ANS achieves its effects via the **endocrine system**, which consists of various ductless glands. Most importantly, the endocrine glands secrete or release **hormones** into the bloodstream—these hormones control ANS activity.

Activities of the autonomic nervous system	
Sympathetic branch	**Parasympathetic branch**
Increased heart rate	Decreased heart rate
Reduced activity within the stomach	Increased activity within the stomach
Saliva production is inhibited (mouth feels dry)	Saliva production increased to aid digestion
Pupil dilation or expansion	Pupil contraction
Relaxation of the bronchi of the lungs	Constriction of the bronchi of the lungs
Glucose is released	Glucose is stored

Nervous system	Endocrine system
• Consists of nerve cells	• Consists of ductless glands
• Acts by transmitting nerve impulses	• Acts by release of hormones
• Acts rapidly	• Acts slowly
• Direct control	• Indirect control
• Specific localised effects of neurotransmitters	• Hormones spread around the body
• Short-lived effects	• Hormones remain in the blood for some time

Hormones can have dramatic effects on our behaviour and emotions, especially stress, which can be regarded in part as an emotional reaction to stressors. Most hormones are slow acting because they are carried around the body relatively slowly by the bloodstream. The effects of hormones last for some time but typically gradually diminish as the situation becomes less stressful.

Homeostasis

The body's internal environment generally remains almost constant in spite of large changes in the external environment. This "steady state" or **homeostasis** is the result of ANS activity and is a fundamental part of the stress response. When an individual is placed under stress, the body strives to return to its normal steady state as soon as possible. The normal body state is controlled by the parasympathetic branch storing and conserving energy. The sympathetic branch produces arousal, which is necessary to deal with emergences.

The take-home message is as follows: we strive for a *balance* between parasympathetic and sympathetic activity. Stress is often experienced when this balance can't be achieved.

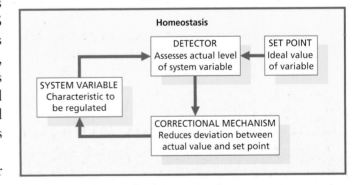

The Body's Response to Stress

It is now time to focus more directly on the ways in which the body responds to stressors, which are events imposing demands on us. It is of key importance to note that stress (our reaction to a

KEY TERMS

Endocrine system: a system of a number of ductless glands located throughout the body that produce the body's chemical messengers, called **hormones**.
Hormones: chemical substances that are produced by one tissue before proceeding via the bloodstream to a second tissue.
Homeostasis: the process of maintaining a reasonably constant internal environment.

See *AS Level Psychology Online* for interactive exercises on this chapter.

stressor) involves an immediate shock response, which is followed by a countershock response. The first or shock response involves the **sympatho-medullary pathway** and depends on what is often called the sympathetic adrenal medullary system (SAM). In what follows, we will use the two terms interchangeably. In contrast, the second or countershock response involves the pituitary–adrenal system or hypothalamic–pituitary–adrenocortical axis (HPA). We will consider each of these systems in turn.

Sympatho-medullary pathway: Sympathetic adrenal medullary system

The initial response to shock involves the sympatho-medullary pathway or sympathetic adrenal medullary system (SAM). In essence, activity in the sympathetic branch of the autonomic nervous system stimulates the adrenal medulla, which forms part of the **adrenal glands**. The adrenal medulla secretes [releases] the hormones **adrenaline** and **noradrenaline** (Americans call these epinephrine and norepinephrine, respectively). Hormones are chemical substances that are produced by one tissue and then travel via the bloodstream to a second tissue. These hormones lead to increased arousal of the sympathetic nervous system and reduced activity in the parasympathetic nervous system.

The measurement of stress

One way to measure stress is to use a lie detector. A lie detector, or more properly a "polygraph", is a machine used to tell if an individual is telling the truth. The machine measures a person's heart rate, blood pressure, breathing rate, and galvanic skin response (GSR). GSR tells us the extent to which your skin can conduct an electrical current because, when you sweat, the conductivity of your skin increases. These are all indicators of arousal of the sympathetic branch of the ANS. When a person is lying, their stress levels are elevated and so is their sympathetic arousal.

It would be nice if we could detect the difference between truth and lies so easily. However, people become sympathetically aroused for many reasons, such as fear of being falsely accused or being in a strange place. The polygraph is an excellent detector of nervousness but not of truthfulness. According to Forman and McCauley (1986) about half of all innocent people "fail" a lie detector test. In addition, many criminals are good liars and do not become aroused.

There are other physiological methods of measuring stress, including checking the size of the adrenal gland, which becomes enlarged under prolonged stress, and checking levels of cortisol in the urine.

Heightened activity of the SAM prepares us for "fight or flight". More specifically, there are the following effects: an increase in energy; increased alertness; increased blood flow to the muscles; increased heart and respiration rate; reduced activity in the digestive system; and increased release of clotting factors into the bloodstream to reduce blood loss in the event of injury. Adrenaline and noradrenaline increase the output of the heart, which can cause an increase in blood pressure.

Evaluation

Activity in the sympatho-medullary pathway forms an important part of the stress response. It is an appropriate reaction of the body, because it prepares us for fight or flight. However, such SAM activity is not *only* associated with stress. For example, we have elevated levels of adrenaline and noradrenaline when we are concentrating hard on a task. There is also the issue of how we *perceive* our internal **physiological** state. Sometimes we perceive heightened activity in the SAM as indicating that we are stressed, but sometimes we interpret such activity as meaning that we are excited or stimulated.

Pituitary–adrenal system: Hypothalamic–pituitary–adrenocortical axis

If someone is exposed to any given stressor for several hours or more, activity within the sympatho-medullary pathway or sympathetic adrenal medullary system increasingly uses up bodily resources. As a result, there is a countershock response designed to minimise any damage that might be caused. As mentioned earlier, this countershock response involves the hypothalamic–pituitary–adrenocortical axis (HPA), also known as the **pituitary–adrenal system**. The details of its functioning are discussed below.

The glands of the endocrine system are distributed throughout the body. Most of this system is controlled by the **hypothalamus**. It is a small structure at the base of the brain producing hormones (e.g. corticotrophin-releasing factor or CRF) that stimulate the anterior **pituitary gland**. The anterior pituitary gland releases several hormones. However, the most important one is **adrenocorticotrophic hormone (ACTH)**. ACTH stimulates the adrenal cortex, which forms part of the adrenal glands. The adrenal cortex produces various glucocorticoids, which are hormones having effects on **glucose** metabolism. The key glucocorticoid with respect to stress is **cortisol**, which is sometimes called the "stress hormone" because excess amounts are found in the urine of individuals experiencing stress.

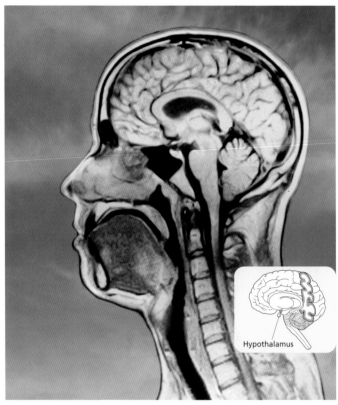

The hypothalamus triggers off the stress response. It is located at the base of the brain.

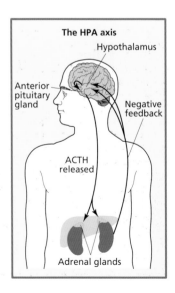

The HPA axis

Hypothalamus

Anterior pituitary gland

Negative feedback

ACTH released

Adrenal glands

KEY TERMS

Physiological: concerning the study of living organisms and their parts.

Pituitary–adrenal system: the second part of the stress response, where the **hypothalamus** activates the pituitary gland, which in turn activates the adrenal cortex to release corticosteroid stress hormones.

Hypothalamus: the part of the brain that integrates the activity of the **autonomic nervous system**. Involved with emotion, stress, motivation, and hunger.

Pituitary gland: an endocrine gland located in the brain. Called the "master gland" because it directs much of the activity of the endocrine system.

Adrenocorticotrophic hormone (ACTH): a hormone produced by the anterior pituitary gland, which stimulates the adrenal cortex.

Glucose: a form of sugar that is one of the main sources of energy for the brain.

Cortisol: a **hormone** produced by the adrenal gland that elevates blood sugar and is important in digestion, especially at times of stress.

EXAM HINT

If you are asked to outline two ways the body responds to stress, you can discuss the dual-stress response:

- The shock response: sympathetic-medullary pathway or sympathetic adrenal medullary system (SAM).
- The countershock response: hypothalamic–pituitary–adrenocortical axis (HPA).

Use examples of how the hormones released on each axis affect the body to ensure you write enough for three marks each, e.g.

- The SAM axis produces adrenaline and noradrenaline, which increases the arousal of the sympathetic nervous system and so leads to increased heart beat, blood pressure, breathing rate, and inhibited digestion.
- The HPA axis produces corticosteroids, which increase glucose release and suppress the immune system.

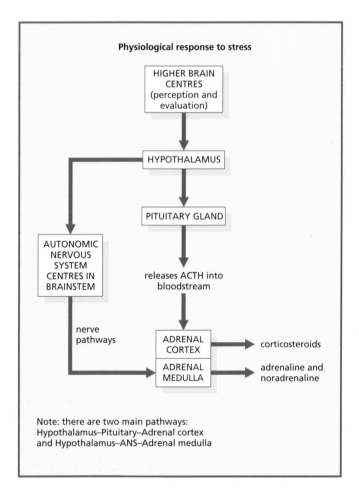

Physiological response to stress

Note: there are two main pathways:
Hypothalamus–Pituitary–Adrenal cortex
and Hypothalamus–ANS–Adrenal medulla

Effects of activity in the pituitary–adrenal system

- Good effect: Cortisol is important for coping with long-term stress, because it maintains a steady supply of fuel.
- Good effects: The secretion of cortisol and other glucocorticoids during the countershock response has various useful functions:
  (i) The glucocorticoids help to conserve glucose for neural tissues.
  (ii) The glucocorticoids elevate or stabilise blood glucose concentrations.
  (iii) The glucocorticoids mobilise protein reserves.
  (iv) The glucocorticoids conserve salts and water.
- Good effect: Cortisol is important in reversing some of the body's initial responses to stress, thus putting bodily systems into a balanced state (Gevirtz, 2000).
- Bad effects: "The blood still has elevated levels of glucose (for energy) and some hormones (including adrenaline and the pituitary hormone ACTH), and the body continues to use its resources at an accelerating rate. Essentially, the organism remains on red alert" (Westen, 1996, p. 427).
- Bad effect: The anti-inflammatory action of glucocorticoids slows wound healing.
- Bad effect: Glucocorticoids suppress the immune system, which has the task of protecting the body against intruders such as viruses and bacteria. When immune responses are low, we are more likely to develop a disease (see Kiecolt-Glaser et al., 1984, 1995) discussed later in the chapter).

Evaluation

As we have seen, the pituitary–adrenal system or HPA is of value in reducing many of the effects of the first or shock response to stress. We can see this by considering people without adrenal glands who can't produce the normal amounts of glucocorticoids. When exposed to a stressor, they must be given additional quantities of glucocorticoid to survive (Tyrell & Baxter, 1981). However, the beneficial effects of HPA activity are achieved at considerable cost, and it cannot continue indefinitely at an elevated level of activity. If the adrenal cortex stops producing glucocorticoids, this eliminates the ability to maintain blood glucose concentrations at the appropriate level.

I have discussed the sympathomedullary pathway or SAM and the pituitary–adrenal system or HPA as if they were different systems. This is basically correct. However, the two systems do *not* operate in complete independence of each other. As Evans (1998, p. 60) pointed out, "At the level of the central nervous system, the crucially important SAM and HPA systems can be considered as one complex: they are as it were the lower limbs of one body."

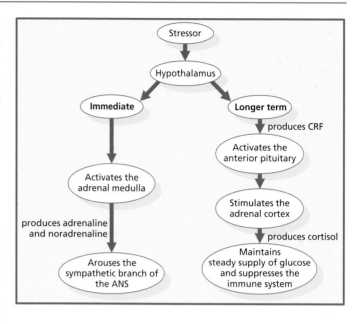

General Adaptation Syndrome

Hans Selye (1936, 1950) was the first person to popularise the term "stress", which had not been used previously as a psychological concept. In 1936, Selye published his first article on the effects of stress, reporting an experiment with rats. When he exposed the rats to "acute nocuous [harmful] agents" (including cold, surgical injury, excessive exercise, severing the spinal cord, or sub-lethal doses of various drugs!), a typical syndrome appeared (discussed below). The same symptoms appeared in response to all of the stimuli. Selye concluded that these symptoms were all due to the general state of what he called "stress".

Selye argued that stress is adaptive in the short term, because it enables us to cope with environmental demands (fight or flight). However, the body's reaction to long-term or prolonged stress can be very damaging. Selye noticed that rats and hospital patients showed a similar pattern of bodily response. He called this pattern the **General Adaptation Syndrome** (GAS), because it represented the body's attempt to cope adaptively with stress. He argued that the GAS consisted of three stages: alarm reaction; resistance; and exhaustion. After the initial alarm reaction, the individual adapts and returns to normal functioning. It is only after prolonged stress that exhaustion occurs. In such extreme cases, stress-related illnesses can develop (see later).

The three stages of the General Adaptation Syndrome (GAS) are described below:

1. *Alarm reaction stage*: This involves increased activity in the sympathetic adrenal medullary system (SAM) and the hypothalamic–pituitary–adrenocortical axis (HPA). However, Selye emphasised the role of the HPA in his account. According to Selye, the alarm reaction develops 6–48 hours after stress (e.g. injury), and includes loss of muscular tone, drop in body temperature, and decrease in size of the spleen and liver.

2. *Resistance stage*: This is the stage of adaptation, and also involves activity in the HPA. The body is adapting or fitting in with the demands of the environment. However, as this stage proceeds, the parasympathetic nervous system (which is involved in energy-storing processes) requires

KEY TERM

General Adaptation Syndrome (GAS): the body's non-specific response to stress that consists of three stages: the alarm reaction, when the body responds with the heightened physiological reactivity of the "fight or flight" response to meet the demands of the stressor; resistance, when the body tries to cope with the stressor and outwardly appears to have returned to normal but inwardly is releasing high levels of stress hormones; and exhaustion, where resources are depleted and the body's defence against disease and illness is decreased.

more careful use of the body's resources in order to cope. The system is being taxed to its limits. This stage is initially marked by an increase in the size of the adrenal glands and a decrease in some pituitary activity, such as the production of growth hormone. If the stress isn't too great (e.g. slight injuries), then the body returns to a near-normal state.

3. *Exhaustion stage*: When stress is very prolonged, the physiological systems used in the previous two stages eventually become ineffective. The initial autonomic nervous system symptoms of arousal re-appear—increased heart rate, sweating, and so on. In extreme cases, the damaged adrenal cortex leads to failure of the parasympathetic system (metabolism and storage of energy) and collapse of the body's immune system. Stress-related diseases (e.g. high blood pressure, asthma, heart disease) become more likely.

? Why do you think the work of Selye has been so influential to the study of stress?

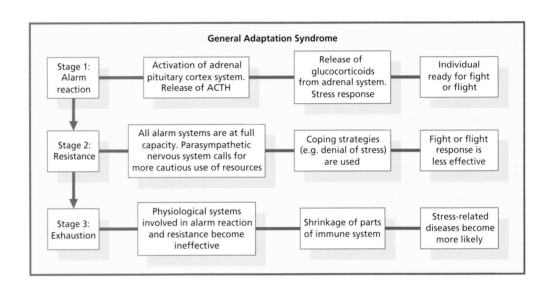

? What are the weaknesses of Selye's work in terms, for example, of the methodology or the ethics?

Evaluation of the General Adaptation Syndrome

Selye correctly focused on what is now called the pituitary–adrenal system or HPA system and on the importance of glucocorticoids. Another key contribution was that he alerted medicine to the importance of stress in disease.

There are several weaknesses with Selye's research. First, he didn't pay much attention to the sympathomedullary pathway or SAM system, and he didn't understand fully the relationship between the HPA and SAM systems. Second, Selye exaggerated when he claimed that stress *always* produces the same physiological pattern. For example, Mason (1975) compared the reactions to stressors varying in how much fear, anger, or uncertainty they created. The various stressors produced *different* patterns of adrenaline, noradrenaline, and cortisol secretion. Third, Selye has been criticised for using non-human animals to support his research on human responses to stress. This may explain why his model exaggerates the importance of physiological factors at the expense of psychological factors such as the role of emotional and cognitive factors in stress. Fourth, Selye assumed that people respond in a *passive* way to stressors. However,

Mason (1975) argued that there is an active process of psychological appraisal when people confront a stressor. Symington et al. (1955) compared the physiological responses of two groups of dying patients, some of whom remained conscious and some of whom were in a coma. There were many more signs of physiological stress in the patients who remained conscious, presumably because they engaged in stressful psychological appraisal of their state.

HOW SCIENCE WORKS: **STRESS AS A BODILY RESPONSE**

Heart rate is one measure that increases in the stress response, and this is easy to monitor by taking the pulse. This can be done manually or by using a pulse monitor, something psychology and biology departments often have in their equipment. This type of data is ratio data and does not depend on opinion, and so it is empirical. The equipment would enable you to measure accurately, and you could record your data methodically, for example by using a simple table.

You could do an experiment on willing participants aged 16 or over, measuring their pulse rate when they are sitting relaxed, and then doing this again when they are in a slightly stressful situation, such as doing a set of puzzles or a simple computer game with a time deadline to create mild stress. Of course, for obvious reasons as well as the BPS Ethical Guidelines, they must not be stressed more than they would be in any normal everyday situation. If you set up this experiment in a special room, a classroom for instance, it would be a laboratory experiment. But if you did it in the participant's own home it would be a field experiment. Each of these situations has strengths and weaknesses, and you could consider, on balance, which situation would give you the most scientific results.

Stress-Related Illness and the Immune System

We now turn to a consideration of the various complex inter-relationships among stress, certain disorders, and the functioning of the immune system. We will start by considering effects of stress on cardiovascular disorders and then focus on other kinds of stress-related illness.

Stress and cardiovascular disorders

It is generally believed that individuals exposed to stress are at greater risk than other people of developing cardiovascular disease. In general terms, it would be expected that chronic stress experienced over a prolonged period of time would pose a much greater risk than acute or short-lasting stress. **Cardiovascular disorders** or diseases consist of all disorders of the heart or blood vessels. Among the conditions covered are coronary artery disease, heart attack, and hypertension (very high blood pressure).

There is good evidence that chronic stress is associated with an increased incidence of cardiovascular disorders and diseases. What mechanisms are involved? The most plausible answer is as follows. The presence of a stressor produces increases in blood pressure and in heart rate, and this happens every time a stressor is experienced. Over time, there is an increase in tonic blood pressure level, and this directly leads on to the development of a cardiovascular disorder or disease.

Findings

Much of the stress experienced by millions of people is work related (see discussion later). Cobb and Rose (1973) found a link between stress and hypertension in

In Cobb and Rose's (1973) study, air traffic controllers were revealed to be suffering from high levels of hypertension, resultant from work-related stress.

a study of men working as air traffic controllers and airmen. The researchers analysed annual medical records and found that hypertension rates were several times higher in the air traffic controllers than in the airmen. In addition, those controllers working in airports with greater traffic density had higher levels of hypertension.

Extreme work-related stress can produce burnout, in which there is emotional exhaustion and physical fatigue (discussed in more detail later). Schuitemaker et al. (2004) carried out a study on adults aged between 41 and 66 years in a Dutch village. Individuals suffering from burnout had three times the risk of fatal and non-fatal heart attacks. Cole et al. (1999) carried out a study on males who didn't suffer from coronary heart disease initially. They were followed up for 12 years. Burnout was associated with a doubling of the risk of coronary heart disease. In their review of the literature on burnout and cardiovascular disease, Melamed et al. (2006) discussed evidence suggesting that burnout causes dysregulation of the pituitary–adrenal system or hypothalamic–pituitary–adrenal axis, increases sympathetic nervous system activation, and impairs immune functions. All of these effects may contribute towards the increased risk that burnout sufferers have of developing cardiovascular disease.

Kuper, Marmot, and Hemingway (2002a) reviewed **prospective studies** concerned with various stress-related factors and coronary heart disease. They were interested in finding out how many studies reported a moderate or strong association between any given factor and coronary heart disease. They considered two main types of studies: (1) those concerned with the risk of developing coronary heart disease in initially healthy participants; (2) those concerned with the outcome for patients suffering from coronary heart disease at the start of the study. There were 13 studies in the former category that focused on work-related stress; of these studies, 10 reported a moderate or strong association with coronary heart disease. There were nine studies on initially healthy participants that considered the effects of inadequate social support; of these, six obtained a moderate or strong association with coronary heart disease. Of the studies on patients with coronary heart disease at the start of the study, two out of four concerned with work-related stress found a moderate or strong association, as did 14 out of 21 concerned with inadequate social support.

Nearly all studies on stress and cardiovascular disorder or disease are limited because individuals weren't *randomly* assigned to the low- and high-stress groups. Consider, for example, studies in which individuals suffering from burnout are compared with individuals not suffering from burnout. Those in the burnout group may have a higher risk of cardiovascular disease because their personalities made them more vulnerable to stress even before they found themselves in a highly stressful work environment. In the absence of random assignment to groups (obviously impossible when comparing burnout and non-burnout groups!), we simply can't be sure that the two groups differ in important ways other than being exposed to (or not exposed to) the chronic stressor of interest.

KEY TERM

Prospective study: a study designed to follow participants forward in time to observe certain events or outcomes (e.g. coronary heart disease) that may happen to them over time.

There is at least a partial solution to the issue raised in the last paragraph. Suppose we consider individuals exposed to a natural disaster such as an earthquake. It is a reasonable assumption that those who were closest to the natural disaster (and so experienced the most stress) are similar in personality and other characteristics to those further away from it. We will consider the Kobe earthquake on 17 January 1995 in which about 6400 people died. The effects of the stress experienced by those exposed to the earthquake were reviewed by Kario et al. (2003). In districts close to the centre of the earthquake there was a 50% increase in heart attacks in the 24 hours after its onset and a 90% increase in sudden death. As Kario et al. pointed out, there were similar increases in cardiovascular deaths following other major earthquakes.

So far we have focused mainly on the effects of stress on fatal and non-fatal heart attacks. However, there are also effects of stress on **hypertension,** a condition in which a person has raised blood pressure consistently for several weeks or more. It is a major risk factor for coronary heart disease. Hypertension is caused by various factors such as obesity, too much salt, coffee (caffeine), or alcohol, lack of exercise, inherited predispositions, and psychosocial factors such as stress, anger, and hostility. As mentioned earlier, Cobb and Rose (1973) produced evidence of a link between stress and hypertension in a study of men working as air traffic controllers and airmen. Hypertension rates were several times higher in the air traffic controllers than in the airmen and controllers working in airports with greater traffic density had higher levels of hypertension.

How does chronic stress lead to cardiovascular disorders? It is generally assumed that exposure to a stressor causes increased heart rate and blood pressure. If these increases occur numerous times over a long period of time, this weakens the cardiovascular system and can produce cardiovascular disorders. It is certainly true that individuals exposed to stressors under laboratory conditions typically show increases in heart rate and blood pressure (reviewed by Schwartz et al., 2003). However, finding that short-lasting stressors in the laboratory influence cardiovascular reactivity does not necessarily mean that individuals suffering from chronic stress will show the same pattern. This issue was addressed by Lucini et al. (2005), who compared individuals with chronic stress with controls. The chronically stressed individuals had higher values of systolic arterial pressure and diastolic arterial pressure than controls and generally impaired autonomic regulation of cardiovascular functions.

The studies we have considered so far have focused on the relationship between some external stressor (e.g. work-related stressors; earthquakes) and cardiovascular disorders. An alternative approach is to consider individual differences in personality. Within this approach, individuals who have a personality that makes them very susceptible to stress are compared with individuals whose personality doesn't make them especially susceptible to stress. Later in the chapter we discuss the Type A personality—individuals with this personality are competitive, impatient, and hostile, and cope poorly with stress. In contrast, Type B individuals are more relaxed and laid-back and cope well with stress. Accordingly, we might expect that Type A individuals would be more likely to have cardiovascular disorders than Type B individuals. The evidence (discussed later in the chapter) is rather inconsistent. Kuper et al. (2002a) discussed 18 studies in which initially healthy Type As and Type Bs were compared. In six of those studies there was a moderate or strong association between being Type A and

? It is normal to have a stress response reaction to a stressor—what change(s) have you noticed in your own body when faced with a stressful situation, such as a test or exam, or being told off? Could you feel your heart beating stronger, your breathing speeding up, or your muscles tensing?

KEY TERM

Hypertension: a condition associated with very high blood pressure.

developing cardiovascular disease. They also discussed 15 studies in which Type A and Type B patients with coronary heart disease were compared. In only two of these studies was there a moderate or strong association between being Type A and having a poor health outcome.

There are very important applications of research on stress and cardiovascular disorders. As Strike and Steptoe (2004, p. 337) pointed out, "Reducing the cardiovascular risk due to psychosocial factors [e.g. chronic stress] will be one of the major health care challenges in the future." They discuss the findings from intervention studies designed to reduce cardiovascular risk, which have so far proved somewhat disappointing.

Evaluation

Individuals exposed to chronic stressors of various kinds are more at risk than other people to cardiovascular disorders or diseases. Some of the most convincing evidence comes from studies on those exposed to natural disasters—the random factor of how close any given individual was to the disaster determines whether he/she is in the high-stress or low-stress group. However, individuals whose personality makes them vulnerable to stress (e.g. Type A individuals) seem to have only a slightly higher risk of cardiovascular disorders than other people. There is also some support for the hypothesis that the main reason why chronic stressors can lead to cardiovascular disorders is because exposure to stressors produces increased cardiovascular reactivity (e.g. increased heart rate).

There are various weaknesses or limitations with the research on stress and cardiovascular disorders:

- In the great majority of studies, participants weren't randomly allocated to the low-stress and high-stress conditions. As a result, the two groups could differ in several ways other than their exposure to chronic stressors. For example, sufferers from burnout may have had more vulnerable personalities and/or poorer physical health than non-sufferers *before* the onset of burnout. However, this is much less of an issue in studies on natural disasters, and the findings from such studies are similar to those from studies on chronic stressors.
- It has been found that several chronic stressors are associated with cardiovascular disorders. However, it is not really clear which stressors have larger or smaller effects on the risk of developing a cardiovascular disorder. It is also not clear precisely *what* it is about any chronic stressor that increases the risk.
- It has been found that chronic stressors increase the probability of an individual developing a wide range of cardiovascular disorders or diseases. More research is needed to clarify which cardiovascular diseases are most and least associated with chronic stress.
- It is generally assumed that stress leads to increased cardiovascular reactivity, and increased cardiovascular reactivity over a long period of time leads to cardiovascular disorder or disease. These assumptions are reasonable. However, most of the research showing an association between stressors and cardiovascular reactivity has used short-lasting laboratory stressors and so may not be very relevant to understanding the effects of chronic stressors in real life.

Stress and other forms of physical illness

Stress has been linked with many other physical illnesses including infectious diseases (e.g. influenza), diabetes, ulcers, asthma, rheumatoid arthritis, and headaches. Much research supports this view. For example, Cohen, Tyrell, and Smith (1991) gave participants nasal drops containing cold viruses. The researchers determined stress levels by recording the number of life changes an individual had recently experienced and also the extent to which they felt "out of control". Both of these factors are associated with increased stress (see Section 13). Those participants with the highest level of stress were almost *twice* as likely to develop colds as those with the lowest level, suggesting a strong link between stress and illness.

There is evidence that stress may be a causal factor in stomach ulcers. The first convincing findings were reported by Brady (1958). Stress often increases the secretion of hydrochloric acid, which plays a role in the development of some ulcers. Stress also weakens the defences of the gastrointestinal tract against this acid, thus permitting gastric ulcers to develop.

Brady (1958) linked high levels of stress to increased hormone production and the development of ulcers. In an early study, he placed monkeys in "restraining chairs" and conditioned them to press a lever. They were given shocks every 20 seconds unless the lever was pressed during the same time period. This study came to an abrupt halt when many of the monkeys died from ulcers caused by raised gastrointestinal hormone levels. The crucial question was whether the ulcers were due to the electric shocks or to the stress. To test this, Brady and his colleagues used yoked controls. One monkey, called the "executive", was responsible for controlling the lever and received the shocks, while at the same time a second monkey received the shocks but had no control over the lever. Thus, only the "executive" monkey had the psychological stress of deciding when to press the lever but both monkeys received the shocks.

After 23 days of 6-hours-on, 6-hours-off schedule, the executive monkey died due to a perforated ulcer. Subsequently, Brady tested the stomachs of executive monkeys on this schedule. He found that stomach acidity was greatest during the rest period. He concluded that it was clearly stress rather than the shocks that created the ulcers. The greatest danger occurred when the sympathetic arousal stopped and the stomach was flooded with digestive hormones, which is a parasympathetic rebound associated with the pituitary–adrenal system.

This study suggested that too much stress at work can lead to ulcers. Brady's findings were supported by Weiner et al. (1957) using army recruits. Prior to basic training, the soldiers were tested and classified on the basis of their release of digestive enzymes as over-secretors or under-secretors. After four months of

> ■ Activity: Cohen et al. (1991) asked participants to list how many of 12 intimate social roles they engaged in, for example as a parent, spouse, child, or close friend. Those who reported fewer than three roles were four times more likely to catch a cold when exposed to the virus under experimental conditions, than those with six or more social roles.
>
> You might try a similar study by asking people to list their social roles and also answer a questionnaire about recent illness (illness can be assessed in terms of, for example, time off work).

? What ethical objections could be raised in connection with this study?

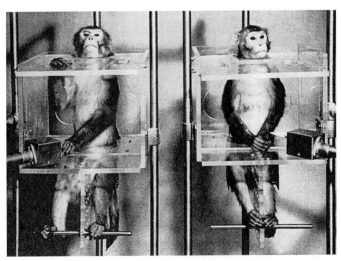

The executive monkey (left) and his yoked control (right). Both animals received shocks at regular intervals but only the executive had control, and only the executive developed the ulcers.

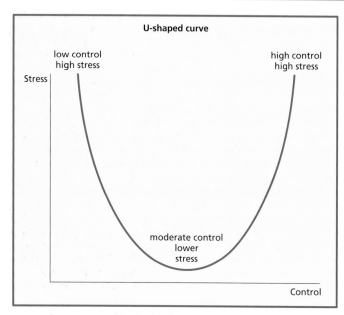

U-shaped curve

low control
high stress

high control
high stress

Stress

moderate control
lower
stress

Control

Research suggests that lack of control may lead to stress (e.g. Cohen et al., 1991) but also that high control may create stress (Brady, 1958). This is a curvilinear realationship as shown in the graph.

stressful training, 14% of the over-secretors had developed ulcers, whereas none of the under-secretors had. This suggests not only that the same principles apply to humans, but also that individual differences may be important in view of the fact that not *all* of the over-secretors developed ulcers.

Evaluation

There is a substantial amount of research showing an association or correlation between stress and several physical illnesses. As with research on stress and cardiovascular disorders, the greatest problem is that participants are typically not *randomly* allocated to low- and high-stress conditions. Consider, for example, the studies by Cohen et al. (1991) and by Weiner et al. (1957). In the former study, those who experienced many life changes may have differed from those with few life changes in personality and/or susceptibility to colds. In the latter study, the groups of under- and over-secretors may have differed in many ways from each other (e.g. general health; physiological functioning) as well as susceptibility to stress.

A second issue is that it remains unclear *which* specific stressors are most strongly associated with any given physical illness. That means that we only have a partial understanding of why and how different stressors influence bodily functioning and physical illness.

Effects of stress on the immune system

It is often believed that stress can cause illness fairly directly by impairing the functioning of the **immune system**. This system is located in various parts of the body including the bone marrow, lymph nodes, tonsils, spleen, appendix, and small intestines. The immune system acts like an army, identifying and killing any intruders to the body. The immune system cells, known as white blood cells or leucocytes, fight any bacteria or viruses that are trying to invade the body. There are various types of leucocytes such as T cells, B cells, and natural killer cells. There is an important distinction between natural immunity and specific immunity (Segerstrom & Miller, 2004). Cells involved in natural immunity (e.g. natural killer cells) are all-purpose cells that can attack **antigens** (foreign bodies) such as viruses and bacteria relatively rapidly. In contrast, cells involved in specific immunity (e.g. T-helper cells; B cells) are much more specific in their effects and take longer to work.

Cells in the immune system have receptors for various chemical substances (hormones and neurotransmitters) involved in the stress response. That means that stress certainly might influence immune system functioning. Evans, Clow, and Hucklebridge (1997, p. 303) argued that we should "think of the immune system as striving to maintain a state of delicate balance". It is plausible to assume that stress can disrupt that "delicate balance".

The field of research in which the links between the immune system and stress and other psychological states are studied is called **psychoneuroimmunology (PNI)**. We will now discuss some of the important findings from PNI.

Findings

One of the first studies to show immunosuppressive effects (something that suppresses the immune system) was carried out by Riley (1981) using mice. Stress was created by placing the mice on a rapidly rotating turntable. Riley measured the lymphocyte count of the mice over a 5-hour period and found a marked decrease. Thus, their immune system response was suppressed, presumably because of the stress caused by sitting on the rotating disc. In a later study, Riley examined the link between stress and tumour growth by implanting cancer cells in mice. One group had 10 minutes of rotation per hour for 3 days (high-stress condition), whereas another group had no stress. Tumour growth stopped in the no-stress group presumably because their intact immune systems could control it. In contrast, the "stressed" mice developed large tumours as a result of their low levels of lymphocytes.

Related findings have been found in humans. For example, Schliefer et al. (1983) studied husbands whose wives had breast cancer. The husbands' immune system functioned less well after their wives had died than before. Segerstrom and Miller (2004) analysed the findings from six studies in which the death of a spouse was the stressor. Overall, losing a spouse was associated with a highly significant reduction in the effectiveness of natural killer cells within the immune system.

By the early 1980s, it was generally accepted that stress can make people more vulnerable to physical illness and psychological disorders. However, there wasn't much evidence concerning *how* stress had these effects. Kiecolt-Glaser et al. (1984) addressed this issue in a study using a naturally occurring stressful situation with which you will be familiar (perhaps too familiar!)—examinations. Blood samples were taken from medical students 1 month before their final examinations and again on the first day of those examinations. Natural killer cell activity *decreased* between the two samples, suggesting that stress is associated with a *reduced* response of the immune system.

Kiecolt-Glaser et al. (1984) also obtained information about psychiatric symptoms, loneliness, and life events on both sampling occasions. They did this because some theories suggest that all of these factors are associated with increased levels of stress. Immune responses were especially weak in those students who felt most lonely, as well as in those experiencing stressful life events or psychiatric symptoms such as depression or **anxiety**. This study suggested that stress could produce a lowered immune response. In addition, several other psychological factors (e.g. psychiatric symptoms; life events) were also associated with impaired functioning of the immune system.

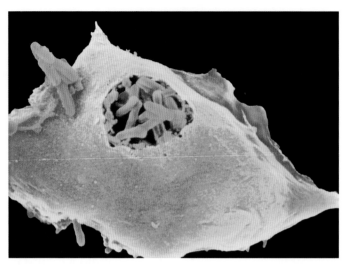

Like some monster in a movie, some cells of the immune system kill "invaders" by engulfing them. In the photograph a macrophage cell is engulfing M. Tuberculosis bacteria.

KEY TERMS

Psychoneuroimmunology (PNI): the study of the effects of both stress and other psychological factors on the immune system.

Anxiety: a normal emotion similar to nervousness, worry, or apprehension, but if excessive it can interfere with everyday life and might then be judged an anxiety disorder.

? This was a natural experiment. What are the advantages and disadvantages of such research?

Further evidence was reported by Kiecolt-Glaser et al. (1995). They tested the hypothesis that a psychological stressor (looking after a relative with Alzheimer's disease) can cause damage to the immune system. It was decided to use slowing of wound healing as a measure of immune system damage. The experimental group consisted of women looking after a relative with Alzheimer's disease, and the control group consisted of women matched in age and family income with the caregivers. The caregivers (who had on average been looking after their relative for almost 8 years) scored much higher than the control women on a perceived stress scale. The functioning of the immune system was studied by creating a small wound on the forearm close to the elbow. The time taken for the wound to heal was assessed by photographing the wound regularly and by observing the response to hydrogen peroxide (an absence of foaming indicated healing).

What did Kiecolt-Glaser et al. (1995) find? The healing time for the caregivers averaged 48.7 days, which was significantly longer than the average of 39.3 days for the control women. In addition, the caregivers had a larger average wound size than the controls, especially during the first few days after the wound had been created. Analysis of the blood collected from the participants revealed that the caregivers produced significantly less interleukin-1β than controls under certain conditions. This may be important because interleukin-1β seems to play a role in speeding up wound healing.

? How well do you feel these results would generalise to all humans?

A strength of the Kiecolt-Glaser et al. (1995) study is that they created the same wound in all the participants, so they could observe effects of stress on the immune system in a controlled way. An application of their findings is that it may assist in developing ways of speeding recovery from surgery. However, there are some weaknesses. Caregivers and controls may have differed in ways other than the level of psychological stress—for example, more caregivers were on medication, and this may have affected their immune system. The role of interleukin-1β in wound healing is somewhat speculative, and Kiecolt-Glaser et al. had no *direct* evidence that it was relevant. There were only 13 participants in each group, and so the study needs to be repeated with a larger sample. In fact, very similar findings were reported by Marucha, Kiecolt-Glaser, and Favagehi (1998). A small wound was created on the hard palate of dental students both 3 days before a major examination and during the summer vacation. Wound healing took 40% longer on average when the students were stressed (i.e. shortly before an examination). Note that stress impaired wound healing even though the stress experienced by the students would have been much less than that experienced by the caregivers in the study by Kiecolt-Glaser et al. (1995).

See *AS Level Psychology Online* for stimulus material relating to this classic study.

We have seen convincing evidence that long-term stressors can impair the functioning of the immune system. However, as Segerstrom and Miller (2004) pointed out, it wouldn't make any sense in evolutionary terms if humans were designed so that even short-term stressors impaired the immune system's functioning. An adaptive response would be for short-term stressors to be associated with enhanced functioning of at least some aspects of the immune system. As mentioned earlier, we need to distinguish between natural immunity and specific immunity. The cells involved in natural immunity have much more general effects than those involved in specific immunity. In addition, the former cells produce effects faster than the latter cells.

Segerstrom and Miller (2004) used meta-analysis to clarify the precise effects of stressors on the immune system. Their key findings were as follows:

- Short-lived stressors (e.g. public speaking) produce *increased* natural immunity (e.g. increased availability of natural killer cells) but don't alter specific immunity.
- Stressful event sequences involving loss of a spouse produce a reduction in natural immunity (e.g. reduced effectiveness of natural killer cells).
- Stressful event sequences involving disasters produce small increases in natural and specific immunity.
- Life events are associated with significant reductions in natural and specific immunity in individuals over 55 years of age. However, life events aren't associated with changes in the immunity system in those under 55.

Segerstrom and Miller (2004) found that short-lived stressors, such as public speaking, increase the availability of natural killer cells.

The take-home message from the very thorough review of Segerstrom and Miller (2004) is as follows: the precise effects of stressors on the immune system depend much more than is generally thought on the specific nature and duration of the stressor.

The focus of nearly all the research on chronic stress and the immune system has been on the notion that stress causes immune suppression. However, there is recent evidence suggesting that what actually happens is more complex than that. Robles, Glaser, and Kiecolt-Glaser (2005) pointed out that the immune system is responsible for producing inflammatory responses that are of great usefulness in resolving infections and in repairing tissue that has been damaged. If chronic stress simply causes immune suppression, we would predict that it would suppress these inflammatory responses. In fact, chronic stress typically leads to an *increase* in inflammatory responses (Robles et al., 2005).

Evaluation

There is good evidence that stress produces changes in the immune system, most of which involve immune suppression. It has become clear that the precise effects of stress on the immune system depend on factors such as whether the stressor is short term or long term, the age of the person involved, and the type of immunity (specific immunity vs natural immunity). There are important practical applications of the research. Basic knowledge about the stressors that impair the immune system and the ways in which they impair it can be used by health professionals and others to anticipate possible problems (e.g. after surgery) and to provide appropriate interventions.

There are several weaknesses and limitations with research on stress and the immune system:

- We know that chronic stress can affect the immune system and can also increase the probability of certain illnesses. However, we still don't know the extent to which the effects of stress on susceptibility to disease depend on changes within the immune system. Bear in mind that stress could be associated with increased probability of various physical illnesses because stressed individuals may have unhealthy lifestyles (e.g. increased smoking and drinking).
- Related to the first point, the functioning of the immune system in many (or even most) stressed individuals is within the normal range (Bachen, Cohen, & Marsland, 1997). When the effects on the immune system are limited, it seems

unlikely that there would be much of an increase in an individual's chances of developing, say, coronary heart disease.

- The immune system is extremely complex, and so it very hard to assess the quality of an individual's immune system. As a result, it is a gross oversimplification to say that stress impairs immune system functioning simply because there are effects of stress on certain small parts of the immune system. For example, Robles et al. (2005) reported that chronic stress *enhanced* some aspects of immune system functioning.

SECTION SUMMARY

What is stress?

❖ Stress is an innate, defensive response to situations that threaten survival.
❖ The bodily response to stress can be explained by looking at:
  - The role of the autonomic nervous system
  - The pituitary–adrenal system or hypothalamic–pituitary–adrenocortical axis
❖ However, the beneficial effects of activity in this system (described below) are achieved at much cost, and it cannot continue indefinitely at an elevated level of activity.
❖ Continued stress can deplete our resources and lead to illness.

The autonomic nervous system (ANS)

❖ The ANS is concerned with involuntary movements and vital bodily functions and is automatic.
❖ It is divided into two branches:
  1. The sympathetic branch, which activates internal organs for flight or fight.
  2. The parasympathetic branch, which conserves energy and promotes metabolism.
❖ These two branches often operate in opposition to each other and maintain homeostasis.
❖ The ANS achieves its effects via the endocrine system, which produces hormones.
❖ In stress situations, the immediate shock response arouses the sympathetic branch (specifically, the sympathomedullary system or sympathetic adrenal medullary system), which prepares the individual for flight or fight.
❖ This is followed by the countershock response, which is designed to minimise any damage caused by the shock response. It involves the pituitary–adrenal system or hypothalamic–pituitary–adrenocortical axis and seeks to return the body to its parasympathetic state.

Sympathomedullary pathway or sympathetic adrenal medullary system

❖ This pathway or system produces an increase in energy and increased alertness in response to a stressor.
❖ It is also associated with increased levels of adrenaline and noradrenaline.
❖ Activity in this pathway or system is sometimes interpreted as indicating stress and sometimes as indicating stimulation.

Pituitary–adrenal system or hypothalamic–pituitary–adrenocortical axis

❖ The pituitary–adrenal system or hypothalamic–pituitary–adrenocortical axis governs the stress response in that:
  1. The hypothalamus directs ANS activity via the corticotrophic releasing factor (CRF).
  2. CRF stimulates the anterior pituitary and this triggers the release of hormones in the endocrine system (a group of ductless glands).

3. The pituitary hormone ACTH stimulates the adrenal cortex, which produces adrenaline and noradrenaline.

4. Both of these hormones are released as a response to stress, and they then create sympathetic arousal (including raised heart rate and sweating).

5. The adrenal cortex also releases hormones such as cortisol producing parasympathetic activity such as suppression of the immune system.

❖ Selye proposed the General Adaptation Syndrome, a model of how the stress response adapts physiological systems to a stressor.

❖ It has three stages:

1. alarm reaction;

2. resistance;

3. exhaustion.

❖ Eventually, resources become depleted and illness ensues.

❖ Selye's model highlighted the importance of stress in illness. However, Selye was wrong in assuming that stress always produces the same physiological pattern, and he almost ignored the sympathetic adrenal medullary system.

General Adaptation Syndrome

❖ Cardiovascular disorders include coronary heart disease, heart attack, and hypertension.

❖ Burnout greatly increases the risk of coronary heart disease by causing dysregulation of the hypothalamic–pituitary–adrenal axis, increasing sympathetic nervous system activation, and impairing immune functioning.

❖ It is hard to evaluate most of the studies because individuals weren't randomly assigned to low- and high-stress groups. However, exposure to natural disasters (e.g. earthquakes) is fairly random, and there are strong associations between stress experienced and subsequent cardiovascular disorders.

❖ Laboratory studies have shown that short-lasting stressors cause increased cardiovascular reactivity. It is often assumed that cardiovascular disorders occur when stress leads to long-term increased cardiovascular reactivity, but strong evidence is lacking.

Stress and cardiovascular disorders

❖ Stress is associated with numerous physical illnesses including diabetes, ulcers, headaches, and arthritis.

❖ It is often difficult to interpret the findings because the participants weren't allocated at random to low- and high-stress conditions.

❖ It remains unclear which specific stressors are most strongly associated with any given physical illness.

Stress and other forms of physical illness

❖ Stress may cause illness by affecting the functioning of the immune system (the activity of lymphocytes, natural killer cells, and endorphins). The field that investigates this is called psychoneuroimmunology.

❖ The evidence indicates that stressful event sequences involving loss of a spouse reduce natural immunity, and that life events reduce natural and specific immunity in people over 55 years of age.

❖ Life events are not associated with changes in the immunity system in individuals under 55. In addition, short-lived stressors produce increased natural immunity but have no effect on specific immunity.

Stress-related illness and the immune system

❖ The extent to which chronic stress increases the probability of certain illnesses because of changes within the immune system is still unclear.

❖ The immune system is very complex, and so it is generally oversimplified to claim that stress has impaired the immune system when all that has been found is that some small part of that system has been adversely affected.

SECTION 13
STRESS IN EVERYDAY LIFE

One of the major ways of considering stress is to examine the factors that affect how much stress we experience. In this section we will consider some of the most important stressors: life events or changes; daily hassles; workplace stress; and personality factors.

In addition to noting many sources of stress (i.e. stressors), we should also consider that there are many different responses to stress. At the start of the last section we considered Selye's definition of stress: "the nonspecific response of the body to any demand". However, this definition suggests that there is only *one* kind of stress response, whereas in fact there are *many* responses, e.g. anxiety, depression, anger, and even happiness (Selye call this last form of response "eustress"). The nature of the stress response depends on various other factors—what we might loosely term "the situation". Selye's definition does not consider adequately the different sources of stress and the responses to it.

Cox (1978) proposed a **transactional model** that described stress in terms of an interaction between the individual and his/her environment. Cox argued that stress is experienced when the perceived environmental demands are greater than the individual's ability to cope. The use of the term "transaction" refers to the *interaction* between the individual and the environment.

After we have discussed various stressors in everyday life, we move to a consideration of some of the main ways in which we try to cope with stress. At a very general level, most of the coping approaches we use can be regarded as either emotion focused or problem focused. Finally, we turn to ways of managing stress. These ways include various psychological and physiological methods.

Cox's transactional model can explain why learners find driving stressful whereas experienced drivers don't. The learner has limited ability to meet the demands of handling a car in traffic, which means that the demands of the environment are greater than their perceived ability to cope. For experienced drivers the perceived demands of the environment are less than their perceived ability to cope.

KEY TERM

Transactional model: an explanation for behaviour, which focuses on the interaction between various factors. The transactional model of stress explains stress in terms of the interaction between the demands of the environment and the individual's ability to cope.

Life Changes and Daily Hassles

Imagine a situation that would make you feel very stressed. Most people imagine some major life event such as discovering that you have a serious illness or that a close family member has died. There has been an enormous amount of research devoted to the stressful effects of numerous **life events**. Many life events (especially the most important or severe ones) produce high levels of stress and alterations in the individual's life patterns—these are known as **life changes**. After we have discussed life events and life changes, we will turn to hassles. **Daily hassles** are the minor challenges and interruptions (e.g. arguing with a friend; malfunctioning computer) of everyday life. On average, people experience at least one hassle on about 40% of the days in each week (Almeida, 2005).

Two medical doctors, Holmes and Rahe (1967), were the first to record systematically the effects of life events. They observed that patients often experienced several life events in the months before the onset of illness, and that these life events seemed to be associated with stress and poor health. In particular, these life events could be characterised as involving change from a steady state, such as getting divorced or moving house. Even positive events such as getting married or going on holiday seemed to be associated with stress. Holmes and Rahe suggested that the changes associated with major life events absorb "psychic [mental] energy", leaving less available for other matters such as physical defence against illness.

Holmes and Rahe (1967) needed some method for measuring life events in order to show associations or correlations between life events, stress, and illness. Accordingly, they developed the Social Readjustment Rating Scale (SRRS) by examining 5000 patient records and making a list of 43 life events that seemed to precede illness. Nearly 400 participants rated each item in terms of the amount of stress it produced, and an arbitrary value of 500 was assigned to marriage as a reference point. The results were averaged and divided by 10 to get a measure of the individual events in terms of life change units (LCUs), representing the degree of stress caused by events. Holmes and Rahe found that there was strong agreement on the ratings across different groups (e.g. male vs female; single vs married; black vs white; younger vs older). Thus, it seemed that the SRRS was a valid measure for all types of people.

LIFE EVENTS

Rank	Life Event	Stress Value
1	Death of a spouse	100
2	Divorce	73
3	Marital separation	65
4	Jail term	63
5	Death of a close family member	63
6	Personal injury or illness	53
7	Marriage	50
8	Fired at work	47
9	Marital reconciliation	45
10	Retirement	45
13	Sex difficulties	39
23	Son or daughter leaving	29
38	Change in sleeping habits	16
40	Change in eating habits	15
41	Vacation	13
42	Christmas	12
43	Minor violations of the law	11

Adapted from Holmes, T., & Rahe, R. (1967). The social readjustment rating scale. *Journal of Psychosomatic Research, 11,* 213–218.

The final scale of the SRRS consisted of 43 items or events, some of which are shown in the table above. Total life events scores were calculated by adding up the LCUs for each event ticked on the scale. The evidence from numerous studies using the Social Readjustment Rating Scale (including the study by Holmes & Rahe, 1967) is that people who have experienced events totalling more than 300 LCUs over a period of 1 year are at greater risk than other people for a wide range of physical and mental illnesses. These illnesses include heart attacks, diabetes, TB, asthma, anxiety, and depression (Martin, 1989). However, the associations or correlations between LCUs and susceptibility to any particular illness tend to be rather low, indicating only a weak association between life events and illness.

KEY TERMS

Life events: events that are common to many people, which involve change from a steady state.

Life changes: significant changes in the pattern of life, such as a divorce or a holiday, that require some kind of social readjustment. Each life change has a score and total scores over a year can predict psychological upset.

Daily hassles: the minor challenges and problems experienced in our everyday lives.

Changes can be stressful, even the usually pleasant ones associated with going on holiday.

The notion that the stressful life events we experience can have effects on our physical health is an important one, because it means we shouldn't only look for physical causes of physical illnesses. Several researchers carried out detailed studies to obtain stronger support for the above notion. In a study discussed in detail below, Rahe, Mahan, and Arthur (1970) found a small but significant positive association between LCUs (life change units) and physical illness. Rahe and Arthur (1977) provided support for the findings of Rahe et al. (1970). They found an increase of various psychological illnesses, athletic injuries, physical illness, and even traffic accidents, when LCUs were high.

Rahe et al. (1970) carried out a study on 2500 male US naval personnel over a period of 6 months. The number of life events was assessed using a self-report questionnaire based on the Social Readjustment Rating Scale (SRRS). Each of the 43 life events had assigned to it a value (or life change unit, LCU) based on how much readjustment the event would require. Participants indicated how many of the life events they had experienced in the past 6 months. A total life change unit score (stress score) was calculated for each participant by adding up the LCUs of each life event. A health record was also kept of each participant during the 6-month tour of duty. A correlational analysis was carried out to test the association between total LCUs and incidence of illness.

Rahe et al. (1970) found a significant positive correlation of +0.118 between the total LCU (life change unit) score and illness. In other words, as total LCUs increased so did the incidence of illness. However, the strength of the association or relationship was weak even though it was significant because the sample size was large (2500). Implications include the importance of using stress management techniques when experiencing life events.

Why is the study by Rahe et al. (1970) important? First, it provided some of the first evidence that there is a genuine association between stressful life events and physical illness. Second, the study was an improvement on previous research, because careful records of physical illness were kept over a 6-month period. Third, the fact that physical health was assessed *after* the life events increases the chances that the life events were helping to cause problems with physical health rather than the other way around.

There are various weaknesses with the study by Rahe et al. (1970). First, the correlational method was used, and so cause and effect can't be inferred—causation can only be inferred when an independent variable has been manipulated directly. Thus, we can't conclude that life events cause illness. Second, it is likely that illness helped to cause certain life events rather than life events helping to cause illness. For example, two of the life-event items on the SRRS are change in eating habits and change in sleeping habits—it is perfectly possible that physical illness would produce such changes. Third, the sample was biased because only American men were studied. Thus, the study was ethnocentric (as only one culture was sampled) and androcentric (as only males were sampled). That means that the findings aren't representative of the wider population (e.g. other cultures; women).

See *AS Level Psychology Online* for stimulus material suggesting how to do a variation of this classic study.

Earlier we mentioned the transactional model (Cox, 1978), according to which an individual's level of stress is determined by an *interaction* between environmental events and the individual. What that means is that the impact of a life event (e.g. major financial problem; break-up of a romantic relationship) depends in part on characteristics of the individual experiencing the life event. Kendler, Kuhn, and Prescott (2004) provide a clear example. They found that individuals who had experienced many severe life events during the preceding year were more likely than those experiencing fewer severe life events to have an onset of major depression. This suggests that life events can cause stress-related psychological problems. However, Kendler et al. also found that the effects of life events on the probability of developing major depression depended strongly on each individual's level of **neuroticism**, a personality dimension that relates to the experience of anxiety, tension, and other negative emotions. The impact of severe life events in increasing the probability of developing major depression was substantially greater in those high in neuroticism than in those low in neuroticism. In other words, there was an interaction between life events and neuroticism.

Evaluation of life change research

The Social Readjustment Rating Scale (and the research associated with it) represented a major breakthrough. It is now generally accepted that life events and changes of many kinds influence our psychological well-being and our physical and mental health. These ideas had been proposed previously by other psychologists, but the development of the SRRS by Holmes and Rahe in 1967 led to a huge increase in life-event research. One application of this research would be the development of techniques to minimise the amount of stress and ill health caused by life events. Another application would be to provide training in ways of controlling those life events that can be controlled.

Here are the main weaknesses of research on life events and life changes:

1. The research is correlational. As a result, it isn't clear whether life events have *caused* some stress-related illness or whether it was stress that caused the life events. For example, divorce can cause stress, but someone who is already stressed may be more likely to behave in ways that lead to divorce. Van Os, Park, and Jones (2001) studied life events in individuals low and high in the personality dimension of neuroticism (involving anxiety, depression, and susceptibility to stress). Neuroticism assessed at the age of 16 predicted the number of stressful life events experienced 27 years later! Thus, individuals with a susceptibility to stress have an increased likelihood of experiencing stressful life events.

2. The impact of most life events depends on the precise situation. For example, marital separation may be less stressful for someone who has already established an intimate relationship with another person. Some measures take account of the *context* in which people experience life events. This is the case with the Life Events and Difficulties Schedule (LEDS; see Harris, 1997). For example, consider the life event of losing your job. That is much more likely to cause stress if you have no other source of money and very poor job prospects than if you have a million pounds in the bank and excellent prospects of finding a very good job in the near future. It is important to take subjective interpretations into account— it is not so much the events themselves but their meaning for us that matters. Cohen (1983) developed a "perceived stress scale" to assess this.

Some people who spend a lot of money on the National Lottery have received stress counselling because their failure to win is making them poor; others receive counselling because of the stress associated with winning large sums of money!

KEY TERM

Neuroticism: a personality dimension proposed by H. J. Eysenck; high scorers experience more intense negative emotional states than low scorers.

3. The SRRS contains very diverse kinds of life events. The assumption built into it that desirable life events can cause stress-related illnesses has not attracted much support. The SRRS also tends to muddle together events over which you have some control and those over which you have no control. The latter may be more stressful.

4. The data on life events are typically collected some time after they have occurred. This can cause unreliability—there is evidence that relatively minor life events can be forgotten within a period of a few months, and stressful events exaggerated once an illness diagnosis is made (Martin, 1989).

5. It has often been assumed that almost any serious life event can play a part in causing almost any type of illness. This has led to a relative ignoring of more *specific* effects. For example, Finlay-Jones and Brown (1981) found that anxious patients were more likely than depressed patients to have experienced danger events (involving future threats). On the other hand, depressed patients were more likely to have experienced loss events (involving past losses). It would be useful to have more such studies.

Daily hassles

Why might daily hassles be a better measure of stress than life events?

In our everyday lives, we often become stressed because of the minor daily hassles we encounter. What are the main categories into which our daily hassles and stressors fall? Almeida (2005) found that 37% involved danger (e.g. potential for future loss), 30% involved some kind of loss (e.g. of money), and 27% were frustrations or events outside the individual's control. (In that last category, I must confess to frequently exhibiting "computer rage" when I can't make my computer do what I want it to!) Almeida found that people reported more psychological distress on days when they encountered hassles than on days without hassles. However, college-educated adults had less psychological distress and fewer physical symptoms than less-educated ones in spite of experiencing more daily hassles. Presumably college-educated people have more effective coping strategies at their disposal.

DeLongis et al. (1982) pointed out that most people experience major life events very infrequently whereas they experience daily hassles dozens and dozens of times every year. They also argued that most studies had found very weak correlations or associations between life events and illness. According to DeLongis et al., the frequently occurring daily hassles are more important than the rare life events in determining how stressed we are. This led them to predict that the correlation between hassles and physical illness would be greater than had previously been found for life events.

DeLongis et al. (1982) used a life events scale and their own hassles scale to see which was the better predictor of later health problems. They also considered how "uplifts"—events that make you feel good—affect health. Participants completed four questionnaires once a month for a year:

- Hassles scale (117 hassles such as concerns about weight, rising prices, home maintenance, losing things, crime, and physical appearance).
- Uplifts scale (135 uplifts such as recreation, relations with friends, good weather, job promotion).
- Life events questionnaire (24 major events).
- A health status questionnaire covering overall health status, bodily symptoms, and energy levels.

Almeida (2005) found that 27% of our daily hassles fall into the "outside of our control" category. Daily hassles such as traffic jams epitomise this kind of stressor.

DeLongis et al. (1982) found that both the frequency and intensity of hassles were significantly correlated with impaired overall health status and bodily symptoms. However, daily uplifts had little effect on health. There was no relationship between life events and health during the study, but there was one for the 2 years before the study.

One of the limitations with DeLongis et al.'s (1982) study is that the original sample consisted of people aged over 45. It may be inappropriate to generalise the findings to younger groups. Khan and Patel (1996) found that older people tended to have less severe (and fewer) hassles than younger people.

Another limitation of the study by DeLongis et al. (1982) was that information about hassles and health was only obtained once a month. This approach placed much reliance on the participants' memory and so may have been unreliable. Stone et al. (1987) adopted a preferable approach that placed less reliance on memory. They considered the hassles and desirable events experienced by participants developing a respiratory illness during the 10 days before its onset. These participants had experienced more hassles and fewer desirable events during that period than had control participants who didn't develop a respiratory illness.

It is important to show that daily hassles are associated with adverse effects on physical health. However, it is also important to try to find out more precisely *how* daily hassles affect us. For example, there is evidence that daily hassles are associated with increased levels of cortisol (a stress-related hormone) (Sher, 2004). This may explain some of the effects of daily hassles on physical health. Twisk et al. (1999) found that people in their 20s who experienced increased numbers of daily hassles showed changes in their health-related behaviour. More specifically, they became more likely to smoke but they had more physical activity.

Finally, the effects of daily hassles may depend on individuals' experience of major life events. The number of psychiatric symptoms reported by students experiencing major life events was greater if they also had substantial numbers of daily hassles (Johnson & Sherman, 1997). The implication is that we should consider both daily hassles *and* life events.

Khan and Patel (1996) found that older people tended to have less severe (and fewer) hassles than younger people.

■ **Activity:** You could conduct your own research into the effects of stress and illness using your own daily hassles index. Some examples are given below from an index that was designed specifically for college students. Illness can be assessed by, for example, checking absenteeism or asking people to keep a diary for a short period.

Hassles scale
Assess yourself by indicating how often each item irritates you, by entering a number between 1 and 10 in the box, where 10 = frequently, 5 = sometimes, and 0 = almost never.

Example items:

☐ Parking problems around campus	☐ Careless bike riders
☐ Library too noisy	☐ Too little time
☐ Too little money	☐ Boring teacher
☐ Not enough close friends	☐ Room temperatures
☐ Conflicts with family	☐ Too little sleep
☐ Writing essays	☐ Fixing hair in the morning

Adapted from Schafer, W. (1992), *Stress management for wellness* (2nd Edn.). New York: Harcourt Brace Jovanovich.

Evaluation of research on daily hassles

It has been found in numerous studies that there is an association between daily hassles and physical health. The fact that minor daily hassles are far more common than major life events suggests the importance of establishing the extent to which stress levels and physical health seem to be affected by daily hassles. It is likely to prove fruitful to consider the combined effects of daily hassles and life events on physical and psychological health, as in the study by Johnson and Sherman (1997). Applications of this research include the provision of training in coping strategies to minimise the adverse effects of daily hassles on stress and health combined with providing individuals with an understanding that daily hassles can have more damaging consequences than is often supposed.

The weaknesses of research on daily hassles are similar to those that apply to research on life events. First, we are dealing with correlational data. Second, there are issues to do with individual differences in the meaning or significance of particular occurrences. For example, a traffic jam may sometimes give you time to relax, whereas at other times it seems highly stressful. For this reason, DeLongis, Folkman, and Lazarus (1988) produced a single "Hassles and Uplifts Scale" on which respondents could indicate the strength of a factor either as a hassle or an uplift. Third, most research doesn't really tell us *how* or *why* daily hassles have adverse effects on physical health. Fourth, there has been much confusion about the distinction between daily hassles and chronic or long-lasting stressors (e.g. poor housing; strains of family life; unsatisfying work). Hahn and Smith (1999) presented participants with items from standard questionnaires designed to measure either daily hassles or chronic stressors, and asked them to decide which category each item belonged to. Many of the items allegedly measuring daily hassles were categorised as chronic stressors and vice versa, suggesting that the distinction is unclear.

HOW SCIENCE WORKS: STRESS IN EVERYDAY LIFE
Scientific research often uses a pilot study to check on the methodology—a small-scale trial run of the method and the data collection to see if they work. You could set up a pilot study for a study of daily hassles in your own age group. First you could print out a list of what you think are the 10 most frequent daily hassles, and ask participants to tick those with which they agree, and to add up to 3 that they feel you have missed out. You would then be able to analyse these data to find the 10 most frequent hassles for your sample. This would allow you, as a researcher, to evaluate your original list and modify it if necessary, before carrying out your main research project (using different participants from the pilot study). This is an illustration of good planning for an investigation into a psychological theory, in this instance the daily hassles theory.

See *AS Level Psychology Online* to download a podcast containing an interview with Adrian Furnham on his workplace stress research.

Workplace Stress

Millions of adults attribute their highly stressed state to the demands of their work. This is unsurprising given that most of them spend nearly 2000 hours a year at work. Cartwright and Cooper (1997) estimated that occupational stress costs American businesses more than 200 billion pounds a year. Both the pressures of work and the work environment itself are potential sources of workplace stress.

Clear evidence of the reality of workplace stress was reported by Johansson, Aronsson, and Lindstgroem (1978). They compared two groups of workers in a highly mechanised production industry. One group was identified as high risk because what they did had the following features: repetitive work; machine regulation of the pace of their work; physical constraints; and requirement to attend continuously. In contrast, the low-risk group carried out their work under more flexible conditions. At work, the high-risk group produced higher levels of adrenaline and noradrenaline (both involving activity in the sympathetic nervous system) than did the low-risk group. This suggests that they experienced more need to mobilise their physiological coping resources. This may help to explain why members of the high-risk group had higher levels of absenteeism and more psychosomatic illness (illness problems such as hypertension thought to be influenced by psychological factors).

According to Melamed et al. (2006), "burnout" is characterised by "emotional exhaustion resulting from prolonged exposure to work-related stress".

The effects of work-related stressors include absenteeism, high job turnover, alcohol and drug abuse, and poor work performance. An extreme stress response is **burnout**, which is characterised by "emotional exhaustion, physical fatigue, and cognitive weariness, resulting from prolonged exposure to work-related stress" (Melamed et al., 2006, p. 327). It was estimated that 4–7% of the Dutch working population had severe burnout (Schaufeli & Enzmann, 1998), which suggests that there may be millions of workers in the world suffering from the condition. It is of particular concern that burnout is a condition that often lasts for several years (Melamed et al., 2006) and is difficult to treat. In their review of the research, Melamed et al. concluded that burnout is associated with failures of regulation of the hypothalamic–pituitary–adrenal axis and activation of the sympathetic nervous system. As a result, sufferers from burnout are at high risk of cardiovascular disease (including sudden cardiac death).

The study by Johansson et al. (1978) and research on burnout indicate clearly that workplace stressors can cause high levels of stress and physical illness. However, the high-risk group studied by Johansson et al. and most sufferers from burnout have been exposed to several different workplace stressors. That means that we can't identify clearly *which* workplace stressors are most dangerous in terms of creating stress. We turn now to a consideration of this issue.

Major workplace stressors

What is it about the work environment that makes people stressed? Several work factors can have a negative effect on workers' stress levels. For example, Warr (1996) identified the following nine factors, all of which influence workers' psychological well-being: opportunity for control; availability of money; opportunity for skills use; work demands; variety; physical security; opportunity for interpersonal contact; environmental clarity; and valued social position. Of these factors, opportunity for control or job control is probably the single most important one. Accordingly, we start with that before considering other factors.

Job control

Spector, Dwyer, and Jex (1988) assessed perceived job control in workers. Low levels of control were associated with frustration, anxiety, headaches,

EXAM HINT

If you are asked to outline two everyday sources of stress, you could describe life changes and workplace stressors. Use research evidence in brief to support your answer:

- Life changes: can absorb "psychic energy" and require psychological adjustment. See Holmes and Rahe (1967) on the development of the SRRS, and Rahe et al.'s (1970) finding of a +0.118 correlation between stress and illness in naval officers.
- Workplace stressors: these can include job insecurity, organisational change, interpersonal conflicts, lack of control. See Marmot et al.'s (1997) study on lack of control.

stomach upsets, and visits to the doctor. Ganster, Fox, and Dwyer (2001) studied occupational stress in a 5-year study on nurses. High perceived control at the start of the study predicted less use of medical services and better mental health over the course of the study.

Some of the most convincing evidence that low control at work can cause high levels of stress and physical illness was reported by Marmot et al. (1997). They studied a sample of 10,308 civil servants aged 35–65, of whom 67% were men and 33% women, in a longitudinal study over 3 years. Research methods included questionnaires and observation. Job control (an aspect of workplace stress) was measured both through a self-report survey and by independent assessments of the work environment by personnel managers. Job control was assessed on two occasions 3 years apart. Records were also kept of stress-related illness. A correlational analysis was carried out to test the association between job control and stress-related illness.

There were several important findings. Workers with low job control were *four* times as likely to die of a heart attack as those with high job control. They were also more likely to suffer from other stress-related illnesses such as cancers, strokes, and gastrointestinal disorders. These findings were consistent on both occasions that job control was measured. The association was still significant after other factors such as employment grade, negative attitude to employment, job demands, social support, and risk factors for coronary heart disease had been accounted for.

The findings of Marmot et al. (1997) seem to show that low job control is associated with high stress as indicated by the amount of stress-related illness. In other words, there is a negative correlation between stress-related illness and job control. Implications include the responsibility of employers to address lack of job control as a source of stress and illness. Giving employees more autonomy (freedom) and control might decrease stress-related illness, which in turn would probably increase the efficiency, productivity, and general well-being of the workforce.

There are various weaknesses with the Marmot et al. (1997) study. First, the self-report method is vulnerable to **investigator effects** and **participant reactivity** bias, which occur when participants are aware they are being observed. The participants may have guessed that an association between job control and stress-related illness was being looked for, and so reported low job control if suffering from illness and high job control if not. Similarly, the observations made by the personnel managers could have been biased by an expectancy effect.

Second, weaknesses of the correlational method mean that there was no control over job control as a variable. This makes interpretation difficult because cause and effect can't be inferred—causation can *only* be inferred when an independent variable has been directly manipulated. Thus, we can't say that low job control causes stress-related illness. It is possible that workers whose health is poor are less likely than

KEY TERMS

Investigator effects: the effects of an investigator's expectations on the response of a participant. Sometimes referred to as experimenter expectancy effect.
Participant reactivity: the situation in which an **independent variable** has an effect on participants merely because they know they are being observed.

healthy workers to achieve career success and to have jobs offering good control. The lack of control over the independent variable (i.e. job control) means that other factors (e.g. personality; coping skills) may be involved in the correlation or association.

Third, the jobs performed by those high and low in job control differed in several ways other than simply control. For example, those having high levels of job control generally earn more money, have more interesting jobs, have more opportunity for interpersonal contact, and so on than those having low levels of job control. The researchers tried to take account of some of these factors, but we simply don't know which of these various factors is most closely associated with heart disease.

Effort–reward imbalance

Severe workplace stress can be created when there is **effort–reward imbalance**, in which the rewards provided at work (e.g. salary, social approval, career opportunities) are very low considering the work efforts that are required. Smith et al. (2005) found that effort–reward imbalance was associated with increased symptoms of cardiovascular disease. This seemed to be the case because workers with effort–reward imbalance experienced much more anger than those not experiencing an imbalance.

Kivimäki et al. (2002) carried out a thorough prospective study in which 812 workers were followed up for an average of 25 years. Workers with effort–reward imbalance were twice as likely as other workers to die from cardiovascular disease during the course of the study. They also considered the effects of high job strain (low job control + high work demands). Workers with high job strain were also twice as likely as other workers to die from cardiovascular disease.

Kuper, Singha-Manoux, Siegrist, et al. (2002b) studied effort–reward imbalance among over 10,000 civil servants who were followed up for an average of 11 years. Effort–reward imbalance was associated with several outcomes suggestive of high levels of stress: non-fatal heart attacks; fatal heart attacks; poor physical functioning; and poor mental functioning.

In sum, there is evidence that effort–reward imbalance is an important workplace stressor that can cause various stress symptoms. These include anger, cardiovascular disease, poor physical functioning, and poor mental functioning. The limitations with the findings are as follows. First, the relative importance of high levels of effort and of poor rewards in producing the stress symptoms is unclear. Second, the evidence obtained is basically correlational, and there was no manipulation of the key variable of effort–reward imbalance. As a result, we don't know that high levels of effort–reward imbalance actually caused the various outcomes obtained.

Personality Factors

So far in this chapter we have focused mainly on the ways in which most or all of us respond when stressed. However, a moment's thought indicates that there are substantial individual differences in stress responses. Of the people you know, I imagine some of them exhibit much more stress than others when exposed to stressful situations. Many of these individual differences can be explained with reference to personality. Researchers have identified several personality factors that are relevant, but we will focus on two that seem especially important: **Type A personality** (sometimes known as Type A behaviour pattern) and hardiness.

See *AS Level Psychology Online* for stimulus material relating to Marmot et al.'s (1997) classic study.

> **KEY TERMS**
>
> **Effort–reward imbalance**: a stressful situation in which workers are required to make considerable efforts at work but receive few rewards in terms of salary, career opportunities, and so on in return.
>
> **Type A personality**: in biopsychology, a personality type who is typically impatient, competitive, time pressured, and hostile.

Type A/B

As recently as the 1950s there was very little scientific evidence suggesting that physical illnesses such as heart disease might be influenced by psychological factors. Many people suspected that there was a link between stress and physical illness, but the view in the medical profession was that we should seek physical causes for physical illnesses. It was in this context that two cardiologists (Meyer Friedman and Ray Rosenman) carried out their well-known research to show that heart disease depends on individual differences in vulnerability to stress.

Friedman and Rosenman (1959) argued that there are *two* important personality types:

- Type As are competitive, ambitious, impatient, hostile, restless, and pressured. They possess "extremes of competitive achievement striving, hostility, aggressiveness, and a sense of time urgency" (Matthews, 1988, p. 373).
- Type Bs lack the characteristics of Type As and are generally more relaxed and laid back.

Friedman and Rosenman (1959, 1974) argued that individuals with the Type A personality are more stressed than Type B individuals. As a result, they are more likely to suffer from cardiovascular disorders. Evidence relating to this prediction is discussed shortly.

[?] Bearing in mind the characteristics of a Type A person, what types of careers would most suit such a personality type?

Evidence

Friedman and Rosenman (1974) carried out a long-term study known as the Western Collaborative Group Study. They used a self-selected sample of nearly 3200 Californian men aged between 39 and 59 at the outset of the study. This was a prospective, longitudinal study in which the participants (all of whom were healthy at the start of the study) were assessed over a period of 8½ years. Part one of the study included the Structured Interview and observation to assess

---

CASE STUDY: DON'T LET IT GET YOU DOWN

"Comfort always, cure rarely" is an old medical motto. And it may be nearer the truth than modern medicine would like to admit. Perhaps if patients were less depressed and more optimistic they might be more likely to recover from stressful operations.

In one study of 100 patients about to undergo bone marrow transplants for leukaemia it was found that 13 of the patients were severely depressed. Of these patients 12 had died within a year of the operation (92%) whereas only 61% of the not-depressed died within 2 years of the study.

Other research has looked at the effects of pessimism and found this to be the biggest single predictor of death from a heart attack. 122 men were evaluated for pessimism or optimism at the time they had a heart attack. Eight years later their state of mind was found to correlate with death more highly than any of the other standard risk factors such as damage to the heart, raised blood

pressure, or high cholesterol levels. Of the 25 men who were most pessimistic, 21 had died whereas only 6 of the most optimistic 25 had died.

Peterson, Seligman, and Valliant (1988) studied optimists and pessimists. They suggested that pessimists tended to explain setbacks in their lives as the result of things within their personality that were unchangeable. In contrast, optimists tended to explain setbacks as the result of things arising from situations within their control, but which were not their own fault. Peterson et al. rated a number of Harvard undergraduates for pessimism and optimism on the basis of essays they wrote about their wartime experiences. After an interval of more than 20 years, the pessimists (aged 45) were more likely to be suffering from some chronic disease.

(Adapted from Goleman, 1991.) ∎

personality type and current health status, respectively. Personality type was determined by the amount of impatience, competitiveness, and hostility reported and observed during the Structured Interview and from participants' answers to questions. During the course of the Structured Interview, the interviewer deliberately interrupted the participants and looked for signs of impatience or irritability when they were interrupted. On the basis of the Structured Interview, participants were classified as A1 (Type A), A2 (not fully Type A), X (equal amounts of Type A and Type B), or B (fully type B). Part two of the study was the follow-up 8½ years later when incidence of coronary heart disease was recorded. A correlational analysis was carried out to test the association between Type A/B personality and coronary heart disease.

Of the original sample of 3200 men, 257 had developed coronary heart disease during the 8½ years of the study. Of crucial importance, 70% of those who had developed coronary heart disease had been classified as Type A, which was nearly twice as many as those who had been classified as Type B. This remained the case even when other factors (e.g. blood pressure, smoking, obesity) known to be associated with heart disease were taken into account. Compared to Type Bs, Type As were found to have higher levels of adrenaline and noradrenaline (both associated with stress) and cholesterol.

What can we conclude from the above study? It appears that the Type A personality is fairly strong linked to coronary heart disease. Friedman and Rosenman (1974) concluded that the Type A behaviour pattern increases the individual's experience of stress, which increases physiological reactivity, which in turn increases vulnerability to coronary heart disease. The stress response inhibits digestion, which leads to the higher level of cholesterol in the blood, and this places Type As at risk of coronary heart disease. A major implication is that it is important to reduce the "harmful" Type A characteristics.

The research of Friedman and Rosenman (1974) is still regarded as important for several reasons. First, they provided some of the earliest scientific evidence that the occurrence of a physical illness such as heart disease can depend on individual differences in personality. Second, this study led to a huge amount of research on the effects of stress on the immune system and various physical illnesses. Third, the study persuaded many people to change their lifestyle so as to have healthier and longer lives.

There are various weaknesses with this study by Friedman and Rosenman (1974). First, the notion of assigning everyone in the world to only four categories seems dubious. Second, the Type A behaviour pattern consists of several aspects, and it wasn't clear which of them were the most important in producing vulnerability to coronary heart disease. As a result, the research lacked internal validity, because it didn't measure precisely what was intended. Third, the correlational method was used. There was no manipulation of an independent variable, which means that there was no clear evidence on cause and effect. It may be that, rather than causing physiological reactivity, the Type A behaviour pattern may be a response to heightened physiological reactivity in some individuals. Fourth, as is discussed shortly, it has proved difficult to replicate the findings of this study.

Some clarification concerning which aspect of the Type A personality is most associated with cardiovascular disease was reported by Matthews et al. (1977). They re-analysed the data obtained by Friedman and Rosenman (1974), and

See *AS Level Psychology Online* for stimulus material relating to Friedman and Rosenman's (1974) classic study.

[?] What are the methodological strengths and weaknesses of this study?

[?] Do you think that the study may have affected the lives of the men taking part? How might that be an ethical issue?

EXAM HINT

A question may ask about the effect of personality on stress, in which case you can obviously use Type A or B personality and hardiness. However, bear in mind that the question could be worded so that you are asked to outline factors that modify the effects of stress. The answer is the same!

found that the hostility component of Type A correlated highest with coronary heart disease. This suggested that hostility rather than Type A in general might explain the findings.

Ganster et al. (1991, p. 145) pointed out that it has often been assumed that "chronic elevations of the sympathetic nervous system (in Type As) lead to deterioration of the cardiovascular system". They put their participants into stressful situations and recorded various physiological measures such as blood pressure and heart rate. Only the hostility component of Type A was associated with high levels of physiological reactivity. These findings, when combined with those of Matthews et al. (1977), suggest that high levels of hostility produce increased activity within the sympathetic nervous system, and this plays a role in the development of coronary heart disease.

The findings of Friedman and Rosenman (1974) were confirmed in the Framingham Heart Study (Haynes et al., 1980). This was a large-scale longitudinal study involving both men and women. However, some researchers have failed to find any relationship between Type A and coronary heart disease. This has led some psychologists to doubt the importance of the Type A behaviour pattern as a factor in causing heart disease. However, Miller et al. (1991) reviewed the literature. They found that many of the negative findings were obtained in studies using self-report measures of Type A behaviour, which may assess Type A inaccurately. Studies using the Structured Interview (which was used by Friedman & Rosenman, 1974) with initially healthy populations reported a mean correlation of +0.33 between Type A behaviour and coronary heart disease. This correlation suggests there is a moderate association or relationship between the two variables.

The relationship or association between type A and coronary heart disease may be becoming smaller as time goes by. Myrtek (2001) reported the findings from meta-analyses including studies published after Miller et al.'s (1991) review. The correlation between Type A and coronary heart disease was very small, as was that between hostility and coronary heart disease. One possibility is that the wide publicity given to the dangers of Type A behaviour have led many Type A individuals to adopt healthy lifestyles (Amelang & Schmidt-Rathjens, 2003).

An important application of the findings on Type A and coronary heart disease is devising interventions that will reduce its harmful effects. De Leon, Powell, and Kaplan (1986) reported on the Recurrent Coronary Prevention Project, which aimed to modify Type A behaviour and so reduce coronary heart disease in participants who had experienced a heart attack. At a 5-year follow-up, those participants who had taken part in a behaviour modification were 44% less likely to have had another heart attack than those who received counselling or no treatment. In addition, they exhibited less Type A behaviour and were less angry and depressed.

Evaluation

Research on Type A and coronary heart disease has been incredibly influential in three ways. First, it has led researchers to consider seriously the relationship between individual differences in personality on the one hand and stress-related symptoms on the other hand. Second, it has led to a broader interest in the effects of stress on physical illness. Third, it has definitely had an effect on the lifestyle adopted by many people. Most people nowadays are aware that components of Type A such as hostility and being excessively motivated can be bad for you.

Do you think there are likely to be cultural differences in the prevalence of Type A and B individuals (i.e. between individualistic and collectivistic cultures)?

The main weaknesses of research on Type A and coronary heart disease are as follows:

- It is clearly oversimplified to assign everyone in the world to a very limited number of categories. The great majority of people are not strongly either Type A or Type B, so the findings apply mainly to a minority of individuals.
- The Type A construct is too broad and consists of a number of somewhat separate components. There is evidence that the hostility component is the most important one, but that is not certain.
- The central weakness with research in this area is that it is correlational in nature. That means that we can't be sure that the relationship between Type A and coronary heart disease occurs because Type A *causes* coronary heart disease. For example, people's hostility may increase when their physical health begins to deteriorate (e.g. in the early stages of heart disease). However, the key point is that we can't rule out alternative explanations of the findings.
- The relationship or association between Type A and coronary heart disease seems to be becoming weaker as time goes by. The optimistic point of view is that this change reflects increasing efforts by Type As to lead healthier lifestyles. The pessimistic point of view is that, with a few exceptions such as Friedman and Rosenman's (1974) Western Collaborative Group Study, the relationship was never very strong.

Hardiness

Kobasa (1979) argued that people differ considerably in their ability to cope with stressors. She used the term **hardiness** to describe a cluster of **traits** possessed by those people best able to cope with stress. According to Kobasa, "hardy" individuals have the following characteristics (the three Cs):

- *Commitment*: They are more involved in what they do and have a direction in life. They find meaning in their work and personal relationships.
- *Challenge*: They view potentially stressful situations as a challenge and an opportunity rather than as a problem or a threat.
- *Control*: They have a stronger sense than other people of personal control. They feel they can influence events in their lives.

Kobasa (1979) argued that hardy individuals experience less stress than other people and as a result are healthier and less inclined to suffer from various physical illnesses. This might show itself in terms of **direct effects**, meaning that there are negative relationships between hardiness on the one hand and stress and physical illness on the other hand. Kobasa also claimed that hardiness has a **buffering effect** on physical illness—that means that hardy individuals cope better than non-hardy ones as the level of stress increases; in other words, they are more resistant to the adverse effects of stress.

> **KEY TERMS**
>
> **Hardiness**: a cluster of traits possessed by those people best able to cope with stress.
> **Trait**: a characteristic distinguishing a particular individual.
> **Direct effect**: occurs when there is a significant relationship or correlation between personality and some other measure (e.g. stress; physical health).
> **Buffering effect**: occurs when a personality characteristic (e.g. **hardiness**) helps to protect or buffer the individual from the adverse effects of stress.

Hardy individuals are less likely to use avoidance coping strategies (such as drinking alcohol) than their less hardy counterparts.

Gentry and Kobasa (1984) developed the ideas of Kobasa (1979), arguing that coping strategies are important in account for the effects of hardiness on health. They made two main assumptions:

1. Hardy individuals encountering stressful life events use more approach coping strategies (e.g. problem solving and planning) and fewer avoidance coping strategies (e.g. denial, becoming angry, drinking alcohol) than non-hardy individuals.
2. Hardy individuals' pattern of coping means that they experience less stress than non-hardy individuals, and also have fewer symptoms of illness.

Evidence

Kobasa (1979) obtained support for her theory in a study on highly stressed male business executives. She divided them into two groups: those who became sick after stressful life events and those who did not. They key finding was that those who didn't suffer from illness were on average more hardy than those who did. Kobasa et al. (1985) carried out a study on male business executives high in stressful events. The three hardiness components (commitment, challenge, control) were assessed and compared against illness scores both at that time and 1 year later. On both occasions, the level and probability of illness were lower for hardy individuals than for non-hardy ones.

Crowley, Hayslip, and Hobdy (2003) studied the effects of hardiness on adjustment among individuals who had either lost their job or whose youngest child had left home. These life events were selected because they differed in terms of predictability. The evidence indicated that job loss was more stressful than the youngest child leaving home. However, there were beneficial effects of hardiness on positive emotions and life satisfaction with respect to both life events, suggesting that hardy individuals can cope better than non-hardy ones with predictable and unpredictable life events.

According to Gentry and Kobasa (1984), hardy individuals are more likely than non-hardy ones to use approach coping strategies such as problem solving. They are less likely than non-hardy individuals to use avoidance coping strategies such as denial or becoming angry. These predictions have been supported several times (e.g. Kobasa et al., 1982; Soderstrom et al., 2000).

One of the most thorough tests of the ideas of Kobasa (1979) and Gentry and Kobasa (1984) was conducted by Klag and Bradley (2004). They assessed hardiness, neuroticism (a personality dimension relating to the experience of negative emotions), stress, symptoms of illness, and approach and avoidance coping in male and female staff at an Australian university. Here are their main findings:

1. Hardiness correlated negatively with stress and physical illness for men and women separately. The same negative correlations were found for both men and women for two of the components of hardiness (commitment and control) but not for the third one (challenge). These are direct effects.
2. *All* of the significant effects listed in (1) became non-significant when neuroticism was controlled for. That indicates that the effects in (1) were due more to neuroticism than to hardiness itself.
3. The adverse effects of stress on physical health were significantly less on hardy men than on non-hardy ones before and after controlling for neuroticism. This is a buffering effect.

4. There was *no* buffering effect of hardiness on the effects of stress on physical health in women.
5. The beneficial effects of hardiness on physical health did *not* depend on the tendency for hardy individuals to use more approach coping strategies and fewer avoidance coping strategies than non-hardy ones.

A major application of research on hardiness is on training programmes designed to increase individuals' hardiness. Khoshaba and Maddi (2001) provided such a training programme known as HardiTraining. It consists of a workbook that includes a focus on hardy coping, on ways to increase social support, and self-care exercises. HardiTraining typically involves several weekly sessions, with trainees carrying out planned exercises to enhance hardy attitudes and behaviour, and then reporting back on their successes and failures. There is evidence (reviewed by Maddi, 2007) that HardiTraining increases job satisfaction, improves health in working adults, and decreases the proportion of workers categorised as having high blood pressure.

Evaluation

There is reasonably good evidence supporting various assumptions made by Kobasa (1979) and by Gentry and Kobasa (1984). First, hardy individuals generally exhibit lower levels of stress and physical illness than non-hardy ones (direct effects). Second, hardiness has been found to buffer the effects of stress on physical illness, at least in men (Klag & Bradley, 2004). Third, hardy individuals make more use of approach coping strategies and less use of avoidance coping strategies than non-hardy ones. Fourth, the success of HardiTraining suggests that the ingredients of hardiness are genuinely important in promoting good psychological and physical health.

Here are the major weaknesses of the hardiness approach to stress:

- Most researchers focus on general hardiness based on combining scores for its three components of commitment, control, and challenge. However, challenge is often irrelevant (e.g. Klag & Bradley, 2004).
- Most of the research findings were based only on male participants. When studies include women as well as men (e.g. Klag & Bradley, 2004), it often turns out that the effects of hardiness are much weaker in women than in men.
- There is a moderate negative correlation or association between hardiness and neuroticism. As a result, it is possible that some of the findings that have been attributed to hardiness are actually due to neuroticism. More specifically, the adverse effects of low hardiness on health may reflect the high levels of neuroticism of non-hardy individuals. As we have seen, some of the apparent effects of hardiness on health disappear when neuroticism is controlled for (Klag & Bradley, 2004).
- There is the important issue that the evidence is essentially correlational and so it is not appropriate to conclude that hardiness has caused certain outcomes. It is possible that the positive correlations between hardiness and physical health occur in part because unhealthy individuals become less hardy as a result. Against that, the success of HardiTraining suggests that manipulations designed to enhance hardiness can be effective.

How would you rate your own hardiness?

Emotion-Focused and Problem-Focused Approaches to Coping with Stress

Stress research is important because it can help us to manage our own stress reactions and those of others. This is an increasingly important application at a time when everyone seems to feel over-stressed. In our everyday lives we spend much of our time trying to find ways of resolving stressful situations and finding ways of feeling less stressed. The term "coping strategies" is used to refer to this process. In this section we will consider two of the main coping strategies. One of these (**problem-focused coping**) involves engaging in purposeful action to improve the situation and reduce stress. The other (**emotion-focused coping**) involves efforts to reduce the negative emotions caused by being stressed.

As we have seen in this chapter, most people have to deal with various stressors. Some of these stressors are major life events (e.g. death of a close relative), others are long-lasting or chronic stressors (e.g. poverty), and still others are more minor (but still stressful) daily hassles that we experience on average on 40% of days in a week (Almeida, 2005).

How do we respond to these stressors? Of key importance, we typically engage in coping. Coping is a broad term that refers to the behavioural and psychological efforts that an individual uses in order to try to reduce, master, or tolerate stressful events. According to Folkman and Moskowitz (2004, p. 745), coping can be defined as "the thoughts and behaviours used to manage the internal and external demands of situations that are appraised as stressful". Most research on coping has been concerned with how people cope with events that have occurred or are occurring in the present. However, coping can also involve preparing to deal with possible future stressors (e.g. increasing your financial and/or social resources).

As you might imagine, individuals use many different forms of coping (coping strategies) to deal with stress. Some idea of the range of coping strategies can be seen if we consider the work of Skinner et al. (2003). They used information from 100 different assessments of coping to identify the most important coping strategies. Their analyses suggested that there are several "families" of coping—each family is a broad category and contains within it several specific coping strategies. Altogether, Skinner et al. identified nine major families of coping:

1. *Problem solving*: various activities including instrumental action, direct action, decision making, and planning.
2. *Support seeking*: comfort seeking, help seeking, and spiritual support.
3. *Escape*: avoidance, disengagement, and denial.
4. *Distraction*: acceptance and engaging in alternative pleasurable activities (e.g. exercise; reading).
5. *Positive cognitive restructuring*: positive thinking and self-encouragement.
6. *Rumination*: intrusive thoughts, negative thinking, self-blame, and worry.
7. *Helplessness*: inaction, passivity, giving up, and pessimism.
8. *Social withdrawal*: social isolation, avoiding others, and emotional withdrawal.
9. *Emotional regulation*: emotional expression, emotional control, and relaxation.

In spite of the large number of coping strategies, many researchers (e.g. Lazarus & Folkman, 1984; Monat & Lazarus, 1991) have argued that problem-focused

---

? How do you cope with stress? What percentage of your coping is problem-focused and what percentage is emotion-focused?

KEY TERMS

Problem-focused coping: involves the use of thoughts or actions to act directly on a stressful situation. It can involve seeking information, purposeful or direct action, decision making, planning, and so on. Generally of most use when the situation can potentially be changed for the better.

Emotion-focused coping: involves the use of thoughts or actions to act directly on the emotional state experienced when faced by a stressful situation. It can involve distraction, avoidance of the situation, seeking social support, emotional control, distancing (detaching oneself from the situation), positive reappraisal of the situation, and relaxation. Generally of most use when the situation probably cannot be changed for the better.

Coping: efforts to deal with demanding and stressful situations by using strategies designed to master the situation, reduce the demands, or tolerate the situation; many coping strategies can be classified as problem-focused or emotion-focused.

coping and emotion-focused coping are of particular general importance. Here are definitions of these two forms of coping:

> Speaking of an alcoholic's two sons: "One was a teetotaller and the other was a drunk. When asked to explain their drinking habits, both replied, 'With a father like that, what do you expect?' This illustrates perhaps the most important moral we can draw from stress research: that it is not what we face but how we face it that matters . . . We do have limited control over ourselves. It is the exercise of this control, or the lack of it, that can decide whether we are made or broken by the stress of life." (Selye, 1980, p.143)

Problem-focused coping refers to efforts to improve the troubled person–environment relationship by changing things, for example, by seeking information about what to do, by holding back from impulsive and premature actions, and by confronting the person or persons responsible for one's difficulty (Monat & Lazarus (1991, p. 6).

Emotion-focused or palliative (relieving without curing) coping refers to thoughts or actions whose goal is to relieve the emotional impact of stress. These are apt to be mainly palliative in the sense that such strategies of coping do not actually alter the threatening or damaging conditions, but make the person feel better (Monat & Lazarus, 1991, p. 6).

Do you think that problem-focused or emotion-focused coping is the more effective strategy? As Lazarus (1993, p. 238) pointed out, "Of the two functions of coping, problem-focused and emotion-focused, there is a strong tendency in western values to venerate [worship] the former and distrust the latter. Taking action against problems rather than re-appraising the relational meaning seems more desirable." We will see how much support there is for that last statement in our discussion of findings involving these coping strategies.

We can identify two major theoretical positions concerning the effectiveness of problem-focused and emotion-focused coping (Zakowski et al., 2001). First, there is the main-effects hypothesis, according to which problem-focused coping is generally more effective than emotion-focused coping in reducing stress. Second, there is the goodness-of-fit hypothesis. According to this hypothesis it is preferable to use problem-focused coping when the stressor is perceived as controllable but to use emotion-focused coping when the stressor is perceived as uncontrollable. Stress levels will be lower when there is a good fit between stressor and coping strategy (problem-focused coping with controllable stressors and emotion-focused coping with uncontrollable stressors) than when there is a poor fit (problem-focused coping with uncontrollable stressors and emotion-focused coping with controllable stressors).

Findings

Folkman et al. (1986) obtained evidence favouring the use of problem-focused coping. Participants indicated the coping strategies they had used to handle stressful events. They were also asked to rate the extent to which the outcome had been satisfactory. Planned problem solving tended to be associated with satisfactory outcomes. In contrast, emotion-focused coping such as confrontative coping (e.g. expressing anger) and distancing (trying to forget about the problem) were associated with unsatisfactory outcomes.

Problem-focused coping sometimes produces a mixture of positive *and* negative outcomes. For example, Wu et al. (1993) found that doctors who accepted responsibility for their own mistakes made constructive changes to their work habits, which was clearly a positive outcome. In addition, however, they experienced more distress (a negative outcome) at the same time.

Many stressful situations change over time. That means that the best coping strategy may also change. For example, Folkman and Lazarus (1985) found

Avoidance-oriented strategy

students faced by a stressful examination sought information (i.e. problem-focused coping) before the examination. Afterwards, while waiting to hear the results, the students typically made use of emotion-focused coping (e.g. forgetting all about the examination).

In a different context, denial (emotion-focused coping) is dangerous when an individual has just suffered a heart attack, but is useful during the subsequent period of hospitalisation (Levine et al., 1987). Denial becomes dangerous again if it continues for a long period of time after discharge from hospital (Levine et al., 1987).

We turn now to evidence relevant to the main-effects and goodness-of-fit hypotheses mentioned earlier. Penley, Tomaka, and Wiebe (2002) obtained support for the main-effects hypothesis. They carried out various meta-analyses on the association between coping strategies and health-related outcomes. Problem-focused coping was positively correlated or associated with physical and psychological health outcomes. In contrast, several forms of emotion-focused coping (e.g. confrontative coping; distancing; avoidance; wishful thinking) were all negatively correlated with physical and psychological health outcomes.

In spite of the findings of Penley et al. (2002), there are many studies in which problem-focused coping was less effective than emotion-focused coping. This is especially the case when there is little or nothing that the individual can do to improve matters. For example, Collins et al. (1983) studied people living close to Three Mile Island shortly after a major nuclear incident. Those using problem-focused coping were significantly more distressed than those using emotion-focused coping.

Some support for the goodness-of-fit hypothesis was reported by Zakowski et al. (2001). They found that participants were more likely to use problem-focused coping when the stressor was perceived as controllable rather than uncontrollable, whereas emotion-focused coping was used more often when the stressor was perceived as uncontrollable. The effects of emotion-focused coping on behavioural and self-report measures of stress was as predicted by the goodness-of-fit hypothesis—this form of coping was more effective with an uncontrollable stressor. However, the effects of problem-focused coping on stress did not vary as a function of stressor controllability, which is inconsistent with the hypothesis.

Forsythe and Compas (1987) studied the effectiveness of problem-focused and emotion-focused coping when dealing with major life events. With respect to major life events, there was support for the goodness-of-fit hypothesis. Individuals had fewer psychological symptoms when problem-focused coping was applied to controllable events and when emotion-focused coping was applied to uncontrollable events than when there was no fit between coping strategy and stressor controllability.

■ Activity: Find out from other people which kind of coping strategy they prefer to use. You might try to devise a suitable questionnaire to collect these data. Are there differences in people who, say, prefer a problem-focused strategy to an emotion-focused one? Do people who experience a lot of stress prefer one strategy more than another, in comparison with people who experience very little stress? Do people vary their strategies depending on the situation? What kinds of strategies are best for which situations?

Evaluation

Problem-focused coping and emotion-focused coping are both generally applicable across a wide range of stressful situations. These two forms of coping are both sufficiently broad that they incorporate the great majority of the specific coping strategies that individuals use in stressful situations. Another strength of this approach to coping is that many of the findings can be accounted for on the goodness-of-fit hypothesis. As predicted by that hypothesis, stressed individuals tend to use problem-focused coping with controllable stressors and emotion-focused coping with uncontrollable ones. In addition, problem-focused coping is generally more effective than emotion-focused coping in reducing stress with controllable stressors, whereas the opposite is the case with uncontrollable ones.

There are various weaknesses with the approach emphasising the importance of problem-focused and emotion-focused coping:

- In spite of the importance of these two types of coping, there are many other types of coping that individuals often use. As we saw earlier, the evidence suggests that there are at least nine families of coping (Skinner et al., 2003).
- It is often implied that problem-focused and emotion-focused coping are quite separate from each other. That isn't really the case. As Skinner et al. (2003, p. 227) pointed out, "Most ways of coping can serve both functions and thus could fit into both categories. For example, making a plan not only guides problem solving but also calms emotion."
- In order to be confident that any differences between problem-focused and emotion-focused coping are genuinely due to the coping strategies themselves, we would have to assign individuals *randomly* to the two forms of coping. In fact, what typically happens is that individuals *choose* which form of coping to use and so the data are basically correlational. This can complicate interpretation of the findings. For example, we saw earlier that hardy individuals tend to use problem-focused coping whereas non-hardy ones tend to use emotion-focused coping (Kobasa, 1982; Soderstrom et al., 2000). That poses the issue of deciding whether any differences between forms of coping are due to the coping strategies themselves or to differences in hardiness.
- Coping strategies are typically assessed by self-report questionnaires. The coping strategies used by individuals in real-life situations may well differ from those they claim to use on questionnaires.
- Self-report questionnaires of coping often focus on individuals' preferred coping strategies in a very *general* way. Such a broad assessment may not allow us to predict how individuals will respond to a *specific* stressor.

Psychological and Physiological Methods of Stress Management

There are many systematic approaches to reducing stress levels that involve **stress management**. We will be considering some of the main approaches in this section. One way of classifying these approaches is in terms of whether they are psychological or physiological methods. **Psychological approaches to stress management** include the following:

1. Cognitive Behavioural Therapy: This approach (discussed in more detail in Chapter 8) has mostly been applied to mental disorders but is also highly

> **KEY TERMS**
>
> **Stress management**: the attempt to cope with stress by reducing the stress response, either by psychological methods (e.g. **Cognitive Behavioural Therapy**) or physiological ones (e.g. drugs).
> **Psychological approaches to stress management**: techniques to control cognitive, social, and emotional responses to stress by attempting to address underlying causes of stress, such as faulty thinking, and inappropriate emotional responses, by changing the person's perceptions of the stressor or their own control.

Research into stress management leads to ways in which we can deal with our stress.

relevant to the management of stress. The key assumption of this approach is that it is desirable to change the behaviour *and* the thoughts or beliefs of anyone who has a mental disorder or is extremely stressed. In this section we will focus on one particular form of Cognitive Behavioural Therapy known as stress inoculation training. It was introduced by Meichenbaum (1977), and has proved an effective way of reducing stress.

Physiological approaches to stress management include the following:

1. *Beta blockers*: These are drugs that decrease heart rate and reduce peripheral blood pressure. They are often used to treat performance anxiety and some of the anxiety disorders.
2. *Anti-anxiety drugs*: These are drugs such as the benzodiazepines and buspirone that are used in the treatment of stress and anxiety.

Cognitive Behavioural Therapy

Psychologists and psychiatrists have developed a huge assortment of psychological treatments for abnormal behaviours, some of which are designed especially for stress disorders. **Cognitive therapy** is especially appropriate for dealing with stress (see Chapter 8). In general terms, its aim is to replace negative and irrational thoughts (e.g. "I am totally incompetent") with positive and rational ones (e.g. "I can achieve many things if I try hard enough"). The assumption lying behind the cognitive approach is that it is the way we think about life's problems and stressors that is **maladaptive**. If we can be trained to restructure our thinking and self-beliefs, the problem itself may simply disappear. As is discussed in Chapter 8, cognitive therapy has increasingly developed into **Cognitive Behavioural Therapy**, in which there is also an emphasis on changing behaviour in desirable ways.

The most important approach to stress management based on Cognitive Behavioural Therapy was devised by Meichenbaum (1977, 1985). He argued that we should use Cognitive Behavioural Therapy before a person becomes very anxious or depressed rather than afterwards. This led him to develop **stress inoculation training**, which is a form of coping and self-management. Stress inoculation training has proved effective, and we will discuss what it is and why it is successful.

There are three main phases in stress inoculation training:

1. *Assessment*: The therapist discusses the nature of the problem with the individual, and asks the individual's views on how to eliminate it.
2. *Stress reduction techniques*: The individual learns various techniques for reducing stress such as relaxation and self-instruction by using coping self-statements (see box opposite for examples). This stage mostly resembles cognitive therapy.

3. *Application and follow-through*: The individual imagines using the stress reduction techniques learned in the second phase in difficult situations and/or engages in role play of such situations with the therapist. After that, he/she starts to use the techniques in real-life situations. This involves changes in behaviour.

In sum, stress inoculation training is very much a form of Cognitive Behavioural Therapy because phase 2 involves changing thoughts and beliefs and phase 3 emphasises changes in behaviour.

Findings

Meichenbaum (1977) compared his stress inoculation training approach with systematic desensitisation (see Chapter 8), in which patients are gradually introduced to the object of their fear while being taught how to relax. In order to compare the two forms of therapy, he treated individuals suffering from both snake phobia and rat phobia. Each patient received treatment for only one phobia involving use of one of the two methods. Both forms of treatment were effective in reducing or eliminating the phobia that was treated, and stress inoculation training also greatly reduced the non-treated phobia. This suggested that self-instruction easily generalises to new situations, which would make it more useful than very specific forms of treatment.

Much of the research on stress inoculation training has used self-report measures to assess the effects of stress inoculation training on stress levels. With such measures, there is always the danger that participants may exaggerate the beneficial effects of the training they have received. One way of reducing this problem is to focus on other kinds of measures. For example, there are several studies in which cortisol levels were assessed—cortisol is often known as the "stress hormone" (see earlier in the chapter). Most of these studies have been concerned with chronic stressors. For example, Antoni et al. (2000) found that stress inoculation training reduced cortisol output and distress symptoms in HIV-positive gay men. Cruess et al. (1999) found that women with breast cancer who received stress inoculation training after surgery had lower levels of evening cortisol levels than those not receiving such training.

Gaab et al. (2003) decided to study the effects of stress inoculation training on cortisol levels when healthy participants were exposed to a brief or acute stressor.

Examples of coping self-statements used in Meichenbaum's stress inoculation training

Preparing for a stressful situation:
What is it you have to do?
You can develop a plan to deal with it.
Just think about what you can do. That's better than getting anxious.
Maybe what you think is anxiety is in fact eagerness to confront it.

Confronting and handling a stressful situation:
Just "psych" yourself up—you can meet this challenge.
One step at a time, you can handle the situation.
This tenseness can be an ally, a cue to cope.
Relax; you're in control. Take a slow, deep breath. Ah, good.

Coping with the feeling of being overwhelmed:
When fear comes, just pause.
Keep the focus on the present; what is it you have to do?
You should expect your fear to rise.
It's not the worst thing that can happen.

Reinforcing self-statements:
It wasn't as bad as you expected.
Wait until you tell your therapist about this.
You made more out of the fear than it was worth.
You did it!

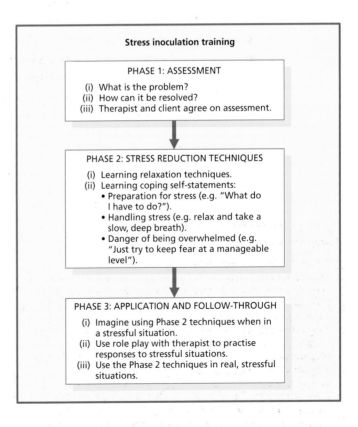

Stress inoculation training

PHASE 1: ASSESSMENT

(i) What is the problem?
(ii) How can it be resolved?
(iii) Therapist and client agree on assessment.

PHASE 2: STRESS REDUCTION TECHNIQUES

(i) Learning relaxation techniques.
(ii) Learning coping self-statements:
• Preparation for stress (e.g. "What do I have to do?").
• Handling stress (e.g. relax and take a slow, deep breath).
• Danger of being overwhelmed (e.g. "Just try to keep fear at a manageable level").

PHASE 3: APPLICATION AND FOLLOW-THROUGH

(i) Imagine using Phase 2 techniques when in a stressful situation.
(ii) Use role play with therapist to practise responses to stressful situations.
(iii) Use the Phase 2 techniques in real, stressful situations.

All of the participants were exposed to a stressful situation (a simulated job interview followed by a mental arithmetic task). Half of them had received stress inoculation training beforehand. The most important finding was that participants who had received stress inoculation training had significantly small cortisol responses in the stressful situation than did controls. In addition, they also appraised the situation as less stressful and showed more competence in dealing with it.

We have seen that stress inoculation training is typically more effective in reducing stress levels than no training at all. However, it would be a more stringent test of the effectiveness of stress inoculation training to compare it against another form of training/treatment known to be effective. Precisely this was done by Foa et al. (1999) in a study on treatment for female clients with post-traumatic stress disorder (PTSD) who had been the victims of sexual or non-sexual assault. They compared the effects of stress inoculation training (including relaxation techniques, guided self-dialogue, and role play) with those of prolonged exposure (in which the traumatic event was repeatedly relived in imagination). The two forms of therapy reduced the severity of PTSD and depression comparably. However, prolonged exposure was more effective than stress inoculation training in reducing anxiety and improving social adjustment.

Lee et al. (2002) compared the effectiveness of stress inoculation training with prolonged exposure to eye-movement desensitisation and reprocessing in the treatment of PTSD. The two treatments were equally effective in reducing scores on global PTSD measures at the end of therapy. However, at follow-up, stress inoculation training was associated with smaller gains than the alternative treatment on all measures.

Evaluation

Stress inoculation training has various strengths. First, it is a form of Cognitive Behavioural Therapy, and that form of therapy is generally regarded as being at least as effective as any other form of therapy (see Chapter 8). Second, stress inoculation training has proved effective in reducing stress levels with stressors that are chronic (long-lasting) or acute (short-lasting). It is impressive that this form of training has proved effective in treating so many kinds of stress from the very serious stress experienced by sufferers from PTSD to the mild stress of short laboratory tasks. Third, stress inoculation training has been shown to reduce stress significantly whether stress is assessed by self-report measures or by cortisol responses. Fourth, it is a valuable idea to provide training in stress management before stress levels become so high that the individual develops a mental disorder.

Listed below are the main limitations of stress inoculation training:

- There are several components to stress inoculation training. As a result, it is often hard to know which component or components are mainly responsible for reducing stress levels. As is often the case with Cognitive Behavioural Therapy, it is unclear

---

EXAM HINT

If you choose to discuss psychological approaches think about the following positive points:

- They are less invasive and do not have side effects.
- The psychological techniques may tackle causes better than the physiological techniques as faulty cognitions may well be the underlying cause of stress given that perception (a cognitive process) is fundamental to the experience of stress.

However, be aware of the following issues:

- A patient in denial may not benefit much from such an approach as the focusing and assessment require the patient to have a high level of self-insight. So they may work better for some patients than others.
- The techniques require commitment and a belief in the approach to be effective. Failure rates may be due to a lack of motivation or belief in the technique. For example, some people may have difficulty using the self-coping statements, as they may find them ridiculous!

whether the cognitive changes or the behavioural changes are more important in benefiting stressed individuals.

- The effects of stress inoculation training have often been compared against no training or treatment. It could be argued that this makes it too easy for stress inoculation training to appear successful—in fact, almost any form of treatment is likely to outperform no treatment at all!

- When stress inoculation training has been compared against another form of treatment it has generally proved less effective than the other treatment (e.g. Foa et al., 1999; Lee et al., 2002) even though still producing some benefits to those receiving it.

- It would be wrong to assume that *all* the beneficial effects of stress inoculation training on reducing stress are due to specific ingredients or components of the training provided. There is substantial evidence (Stevens et al., 2000) that factors common to most forms of therapy (e.g. therapist warmth; alliance between therapist and client) often play a sizeable role. Thus, it is possible that most of the benefits deriving from use of stress inoculation training owe little or nothing to the specific ingredients incorporated into the training programme.

EXAM HINT

If you are to outline and/or evaluate one method of stress management, you can use either

- drugs (a physiological approach), or
- Cognitive Behaviour Therapy (a psychological approach).

Note that the evaluation for either can be drawn partly from considering what an individual would *not* get by not having the other type of therapy.

Drugs

One of the main ways in which people's level of stress can be reduced is by giving them drugs that reduce stress and anxiety. This is directly related to our understanding of the body's responses to stress (discussed in Section 12). The body produces chemicals (hormones) that create anxiety, which can be countered using other chemical substances (i.e. drugs) that reduce anxiety. Several different types of drugs work via different mechanisms. We will consider two categories of drugs: beta blockers and anti-anxiety drugs.

Beta blockers

Among the drugs used to reduce stress and anxiety are the **beta blockers**, which reduce activity in the sympathetic nervous system. Beta blockers have a direct action on the heart and circulatory system, and so decrease heart rate and lower peripheral blood pressure. Their effects are on the body, and they do not have direct effects on brain activity.

Findings. Beta blockers have proved useful in reducing blood pressure and in treating patients with heart disease. For example, Lau et al. (1992) considered the findings from numerous studies in a meta-analysis (combining data from many studies). They found that beta blockers reduced the risk of death by about 20% in patients suffering from heart disease. Metra et al. (2000) reviewed findings from almost 10,000 patients with heart failure. The use of beta blockers was associated with a highly significant reduction in the number of subsequent heart attacks and mortality.

Beta blockers have been used in the treatment of performance anxiety, and have become increasingly popular in recent years. Much of the research has focused on music performance anxiety (reviewed by Kenny, 2006). Lockwood (1989) found that 27% of orchestral musicians used a beta blocker, and 19% of

KEY TERM

Beta blockers: drugs reducing stress by reducing activity in the sympathetic nervous system.

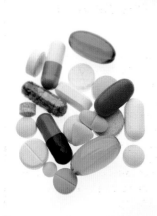

Stress can be treated with anti-anxiety drugs such as Valium that reduce the effects of stress but not the problems that cause it. Such drugs often have undesirable side effects.

? To what extent can patients give fully informed consent to taking medication?

those using beta blockers used the drug every day. Beta blockers are generally preferred to anti-anxiety drugs because they have much less effect on brain functions such as mental alertness and other cognitive functions. Since beta blockers work on the body, they seem to most effective for those musicians reporting mainly bodily symptoms of stress and anxiety (e.g. palpitations, hyperventilation, tremor, sweating palms).

How effective are beta blockers in treating music performance anxiety? It has often been found that they improve performance quality (e.g. Berens & Ostrosky, 1988; Brantigan, Brantigan, & Joseph, 1982). In the study by Brantigan et al. (1982), beta blockers enhanced the quality of musical performance as evaluated by experienced music critics. The drugs seemed to eliminate the bodily symptoms that can impair performance and also eliminated dry mouth. However, other studies have failed to report clear evidence that beta blockers improve judges' ratings of performance quality or reduce self-reported anxiety among singers (Gates et al., 1985).

Performance anxiety is related to social phobia, in which individuals have intense fear of certain social situations that almost always trigger anxiety. The difference is that individuals with social phobia typically fear a much wider range of situations than those with performance anxiety. The evidence suggests that beta blockers have little effect in reducing anxiety in individuals with social phobia (Bruce & Saeed, 1999). This may be because people with social phobia have psychological symptoms (e.g. self-esteem) rather than the bodily symptoms affected by beta blockers.

There are some disadvantages with the use of beta blockers. First, there can be problems with drug withdrawal. Second, there can be various unwanted side effects, including sleep disturbance, muscle fatigue, and gastrointestinal upset.

Anti-anxiety drugs

Drugs can intervene in natural processes by controlling the action of neurotransmitters. **Benzodiazapines** such as Valium and Librium increase the activity of the neurotransmitter GABA. This decreases **serotonin** activity, which in turn reduces arousal. Benzodiazepines are very effective at reducing anxiety, and are used by hundreds of millions of people around the world. These drugs have several strengths. First, they have a rapid onset of action, which means that very high levels of stress and anxiety can be reduced in a short period of time. Second, they are effective with the great majority of people and are generally well tolerated. Third, when used over short periods of time, benzodiazepines rarely produce serious side effects.

In spite of the effectiveness of the benzodiazepines, they can produce several unwanted side effects especially when used long term. Some of these side effects (e.g. drowsiness; feelings of depression; unpredictable interactions with alcohol) are linked to the reduced serotonin levels produced by the drugs. These side effects mean that individuals taking benzodiazepines are more likely to be involved in accidents.

There are two other side effects associated with the long-term use of benzodiazepines (Ashton, 1997). First, many people become dependent on benzodiazepines, and their sudden withdrawal can lead to a return of the original symptoms of intense stress and anxiety. Second, there is the problem of drug escalation—many individuals find that they need to take increasingly large doses of benzodiazepines in order to reduce their levels of stress and anxiety.

There has been controversy concerning the effects of long-term treatment with benzodiazepines on cognitive functioning. As Stewart (2005, p. 9) pointed out, it has been claimed that long-term use of these drugs causes impairment in "visuospatial ability, speed of processing, and verbal learning". On the other hand, it has been argued that any apparent adverse effects on cognitive functioning are only temporary and reflect sedation or inattention. In view of this controversy, Stewart (2005) carried out a meta-analysis including all relevant studies. There was clear evidence that long-term use of benzodiazepines leads to cognitive impairments. Cognitive performance typically improves when benzodiazepines are withdrawn, but it still remains below the level of controls who have never taken benzodiazepines. There is some reassurance in the finding that individuals given benzodiazepines over long periods of time don't show any evidence of brain abnormalities.

A more recent anti-anxiety drug, **buspirone**, offers some advantages over benzodiazepines. It is a serotonin agonist, meaning that it helps or "facilitates" the effects of serotonin. It has proved effective in treating clients with anxiety disorders. In one study (Davidson et al., 1999), buspirone was used with clients suffering from generalised anxiety disorder (a condition involving excessive worrying about major areas of life). Those treated with buspirone showed greater improvement than controls on a scale of clinical global impressions. However, buspirone proved to be less effective than an anti-depressant drug that was administered to other individuals suffering from generalised anxiety disorder.

Buspirone doesn't have the sedative effect of benzodiazepines and there are typically no withdrawal symptoms. In addition, buspirone doesn't have the adverse effects on cognitive functioning found with benzodiazepines. For example, Chamberlain et al. (2007) found that participants who had taken buspirone performed as well as non-drug controls on tests of memory, planning, decision making, and cognitive flexibility. However, buspirone produces other side effects such as headaches and depression (Goa & Ward, 1986).

Evaluation. Anti-anxiety drugs can be very effective at reducing intense feelings of stress and anxiety. However, they don't address the problems that are causing the stress. In that sense, we could say that the use of these drugs is an emotion-focused coping strategy.

As we have seen, anti-anxiety drugs can have unfortunate side effects. The recommendation is that benzodiazepines should generally be limited to short-term use of no more than about 4 weeks (Ashton, 1997), and that they should only be given to individuals with severe anxiety symptoms. In addition, they should be given in the minimal effective dose. Individuals who have become dependent on benzodiazepines should have their dosage reduced gradually. The good news is that about 70% of dependent users of benzodiazepines who are motivated to give them up manage to do so for periods of several years or more.

CASE STUDY: SEROTONIN AND ECSTASY

If you have heard of serotonin, it is probably because you have read articles about the antidepressant Prozac, which increases levels of serotonin in the brain. Less well known is the fact that the ecstatic "rush" experienced by users of the drug Ecstasy is partly a result of a dramatic increase in serotonin levels in the brain.

Ecstasy causes long-term damage because it is thought to kill serotonin receptors. People with low levels of serotonin are thought to suffer from a host of problems including depression, impulsive violence, eating disorders, and sleep problems.

(Taken from Oliver James, 1997, Serotonin: A chemical feel-good factor. *Psychology Review, 4,* 34.) ∎

EXAM HINT

If you choose to discuss physiological approaches remember:

- They generally work better than a psychological approach if the individual is highly stressed and assessment and focusing would be difficult.

If you are asked to discuss psychological methods of stress management remember:

- A key strength is the multi-dimensional approach, e.g. hardiness training and stress inoculation therapy combine cognitive and behavioural approaches.

KEY TERM

Buspirone: a more recent anti-anxiety drug, which increases the production of **serotonin** and has fewer side effects than **benzodiazepines**.

SECTION SUMMARY

Life changes and daily hassles

❖ Holmes and Rahe were the first to record the effects of life events or changes in a systematic way. They developed the Social Readjustment Rating Scale, which has been used to measure life change units.

❖ There is an association between the number and intensity of life changes or events and physical illness. However, this is a correlation and so doesn't prove that life changes cause illness. There is some evidence that individuals with a susceptibility to stress have an increased likelihood of experiencing life changes.

❖ The impact of most life changes depends on the precise situation and on how the changes are interpreted.

❖ The assumption that almost any serious life change can help to cause almost any type of illness is oversimplified.

❖ The frequency and intensity of daily hassles are associated with impaired physical health. Daily hassles can produce increased levels of cortisol and changes in health-related behaviour (e.g. more smoking).

❖ Correlations between daily hassles and physical health don't prove that hassles cause poor physical health.

❖ The distinction between life events or changes and daily hassles is often somewhat unclear.

Workplace stressors

❖ Research on burnout indicates clearly that workplace stressors can cause high levels of stress and physical illness.

❖ Workers with low job control are more likely than those with high job control to die of a heart attack, or to suffer from cancer, strokes, and gastrointestinal disorders. This evidence is basically correlational, and the jobs performed by those high and low in job control differ in several ways other than simply control (e.g. salary; job variety).

❖ Workers with effort–reward imbalance tend to have worse physical health (including cardiovascular disease) than other workers. However, the evidence is only correlational, and the relative importance of high effort levels and poor rewards in producing stress is unclear.

Personality factors

❖ Friedman and Rosenman (1959) argued that Type As (competitive, hostile, driven) suffer more than Type Bs (relaxed, laid back) from cardiovascular disorders. Their evidence supported this argument, but was only correlational in nature.

❖ Matthews et al. (1977) re-analysed Friedman and Rosenman's data, and argued that the hostility component of Type A was of most importance in producing cardiovascular disease.

❖ More recent research has reported much smaller associations between Type A and cardiovascular disorders, possibly because Type As are adopting healthier lifestyles.

❖ Hardy individuals are high in commitment, challenge, and control. According to Gentry and Kobasa (1984), hardy individuals experience less stress than other people because they use approach coping strategies and don't use avoidance coping strategies.

❖ Hardy individuals have lower levels of stress and physical illness than non-hardy ones, and they make more use of approach coping strategies.

- Limitations of hardiness research:
  - the challenge component of hardiness seems to be irrelevant;
  - the effects of hardiness seem to be weaker in women than in men;
  - some of the effects attributed to hardiness are probably due to neuroticism instead;
  - most of the evidence is only correlational, and so doesn't show that hardiness reduces stress and illness.

- Coping refers to behavioural and psychological efforts to reduce, master, or tolerate stressful events.
- Problem-focused coping involves changing things, whereas emotion-focused coping involves relieving the emotional impact of stress.
- According to the goodness-of-fit hypothesis, problem-focused coping is preferable when the stressor is controllable, whereas emotion-focused coping is preferable when it isn't controllable. The evidence generally supports this hypothesis.
- Approaches based on emotion-focused and problem-focused coping have the following limitations:
  - the evidence relating coping strategies to stress is mostly only correlational;
  - problem-focused coping and emotion-focused coping are less separate than is generally assumed;
  - coping strategies are typically assessed by self-report measures that focus on individuals' coping strategies in a very general way—this doesn't really allow us to predict their coping in response to a specific stressor.

Emotion-focused and problem-focused coping

- Cognitive Behavioural Therapy, which involves techniques for changing thoughts, beliefs, and behaviour, has been applied to the management of stress. A particularly important form of Cognitive Behavioural Therapy for stress management is stress inoculation training.
- Stress inoculation training involves three phases: assessment; stress reduction techniques (e.g. relaxation; coping self-statements); and application and follow-through.
- Stress inoculation training has proved effective in treating stress ranging from mild to very serious.
- There are several components to stress inoculation training, and it is hard to know whether the changes in thoughts and beliefs or those in behaviour are more important in reducing stress levels.
- Some of the beneficial effects of stress inoculation training are probably due to factors (e.g. therapist warmth; alliance between therapist and client) owing little or nothing to the specific ingredients of the training.

Cognitive Behavioural Therapy

- Beta blockers decrease heart rate and lower peripheral blood pressure but don't have direct effects on brain activity.
- Beta blockers have been found to reduce performance anxiety and enhance performance. However, they have failed to reduce anxiety levels in people with social phobia.
- Benzodiazepines are very effective at reducing anxiety. They have a rapid onset of action, and have few side effects when used over short periods of time.

Drugs

❖ However, benzodiazepines can produce drowsiness and cause dependence if used over long periods of time.

❖ Buspirone has proved effective in the treatment of anxiety disorders. It doesn't have the sedative effect of the benzodiazepines, but it has side effects including headaches and depression.

> You have reached the end of the chapter on biological psychology. Biological psychology is an approach or perspective in psychology. The material in this chapter has exemplified the way that biological psychologists explain behaviour. They look at behaviour in terms of the way the bodily systems work (for example, nerves and hormones, parts of the brain and bodily organs). This is often regarded as a "reductionist" approach because it reduces complex behaviour and experiences to simpler processes and explanations.

FURTHER READING

There is good coverage of stress research in J. Ogden (2000) *Health psychology: A textbook (2nd. Edn.)* (Buckingham, UK: Open University Press). E.P. Sarafino (1990) *Health psychology* (New York: Wiley & Sons) discusses many aspects of stress and stress management. There is a thorough review of what is known about the effects of different forms of coping in S. Folkman and J.T. Moskowitz (2003) Coping: Pitfalls and promises. *Annual Review of Psychology, 55*, 745–774. Most of the main issues in stress research are discussed in C. Belaise, with contributions by S. Acharya, R.A. Askew, E. Caffo, D.G. Cruess, & K.V. Oxington (2005) *Psychology of stress* (Hauppauge, NY: Nova Biomedical Books). S.C. Segerstrom and G.E. Miller (2004) Psychological stress and the human immune system: A meta-analytic study of 30 years of inquiry. *Psychological Bulletin, 130*, 601–630, provides an excellent analysis of what is known about the effects of psychological stress on the workings of the immune system and on disease.

WEBSITES

http://www.apa.org/monitor/oct07/armor.html
  Workplace stressors: A site describing a special programme that helps soldiers manage stress in combat and deployment better.

http://www.apa.org/monitor/oct06/stress.html
  The stress response: A description of the initial protective function of the response.

http://www.apa.org/releases/religious06.html
  Managing stress: An outline of a research study which suggests that religious beliefs can reduce the harmful effects of stress.

http://www.sciencedaily.com/releases/2007/05/070510194055.htm
> Cognitive therapy and stress: How cognitive therapy can help people who have post-traumatic stress disorder as a result of being victims of terrorism.

http://technology.newscientist.com/channel/tech/mg19626285.800-smilehunting-game-makes-for-happy-workers.html
> Resistance to stress: Discussing how a simple computer game seems to give protection against daily hassles.

http://www.bbc.co.uk/health/interactive_area/assessments_stresstest1.shtml
> Stress test!: Assess your own stress levels, but be aware that this is a guide to one's own stress and not a definitive diagnostic tool!

See Chapter 5 of the revision guide for guidance on revising this chapter for the exam.

REVISION QUESTIONS

The examination questions aim to sample the material in this whole chapter. For advice on how to answer such questions refer to Chapter 1, Section 2.

When you are provided with a stimulus question do not panic if you have not seen that specific question before. Stimulus questions require you to apply your knowledge to a specific scenario. Whilst you may not have seen such a scenario before, if you have revised everything you *will* have the knowledge needed to answer the question.

Question 1
a. Outline **two** ways the body responds to stress. (6 marks)
b. Outline research into the relationship between stress and the immune system. (6 marks)
c. Explain why this research does not establish cause and effect. (4 marks)

Question 2
a. Using your knowledge of personality factors and stress to explain how these can modify the body's response to stress. (6 marks)
b. Outline **one** source of stress. (4 marks)

Question 3
a. Outline **one** psychological approach to stress management. (6 marks)
b. Discuss the use of drugs to manage the negative effects of stress. (8 marks)

Social psychology is an approach or perspective in psychology. "Social" refers to any situation involving two or more members of the same species. Social psychologists are interested in the ways people affect each other. Social psychology differs from sociology in that it places greater emphasis on the individual as a separate entity—sociologists are interested in the structure and functioning of groups, whereas social psychologists look at how these processes influence the individual members of a social group.

SECTION 14
Social influence p. 264

Individuals in groups are often influenced by other members of the group and show conformity to their behaviour. Majority influence (in which the majority influences the minority) is more common than minority influence (in which the minority influences the majority), but the latter has been observed many times. Why do people conform by yielding to both majority and minority influence? To what extent do people behave in ways they believe are expected of them? Individuals show obedience to authority when they (often unthinkingly) follow the orders of authority figures. Why do people show obedience to authority? What are the psychological processes involved in obedience?

Specification content: Types of conformity, including internalisation and compliance. Explanations of why people conform, including informational social influence and normative social influence. Obedience, including Milgram's work and explanation of why people obey.

SECTION 15
Social influence in everyday life p. 296

In spite of much evidence that many people show majority and minority influence and are obedient to authority, some people manage to withstand the social pressures they face. Such individuals are said to show independent behaviour. What kinds of individuals are most likely to behave in an independent fashion?

Specification content: Explanations of independent behaviour, including how people resist pressures to conform and pressures to obey authority. The influence of individual differences on independent behaviour, including locus of control. Implications of research into conformity, obedience, and independence for social change.

SOCIAL PSYCHOLOGY
Social Influence

This chapter explores one very important topic in social psychology—social influence. What we say and how we behave are heavily influenced by other people. They possess useful knowledge about the world, and it is often sensible to pay attention to what they say. In addition, we want to be liked by other people, and to fit into society. As a result, we sometimes hide what we really think, and behave in ways that will earn the approval of others. All these issues relate to **social influence**, which can be defined as "the process whereby attitudes and behaviour are influenced by the real or implied presence of other people" (Hogg & Vaughan, 2005, p. 655).

This chapter examines three of the most common kinds of social influence: conformity produced by majority influence; conformity produced by minority influence; and obedience. **Majority influence** is when a majority within a group changes the expressed attitudes or behaviour of a minority. **Minority influence** is when a minority within a group changes the attitudes or behaviour of the majority. Majority influence and minority influence both involve **conformity**, which can be defined as yielding to group pressures in terms of our expressed attitudes or behaviour. Obedience involves behaving as instructed, usually in response to individual rather than to group pressures. Finally, the chapter considers the reasons why some people are more independent than others in their behaviour. Although most people show some tendency to conform to the wishes of others and show **obedience to authority**, some individuals are much less affected by these social influences towards conformity. The personality (and other) characteristics of those who resist pressures to conform and to obey authority are discussed in this final section.

KEY TERMS

Social influence: how we are influenced by others, either by a group (**majority influence**) or an individual (**minority influence** or **obedience**), to change our behaviour, thinking, and/or attitudes.

Majority influence: occurs when people adopt the behaviour, attitudes, or values of the majority (dominant or largest group) after being exposed to their values or behaviour.

Minority influence: a majority being influenced to accept the beliefs or behaviour of a minority.

Conformity: changes in behaviour and/or attitudes occurring in response to group pressure.

Obedience to authority: behaving as instructed, usually in response to individual rather than group pressure, often in a hierarchy where the instructor is of higher status so the individual feels unable to resist or refuse to obey, though their private opinion is unlikely to change.

SECTION 14
SOCIAL INFLUENCE

Even the most independent of individuals can feel the need to conform under social pressure from peers.

Group decisions can lead people to deny the evidence in front of their eyes. This picture shows Rodney King, victim of a videotaped beating by Los Angeles police officers in 1992. The police officers involved were acquitted.

KEY TERM

Autokinetic effect: a visual illusion where a small spot of light in a darkened room appears to be moving when in fact it is stationary.

Types of Conformity: Majority Influence

Conformity (which typically takes the form of majority influence) can be defined as yielding to group pressures in terms of our expressed attitudes or behaviour, something that nearly all of us do at least some of the time. For example, if all your friends think a film is wonderful, you may pretend to agree with them rather than saying how boring you found the film. Majority influence occurs much more often than most people imagine.

Is majority influence undesirable?

As you read through this section, you may find yourself thinking that majority influence and conformity are undesirable. That is often true. For example, Rodney King (a black man) was assaulted by four Los Angeles police officers. The assault was videotaped by a local resident, and shown in court to the jurors. In spite of the fact that the videotape indicated that Rodney King was a victim of police brutality, the police officers were acquitted. Afterwards, Virginia Loya (one of the jurors) admitted she had changed her vote from guilty to not guilty because of pressures to conform to the views of other jury members.

However, it isn't clear that majority influence and conformity are always undesirable. Majority influence often leads to desirable behaviour. People live together and abide by social rules to facilitate their interactions—think of the rule that you must stop for a red traffic light! We also know that other people possess useful knowledge about the world, and it is often sensible to heed what they say. In addition, most people want to be accepted by other people.

Sherif's study

The first major study of majority influence or conformity was carried out by Muzafer Sherif (1935), who studied the **autokinetic effect**. If we look at a stationary spot of light in a darkened room, very small movements of the eyes make the light seem to move. Participants were tested one at a time, and then in small groups of three. They had to say how much the light seemed to move and in what direction. Each participant rapidly developed his/her own personal norm or standard, which varied considerably between individuals. When three individuals with very different personal norms were put together into a group, they typically produced very similar judgements. In other words, a group norm rapidly replaced the personal norms of the group members, indicating the existence of social influence.

Sherif (1935) also used a condition in which individuals started the experiment in groups of three and were then tested on their own. Once again, a group norm developed within the group. When the group members were then tested on their own, their judgements continued to reflect the influence of the group.

You could argue that Sherif's findings are not particularly surprising. After all, the participants had no way of knowing what the "right" answer was, and so it made sense to take account of the views of others. Solomon Asch (1951, 1956) wondered whether there would be majority influence when the answer was obvious but the majority gave the wrong answer. If so, that would be surprising. Asch's notion that individuals are most likely to give way to pressure when several people are united against them reminds me of the old Spanish saying, "If three people call you an ass, put on a bridle!"

Norms are a set of rules established by the behaviour of a group of people. Conforming to group norms is a part of group membership. At a football game, different people are conforming to different norms—the home team has prescribed behaviours (clothes, songs, slogans), and so has the away team (such as unwritten "rules" for how to behave at an away match).

Asch's (1951) study on majority influence

Asch (1951) was interested in seeing whether a majority can influence a minority even when the situation is unambiguous and the correct answer is obvious. He aimed to find out whether the effects of majority influence, previously found in situations in which the stimulus was ambiguous, are so great that they are still present even when it is apparently obvious that the majority have responded incorrectly.

Asch set up a situation in which (in some of his experiments) seven people all sat looking at a display. In turn, they said out loud which one of three lines A, B, or C was the same length as a given stimulus line X (see illustration on the right). All but one of the participants were confederates of the experimenter, that is, they were behaving as the experimenter had told them to behave beforehand. On some "critical" trials, the confederates were instructed to give the same wrong answer unanimously. The one genuine participant was the last (or the last but one) to offer his/her opinion on each trial. The performance of participants exposed to such group pressure was compared to performance in a control condition in which there were no confederates.

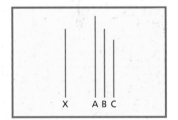

X   A B C

? Asch's participants weren't told the true nature of the study. Was this ethical?

What did Asch (1951) find? On the critical trials on which all the confederates gave the same wrong answer, the genuine participants showed majority influence by also giving the same wrong answer on approximately 37% of trials. We need to compare this figure against the error rate in the control condition (with no group), which was only 0.7%. In other words, participants answered correctly over 99% of the time when there was no social pressure. Many of the participants who gave wrong responses admitted that they had yielded to majority influence because they didn't want to stand out. Individuals who gave only correct answers said they were confident in the accuracy of their own judgement or focused on performing the task as directed (i.e. striving to be accurate and correct).

The main conclusion of Asch's study is that a majority can influence a minority even in an unambiguous situation in which the correct answer is obvious

? Asch carried out his research in the United States. Why might the findings be different in other cultures?

EXAM HINT

Take note of the reasons why some people did NOT conform. In all, 25% of people never conformed in this study (that is, they always gave the correct line length). The reasons why they did this are mentioned in the study—make sure you know these, so you can use them when discussing independent behaviour, a topic that comes later in the chapter.

See *AS Level Psychology Online* for stimulus material relating to Asch's (1951) classic study . . .

? What does Asch's study tell us about non-conformity?

. . . and an interactive exercise.

(as shown by the almost perfect performance in the control condition). Asch showed convincingly that group pressure to conform in terms of majority influence is much stronger than had been thought previously. However, remember that the genuine participant actually gave the correct answer on about two-thirds of the crucial trials. That means that many people can successfully resist majority influence.

There are various weaknesses with Asch's study on conformity:

- Asch's research was carried out in the United States in the late 1940s and early 1950s. This was a time at which conformity was high and "doing your own thing" was much less socially acceptable than in the 1960s and afterwards.
- Asch's research on conformity is among the most famous in the whole of social psychology. Oddly, however, there was nothing very social about it because he used groups of strangers! The effects of majority influence are actually much stronger when participants really care about the opinions of the other group members. For example, Williams and Sogon (1984) found that majority influence was significantly greater among friends than among strangers. Abrams et al. (1990) argued that their first-year psychology participants would show more conformity if the other group members were perceived as belonging to an ingroup (other first-year psychology students from a nearby university) than if they were perceived as belonging to an outgroup (students of ancient history from the same university). This manipulation had a dramatic effect—there was conformity on 58% of trials in the presence of an ingroup compared to only 8% with an outgroup. Asch failed to realise that he could have obtained much stronger majority influence if he had replaced groups of strangers with an ingroup of friends of the genuine participants.
- Asch obtained some relevant evidence from questioning his participants. However, he didn't really explain *why* there was so much majority influence. He also failed to explain clearly *why* there were individual differences in the tendency to submit to majority influence (we consider this issue later).
- Asch's research raises important ethical issues. His participants didn't provide fully informed consent because they were misled about key aspects of the experimental procedures (e.g. the presence of confederates). In addition, they were placed in a difficult and embarrassing position—many of them seemed to be very anxious and distressed.

Asch (1956) extended his original research. He manipulated various aspects of the situation to understand more fully the factors underlying conformity in terms of majority influence. For example, he found that majority influence increased as the number of confederates went up from one to three, but there was no increase between three and sixteen confederates. Note, however, that a small increase in conformity has sometimes been found as the number of confederates goes up above three (see van Avermaet, 2001). In addition, the precise effects of adding to the number of confederates depend on whether participants respond publicly or privately (Bond, 2005).

Asch (1956) found that another important factor was whether the genuine participant had a supporter in the form of a confederate who gave the correct answer on all trials, and who gave his answers before the genuine participant.

Participants who had a supporter showed majority influence on only 5% of crucial trials—this is a dramatic reduction from the 37% found by Asch (1951) when there was no supporter.

Types of Conformity: Minority Influence

Nearly all the early research on conformity focused on how the majority can influence the thinking and behaviour of a minority. This happened at least in part because social psychologists assumed that it was very hard for a minority to have *any* real influence on the majority. However, Moscovici disagreed with that assumption, and it is certainly true that minorities such as revolutionary groups and leaders have sometimes changed the course of history. Below we consider some of his research.

Moscovici, Lage, and Naffrenchoux (1969) investigated whether a minority can influence a majority of naive participants and so reverse the usual direction of social influence. Their participants were asked to describe various colours, and so they were pre-tested to ensure that they weren't colour blind. The participants were assigned to a consistent, inconsistent, or control condition. Each condition involved six participants being present at the same time: four naive participants (the majority) and two confederates (the minority). Participants were asked to describe the colours of 36 slides. All of the slides were blue, but varied in brightness due to different filters. In the consistent condition, the two confederates described all 36 slides as green. In the inconsistent condition, the two confederates described 24 of the 36 slides as green and the other 12 as blue. In the control condition, there were no confederates. Minority influence was measured by the percentage of naive participants who yielded to the confederates by calling the blue slides green.

What did Moscovici et al. (1969) find? In the consistent condition, 8.42% of the participants answered "green" and 32% yielded to minority influence at least once. In the inconsistent condition, 1.25% of the participants answered "green". In the control condition, only 0.25% of the participants answered "green". Thus, the consistent condition showed the greatest yielding to minority influence. In a follow-up study, both experimental groups were more likely than the control group to report ambiguous blue/green slides as green.

We can conclude from this study that a minority can have influence over a majority. This minority influence is much greater when the minority is consistent in its opinions. The fact that minorities are more persuasive when they are consistent has implications for people in leadership positions who hope to influence the majority. *Why* is it important for members of a minority to be consistent in their responses? Suppose you are in a group and someone consistently expresses a point of view differing from that of everyone else in the group. You would probably interpret that person's behaviour as indicating that they were expressing their genuine beliefs. As a result, their views deserve to be taken seriously.

The study by Moscovici et al. (1969) can be criticised for various reasons. First, it lacked experimental realism, because the experimental set-up was not very believable. The slide test was artificial and may have yielded demand characteristics because it wasn't believable.

Second, the research lacked mundane realism, that is, the research set-up had no relevance to real life. Identifying the colour of a slide is trivial compared to

See *AS Level Psychology Online* to download a podcast containing an interview with Robin Martin on his research on minority influence.

How do the results of this study compare with the studies that looked at majority influence?

To what extent can we generalise about human behaviour from these studies?

See *AS Level Psychology Online* for an interactive exercise on this topic.

Minority influence is probably of more importance than majority influence in terms of social change. Can you think of an example where a minority of one changed the course of human history?

real-life instances of minority influences such as the views of political leaders or decision making by juries. As a result, the findings have low external validity, because they can't be generalised to real-life settings. Indeed, real-life studies often (but by no means always) show very little impact of minorities on issues of importance.

Third, Moscovici et al. (1969) focused on the distinction between the majority and the minority. In the real world the distinction is generally more complex, because most minorities have less power and status than majorities. This may explain why minorities rarely prevail in the real world.

Nemeth, Swedlund, and Kanki (1974) confirmed that consistency is necessary for a minority to influence the majority. However, it isn't always sufficient. They essentially replicated the study by Moscovici et al. (1969) except that their participants could respond with all the colours they saw in the slides rather than only a single colour. There were three main conditions:

1. The two confederates of the experimenter said "green" on 50% of the trials and "green-blue" on the other 50% in a random way.
2. As (1), except that the confederates said "green" to the brighter slides and "green-blue" to the duller ones, or vice versa.
3. The two confederates said "green" on every trial.

Nemeth et al. (1974) found that nearly 21% of the responses of the majority were influenced by the minority in condition 2, but the minority had no influence at all in conditions 1 and 3. The minority had no effect in condition 1 because it didn't respond consistently. The minority in condition 3 responded consistently, but its refusal to use more complex descriptions of the stimuli (e.g. "green-blue) made its behaviour seem rigid and unrealistic.

We will consider additional studies on minority influence later in the chapter.

Cultural and personality factors

Nearly all the research discussed so far has focused on majority and minority influence in American participants. It would be unwise to assume that findings obtained in the American culture will necessarily be obtained in other cultures. Even within any given culture, there have been considerable changes in views and behaviour in the decades since Asch's pioneering research. In addition, it is very likely that individual differences in personality help to determine the extent of majority and minority influence. In this section we will discuss cultural and personality factors.

Cultural factors

Why might engineering students be less likely to conform in these kinds of studies than other students?

Perrin and Spencer (1980) repeated Asch's study in England in the late 1970s. They found very little evidence of majority influence, leading them to conclude that the Asch effect was "a child of its time". However, the low level of majority influence in their study may have occurred because they used engineering students. These students had been given training in the importance of accurate measurement and so had more confidence in their own opinions about the length of the lines. Smith and Bond (1993) carried out an analysis of studies that had used Asch's task in the United States. They concluded (1993, p. 124) that, "Levels of conformity in general had steadily declined since Asch's studies in the early 1950s." However, even the most recent studies still nearly all showed clear evidence of majority influence.

 What are some of the limitations of cross-cultural studies?

Perrin and Spencer (1980) carried out two more studies. In one study, the participants were young men on probation. Mixed in with these genuine participants were confederates of the experimenter primed to give the same wrong answers. The level of conformity shown was about the same as in the Asch studies. In the other study, the participants and the confederates were both young unemployed men with Afro-Caribbean backgrounds. Once again, conformity levels were similar to those reported by Asch (1951).

Bond and Smith (1996) reported a meta-analysis of cross-cultural studies of conformity using Asch's experimental design. The participants gave the wrong answer on average on 31.2% of trials across these studies, only slightly lower than the figure obtained by Asch. The highest figure was 58% wrong answers for Indian teachers in Fiji, and the lowest figure (apart from Perrin & Spencer, 1980) was 14% among Belgian students.

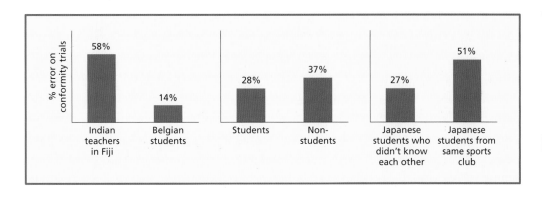

When Asch's study was replicated, cross-cultural differences emerged.

 Why do you think students were less likely to conform (28%) than non-students (37%)

Social psychologists distinguish between individualistic and collectivistic cultures. **Individualistic cultures** (e.g. the United Kingdom and the United States) emphasise the desirability of individuals being responsible for their own well-being and having a sense of personal identity. In contrast, **collectivistic cultures** emphasise the priority of group needs over individual ones, and value the feeling of group identity and solidarity. Kim and Markus (1999) found that a failure to show majority influence is seen positively as uniqueness in individualistic cultures but negatively as deviance in collectivistic ones. Bond and Smith (1996) analysed numerous Asch-type studies in several countries. As we would expect, majority influence was greater in collectivistic cultures in Asia, Africa, and elsewhere (37.1% of trials) than in individualistic cultures in North America and Europe (25.3%). Thus, majority influence is about 50% greater in collectivistic cultures.

Personality

Some individuals are affected more than others by majority and minority influence because of their biology or experience. Students made errors on 29% of crucial trials in the Asch task compared to 37% for non-students, perhaps because students are more independent than non-students in their thinking. Alternatively, their higher level of intelligence may make them more confident in their opinions.

> **KEY TERMS**
>
> **Individualistic cultures**: cultures that emphasise individuality, individual needs, and independence. People in these cultures tend to live in small nuclear families.
>
> **Collectivistic cultures**: cultures where individuals share tasks, belongings, and income. The people may live in large family groups and value interdependence.

Some studies have found gender differences, with women being more affected by majority influence than men (Eagly & Carli, 1981). Eagly (1978) suggested that many of the studies are biased because of their focus on "masculine" content, i.e. issues on which it is generally accepted that men are more knowledgeable than women. It would be expected that individuals who are very knowledgeable would be less open to influence than those who aren't. Maslach, Santee, and Wade (1987) used an equal number of feminine-relevant and masculine-relevant stories, and found no gender difference in conformity via majority influence.

Other research has also failed to find gender differences. For example, Kurosawa (1993) studied majority influence in the Asch situation with two or four confederates. There was no gender effect in either condition. However, those low in self-esteem showed more majority influence than those high in self-esteem when there were four confederates.

Types of Conformity: Compliance, Internalisation, and Identification

Do some individuals and groups have more influence over you than others? If so, why do you think this might be the case?

We have seen that conformity can occur through either majority influence or minority influence. Kelman (1958) argued that it is more important to distinguish between social influence in which individuals conform publicly but not privately and social influence in which their private beliefs change to agree with others. He used this distinction to outline three different kinds of social influence, discussed below. His approach was relatively broad, in that he considered social influence within society as well as within the laboratory.

1. Compliance (or group acceptance) occurs "when an individual accepts influence because he hopes to achieve a favourable reaction from another person or group. He adopts the induced behaviour because . . . he expects to gain specific rewards or approval and avoid specific punishments or disapproval by conforming" (Kelman, 1958, p. 53). As the influence is only superficial, compliance stops when there are no group pressures to conform. Compliance is most likely to be found when the person or group providing the influence is powerful and controlling. Of crucial importance, compliance typically involves conformity at a public but not at a private level—the individual's behaviour shows conformity but their private beliefs haven't changed.

2. Internalisation (or genuine acceptance of group norms) occurs "when an individual accepts influence because the content of the induced behaviour—the ideas and actions of which it is composed—is intrinsically rewarding. He adopts the induced behaviour because it is congruent [consistent] with his value system" (Kelman, 1958, p. 53). Internalisation is involved when someone shows influence from other group members because he/she is really in agreement with their views. Since the content of the message matters with internalisation, there is likely to be thorough processing of it. Internalisation is most likely to be found when the person or group providing the influence is credible and communicates what appears to be valuable information. Of crucial importance, there is private as well as public conformity.

KEY TERMS

Compliance: conforming to the majority view in order to be liked, or to avoid ridicule or social exclusion. Compliance occurs more readily with public behaviour than private behaviour, and is based on power.

Internalisation: conformity behaviour where the individual has completely accepted the views of the majority.

3. **Identification** (or group membership) occurs "when an individual accepts influence because he wants to establish or maintain a satisfying self-defining relationship to another person or a group" (Kelman, 1958, p. 53). Identification is found when someone shows influence with respect to the demands of a given role in society, conforming to what is expected of them. It is seen in the behaviour of nurses, traffic wardens, and air hostesses regardless of how they may actually be feeling.

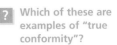 Which of these are examples of "true conformity"?

CASE STUDY: GROUPTHINK

Conformity to group opinion has many important applications, such as in juries and in the management committees of large organisations. The way individuals behave in these groups is likely to matter a lot. Janis (1972) coined the term "groupthink" to describe how the thinking of people in these situations is often disastrously affected by conformity.

Janis was describing the "Bay of Pigs" disaster to his teenage daughter and she challenged him, as a psychologist, to explain why such experts could make such poor decisions. (The Bay of Pigs invasion took place in 1961. President Kennedy and a group of government advisers made a series of bad decisions that resulted in this extremely unsuccessful invasion of the Bay of Pigs in Cuba—disastrous because 1000 men from the invasion force were only released after a ransom payment of fifty-three million dollars-worth of food and medicine, and

also because ultimately the invasion resulted in the Cuban missile crisis and a threat of nuclear war.) Janis suggested that there are a number of group factors that tend to increase conformity and result in bad decision-making:

- Group factors. People in groups do not want to be ostracised, they want to be liked and therefore tend to do things to be accepted as one of the group.
- Decisional stress. A group feels under pressure to reach a decision. To reduce this sense of pressure they try to reach the decision quickly and with little argument.
- Isolation. Groups often work in isolation, which means there are no challenges to the way they are thinking.
- Institutional factors. Often people who are appointed to higher positions are those who tend to conform, following the principle that a good soldier makes a good commander. ■

Findings

Kelman (1958) provided support for the distinction between compliance and internalisation. Black American students were presented with a message indicating it was important to maintain some private black colleges as all-black institutions to preserve black culture. This was a message initially opposed by most of the students. In the compliance condition, the students were told that the message came from a very powerful man who would withdraw funds from any college that disagreed with his position. In the internalisation condition, the same message was allegedly from a very credible source (a top expert on the problems of minority groups). After the message had been presented, the participants completed a questionnaire concerning the relevant issues. Some students were told their answers would be shown to the person delivering the message (public responding), whereas others were told their answers were anonymous (private responding).

Kelman (1958) found in the compliance condition that students claimed to be significantly more influenced by the message with public than with private responding. That suggests their private views hadn't really changed as a result of exposure to the message. In contrast, in the internalisation condition, the views expressed were very similar with public and private responding, suggesting that they had been influenced by the message privately as well as publicly. Thus, the findings were consistent with Kelman's theoretical predictions.

We will consider Kelman's notions about identification a little later in the chapter. For now we will consider compliance and internalisation in more detail, relating them to research on majority and minority influence. Majorities tend to be powerful and controlling, and can administer rewards and punishments.

KEY TERM

Identification: conforming to the demands of a given role because of a desire to be like a particular person in that role.

Accordingly, we might expect that majority influence would generally involve compliance (public but not private conformity). In contrast, minorities typically don't command much power and aren't in a position to administer rewards and punishments to the majority. Thus, we might expect that any influence they have would depend on providing credible and convincing messages. If so, minority influence should generally involve internalisation (private and public conformity).

As is discussed next, Moscovici's conversion theory built on Kelman's foundations and involves predictions resembling those we have just mentioned.

Conversion theory

What is the difference between compliance and conversion?

Moscovici (1980, 1985) distinguished between compliance and conversion. Compliance occurs when an individual goes along with the majority view to be liked (reward), avoid ridicule (punishment), or avoid social exclusion (punishment). It occurs more often with public behaviour than with private behaviour. It is clear that Moscovici's definition of compliance is rather similar to that of Kelman (1958). Remember that Kelman emphasised the importance of the persuaders' ability to control rewards and punishments in producing compliance. Generally speaking, majorities are much more likely than minorities to possess that ability.

In contrast, conversion occurs when the majority is influenced by the views of the minority. **Conversion** (which resembles what Kelman, 1958, called internalisation) typically affects private beliefs more than public behaviour. The difference is that Kelman argued that internalisation affects *both* private beliefs and public behaviour.

In sum, compliance involves public (but not internal or private) changes in expressed attitudes or behaviour in response to social influence from a majority. In contrast, conversion involves internal and private changes in attitudes in a majority due to minority influence. Individuals within the majority might still appear to go along with the majority (perhaps for their own safety), but privately their opinions have changed.

According to Moscovici, majority influence typically occurs after relatively brief and superficial processing of the majority's views, whereas minority influence generally occurs after detailed and thorough processing of the minority's views. Remember that Kelman argued that credibility and providing useful information are what allow persuaders to produce internalisation. In view of the very limited power of most minorities, these are the main routes open to minorities to produce conformity.

There is much overlap between Moscovici's views and those of Kelman. However, bear in mind that Moscovici's theory is more extensive than Kelman's, and that he was much more interested than Kelman in differences between majority and minority influence.

Moscovici (1985) argued that conversion (what Kelman called internalisation) is most likely to occur under certain conditions:

1. *Consistency*: The minority must be consistent in their opinion.
2. *Flexibility*: the minority mustn't appear to be rigid and dogmatic.
3. *Commitment*: A committed minority will lead people to re-think their position and so produce conversion.
4. *Relevance*: The minority will be more successful if their views are in line with social trends.

KEY TERM

Conversion: the influence of the minority on the majority. This is likely to affect private beliefs more than public behaviour.

Moscovici also suggested some behavioural styles that minorities should have if they want to exert an influence. These include being consistent in order to demonstrate certainty, convey an alternative view, disrupt the norm, and draw attention to their views. In addition, they should act on principles rather than just talking about them, and should make sacrifices to maintain the view they hold. It also helps if they are similar in terms of age, class, and gender to the people they are trying to persuade.

An important real-life example of a minority influencing a majority was the suffragette movement in the early years of the 20th century. A relatively small group of suffragettes argued strongly for the initially unpopular view that women should be allowed to vote. The hard work of the suffragettes, combined with the justice of their case, finally led the majority to accept their point of view.

Findings

We will start by considering findings of direct relevance to Kelman's distinction between compliance and internalisation and then move on to other findings mostly of relevance to Moscovici's approach. Maass and Clark (1983) carried out a study on attitudes to gay rights. In one condition, the majority favoured gay rights and the minority did not. In another condition, the majority opposed gay rights and the minority favoured gay rights. As predicted by conversion theory, publicly expressed attitudes generally conformed to the majority view indicating compliance. Also as predicted, privately expressed attitudes tended to agree with those of the minority indicating conversion or internalisation.

Wood et al. (1994) identified three conformity effects predicted by Moscovici (see Figure):

1. *Public influence*, in which the individual's behaviour in front of the group is influenced by the views of others. This should occur mostly when majorities influence minorities and generally indicates compliance.
2. *Direct private influence*, in which there is a change in the individual's private opinions about the issue discussed by the group. This should be found

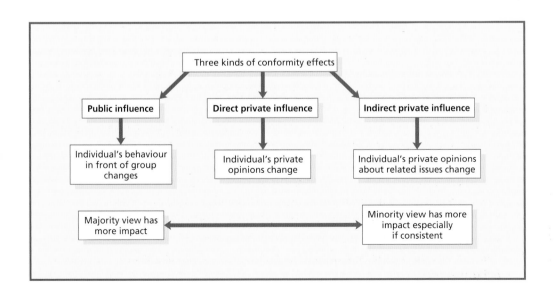

mainly when minorities influence majorities and indicates conversion or internalisation.

3. *Indirect private influence*, in which the individual's private opinions about related issues change. This should also be found mostly when majorities are influenced by minorities and also indicates conversion or internalisation.

Wood et al. (1994) carried out various meta-analyses to test for the existence of these three effects. As predicted, majorities in most studies had more public influence than minorities. Also as predicted, minorities had more indirect private influence than majorities, especially when their opinions were consistent. These findings indicate that majorities generally produced compliance, whereas minorities produced conversion or internalisation. However, majorities had more direct private influence than minorities, which is opposed to the prediction from Moscovici's theory.

We turn now to specific predictions from Moscovici's theory. Martin, Hewstone, and Martin (2003) gave their participants two messages, the second of which argued for the opposite position to the first one. According to Moscovici, resistance to changing participants' opinions when given the second message should have been greater when the first message was endorsed by a minority, because it should have been processed more thoroughly. That was precisely what was found.

Meyers, Brashers, and Hanner (2000) studied patterns of communication in small group decision making. When they compared minorities that were successful in influencing majorities with those that weren't, they found that the former argued in a more consistent way than the latter. That is as predicted by Moscovici.

Evaluation

Moscovici's conversion theory (which is mostly consistent with Kelman's views on compliance and internalisation) has many successes to its credit. First, as predicted by the theory, minorities often influence majorities. Second, the influence of minorities on majorities is mainly in the form of private agreement, with the opposite pattern being found when majorities influence minorities. These finding are entirely consistent with Kelman's (1958) approach based on compliance and internalisation. Third, there is evidence (e.g. Martin et al., 2003) that the opinions of the minority are often processed more thoroughly than those of the majority. This fits with Kelman's assumption that internalisation often involves detailed processing of information.

There are various weaknesses with conversion theory:

- Minorities are often less influential than majorities on direct private measures (e.g. Erb et al., 2002; Wood et al., 1994). This finding is not readily explained by Moscovici's theory. In terms of Kelman's approach, it would appear that majorities can produce internalisation as well as compliance.
- Moscovici exaggerated the differences between the ways in which majorities and minorities exert influence. As Smith and Mackie (2000, p. 371) concluded, "Minorities are influential when their dissent offers a consensus, avoids contamination [i.e. obvious bias], and triggers private acceptance— the same processes by which all groups achieve influence." With respect to

Kelman's views the implication is that a mixture of compliance and internalisation may be found with both majority and minority influence.

- Majorities generally differ from minorities in several ways (e.g. power; status) largely ignored by Moscovici. Differences in the social influence exerted by majorities and minorities may depend on power and status rather than on their majority or minority position within the group.

The Stanford prison experiment: Identification

In the 1960s, there were numerous reports of brutal attacks by prison guards on prisoners in American prisons. Why did this brutality occur? Perhaps those who put themselves in a position of power by becoming prison guards have aggressive or sadistic personalities. Alternatively, the behaviour of prison guards may be due mainly to the social environment of prisons (e.g. the rigid power structure). In other words, prison guards behave in ways they feel are expected of them in their particular role—this is what Kelman (1958) called identification. These two explanations can be regarded as **dispositional** and **situational explanations**, respectively.

Philip Zimbardo (1973) studied this important issue in the Stanford prison experiment, carried out in the basement of the psychology department at Stanford University. Emotionally stable individuals acted as "guards" and "prisoners" in a mock prison. Zimbardo wanted to see whether the hostility found in many real prisons would also be found in his mock prison. If hostility were found in spite of not using sadistic guards, this would suggest it is the power structure that creates hostility.

The events in the prison were so unpleasant and dangerous that the entire experiment was stopped 8 days early! Violence and rebellion broke out within 2 days. The prisoners ripped off their clothing and shouted and cursed at the guards. In return, the guards violently put down this rebellion by using fire extinguishers. One prisoner showed such severe symptoms of emotional disturbance (disorganised thinking and screaming) that he had to be released after only 1 day. Over time, the prisoners became more subdued and submissive, often slouching and keeping their eyes fixed on the ground. At the same time, the use of force, harassment, and aggression by the guards increased steadily, and were clearly excessive reactions to the prisoners' submissive behaviour. For example, the prisoners were put in solitary confinement and had to clean the toilets with their bare hands.

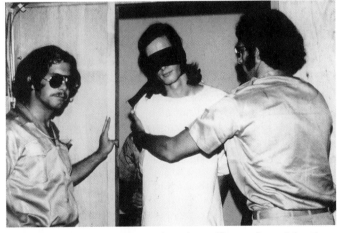

Zimbardo tried to minimise the after-effects of participation in his Stanford prison experiment by asking the participants to sign an informed consent form before the experiment began. Even so, some of the mock guards became very aggressive during the experiment, and four of the mock prisoners had to be released early.

What conclusions can we draw? First, the study suggested that brutality and aggression in prisons are due mainly to the power structure. Thus, the study seems to show conformity by identification at work. However, real prison guards may be more sadistic than other people. Second, the situation within the mock prison had such a strong influence that

KEY TERMS

Dispositional explanation: deciding that other people's actions are caused by their internal characteristics or dispositions.

Situational explanation: deciding that people's actions are caused by the situation in which they find themselves rather than by their personality.

Wearing a uniform may lead individuals to conform to an expected role, as they did in Zimbardo's prison study.

? How can the concept of "demand characteristics" be used to explain the behaviour of the participants in this study?

aggressive behaviour shown by the guards increased progressively. Third, the study showed how stereotypes about the kinds of behaviour expected of guards and prisoners influenced the participants' actions. According to Haney, Banks, and Zimbardo (1973, p. 12), guard aggression "was emitted [shown] simply as a 'natural' consequence of being in the uniform of a 'guard' and asserting the power inherent in that role."

How does this experiment relate to other research on conformity and obedience? In our everyday lives we often show conformity by acting out a role in ways expected by society. This is known as identification, and was shown by the guards and prisoners, who both conformed closely to expected forms of behaviour.

In addition, the guards all tended to behave in similar ways, and the same was true of the prisoners. This indicates a conformity effect, and may reflect the participants' need to be accepted by their fellow guards or prisoners.

Obedience to authority was also clearly at work. There was a definite power structure in the prison, with the guards having the power to force the prisoners to behave in ways they didn't want to. This corresponds closely to the kinds of obedience to authority observed by Milgram (discussed later).

Various criticisms can be made of the Stanford prison experiment. First, the mock prison was very different from a real prison. For example, the participants knew they hadn't committed any crime and could ask to leave at any time.

Second, the artificial set-up may have produced effects due to **participant reactivity**, with the guards and prisoners merely play-acting. However, the physical abuse and harassment shown by the prison guards went far beyond play-acting.

Third, some of the hostility and aggression displayed by the guards was due to following the instructions of the experimenter rather than simply identifying with their role. When Zimbardo briefed the guards, he told them:

CASE STUDY: ZIMBARDO'S DEFENCE

Zimbardo pointed out that all of his participants had signed a formal informed consent form, which indicated that there would be an invasion of privacy, loss of some civil rights, and harassment. He also noted that day-long debriefing sessions were held with the participants, so that they could understand the moral conflicts being studied. However, Zimbardo failed to protect his participants from physical and mental harm. It was entirely predictable that the mock guards would attack the mock prisoners, because that is exactly what had happened in a pilot study that Zimbardo carried out before the main study. ■

You can create in the prisoners feelings of boredom, a sense of fear to some degree, you can create a notion of arbitrariness that their life is totally controlled by us, by the system, you, me—and they'll have no privacy . . . they can do nothing, say nothing that we don't permit. We're going to take away their individuality (Zimbardo, 1989).

In December 2001, British researchers carried out a similar study, parts of which were subsequently broadcast by the BBC. Their findings (Reicher & Haslam, 2006) were very different from those of the Stanford prison experiment. There were 5 guards and 10 prisoners, all selected to be well adjusted. The key finding was that the guards failed to identify with their role, whereas the prisoners increasingly *did* identify with their role. As a result, the guards were overcome by the prisoners. As Reicher and Haslam (2006, p. 30) concluded, "People do not automatically assume roles that are given to them in the manner suggested by the role account that is typically used to explain events in the SPE [Stanford prison experiment] (Haney et al., 1973)." Thus, identification is *not* always found.

KEY TERM

Participant reactivity: the situation in which an **independent variable** has an effect on participants merely because they know they are being observed.

Why were the findings so different from those of the Stanford prison experiment? Participants in the BBC prison study knew that what they said and did might be shown to millions of television viewers. This might have encouraged the guards to behave gently. However, this doesn't explain why the guards failed to become more aggressive over time as their awareness of being filmed diminished. Perhaps 30 years on from the Stanford prison experiment people were more aware of the dangers of conforming to stereotyped views, in part because of the wide publicity given to the Stanford prison experiment.

Deindividuation

Deindividuation is another factor that may affect the amount of conformity through majority influence. The term refers to the loss of a sense of personal identity that can occur when we are, for example, in a crowd or wearing a mask. Zimbardo (1969) conducted a Milgram-type obedience experiment (described on p. 283). Female participants were told to give electric shocks to other women. Deindividuation was produced in half of the participants by having them wear laboratory coats and hoods that covered their faces, and the experimenter addressed them as a group rather than as individuals. The intensity of electric shocks given by the deindividuated individuals was twice as great as that given by participants who wore their own clothes and were treated as individuals. Why was that? Presumably the deindividuated participants felt more able simply to follow the experimenter's instructions, conforming to the stereotypical role of obeying a person in authority.

Johnson and Downing (1979) were not convinced that deindividuation was really responsible for the findings of Zimbardo. They pointed out that the clothing worn by the deindividuated participants resembled that worn by the Ku Klux Klan (a secret organisation in the United States that carried out many violent acts against American black people). Johnson and Downing found that deindividuated individuals dressed as nurses actually gave fewer electric shocks than did those wearing their own clothes. Thus, the participants in both studies were showing conformity to a role.

Johnson and Downing (1979) pointed out the similarity between the clothes of Zimbardo's deindividuated participants and another uniform, that of the Ku Klux Klan.

? If you feel deindividuated, do you think this makes you more or less likely to conform to group norms or to follow orders?

Explanations of Why People Conform

Several theories have been put forward to explain conformity in the Asch and other situations. We will focus on the two-process theory put forward by Deutsch and Gerard (1955), according to which conformity can depend on informational social influence or on normative social influence. Note that Moscovici's theoretical approach also provides a detailed explanation of why people conform.

Informational social influence and normative social influence

One of the most influential attempts to identify the factors responsible for *majority* influence was that of Deutsch and Gerard (1955). It should be emphasised that they did *not* try to explain conformity due to *minority* influence—one good

KEY TERM

Deindividuation: losing one's sense of personal identity.

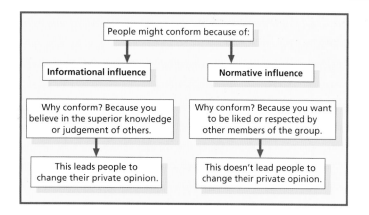

[?] What is the difference between informational and normative social influence?

reason for this is that in 1955 there had been practically no research on minority influence at all! They proposed two possible explanations:

- **Informational social influence:** This is "an influence to accept information obtained from another as *evidence* about reality" (Deutsch & Gerard, 1955, p. 629). It generally involves majority influence due to the perceived superior knowledge or judgement of others, as in Sherif's (1935) study. It generally leads to a change in private opinion.

- **Normative social influence:** This is "an influence to conform with the positive expectations of another" (Deutsch & Gerard, 1955, p. 629). It involves majority influence due to wanting to be liked by the other members of the group and to avoid being rejected. It undoubtedly played a major role in Asch's (1951, 1956) research. For example, when Asch (1956) had one confederate in a group of genuine participants give the wrong answer, the group laughed out loud at the confederate. Many people are motivated to avoid such embarrassment. Normative social influence affects public opinions but isn't likely to change private opinions.

It is easy to imagine that what Deutsch and Gerard (1955) had in mind was that one or other of the two forms of influence (but not both) would be operative at any given time. However, that was *not* their intention. Deutsch and Gerard (1955, p. 629) argued that "Commonly these two types of influence are found together." However, Deutsch and Gerard (1955) predicted that normative social influence would be especially important in the Asch-type situation in which the correct answer was unambiguous and clear cut.

Findings

A useful starting point for understanding why participants often conform in the Asch situation is to ask them. That is what Asch (1951) did. Their self-reports focused on factors such as feeling self-conscious, having fear of disapproval, and feelings of anxiety, suggesting that normative social influence was at work. Self-reports provide interesting data, but we can't be sure that they accurately identify the reasons why people conform.

We could explain the level of conformity found in Asch's (1951) basic situation by assuming that the requirement to give their judgements out loud in front of the group maximised normative social influence. If that is the case, then it should be possible to reduce conformity by having participants write down their judgements privately. Asch (1951) did precisely that, and found that conformity dropped to 12.5%. This happened because there is much less normative social influence when other group members are unaware of your judgements.

Bond (2005) carried out a meta-analysis of Asch-type studies in which the number of confederates varied. He compared studies in which participants responded publicly or privately. As expected, conformity increased in line with increasing number of confederates with public responding. However, the *opposite* was found with private responding—in other words, the more confederates there

KEY TERMS

Informational social influence: when someone conforms because others are thought to possess more knowledge.

Normative social influence: when someone conforms in order to gain liking or respect from others.

were, the *less* private conformity there was! These findings suggest that increased public conformity with increasing numbers of confederates is mainly due to normative social influence.

Deutsch and Gerard (1955) assessed the role of normative social influence by extending Asch's research. They used several conditions varying in the likely importance of normative social influence but with the same information about the judgements of other group members available to them. Thus, any group differences should depend mainly on differences in normative social influence. The main conditions were as follows:

1. Face-to-face situation: this was very similar to Asch's situation with three confederates and the genuine participant announcing his/her judgements publicly.
2. Anonymous situation: the genuine participant gave his/her judgements anonymously in an isolated cubicle by pressing a button, believing that there were three other participants.
3. Group situation: this was like the anonymous situation except that the experimenter said a reward would be given to the groups making the most accurate decisions.

What would we expect to find in this experiment? Normative social influence (and so conformity) should be greatest in the third condition (social pressure to conform) and least in the second condition. That was precisely what Deutsch and Gerard (1955) found. They also used a variation of the anonymous situation in which participants wrote their judgements on a sheet of paper and subsequently threw them away. In this situation (designed to minimise normative social influence) participants conformed on only 5% of trials.

Earlier we mentioned that Asch found that conformity decreased from 37% to 5% when there was a single confederate who consistently gave the correct judgements. This could be due to a reduction in normative social influence (e.g. "Thank goodness I have some social support!") or to informational social influence (e.g. "Here is information suggesting there is no problem with my eyesight!"). Asch also found that a confederate of the experimenter who gave judgements even more incorrect than the majority was as effective as an accurate confederate in reducing conformity. It is likely that an inaccurate confederate reduced normative social influence more than informational social influence, because the confederate wasn't providing accurate information.

There is evidence from the Asch-type situation that informational social influence *can* be an important factor. Allen and Levine (1971) asked participants to make visual and other judgements in a group setting. There were three conditions: (1) participants had no support; (2) participants had a valid supporter with normal vision; and (3) participants had an invalid supporter with very poor vision who wore very thick glasses. There was a very high level of conformity in the first condition (97%) and a much lower level when there was a valid supporter (36%). The most interesting condition was the one involving the invalid

Refer back to the case of Kitty Genovese (see Chapter 2, Section 3), who was fatally stabbed, despite there being 38 witnesses to the attack. The reason no one answered her pleas for help can be explained in terms of conformity and informational social influence. The fact that each individual did nothing sent a message to the others that everything was OK and there was no need to do anything. Everyone conformed to the behavioural norm of the majority by not acting (Rosenthal, 1964).

If a participant is told that a "counting the jelly beans" task is very important, he or she would be more likely to rely on, and be influenced by, the information provided by other group members.

supporter, in which conformity was observed on 64% of critical trials. The lower conformity with a valid supporter than an invalid one presumably occurred because the valid supporter reduced the group's informational social influence more than did the invalid supporter. However, the lower conformity with an invalid supporter than with no supporter is likely to reflect a reduction in the group's normative social influence in the former condition.

When might we expect normative social influence to be important? Suppose that you were given a difficult task and told that it was very important. In those circumstances, you might very well rely on the information provided by other group members (i.e. informational social influence). That is exactly what was found by Baron, Vandello, and Brunsman (1996). Participants were given easy and difficult versions of the same task and were told it was very important or unimportant. Substantial conformity effects were only found when the task was difficult and very important.

So far we have focused mainly on the Asch situation. However, the processes involved seem to be somewhat different in the Crutchfield situation (Crutchfield, 1955). What Crutchfield did was to have groups of five individuals sitting side by side in individual booths. They were presented with slides containing multiple-choice questions and given the following instructions:

The slides call for various kinds of judgements—lengths of lines, areas of figures, logical completion of number series, vocabulary items, estimates of the opinions of others, expression of his own attitudes on issues, expression of his personal preferences for line drawings . . .

There are two major differences between the Crutchfield situation and the Asch one. First, there is a less obvious group, in that participants in the Crutchfield situation can't see any of the other members of the group. Second, it is much harder to be confident of the correct answers in the Crutchfield situation, because many of the questions involve specialised knowledge or are based on opinions. Thus, participants are far more likely to be seeking information than in the Asch situation, and so informational social influence should be more important than in Asch-type studies. Crutchfield (1955) found that less intellectually effective participants showed more conformity, perhaps because they were more affected by informational social influence.

Lucas et al. (2006) also found evidence for informational social influence. Students were asked to give the answers to easy and hard problems in mathematics. There was more conformity to the incorrect answers of others with hard problems than with easy ones, and this was especially the case among students who doubted their mathematical ability. It seems reasonable to assume that informational social influence would be greatest when individuals are given difficult problems and doubt their ability to solve them.

Evaluation

Conformity generally depends on some mixture of normative social influence (involving emotional processes) and informational social influence (involving cognitive processes). Thus, Deutsch and Gerard (1955) successfully identified two key processes underlying conformity behaviour. In addition, some of the factors increasing or decreasing these types of social influence have been studied.

HOW SCIENCE WORKS: RESISTING PRESSURE

Does personal experience fit in with psychological explanations? You could try to test psychological models about resisting pressure. It could be interesting to ask a few participants each to draw up a table, with clear headings. The left-hand column could be for real examples of resisting pressure from their individual personal experiences, e.g. choosing not to go to the cinema with friends as they'd already seen the film. The right-hand column could be for their explanation of how they resisted the pressure to conform or join in. When each person has given three or four examples you could look again at the theories and evaluate their usefulness in explaining these real-life behaviours. You could then work out which explanation or explanations seem to have more validity in the real world.

NB This exercise could raise some ethical issues if people have felt under pressure to conform in the past. Therefore all responses should be anonymous, and participants should have the right to withdraw and withhold their contribution at any time.

In general terms, normative social influence is reduced when participants' judgements are anonymous and private, participants are permitted to throw away information about their judgements, or they have social support in the form of at least one supporter or dissenter from the majority. Informational social influence is greater when the situation is ambiguous, accuracy is crucial, a supporter is likely to possess valid information, and the participants have doubts about their knowledge or ability.

What are the limitations with the two-process approach based on normative and informational social influence? First, the approach was really designed to apply to majority influence. It also has some relevance to minority influence, but its precise relevance is not clear. However, the evidence is mostly consistent with the notion that minorities typically produce conformity through informational social influence rather than normative social influence.

Second, it is often not possible to decide whether the effects of any given factor on conformity behaviour are due to normative social influence, informational social influence, or some mixture of both. For example, we have seen that conformity is markedly reduced if the genuine participant has one supporter. That supporter may provide social support (reducing the group's normative influence) and/or useful information (reducing the group's informational influence). The problem is that we have no easy way of telling which type of social influence is more important.

Third, Deutsch and Gerard (1955) seem to have assumed that normative social influence would be extremely common, because it occurs whenever individuals seek social approval and acceptance. However, there is more to normative social influence than that. As discussed earlier, Williams and Sogon (1984) found that there was much more conformity when the other group members were friends rather than strangers, and Abrams et al. (1990) found *seven* times as much conformity when the other group members belonged to one of the participants' ingroup rather than to an outgroup. These findings suggest that group belongingness is much more powerful than simply the need for social approval.

Fourth, the extent of conformity behaviour depends on both the situation in which an individual finds himself/herself *and* his/her personal characteristics. For example, highly intelligent and knowledgeable individuals are less affected by informational social influence than those of lesser intelligence and knowledge. In addition, individuals who have a great need to be positively regarded by others will be more affected by normative social influence than those with a lesser need.

Differences between obedience and conformity

OBEDIENCE	CONFORMITY
Occurs within a hierarchy. Actor feels the person above has the right to prescribe behaviour. Links one status to another. Emphasis is on power.	Regulates the behaviour among those of equal status. Emphasis is on acceptance.
Behaviour adopted differs from behaviour of authority figure.	Behaviour adopted is similar to that of peers.
Prescription for action is explicit.	Requirement of going along with the group is often implicit.
Participants embrace obedience as an explanation for their behaviour.	Participants deny conformity as an explanation for their behaviour.

How does obedience differ from conformity?

Both obedience and conformity involve social pressure. In obedience the pressure comes from behaving as you are instructed to do, whereas in conformity the pressure comes from group norms. A further distinction can be made in terms of the effects on private opinion. Obedience is more likely to involve public behaviour only.

Research on obedience to authority differs in at least three ways from research on conformity. First, the participants are ordered to behave in certain ways rather than being fairly free to decide what to do. Second, the participant is of lower status than the person issuing the orders, whereas in studies of conformity the participant is usually of equal status to the group members trying to influence him or her. Third, participants' behaviour in obedience studies is determined by social power, whereas in conformity studies it is influenced mostly by the need for acceptance.

Unquestioning obedience to authority may have catastrophic consequences. The picture shows survivors of the Auschwitz concentration camp at the end of the war in 1945, following a decade of persecution, imprisonment, and genocide.

Most research has focused on situational determinants of social influence, and as yet we lack a clear idea of how situational and personal factors interact to determine conformity behaviour.

Obedience to Authority

This section is concerned with obedience to authority. What is obedience? According to Franzoi (1996, p. 259), "Obedience is the performance of an action in response to a direct order. Usually the order comes from a person of high status or authority."

In nearly all societies, certain people are given power and authority over others. In our society, for example, parents, teachers, and managers are invested with varying degrees of authority. Most of the time this doesn't cause any problems. If the doctor tells us to take some tablets three times a day, we accept that he/she is the expert. If the school crossing attendant says "Cross now", it would be foolish not to obey—except if you could see a car approaching rapidly. The desirability of obeying authority is related to the reasonableness of their commands.

Obedience to unjust commands: Milgram

An issue that has been of interest to psychologists for many years is to work out how far most people are willing to go in their obedience to authority. What happens if you are asked by a person in authority to do something that you think is wrong? What we should do in those circumstances is to refuse to obey. However, the lesson of history (e.g. Nazi Germany) seems to be that many ordinary people are willing to do terrible things when ordered to do so.

Many people argue that only sadistic or psychopathic individuals would be so obedient to authority as to be prepared to do appalling things to another human being. Other people argue that most of us would probably be prepared to treat someone else very badly if ordered to do so by an authority figure. The famous (some would say infamous!) research of Stanley Milgram was designed to find out how far most people are willing to go to obey an authority figure. His first study was conducted in 1963 at the prestigious Yale University. In this study, he aimed to see whether he could set up a situation in which participants were more obedient to authority than was generally believed to be the case.

Forty male volunteers (a self-selected sample) took part in a controlled observational study, which they were deceived into thinking was a test of learning. The naive participant was always assigned the role of "teacher" and a middle-aged confederate "Mr Wallace", played the role of "learner". Mr Wallace was said to have a heart condition. A word association test was the learning task, and the naive participant was instructed to deliver an electric shock to the learner for each incorrect answer. If the teacher was unwilling to administer the shocks, the experimenter told him/her to continue. The teacher and the learner were in separate rooms with no voice contact. The measure of obedience was the strength of the electric shock administered by the participants on a scale of 15 to 450 volts with 15-volt increments for each wrong answer. The participants understood that the highest levels of shock might be fatal, especially to a man with a heart condition. At 180 volts, the learner yelled, "I can't stand the pain", and by 270 volts the response had become an agonised scream. The participants didn't know until the end of the experiment that no shocks were actually administered. (The fact that no shocks were delivered shows that psychologists are not as sadistic as you may have started to believe!)

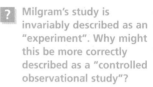

? Milgram's study is invariably described as an "experiment". Why might this be more correctly described as a "controlled observational study"?

See *AS Level Psychology Online* for an interactive exercise on this topic.

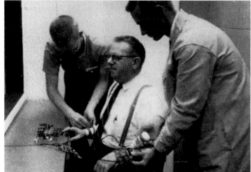

The photographs show the electric shock machine used in Milgram's classic experiment where 65% of the participants gave a potentially lethal shock to the "learner", shown in the bottom photograph. The learner was actually a confederate of the experimenter, a 47-year-old accountant called "Mr Wallace". The photographs show the experimenter (in the overall) and the true participant, the "teacher".

Would you have been willing to give the maximum (and potentially deadly) 450-volt shock? Milgram found that everyone he asked denied that they personally would do any such thing. He also found that 110 experts on human behaviour (e.g. psychiatrists) predicted that no one would go to the 450-volt stage. In fact, all of the participants gave shocks up to the 300-volt level, and 65% of them (there was no gender difference) continued through to the highest level of 450 volts. As you can see, this was hugely different from expert predictions!

? Do most people simply obey authority in a rather mindless way?

Milgram's initial hypothesis was that German obedience during the Second World War was a facet of German culture. He was going to compare how Americans behaved with how Germans behaved but he found, to his astonishment, that Americans were extremely obedient—and therefore concluded that obedience was in human nature, not just German nature.

See *AS Level Psychology Online* for stimulus material relating to Milgram's (1963) classic study.

EXAM HINT
Notice how the terms experimental realism and mundane realism apply to an evaluation of Milgram's study. Make sure that you can link these issues appropriately to internal and external validity, i.e. you should be able to assess how experimental realism questions internal validity and how mundane realism questions external validity.

Milgram's (1963) research suggested that obedience to authority is due more to situational factors (the experimental setting, the status of the experimenter, and the pressure exerted on the participant to continue) than to "deviant" personality. Implications include the relevance of this research to the real-life atrocities of the Second World War and the need to identify ways of preventing people from showing misplaced obedience to authority.

Evaluation

Many psychologists (including the author) regard Milgram's (1963) study as one of the most important ever carried out in social psychology for various reasons. First, Milgram studied a phenomenon (i.e. obedience to authority) of massive importance within most societies. For example, obedience to authority can be seen every day in the interactions between doctors and nurses or between teachers and students. Second, his findings were so strikingly different from prediction that they showed that psychologists' ideas about obedience to authority needed to be re-thought. Third, they appeared to demonstrate that obedience to authority depends primarily on situational pressures and is due surprisingly little to an individual's personality.

In spite of the importance of Milgram's (1963) research, various criticisms that can be made of it:

- Orne and Holland (1968) argued that the research lacked experimental realism, meaning that the experimental set-up was simply not believable. More specifically, they thought many of the participants realised that the electric shocks were not genuine because they were not a credible punishment for making mistakes on a test. However, many of the participants became very anxious and upset during the experiment, which hardly suggests that they didn't believe they were administering electric shocks.
- Orne and Holland (1968) also argued that the research lacked mundane realism because the research set-up was in an artificial controlled environment unlike real life. However, experimental realism can compensate for a lack of mundane realism, and it can be argued that that is the case with this study.
- Milgram (1963) didn't really tell us in detail what was different about the 35% of the participants who refused to give the strongest electric shock.
- Milgram's research was very dubious ethically. For example, he tried to prevent participants from leaving the experiment and they were placed in a very stressful situation. One of the most serious ethical problems is that Milgram totally failed to obtain informed consent from his participants, who simply didn't know what was in store for them. In addition, the participants weren't really free to leave the experiment if they wanted to—the experimenter urged them to continue when they indicated that they wanted to stop.

Milgram (1974)

Milgram (1974) extended our knowledge about obedience to authority by carrying out several variations on his original experiment. He found that there were two main ways in which obedience to authority could be reduced. The first way was to increase the obviousness of the learner's plight, which was done by comparing four situations (the percentage of totally obedient participants is in brackets):

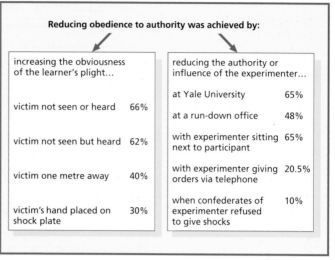

Reducing obedience to authority was achieved by:	
increasing the obviousness of the learner's plight...	**reducing the authority or influence of the experimenter...**
	at Yale University 65%
victim not seen or heard 66%	at a run-down office 48%
	with experimenter sitting next to participant 65%
victim not seen but heard 62%	
	with experimenter giving orders via telephone 20.5%
victim one metre away 40%	
	when confederates of experimenter refused to give shocks 10%
victim's hand placed on shock plate 30%	

- *Remote feedback*: The victim couldn't be heard or seen (66%).
- *Voice feedback*: The victim could be heard but not seen (62%).
- *Proximity*: The victim was only one metre away from the participant (40%).
- *Touch-proximity*: This was like the proximity condition except that the participant had to force the learner's hand onto the shock plate (30%).

The other main way in which obedience to authority could be lessened was by reducing the authority or influence of the experimenter in the following ways:

- Staging the experiment in a run-down office building rather than at Yale University (48%).
- Orders given by telephone rather than having the experimenter sitting close to the participant (20.5%). (The effect of distance may help to explain why it is less stressful to kill people by dropping bombs from a plane than by shooting them at close range.)
- The experimenter was an ordinary member of the public rather than a white-coated scientist (20%).
- Giving the participant two confederates (individuals working for the experimenter) who refused to give shocks (10%).

See *AS Level Psychology Online* for an interactive exercise on this topic.

Milgram's (1974) variations on the original study give us greater insight into the conditions under which people obey unjust requests. They also show us something about independent behaviour, because in many situations a majority of participants behaved independently.

The main criticisms of Milgram's research approach concern the lack of internal and external validity, and the unethical nature of what he did. We will consider these criticisms now.

Validity of obedience research

The validity of any research refers to the extent to which it meets certain standards. An experiment may produce a significant finding and so apparently "prove" the researcher's initial hypothesis, but that doesn't mean that the finding is necessarily valid or genuine.

There are several types of validity. One is internal validity, which is a measure of the extent to which the experimental design actually did the job it was supposed to do. If the experimental set-up wasn't believable then the participants probably wouldn't behave as they would generally do in such situations. It is called *internal* validity because it concerns what goes on inside the experiment. Another form of validity is external validity, which is the extent to which the results of a study can be applied to other situations and other individuals.

EXAM HINT

You need to be able to outline two factors that influence resistance to obedience so identify the following:

- Increasing the obviousness of the learner's distress.
- Reducing the influence of the experimenter.

Use the later variations that Milgram conducted to support each factor. If possible memorise the % rates of obedience to show how much obedience dropped from the original 65%.

? What is the difference between internal and external validity?

It is called *external* validity because it concerns issues outside the specific context of the study. We will consider both of these forms of validity in relation to obedience research.

Internal validity

To what extent did Milgram's participants actually believe they were giving electric shocks to the "learner"? As we have seen, Orne and Holland (1968) claimed that Milgram's experiment lacked experimental realism because the participants may have found it hard to believe in the set-up. For example, they might well have questioned why the experimenter wasn't giving the shocks himself—why employ someone else if there wasn't some kind of trickery going on? However, in a replication of Milgram's experiment by Rosenhan (1969), nearly 70% of participants reported that they believed the whole set-up. Milgram's own response was that there is evidence that participants will believe in (and comply with) almost anything. In a study by Turner and Solomon (1962), participants were willing to be *given* strong shocks, and so must have believed the experimental task. Coolican (1996) agrees with Milgram on the basis of film showing that the participants in Milgram's (and Asch's) studies were taking the situation very seriously and appeared to be experiencing real distress.

Orne and Holland (1968) also considered the issue of demand characteristics in relation to internal validity. Demand characteristics are those cues in an experiment that "invite" participants to behave in certain predictable ways. One demand characteristic of any experiment is that participants should obey the experimenter's instructions. So, in Milgram's experiment, the reason the participants obeyed so completely was not necessarily because they were very obedient but perhaps more because this is how one should behave in an experiment. If that were the case, then Milgram's findings lack validity—they do not tell us about human obedience behaviour in general but only about how willing participants are to obey in experiments.

Milgram's approach may also lack validity as a consequence of the fact that the participants behaved as they did because they had entered into a social contract with the experimenter. In exchange for payment ($4.50), participants might have felt that they should obey the instructions they received—their behaviour didn't show obedience within the real world but only within a contractual relationship. They were told they could leave and still be paid but, at the same time, the instructions "You must continue" must have made it quite difficult to leave. However, Milgram (1992) argued that experiments generally follow similar rules to social situations and in this sense they are true to life.

External validity

External validity concerns the extent to which we can generalise the findings of a study to other situations. The main challenge to external validity in all of Milgram's research is that it was carried out in laboratory situations, and so we might not be able to generalise the findings to the real world. However, consider the point made earlier that experiments are like real-life social situations. Another way to answer the external validity criticism is by reference to the distinction between experimental and mundane realism (Carlsmith et al., 1976). Any research set-up that is like real life can be said to have mundane realism in so far as it

? Why do you think that the setting in which the experiments took place made such a difference?

appears real rather than artificial to the participants. Some experiments lack mundane realism. However, experimental realism can compensate for this when the way the experiment is conducted is so involving that the participants are fooled into thinking the set-up is real rather than artificial.

Milgram argued that his research had both mundane realism and experimental realism. It had mundane realism because the demands of an authority figure are the same regardless of whether the setting is artificial or occurring more naturally outside the laboratory. It also had experimental realism because the experiment must have been highly involving and engaging for the participants to have behaved as they did.

External validity can be shown through attempts to replicate or repeat the research in more natural situations. For example, Bickman (1974) used the realistic setting of the streets of New York and had pedestrians as participants. Three male experimenters (one dressed in a sports coat and tie, one dressed as a milkman, and one dressed in a guard's uniform that made him look like a police officer) gave one of three orders to the pedestrians:

1. Pointing to a bag on the street, "Pick up this bag for me."
2. Nodding in the direction of a confederate, "This fellow is overparked at the meter but doesn't have any change. Give him a dime."
3. Approaching a participant at a bus stop, "Don't you know you have to stand on the other side of the pole? This sign says 'No standing'."

[?] What ethical codes are infringed by Bickman's study?

Bickman found that participants were more likely to obey the experimenter dressed as a guard than the milkman or civilian. This supports one of the variations of Milgram's findings, that obedience is related to the amount of perceived authority. However, what Bickman asked participants to do was much more trivial than what was expected of participants in Milgram's research, and so his findings are of only partial relevance.

Probably the best-known replication of obedience research is a real-life study by Hofling et al. (1966). In this study, 22 nurses were phoned up by someone claiming to be "Dr Smith". The nurses were asked to check that a drug called Astroten was available. When the nurses did this, they saw on the bottle that the maximum dosage was 10 mg. When they reported back to Dr Smith, he told them to give 20 mg of the drug to a patient.

Obedience can be related to the amount of perceived authority.

There were two good reasons why the nurses should have refused to obey. First, the dose was double the maximum safe dose. Second, the nurses didn't know Dr Smith, and they were supposed to take instructions only from doctors they knew. However, the nurses' training had led them to obey instructions from doctors. There is a clear power structure in medical settings, with doctors in a more powerful position than nurses. The nurses were more influenced by the power structure than by the hospital regulations: all but one did as Dr Smith instructed. However, when they were asked what other nurses would have

Uniforms, such as those worn by nurses, increase an individual's sense of anonymity and make it more likely that they will conform to the role associated with the uniform.

done in the same circumstances, they all predicted that others would *not* have obeyed the instructions. This indicates that the pressures to show obedience to authority are greater than most people imagine. This study raised important issues about hospital practices.

Many people have argued that Hofling et al.'s study had greater external validity than Milgram's. However, attempts to replicate Hofling et al.'s study have produced variable results. Similar findings were reported by Lesar, Briceland, and Stein (1997) in a study on actual medication errors in American hospitals. Nurses typically carried out doctors' orders even when they had good reasons for doubting the wisdom of those orders. However, Rank and Jacobsen (1997) found that only 11% of nurses obeyed a doctor's instructions to give too high a dose to patients when they talked to other nurses beforehand. This finding suggests that social support can reduce the tendency to be obedient to authority. As such, it seems somewhat similar to Milgram's (1974) finding that obedience was much less when the genuine participants were accompanied by a confederate who refused to give electric shocks.

Overall, there is good support for external validity. Milgram's main findings have been repeated literally dozens of times in other situations and other countries. Remember that the criterion for external validity is that the findings should be replicable in other settings.

Cross-cultural support for external validity. Milgram's studies were carried out in the United States during the 1960s and 1970s. Those limitations pose issues about the external validity of his research that have been addressed by numerous studies in other cultures in recent decades. The relevant cross-cultural evidence has been collected by Smith and Bond (1993). Unfortunately, key aspects of the procedure varied from one culture to another, and so it is very hard to interpret cross-cultural differences in obedience. However, the percentages of participants willing to give the most severe shock were very high in several countries: 80% or higher in studies carried out in Italy, Spain, Germany, Austria, and Holland, suggesting substantial obedience to authority.

Ancona and Pareyson (1968) replicated Milgram's study in Italy. They found a total obedience rate of 80%. In Austria, Schurz (1985) obtained an obedience rate of 85%.

Meeus and Raaijmakers (1995) carried out an interesting series of studies in Holland. They told participants they were carrying out a study to see how job applicants would handle stress in an interview. Each participant was given the role of being the interviewer, and the job applicants were actually confederates of the experimenter. The interviewer was told to create stress for the interviewee, and was given a set of negative statements to do this ranging from mild to utterly humiliating (e.g. "This job is too difficult for you").

At the time of the study, unemployment rates in Holland were very high, and so the participants would have felt bad about making an interview more difficult

EXAM HINT
The issue of ethics is important in all psychological studies but ethics are particularly relevant to studies of conformity and obedience. In an exam they can be useful in evaluating studies such as Asch, Milgram, Zimbardo's prison study, and Hofling. Just consider how issues such as deception, informed consent, protection of participants from harm, and right of withdrawal apply to these studies.

for someone trying to get a job. Thus, we might have expected them to refuse to obey. The confederates were told to start off behaving confidently but to gradually appear more and more distressed as the interviewer's statements became more humiliating. Eventually the applicants pleaded with the interviewer to stop interrupting and then they refused to answer any more questions. In spite of the obvious distress caused to the job applicant, 22 out of 24 participants (interviewers) delivered all 15 "stress remarks". They clearly felt stressed themselves but tried to hide this from the interviewee and to act as if nothing was wrong. Thus, about 90% of the participants were fully obedient to the experimenter.

The study by Meeus and Raaijmakers (1995) shows once again the willingness of individuals to obey an authority figure even when both their stress and that of the recipient is obvious. The explanation for the high level of obedience may lie in the Dutch attitude to social institutions and their ways of relating to their fellow citizens.

Explanations of why people obey

People may obey because the situation they find themselves in somehow puts pressure on them to be obedient. Alternatively, Erikson concluded that people obey because obedience is a feature of human nature. Below we consider situational and personality/dispositional explanations of obedience.

Gross (1999) used the example of the Ik who are a society of hunter-gatherers forced to live in a confined territory with few resources because of the changes that have occurred in their native Uganda. Their harsh living environment has forced them not to have many of the values that we Europeans hold. For example, the Ugandan government took away the Ik tribe's traditional hunting, as a result of which obtaining sufficient food is now very difficult. In this harsh, survival-of-the-fittest environment children as young as 3 or 4 are expected to fend for themselves. They often join gangs of other children, but receive very little support from their parents. Those who become too weak or ill to support themselves are often left to die. The conclusion is that, in certain situations, people are "forced" to behave in anti-social ways.

Situational explanations

Why were Milgram's participants so markedly more obedient than most people would have expected? It is likely that the **fundamental attribution error** (the tendency to overestimate the importance of other people's personality in determining their behaviour) is involved. When we decide how many people would show total obedience in Milgram's situation, we think as follows: "Only a psychopath would give massive electric shocks to another person. There are very few psychopaths about, and so practically no one would be totally obedient." This line of reasoning focuses only on the role of personality. In fact, Milgram's participants were strongly influenced by situational factors such as the experimenter's insistence that the participant continue to give shocks, the scientific expertise of the experimenter, and so on. As we will see, it is actually unclear that we can gain much of an understanding of the high level of obedience to authority in the Milgram situation by focusing on the fundamental attribution error.

? To what extent can the same criticisms be applied to Meeus and Raaijmakers' study as were raised against Milgram's original experiment?

? In what way does Meeus and Raaijmakers' study have greater validity than Milgram's study?

? What are the main factors determining whether or not there is obedience to authority?

? Why do you think situational explanations may be more common in some cultures than others?

KEY TERM

Fundamental attribution error: the tendency to explain the causes of another person's behaviour in terms of dispositional rather than situational factors.

Milgram (1974) argued there are three main features of the situation he used that were conducive to obedience:

1. Experience has taught us that authorities are generally trustworthy and legitimate, and so obedience to authority is often appropriate. For example, it would be disastrous if those involved in carrying out an emergency operation refused to obey the surgeon's orders!
2. The orders given by the experimenter moved gradually from the reasonable (small shocks) to the unreasonable (harmful shocks). This made it difficult for participants to notice when they began to be asked to behave unreasonably. Think of the "foot-in-the-door" technique used by salespeople. They start with a minor request such as "Can I ask you a few questions?" (getting their foot metaphorically in the door) and then gradually make larger requests. Before you know it, you have bought some item you couldn't afford!
3. **Buffers.** These are aspects of the situation that prevent the person from seeing the consequences of their actions. In Milgram's study, this occurred when the participants couldn't see the victim.

According to Milgram (1974), these various aspects of his situation led to the participants being put into an **agentic state**. In this state, they became the instruments of an authority figure and so ceased to act according to their conscience. Someone in the agentic state thinks, "I am not responsible, because I was ordered to do it." In essence, Milgram was arguing that we have an unfortunate tendency to do as we're told provided that the person doing the telling is an authority figure. This contrasts with our everyday lives, where we are generally in the **autonomous state**, in which we are aware of the consequences of our actions and feel in control of our own behaviour.

Milgram (1974) claimed that the tendency to adopt the agentic state "is the fatal flaw nature has designed into us". This led him to stress the links between his findings and the horrors of Nazi Germany.

Evaluation. All of the situational factors identified by Milgram do play a part in producing obedience to authority. As we saw earlier, Milgram (1974) found that obedience to authority was greatest when the authority of the experimenter was reduced and when the obviousness of the learner's plight was maximised. Some of these situational factors have powerful effects. For example, full obedience to authority was reduced substantially from 65% in the standard condition to only 10% when the participant had a confederate who wouldn't give shocks. There is also some validity in the notion that a number of participants in the Milgram situation find themselves in an agentic state.

There are several weaknesses in Milgram's theoretical approach:

- It is not really correct that most participants found themselves in an agentic state. Most obedient participants experienced a strong conflict between the experimenter's demands and their own conscience. They seemed very tense and nervous, they perspired, they bit their lips, and they clenched and unclenched their fists. Such behaviour does *not* suggest they were in an agentic state.
- Milgram (1974) didn't emphasise one of the most important factors in producing obedience to authority. The experimenter repeatedly told

concerned participants that he took full responsibility for what happened in the Milgram situation, which persuaded many of them to continue with the experiment. Tilker (1970) found that there was a substantial reduction in obedience when participants were told that they (rather than the experimenter) were responsible for their actions.

- Milgram (1974) didn't focus much on the role of individual differences in personality in determining the extent to which participants were obedient. The fact that 35% of participants weren't fully obedient in the standard Milgram situation indicates that the situational pressures didn't influence all participants in the same way. We will shortly consider the personality characteristics of those most likely to resist the pressures to be obedient to authority.

- Milgram exaggerated the links between his findings and Nazi Germany. The values underlying Milgram's studies were the positive ones of increasing our understanding of human behaviour in contrast to the vile ideas prevalent in Nazi Germany. Most participants in Milgram's studies had to be watched closely to ensure their obedience, which wasn't necessary in Nazi Germany. Finally, most of Milgram's participants experienced great conflict and agitation, whereas those who carried out atrocities in Nazi Germany often seemed unconcerned about moral issues.

> **CASE STUDY: WAR CRIMINALS**
>
> After the Second World War, the Allies tried many of the high-ranking Nazi officers at Nuremberg. Adolf Eichmann argued that he had only been obeying orders. He said he was not the "monster" that the newspapers described but simply an ordinary person caught up in an extraordinary situation. Eichmann was described as having no violent anti-Jewish feelings (Arendt, 1963). The argument was that he was an autonomous individual who became agentic when he joined the SS and subscribed to the military code of obedience to those in authority. ∎

Situational factors: Soft influences. Some researchers (e.g. Blass & Schmitt, 2001) have drawn a distinction between social power based on harsh *external* influences (e.g. hierarchy-based legitimate power) and social power based on soft influences *within* the authority figure (e.g. expertise; credibility). Milgram emphasised the importance of harsh influences, but soft influences are also important. Blass and Schmitt presented participants with a 12-minute edited version of Milgram's documentary film, *Obedience*. They had to choose the best explanation for the strong obedience to authority shown in the film from the following choices based on various sources of power:

- *Legitimate*: experimenter's role as authority figure.
- *Expert*: experimenter's superior expertise and knowledge.
- *Coercive*: the power to punish the participant for non-compliance.
- *Informational*: the information conveyed to the participant was sufficient to produce obedience.
- *Reward*: the power to reward the participant for compliance.
- *Referent*: the power occurring because the participants would like to emulate the authority figure.

The sources of power most often chosen were in the order given above. That is to say, legitimate power (a harsh influence) and expertise (a soft influence) were chosen most frequently, followed by coercive power (a harsh influence) and informational power (a soft influence). These findings are important in two ways. First, they show that Milgram was only partially correct when explaining obedience to authority in terms of legitimate power. Second, they indicate that obedience to authority in the Milgram situation depends on at least two different sources of power.

CASE STUDY: THE MY LAI MASSACRE

The My Lai massacre has become known as one of the most controversial incidents in the Vietnam War. On 14 December 1969 almost 400 Vietnamese villagers were killed in under 4 hours. The following transcript is from a CBS News interview with a soldier who took part in the massacre.

Q. How many people did you round up?
A. Well, there was about forty, fifty people that we gathered in the center of the village. And we placed them in there, and it was like a little island, right there in the center of the village, I'd say . . . And . . .
Q. What kind of people—men, women, children?
A. Men, women, children.
Q. Babies?
A. Babies. And we huddled them up. We made them squat down and Lieutenant Calley came over and said, "You know what to do with them, don't you?" And I said yes. So I took it for granted that he just wanted us to watch them. And he left, and came back about ten or fifteen minutes later and said, "How come you ain't killed them yet?" And I told him that I didn't think you wanted us to kill them, that you just wanted us to guard them. He said, "No. I want them dead." So—
Q. He told this to all of you, or to you particularly?
A. Well, I was facing him. So, but the other three, four guys heard it and so he stepped back about ten, fifteen feet, and he started shooting them. And he

told me to start shooting. So I started shooting, I poured about four clips into the group.
Q. You fired four clips from your . . .
A. M-16.
Q. And that's about how many clips—I mean, how many—
A. I carried seventeen rounds to each clip.
Q. So you fired something like sixty-seven shots?
A. Right.
Q. And you killed how many? At that time?
A. Well, I fired them automatic, so you can't—You just spray the area on them and so you can't know how many you killed 'cause they were going fast. So I might have killed ten or fifteen of them.
Q. Men, women and children?
A. Men, women and children.
Q. And babies?
A. And babies.

William Calley stood trial for his involvement in this massacre. His defence was that he was only obeying orders. Before the massacre Calley showed no criminal tendencies and afterwards he returned to a life of quiet respectability. His behaviour was that of a "normal" person. Kelman and Lawrence (1972) conducted a survey after the trial and found that half of the respondents said that it was "normal, even desirable" to obey legitimate authority. ■

Personality/dispositional explanations

Adorno et al. (1950) argued that obedience to authority could be mostly explained in terms of personality. According to them, some people have an **authoritarian personality**, as a result of which they are very likely to be obedient and also prejudiced. Such individuals have the following characteristics:

- Rigid beliefs in conventional values.
- General hostility towards other groups.
- Intolerance of ambiguity.
- Submissive attitude towards authority figures.

Why are individuals with an authoritarian personality so obedient? Adorno et al. (1950) claimed that they were treated harshly as children, causing them to have much hostility towards their parents. This hostility remains unconscious, with the child seeming to idealise his/her parents. In later life, such children act in a submissive way towards authority figures, and displace their hostility onto

KEY TERM

Authoritarian personality: identified by Adorno et al. as someone who is more likely to be obedient. These people tend to hold rigid beliefs, and to be hostile towards other groups and submissive to authority.

minority groups in the form of prejudice. These characteristics of the authoritarian personality make people especially likely to obey the orders of an authority figure.

Adorno et al. devised various questionnaires relating to their theory. The most important one was the **F (Fascism) Scale**, which was designed to measure the attitudes of the authoritarian personality (look at the box below). Adorno et al. gave the test to about 2000 people and found that those who scored high on the F Scale also scored high on a scale that measured prejudice. This confirmed the validity of the scale.

Are we more likely to assume that this man is sleeping rough because of situational factors (he's been taken ill, forgotten his house keys) or dispositional factors (he can't keep a job, he's drunk and rowdy in accommodation, for example)?

Items from the F scale devised by Adorno et al.

Indicate whether you hold slight, moderate, or strong support OR slight, moderate, or strong opposition to the following:

"Obedience and respect for authority are the most important virtues children should learn."

"Most of our social problems would be solved if we could somehow get rid of the immoral, crooked, and feeble-minded people."

"What the youth needs most is strict discipline, rugged determination, and the will to work for family and country."

"Familiarity breeds contempt."

"Sex crimes, such as rape and attacks on children, deserve more than mere imprisonment, such criminals ought to be publicly whipped."

Milgram (1974) found that high scorers on the F Scale gave stronger shocks than low scorers when ordered to do so by an authority figure, thus indicating that personality plays a part in determining obedience to authority. However, the fact that about two-thirds of the participants in Milgram's experiments were fully obedient but far fewer people than that have an authoritarian personality means that this approach only provides a partial explanation.

Other studies have produced similar findings. Miller (1975) studied obedience to an order that the participants should grasp live electric wires for 5 minutes while working on some problems in arithmetic. Those scoring high on the F Scale were more likely to obey this order. Altemeyer (1981) used his own scale to assess authoritarianism, and found that high scorers tend to give more intense electric shocks than low scorers on a verbal learning task.

Some of the strongest evidence of the importance of individual differences in personality in determining the extent of obedience to authority was reported by Haas (1966). Top management in a company ordered lower-level management staff to indicate which one of their superiors should be fired. They were told that their recommendation would serve as "the final basis for action". There was a fairly high correlation of +0.52 between hostility as a personality dimension and participants' degree of obedience.

KEY TERM

F (Fascism) Scale: a test of tendencies towards fascism. High scorers are prejudiced and racist.

SECTION SUMMARY

❖ Social influence involves an individual's attitudes and/or behaviour being affected by other people.

Types of conformity: Majority influence

❖ Majority influence occurs when individuals in groups adopt the behaviour, attitudes, or values of the majority.

❖ Asch found majority influence on about one-third of trials even when the correct response was obvious. Others have found that the effects of majority influence can be even greater when the majority is an ingroup.

❖ There are various reasons for majority influence:
  – Informational social influence: people conform to gain information or because they are uncertain what to do.
  – Normative social influence: people conform to be liked or to avoid ridicule.
  – People conform to perceived social roles.

❖ Majority influence may be the result of:
  – Compliance: group acceptance.
  – Identification: group membership.
  – Internalisation: acceptance of group norms and changing of private opinions.

Types of conformity: Minority influence

❖ Minority influence occurs when the minority changes the beliefs and opinions of the group majority.

❖ The likely conditions for minority influence include:
  – Consistency
  – Flexibility
  – Commitment
  – Relevance of minority argument

❖ Minority influence is generally weaker than majority influence. This is probably due mainly to the smaller number of individuals in minorities, but may also reflect the greater power and status of majorities.

Types of conformity: Internalisation, compliance, and identification

❖ Kelman distinguished among compliance, internalisation, and identification. Compliance involves public conformity without internal agreement with other group members; internalisation involves conformity with internal agreement with others; and identification is conformity based on adhering to a given role in society.

❖ According to Moscovici, compliance is typically found when a majority influences a minority. In contrast, conversion (which closely resembles internalisation) occurs when a minority influences a majority.

❖ Conversion generally requires consistency, flexibility, commitment, and relevance from the minority.

❖ Much of the evidence provides good support for Moscovici's theory. However, differences in social influence of majorities and minorities are often more complicated than suggested by Moscovici, and these differences may depend on the majority's status and power rather than on sheer numbers.

❖ The Stanford prison experiment provides evidence for identification with the roles of prison guards and prisoners. However, the key findings have proved hard to replicate.

❖ Deindividuation is one reason why individuals conform to majority influence. It can involve conforming to an expected role.

Explanations of why people conform

❖ According to Deutsch and Gerard (1955), conformity via majority influence depends on informational and normative social influence. These two forms of influence generally operate at the same time.

❖ Normative social influence is less when participants' judgements are made in private or they have social support. Informational social influence is greater when the situation is ambiguous or participants have doubts about their knowledge or ability.

❖ Many factors affect both forms of social influence, but it is very hard to assess their relative importance.

❖ The situation and personal characteristics interactively determine the extent to which any given individual conforms, but the processes involved are poorly understood.

Obedience to authority

❖ Obedience to authority is behaving as instructed, usually in response to one individual.

Milgram's research

❖ Milgram's classic research showed that about two-thirds of people were prepared to administer potentially fatal electric shocks to another person. Similar findings have been obtained in several other cultures.

❖ Milgram discovered two ways in which obedience to authority could be reduced:
   1. Increasing the obviousness of the learner's plight;
   2. Reducing the authority or impact of the experimenter.

❖ There are issues of internal validity (believability of the set-up) and of external validity (generalising to real life). The fact that many participants were obviously distressed suggests reasonable internal validity. Replication of Milgram's findings when nurses were ordered to obey doctors suggests reasonable external validity.

Explanations of obedience

❖ Milgram argued that his situation placed participants in an agentic state in which they surrendered responsibility for their actions to the experimenter, who was perceived as a legitimate source of power.

❖ The fact that many participants became distressed doesn't suggest that they surrendered all responsibility.

❖ Milgram argued that the experimenter exerted harsh influence because he was regarded as a high-status power figure. However, there is evidence that much of the experimenter's power is via soft influence as a recognised expert.

❖ It is important to consider factors within the individual as well as those within the situation. For example, individuals having an authoritarian personality are more likely than other people to be fully obedient in the Milgram situation.

Independent Behaviour

We have seen that social pressures to conform or to obey authority can exert powerful effects on people's behaviour. Indeed, in Milgram's (1963) initial research on obedience to authority, he found that 65% (almost two-thirds) of participants were fully obedient. However, in virtually every experiment on majority influence and obedience to authority some people managed to resist the pressures to conform or to obey and so exhibited **independent behaviour**. Even in Milgram's original research as many as 35% of participants behaved in an independent way. In experiments in the Asch situation, independent behaviour was exhibited on about two-thirds of the critical trials.

What factors explain the existence of such independent behaviour? At the most general level, there are two major types of factors that might be important. First, there are aspects of the situation (situational factors) that may make it easier or harder to behave independently. Second, there are individual differences in personality. It seems reasonable to assume that some individuals have personalities that cause them to stick to their own opinions and resist behaving in line with a majority or in response to the instructions of an authority figure. We will discuss these explanations in turn.

> ### CASE STUDY: STANLEY MILGRAM'S OTHER RESEARCH
>
> Milgram's name is synonymous with obedience research, however he did conduct a number of other studies and was always seeking to test new ideas. Tavris (1974) called him "a man with a thousand ideas". He wrote songs, including a musical, and devised light-shows and machines.
>
> In relation to conformity, he tried the following with a group of students (Tavris, 1974). He asked them to go up to someone on an underground train and say "Can I have your seat?" They all recoiled in horror at the idea. Why were they so frightened? Milgram tried the task himself, assuming that it would be easy, but when he tried to say the actual words to a stranger on the underground he froze. He found he was overwhelmed by paralysing inhibition, and suggested that this shows how social rules exert extremely strong pressure. ■

Explanations of How People Resist Pressures to Conform and to Obey Authority

We will start by considering some of the situational factors that increased independent behaviour in Milgram's studies. As Milgram (1974) pointed out, there are two ways in which we can manipulate the situation so as to reduce obedience to authority. First, the harm being done to the victim can be made very clear. Milgram did this by using a condition in which participants had to force the learner's hand onto the shock plate. This approximately halved the percentage of participants who were totally obedient compared to the standard condition (30% vs 65%, respectively).

Second, steps can be taken to reduce the perceived authority of the person issuing the orders. Milgram did this in various ways. One effective method was to reduce the status of the experimenter from a white-coated scientist to an ordinary member of the public. This reduced total obedience from 65% in the standard condition to 48% in a run-down office. Much more effective at undermining the authority and power of the experimenter was providing the participant with a confederate who refused to give electric shocks. Only 10% of participants were fully obedient in this condition, which shows that people are much better able

> ### KEY TERM
>
> **Independent behaviour**: resisting the pressures to conform or to obey authority.

to exhibit independent behaviour when they feel they have someone's support. Note also that Rank and Jacobsen (1997) found that very few nurses (11%) obeyed an unreasonable request from a doctor when they had had the opportunity to discuss this request with other nurses.

If we develop a good understanding of obedience, then we should be able to make people more capable of resisting obeying others when their orders are unreasonable. Based on our knowledge, it seems likely that the following methods would work:

- Educate people about the problems of "blind obedience".
- Remind people that they should take responsibility for their own actions.
- Provide role models who refuse to obey.
- Question the motives of authority figures when they issue unreasonable orders.

We turn now to research on conformity. It is important to note that there were reasonably high levels of independence in Asch's (1951) original study. About two-thirds of the responses on critical trials involved resisting conformity pressures, and 26% of his participants never agreed with the majority.

How can we reduce majority influence or conformity behaviour? Asch (1951, 1956) identified two important factors. First, he found that conformity dropped dramatically from 37% to 5% when one confederate gave the correct answer on all trials. As with obedience to authority, the presence of support from someone else makes it much easier to resist social pressure—you're not being left completely isolated. Second, it is easier to avoid conforming when the number of people ranged against you is relatively small than when it is large. However, it is a matter of diminishing returns—there is little increase in conformity as that number goes up above three.

There are important social and cultural factors that help to determine whether people will resist pressures to conform. As we saw earlier, participants in the Asch situation are considerably more likely to display independent behaviour and resist majority influence when the others are not perceived as members of their ingroup. For example, Abrams et al. (1990) found that their participants resisted pressures to conform on 92% of trials when the other group members were seen as belonging to an outgroup. There was a substantial decrease in resistance to conformity to only 42% of trials when the others belonged to the participants' ingroup. In similar fashion, Williams and Sogon (1984) found that participants were significantly more likely to resist pressures to conform when the other group members were strangers rather than friends. It is more embarrassing to appear incompetent in front of ingroup members or friends than outgroup members or strangers.

Participants in the Asch situation face severe pressures to conform from the other members of the group. However, there are also pressures to conform or to be independent that depend on the culture from which the participants come. It makes sense to assume that people would be better able to resist pressures to conform if they belonged to a culture that valued independent behaviour than if they belonged to a culture that valued group-focused behaviour. As we saw earlier, Bond and Smith (1996) found in a meta-analysis that the extent of non-conformity varies across cultures. More specifically, participants resisted conformity pressures on average 75% of the time in individualistic cultures compared to only 63% of the time in collectivistic cultures. The take-home message is that it is easier to avoid conformity if you feel you have the support of your culture in doing so.

We conclude by considering an interesting study by Gamson, Fireman, and Rytina (1982). As we will see, they found that rebellion in a group situation can create disobedience. Gamson et al. set up a fictitious public relations firm called MHPC. Participants were employed to help the company to collect opinions on moral standards. They met at a motel, and engaged in a videotaped discussion. The discussion was about Mr C, who had managed a service station for an oil company. However, his franchise had been revoked because the company claimed he had behaved immorally and this made him unfit to be their local representative (he was living with a young woman and they weren't married). Mr C was suing the company for unfair dismissal. It also transpired that Mr C had spoken out on TV against higher petrol prices. The participants were told to discuss their attitudes towards Mr C's lifestyle, during which the co-ordinator switched the cameras on and off at various times while instructing the groups to argue as if they were offended by Mr C's behaviour. The groups quickly realised they were being manipulated to produce evidence supporting the oil company's position. In some of the groups, the participants threatened to confiscate the videotapes of the discussion, and to expose the oil company to the media. There was some rebellion in all 33 groups. All but four of the groups (i.e. 29 out of 33) refused to sign an affidavit giving MRHC permission to use the videotape in a trial.

Why were the findings of Gamson et al. (1982) so different from those obtained by Milgram? Why did rebellion occur instead of obedience? What happened in each group was that one member in each group spontaneously rebelled and this minority opinion swayed most of the groups. This change from Milgram's research may reflect the fact that Americans were generally more willing to challenge authority in the early 1980s than the early 1960s. It may also be that the MHRC co-ordinator had less authority than the experimenter in Milgram's study. Finally, it may be because the MHRC study involved groups. Groups often behave differently from individuals because there is the possibility of group action—everyone knows they can group together to resist authority.

■ **Activity:** You might try out Gamson et al.'s technique with various people. Pretend that you are about to conduct an experiment and ask the potential participants whether they are willing to take part in any of the following kinds of research. Show them the list from Gamson et al.'s study (on page 187). Afterwards, debrief them by telling them the true purpose of your research and ask what they felt about the deception and the use of prior general consent.

? How would you explain the findings of Gamson et al.'s research?

? In the light of Gamson et al.'s 1982 study how can we re-interpret Asch's research (see page 265)?

The Influence of Individual Differences on Independent Behaviour

There are large individual differences between participants in their responses to situations such as those devised by Asch and by Milgram. It is therefore an important issue to try to identify the personality and other characteristics of those individuals whose behaviour in such situations is independent. However, Milgram (1974, p. 205) was sceptical about the importance of individual differences: "The disposition a person brings to the experiment is probably less important a cause of his behaviour than most readers assume. For the social psychology of this century reveals a major lesson: often, it is not so much the kind of person a man is as the kind of situation in which he finds himself that determines how he will act."

Modigliani and Rochat (1995) identified one very important feature of those individuals who were independent in the Milgram situation. They re-analysed Milgram's own data based on audio recordings of conversations between the experimenter and the teacher. Of participants who protested verbally at an early stage, not one administered the maximum shock, and only 17% delivered more than 150 volts. These are strikingly high levels of independent behaviour given that about two-thirds of Milgram's participants administered the maximum shock. There was considerably less disobedience among participants who only began to protest later in the experiment. Thus, it was important for participants to "break the ice" by voicing their concerns very early in the experiment if they were to refuse to obey the experimenter's instructions.

Locus of control: Attribution theory

According to attribution theorists (e.g. Ross & Nisbett, 1991), people's behaviour in any situation can be caused externally (by situations) or it can be caused internally (by dispositions, including personality). According to this approach, there is substantial obedience to authority in Milgram's situation because behaviour is under external or situational control rather than internal or dispositional control. More specifically, most participants' behaviour was determined by what the experimenter ordered them to do (an external or situational factor) rather than by what their conscience told them to do (an internal or dispositional factor).

Nearly everyone greatly underestimates the extent to which participants will be obedient because of the fundamental attribution error—this is the tendency to underestimate the degree to which behaviour is externally or situationally determined. Thus, the fundamental attribution error explains why most people are very surprised when they discover that only about one-third of Milgram's participants were fully obedient—most people assume that practically no one would be.

The fundamental attribution error is the tendency to underestimate the influence of external factors on obedience. Many of Hitler's followers' levels of obedience may have been determined by situational factors (following orders) rather than dispositional factors (following internal moral resistance).

A similar account can be offered of conformity in the Asch situation. We could argue that participants in Asch's experiments were strongly influenced by an external factor (the opinions of other group members) but were sometimes not influenced by an internal factor (what they genuinely believed). Other attributional hypotheses are possible. For example, Ross, Bierbrauer, and Hofman (1976) argued that participants in the Asch situation have to grapple with two questions: (1) To what can I attribute the strange behaviour of the majority? (2) If I resist the majority, to what will they attribute my behaviour? If participants go along with the majority they will appear weak to themselves, but if they dissent they will appear incompetent to others. If they would rather appear weak to themselves than incompetent to others, they conform to the majority.

Locus of control

? Can you think of a recent situation where you went against what you would have decided because of the "power of the situation"? This is an example of, in that instance, an external locus of control.

The attribution theory approach provides a way of predicting the kind of person who would be most likely to resist majority influence and pressures to obey authority. We can distinguish between individuals who believe that their behaviour is determined mainly by external factors (e.g. luck) and those who believe that their behaviour is determined mainly by internal factors (e.g. their own ability and effort). According to the attribution approach, we would expect those whose behaviour is most under the influence of internal factors to be more independent in their behaviour than those whose behaviour is strongly influenced by external factors. This could explain the behaviour of participants in both the Asch and Milgram situations.

Rotter (1966) devised a questionnaire that assessed people's perceptions of control over personal outcomes, their generalised expectancies about the rewards they receive, and perceptions of control over entities such as governments. This questionnaire assessed **locus of control** (a personality dimension concerned with perceptions about the factors controlling what happens to us). More specifically, this questionnaire indicates whether we perceive that what happens to us is under our own control (internal locus of control) or whether it is determined mainly by situational factors (external locus of control). The prediction that follows from the attribution theory approach is that individuals with internal locus of control would be more likely than those with external locus of control to show independent behaviour in the Asch and Milgram situations. In addition, we might expect that the difference in independent behaviour between internals and externals might be greater when the external pressures to conform or to be obedient are very strong than when they are weak—increasing external pressures should only have much effect on externals who are very influenced by situational factors.

The evidence generally supports the prediction that those with internal locus of control will be more independent in their behaviour than those with external locus of control. For example, Shute (1975) studied the effects of peer pressure on attitudes to drugs. As predicted, participants with internal locus of control showed a smaller conformity effect than those with external locus of control. London and Lim (1964) found that internals were more independent than externals on a conformity task. The most convincing evidence was reported by Avtgis (1998), who carried out a meta-analysis of studies on the effects of locus of control on social influence and conformity or majority influence. Those with internal locus of control showed a moderately strong tendency to show less social influence and majority influence than those with external locus of control.

In spite of several positive findings, there have been some failures to find any relationship between locus of control and majority influence. For example, Williams and Warchal (1981) identified individuals having low and high scores for majority influence on Asch-type tasks. The two groups didn't differ in locus of control.

KEY TERM

Locus of control: a personality dimension concerned with perceptions about the factors controlling what happens to us.

Locus of control is relevant to predicting the extent to which individuals will conform in the Milgram situation (reviewed by Blass, 1991). For example, Holland (1967) carried out three versions of the Milgram experiment with participants with internal or external locus of control. Overall, 37% of the internals were disobedient in that they didn't administer the strongest electric shocks, compared to only 23% of externals.

Miller (1975) carried out a study in which the participants were told by the experimenter to give themselves electric shocks by grasping live electric wires (!) and to perform other tasks. The experimenter's apparent social status was manipulated—he seemed to have either a low or a high bureaucratic authority. Participants with external locus of control were more obedient when told what to do by a high than a low bureaucratic authority. In contrast, those with internal locus of control weren't affected by the experimenter's social status. Thus, internals were more resistant than externals to the external pressure of receiving orders from a high bureaucratic authority.

Other kinds of individual differences related to locus of control are also associated with independent behaviour. In conformity studies, participants who exhibit much independent behaviour tend to have higher self-esteem than those who display less independent behaviour. For example, Kurosawa (1993) studied independent behaviour in an Asch-type situation with low conformity pressure (two confederates) or high conformity pressure (four confederates). Self-esteem didn't affect independent behaviour in the low pressure situation. However, those high in self-esteem showed more independent behaviour than those low in self-esteem in the high pressure situation. Santee and Maslach (1982) found that students with high self-esteem were less likely than those with low self-esteem to agree with the solutions to a problem put forward by other students. Note that individuals high in self-esteem tend also to have internal locus of control (Sterbin & Rakow, 1996). Thus, individuals high in self-esteem may show independent behaviour mainly because they have internal locus of control.

As we saw earlier, individuals who are high in authoritarianism are more likely than other people to be fully obedient in the Migram situation (e.g. Altemeyer, 1981; Milgram, 1974; Miller, 1975). The other side of that coin is that those low in authoritarianism are relatively likely to exhibit independent behaviour. It is of interest that those low in authoritarianism tend to have an internal locus of control (de Man, Morrison, & Drumheller, 1993). Thus, their behaviour may be independent because they are influenced mainly by internal factors.

? Why is it that people high in self-esteem are more likely to resist orders to obey?

Evaluation

The attribution theory approach as tested through focusing on locus of control has proved successful in various ways. First, it seems reasonable to argue that there is so much obedience to authority and so much conformity because most people are strongly influenced by situational factors. Second, the fundamental attribution error seems to explain why most people grossly underestimate the amount of obedience in the Milgram situation. Third, it follows theoretically that individuals influenced mainly by internal factors (i.e. those with internal locus of control) should show more independent behaviour than those influenced mainly by external factors (i.e. those with external locus of control) and that prediction has been supported in both the Milgram and Asch situations. Fourth, there is some support (Miller, 1975) for the prediction that the difference in independent behaviour between internals and externals should be greater when situational pressures are greater than when they are weaker. Fifth, other personality factors (e.g. self-esteem; low authoritarianism) that predict independent behaviour are correlated in expected ways with measures of locus of control.

There are various weaknesses with the attribution theory approach to understanding why people resist (or fail to resist) the pressures they are exposed to in the Asch and Milgram situations:

- Locus of control has typically been assessed by the Rotter scale, which provides a very *general* measure of whether a given individual has an external or internal locus of control. It is unlikely that such a general measure would allow us to predict accurately individuals' behaviour in the *specific* Asch and Milgram situations.

- The assumption that individuals whose behaviour is mainly controlled by internal factors will *always* show more independent behaviour is dubious. Nearly everyone agrees that psychopaths (who are very aggressive and uncaring) would not only administer the maximum shock in the Milgram situation, but would probably enjoy doing so. Psychopaths in the Milgram situation would be driven by internal factors (e.g. desire to hurt others) and so their total obedience is completely inconsistent with the attribution theory approach!

- *Several* internal and external factors could be involved in the Asch and Milgram situations. As Sabini, Siepman, and Stein (2001) pointed out, we could argue that independent behaviour involves a dominance of external factors over internal factors—precisely the opposite to the usual assumption. In the Milgram situation, independent individuals who don't show obedience to authority may be strongly influenced by an external or situational factor (the suffering of others) but relatively unaffected by an internal factor (the disposition to obey authority). In the Asch situation, independent individuals who are unaffected by majority influence may be more influenced by an external or situational factor (the experimenter's instructions to give correct answers) than by an internal factor (the need not to look like a fool). The desire to avoid embarrassment seems very likely to influence behaviour in the Asch situation.

- In essence, attribution theory as applied to individual differences in locus of control focuses on situational factors leading to obedience/conformity and internal factors leading to disobedience/failure to conform. However, there are situational factors that could lead to disobedience/failure to conform and internal factors that could lead to obedience/conformity.

- The notion that internal and external factors are entirely separate from each other is incorrect. For example, consider addicts. It is generally assumed that they are driven by their internal cravings. However, their lives are very controlled by whatever it is that they crave. As Sabini et al. (2001, p. 8) pointed out, "The more internally controlled they [addicts] are, the more externally controlled they are." In similar fashion, psychopaths have very powerful internal desires to hurt others, and these desires cause them to seek situations in which these desires can be expressed (an external factor).

- Most of the research has focused simply on showing that internals display more independent behaviour than externals in a particular version of the Milgram or Asch situation. However, it follows from attribution theory that there should be larger differences between the groups in independent behaviour when the situational pressures are small than when they are great—in other words, the effects of locus of control on independent behaviour depends on the strength of the situational factors. However, this prediction has only rarely been tested.

Implications for Social Change of Research into Conformity, Obedience, and Independence

As you have read this chapter, you may have found yourself worrying about the implications of the research for society. As a result of his research on obedience to authority, Milgram (1974) became extremely pessimistic about the future: "The capacity for man to abandon his humanity, indeed the inevitability that he does so, as he merges his unique personality into the large institutional structures . . . is the fatal flaw nature has designed into us, and which in the long run gives our species only a modest chance for survival." In a similar vein, Milgram (1974) also referred to "the extreme willingness of adults to go to almost any lengths on the command of an authority".

The notion that evil behaviour is not confined to a few psychopaths and other mentally ill individuals is one that has been expressed by many other experts. For example, the philosopher Hannah Arendt argued that what was most horrifying about the Nazis was that they were "terrifyingly normal" rather than being extremely deviant.

In this section, we will consider the extent to which the bleak picture painted by Milgram and by Arendt is supported by research on conformity, obedience, and independence. After that, we will turn to the issue of what (if anything) can be done to minimise the dangers of blind obedience and conformity. For example, we will consider whether Milgram (1974) was right that there is a real need "to invent political systems that give conscience a better chance over errant authority".

Conformity research

On the face of it, it seems very worrying that participants in Asch-type experiments give the wrong answer on about one-third of trials even though the correct answer is obvious. Such findings suggest that people's behaviour is much more easily manipulated by the views of others than might have been thought to be the case. It could also be argued that it is worrying that conformity to a mistaken majority in the Asch situation is very high when the majority belongs to the same ingroup as the participant (58% conformity in the Abrams et al., 1990, study). The reason why that is worrying is because most of us spend a lot of our time in the presence of one or more of the ingroups to which we belong.

What grounds are there for optimism based on research on conformity? First, it is important to note that the Asch situation is very artificial—in your entire life, you have almost certainly never been in a situation in which several other people have deliberately lied to you in order to influence your behaviour! Second, it is rather unusual in everyday life to have no chance to discuss what you consider the wrong-headed approach of a group with friends and acquaintances. Third, we can turn the findings around and point out (totally accurately) that participants successfully ignore the views of the majority on approximately two-thirds of trials. That hardly suggests that we can't stop ourselves conforming to majorities. Fourth, the fact that majority influence generally operates much more strongly on public judgements than on private ones means that most individuals are not convinced of the rightness of the group's judgements. Fifth, there is evidence from studies in the United States that conformity in the Asch situation has been diminishing (Smith & Bond, 1993).

Obedience research

Milgram's findings seem to indicate that most people are prepared to ignore the dictates of their own conscience if an authority figure orders them to behave in a morally unacceptable way. Since the participants were told that the victim had a heart condition, they knew that administering high levels of shock could prove fatal. These findings seem to confirm Milgram's (1974) claim that people can be persuaded to abandon their consciences and moral values if ordered to do so by an authority figure. This pessimistic view appears to find confirmation in Milgram's finding that some participants justified administering the maximum electric shock by blaming the victim rather than accepting responsibility: "Once having acted against the victim, these subjects found it necessary to view him as an unworthy individual whose punishment was made inevitable by his own deficiencies of intellect and character" (Milgram, 1974, p. 10).

It could be argued that Milgram's set-up was so artificial that his findings don't have any real relevance to everyday life. However, that argument doesn't stand up very well to scrutiny. We have seen that nurses in real-life situations will give patients too high doses of drugs if ordered to do so by a doctor (Hofling et al., 1966; Lesar et al., 1997). In addition, there is the Strip Search Prank Call Scam (Wolfson, 2005). Fast-food workers in the United States received phone calls from a prankster (not a researcher!) claiming to be a policeman. He persuaded many of the workers to strip and sexually abuse other workers.

For many people, the most compelling evidence that Milgram was right in assuming that we are nearly all willing to ignore our consciences in the face of authority comes from world history. The horrors of Nazi Germany perhaps provide the most obvious example, but the genocide in Rwanda, the mass

Events such as the torture that was carried out on prisoners in Abu Ghraib support Milgram's findings that most people are prepared to ignore their own conscience in the face of authority.

murders in Stalin's Russia, and the torture and abuse at Abu Ghraib prison in Iraq are just a few other striking cases of immoral behaviour and obedience to authority.

? Can you think of an example where conformity and/or obedience are very useful or essential, and an example of where they should be challenged?

What grounds for optimism emerge from research on obedience? Milgram (1974) believed that his findings had direct relevance to the horrors of Nazi Germany. However, there are various reasons for believing that Milgram exaggerated the similarities. First, as mentioned earlier, Milgram emphasised to his participants that the experiment was designed to achieve positive goals such as increasing our knowledge of human learning and memory. In contrast, the goals that the Nazis had in mind were totally negative, including the systematic murder and eventual extermination of Jews, gypsies, and homosexuals.

Second, Milgram (1974) argued that people who behave in an ethically unacceptable way when obeying an authority figure do so because they have entered an agentic state in which they forget their own consciences and absolve themselves of all personal responsibility. That may well have been true of many Nazis working in concentrations camps, but it is certainly not true of the overwhelming majority of participants in Milgram's research. The most common reaction was for participants to show obvious signs of tension and unease and to give every appearance of being in emotional turmoil. In addition, most of the participants seemed reluctant to look at the learner, which suggests that they experienced some concern and guilt about the shocks they were inflicting on him. For example, Milgram (1974) found that a mature and initially poised businessman doing the experiment was rapidly "reduced to a twitching stuttering wreck, who was rapidly approaching nervous collapse".

Third, most of the Nazis who committed atrocities against the Jews and others did so in the absence of any minute-by-minute surveillance. In contrast, the participants in Milgram's experiments were much more obedient when the experimenter could see what they were doing than when he could not. This difference strongly suggests that the Nazis had a much stronger commitment to obey authority than did Milgram's participants.

One of the important features of Milgram's basic experiment was that the participant had to decide whether or not to obey the authority figure in the absence of any social support. In the real world, people rarely have to make moral decisions when isolated from other people—they generally have at least some opportunity to discuss what they should do when an authority figure orders them to do something they feel strongly is wrong. There is plenty of evidence indicating that social support can drastically reduce obedience to authority. For example, Rank and Jacobsen (1997) found that only 11% of nurses obeyed a doctor's instructions to give too high a dose of medication to patients when they had the chance to talk to other nurses beforehand.

Independence research

The research on individual differences in independent behaviour can be regarded from a pessimistic perspective. There are millions of individuals in the world whose personalities equip them poorly to avoid immoral obedience to authority or conformity to mistaken majorities. For example, the evidence suggests that those with an external locus of control, or who are high in authoritarianism, or lacking self-esteem, are all vulnerable. However, this pessimistic perspective is very much like arguing that the glass is half empty rather than half full.

There are various encouraging findings that have emerged from research into independence. First, individuals in studies on obedience to authority who protest at an early stage about the unreasonableness of what they are being asked to do are very much more likely than other individuals to refuse to give large electric shocks (Modigliani & Rochat, 1995). Second, individuals who have an internal locus of control generally seem less likely than those with an external locus of control to conform to mistaken majority views. Third, individuals high in self-esteem show less conformity than those low in self-esteem. Fourth, individuals low in authoritarianism tend to show less obedience to authority than those high in authoritarianism.

The findings discussed above have important implications. They suggest that independent behaviour can be fostered by training programmes designed to increase internal locus of control, increase self-esteem, and reduce authoritarianism. In addition, it seems likely that the assertiveness training programmes that are available might prove useful in view of the evidence that assertive individuals have been shown to exhibit less conformity than non-assertive ones in the Asch situation (Williams & Warchal, 1981).

How can we promote social change?

The impressive research that psychologists have carried out on conformity, obedience to authority, and independence can provide the basis for promoting **social change** in several ways. First, individuals are much less likely to obey immoral orders or to be persuaded to conform to the mistaken views of a majority if they have at least some social support. This point was well made by Milgram (1974): "When an individual wishes to stand in opposition to authority, he [sic!] does best to find support for his position from others in his group. The mutual support provided by men for each other is the strongest bulwark against the excesses of authority."

Some of the evidence we have discussed in this chapter fits neatly with the notion that social support can have very beneficial effects. Asch (1956) found that participants who had one supporter conformed on only 5% of trials rather than 37% as happened when they lacked support. In similar fashion, Milgram (1974) found that only 10% of participants showed complete obedience when there were confederates who refused to administer electric shocks. This figure should be compared against 65% when the experiment was conducted under standard conditions with no social support.

Second, most individuals are less likely to exhibit morally undesirable behaviour if they spend some time reflecting on moral issues. Evidence for this was reported by Sherman (1980). He asked a colleague to phone several people apparently just to find out their opinions on various issues. They were asked to indicate what they would do if they were ordered to perform a certain act that was morally and/or socially undesirable, and there was some discussion of the issues over the phone. Several weeks later, the same individuals were asked by an authority figure to carry out that particular act. Two-thirds of the participants refused to obey, which is far higher than the number refusing to obey in Milgram's research.

KEY TERM

Social change: the process of changing social norms such as attitudes and beliefs.

Third, we have seen that conformity to the mistaken views of the majority is approximately 50% more common in collectivistic cultures than in individualistic ones (Bond & Smith, 1996). There are grounds for assuming that there will be a steady increase in the number of individualistic cultures over time because increasing affluence is associated with a move towards individualism (Kashima & Kashima, 2003). Since most countries (with the exception of those in Africa) are becoming more affluent, it seems likely that many countries are becoming more individualistic and thus perhaps less conforming.

Fourth, we have seen that individuals with high self-esteem are more independent in their behaviour than those with low self-esteem (Kurosawa, 1993; Santee & Maslach, 1982). Arndt et al. (2002) argued that people will tend to be independent and less conforming when they focus on one aspect of the self that is unchanging and makes them feel good about themselves. As predicted, participants told to think of such an aspect of the self were more independent than controls when rating an abstract painting in the knowledge of the ratings of others.

Fifth, conformity is greater when the other group members are of higher status than the participant and obedience to authority is similarly greater when the participant is of lesser status than the authority figure. An implication is that there will be more conformity and obedience to authority in hierarchical organisations or groups with large status differences than in organisations or groups that are non-hierarchical. It is no coincidence that many of the tragic situations that have occurred through undue obedience to authority (e.g. Nazi Germany; Abu Ghraib) have occurred in military groups, in which there is a very strong hierarchy.

Subbotsky (1994) found that young children tended to show conformity by imitating the incorrect actions of an adult experimenter, and argued that this occurred because children feel themselves in a submissive position relative to adults. As predicted, the children displayed much less conformist behaviour when the adult occupied the position of a "child" when interacting with the children participants. This occurred because the children perceived themselves as equal partners with the adult.

Sixth, we can reduce unthinking obedience to authority and conformity by means of education and learning. Many of the participants in the research carried out by Asch and by Milgram reported afterwards that they had learned much from the experience. Of most immediate relevance, they felt that they had learned more about themselves and were determined in future to be very careful not to conform or obey an authority figure in an unthinking way. In similar fashion, your knowledge of research in this area may well prove helpful when you find yourself confronted by a moral conflict or dilemma.

Evaluation

Research on conformity, obedience to authority, and independence can be used in several ways to produce desirable social change. More specifically, the provision of social support, providing individuals with time to reflect on complex moral issues, fostering personal responsibility (e.g. in individualistic cultures), enhancing self-esteem, avoiding hierarchical organisations with large status differentials, and

? Why is it that collectivist cultures are more likely to conform to a mistaken view?

■ **Activity:** On the basis of the psychological evidence, what advice would you give to the management committee of a children's home for difficult children? They want to know how to increase obedience and reduce group conformity. List three things for obedience and three things for conformity, citing the relevant evidence to support your argument.

providing information about the dangers of obedience to authority and conformity are all very useful.

From time to time in this chapter, I have pointed out that it is dangerous to think that conformity and obedience to authority should *always* be avoided. So far as conformity is concerned, Deutsch and Gerard (1955) argued that people generally conform either because they acknowledge the superior knowledge of other group members or because they want to be liked and/or to avoid embarrassment. It is important to note that these are not unworthy motives. It is often absolutely right to defer to the greater knowledge of others, and we should be very suspicious of anyone who has no desire to be liked or to avoid embarrassment!

So far as obedience is concerned, it is generally advisable to obey authority figures. If your doctor strongly urges you to follow a particular treatment regime, you may endanger your health by not doing as he/she tells you. In similar fashion, if your boss orders you to carry out a given piece of work, the order is generally perfectly reasonable and obeying is the correct response.

In sum, we can sometimes find it hard to know in a given situation whether conformity or obedience to authority is appropriate or whether we should display independent behaviour. One of the most important factors is whether we are asked to behave in a morally or socially undesirable way, in which case independent behaviour is obviously much preferable.

HOW SCIENCE WORKS: SOCIAL INFLUENCE IN EVERYDAY LIFE
You could do a naturalistic observation of obedience or conformity in everyday life. This would comply with BPS Ethical Guidelines if you were careful to observe in a public place, and to respect your participants. How might you assess conformity to social norms? And how might you adjust your observation and data collection to reduce the chance of people feeling spied on, and in consequence becoming suspicious or agitated?

You could observe other customers in a fast food place, by sitting chatting with a friend and having a coffee so you look very ordinary. You could also have a magazine or newspaper on your table, and hidden in it a ready-drawn simple two-column grid on which you could tick the columns, one for conforming (people who clear away their own rubbish) and one for not conforming (people who leave their own rubbish). You would record no personal data at all, just ticks, and at the end of your observation you would total each column. Then you could see whether your prediction, your hypothesis, was supported by your data or not.

SECTION SUMMARY

Reducing obedience and conformity

❖ One of the most effective ways of reducing obedience is to provide individuals with a disobedient confederate.

❖ Obedience to authority can be reduced by emphasising the harm being done to the victim or reducing the perceived authority of the person who issues the orders.

❖ A confederate who always gives the right answer greatly reduces conformity in the Asch situation.

❖ Independent behaviour in the Asch situation is more common in individualistic cultures than in collectivistic ones.

❖ According to attribution theorists, individuals are most likely to display independent behaviour if they focus on internal or dispositional factors rather than situational ones.

❖ It follows from the above that individuals with an internal locus of control should show more independent behaviour than those with external locus of control. There is some support for this prediction in the Asch and Milgram situations.

❖ High self-esteem and low authoritarianism (both associated with internal locus of control) are both predictive of independent behaviour.

❖ Attribution theory is wrong in assuming that individuals whose behaviour is mainly controlled by internal factors will always show relatively independent behaviour. For example, psychopaths might focus on their internal desire to hurt other people, which would make them very inclined to be obedient in the Milgram situation.

❖ Attribution theory is also wrong in drawing a sharp distinction between internal and external factors.

Locus of control: Attribution theory

❖ People's apparent willingness to inflict harm on others when ordered to do so, and to conform when they know the group is wrong, may seem very worrying.

❖ In fact, Milgram and Asch both used very artificial situations, and many participants refused to obey or to conform.

❖ Milgram compared his situation to that of Nazi Germany, but there are several major differences. For example, the research goals were worthy, whereas those of Nazi Germany were morally vile.

❖ Training can be provided to make individuals more assertive and have more self-esteem—this should reduce obedience and conformity.

Implications for social change of research into conformity, obedience, and independence

❖ Social support is very effective at reducing unreasonable obedience to authority and conformity.

❖ There is less obedience and conformity when individuals have the chance to reflect on moral issues.

❖ Obedience to authority and conformity can be reduced by fostering individualistic societies in which there are non-hierarchical and democratic mechanisms for making important decisions.

❖ Education and training (including providing information about psychological research on obedience and conformity) would have beneficial effects.

How can we promote social change?

> You have reached the end of the chapter on social psychology. Social psychology is an approach or perspective in psychology. The material in this chapter has exemplified the way that social psychologists explain behaviour. They look at behaviour in terms of the ways in which other people affect our behaviour. Nowhere is this clearer than in social influence research. Ancient astrologers believed that people's actions were affected by an airy fluid that flowed down from the heavenly bodies. This fluid force-field was called *"influentia"*. The concept of influences comes from this—they are both invisible and very powerful, as we have seen.

See Chapter 6 of the revision guide for guidance on revising this chapter for the exam.

FURTHER READING

The whole topic of social influence is discussed in detail in M.W. Eysenck (2008). *Fundamentals of Psychology* (Hove, UK: Psychology Press). Most of the topics discussed in this chapter are dealt with in various chapters in M. Hewstone and W. Stroebe (Eds.) (2001) *Introduction to social psychology (3rd Edn.)* (Oxford: Blackwell). R.S. Baron and N. Kerr (2003) *Group process, group decision, group action (2nd Edn.)* (Buckingham, UK: Open University Press) provide an accessible introduction to topics relating to social influence. If you want a thorough and up-to-date account of research and theory on social influence, it is to be found in R.B. Cialdini and N.J. Goldstein (2004). Social influence: Compliance and conformity. *Annual Review of Psychology, 55,* 591–621.

WEBSITES

http://news.bbc.co.uk/1/hi/magazine/3300635.stm
   Conformity and obedience over-view: A snapshot about the research of Asch, Milgram, and Zimbardo.

http://www.newscientist.com/channel/life/dn7881-copycat-chimps-are-cultural-conformists.html
   Is conformity genetic?: Discusses how our chimpanzee relatives also conform.

http://www.bbc.co.uk/science/humanbody/mind/articles/psychology/psychology_9.shtml
   Independence and peer pressure.

http://www.stanleymilgram.com/milgram.php
   Stanley Milgram: Links to more snapshots of Milgram's work.

http://www.jewishcurrents.org/2004-jan-dimow.htm
   Resisting authority: A personal account of one of Milgram's participants.

http://bps-research-digest.blogspot.com/2007/05/can-good-people-really-turn-bad-re.html
   Zimbardo's prison simulation revisited: Discusses how a biased sample may have been an important factor.

REVISION QUESTIONS

The examination questions aim to sample the material in this whole chapter. For advice on how to answer such questions refer to Chapter 1, Section 2.

When you are provided with a stimulus question do not panic if you have not seen that specific question before. Stimulus questions require you to apply your knowledge to a specific scenario. Whilst you may not have seen such a scenario before, if you have revised everything you *will* have the knowledge needed to answer the question.

Question 1
a. Using your knowledge of obedience explain why people obey. (6 marks)
b. Explain why studies of obedience have been criticised as lacking validity. (5 marks)

Question 2
a. Using your knowledge of obedience explain two ways the situation would have to change to increase resistance to obedience. (6 marks)
b. Discuss research into the individual differences that influence independent behaviour (12 marks)

Question 3
a. Outline **two** types of conformity. (4 marks)
b. Explain why studies of conformity have been criticised in terms of the ethical issues raised. (5 marks)

Individual differences is an approach or perspective in psychology. The study of individual differences is literally the study of the ways that individuals differ in terms of their psychological characteristics. Individuals differ *physically* in terms of, for example, height and hair colour. They differ *psychologically* in terms of intelligence, aggressiveness, willingness to conform, masculinity and femininity, and just about every other behaviour that comes to mind. An important individual difference is the extent to which a person is mentally healthy. This is specifically referred to as the study of abnormal or atypical psychology.

SECTION 16
Defining and explaining psychological abnormality p. 313

This section explores the question "What is abnormality?" by looking at various possible definitions. What are the limitations of these definitions of abnormality? It may be possible to explain mental disorders in the same way that we explain physical illnesses—in terms of biological or physical causes. This is called the biological (or medical) model. Alternatively, we could use psychological explanations, such as those based on learning theory (the behavioural model) or on Freud's views (the psychodynamic model), or we could use a cognitive approach. What are the implications of these models for treatment?

Specification content: Definitions of abnormality, including deviation from social norms, failure to function adequately and deviation from ideal mental health, and limitations associated with these definitions of psychological abnormality. Key features of the biological approach to psychopathology. Key features of psychological approaches to psychopathology including the psychodynamic, behavioural, and cognitive approaches.

SECTION 17
Treating abnormality p. 341

Various forms of therapy for the treatment of mental disorders have been developed over the past hundred years. Most of these therapies are based on the biological and psychological models of abnormality discussed in Section 16. The effectiveness of the major biological and psychological therapies are discussed.

Specification content: Biological therapies: including drugs and ECT (electroconvulsive therapy). Psychological therapies, including psychoanalysis, systematic de-sensitisation, and Cognitive Behavioural Therapy.

INDIVIDUAL DIFFERENCES
Psychopathology (Abnormality)

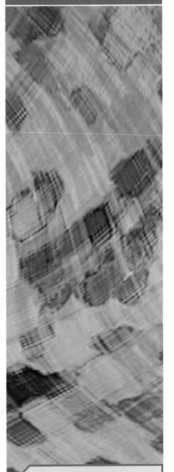

This chapter explores one major topic in the study of individual differences—abnormality. What is **abnormality**? If clinicians are to treat patients with mental disorders, they need to distinguish between normal and abnormal behaviour. However, first they must define abnormality. Mental disorder has been likened to physical illness—for example, having a cold is an abnormal and undesirable state. We will consider that definition a little later in the chapter.

Why do some people have mental disorders and others don't? Are mental disorders "caught" in the same way that you catch a cold, or do they depend on genetic factors and/or personality? We will explore mental abnormality and its potential undesirability in this chapter.

Most of our definitions of abnormality and our explanations for mental disorder are based on Western beliefs. In recent years, however, there has been a growing recognition that it is very important to take account of cultural and sub-cultural differences. This chapter takes account of these issues.

In the final section of the chapter, we consider the main therapeutic approaches that are used to treat individuals suffering from mental disorders. In general terms, we can place these therapies in two main categories: those that are mostly biological in emphasis and those that are primarily psychological.

SECTION 16
DEFINING AND EXPLAINING PSYCHOLOGICAL ABNORMALITY

Definitions of Abnormality

What is abnormality? The term "abnormal" is defined as "deviating from what is normal or usual". What, then, is meant by the term "normal"? Conforming to a standard of some sort. But how do we establish the standard? Several approaches will be considered here—all of which have something in their favour:

1. The standard can be defined in statistical terms—what most people are doing.
2. The standard can be defined in social terms—what is considered socially acceptable or deviant.
3. We might use the function of "adequate functioning"—being able to cope reasonably well with the demands of daily life.
4. There is the concept of **ideal mental health**—a state of contentment we all strive to achieve.

KEY TERMS

Abnormality: an undesirable state producing severe impairment in a person's social and personal functioning, often causing anguish. Abnormal behaviour deviates from statistical or social norms, causes distress to the individual or others, and is seen as a failure to function adequately.
Ideal mental health: a state of contentment that we all strive to achieve.

Statistical deviation from a normal distribution

If you measure any aspect of human behaviour, such as height or intelligence or aggressiveness, you should find that people with varying degrees of the behaviour are normally distributed around the mean. For example, there are a lot of people who are "averagely" tall or aggressive, whereas there are very few who are very small or highly aggressive. The shape of this distribution is shown in the figure on the right. The majority of individuals are clustered round the mean, which is why the curve is highest at this point. The further away you go from the mean, the fewer individuals there are. There are as many people above and below the mean. In other words (theoretically) there are as many non-aggressive as there are very aggressive people, and as many people who are taller than average as there are people who are shorter than average. Furthermore, we can specify the percentage of people who are within one or two standard deviations of the mean (this concept is explained further in Chapter 5 Section 11). Basically, a standard deviation is a measure of "average" distance from the mean. A very unusual behaviour will be more than 2 standard deviations from the mean, that is it will be found in less than 5% of the population. With reference to the normal curve in the figure, you can see that only very few people are in the "tail" regions.

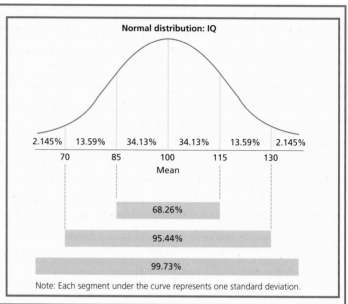

Note: Each segment under the curve represents one standard deviation.

? In what ways are you abnormal?

Statistical infrequency

The statistical approach is based, not surprisingly, on the idea that certain behaviours are statistically rare in the population. Consider, for example, trait anxiety (a personality characteristic relating to the tendency to experience high levels of anxiety) as assessed by Spielberger's State-Trait Anxiety Inventory. The mean score for trait anxiety is about 40. Only 2% of the population will have a score higher than 55, so these people can be regarded as abnormal in the sense that their scores deviate from the majority in terms of the *normal distribution*, which is discussed in the box above.

Limitations of the statistical approach

There are problems with this approach. In terms of a personality characteristic such as trait anxiety we would expect to find a normal distribution within the great majority of populations. Most people cluster around the mean score with just a few scoring very high or very low. An "abnormally" high score on trait anxiety would suggest that treatment might be helpful. A low score on trait anxiety (scores of 25 or less) would also be statistically abnormal. However, it would hardly indicate clinical abnormality—it might even be fairly desirable.

A similar argument could be applied to intelligence. Only 2% of the population have an IQ (intelligence quotient) in excess of 130 (see the box). Such individuals are abnormal in terms of statistical infrequency, but most people would be very pleased to discover that they had a really high IQ!

We have seen that the concept of **statistical infrequency** in relation to abnormality is of importance, but it doesn't allow us to identify *what* behaviours require treatment. In other words, it overlooks *desirability*. Some statistically abnormal behaviours are undesirable (e.g. high trait anxiety), whereas others are desirable (e.g. low trait anxiety or genius). To treat mental disorder we need a definition to include behaviours that are not only statistically rare but also undesirable and damaging.

A second problem with the statistical approach is deciding by how much a behaviour must deviate from the norm or average before it should be considered abnormal. Statistical definitions rely on an arbitrary cut-off point, which might be

KEY TERM

Statistical infrequency/deviation from statistical norms: behaviours that are statistically rare, or deviate from the average/statistical norm as illustrated by the normal distribution curve, are classed as abnormal.

in terms of standard deviations (discussed in the box on the previous page). A third problem is that our cut-off point might not apply to another cultural group in which trait anxiety is rather differently distributed. A fourth problem with statistical definitions is that they are related to a standard set by a particular population, which may not apply to people in different age groups or cultures. For example, very few middle-aged people have clothes everywhere in their bedroom, but the same can't be said for teenagers! On the positive side, the statistical approach is less affected by value judgements than some of the other approaches we will be considering. A fifth problem is that we sometimes find that behaviours are not rare at a given time in a particular culture even though they are clearly "abnormal" in the sense of being undesirable. A clear example is the genocide in Rwanda several years ago in which hundreds of thousands of people were systematically murdered.

> **KEY TERM**
>
> **Deviation from social norms**: behaviour that does not follow accepted social patterns, or unwritten social rules. Such violation is considered abnormal. These norms vary from culture to culture and from era to era.

Deviation from social norms

An important part of what is missing from the statistical approach to abnormality is any consideration of the *impact* of an individual's behaviour on others. A different approach is that people who behave in a socially deviant and apparently incomprehensible way should be regarded as abnormal.

The social norms approach also allows us to account for desirability of a behaviour, both for the individual and for society as a whole. **Deviation from social norms** is abnormal and undesirable. Many people labelled as clinically abnormal do behave in a socially deviant way. For example, anti-social personality disorder describes individuals who lack a conscience and behave aggressively towards others because they experience little or no guilt. Consider also the Case Studies described below and on the following page.

> **Moral codes**
>
> The subjective judgements we make when deciding whether or not a particular form of behaviour is normal are derived from the moral codes or standards that we have observed in the behaviour of significant others. We never become entirely independent in our moral thinking. Even as adults our thinking about morality often refers to a collective understanding of the right way to behave in a given situation. Someone who demonstrates a deviation from this may be perceived as either "mad" or "bad".

CASE STUDY: SIMON, A BOY WITH ACUTE SCHIZOPHRENIA

Simon lived at home with his parents. Over some months his parents had become increasingly concerned about his behaviour. He had grown reclusive, spending a lot of time in his room, and he had lost contact with his friends. His parents feared he might be taking drugs. They decided to call the doctor when they found that he had scratched the words "good" and "evil" on his arms, along with other unusual symbols. The GP was also concerned and contacted a psychiatrist who visited Simon at home. Simon at first pretended to be out. After some negotiation, he agreed to let the psychiatrist in. Initially, Simon was very suspicious and denied that there was a problem. Eventually, he told the psychiatrist that he was very worried about all the evil in the world, and had discovered that he could tell whether people were good or evil just by looking at them. He described receiving messages from the radio and TV.

The psychiatrist was concerned when Simon said that he left the house at night to look for evil people,

believing it was his duty to fight them. The psychiatrist found that Simon's bedroom was painted black and the curtains were taped shut. The walls were covered with crucifixes and mystical symbols, and Simon slept with a large knife near his bed in case he was confronted by evil people at night.

Simon was asked if he was willing to be admitted to a local hospital. He refused, saying he did not need help. The psychiatrist was sufficiently concerned about the possible risks to Simon or others that he arranged for Simon to be admitted under the Mental Health Act. For the first few weeks in hospital, Simon continued to claim that he was not ill and did not need treatment. Drug therapy resulted in significant improvements and he eventually returned home, continuing with his medication.

(Adapted from J.D. Stirling & J.S.E. Hellewell, 1999, *Psychopathology*. London: Routledge.) ■

CASE STUDY: SARAH: A CASE OF AGORAPHOBIA

Sarah, a woman in her mid-thirties, was shopping for bargains in a crowded department store during the January sales. Without warning and without knowing why, she suddenly felt anxious and dizzy. She worried that she was about to faint or have a heart attack. She dropped her shopping and rushed straight home. As she neared home, she noticed that her feelings of panic lessened.

A few days later she decided to go shopping again. On entering the store, she felt herself becoming increasingly anxious. After a few minutes she had become so anxious that a shopkeeper asked her if she was alright and took her to a first aid room. Once there her feelings of panic became worse and she grew particularly embarrassed at all the attention she was attracting.

After this she avoided going to the large store again. She even started to worry when going into smaller shops because she thought she might have another panic attack, and this worry turned into intense anxiety.

Eventually she stopped shopping altogether, asking her husband to do it for her.

Over the next few months, Sarah found that she had panic attacks in more and more places. The typical pattern was that she became progressively more anxious the further away from her house she got. She tried to avoid the places where she might have a panic attack but, as the months passed, she found that this restricted her activities. Some days she found it impossible to leave the house at all. She felt that her marriage was becoming strained and that her husband resented her dependence on him.

Clearly Sarah's behaviour was abnormal, in many of the ways described in the text. It was statistically infrequent and socially deviant. It interfered with her ability to function adequately, both from her own point of view and from that of her husband. She did not have many of the signs of mental healthiness.

(Adapted from J.D. Stirling & J.S.E. Hellewell, 1999, *Psychopathology*. London: Routledge.) ■

Sitting in the road may be considered an abnormal behaviour in our society, but it is acceptable to those involved in a road protest.

Limitations of the social deviance approach

1. The concept of social deviancy is related to moral codes or standards, subjectively defined by a society, and these vary with prevailing social attitudes. For example, until fairly recently in Britain it was regarded as unacceptable for an unmarried woman to have a child. Single women who became pregnant were seen as social deviants and some were even locked up in psychiatric institutions as a result. In Russia throughout much of the 20th century, individuals who disagreed with the communist government were called dissidents. Their attitudes were seen as symptoms of mental derangement and they were confined in mental hospitals. Using social deviancy to establish a standard allows serious abuses of human rights to occur. Szasz (1960) suggested that the concept of mental illness is a myth used by the state as a means of control. It is certainly open to such abuse.

2. Social deviance is defined by the context in which a behaviour occurs. Wearing very few clothes is acceptable on a beach but not in the high street. Cultural context is also important. For example, the Kwakiutl Indians engage in a special ceremony in which they burn valuable blankets to cast shame on their rivals. If someone in our society deliberately set fire to his/her most valuable possessions, they would be regarded as very odd or mentally ill (Gleitman, 1986). Even within societies there are sub-cultural differences in relation to, for example, different religious groups that have different norms—the Mormons believe it is acceptable for a man to have several wives.

3. Social deviancy is not necessarily a bad thing. Some people are socially deviant because they have chosen a non-conformist lifestyle and others because their behaviour is motivated by high principles. For example, consider those "deviants" in Nazi Germany who spoke out against the atrocities that were being committed or risked their lives to help the Jews.

The fact that social deviance should be rejected as the only criterion of abnormality doesn't mean that it is entirely irrelevant. After all, people derive much of their pleasure in life from their interactions with other people. As a result, most people find it important for a contented existence to avoid behaving in socially deviant ways that bemuse or upset others.

Failure to function adequately

The next possible way of defining abnormality is as a **failure to function adequately**. Most people who seek help from a clinical psychologist or psychiatrist are suffering from a sense of psychological distress or discomfort (Sue et al., 1994). We could say that this recognition of not functioning adequately could act as a standard of abnormality.

In most societies we have expectations about how people should live their lives and how they should contribute to the social groups around them. When an individual can't meet these obligations, then both we and they usually feel they aren't functioning adequately. Rosenhan and Seligman (1989) suggested that the concept of distress and failure to function adequately can be extended to include a number of behaviours.

According to Rosenhan and Seligman (1989), the most suitable approach to defining mental abnormality may be to identify a set of seven abnormal characteristics. Each of them on its own may not be sufficient to cause a problem. However, when several are present, then they are symptomatic of abnormality. The fewer features that are displayed, the more an individual can be regarded as normal. This approach enables us to think in terms of *degrees* of normality and abnormality rather than whether or not a behaviour or person is abnormal. Here are the seven features identified by Rosenhan and Seligman:

Abnormal behaviour...?

...Not when rescuing a cat!

- *Suffering*. Most abnormal individuals report that they are suffering, and so this is a key feature of abnormality. However, nearly all normal individuals grieve when a loved one dies, and some abnormal individuals (e.g. psychopaths or those with anti-social personality disorder) treat other people very badly but don't suffer themselves.
- *Maladaptiveness*. Maladaptive behaviour prevents an individual from achieving major life goals such as enjoying good relationships with other people or working effectively. Most abnormal behaviour is maladaptive in this sense. However, maladaptive behaviour can also be due to a lack of relevant knowledge or skills.
- *Vividness and unconventionality of behaviour*. The ways in which abnormal individuals behave in various situations differ substantially from how most people behave. However, the same is true of non-conformists and eccentrics.
- *Unpredictability and loss of control*. Abnormal individuals' behaviour is often very variable and uncontrolled, and is also inappropriate. However, most people sometimes behave like this (e.g. after binge drinking).
- *Irrationality and incomprehensibility*. A common feature of abnormal behaviour is that it isn't clear why anyone would choose to behave in that way. However, we might simply not know the reasons for it.
- *Observer discomfort*. Those who see the unspoken rules of social behaviour being broken by others often experience some discomfort. However, observer

KEY TERM

Failure to function adequately: a model of abnormality based on an inability to cope with day-to-day life caused by psychological distress or discomfort.

discomfort may reflect cultural differences in behaviour and style rather than abnormality.

- *Violation of moral and ideal standards.* Behaviour may be judged to be abnormal when it violates established moral standards. However, the majority of people may fail to maintain those standards, which may be out of date or imposed by minority religious or political leaders. For example, various common sexual practices are illegal in some parts of the United States.

■ **Activity:** The seven features of abnormality

Imagine a continuum from extremely abnormal behaviour at one end to normality at the other. At what point does our behaviour become unacceptable? Bearing in mind Rosenhan and Seligman's definitions, consider the experiences described below. For each one describe what would be acceptable behaviour and what would be regarded as abnormal. For example, what kind of expression of grief would go beyond the bounds of normality?

Suffering: Grief at the loss of a loved one.
Maladaptiveness: Disregard for one's own safety, e.g. taking part in extreme sports.
Vividness and unconventionality: Tattooing or body piercing.

Unpredictability and loss of control: Losing one's temper.
Irrationality and incomprehensibility: Remaining friendly towards someone who is hostile.
Observer discomfort: Laughing at inappropriate times, e.g. when someone is describing a sad event.
Violation of moral and ideal standards: Removing one's clothes to sunbathe on the beach.

- Are the criteria we use influenced by our cultural and personal backgrounds?
- Try to think of other examples for each standard.

One serious problem with Rosenhan and Seligman's features is that most of them involve making subjective judgements. For example, behaviour causing severe discomfort to one observer may have no effect on another observer. Behaviour that violates one person's moral standards may be consistent with another person's moral standards. Another problem with some of the features is that they also apply to people who are non-conformists or who simply have their own idiosyncratic style. However, there are no clear objective measures of abnormality that we can use.

Limitations of the "failure to function" approach

The main problem with this way of defining abnormality is that not all people who experience mental disorder are aware of their failure to function. For example, individuals suffering from schizophrenia often deny they have a problem (see the Case Study on page 315). It is distressing to others, who may be able to judge that the individual isn't functioning adequately and seek help on his/her behalf.

On the positive side, it is relatively easy to assess the consequences of dysfunctional behaviour (e.g. absenteeism from work; inadequate work performance) to measure the level of functioning. However, value judgements are still required. That means that the "failure to function adequately" model is tied to the social deviancy one.

The model doesn't recognise the individual's subjective experience. Inevitably, however, such judgements are made by others, and those judgements are influenced by social and cultural beliefs and biases.

Deviation from ideal mental health

If we take the view that abnormality is related to the lack of a "contented existence", then we might seek a definition in terms of deviation from ideal mental health. This is the view taken by **humanistic psychologists** such as Carl Rogers and Abraham Maslow. They both felt that **self-actualisation** (fulfilment of one's potential) was a key standard and goal for human endeavour. Very few people are fully self-actualised, so don't worry if you feel that you are only partially fulfilling your potential!

Rogers (1959) was the founder of **client-centred therapy**. This has been extremely influential and has played a major role in the development of counselling. Rogers believed that maladjustment or abnormal development occurred when a child received only conditional love from his/her parents. What this means is that the child will only receive love from his/her parents if the child behaves in certain ways. The resulting conflict between the self-concept and the ideal self means that the individual will try to be someone else in order to receive the love he/she wants. Healthy psychological development occurs through receiving *unconditional* positive regard from significant others (i.e. love is given

According to Rogers, young children should receive unconditional positive regard from their parents.

regardless of the child's behaviour). This leads to high **self-esteem** and self-acceptance. It frees the individual from seeking social approval and enables him/her to seek self-actualisation.

Maslow (1954) was interested in the factors driving or motivating individuals. He claimed that we seek first to have our basic needs satisfied (e.g. hunger; safety). After that, people are driven by "higher" motives such as love, belonging, and knowledge. The highest motive of all is to seek self-actualisation (see diagram).

Humanists wanted to define the ultimate goals of human behaviour. Normal people would strive for these goals, and abnormality results from a failure to achieve them.

Jahoda (1958) argued that the concepts of abnormality and normality were useless because their definition varies as a function of the group or culture we are considering. She suggested that it was preferable to identify the criteria for positive mental health and then look at the frequency of their distribution in any population. Jahoda tried to identify common concepts that were used when describing mental health. She proposed that there were six categories that **clinicians** typically related to mental health:

1. *Self-attitudes*. High self-esteem and a strong sense of identity are related to mental health.
2. *Personal growth*. The extent of an individual's actual growth, development, or self-actualisation is important.

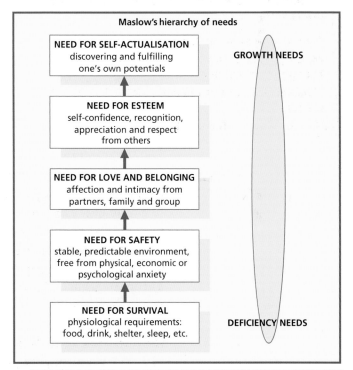

Maslow's hierarchy of needs

NEED FOR SELF-ACTUALISATION
discovering and fulfilling one's own potentials

NEED FOR ESTEEM
self-confidence, recognition, appreciation and respect from others

NEED FOR LOVE AND BELONGING
affection and intimacy from partners, family and group

NEED FOR SAFETY
stable, predictable environment, free from physical, economic or psychological anxiety

NEED FOR SURVIVAL
physiological requirements: food, drink, shelter, sleep, etc.

GROWTH NEEDS

DEFICIENCY NEEDS

KEY TERMS

Humanistic psychology: an approach to psychology that focuses on higher motivation, self-development, and on each individual as unique.
Self-actualisation: fulfilling one's potential in the broadest sense.
Client-centred therapy: a form of humanistic therapy introduced by Rogers and designed to increase the client's self-esteem and reduce incongruence between self and ideal self.
Self-esteem: the feelings that an individual has about himself or herself.
Clinician (or clinical psychologist): a person who works in clinical psychology, concerned with the diagnosis and treatment of abnormal behaviour.

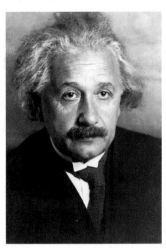

Maslow characterised Einstein as a famous individual who demonstrated "self-actualisation"— including characteristics such as self-acceptance, resistance to cultural influences, empathy, and creativeness.

3. *Integration*. This is a "synthesising psychological function" that integrates or combines the above two concepts. It can be assessed in terms of the individual's ability to cope with stressful situations.
4. *Autonomy*. This is the degree to which an individual is independent of social influences. We need to be careful here, because ignoring social influences can be a sign of mental illness!
5. *Perception of reality*. A prime factor in mental health. Individuals with good mental health don't need to distort their perception of reality, and they exhibit empathy and social sensitivity.
6. *Environmental mastery*. The extent to which an individual is successful and well-adapted, including the ability to love, adequacy at work and at play, good interpersonal relations, efficiency in meeting situational requirements, capacity for adaptation and adjustment, and efficient problem solving. Most of us probably don't succeed in all these areas!

Jahoda's approach has the advantage of being positive. It seeks to identify the characteristics that people need in order to be mentally or psychologically healthy rather than identifying the problems. As a result, the six categories she identified could be translated into useful therapeutic aims (treatment goals). However, Jahoda's approach may not provide useful criteria for identifying what constitutes abnormality. A psychological scale that measures psychological concepts (e.g. a person's level of self-esteem) can't provide an objective measurement.

It is important to note that any set of values is inevitably linked to a given culture and a given historical period. Many psychologists (e.g. Oyserman et al., 2002) have drawn a distinction between individualistic cultures and collectivistic ones. Individualistic cultures (e.g. the United Kingdom; the United States) emphasise independence and personal control. In contrast, collectivistic cultures (e.g. China; Japan) focus on interdependence and considering oneself as a member of a group. Jahoda's list of mentally healthy behaviours such as self-attitudes, autonomy, and personal growth makes more sense in individualistic cultures than in collectivistic ones. For example, Heine et al. (1999) discussed research in which European Canadian and Japanese students ranked 20 traits in terms of how much they ideally would like to possess them. European Canadians rated self-confidence as the trait they would *most* like to possess, whereas the Japanese rated it as the trait they would *least* like to possess.

Limitations of the ideal mental health approach

The ideal mental health approach has the benefit of focusing on positive characteristics—on health rather than on illness. However, the criteria used are hard to define because they are abstract ideals and are related to our particular culture. For example, consider self-attitudes—high self-esteem is regarded as extremely important within the American culture but is not at all highly regarded within the Japanese culture. Not all societies feel that these are the ultimate aims for psychological health. As we have seen, collectivistic societies strive for the greater good of the community rather than for self-centred goals.

The vague criteria for ideal mental health are also hard to measure. How can we rate positive interpersonal relations or self-acceptance?

Finally, we should consider the fact that these "healthy behaviours" are ideals. Very few people ever achieve them, so many of us could be classified as abnormal. It could be argued that abnormality involves a substantial falling short on most or all of the criteria for ideal mental health. However, that raises the tricky issue of how much of a falling short is required for behaviour to be regarded as abnormal.

Cultural relativism

A fundamental limitation with all of the definitions of abnormality that we have examined is that they are culturally specific. The notion of **cultural relativism** means that value judgements are *relative* to individual cultural contexts. As a result, we can't make absolute statements about what is normal and abnormal in human behaviour. This is very clear if we consider culture-bound syndromes, which are patterns of abnormal behaviour that are typically found only in a single culture. For example, dhat syndrome is a culture-bound syndrome found among males of the Indian subcontinent. Sufferers have multiple somatic complaints, and blame their physical and mental exhaustion on the presence of semen in their urine. The origins of this lie in the Hindu belief that semen is produced in the blood, and that the loss of semen will result in illness. Chadda and Ahuja (1990) examined various patients with dhat and concluded they were suffering from either neurotic depression or anxiety neurosis. Thus, a single underlying disorder (e.g. depression) may be expressed in different ways from one culture to another.

There are many other culture-bound syndromes, and we will briefly mention three more here. Ghost sickness, which is common in Native American tribes, has as its main symptom an excessive focus on death and on those who have died. Koro involves extreme anxiety that the penis or nipples will recede into the body and possibly cause death. It is found in south and east Africa. Finally, there is amok (originally identified in Malaysia), which involves brooding followed by a violent outburst.

Notions of abnormality not only vary from one culture to another, they also vary *within* any given culture at different periods in history. For example, the way in which homosexuality is regarded within American culture has altered over successive editions of DSM (*Diagnostic and Statistical Manual of Mental Disorders*). This is the system used to classify mental illness in America. It is used by clinicians to diagnose mental disorders. In DSM-II, which was published in 1968, homosexuality was classified as a sexual deviation. In DSM-III, published in 1980, homosexuality was no longer categorised as a mental disorder. However, there was a new category of "ego-dystonic homosexuality" that was used only for homosexuals wishing to become heterosexual. In DSM-III-R, this last category had disappeared. However, a category of "sexual disorder not otherwise specified" with "persistent and marked distress about one's sexual orientation" was added. This remained

Homosexuality ceased to be categorised as a mental disorder in the 1980 edition of DSM.

KEY TERMS
Cultural relativism: the view that to understand and judge a culture it must be viewed from within that culture, and not from the perspective of the observer's own culture if that is a different one.
Culture-bound syndromes: patterns of abnormal behaviour that are only found in one or a small number of cultures.

EXAM HINT

- You are most likely to be asked to give ONE criticism of any of the definitions of abnormality, however as there are many you should know at least two to be fully prepared for all possible types of question. You must be able to ELABORATE the criticism sufficiently for 3 marks.
- Culture bias works well for all four definitions. Use examples of social norms changing across cultures and examples of how the criteria in failure to function and ideal mental health can be viewed differently across cultures to make sure your answer is DETAILED and FOCUSED on the definition specified in the question.

the case in DSM-IV, which was published in 1994. However, even today many people continue to view homosexuality as an aberrant mental state.

The importance of the cultural context can be seen if we go back to the seven features of abnormality proposed by Rosenhan and Seligman (1989; see pages 317–318). Many of those features refer to behaviour that is defined by the social norms or expectations of the culture. That is certainly true of vividness and unconventionality of behaviour; irrationality and incomprehensibility; and observer discomfort. In other words, abnormality has a somewhat different meaning across cultures. For example, hallucinations are considered normal in certain situations in some societies, but in the West they are seen as a manifestation of a mental disorder (Sue et al., 1994).

Finally, it is important to strike the right balance. Some of the features identified by Rosenhan and Seligman can be thought of as universal indicators of undesirable behaviour for the individual concerned and those around them. Examples include a refusal to eat, chronic depression, a fear of going outdoors, and anti-social behaviour. Thus, there do appear to be some universal indicators of abnormality, even though far more behavioural signs of abnormality are culture-specific.

Conclusions

Concepts differ very much in their precision. "Abnormality" is an imprecise concept. Abnormal behaviour can take different forms and can involve different features. Moreover, there is no single feature that can always be relied on to distinguish between normal and abnormal behaviour. What is needed is to identify the main features that are *much more likely* to be found in abnormal than in normal individuals. The seven features proposed by Rosenhan and Seligman (1989) may offer a combined and realistic approach. The more of these features possessed by an individual, the greater the likelihood that he/she will be categorised as abnormal.

Labels and symptoms

Imagine that you are in a situation where you have been wrongly diagnosed as suffering from a mental disorder such as schizophrenia. How would you react to such a situation? Would you be incredulous? Furious? Tearful? Shocked and withdrawn? How could all those emotions be interpreted by those people whose job it is to assess your mental condition?

Biological and Psychological (Including Psychodynamic, Behavioural, and Cognitive) Approaches to Psychopathology

A different way to approach abnormality is to consider explanations of *why* it happens. Several models of abnormality have been put forward over the years. These models have been very influential, because the form of treatment for any given mental disorder is based in part on our understanding of the causes of that disorder.

The dominant model at one time was the biological (medical) model, in which mental disorders are regarded as illnesses. Most **psychiatrists** accept this model, whereas most clinical psychologists reject it in favour of psychological models. There are also numerous psychologically based models of abnormality, focusing on different factors and/or attitudes to life.

> **EXAM HINT**
> Whichever approach you are evaluating—biological, psychodynamic, behavioural, or cognitive—you can use the diathesis–stress model in your evaluation. This is because all these models are one-dimensional, but the diathesis–stress model is multi-dimensional and is therefore less simplistic because it takes account of multiple factors and their interaction.

We can distinguish between one-dimensional and multi-dimensional causal models (Durand & Barlow, 2006). According to one-dimensional models, the origins of a mental disorder can be traced to a *single* underlying cause. For example, severe depression might be caused by a major loss (e.g. death of a loved one) or schizophrenia by genetic factors. In practice, one-dimensional models have been replaced by multi-dimensional models assuming that any given mental disorder is typically caused by *several* factors in interaction.

One way of expressing the multi-dimensional approach is in terms of the **diathesis–stress model**. According to this model, the occurrence of psychological disorder depends on two factors:

1. Diathesis: a genetic vulnerability or predisposition to disease or disorder.
2. Stress: some severe or disturbing environmental event.

If the multi-dimensional approach is correct, it follows that we may need to combine the insights of the biological and psychological models. That is the position we adopt here. We assume that each of the models is partially correct, and that a full understanding of the origins of mental disorders requires us to combine information from all of them. Here we will focus on the four most important ones: biological, psychodynamic, behavioural, and cognitive models.

The biological approach

The essence of the biological (medical) approach or model is that "abnormal behaviours result from physical problems and should be treated medically". In other words, mental disorders are illnesses with a physical cause, so we should approach mental disorders from the perspective of medicine.

There are four kinds of medical explanation that can be used to explain the cause of abnormality.

Infection

Germs or micro-organisms such as bacteria or viruses are known to produce disease states. Many common physical illnesses (e.g. measles, influenza) are caused in this way. Some mental illnesses have also been linked to known micro-organisms. However, this approach doesn't make much sense, because most mental disorders don't form distinct syndromes nor do they have one cause. However, this is the aim of the medical approach—if we can diagnose a syndrome then we might find a cure. The one relies on the other. For example, micro-organisms have been suggested as a cause of schizophrenia. Barr et al. (1990) found that there was an increased incidence of schizophrenia in children whose mothers had flu when they were pregnant, suggesting that the disorder

> **KEY TERMS**
> **Biological (medical) model**: a model of abnormality that regards mental disorders as illnesses with a physical cause.
> **Psychiatrist**: a medically trained person who specialises in the diagnosis and treatment of mental disorders.
> **Diathesis–stress model**: the notion that psychological disorders occur when there is a genetically determined vulnerability (diathesis) and relevant stressful conditions.

Identical twins offer the opportunity of conducting a natural experiment. They are the same genetically so any differences in their behaviour should be due to the environment. However, they usually share the same environment as well.

might be a disease. However, this approach to schizophrenia is very limited and ignores several important factors. For example, people with schizophrenia tend to have experienced a high number of stressful life events in the few weeks before its onset (Day et al., 1987), a finding that can't be explained in terms of infection.

Genetic factors

Individuals may inherit predispositions to certain illnesses. These predispositions are carried by genes that pass from one generation to the next. One way to show the inheritance of mental disorder is by looking at patterns of such disorders within families or within twin pairs. If a disorder is caused genetically, then we would expect individuals who are closely related (and so share many genes) to be more likely to have it. However, there is a problem here—individuals within a family who are closely related are likely to experience more similar environments (e.g. living in the same home) than those who aren't closely related. That can make it hard to decide whether the presence of a given mental disorder in two closely related individuals is due to the similarity of their genes or to the similarity in their environment.

In practice, the most useful way of deciding whether genetic factors are important is to carry out twin studies. Identical or monozygotic twins share 100% of their genes whereas fraternal or dizygotic twins share only 50% of their genes. For any given disorder, the key measure is the **concordance rate**: this is the likelihood that, if one twin has the disorder, the other twin also has it. If genetic factors are important, the concordance rate should be higher in identical than in fraternal twins. That is what has been found for several disorders (especially schizophrenia). Gottesman (1991) summarised the findings from about 40 twin studies on schizophrenia, finding that the concordance rate was 48% for identical twins but only 17% for fraternal twins. McGuffin et al. (1996) found that the concordance rate for major depression was 46% for identical twins and 20% for fraternal twins.

? How might research on gene-mapping be of use when counselling prospective parents?

The biological approach to abnormality: Genes

How much of our behaviour is determined by our personal mix of genes is uncertain, but it is a fact that they do affect behaviour. A very unique example of this is in the Batista family in the Dominican Republic. For example, out of ten children in this family there were four boys born with normal *female* genitalia, but at puberty, about age 12, the vaginas of these four closed and healed over, two testicles descended, and normal penises grew. Similar physical changes have occurred in related families in the village and these have been found to be the result of a homozygous recessive pair of genes. The question is whether this clearly unusual physical development could be classed as psychological abnormality—what do you think, and why?

KEY TERMS

Concordance rate: in twin studies, the probability that if one twin has a given disorder the other twin also has the same disorder.
Genetic: information from genes, the units of inheritance.
Gene mapping: determining the effect of a particular gene on physical or psychological characteristics.

Another way to study **genetic** influences is to identify particular genes and show they are more likely to be present in individuals with a disorder than in those without the disorder. This can be more informative than simply showing that genetic factors are involved in producing a given disorder. **Gene-mapping** studies have found several genes that may be involved in particular disorders. For example, Berrettini (2000) linked bipolar disorder (a disorder in which there are depressive and manic episodes) to genes on chromosomes 4, 6, 11, 12, 13, 15, 18, and 22.

Biochemistry

A third possible cause of abnormality lies in the patient's **biochemistry**. For example, several theorists have argued that one of the factors involved in schizophrenia is an excessive amount of dopamine, a chemical substance in the brain. However, research has only identified *correlations* between the disorder and the raised biochemical levels. What this means is that we can't be certain whether the excessive amount of dopamine is *cause* or *effect*. It is possible that having schizophrenia causes dopamine levels to rise rather than excessive dopamine levels playing a role in the onset of schizophrenia.

Some evidence that biochemical changes can have significant effects on the symptoms of abnormality comes from drug studies using patients. For example, it has been suggested that depression is associated with low levels of the neurotransmitter serotonin. Prozac, a well-known drug that increases serotonin activity, has been found to reduce significantly the symptoms of depression (Hirschfeld, 1999). This is consistent with the hypothesis that abnormal levels of serotonin play a role in producing depression.

Neuroanatomy

A fourth possible cause lies in **neuroanatomy**—the structure of the nervous system. For example, many brain-imaging studies have shown that the brains of people with schizophrenia differ from those of normal individuals. Lawrie and Abukmeil (1998) reviewed 40 brain-imaging studies. On average, people with schizophrenia have smaller brain volume than normals, but the lateral ventricles were about 40% larger in people with schizophrenia. Once again, we can't be sure whether the brain differences partly caused the schizophrenia or whether schizophrenia caused the neuroanatomical changes. However, neuropathology (abnormal neuroanatomy) has been found in recently diagnosed untreated schizophrenic patients, suggesting that there is a link between neuropathology and schizophrenia.

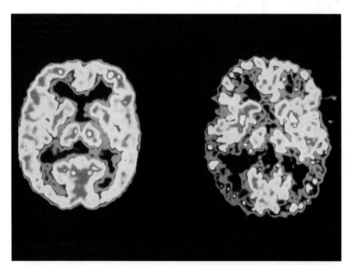

PET scans of a normal (left) and schizophrenic human brain.

Evaluation of the biological model

The biological (medical) model has had an enormous influence on the terms used to refer to mental disorder and their treatment. As Maher (1966, p. 22) pointed out, deviant behaviour

> is termed pathological and is classified on the basis of symptoms, classification being called diagnosis. Processes designed to change behaviour are called therapies, and are [sometimes] applied to patients in mental hospitals. If the deviant behaviour ceases, the patient is described as cured.

The biological model approach is clearly successful in the case of some psychological conditions. For example, phenylketonuria (PKU), which is a cause of mental retardation, can be treated simply and effectively by physical means. It is a condition in which an individual is born with an inability to metabolise

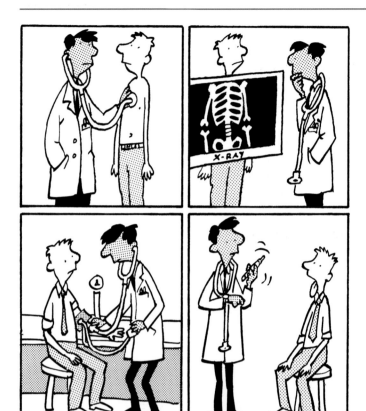

Results of medical tests provide more precise information than is available to psychiatrists and clinical psychologists.

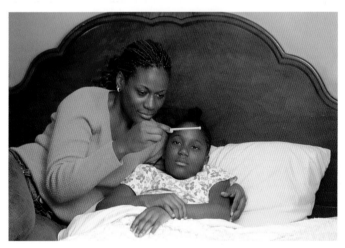

It may not be appropriate to think that mental illnesses are the same as physical ones.

(process) the amino acid phenylalanine. As a result, the concentration of phenylalanine increases, and there is permanent brain damage. In addition, there are usually seizures and behaviour problems. PKU is preventable if it is detected early enough. Infants are given a special diet low in phenylalanine and this has proved very successful in preventing the development of PKU.

How useful is the biological model approach to most mental disorders? It has the merit of being based on well-established sciences such as medicine and biochemistry. Some forms of mental disorder can be understood from the perspective of the biological model, and numerous mental disorders are caused *in part* by genetic factors. Drug therapies based on the biological model have often proved effective in at least reducing symptoms.

There are several weaknesses of the biological model approach:

- There is generally only a loose analogy between physical and mental illness. It is easier to establish the causes of most physical illnesses than mental ones, and symptoms of mental disorders are often more subjective.
- The biological model applies much better to some mental disorders (e.g. schizophrenia) than to others (e.g. phobias). Genetic factors are especially important in schizophrenia, but note that Gottesman (1991) reported a concordance rate of 48% for identical twins. If schizophrenia were caused *only* by genetic factors, the concordance rate would be 100%.
- When biological differences (e.g. in biochemistry, in brain structure) are found between individuals with a given mental disorder and those without the disorder, it is tempting to conclude that the biological differences caused the mental disorder. In fact, however, since we only have correlational evidence, we don't know whether the biological differences caused the mental disorder or whether the biological differences are a by-product of having the disorder.
- The biological model is too narrow in its focus. It focuses on biological causes of mental disorder but ignores cultural factors, social factors (e.g. severe life events; inadequate social support), and psychological factors (e.g. distorted beliefs about oneself and the world).
- Thomas Szasz (pronounced "sas") was one of the greatest critics of the medical approach. He claimed that mental illnesses are more appropriately

described as "problems in living" than as disease. In his own words:

It is customary to define psychiatry as a medical speciality concerned with the study, diagnosis, and treatment of mental illness. This is a worthless and misleading definition. Mental illness is a myth. Psychiatrists are not concerned with mental illnesses and their treatment . . . In actual practice they deal with personal, social and ethical problems in living . . . the notion of a person "having a mental illness" is scientifically crippling. It provides professional assent to a popular rationalisation, namely that problems of living . . . expressed in terms of so called psychiatric symptoms are basically similar to bodily diseases . . . We must recast and redefine the problem of "mental illness" so that it may be encompassed in a morally explicit science of man (1960, p. 269).

Szasz's objections to the medical or biological model are not made very clear in the above quotation (as you will probably agree!), so I will try to clarify what he had in mind. First, he pointed out that we generally don't hold someone responsible if they have a physical illness and we tend to do the same if they have a so-called mental illness. He felt this was very undesirable ethically, because it stops people accepting responsibility for themselves and for their own lives. Second, putting a label on someone (e.g. "You're a schizophrenic!") can create problems for the individual concerned. People who are identified as suffering from a mental illness are often rejected by others in the same way as someone who is identified as a prostitute or criminal. In Szasz's view, it is unfair to add to someone's problems in this way.

> **Assumptions of the biological model**
> - All mental disorders have a physical cause (micro-organisms, genetics, biochemistry, or neuroanatomy).
> - Mental illnesses can be described in terms of clusters of symptoms.
> - Symptoms can be identified, leading to the diagnosis of an illness.
> - Diagnosis leads to appropriate physical treatments.

Ethical implications of the biological model

We could turn Szasz's argument on its head. The notion that individuals with mental disorders are suffering from an illness could be regarded as ethically desirable—it suggests that they aren't responsible for their condition and so shouldn't feel guilty. However, it may be undesirable to encourage individuals with mental disorders to hand over complete responsibility for their recovery to experts trained in treating "mental illness".

The notion that genetic factors often play a significant role in the development of mental disorders raises ethical issues. The relatives of an individual diagnosed as suffering from such a disorder may well become very anxious, which could increase their chances of developing the disorder. On the other hand, it could be regarded as unethical not to provide full and accurate information to the relatives! For example, if they are at high risk of developing an anxiety disorder, they could take action to reduce the risk by trying to lead a predictable and safe existence.

Many of the forms of treatment based on the biological model raise important ethical issues. Drugs can have serious side effects and lead to drug dependence. However, a failure to use drugs may increase the suffering of those with mental disorders.

Finally, most people would argue that the best approach to diagnosis is to take account of all the factors that might be relevant, including environmental factors

Sigmund Freud, 1856–1939.

See *AS Level Psychology Online* for interactive exercises on this topic.

Defence mechanisms

Another example of a defence mechanism is reaction formation, e.g. in an adult who has developed a fear of close, intimate relationships due to a disappointment or hurt experienced during childhood. As a consequence, when this adult meets someone to whom they feel a strong attraction, they may sub-consciously experience the opposite emotion of dislike, or even hatred.

KEY TERMS

Psychodynamic model: a model of abnormality that regards the origin of mental disorders as psychological rather than physical, and suggests that mental illness arises out of unresolved unconscious conflicts.
Repression: a main ego defence mechanism suggested by Freud, where anxiety-causing memories are kept out of conscious memory to protect the individual. This is a type of motivated forgetting, and the repressed memories can sometimes be recalled during **psychoanalysis**.
Projection: attributing one's undesirable characteristics to others, as a means of coping with emotionally threatening information and protecting the ego.
Displacement: one of the defence mechanisms identified by Freud in which impulses are unconsciously moved away from a very threatening object towards a non-threatening one.

---

such as close relationships and employment. It could be regarded as unethical to focus *exclusively* on biological factors.

The psychodynamic model

The term "psychodynamic" refers to a group of explanations that tries to account for the *dynamics* of behaviour, or the forces that motivate it. Sigmund Freud's theory is the best-known example. He put forward the first psychodynamic model, which he called psychoanalysis. He has been the most influential person in the history of clinical psychology (and psychology generally). Freud's view was that mental illness doesn't have a physical origin. Instead, he suggested that it arises out of unresolved, unconscious conflicts that form in early childhood.

To understand the psychodynamic model, we need to look again briefly at Freud's theory of personality development (see Chapter 2, Section 4). Freud argued that the mind is divided into three parts: the id, the ego, and the superego, which are often in conflict with each other.

The **psychodynamic model** proposed by Freud was based on his theory of psychosexual development. According to this theory, the child passes through a series of stages (oral, anal, phallic, latency, and genital). Major conflicts (or excessive gratification) at any of these stages can mean that the child spends an unusually long time at that stage of development—this is known as fixation. Conflicts cause anxiety, and the ego defends itself against anxiety by using several defence mechanisms to prevent traumatic thoughts and feelings reaching consciousness. These defence mechanisms include **repression** (forcing distressing memories into the unconscious), **projection** (attributing one's own undesirable characteristics to others), and **displacement** (transferring one's impulses away from a threatening object and towards a less threatening one, as when someone made angry by their boss goes home and kicks the cat).

There has been much research on repression. The most relevant studies on repression are those on clinical patients with recovered previously repressed memories of child abuse. Several of these studies support the notion of repression. There has also been much research on displacement. Marcus-Newhall et al. (2000) carried out a meta-analysis of 82 studies concerned with displaced aggression. They defined displaced aggression as aggressive behaviour directed towards someone not responsible for the provocation that the participants had experienced. Displaced aggression was a moderately strong and replicable finding. The main limitation of the findings was that the time interval between the provocation and the opportunity to show displaced aggression was typically only a few minutes. In contrast, Freud argued that displaced aggression can be found at much longer time intervals, but we don't have the necessary evidence for this.

According to Freud, mental disorders can arise when an individual has unresolved conflicts and traumas from childhood. Defence mechanisms may be used to reduce the anxiety caused by such unresolved conflicts, but they act more as sticking plaster than as a way of sorting out an individual's problems.

As we have seen, Freud assumed that most adult mental disorders have their roots in either childhood experiences or personality development in childhood. The evidence is mixed, but there is some support for this assumption. Kendler et al. (1996) considered the role of childhood experiences. They studied adult female twins who had experienced parental loss through separation in childhood. These twins showed an above-average tendency to suffer from depression and alcoholism in adult life. Caspi et al. (1996) considered the role of childhood personality in subsequent problems. They studied 3-year-olds, and then carried out a follow-up 18 years later. Children who had an introverted personality at the age of 3 tended to be depressed at the age of 21. Children who were under-controlled at the age of 3 were more likely to have developed anti-social personality disorder by the time they reached 21.

> **Positive aspects of the Freudian approach**
>
> Freud's work is often criticised, and it is true that it is difficult to verify the workings of the subconscious mind through scientific investigations. However, post-Freudian study of the importance of subjective feelings and experience has been a major undertaking in both psychology and other dissociated fields such as creative writing, literary theory, and art history. Freud's ideas about the importance of the subconscious mind were one of the most profound influences on human thought of the 20th century, leading to in-depth questioning of human motives and intentions. It is hard for us to think about the world without employing Freudian concepts.

Evaluation of the psychodynamic model

Psychoanalysis, the psychodynamic model proposed by Freud, was the first systematic model of abnormality that focused specifically on *psychological* factors as the cause of mental disorder and on psychological forms of treatment. Before Freud, nearly all explanations of mental illness were in terms of physical causes or ideas such as possession by evil spirits. Psychoanalysis paved the way for later psychological models and forms of therapy. In essence, Freud focused very much on the individual and his/her personal conflicts dating back to childhood. In contrast, later psychodynamic therapists put more emphasis on the patient's current social and relationship problems.

A strength of the psychodynamic model concerns the notion of defence mechanisms. Some of the evidence is controversial, but there is clear support for the existence of defence mechanisms such as repression and displacement.

Another strength of the psychodynamic model is that it identified traumatic childhood experiences as a factor in the development of adult disorders. There is reasonable evidence for this (Comer, 2001), but Freud may have exaggerated the role played by such experiences. More generally, the notion that childhood experiences and childhood personality development play a role in adult mental disorder has received some support (Caspi et al., 1996; Kendler et al., 1996). Note, however, that finding that there is an association between having had a troubled childhood and adult mental disorder doesn't prove that the troubled childhood helped to *cause* the adult mental disorder.

We turn now to the weaknesses of the psychodynamic model:

- Freud was relatively uninterested in the *current* problems his clients were facing. Even if childhood experiences stored in the unconscious play a part in the development of mental disorders, that does *not* mean that adult experiences can be ignored. Modern psychodynamic therapy has evolved from Freud's approach, but places more emphasis on current problems.

Assumptions of the psychodynamic model

- Much of our behaviour is driven by unconscious motives.
- Childhood is a critical period in development.
- Mental disorders arise from unresolved, unconscious conflicts originating in childhood.
- Resolution occurs through accessing and coming to terms with repressed ideas and conflicts.

- Freud focused too much on sexual factors as the cause of mental disorders. In contrast to his approach, most psychodynamic therapists nowadays regard interpersonal and social factors as important. Most modern psychodynamic therapists believe that sexual problems are a *result* of poor relationships with others rather than a direct cause of disorder.
- The psychodynamic model isn't based on a solid foundation of scientific research. Freud's theoretical views emerged mainly from his interactions with clients in the therapeutic situation. This provided a weak form of evidence contaminated by his biases and preconceptions.
- The psychodynamic approach is limited because it tends to ignore genetic factors involved in the development of mental disorder.
- The psychodynamic approach has a strong emphasis on neuroses (what are now called the anxiety disorders) and on depression. As a result, the psychodynamic model has been applied mainly to clients suffering from anxiety disorders or depression rather than from more severe disorders such as schizophrenia.
- Many of the key concepts used by Freud (e.g. id, ego, superego, fixation) are imprecise, which makes it hard to assess their usefulness.

Ethical implications of the psychodynamic model

One of the implications of the psychodynamic model is that individuals aren't really responsible for their own mental disorders because those disorders depend on unconscious processes. However, the notion that adult mental disorders have their basis in childhood experiences suggests that parents or other caregivers are at least partly to blame. This can easily cause them distress if they are led to believe that they are responsible for their child's disorder.

Very serious issues are raised by numerous recent cases of **false memory syndrome**. In these cases, clients undergoing psychotherapy have made allegations about childhood physical or sexual abuse that have sometimes turned out to have no basis in fact. Do note, however, that this is a very controversial area, and many memories of abuse are undoubtedly genuine.

Freud argued that males and females have their own biologically determined sexual natures, and anxiety disorders or depression can develop when the natural course of their sexual development is thwarted. This approach is dubious because it ignores the importance of cultural differences in sexual attitudes and behaviour. It is also very sexist in its emphasis on the notion that behavioural differences between men and women stem from biology rather than from social and cultural factors.

The behavioural model

The **behavioural model of abnormality** was developed out of the behaviourist approach to psychology put forward mainly by John Watson and Fred Skinner. According to this model, individuals with mental disorders possess maladaptive forms of behaviour, which they have learned. Most of this learning takes the form

John Watson, 1878–1958.

of classical conditioning or operant conditioning (see Chapter 2, Section 4). Subsequent neo-behaviourists such as Bandura (1965) identified another basic form of learning known as observational learning. This occurs when an individual learns certain responses simply by observing someone else and then imitating their behaviour.

The behavioural model is defined in part by what it doesn't emphasise as well as by what it does. The model differs from most others in that there is very little consideration of the client's internal thoughts and feelings, and the underlying cause of the client's disorder isn't explored. Instead, the focus is mainly on the client's behavioural symptoms.

Classical conditioning

Classical conditioning is a form of learning first shown by Ivan Pavlov. In essence, a neutral or conditioned stimulus (e.g. a tone) is paired repeatedly with a second or unconditioned stimulus (e.g. presentation of food). After a while, the natural or unconditioned response to the second or unconditioned stimulus (e.g. salivation) comes to be made to the neutral stimulus when it is presented on its own. This learned response is known as the conditioned response.

John B. Watson and Rosalie Rayner (1920) showed in a classic study that emotions could be classically conditioned in the same way as any other response is conditioned. Their participant was an 11-month-old boy called "Little Albert", who was reared almost from birth in a hospital. At the start of the experiment, Watson and Rayner found out that items such as a white rat, a rabbit, and white cotton wool didn't trigger any fear response. In other words, they could all be regarded as neutral stimuli. Watson and Rayner then induced a fear response (unconditioned response) by striking a steel bar with a hammer (unconditioned stimulus). This startled Albert and made him cry. After that, they gave him a white rat to play with. As he reached to touch it, they struck the bar to make him frightened. They repeated this three times, and did the same 1 week later. After that, when they showed the rat to Albert he began to cry, rolled over, and started to crawl away quickly. Classical conditioning had occurred, because the previously neutral or conditioned stimulus (i.e. the rat) produced a conditioned fear response.

Watson and Rayner found that now the sight of any object that was white and furry (e.g. a white fur coat; a Father Christmas beard) provoked a fear response. This is called **generalisation**—Albert had learned to generalise his fear of the white rat to other similar objects. They intended to "re-condition" Albert to eliminate these fearful reactions. However, he was taken away from the hospital before this could happen.

It is possible that Little Albert developed a *phobia*, which is an extreme fear causing the individual concerned to avoid the feared stimulus. Mowrer (1947) developed a two-process theory to explain the origins of phobias. The first stage involves classical conditioning (e.g. linking the white rat and the loud noise). The second stage involves operant conditioning. What happens here is that avoidance of the phobic stimulus reduces fear and this reduction in fear is reinforcing or rewarding. It should be noted that **specific phobia**, in which there is an extreme fear reaction to a specific type of stimulus (e.g. snakes; spiders), is recognised as a mental disorder even though it is nothing like as serious as most other mental disorders.

Watson and Rayner taught a boy ("Little Albert") to fear white fluffy objects by striking a metal bar (unconditioned stimulus) every time he touched the previously unfeared object (neutral stimulus). Thus, they demonstrated that fears could be learned through classical conditioning.

KEY TERMS

Generalisation: in classical conditioning, the tendency to transfer a response from one stimulus to another that is quite similar.

Specific phobia: extreme fear and avoidance of specific kinds of stimuli (e.g. snakes, spiders).

Classical conditioning

- Unconditioned stimulus (US) e.g. food → causes → reflex response e.g. salivation.
- Neutral stimulus (NS) e.g. bell → causes → no response.
- NS and US are paired in time (they occur at the same time).
- NS (e.g. bell) is now a conditioned stimulus (CS) → which produces → a conditioned response (CR) [a new stimulus–response link is learned, the bell causes salivation].

Operant conditioning

- A behaviour that has a positive effect is more likely to be repeated.
- Positive and negative reinforcement (escape from aversive stimulus) are agreeable.
- Punishment is disagreeable.

CASE STUDY: JOHN WATSON

At the time the "Little Albert" study was conducted, Watson was a major figure in behaviourism and psychology. In 1913 he published a key paper arguing that psychology had to throw out introspection as a research method, and dismiss vague concepts such as "the mind" in order to become a respectable science. Psychologists, he suggested, should instead focus on observable, directly measurable behaviours. In short, he was largely responsible for founding the behaviourist movement, drawing on the ideas of Pavlov.

At the time he was the Professor of Psychology at Johns Hopkins University, Baltimore, USA, where he conducted research into animal behaviour until 1918 when he turned his attention to conditioning infants. However in 1920 he was involved in a rather sensational divorce as a result of his affair with his research assistant Rosalie Rayner, whom he subsequently married. This led him to resign from his job and he went into the advertising business. He continued to have an interest in psychology, publishing a book on infant and child care, but for the most part devoted himself entirely to business where he applied the principles of behaviourism to the world of advertising. In fact he probably was the first applied psychologist and had an extremely successful second career. ∎

Try to use classical conditioning to explain some other abnormal behaviour.

The research of Watson and Rayner (1920) is very relevant to the behavioural model of abnormality. It showed how high levels of fear and anxiety could occur through a learning process. As we have seen, this could help to explain how phobias arise. More generally, their research suggested that classical conditioning might be involved in several other anxiety disorders (e.g. panic disorder).

There are various weaknesses with this approach to phobias. First, it has proved hard to repeat the findings on Little Albert when attempts were made to condition people to fear neutral stimuli by pairing them with unpleasant ones in the laboratory (Davison, Neale, & Kring, 2004). Second, research into phobias has found that many phobic people have not had prior traumatic experiences with the objects (e.g. snakes) of which they are frightened. Menzies and Clarke (1993), in a study on child participants suffering from water phobia, found that only 2% of them reported a direct conditioning experience involving water. DiNardo et al. (1988) found that about 50% of dog-phobic people had become very anxious during an encounter with a dog, which might seem to support conditioning theory. However, about 50% of normal controls without dog phobia had also had an anxious encounter with a dog!

Social learning theory

Operant conditioning involves learning a new response because that response has previously resulted in a reward or reinforcement. Bandura (1986) further developed conditioning theory (see Chapter 2). He argued that observational learning or modelling is important—learning by imitating the behaviour of someone else. Observational learning is especially likely to influence behaviour when the other person's behaviour is rewarded or reinforced (vicarious reinforcement). One of Bandura's key insights was that the early behaviourists (e.g. Skinner, 1938) were wrong to attach so much importance to the need to produce *responses* that are then rewarded if learning is to occur. In our everyday lives we learn much by watching and observing others rather than responding.

Observational learning may be relevant to several mental disorders. For example, Mineka et al. (1984) found that monkeys could develop snake phobia simply by watching another monkey experience fear in the presence of a snake. We might assume that the

Reinforcement increases the likelihood that the behaviour will be repeated...

same principle applies to humans. Some evidence that we do was reported by Bandura and Rosenthal (1966). Participants observed someone responding to a buzzer by pretending to be in pain (e.g. twitching; shouting). After the participants had observed this reaction several times, they experienced a fear whenever they heard the buzzer.

Evaluation of the behavioural model

The basic concepts in the behavioural model (stimulus; response; reinforcement; modelling) are easier to observe and to measure than the concepts emphasised in other models. Conditioning experiences may play a role in the development of some mental disorders (e.g. phobias). In addition, there is compelling evidence that much human learning is based on operant conditioning and observational learning, and it is entirely likely that this accounts for some of the maladaptive learning shown by individuals with mental disorders. More generally, the experiences that people have in life (including the forms of conditioning to which they have been exposed) do play a part in the development of mental disorders. It could be argued that the behavioural model has the advantage over the psychodynamic model in that it focuses on the symptoms that concern the client (i.e. maladaptive patterns of behaviour) rather than what happened to the client many years earlier.

We will now consider some of the main weaknesses of the behavioural model:

- It is hard to apply the findings of laboratory studies to explain the origins of mental disorders. As Comer (2001, p. 63) pointed out, "There is still no indisputable evidence that most people with psychological disorders are victims of improper conditioning." The sad fact is that we are rarely in a position to know for sure the details of the learning experiences of anyone suffering from a mental disorder, and this makes it hard to test the behavioural

See *AS Level Psychology Online* for an interactive exercise on this topic.

model thoroughly. To show that a patient's reinforcement history was responsible for his/her disorder, we would need to have detailed information about rewards or reinforcements received over a period of years.

- The behavioural model exaggerates the importance of environmental factors in causing disorders and minimises the role played by genetic factors. As a result, it is of little value in explaining disorders such as schizophrenia in which genetic factors are important.

- The behavioural model also minimises the role played by internal processes (e.g. thinking, feeling). This makes it more relevant to disorders with easily observed behavioural symptoms (e.g. the avoidance of certain stimuli in people with phobias) rather than to disorders with few clear behavioural symptoms (e.g. generalised anxiety disorder in which the central symptom is excessive worrying).

- Much of the learning research on conditioning has involved the use of non-human species. The findings obtained can be misleading, because conditioning is generally less important in humans than it is in other species. This is because language and complex cognitive processes are much more important in humans than in any other species.

- In general terms, the behavioural model is oversimplified and rather narrow in scope. On the basis of the available evidence, it seems that only a small fraction of mental disorders depend to any great extent on the individual's conditioning history.

Assumptions of the behavioural model

- All behaviour is learned, and maladaptive behaviour is no different.
- This learning can be understood in terms of the principles of conditioning and modelling.
- What was learned can be unlearned, using the same principles.
- The same laws apply to human and non-human animal behaviour.

Ethical implications of the behavioural model

The behavioural model has some advantages from the ethical perspective:

1. It is assumed that mental disorders result from maladaptive learning and thus shouldn't be regarded as "illnesses".
2. The focus on each individual's particular experiences and conditioning history means that the behavioural model is potentially sensitive to cultural and social factors.
3. The behavioural approach tends to be non-judgemental, in the sense that treatment is recommended only when an individual's behaviour causes severe problems to that person or to other people.
4. It is assumed within the behavioural model that abnormal behaviour is determined mainly by environmental factors—that means that individuals who develop mental disorders shouldn't be held responsible for those disorders.

There are ethical problems with some of the forms of treatment based on the behavioural model. Aversion therapy involves giving very unpleasant stimuli (e.g. electric shocks or nausea-inducing drugs) to clients in order to stop some undesirable form of

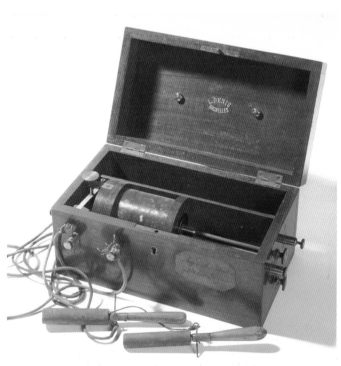

A very early example of an induction coil device used in 18th-century electric-shock therapy. Today, aversion therapy utilises much more sophisticated methods and equipment.

behaviour such as drinking in alcoholics. There has been much controversy about the morality of causing high levels of pain and discomfort. Most forms of treatment focus mainly on changing behaviour, and it could be argued that it is dehumanising to neglect the client's internal experiences and feelings. Therapies derived from the behavioural model can be seen as manipulative.

The cognitive model
The **cognitive model of abnormality** grew out of dissatisfaction with the behavioural model and its major focus on external factors (stimuli and responses). According to the cognitive model, we need to consider internal, mental influences, and the power of the individual to shape his/her own thinking. The central notion in the cognitive model is that individuals suffering from mental disorders have distorted and irrational thinking—they suffer from maladaptive thinking rather than maladaptive behaviour as in the behavioural model. Warren and Zgourides (1991) pointed out that many of these thoughts have a "must" quality about them. For example, "I *must* perform well and/or win the approval of others, or else it's awful", "You *must* treat me fairly and considerately and not unduly frustrate me, or it's awful", "My life conditions *must* give me the things I want easily and with little frustration . . . or else life is unbearable." These distorted thoughts can play an important role in the development of mental disorders.

In practice, the cognitive model has been applied most often to individuals suffering from anxiety and depression. There is reasonable evidence that such individuals do have irrational thoughts. For example, Newmark et al. (1973) found that 65% of anxious clients (but only 2% of normals) agreed with the statement, "It is essential that one be loved or approved by virtually everyone in his [sic!] community." The statement "One must be perfectly competent, adequate, and achieving to consider oneself worthwhile", was agreed to by 80% of anxious patients compared with 25% of normals.

Nearly everyone agrees that anxious and depressed patients have distorted views and attitudes about themselves and the world around them. For example, those with panic disorder often have catastrophic beliefs (e.g. that when they perceive their heart racing, this indicates they are about to have a heart attack) (Clark, 1986). Those with social phobia (involving excessive fear about social situations) often believe that they are in imminent danger of social disgrace and humiliation.

Beck (1976) used the term *cognitive triad* to refer to the typically unrealistic negative thoughts of depressed patients in the three areas of themselves, the world, and the future. The crucial issue (and one that is still not resolved) is whether the distorted and

 HOW SCIENCE WORKS: DEFINING AND EXPLAINING PSYCHOLOGICAL ABNORMALITY
The various psychological approaches' explanations of psychological abnormality really are different. You can demonstrate this by producing a set of four posters, one for each approach. Each one should identify the key assumptions of the approach, the actual explanation the approach offers, and a summary of the main strengths and weaknesses of that explanation. Make your posters as lively as possible. Finally you could use your analysis of the models, i.e. your posters, to evaluate the different models' explanations of abnormality. The posters will be useful revision tools too!

 Behavioural approaches to the treatment of mental disorders have been successful but they assume that the patient and therapist share the same goals for behaviour. In what way might such treatments be seen as "social manipulation"?

KEY TERM
Cognitive model of abnormality: a model of abnormality which considers that individuals who suffer from mental disorders have distorted or irrational thinking.

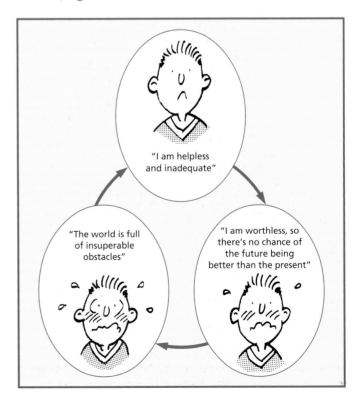

? Think of an occasion when you felt helpless or worthless. Could you try to re-interpret the occasion in a more positive way?

unrealistic thoughts of clients with various mental disorders actually played a part in the development of the mental disorder. It is entirely possible that clients only start having these unrealistic thoughts *after* they have developed an anxiety disorder or depression. If so, this is a real problem—it would mean that distorted thoughts have nothing to do with causing mental disorders!

Some support for the notion that unrealistic thoughts may occur *before* a disorder develops and may play a part in its occurrence was reported by Lewinsohn et al. (2001). They identified one group of adolescents who had unrealistic negative thoughts (e.g. "My life is wasted unless I am a success"; "I should be happy all the time") at the start of the study and another group who did not. Lewinsohn et al. then had a look 12 months later to see how many of these adolescents had developed major depression. Those who had had unrealistic negative thoughts 12 months earlier were significantly more likely to have become clinically depressed than those whose thoughts 1 year earlier were realistic. These findings don't prove that unrealistic negative thoughts help to cause depression, but they are entirely consistent with that possibility.

A key question raised by the cognitive model is the following: Why do individuals with anxiety disorders or depression maintain distorted and irrational thoughts and beliefs year after year in the face of contrary evidence from the world around them? I will answer this question with respect to social phobia. Social-phobic people fear they will experience catastrophe (e.g. public humiliation) in social situations even though they haven't actually experienced any such catastrophes. According to Clark and Wells (1995), they do so because they make use of **safety-seeking behaviours** designed to reduce the anxiety experienced in social situations. These safety-seeking behaviours include avoiding eye contact, talking very little, ignoring other people, and avoiding talking about themselves. People with social phobia mistakenly believe that these safety-seeking behaviours are all that stands between them and social catastrophe.

Assumptions of the cognitive model

- Maladaptive behaviour is caused by faulty and irrational cognitions.
- It is the way you think about a problem, rather than the problem itself, that causes mental disorder.
- Individuals can overcome mental disorders by learning to use more appropriate cognitions.
- Aim to be positive and rational.

KEY TERM

Safety-seeking behaviours: actions taken by individuals with anxiety disorders to reduce their anxiety level and prevent feared consequences.

Patients with panic disorder have catastrophic cognitions about fainting, having a heart attack, or being paralysed with fear. According to such patients, these catastrophes haven't happened because they use safety-seeking behaviours such as holding on to people, distracting themselves, or trying to exercise during a panic attack (Salkovskis, Clark, & Gelder, 1996).

Evaluation of the cognitive model

The cognitive model of abnormality has become very influential in recent years. Distorted and irrational beliefs are very common among patients with mental disorders, and seem to be of central importance in anxiety disorders and depression (Beck & Clark, 1988). There is some evidence that distorted beliefs may play a part in the development of depression (Lewinsohn et al., 2001). Of major importance in Cognitive Behavioural Therapy (discussed later) is the attempt to eliminate the biased and distorted beliefs of individuals with mental disorders. The fact that Cognitive Behavioural Therapy is effective and may even be more effective than other forms of therapy suggests that an emphasis on distorted beliefs is justified.

Here are some of the main weaknesses of the cognitive model of abnormality:

- We know that individuals suffering from anxiety or depression have numerous distorted beliefs. However, it remains unclear whether distorted beliefs help to cause the disorder (as predicted by the cognitive model) or whether they are merely a consequence of having a mental disorder.
- Related to the above point, it can be argued that the cognitive model isn't very explanatory. As Davison and Neale (1998, p. 46) pointed out, "That a depressed person has a negative schema [organised knowledge] tells us that the person thinks gloomy thoughts. But everyone knows that such a pattern of thinking is actually part of the diagnosis of depression."
- Little attention is paid to the role of social and interpersonal factors or of individuals' life experiences in producing mental disorders.
- The cognitive approach is limited in that genetic factors are ignored; indeed, all the factors emphasised within the biological model approach are ignored.
- The cognitive model has been applied to many mental disorders, but it has mainly been applied to anxiety and depression. Its potential relevance to other disorders is unclear.

Ethical implications of the cognitive model

According to the cognitive model, individuals with mental disorders have distorted thoughts and beliefs, and so the disorders are mainly their own fault. That notion raises various ethical issues. First, patients may find it stressful to accept

See *AS Level Psychology Online* for an interactive exercise on this topic.

> **EXAM HINT**
> You may be asked to specify the assumptions of one of the following models of abnormality: biological/ behavioural/ cognitive/ psychodynamic in relation to the causes of abnormality. In your answer you should give the general assumption of the model (e.g. the biological model assumes mental illness has a physical basis) and then describe two possible causes for each model to illustrate this. Here are two possible causes for each model:
>
> - Biological: genes, biochemical imbalance.
> - Behavioural: classically conditioned associations, reinforcement.
> - Cognitive: cognitive dysfunction, breakdown in information processing.
> - Psychodynamic: unconscious conflicts, regression.

> **EXAM HINT**
> All of the models of abnormality can be evaluated as:
>
> - *Reductionist* because they are oversimplified and ignore other explanations.
> - *Deterministic* because they ignore the free will of the individual to control their own behaviour.
>
> Each of these can be further elaborated for 3 marks so do this for each model or choose alternative criticisms but make sure you elaborate for 3 marks.

responsibility for their mental disorders. Second, it may be unfair to "blame" individuals for their mental disorder, because others around them may be mainly responsible. It is suggested that the root of maladaptive beliefs may be childhood experiences. Third, the negative thoughts and beliefs of those with mental disorders are often entirely rational and reflect all too accurately the unfortunate circumstances in which an individual is living. Attempts to put the blame on to the patient may inhibit his/her efforts to produce desirable changes.

SECTION SUMMARY

The statistical infrequency approach

❖ This is one way of defining abnormality. According to this approach, abnormality can be defined in terms of behaviour or beliefs that are statistically rare in a population.

❖ The normal distribution is one way to describe a statistical distribution.

❖ While this approach suffers less from value judgements than the other approaches, it has been criticised as follows:
  – It doesn't distinguish between desirable deviation and undesirable deviation.
  – It doesn't define the level or percentage at which statistical deviancy is decided.
  – It doesn't allow for cultural and sub-cultural differences.

Deviation from social norms

❖ This is another way of defining abnormality. Social groups have norms of what is considered to be socially acceptable behaviour. Deviation from these is abnormal and undesirable.

❖ This approach has been criticised as follows:
  – The perception of deviance may change over historical time, and what is socially deviant varies across cultures with ethnic or religious differences.
  – The definition ignores the role of social context. In some cases (e.g. Nazi Germany) it may be desirable to be socially deviant.
  – The concept of social deviance could lead to an abuse of human rights.

Failure to function adequately

❖ The third approach suggests that abnormality can be defined in terms of an inability to function adequately in day-to-day life and social interactions.

❖ An absence of distress and the ability to function are standards of normal behaviour.

❖ This approach has the benefit of taking the individual's experience into account. However, it has been criticised as follows:
  – How do we determine whether a person is functioning adequately?
  – Not all those with mental disorders are aware of their own distress or dysfunction.
  – The definition raises concerns about cultural bias and subjectivity as judgements by others on their behalf may be biased.

- Rosenhan and Seligman have extended the "failure to function" model to cover seven features associated with abnormality, but these also rely on making subjective judgements.

- ❖ Another approach suggests that abnormality can be defined in terms of deviation from ideal mental health.
- ❖ Humanistic psychologists consider the factors that may be important for normal development such as unconditional positive regard. They also see self-actualisation as an ultimate goal.
- ❖ This approach has been criticised as follows:
  - It is based on abstract and culturally relative ideals not shared by collectivistic societies. There are cultural variations in how to identify psychological health.
  - Unlike physical health, it is difficult to measure psychological health.

Deviation from ideal mental health

- ❖ Cultural relativism is a problem in all four of the approaches described. The definitions inevitably refer to some subjective, culturally determined set of values.
- ❖ However, there are also cultural universals—behaviours such as anti-social behaviour or chronic depression are universally viewed as abnormal and undesirable.
- ❖ The resolution may lie in using a combined approach that focuses on which features are more likely to be associated with abnormality.

Limitations with all these approaches

- ❖ There are five major models of abnormality, each of which provides explanations for the treatment of mental disorders. They are:
  - Biological (medical) model
  - Psychodynamic model
  - Behavioural model
  - Cognitive, and now cognitive behavioural, model
  - Diathesis–stress model
- ❖ These models are not mutually exclusive, and all of them have contributed to our understanding of the causes of mental disorders.

Models of abnormality

- ❖ This model suggests that the causes of mental disorders resemble those of physical illness.
- ❖ Clusters of symptoms can be identified and a diagnosis made, followed by suitable treatment.
- ❖ There is some evidence that the following may account for mental disorders:
  - genetics
  - biochemistry
  - neuroanatomy
  - infections
- ❖ While this approach has received some scientific support and has contributed to treatments, it has been criticised in that:
  - It focuses on symptoms rather than the person's thoughts and feelings.
  - It is less appropriate for disorders with psychological symptoms such as the anxiety disorders.

Biological model of abnormality

– There is some debate as to whether mental disorders are basically similar to physical illnesses.
– The treatments based on the medical model (e.g. drugs, ECT, psychosurgery) may have unpleasant side effects and their effectiveness has been challenged.

Psychodynamic model of abnormality

❖ This model suggests that the causes of mental disorders arise from unresolved unconscious conflicts and traumas of early childhood and in problems with personality development.
❖ Although this model has offered insights into anxiety disorders and has changed the perception of mental illness, it has been criticised in that:
– It is hard to disprove and has thus been criticised for being unscientific.
– It may focus too much on sexual problems rather than interpersonal and social issues.
– It raises ethical concerns about the problems of false memory syndrome, sexism, and parental blame.

Behavioural model

❖ This model suggests that mental disorders are caused by learning maladaptive behaviour via conditioning or observational learning.
❖ This model offers people with mental disorders hope, in that it implies that their behaviour can be changed—anything that is learned can be unlearned using the same techniques.
❖ The approach is most suited to explaining and treating those disorders in which the emphasis is on external behaviour (e.g. phobias).
❖ Ethically, there are advantages such as the lack of blame attached to a person with a mental disorder. However, the model has been criticised in that:
– It is somewhat oversimplified and ignores individual differences.
– It is based on animal research.
– The treatments developed from this model can be painful and manipulative (e.g. aversion therapy).

Cognitive model

❖ This model suggests that mental disorders stem from distorted and irrational beliefs, and there is no doubt that patients with anxiety disorders and depression have distorted beliefs.
❖ This model has been criticised in that:
– It is generally not clear whether the distorted thinking is an effect of the disorder or the cause.
– Another issue is that the cognitive model has been applied mainly to anxiety and depression, and its relevance to other mental disorders is largely unknown.
– It implies that individuals are somehow to blame for their problems.
❖ Over the past 30 years or so, a cognitive behavioural model has been suggested that combines the cognitive and behavioural approaches.

The diathesis–stress model

❖ This model offers a multi-dimensional approach.
❖ It suggests that individuals may have a genetic vulnerability (diathesis) that can be triggered by environmental factors (stress).

SECTION 17
TREATING ABNORMALITY

Individuals with mental disorders exhibit a wide range of symptoms. There may be problems associated with thinking (e.g. the distorted beliefs of anxious and depressed individuals), with behaviour (e.g. the avoidance behaviour of the phobic person), or with physiological and bodily processes (e.g. the highly activated physiological system of someone with post-traumatic stress disorder). Note, however, that thinking, behaviour, and physiological processes are all highly *interdependent*.

Therapeutic approaches to mental disorder could focus on producing changes in thinking, in behaviour, or in physiological functioning. At the risk of over-simplification, this is precisely what has happened. The psychodynamic approach was designed to change thinking, and the same is true of cognitive therapy. Behaviour therapy, as its name implies, emphasises the importance of changing behaviour. Cognitive Behavioural Therapy, which represents a combination of cognitive and behaviour therapy, aims to change clients' thinking *and* their behaviour. Biological therapies (e.g. drug therapy; electroconvulsive therapy) focus on physiological and biochemical changes.

When considering various forms of therapy, we must avoid making the treatment aetiology fallacy (MacLeod, 1998). This is the mistaken notion that the success of a given form of treatment reveals the cause of the disorder. For example, aspirin is an effective cure for headache. However, that doesn't mean that a lack of aspirin causes headaches!

HOW SCIENCE WORKS: TREATING ABNORMALITY
It would be interesting to analyse and evaluate a specific model for treating psychological abnormality. For instance, you could produce a PowerPoint presentation, using notes and downloaded images, showing the stages of either a systematic desensitisation therapy programme for un-learning a fear of heights, or of a Cognitive Behavioural Therapy for reducing that same fear. When you present this to your class or group you could ask them to produce arguments based on psychological theory or theories for and against each therapeutic approach. You could also ask them to generate therapeutic programmes for other psychopathologies—you provide the necessary details of the pathology, and they apply what they have learned to a novel or unfamiliar psychological problem.

Biological Therapies

Biological therapies are those forms of treatment that involve manipulations of the body. Biological therapies mostly involve the administration of drugs and they are associated with the biological model. According to the biological model, mental disorders develop because of abnormalities in bodily functioning (especially within the brain), and drugs can often be used to reduce or eliminate those abnormalities.

Apart from drug therapy, two other main forms of biologically based therapy are electroconvulsive therapy (ECT) and psychosurgery. I will discuss drug therapy and ECT in detail shortly, but will first briefly refer to psychosurgery. Psychosurgery involves carrying out brain surgery to treat mental disorders. Pioneering work was carried out by Antonio Egas Moniz. He carried out

KEY TERM

Biological therapies: forms of treatment that involve manipulations of the body, e.g. drugs or ECT.

In the film One Flew Over the Cuckoo's Nest, Jack Nicholson played Randle Patrick McMurphy, who inspired and awakened his fellow patients, while falling out with the authorities. Eventually, the character is lobotomised, and becomes calmer and easier to handle, but loses all his intellectual spark and energy.

prefrontal lobotomies, in which fibres running from the frontal lobes to other parts of the brain were cut. In the film *One Flew Over the Cuckoo's Nest*, a lobotomy operation ends Randle Patrick McMurphy's rebellion against the hospital authorities. Moniz claimed that such operations made schizophrenic and other patients less violent and agitated. However, lobotomies have very serious side effects, including apathy, diminished intellectual powers, and even coma and death. In addition, psychosurgery poses immense ethical issues. As a result, lobotomies stopped being performed many years ago in most countries.

Early somatic therapy

There have been many bizarre treatments for mental illness over the course of history, from blood-letting and purging (use of laxatives), to ice baths. In 1810, Dr Benjamin Rush invented the restraining chair illustrated here. Herman and Green (1991) quote his description of its effectiveness:

> I have contrived a chair and introduced it to our Hospital to assist in curing madness. It binds and confines every part of the body. By keeping the trunk erect, it lessens the impetus of blood toward the brain . . . It acts as a sedative to the tongue and temper as well as to the blood vessels.

Rush coined the word *Tranquiliser* as a name for his apparatus and patients were confined in it for up to 24 hours at a time. No one today would be surprised that this would subdue anyone, regardless of their mental state.

Drug therapy

How can we show that any given drug is effective in treating a particular disorder? It might seem as if all we need to do is to assign patients to two groups, one of which receives the drug and the other of which receives nothing. In fact, that is *not* an adequate approach because of what is known as the placebo effect. The **placebo effect** occurs when patients given an inactive substance or placebo (e.g. a salt tablet) show significant reductions in their symptoms. In other words, if you think something is going to make you better, it may do so simply through "the power of the mind". The ideal is a double-blind study in which neither the patient nor the therapist knows whether the patient is receiving an active drug or a placebo. In such a study, the expectations of the patient and therapist can't influence the outcome. In what follows, we will consider drug therapy for depression, anxiety, and schizophrenia in turn.

Depression

There are two main forms of depression. First, there is **major depressive disorder**, which is characterised by sadness, depressed mood, tiredness, and loss of interest in various activities. Second, there is bipolar disorder, which is a mood disorder characterised by depressive and manic (elated) episodes. **Bipolar disorder** is the more serious condition and is hard to treat.

Individuals with major depressive disorder often have low levels of the neurotransmitters serotonin and noradrenaline. Accordingly, drugs to treat that disorder are designed to rectify these low levels. There are three main types of antidepressant drugs used to treat major depressive disorder: (1) monoamine oxidase inhibitors (MAOIs); (2) tricyclic anti-depressants (TCAs); and selective serotonin re-uptake inhibitors (SSRIs). The MAOIs were developed during the 1950s and the SSRIs were developed more recently.

The MAOIs block monoamine oxidase and by so doing help to prevent the destruction of noradrenaline. As a result, depressed patients taking MAOIs have increased noradrenaline activity leading to a reduction in depressive symptoms. The MAOIs are reasonably effective in reducing depression, but they do produce various side effects. They block the production of monoamine oxidase in the liver, leading to the accumulation of tyramine. This is dangerous, because high levels of tyramine cause high levels of blood pressure. Accordingly, depressed patients taking MAOIs have to follow a careful diet, making sure to avoid foods (e.g. cheese, bananas) containing tyramine. Newer drugs (reversible inhibitors of monoamine oxidase type A or RIMAs) create fewer problems.

Tricyclic anti-depressant drugs appear to increase the activity of those neurotransmitters, and generally reduce the symptoms of depression. In a large-scale study (Elkin, 1994), a tricylic (imipramine) was as effective as cognitive therapy and interpersonal psychotherapy in treating depression. However, there can be a high relapse rate unless drug therapy is continued over a long period of time (Franchini et al., 1997). The tricyclics are less dangerous than the MAOIs, but they can impair driving to a dangerous extent.

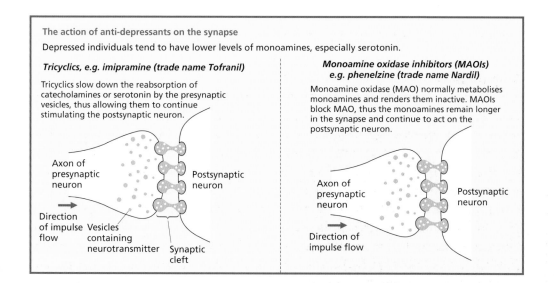

The action of anti-depressants on the synapse

Depressed individuals tend to have lower levels of monoamines, especially serotonin.

Tricyclics, e.g. imipramine (trade name Tofranil)

Tricyclics slow down the reabsorption of catecholamines or serotonin by the presynaptic vesicles, thus allowing them to continue stimulating the postsynaptic neuron.

Axon of presynaptic neuron

Postsynaptic neuron

Direction of impulse flow

Vesicles containing neurotransmitter

Synaptic cleft

Monoamine oxidase inhibitors (MAOIs) e.g. phenelzine (trade name Nardil)

Monoamine oxidase (MAO) normally metabolises monoamines and renders them inactive. MAOIs block MAO, thus the monoamines remain longer in the synapse and continue to act on the postsynaptic neuron.

Axon of presynaptic neuron

Postsynaptic neuron

Direction of impulse flow

The most common drugs used to treat depression are the serotonin re-uptake inhibitors (SSRIs), of which Prozac is the best known. These drugs are more selective in their functioning than the tricylics, in that they increase serotonin activity without influencing other neurotransmitters such as noradrenaline. The SSRIs are as effective as the tricyclics (Hirschfeld, 1999), but they possess some advantages.

? Why do you think that many people won't take drugs for mental problems?

KEY TERM

Bipolar disorder: a mood disorder in which there are depressive and manic (elated) episodes.

[?] It has sometimes been suggested that manic depression is higher among very creative people, and that the manic phase of the disorder can particularly heighten creativity. How might this affect some sufferers' decisions about whether or not to take drug treatment such as lithium carbonate?

Depressed patients taking SSRIs are less likely to suffer from dry mouth and constipation than those taking tricyclics, and it is harder to overdose on SSRIs. However, SSRIs conflict with some other forms of medication.

The most commonly used drug for bipolar disorder is lithium. Various suggestions have been made as to the mechanism by which it has its effects. One notion is that lithium alters potassium and sodium ion activity in neurons and hence transmission of nerve impulses. Lithium has beneficial effects in about 80% of patients, especially in reducing the symptoms associated with manic episodes (Prien & Potter, 1993). Geddes et al. (2004) carried out a meta-analysis of studies on lithium therapy for bipolar disorder. Overall, lithium was effective in preventing relapses after most of the symptoms had been eliminated. However, its effectiveness was significantly greater in preventing relapses of manic symptoms than of depressive symptoms.

There are some problems with the use of lithium to treat bipolar disorder. First, it produces various side effects (e.g. impaired coordination, tremors, and digestive problems). Second, up to about 40% of patients with bipolar disorder fail to take the prescribed dosage of the drug (Basco & Rush, 1996).

CASE STUDY: VIRGINIA WOOLF

The author Virginia Woolf, who committed suicide in 1941 at the age of 59, was plagued by an intermittent form of depression. This affliction appears to have been bipolar depression, but was accompanied by extreme physical symptoms and psychotic delusions. In her biography of Woolf, Hermione Lee (1997) unravels the series of treatments administered to Woolf between 1895, when she experienced her first breakdown, and the 1930s. Later, Woolf's husband Leonard made detailed notes on her breakdowns (Lee, 1997, pp.78–179):

In the manic stage she was extremely excited; the mind raced; she talked volubly and, at the height of the attack, incoherently; she had delusions and heard voices . . . During the depressive stage all her thoughts and emotions were the exact opposite . . . she was in the depths of melancholia and despair; she scarcely spoke; refused to eat; refused to believe that she was ill and insisted that her condition was due to her own guilt.

During the period from 1890 to 1930, Woolf consulted more than 12 different doctors, but the treatments barely altered during this time. They tended to consist of milk and meat diets to redress her weight loss; rest to alleviate her agitation; sleep and fresh air to help her regain her energy. Lithium had not yet been discovered as a treatment for manic depression. Instead, bromide, veronal, and chloral, most of which are sedatives, were prescribed. Lee points out that there is great uncertainty about the neuropsychiatric effects of some of these drugs, and Woolf's manic episodes may well have been the result of taking these chemicals. ∎

Anxiety disorders

Patients with anxiety disorders (especially generalised anxiety disorder in which excessive worrying is the central symptom) are often given drugs. Many of these drugs are also given to people suffering from high levels of stress (see Chapter 6). The most popular anti-anxiety drugs are the benzodiazepines (e.g. Librium and Valium), which are often used to treat anxiety disorders. In 2003, over 13 million prescriptions for benzodiazepines were written in the UK (Garfield, 2003). These drugs bind to receptor sites in the brain that generally receive the neurotransmitter GABA. The benzodiazepines increase the ability of GABA to bind to these sites, which enhances the ability of GABA to inhibit bodily arousal and anxiety.

The benzodiazepines are reasonably effective in the treatment of generalised anxiety disorder (Rickels, DeMartinis, & Aufdrembrinke, 2000), and have also been used to treat social phobia. Mitte (2005) found in a meta-analysis of 65 studies that drug-based approaches to the treatment of generalised anxiety disorder are mostly effective. Indeed, they are comparably effective to Cognitive Behavioural Therapy, which is well established as a successful form of treatment.

In spite of the successes associated with the use of benzodiazepines in the treatment of the anxiety disorders, they can produce several unwanted effects:

- Anxious symptoms often return when patients stop taking the drugs.
- There are various side effects (e.g. lack of coordination; poor concentration; memory loss; sedative effects).
- Stewart (2005) found in a meta-analysis that long-term use of benzodiazepines was associated with various cognitive impairments. There was some improvement after the drugs were withdrawn, but cognitive performance was still somewhat below normal.
- There is the danger of drug escalation, with patients taking progressively larger doses of the drug to achieve the same effect.
- There can be physical dependence, with patients finding it difficult to manage without drugs.

[?] In what instances might a GP feel justified in prescribing drugs such as Valium or Librium? What other forms of treatment would benefit an anxious patient, together with or instead of drugs?

Disorder	Drug/group of drugs	How they work	Drawbacks
Depression (major)	Monoamine oxidase inhibitors (MAOIs)	Inhibit oxidation of monoamines (neurotransmitters, including dopamine, serotonin, and nor-adrenaline), so that levels increase	A range of side-effects
	Tricyclics	As MAOIs	Dizziness, blurred vision, dry mouth
	SSRIs (e.g. Prozac)	As MAOIs, but mainly affect levels of serotonin	Preoccupation with suicide and violence
Depression (bipolar)	Lithium carbonate	Anti-mania, but mechanism is imperfectly understood	Side-effects on CNS, cardiovascular, and digestive systems. Overdose can be fatal
Anxiety disorders	Barbiturates	Treat symptoms of anxiety: palpitations, shortness of breath, accelerated heart rate, feeling of choking, nausea, dizziness, etc.	Problems of concentration, lack of co-ordination, slurred speech. Addictive. Withdrawal symptoms include delirium, irritability
	Benzodiazepines (e.g. Valium, Librium)	Have a sedative effect on the CNS	Drowsiness, lethargy, impairments of long-term memory. Withdrawal symptoms and possible addiction
	Buspirone	Affects dopamine receptors in the brain	Doesn't appear to have sedative effect, but other side-effects not yet established
Schizophrenia	Neuroleptic drugs (e.g. phenothiazines butyrophenones, thioxanthenes)	Reduce delusions, hallucinations	Little effect on lack of motivation and emotion, social withdrawal. Some patients report grogginess, sedation, difficulty concentrating, dry mouth, blurred vision
	Atypical anti-psychotic drugs (e.g. clozapine)	As neuroleptics, but with fewer side-effects	Expensive. May produce fatal blood disease in 1–2% of patients

? Which other disorder is also linked to abnormal levels of serotonin?

Buspirone, a drug that started to be used about 20 years ago, doesn't have the potentially dangerous sedative effects of the benzodiazepines. It acts differently from the benzodiazepines, by stimulating serotonin receptors in the brain. Buspirone is as effective as the benzodiazepines in treating generalised anxiety disorder (Lader & Scotto, 1998), and it has the advantage of rarely leading to physical dependence. Chamberlain et al. (2007) found that short-term use of buspirone was not associated with any impairments of cognitive functions such as planning, memory, and decision making. However, there is evidence (e.g. Goa & Ward, 1986) that buspirone can cause depression and headaches.

Tricyclic drugs (generally used to treat major depression) have been used successfully to treat panic disorder. Barlow et al. (2000) found that tricyclic drugs were as effective as Cognitive Behavioural Therapy in reducing the symptoms of panic disorder. However, they were less effective at 6-month follow-up.

Schizophrenia

When discussing drug effects on **schizophrenia**, it is important to distinguish between the positive and negative symptoms of schizophrenia. The positive symptoms include the presence of delusions and hallucinations, whereas the negative symptoms include lack of motivation, lack of emotion, and social withdrawal. Some drugs are more effective at reducing the positive symptoms than the negative ones. There are two main categories of drugs: (1) conventional or neuroleptic drugs; and (2) the newer atypical drugs.

Neuroleptic drugs (drugs reducing psychotic symptoms but producing some of the symptoms of neurological diseases) are conventional drugs often used in the treatment of schizophrenia. Common neuroleptic drugs include Thorazine, Prolixin, and Haldol. These drugs block the activity of the neurotransmitter dopamine within 48 hours, and their effects on dopamine are believed to be important in therapy. However, it takes several weeks of drug therapy before schizophrenic symptoms show substantial reduction. The major neuroleptic drugs are of real value in treating

KEY TERM

Schizophrenia: a very severe disorder characterised by hallucinations, delusions, lack of emotion, and very impaired social functioning.

CASE STUDY: CHEMOTHERAPY SAVES LIVES

Novelist blames depression in son's apparent overdose
Danielle Steel says he was manic-depressive

When Nicholas Traina was found dead of an apparent overdose during the weekend, his mother, novelist Danielle Steel, was heartbroken but not entirely surprised. Though her 19-year-old son had a history of drug use, the problem was much deeper: for his entire short life, Traina was tormented by mental illness. "The only time he messed around with drugs was when his medications failed him and he was desperate," Steel told *The Chronicle* in the first interview she has given since her son's death on Saturday. "This was not some wild kid, this was a very sick kid. The awful thing is I knew for years. He was manic-depressive, and wrestled with mental illness all his life. The biggest agony of my life is that for years, no one would listen to me that he was sick until we found a doctor in LA about 4 years ago who gave him amazing medication. He understood because he was manic-depressive, too."

Adapted from an article in the *San Francisco Chronicle* 17 September 1997.

To Dad, girl was Satan and thought he was Messiah when he killed daughter, 6, court told

Paranoid schizophrenic Ron England believed he was the Messiah ridding the world of evil when he murdered his mother and 6-year-old daughter, a psychiatrist says.

Dr Ian Jacques told a coroner's inquest yesterday England still does not believe his daughter, Jenny, and her grandma, Marian Johnston, are dead.

Jacques said England—who'd sworn off medication treating his severe mental illness—was "almost functioning on auto-pilot and getting his instructions (to kill) from television." England called 911 on April 2, 1996, to report he'd killed his mother and daughter at their home in Bowmanville. Marian Johnston, 79, was found slumped on her bed in pyjamas, housecoat and black boots. The former public health nurse, who'd helped England win supervised custody of Jenny over her biological parents, had been stabbed 34 times. On the floor lay Jenny with a knife embedded in her heart. She'd been stabbed 89 times.

Adapted from an article in the *Toronto Sun*. ■

schizophrenia. However, their effectiveness is greater in reducing positive symptoms than negative ones. Overall, these drugs "reduce schizophrenic symptoms in the majority of patients . . . the drugs appear to be a more effective treatment for schizophrenia than any of the other approaches used alone" (Comer, 2001).

Neuroleptic drugs produce some side effects. Windgassen (1992) found that 50% of schizophrenic patients taking neuroleptics reported grogginess or sedation, 18% reported problems with concentration, and 16% had blurred vision. In addition, many schizophrenic patients on neuroleptic drugs develop symptoms closely resembling those of Parkinson's disease (e.g. muscle rigidity, tremors, foot shuffling).

Most of the above side effects occur within a few weeks of the start of drug therapy. However, more than 20% of patients who take neuroleptic drugs for over a year develop the symptoms of **tardive dyskinesia**. These symptoms include involuntary sucking and chewing, jerky movements of the limbs, and writhing movements of the mouth or face, and the effects can be permanent.

Schizophrenia is increasingly treated with atypical anti-psychotic drugs (e.g. Clozaril; Risperdal; Zyprexa). These drugs have various advantages over the conventional drugs. First, they have fewer side effects than the neuroleptic drugs. Second, they benefit 85% of schizophrenic patients compared to 65% given neuroleptic drugs (Awad & Voruganti, 1999). Third, the atypical drugs are of much more use in helping schizophrenic patients suffering mainly from negative symptoms (Remington & Kapur, 2000). Fourth, many side effects of the conventional drugs (especially tardive dyskinesia) are absent with the atypical drugs.

The atypical drugs can produce serious side effects. For example, schizophrenic patients who take clozapine have a 1–2% risk of developing agranulocytosis. This involves a substantial reduction in white blood cells, and the condition can be life threatening. However, olanzapine (an atypical anti-psychotic drug) doesn't seem to cause agranulocytosis.

Overall evaluation

Drug therapy has many successes to its credit. It often produces rapid beneficial effects when used to treat depression, anxiety, and schizophrenia. This can be extremely important, for example, if a severely depressed individual is in danger of committing suicide. As we have seen, drug therapy is as effective as Cognitive Behavioural Therapy in the treatment of generalised anxiety disorder (Mitte, 2005) and tricyclic drugs are almost as effective as Cognitive Behavioural Therapy in the treatment of panic disorder (Barlow et al., 2000). In the treatment of schizophrenia, the atypical drugs are not only more effective than the neuroleptic drugs (Awad & Voruganti, 1999), but are also probably more effective than any other form of treatment (Comer, 2001). This is especially impressive given that schizophrenia is notoriously hard to treat.

There are various weaknesses of the drug therapy approach:

- Relapse is more common after drug therapy than after other types of therapy. This is probably because drugs don't deal directly with the problems underlying any given mental disorder.
- It is often difficult to know precisely *why* any given drug is effective in the treatment of a particular disorder because of our limited understanding of the underlying biochemical factors.

? To what extent should practical concerns take precedence over ethical issues?

KEY TERM

Tardive dyskinesia: some of the long-term effects of taking neuroleptic drugs, including involuntary sucking and chewing, jerky movements, and writhing movements of the mouth or face.

See *AS Level Psychology Online* for an interactive exercise on this topic.

- There can be problems of drug dependence, with patients finding it very hard to cope without drugs.
- The drop-out rate is often rather high when drug therapy is used.
- Nearly all drugs have unwanted side effects. Some of these side effects (e.g. tardive dyskinesia; agranulocytosis) can be very serious and even life threatening.

Electroconvulsive therapy (ECT)

Electroconvulsive therapy (ECT) is used mainly in the treatment of major depressive disorder. What happens in ECT is that an electric current is passed through the head in order to produce a convulsion. In the past, ECT used to produce broken bones, patient terror, and memory loss. However, various changes in treatment have been introduced so that these problems have been almost eliminated. First, strong muscle relaxants are given to patients to prevent or minimise convulsions. Second, the current is generally only passed through the non-dominant brain hemisphere rather than through both hemispheres. This reduces the danger of memory loss, but on average reduces the effectiveness of treatment. Third, anaesthetics are used to put patients to sleep during ECT, thus reducing substantially the chances of experiencing terror.

Many studies designed to assess the effectiveness of ECT have compared it against simulated ECT, in which patients are exposed to the equipment and believe falsely that they have received ECT. This is done to ensure that the beneficial effects of ECT are genuine and not simply a placebo effect—seeing the equipment and believing that you are receiving shocks might be enough to reduce symptoms in the absence of any actual shocks.

When is ECT used rather than anti-depressant drugs in the treatment of major depressive disorder? The great majority of patients are initially treated by anti-depressant drugs rather than by ECT. However, some patients have poor tolerance of anti-depressant drugs or don't respond when given them, and such patients are sometimes given ECT. ECT is also often the treatment of choice in the case of patients with very severe depression when rapid reduction in symptoms is especially important. This can be essential in cases of severe depression in which attempts at suicide are possible.

How effective is ECT in the treatment of depression? Most of the findings are encouraging. For example, Petrides et al. (2001) reported that between 65% and 85% of depressed patients had a favourable response to ECT. Pagnin et al. (2004) carried out a meta-analysis in which the effectiveness of ECT was compared against various types of

---

ECT and psychosurgery

Some forms of treatment based on the biological model include fairly drastic methods such as electroconvulsive therapy (ECT) and brain surgery. However, ECT is not the barbaric treatment it once was. Patients are given sedatives before treatment and then brief shocks are applied to the non-dominant hemisphere of the brain. The treatment has been found to be successful for patients suffering from chronic depression, and long-term side effects are unusual (Stirling & Hellewell, 1999).

Brain surgery (psychosurgery) is used in extremely rare conditions, where no other treatment seems appropriate. Sections of the brain are removed or lesions are made separating regions of the brain. The technique was first pioneered by Antonio Egas Moniz (1937) who performed prefrontal lobotomies, in which fibres running from the frontal lobes to other parts of the brain were cut. Lobotomies typically make patients calmer, but side effects include apathy, diminished intellectual powers, impaired judgement, and even coma and death. In view of the dangers of lobotomies, it is ironic that Moniz was shot by one of his own lobotomised patients!

KEY TERM

Electroconvulsive therapy (ECT): a form of therapy used to treat depressed patients, in which brain seizures are created by passing an electric current through the head.

anti-depressant drugs and simulated ECT. ECT was more effective in the treatment of depression than anti-depressant drugs or simulated ECT. The findings led Pagnin et al. (2004, p. 13) to conclude that "ECT is a valid therapeutic tool for treatment of depression, including severe and resistant forms." Grunhaus et al. (2002) compared the effectiveness of ECT in patients with major depressive disorder and with bipolar disorder. They found that 57% of the patients responded positively to ECT and both groups of patients benefited equally.

What kinds of patients benefit most from ECT? This issue was addressed by de Vreede, Burger, and van Vliet (2005) in a study on patients with major

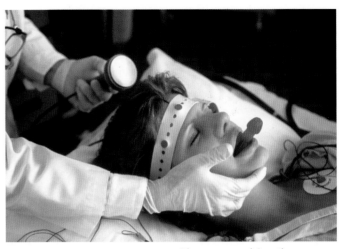

Electroconvulsive therapy has been found to be quite effective in cases of severe depression, though the reasons why it might be effective are uncertain.

depression. They identified four patient factors that predicted good response to ECT: age above 65 years; the absence of a psychotic depression (involving more severe symptoms); the absence of a personality disorder; and responding well to anti-depressants.

ECT is also used in the treatment of schizophrenia (one of the most serious mental disorders), but much less frequently than in the treatment of depression. Tharyan and Adams (2005) carried out a meta-analysis on the effects of ECT in treating schizophrenia. It has beneficial effects in the short term, but these effects are smaller than those obtained with drugs. ECT can be useful when used in combination with drugs, especially when it is thought important to produce rapid reductions in symptoms. It is less clear that ECT produces long-term benefits to patients with schizophrenia.

There are various problems with the use of ECT. First, there is still no detailed understanding of precisely why ECT is effective. It has numerous effects on the brain, including affecting neurotransmission and probably producing structural changes in neuronal networks. However, it is hard to establish *which* effects are the important ones in reducing the symptoms of depression. Second, ECT is associated with various side effects including memory loss and other cognitive impairments, although most of these problems seem to be short term rather than long term. Third, ECT is generally most effective at reducing symptoms when it is given to both hemispheres at a high dose. However, those are the conditions in which side effects are most common. Fourth, ECT seems to be less effective in the treatment of depression among patients who are below 65 years of age, who respond poorly to anti-depressants, and who have a psychotic depression and a personality disorder (de Vreede et al., 2005). Fifth, while ECT has been shown to benefit people with schizophrenia in the short term, it is less clear that it conveys long-term benefits to them.

? Given that the full implications of ECT are poorly understood, do you think it is ever right to administer such treatments to vulnerable patients?

Psychological Therapies

Psychological therapies involve the use of various psychological techniques to produce beneficial changes in individuals suffering from mental disorders. There are many psychological therapies, but we will be focusing on only a few

KEY TERM

Psychological therapies: forms of treatment that involve the use of various psychological techniques, e.g. psychoanalysis.

of the main ones. First, we consider psychoanalysis, which was developed by Sigmund Freud about 100 years ago. Psychoanalysis influenced the development of many other psychodynamic therapies subsequently. Second, we consider behaviour therapy, which was developed mainly in the United States and in the United Kingdom in the middle of the 20th century. More specifically, we will discuss in detail one of the techniques used in behaviour therapy—systematic de-sensitisation. Third, we consider Cognitive Behavioural Therapy. That form of therapy developed out of behaviour therapy, and started becoming influential from the 1970s onwards.

Psychoanalysis

Psychoanalysis was the first fully developed psychological therapy for the treatment of mental disorders. It was first proposed by Sigmund Freud in the early years of the 20th century. Psychoanalysis has been used to treat individuals with a wide range of mental disorders, but it has mostly been used to treat those suffering from neuroses, such as the anxiety disorders, or from depression. In general terms, psychoanalysis has been incredibly successful—the whole notion of "talking cures", which is very widely accepted nowadays, owes its origins to Freud.

According to Freud, neuroses occur because of conflicts among the three parts of the mind: the ego (rational mind), the id (sexual and other instincts), and the superego (conscience). Most of these conflicts are between the id and the superego—the id wants immediate gratification, whereas the superego is concerned about social and moral values. These conflicts cause the ego to use various defence mechanisms to defend itself. The most important defence mechanism is repression. Repression involves forcing painful, threatening, or unacceptable thoughts and memories out of consciousness into the unconscious mind. Repressed memories mostly refer to childhood and to the conflicts between the instinctive (e.g. sexual) motives of the child and the restraints imposed by his/her parents.

Freud argued that adults who experience great personal problems tend to show regression. Regression involves going backwards through the stages of psychosexual development the person went through in childhood (see Chapter 2). Children often fixate or spend an unusually long time at a given stage of psychosexual development if it was associated with conflicts or with excessive gratification. Regression typically occurs back to a stage at which the person had previously fixated. In general, more serious mental disorders are associated with regression further back into childhood. Thus, for example, individuals suffering from schizophrenia (which involves a loss of contact with reality) would regress to an earlier age of their lives than individuals suffering from neuroses or anxiety disorders.

Freud argued that the best way to cure neuroses was to allow the client to gain access to his/her repressed ideas and conflicts and to face up to whatever emerged from the unconscious. The client should focus on the feelings associated with the previously repressed ideas, and shouldn't simply regard them unemotionally. Emotional involvement is necessary for the client to appreciate the full significance of the events and ideas recovered from

KEY TERMS

Psychoanalysis: the form of therapy derived from psychoanalytic theory.
Ego: the conscious, rational part of the mind, which is guided by the reality principle.
Id: in Freudian theory, that part of the mind motivated by the pleasure principle and sexual instincts.
Superego: in Freud's theory, the part of the mind that embodies one's conscience. It is formed through identification with the same-sex parent.

the unconscious and thus to gain insight. **Insight** "involves a conscious awareness of some of the wishes, defences, and compromises . . . that have interacted to produce emotional conflict or deficits in psychological development" (Kivlighan, Multon, & Patton, 2000, p. 50).

How can we uncover repressed memories and permit the client to gain insight into some of the causes of his/her mental disorder? Freud made use of three main methods in psychoanalysis. The first method, and one that he initially used extensively, was hypnosis. Freud and Breuer (1895) treated a young woman called Anna O, who suffered from several neurotic symptoms (e.g. paralysis; nervous coughs). Hypnosis uncovered a repressed memory of Anna hearing the sound of dance music coming from a nearby house while she was nursing her dying father, and feeling guiltily that she would rather be dancing. Her nervous coughing stopped after that repressed memory came to light.

Freud gradually lost interest in hypnosis, partly because many clients were hard or impossible to hypnotise. Another problem is that individuals under hypnosis become very suggestible. As a result, little reliance can be placed on the accuracy of what they claim to remember when hypnotised.

> ### KEY TERM
>
> **Insight**: in Freud's theory this involves recovering traumatic and other distressing memories from the unconscious and considering them in terms of their true emotional significance. Insight allows the client to recognise how these traumatic and other events have adversely affected their lives, which provides a basis for him/her to recover from mental illness.

CASE STUDY: ANNA O

Freud's theory was largely based on the observations he made during consultations with patients. He suggested that his work was similar to that of an archaeologist, who digs away layers of earth before uncovering what he or she was seeking. In a similar way, the psychiatrist seeks to dig down to the unconscious and discover the key to the individual's personality dynamic.

"Anna O. was a girl of twenty-one, of a high degree of intelligence. Her illness first appeared while she was caring for her father, whom she tenderly loved, during the severe illness which led to his death. The patient had a severe paralysis of both right extremities, disturbance of eye-movements, an intense nausea when she attempted to take nourishment, and at one time for several weeks a loss of the power to drink, in spite of tormenting thirst. She occasionally became confused or delirious and mumbled several words to herself. If these same words were later repeated to her, when she was in a hypnotic state, she engaged in deeply sad, often poetically beautiful, day dreams, we might call them, which commonly took as their starting point the situation of a girl beside the sick-bed of her father. The patient jokingly called this treatment 'chimney sweeping'.

Dr. Breuer [Freud's colleague] soon hit upon the fact that through such cleansing of the soul more could be accomplished than a temporary removal of the constantly recurring mental 'clouds'.

During one session, the patient recalled an occasion when she was with her governess, and how that lady's little dog, that she abhorred, had drunk out of a glass. Out of respect for the conventions the patient had remained silent, but now under hypnosis she gave energetic expression to her restrained anger, and then drank a large quantity of water without trouble, and woke from hypnosis with the glass at her lips. The symptom thereupon vanished permanently.

Permit me to dwell for a moment on this experience. No one had ever cured an hysterical symptom by such means before, or had come so near understanding its cause. This would be a pregnant discovery if the expectation could be confirmed that still other, perhaps the majority of symptoms, originated in this way and could be removed by the same method.

Such was indeed the case, almost all the symptoms originated in exactly this way, as we were to discover. The patient's illness originated at the time when she was caring for her sick father, and her symptoms could only be regarded as memory symbols of his sickness and death. While she was seated by her father's sick bed, she was careful to betray nothing of her anxiety and her painful depression to the patient. When, later, she reproduced the same scene before the physician, the emotion which she had suppressed on the occurrence of the scene burst out with especial strength, as though it had been pent up all along.

In her normal state she was entirely ignorant of the pathogenic scenes and of their connection with her symptoms. She had forgotten those scenes. When the patient was hypnotized, it was possible, after considerable difficulty, to recall those scenes to her memory, and by this means of recall the symptoms were removed."

(Adapted from Sigmund Freud, 1910, The origin and development of psychoanalysis. *American Journal of Psychology, 21*, 181–218.) ■

The client is reluctant to say what he or she is really thinking.

Dream analysis

There are various schools of thought on the significance of dreams and their possible biological function. Freud and Jung believed that dreams signified the thoughts and feelings of the unconscious mind and are therefore necessary to allow the mind to explore them. Others have suggested that dreams perform no concrete function, but this view has been contested by referring to examples of sleep deprivation. Sleep-deprived participants tend to experience an increase in dreaming sleep when they are finally permitted to sleep.

What is your view on the role of dreams? How might psychologists test your views scientifically?

The second method was **free association**. In this method, the therapist tells the client to respond with the first thing that comes into his/her mind when presented with certain words or ideas. Free association is ineffective if the client shows resistance and is reluctant to say what he/she is thinking. Nevertheless, the presence of resistance (revealed by long pauses) suggests that the client is getting close to an important repressed idea, and that further probing by the therapist is needed.

The third method used by Freud to uncover repressed memories was the analysis of dreams, which he described as "the via regia [royal road] to the unconscious". Freud argued that the mind has a censor that keeps repressed material out of conscious awareness. This censor is less vigilant (it nods off?) during sleep, and so repressed ideas from the unconscious are more likely to appear in dreams than in waking thought. However, these repressed ideas usually emerge in disguised form because of their unacceptable nature. As a result, the therapist has to work with the client to decide on the true meaning of each dream.

Progress in therapy depends partly on **transference**. This involves the client transferring onto the therapist the powerful emotional reactions previously directed at his/her own parents or other highly significant others. These intense feelings can be negative or positive and the client is usually unaware of what is happening. Transference often provides a direct link back to the client's childhood by providing a re-creation of dramatic conflicts that were experienced at that time. As a result, transference can facilitate the uncovering of repressed memories.

Evidence

One of the main assumptions underlying psychoanalysis (and a very controversial one!) is that many adult mental disorders have their origins in childhood. There is evidence that this may well be true at least in some cases. For example, Kendler et al. (1996) studied adult female twins who had experienced parental loss through separation in childhood. These twins tended to suffer from depression and alcoholism in adult life. Caspi et al. (1996) found that children who were inhibited at the age of 3 were more likely than other children to suffer from major depression at the age of 21. They were also more likely to have attempted suicide. However, these effects were not large. Reinherz et al. (2000) assessed children's personal and familial characteristics between the ages of 5 and 9. Those who experienced high levels of anxiety and depression at that time were more likely than other children to have suffered from major depression by the age of 21.

It is important not to exaggerate the importance of early childhood in causing adult mental disorder. The onset of mental disorder is often triggered by *recent* events rather than those of childhood. For example, Kendler, Karkowski,

KEY TERMS

Free association: a technique used in psychoanalysis, in which the patient says the first thing that comes into his/her mind.

Transference: the transfer of the patient's strong feelings concerning one or both parents onto the therapist.

and Prescott (1998) studied the probability of female adults developing major depression as a function of the number of stressful life events in the preceding month. The percentages were as follows: 0.9% (0 events); 3.4% (1 event); 6.8% (2 events); and 23.8% (3 events).

It is hard to test Freud's notion that insight is of crucial importance if clients are to recover. The reason is that the concept is rather vague and imprecise. For example, Høglend et al. (1994) found that psychiatrists showed poor agreement among themselves concerning the insight levels shown by anxious and depressed patients in therapy. However, Høglend et al. (2000) used a scale to assess insight in clients with a range of problems (mostly anxiety or depression) who received psychotherapy for an average of 1 year. They found that 46% of the clients showed a significant increase in insight during the course of therapy. However, that doesn't necessarily mean that the recovery shown by the clients was due to the increases in insight.

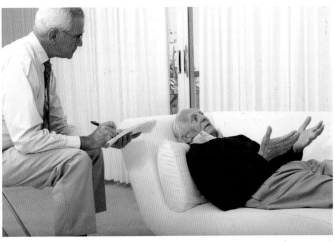

The findings of Kivlighan et al.'s (2000) study supported Freud's prediction that the levels of insight demonstrated by clients would increase as the psychoanalytic sessions progress.

Impressive findings on the value of insight in therapy using the Insight Rating Scale (in which experts evaluate clients' reports of the counselling session just finished) were reported by Kivlighan et al. (2000). They studied 12 clients who received 20 sessions in psychoanalytic counselling. There were steady decreases in symptoms across sessions and progressive increases in insight. Of key importance, clients showing an increase in insight had reduced symptoms over the following week. This suggests (as predicted by Freud) that insight plays a role in causing symptom reduction.

According to Freud, transference is very important in psychoanalysis because it provides a major way for the client to recover repressed memories and so achieve insight. Most of the evidence doesn't support Freud's views on transference. Høglend (2004) reviewed 10 studies on psychotherapy concerned with the relationship between transference and therapy outcome. Sessions were audiotaped for subsequent analysis to determine the amount of transference. It follows from Freud's views that therapy outcome should be *positively* correlated or associated with the amount of transference. In fact, the correlation was significantly *negative* in seven of the studies and only significantly positive in one.

The studies reviewed by Høglend (2004) were limited in that they were correlational and so couldn't indicate causality. Accordingly Høglend et al. (2006) carried out an experimental study. Clients, most of whom suffered from anxiety or depression, received psychotherapy over a 1-year period. They were assigned at random to two groups, in one of which there was much more focus on transference than in the other. The two groups didn't differ in terms of therapy outcome, suggesting that transference is not an important factor in producing recovery from mental disorder.

How effective is psychoanalysis? It is hard to answer that question, because psychoanalysis as originally practised has increasingly been replaced by various psychodynamic therapies based in part on Freud's ideas. In general terms, it appears that psychodynamic therapy is moderately effective. For example, Matt and Navarro (1997) considered the amazing number of 63 meta-analyses in

? How can you account for the appeal of psychoanalysis?

See *AS Level Psychology Online* for stimulus material relating to Matt and Navarro's (1997) classic study.

? Freud developed his theory in the early part of the twentieth century when attitudes to sex and sexuality were very different from today. What effect do you think this might have on the development of psychodynamic therapy?

which different types of therapy had been compared. On average, 75% of clients receiving treatment improved more than the average untreated control person. Behaviour therapy and cognitive therapy (discussed shortly) tended to be more effective than psychodynamic therapy. However, Matt and Navarro argued that those differences were more apparent than real. Clients treated by behaviour or cognitive therapy often had less serious symptoms than those treated by psychodynamic therapy. A counterargument is that there are remarkably few studies in which psychodynamic therapy has been shown to be significantly more effective than alternative forms of therapy (Fonagy et al., 2005).

Evaluation

Psychoanalysis has a very important place in the history of therapy. It was the first systematic form of psychological treatment for mental disorders, and it has strongly influenced several subsequent forms of therapy. In addition, it has proved moderately effective (Matt & Navarro, 1997). Some critics (e.g. H.J. Eysenck, 1985) are unimpressed by psychoanalysis and emphasise that it may be less effective than later forms of therapy. The obvious counterargument is that it is truly remarkable that a form of therapy originally put forward 100 years ago is almost as effective as forms of therapy put forward several decades later. Another possible strength of psychoanalysis is that some evidence suggests insight may play an important role in promoting recovery from mental illness.

There are various weaknesses with Freud's psychoanalysis:

- Most clients treated by psychoanalysis have reported repressed memories of childhood as predicted by Freud. However, there is a real danger that much of what the client says is influenced by suggestions implanted previously by the therapist and so may not reflect his/her genuine views.
- Some of the concepts of central importance to Freud's therapeutic approach are very vague. For example, it has proved hard to find valid ways of measuring concepts such as "insight" and "transference".
- Studies in which attempts have been made to manipulate or to measure transference have mostly failed to find any evidence that it facilitates recovery from mental illness.
- Psychoanalysis has too narrow a focus. Insufficient attention is paid to the individual's *current* problems and the difficulties he/she has at the social and interpersonal level.
- It is assumed that insight produces recovery. It seems about as likely that recovery leads to insight.

Systematic de-sensitisation

Systematic de-sensitisation (often written without a hyphen) is one of the main techniques within **behaviour therapy**. Accordingly, we will briefly consider some of the main assumptions of behaviour therapy before discussing systematic de-sensitisation in detail. Behaviour therapy was developed during the 1950s and 1960s, but its origins go back several decades before that. The underlying notions are that most mental disorders are caused by maladaptive learning, and that the best treatment consists of appropriate new learning.

Behaviour therapists believe that abnormal behaviour develops through conditioning (see Chapter 2). There are two main forms of conditioning: (1) classical conditioning involving learning by association; and (2) operant conditioning involving learning by reinforcement or reward. Behaviour therapists argue that classical and operant conditioning can change unwanted behaviour into a more desirable pattern of behaviour.

Consider how behaviour therapists might treat someone suffering from alcoholism. According to behaviour therapists, what we need to do is to replace the undesirable response of drinking alcohol when it is presented, with the response of avoiding it. This can be done by means of aversion therapy. For example, an alcoholic is given a drug (e.g. Antabuse) that causes him/her to vomit or have great difficulty in breathing if he/she starts to drink alcohol. This often causes the alcoholic to change his/her behaviour and cease drinking in the short term, but tends to be less effective in the long term (Roth et al., 2005).

Systematic de-sensitisation is a technique developed by Joseph Wolpe (1958, 1969) to treat individuals suffering from phobias involving excessive fear of certain stimuli (e.g. snakes; spiders). According to behaviour therapists, phobias develop through classical conditioning, with the phobic object being associated with some aversive or unpleasant event (discussed earlier in this chapter). The obvious prediction from this account is that phobic individuals would be much more likely than other people to have had a frightening experience with the phobic object. In fact, however, dog-phobic people were no more likely than anyone else to report frightening experiences with a dog (DiNardo et al., 1988). As discussed earlier, only 2% of water-phobic children claimed to have had a direct conditioning experience involving water (Menzies & Clarke, 1993).

What is involved in systematic de-sensitisation? The first stage is to provide clients with relaxation training in which they learn how to engage in deep muscle relaxation.

Second, clients construct a fear hierarchy with the assistance of their therapist. A **fear hierarchy** consists of a list of situations or objects that produce fear in the client, starting with those that cause only a small amount of fear and moving on to those that cause increasingly great levels of fear. For example, the first item on the list of a snake-phobic person might be a small, harmless snake 50 feet away, with subsequent items featuring larger and more dangerous snakes closer to the client.

Third, clients learn how to use their relaxation techniques while imagining the objects or situations they fear, starting with those at the bottom of the fear hierarchy. The therapist describes the object or situation, and the client then tries to form as clear an image of it as possible. What often happens is that the client engages in covert de-sensitisation during therapy sessions and places himself/

What is unwanted behaviour?

The term "unwanted behaviour" leads to questions about who decides which behaviour is disliked, unwanted, or abnormal. Usually the client himself or herself will decide that symptoms (e.g. phobic reactions) need treatment. Some behaviour is so anti-social that everyone agrees it is undesirable. However, it is possible for behaviour that those in authority decide is unacceptable to be labelled as "mental illness". Could the behaviour of rebellious young people, trade union activists, or lonely old people be construed as "undesirable" and in need of modification? Has this ever happened as far as you know?

Aversion therapy

- (UCS) Electric shock → (UCR) fear
- (NS) Pornographic pictures → pleasure

Conditioning: Pornographic pictures associated with electric shock

- (CS) Pornographic pictures → (CR) fear
- (UCS) Vomiting → (UCR) displeasure
- (NS) Alcohol → pleasure

Conditioning: Alcohol associated with vomiting

- (CS) Alcohol → (CR) displeasure

Fear of dogs

If an individual has a fear of dogs, systematic de-sensitisation could be used to overcome this. The client might have learned their fear in the following way:

- Child is bitten by dog. Unpleasant bite (UCS) → fear (UCR).
- Dog (NS) paired with UCS, becomes CS → fear (now CR).

This can be overcome by associating the dog with a new response—relaxation.

- Dog (CS) → fear (CR).
- Dog paired with new UCS (relaxation) → pleasant feelings (CR).

KEY TERM

Fear hierarchy: a list of feared situations or objects, starting with those creating only small amounts of fear and moving on to those creating large amounts of fear; used in the treatment of **phobias**.

You know, a large spider five metres away doesn't seem scary at all any more.

? What are the two main explanations for how systematic desensitisation works in treating phobias?

herself in progressively more frightening real-life situations between sessions. An alternative approach that is sometimes used is to present the actual object or situation itself (known as in vivo de-sensitisation).

When the client can imagine the less feared items in the fear hierarchy without experiencing fear, he/she moves on to the next items. Eventually, the client can confront the most feared object or situation in the fear hierarchy without fear, at which point he/she is regarded as cured.

Systematic de-sensitisation is a technique that puts demands on the expertise of the therapist. For example, it is essential to the success of systematic de-sensitisation that the therapist identifies the reasons for the client's anxiety. Consider someone who is very fearful of social situations. This fear may be totally irrational or it may occur because the individual concerned lacks social skills. If the latter is the case, then training in social skills is required in addition to systematic de-sensitisation.

As we will see shortly, systematic de-sensitisation has proved to be a moderately effective form of treatment for phobia. How does it work? Several answers have been proposed to that question. Wolpe (1958), the inventor of the technique, argued that individuals learn through a process of conditioning to associate certain specific stimuli (e.g. snakes) with anxiety. What is needed is for the individuals to learn to produce a response incompatible with anxiety (e.g. deep muscle relaxation) in the presence of the anxiety-evoking stimulus. Wolpe used the term **reciprocal inhibition** to refer to this process of inhibiting anxiety by substituting some competing response. If relaxation is going to be successful in inhibiting the client's anxiety, it is necessary that the amount of anxiety triggered by imagining the phobic stimulus is not too great. That explains why systematic de-sensitisation starts with stimuli that create only a small amount of anxiety.

Another possible explanation of the effectiveness of systematic de-sensitisation was proposed by Wilson and Davison (1971). According to them, the crucial process is one of **extinction**, which occurs when a response that is repeatedly produced in a given situation in the absence of reinforcement loses its strength. More specifically, imagining the phobic stimulus produces the anxiety response but there are no adverse consequences (e.g. being bitten by a snake). This lack of consequences eventually leads to a reduction in the strength of the anxiety response. According to this explanation, *all* that matters is repeated non-reinforced exposure to the phobic stimulus. There is a crucial difference in prediction between the reciprocal inhibition and extinction accounts—according to the former, deep muscle relaxation is essential, whereas it is almost irrelevant according to the latter.

Evidence

Choy, Fyer, and Lipsitz (2007) reviewed the literature on the effectiveness of systematic de-sensitisation in the treatment of phobias. Choy et al. reported that systematic de-sensitisation was generally moderately effective in reducing anxiety levels. However, its effects on avoidance of the feared object or situation were less consistent. For example, Rosen, Glasgow, and Barrera (1976) found in

KEY TERMS

Reciprocal inhibition: the process of inhibiting anxiety by substituting a competing response.

Extinction: elimination of a conditioned response when the conditioned stimulus is not followed by the unconditioned stimulus or a response is not followed by a reward.

a study on animal phobia that clients treated with systematic de-sensitisation were as likely as controls to continue to avoid the feared animals.

Four studies have assessed the long-term effects of systematic de-sensitisation by carrying out a follow-up at least 6 months after the end of treatment. According to Choy et al. (2007), the treatment gains (decreased anxiety and avoidance) present at the end of treatment were maintained at the time of follow-up. For example, Denholtz, Hall, and Mann (1978) found that 60% of clients who were treated for flying phobia continued to fly during the 3½-year follow-up period.

Does systematic de-sensitisation work because of reciprocal inhibition (with muscle relaxation inhibiting the anxiety response) or because of extinction (non-reinforced exposure to the feared stimulus)? The most direct approach to answering this question is to compare systematic de-sensitisation with and without relaxation. Levin and Gross (1985) reviewed the relevant literature. The picture was a confused one. In 10 studies, systematic de-sensitisation without relaxation was as effective as de-sensitisation with relaxation. However, there were a further 15 studies in which relaxation did contribute to the success of systematic de-sensitisation!

In exposure therapy, individuals are exposed to the source of their anxiety for a prolonged period until their fear subsides.

McGlynn et al. (1981) shed some light on the apparently inconsistent findings. They pointed out that extinction is a process that occurs only slowly over time. Thus, there would be very little extinction of anxiety if clients spent only a short period of time imagining each item in the fear hierarchy and if there were only a few treatment sessions. In such circumstances, any beneficial effects of systematic de-sensitisation would depend on relaxation and reciprocal inhibition. As they predicted, relaxation was generally important in treatment when there was little opportunity for extinction to occur.

We can pursue this issue further by considering exposure therapy. In **exposure therapy**, phobic individuals are exposed to the object or situation they fear for lengthy periods of time until their anxiety level is substantially reduced. In recent years, this form of therapy has been developed into virtual reality exposure therapy. What happens with virtual reality exposure is that a computer program produces a virtual environment that simulates the phobic situation. Exposure therapy provides maximal scope for extinction to occur but doesn't involve muscle relaxation. If extinction is the crucial process in curing phobias, exposure therapy should be very effective. However, if muscle relaxation is essential, then exposure therapy shouldn't be effective. In fact, exposure therapy has consistently been found to be effective, with traditional exposure therapy and virtual reality exposure therapy producing similar success rates. Both forms of exposure therapy are often more effective than systematic de-sensitisation (Choy et al., 2007). However, there is one problem with exposure therapy—prolonged exposure to feared stimuli can create intense levels of anxiety, and so the dropout rate with this form of therapy is sometimes rather high.

KEY TERM

Exposure therapy: a form of therapy in which patients are exposed to the object or situation they fear for lengthy periods of time until their anxiety level is substantially reduced.

Evaluation

Systematic de-sensitisation is a form of therapy that possesses various strengths:

- It was one of the first techniques within behaviour therapy to be developed. The success of systematic de-sensitisation played some role in the subsequent development of related techniques such as exposure therapy and virtual reality exposure therapy.

- It is based on solid theoretical grounds, namely the notion that through conditioning individuals could learn to replace the anxiety response to feared stimuli with a relaxation response.

- The basic ingredients of systematic de-sensitisation (muscle relaxation; fear hierarchy; association of phobic stimuli with relaxation responses) can easily be manipulated to see whether each one is important in successful treatment.

- Systematic de-sensitisation is of proven effectiveness. In the great majority of studies, individuals treated with systematic de-sensitisation improved more than those receiving no treatment (Choy et al., 2007).

There are various limitations with systematic de-sensitisation:

- It is a form of therapy that is specifically designed to reduce anxiety, and so it is only of relevance to the anxiety disorders. Even within the anxiety disorders, it can only be used when the stimuli producing a client's anxious state can be identified. For example, it wouldn't be appropriate to use systematic de-sensitisation with someone suffering from generalised anxiety disorder, because that condition involves excessive worrying about numerous, ill-defined situations.

- Many of the phobias (e.g. snake phobia; spider phobia) that have been treated by systematic de-sensitisation are relatively trivial, in the sense that they don't have the crippling effects on everyday life of other mental disorders such as depression or schizophrenia. However, systematic de-sensitisation has been used successfully in the treatment of social phobia (excessive fear of social situations), and social phobia can severely disrupt people's lives.

- Most of the evidence (e.g. Choy et al., 2007) indicates that exposure therapy tends to be more effective than systematic de-sensitisation in the treatment of phobias. This helps to explain why there has been a pronounced reduction in the use of systematic de-sensitisation over the years (McGlynn, Smitherman, & Gothard, 2004).

- There has been a lack of clarity about the precise reasons why systematic de-sensitisation is effective. However, there are good grounds for arguing that Wolpe exaggerated the importance of muscle relaxation. Muscle relaxation often adds nothing to the effectiveness of systematic de-sensitisation, and exposure therapy is effective without making any use of muscle relaxation.

Cognitive Behavioural Therapy

What is Cognitive Behavioural Therapy? As the name implies, Cognitive Behavioural Therapy involves elements of cognitive therapy and behaviour therapy. The basic notion is that the client needs to change his/her inappropriate behaviour *and* his/her dysfunctional thoughts. It is claimed that changing behaviour and thoughts produces more effective therapy than focusing primarily on behaviour (behaviour therapy) or on beliefs (cognitive therapy).

What are the defining characteristics of Cognitive Behavioural Therapy? According to Kendall and Hammen (1998), *four* basic assumptions underlie Cognitive Behavioural Therapy:

1. Clients typically respond on the basis of their *interpretations* of themselves and the world around them rather than on the basis of what is *actually* the case. Of central importance here is the notion of **interpretive bias**—this is the tendency shown by most anxious and depressed patients to interpret ambiguous stimuli and situations in a negative or threatening way. Interpretive biases are especially common with respect to interpretations concerning the individual himself or herself.
2. Thoughts, behaviours, and feelings are all inter-related, and all influence each other. Thus, no single factor is more important than the others.
3. In order for therapeutic interventions to be successful, therapists must clarify and change how people think about themselves and about the world around them. A major part of this involves reducing or eliminating their interpretive biases about themselves and the world around them.
4. It is important to change both the client's cognitive processes and his/her behaviour. The reason is that the benefits of therapy are likely to be greater than when only cognitive processes or behaviour change.

Beck (1976) proposed a form of Cognitive Behavioural Therapy. He argued that therapy should involve more than simply changing dysfunctional thoughts and replacing them with more appropriate and positive ones. He emphasised the use of homework assignments requiring clients to behave in certain ways they found hard. For example, a client suffering from social anxiety might be told to initiate a conversation with everyone in his/her office over the following few days. A crucial ingredient in such homework assignments is hypothesis testing. Clients typically predict that carrying out their homework assignments will make them feel anxious or depressed, and so they are told to test their predictions. The clients' hypotheses are generally shown to be too pessimistic. Discovering that many of their fears are groundless speeds recovery.

■ **Activity:** Devise a situation like the following example and describe how the thoughts, emotions, and behaviour that result from it could be changed.

It is your birthday and you are given a surprise invitation to meet your friends at lunchtime to celebrate. You are disappointed to find that your best friend does not join you and gives no reason or apology.

	Irrational/negative	Rational/positive
Thoughts	He/she is annoyed with you but won't say why	Maybe he/she was under pressure with work, etc.
Emotions	Hurt and upset. Perhaps you aren't friends after all	Disappointed, but sure you'll get together soon to celebrate
Behaviour	Treat him/her with cool detachment next time you meet	Ring him/her to arrange to meet

KEY TERM

Interpretive bias: the tendency shown by most anxious and depressed patients to interpret ambiguous stimuli and situations in a negative or threatening way.

? In what ways might a person's thoughts about themselves influence the way they react in a particular situation?

Here is a concrete example of Cognitive Behavioural Therapy (Clark, 1996) involving a 40-year-old man with panic disorder (a disorder involving frequent panic attacks). The client tried to protect himself against having a heart attack during panic attacks by taking paracetamol and by taking deep breaths. The hypothesis that this was what prevented him from having a heart attack was tested by the therapist and the client alternately sprinting and jogging around a football pitch. In addition, the client was given the homework of taking strenuous daily exercise without trying to control his breathing. The client rapidly accepted that his problem centred on his own mistaken beliefs.

Earlier in the chapter we considered the issue of how anxious individuals maintain their mistaken beliefs and interpretations of the world over long periods of time. Part of the answer is safety-seeking behaviours which are used to reduce the level of anxiety. For example, patients with panic disorder often have the mistaken belief that they are in danger of having a heart attack and are dying when they have a panic attack. They may maintain this belief by adopting the safety-seeking behaviour of keeping very still when they experience a panic attack, imagining that this behaviour protects them against having a heart attack. It follows from this analysis that preventing patients from using safety-seeking behaviours should assist in eliminating their mistaken beliefs.

Findings

How effective is Cognitive Behavioural Therapy? The most thorough attempt to answer that question was made by Butler et al. (2006). They considered the findings from 16 meta-analyses concerned with the therapeutic value of Cognitive Behavioural Therapy based on a total of almost 10,000 patients. This form of therapy was notably successful in treating major depressive disorder, generalised anxiety disorder, panic disorder with or without agoraphobia, social phobia, and post-traumatic stress disorder.

In addition, Cognitive Behavioural Therapy was more effective than anti-depressants in the treatment of major depressive disorder especially in terms of the long-term persistence of its beneficial effects. Finally, it seems to be useful in the treatment of schizophrenia, and would be valuable if used in conjunction with atypical anti-psychotic drugs.

According to advocates of Cognitive Behavioural Therapy, it is important to identify and to eliminate the interpretive biases (unduly negative interpretations) possessed by clients. For example, individuals with social anxiety or social phobia typically interpret their own social behaviour as being less skilled and more inept than is actually the case. One effective way of reducing this interpretive bias involves the use of video feedback. For example, Harvey et al. (2000) asked socially anxious individuals to give a speech while being videoed. They were then asked to predict what they would see when the video was shown to them. Nearly all of them showed interpretive bias—they discovered when viewing the video that their social performance was much better than they had predicted. The reduction in this interpretive bias has been found to assist in treatment (see Eysenck, 1997, for a review).

It is assumed within Cognitive Behavioural Therapy that safety-seeking behaviours may help to maintain anxious patients' mistaken beliefs and so reduce the value of therapy. For example, exposure therapy (putting patients in feared situations) is assumed to be effective with social-phobic people because it allows them to disconfirm their unrealistically negative views about the dangers of social situations. Safety-seeking behaviours (e.g. avoiding eye contact; keeping quiet) may prevent effective disconfirmation of those negative views. Evidence supporting these assumptions was reported by Morgan and Raffle (1999). They instructed some social-phobic people receiving exposure therapy (e.g. giving talks in public) to avoid safety-seeking behaviours, whereas others weren't given those instructions. As predicted, those patients instructed to avoid safety-seeking behaviours showed more improvement from therapy.

In similar fashion, Salkovskis et al. (1999) put patients suffering from panic disorder with agoraphobia (fear of crowded places) in an exposure situation, during which they were told to use or avoid using safety-seeking behaviours (e.g. distracting themselves; holding on to people). Those patients who had avoided using safety-seeking behaviours showed a greater reduction in catastrophic beliefs and in anxiety.

Evaluation

Cognitive Behavioural Therapy has established itself over the past 20 years or so as one of the most important and most commonly used forms of treatment for several mental disorders. Here are some of the main strengths of Cognitive Behavioural Therapy:

? Why has cognitive behavioural therapy become such a popular therapeutic treatment for many mental disorders?

- Cognitive Behavioural Therapy combines features of cognitive therapy and of behaviour therapy. As such, it is broader and more effective than either of the forms of therapy from which it arose.
- Cognitive Behavioural Therapy is based on research carried out by behaviourists and by cognitive psychologists (see earlier in this chapter). As a result, it is based on a solid foundation.
- Cognitive Behavioural Therapy has shown itself to be clearly effective (and generally more effective than other forms of therapy) in the treatment of major depression, generalised anxiety disorder, panic disorder with agoraphobia, and post-traumatic stress disorder (Roth & Fonagy, 2005). That is a considerable achievement. Of importance, the beneficial effects of Cognitive Behavioural Therapy when used with panic disorder patients or people with schizophrenia are more long lasting than the effects of drug therapy (Butler et al., 2006).
- The effectiveness of exposure therapy (used in behaviour therapy) is increased when patients avoid safety-seeking behaviours as predicted by cognitive-behaviour therapists (e.g. Salkovskis et al., 1999).

Here are the main weaknesses or limitations of Cognitive Behavioural Therapy:

- There are many mental disorders for which it may have less to offer than other forms of therapy. For example, it is less effective in treating schizophrenia than are family intervention programmes involving the families of schizophrenic patients, or drug therapy. However, there are encouraging signs that Cognitive Behavioural Therapy is of some value in treating schizophrenia (Butler et al., 2006).

- Those who advocate Cognitive Behavioural Therapy may exaggerate the importance of cognitive processes. Many clients develop more rational and less distorted ways of thinking about important issues with no beneficial changes in their maladaptive behaviour. In addition, many of the beliefs of anxious and depressed patients simply reflect the reality of their difficult everyday lives, rather than being distortions of that reality!

- Cognitive Behavioural Therapy tends to de-emphasise factors that are regarded as important in other forms of therapy. For example, little attention is paid to physiological or biological processes, and the emphasis is on current problems rather than traumatic childhood experiences.

- Cognitive Behavioural Therapy often involves a complex mixture of cognitive and behavioural ingredients. As a result, it can be hard to determine precisely *which* ingredients are more and less responsible for the success of treatment.

You have reached the end of the chapter on individual differences. Individual differences is an approach or perspective in psychology. The material in this chapter has exemplified this approach in so far as abnormal behaviour is one of the ways that individuals vary. Individual differences can be explained in terms of biological (physiological), behaviourist (learning theory), psychoanalytic, and cognitive explanations. All of these explanations have also appeared elsewhere in this book and are important "tools" for explaining behaviour.

SECTION SUMMARY

Biological therapies

- ❖ Biological therapies involve manipulation of the body.
- ❖ Major depressive disorder is treated with various drugs, of which the serotonin re-uptake inhibitors are the ones most commonly used.
- ❖ Lithium is the drug most commonly used to treat bipolar disorder. It is effective but can produce tremors and digestive problems.
- ❖ Anxiety disorders are often treated with the benzodiazepines. These drugs are moderately effective but can produce poor concentration, sedative effects, and physical dependence.
- ❖ Buspirone is also used to treat anxiety disorders. It has fewer unwanted side effects than the benzodiazepines.
- ❖ Schizophrenia is treated by neuroleptic and atypical anti-psychotic drugs. The latter drugs have fewer side effects and are generally more effective.
- ❖ Problems with drug therapy include the following:
  - Fairly frequent relapse
  - Limited understanding of *why* drugs are effective
  - Drug dependence
  - High drop-out rates
  - Unwanted side effects

❖ ECT is mostly used to treat major depressive disorder but is also used to treat schizophrenia.

❖ ECT is generally effective and can produce rapid symptom reduction in depression. However, it is less effective in patients under the age of 65.

❖ ECT can produce memory loss and other cognitive impairments.

❖ A central goal in psychoanalysis is for the client to gain insight into the emotional significance of his/her traumatic and distressing childhood experiences.

❖ Insight can be produced by hypnosis, free association, dream analysis, and transference.

❖ Psychoanalysis has proved moderately effective and is of huge historical significance.

❖ Problems with psychoanalysis include the following:
- Many traumatic childhood memories may be distorted by the therapist's influence.
- Concepts such as "insight" and "transference" are very vague.
- Transference doesn't seem to promote recovery in the way that Freud claimed.
- Freud assumed that insight helped to cause recovery, but it may well be that recovery causes insight.
- This form of therapy is too narrow—it tends to focus on childhood experiences while ignoring the client's current social and interpersonal difficulties.

Psychoanalysis

❖ Systematic de-sensitisation is used in the treatment of phobias. It involves muscle relaxation, the construction of a fear hierarchy, and the replacement of an anxious response to phobic stimuli with relaxation.

❖ Systematic de-sensitisation was one of the first techniques developed within behaviour therapy. It is based on solid theoretical grounds and is moderately effective.

❖ Problems with systematic de-sensitisation include the following:
- It is only of much relevance to the anxiety disorders.
- Even within the anxiety disorders, it is hard to use with generalised anxiety disorder, because that disorder involves numerous general worries and concerns rather than fears of specific stimuli.
- Exposure therapy is generally more effective than systematic de-sensitisation. This suggests that muscle relaxation is not needed to treat phobias successfully.

Systematic de-sensitisation

❖ Cognitive Behavioural Therapy evolved out of behaviour therapy and cognitive therapy.

❖ It involves changing the client's cognitive processes and behaviour in order to eliminate his/her interpretive biases and mistaken beliefs.

❖ It is assumed that mistaken interpretations and beliefs are maintained by safety-seeking behaviours.

❖ Cognitive Behavioural Therapy is very effective in treating anxiety disorders and depression.

Cognitive Behavioural Therapy

❖ Problems with this form of therapy include:
– It is less effective than other therapies in treating schizophrenia.
– It exaggerates the importance of cognitive processes in changing people's behaviour.
– Cognitive Behavioural Therapy tends to ignore biological factors and the events of childhood.
– The complexity of therapy means that it is hard to know precisely which ingredients are most effective.

FURTHER READING

There are several excellent and thorough textbooks on abnormal psychology. The main issues within abnormal psychology are discussed in an accessible and reader-friendly way in P. Bennett (2003) *Abnormal and clinical psychology: An introductory textbook*. Another textbook providing good and up-to-date coverage of the topics discussed in this chapter is R.J. Cromer (2007) *Abnormal psychology (6th Edn.)* (New York: Worth). A third textbook that can be recommended because of its focus on the main issues in abnormal psychology is V.M. Durand and D.H. Barlow (2006) *Essentials of abnormal psychology (4th Edn.)* (New York: Thomson/Wadsworth). There is detailed coverage of major forms of therapy and an assessment of their effectiveness in A. Roth and P. Fonagy (2005) *What works for whom?: A critical review of psychotherapy research (2nd Edn.)* (New York: Guilford Press).

See Chapter 7 of the revision guide for guidance on revising this chapter for the exam.

WEBSITES

http://www.newscientist.com/channel/health/dn9578-emotion-centre-of-autistic-brains-have-fewer-cells.html
Brain structure and abnormality: Research showing that autism may be caused by an abnormality in the emotional brain.

http://www.bbc.co.uk/health/conditions/mental_health/disorders_index.shtml
Common psychological disorders: A menu for accessing information about more common disorders.

http://www.apa.org/monitor/may06/perfectionists.html
Individual differences and depression: Discusses how perfectionists are more susceptible to depression.

http://abcnews.go.com/Health/OnCallPlusLiving/story?id=3738082&page=1
Therapy for anxious children: A programme for children who are anxious about their mothers' chemotherapy.

REVISION QUESTIONS

The examination questions aim to sample the material in this whole chapter. For advice on how to answer such questions refer to Chapter 1, Section 2.

When you are provided with a stimulus question do not panic if you have not seen that specific question before. Stimulus questions require you to apply your knowledge to a specific scenario. Whilst you may not have seen such a scenario before, if you have revised everything you *will* have the knowledge needed to answer the question.

Question 1
a. Outline **two** definitions of abnormality.   (3 + 3 marks)
b. Explain **one** limitation of each of the definitions answered in (a.)   (2 + 2 marks)

Question 2
a. Explain **one** way in which psychologists have investigated the genetic basis of abnormality.   (4 marks)
b. Outline key features of the cognitive approach to psychopathology.   (6 marks)

Question 3
Discuss the usefulness of biological treatments of psychopathology.   (12 marks)

GLOSSARY

Abnormal or atypical psychology: the study of individuals who differ from the norm, such as those with mental disorders.

Abnormality: an undesirable state producing severe impairment in a person's social and personal functioning, often causing anguish. Abnormal behaviour deviates from statistical or social norms, causes distress to the individual or others, and is seen as a failure to function adequately.

Acoustic coding: encoding words in terms of their sound using information stored in long-term memory.

Adaptive: the extent to which a behaviour increases the reproductive potential of an individual and survival of its genes.

Adrenal glands: the endocrine glands that are located adjacent to, and covering, the upper part of the kidneys.

Adrenaline: one of the hormones (along with **noradrenaline**) produced by the adrenal glands, which increases arousal by activating the sympathetic nervous system and reducing activity in the parasympathetic system.

Adrenocorticotrophic hormone (ACTH): a hormone produced by the anterior pituitary gland, which stimulates the adrenal cortex.

Agentic state: a state of feeling controlled by an authority figure, and therefore lacking a sense of personal responsibility.

Aims: the purpose of a research study.

Alternative hypothesis: another term for the experimental hypothesis. The experimental hypothesis is the alternative to the null hypothesis.

Amae: a Japanese word referring to a positive form of attachment that involves emotional dependence, clinging, and attention-seeking behaviour. Such behaviour is regarded more negatively in Western countries.

Anaclitic depression: a severe form of depression in infants who experience prolonged separations from their mothers. The term "anaclitic" means "arising from emotional dependency on another".

Animal behaviour: the study of non-human animals in their own right.

ANS (autonomic nervous system): that part of the nervous system that controls vital body functions, which is self-regulating and needs no conscious control (automatic).

Antigens: foreign substances such as bacteria or viruses that can cause disease and that trigger an immune response.

Anxiety: a normal emotion similar to nervousness, worry, or apprehension, but if excessive it can interfere with everyday life and might then be judged an anxiety disorder.

Attachment: a strong, emotional bond between an infant and his or her caregiver(s) that is characterised by a desire to maintain proximity. Such bonds may be secure or insecure.

Authoritarian personality: identified by Adorno et al. as someone who is more likely to be obedient. These people tend to hold rigid beliefs, and to be hostile towards other groups and submissive to authority.

Autokinetic effect: a visual illusion where a small spot of light in a darkened room appears to be moving when in fact it is stationary.

Autonomic nervous system: see **ANS**.

Autonomous state: being aware of the consequences of our actions and therefore taking voluntary control of our behaviour.

Bar chart: like a histogram, a representation of frequency data, but the categories do not have to be continuous; used for nominal data.

Behaviour therapy: therapy based on the assumption that the best way to treat mental disorders is through techniques that allow the individual to learn new forms of behaviour more appropriate than their current behaviour. More specifically, **classical** and **operant conditioning** are used to replace unwanted patterns of behaviour.

Behavioural model of abnormality: a model of abnormality which considers that individuals who suffer from mental disorders possess maladaptive forms of behaviour, which have been learned.

Benzodiazepines: anti-anxiety drugs such as Valium and Librium. They work by reducing **serotonin** levels.

Beta blockers: drugs reducing stress by reducing activity in the sympathetic nervous system.

Bimodal: a distribution with two modes.

Biochemistry: the study of the chemical processes of living organisms.

Biological (medical) model: a model of abnormality that regards mental disorders as illnesses with a physical cause.

Biological therapies: forms of treatment that involve manipulations of the body, e.g. drugs or ECT.

Bipolar disorder: a mood disorder in which there are depressive and manic (elated) episodes.

Black box: the term used by behaviourists to refer to the mind. Their focus was on what goes in (a stimulus) and what comes out (a response).

Bond disruption: occurs when a child is deprived of their main attachment object, in the short or long term, and receives no substitute emotional care.

Bonding: the process of forming close ties with another.

Buffering effect: occurs when a personality characteristic (e.g. **hardiness**) helps to protect or buffer the individual from the adverse effects of stress.

Buffers: aspects of situations that protect people from having to confront the results of their actions.

Burnout: physical and/or emotional exhaustion produced especially by stress.

Buspirone: a more recent anti-anxiety drug, which increases the production of **serotonin** and has fewer side effects than **benzodiazepines**.

Cardiovascular disorders: disorders of the heart and circulatory system; for example atherosclerosis, where the arteries start to block up, and hypertension, or very high blood pressure.

Case study: detailed study of a single individual, event, or group.

Categorical clustering: the tendency for categorised word lists (even with the words presented in random order) to be recalled category by category.

Central executive: the key component of working memory. It is a modality-free system (i.e. not visual or auditory) of limited capacity and is similar to "paying attention" to something.

Central nervous system: see **CNS**.

Chunking: the process of combining individual items (e.g. letters; numbers) into larger, meaningful units.

Chunks: integrated units of information.

Classical conditioning: learning through association; a neutral stimulus becomes associated with a known stimulus–reflex response.

Client-centred therapy: a form of humanistic therapy introduced by Rogers and designed to increase the client's self-esteem and reduce incongruence between self and ideal self.

Clinician (or clinical psychologist): a person who works in clinical psychology, concerned with the diagnosis and treatment of abnormal behaviour.

CNS (central nervous system): part of the nervous system that consists of the brain and the spinal cord.

Cognitive Behavioural Therapy: a development of cognitive therapy in which attempts to change behaviour directly are added to thought and belief restructuring.

Cognitive interview: an interview technique that is based on our knowledge about the way human memory works; paying attention, for example, to the use of retrieval cues.

Cognitive model of abnormality: a model of abnormality which considers that individuals who suffer from mental disorders have distorted or irrational thinking.

Cognitive therapy: a form of treatment that involves attempts to change or restructure the client's thoughts and beliefs.

Collectivistic cultures: cultures where individuals share tasks, belongings, and income. The people may live in large family groups and value interdependence.

Comparative psychology: the study of non-human animals, in which comparisons are made between animals of different species to find out more about human behaviour.

Compliance: conforming to the majority view in order to be liked, or to avoid ridicule or social exclusion. Compliance occurs more readily with public behaviour than private behaviour, and is based on power.

Concordance rate: in twin studies, the probability that if one twin has a given disorder the other twin also has the same disorder.

Conditioning: simple forms of learning in which certain responses become more or less likely to occur in a given situation.

Confidentiality: the requirement for ethical research that information provided by participants in research is not made available to other people.

Conformity: changes in behaviour and/or attitudes occurring in response to group pressure.

Confounding variables: variables that are mistakenly manipulated or allowed to vary along with the **independent variable** and therefore affect the **dependent variable**.

Content analysis: A qualitative research method involving the analysis of behaviours or the written or spoken word into pre-set categories, a process known as coding, to produce an overview of the research area.

Control group: the group of participants who receive no treatment and act as a comparison to the experimental group to study any effects of the treatment.

Controlled observations: observations in which the researcher exercises control over some aspects of the environment in which the observations are made.

Conversion: the influence of the minority on the majority. This is likely to affect private beliefs more than public behaviour.

Coping: efforts to deal with demanding and stressful situations by using strategies designed to master the situation, reduce the demands, or tolerate the situation; many coping strategies can be classified as problem-focused or emotion-focused.

Correlation: an association that is found between two variables.

Correlation coefficient: a number that expresses the extent to which two variables are related or vary together.

Correlational analysis: testing a hypothesis using an association that is found between two variables.

Cortisol: a **hormone** produced by the adrenal gland that elevates blood sugar and is important in digestion, especially at times of stress.

Cost–benefit analysis: a comparison between the costs of something and the related benefits, in order to decide on a course of action.

Counterbalancing: used with repeated measures design to overcome the problems of practice and order effects, and involves ensuring that each condition is equally likely to be used first and second by participants.

Co-variables: the variables involved in a correlational study that may vary together (co-vary).

Critical period: a biologically determined period of time during which an animal is exclusively receptive to certain changes.

Cultural relativism: the view that to understand and judge a culture it must be viewed from within that culture, and not from the perspective of the observer's own culture if that is a different one.

Culture-bound syndromes: patterns of abnormal behaviour that are only found in one or a small number of cultures.

Daily hassles: the minor challenges and problems experienced in our everyday lives.

Day care: care that is provided by people other than the parent or relatives of the infant, for example, nurseries, childminders, play groups, etc. A temporary alternative to the caregiver, day care is distinct from institutionalised care, which provides permanent substitute care.

Debriefing: attempts by the experimenter at the end of a study to provide detailed information for the participants about the study and to reduce any distress they might have felt.

Deception: in research ethics, deception refers to deliberately misleading participants, which was accepted in the past. Currently the view is that deception should be avoided wherever possible, as it could lead to psychological harm or a negative view of psychological research.

Declarative knowledge: knowledge related to "knowing that", including episodic and semantic memory.

Defence mechanisms: strategies used by the ego to defend itself against anxiety.

Deindividuation: losing one's sense of personal identity.

Demand characteristics: features of an experiment that help participants to work out what is expected of them, and lead them to behave in certain predictable ways.

Dependent variable (DV): an aspect of the participant's behaviour that is measured in the study.

Deprivation: to lose something, such as the care of an attachment figure, for a long period of time.

Deviation from social norms: behaviour that does not follow accepted social patterns, or unwritten social rules. Such violation is considered abnormal. These norms vary from culture to culture and from era to era.

Diathesis–stress model: the notion that psychological disorders occur when there is a genetically determined vulnerability (diathesis) and relevant stressful conditions.

Direct effect: occurs when there is a significant relationship or correlation between personality and some other measure (e.g. stress; physical health).

Directional (one-tailed) hypothesis: a prediction that there will be a difference or correlation between two variables and a statement of the direction of this difference.

Discourse analysis: a qualitative method involving the analysis of meanings expressed in various forms of language (e.g. speeches; writings). The emphasis is often on effects of social context on language use.

Displacement: one of the defence mechanisms identified by Freud in which impulses are unconsciously moved away from a very threatening object towards a non-threatening one.

Dispositional explanation: deciding that other people's actions are caused by their internal characteristics or dispositions.

Double blind: a procedure where neither the participant nor the experimenter knows the precise aims of the study. This reduces experimenter effects.

Dysexecutive syndrome: a condition caused by brain damage (typically in the frontal lobes) in which there is severe impairment of the functioning of the central executive component of working memory.

Effort–reward imbalance: a stressful situation in which workers are required to make considerable efforts at work but receive few rewards in terms of salary, career opportunities, and so on in return.

Ego: the conscious, rational part of the mind, which is guided by the reality principle.

Electroconvulsive therapy (ECT): a form of therapy used to treat depressed patients, in which brain seizures are created by passing an electric current through the head.

Emotion-focused coping: involves the use of thoughts or actions to act directly on the emotional state experienced when faced by a stressful situation. It can involve distraction, avoidance of the situation, seeking social support, emotional control, distancing (detaching oneself from the situation), positive reappraisal of the situation, and relaxation. Generally of most use when the situation probably cannot be changed for the better.

Encoding: involves the transfer of information into code, leading to the creation of a memory trace, which can be registered in the memory store.

Endocrine system: a system of a number of ductless glands located throughout the body that produce the body's chemical messengers, called **hormones**.

Ethical committees: committees of psychologists and lay individuals who consider all research proposals from the perspective of the rights and dignity of the participants.

Ethical guidelines: written codes of conduct and practice to guide and aid psychologists in planning and running research studies to an approved standard, and dealing with any issues that may arise.

Ethics: a set of moral principles used to guide human behaviour.

Ethologists: individuals who study animal behaviour in its natural environment, focusing on the importance of innate capacities and the functions of behaviours.

Evaluation apprehension: concern felt by research participants that their performance is being judged.

Event sampling: a technique for collecting data in an observational study. The observer focuses only on actions or events that are of particular interest to the study.

Experiment: a procedure undertaken to make a discovery about causal relationships. The experimenter manipulates one variable to see its effect on another variable.

Experimental group: the group receiving the experimental treatment.

Experimental hypothesis: the hypothesis written prior to conducting an experiment, which usually specifies the independent and dependent variables.

Experimental realism: the use of an artificial situation in which participants become so involved that they are fooled into thinking the set-up is real rather than artificial.

Experimental treatment: the alteration of the independent variable.

Experimenter bias: the effect that the experimenter's expectations have on the participants and therefore the results of the study.

Experimenter expectancy: the systematic effects that an experimenter's expectations have on the performance of the participants.

Exposure therapy: a form of therapy in which patients are exposed to the object or situation they fear for lengthy periods of time until their anxiety level is substantially reduced.

External validity: the validity of an experiment outside the research situation itself; the extent to which the findings of a research study are applicable to other situations, especially "everyday" situations.

Externalising problems: various types of behaviour problems such as aggression, assertiveness, and disobedience.

Extinction: elimination of a conditioned response when the conditioned stimulus is not followed by the unconditioned stimulus or a response is not followed by a reward.

Eyewitness testimony: an account or evidence provided by people who witnessed an event such as a crime, reporting from their memory. Research suggests that this evidence may not be factually accurate.

F (Fascism) Scale: a test of tendencies towards fascism. High scorers are prejudiced and racist.

Failure to function adequately: a model of abnormality based on an inability to cope with day-to-day life caused by psychological distress or discomfort.

False memory syndrome: a condition where an adult "recovers" apparently repressed memories. In fact the memories are for events that did not happen, thus "false memory".

Fear hierarchy: a list of feared situations or objects, starting with those creating only small amounts of fear and moving on to those creating large amounts of fear; used in the treatment of **phobias**.

Field experiment: a study in which the experimental method is used in a more naturalistic situation.

Fixation: in Freudian terms, spending a long time at a given stage of development because of over- or under-gratification.

Free association: a technique used in psychoanalysis, in which the patient says the first thing that comes into his/her mind.

Fundamental attribution error: the tendency to explain the causes of another person's behaviour in terms of dispositional rather than situational factors.

Gene: a unit of inheritance that forms part of a chromosome. Some characteristics are determined by one gene whereas for others many genes are involved.

Gene mapping: determining the effect of a particular gene on physical or psychological characteristics.

General Adaptation Syndrome (GAS): the body's non-specific response to stress that consists of three stages: the alarm reaction, when the body responds with the heightened physiological reactivity of the "fight or flight" response to meet the demands of the stressor; resistance, when the body tries to cope with the stressor and outwardly appears to have returned to normal but inwardly is releasing high levels of stress hormones; and exhaustion, where resources are depleted and the body's defence against disease and illness is decreased.

Generalisability: the extent to which the findings of a study can be applied to other settings, populations, times, and measures.

Generalisation: in classical conditioning, the tendency to transfer a response from one stimulus to another that is quite similar.

Genetic: information from genes, the units of inheritance.

Glucose: a form of sugar that is one of the main sources of energy for the brain.

Hardiness: a cluster of traits possessed by those people best able to cope with stress.

Hindsight bias: the tendency to be wise after the event, using the benefit of hindsight.

Histogram: a graph in which the frequencies of scores in each category are represented by a vertical column; data on the y-axis must be continuous with a true zero.

Homeostasis: the process of maintaining a reasonably constant internal environment.

Hormones: chemical substances that are produced by one tissue before proceeding via the bloodstream to a second tissue.

Humanistic psychology: an approach to psychology that focuses on higher motivation, self-development, and on each individual as unique.

Hypertension: a condition associated with very high blood pressure.

Hypothalamus: the part of the brain that integrates the activity of the **autonomic nervous system**. Involved with emotion, stress, motivation, and hunger.

Hypothesis: a statement of what you believe to be true.

Id: in Freudian theory, that part of the mind motivated by the pleasure principle and sexual instincts.

Ideal mental health: a state of contentment that we all strive to achieve.

Identification: conforming to the demands of a given role because of a desire to be like a particular person in that role.

Immune system: a system of cells (white blood cells) within the body that is concerned with fighting disease. The white blood cells, called leucocytes, include T and B cells and natural killer cells. They help prevent illness by fighting invading **antigens** such as viruses and bacteria.

Imposed etic: the use of a technique developed in one culture to study another culture.

Imprinting: a restricted form of learning that takes place rapidly and has both short-term effects (e.g. a following response) and long-lasting effects (e.g. choice of reproductive partner).

Independent behaviour: resisting the pressures to conform or to obey authority.

Independent groups design: a research design in which each participant is in one condition only. Each separate group of participants experiences different levels of the IV. Sometimes referred to as an unrelated or between-subjects design.

Independent variable (IV): some aspect of the research situation that is manipulated by the researcher in order to observe whether a change occurs in another variable.

Individual differences: the characteristics that vary from one individual to another.

Individualistic cultures: cultures that emphasise individuality, individual needs, and independence. People in these cultures tend to live in small nuclear families.

Informational social influence: when someone conforms because others are thought to possess more knowledge.

Informed consent: relates to an ethical guideline which advises that participants should understand what they are agreeing to take part in. They should be aware of what the research involves, and their own part in this.

Innate: inborn, a product of genetic factors.

Insecure attachment: a weak emotional bond between child and caregiver(s) leading to an anxious and insecure relationship, which can have a negative effect on development.

Insight: in Freud's theory this involves recovering traumatic and other distressing memories from the unconscious and considering them in terms of their true emotional significance. Insight allows the client to recognise how these traumatic and other events have adversely affected their lives, which provides a basis for him/her to recover from mental illness.

Institutionalisation: the adverse effects on children of being placed in an institution; these effects can influence cognitive and social development.

Internal validity: the validity of an experiment in terms of the context in which it is carried out. Concerns events within the experiment as distinct from **external validity**.

Internal working model: a mental model of the world that enables individuals to predict, control, and manipulate their environment. The infant has many of them, some of which will be related to relationships.

Internalisation: conformity behaviour where the individual has completely accepted the views of the majority.

Interpretive bias: the tendency shown by most anxious and depressed patients to interpret ambiguous stimuli and situations in a negative or threatening way.

Interquartile range: the spread of the middle 50% of an ordered or ranked set of scores.

Interview: a verbal research method in which the participant answers a series of questions.

Interviewer bias: the effects of an interviewer's expectations on the responses made by an interviewee.

Introspection: the process by which a person considers their inner thoughts as a means of understanding how the mind works.

Investigator effects: the effects of an investigator's expectations on the response of a participant. Sometimes referred to as experimenter expectancy effect.

IV: see **independent variable**.

Laboratory experiment: an experiment conducted in a laboratory setting or other contrived setting away from the participants' normal environments. The experimenter is able to manipulate the IV and accurately measure the DV, and considerable control can be exercised over confounding variables.

Learning: a relatively permanent change in behaviour, which is not due to maturation.

Learning theory: the explanation of behaviour using the principles of classical and operant conditioning; the view that all behaviour is learned.

Life changes: significant changes in the pattern of life, such as a divorce or a holiday, that require some kind of social readjustment. Each life change has a score and total scores over a year can predict psychological upset.

Life events: events that are common to many people, which involve change from a steady state.

Locus of control: a personality dimension concerned with perceptions about the factors controlling what happens to us.

Longitudinal: over an extended period of time, especially with reference to studies.

Long-term memory: a relatively permanent memory store with an unlimited capacity and duration, containing different components such as episodic (personal events), semantic (facts and information), and procedural (actions and skills) memory.

Major depressive disorder: a disorder characterised by symptoms such as sad depressed mood, tiredness, and loss of interest in various activities.

Majority influence: occurs when people adopt the behaviour, attitudes, or values of the majority (dominant or largest group) after being exposed to their values or behaviour.

Maladaptive: the extent to which a behaviour is not adaptive.

Matched pairs design: a research design that matches participants on a one-to-one basis rather than as a whole group.

Maternal deprivation hypothesis: Bowlby's view that separation from the primary caregiver leads to disruption and perhaps breaking of the attachment bond, with long-term adverse and possibly permanent effects on emotional development.

Maternal sensitivity hypothesis: the notion that individual differences in infant attachment are due mainly to the sensitivity (or otherwise) of the mother.

Mean: an average worked out by dividing the total of participants' scores by the number of participants.

Measures of central tendency: any means of representing the mid-point of a set of data, such as the mean, median, and mode.

Measures of dispersion: any means of expressing the spread of the data, such as range or standard deviation.

Median: the middle score out of all the participants' scores.

Memory: the mental processes involved in encoding, storage, and retrieval of information. Encoding depends on which sense provides the input; storage is the information being held in memory; retrieval involves accessing the stored information.

Memory span: an assessment of how much can be stored in short-term memory (STM) at any time.

Mental rotation: a type of task in which participants imagine rotating two- or three-dimensional objects in order to perform some task.

Meta-analysis: a form of analysis in which the data from several related studies are combined to obtain an overall estimate.

Metabolism: all the chemical processes within the living organism.

Method of loci: a **mnemonic technique** in which various items of information are remembered by associating them with successive locations (e.g. along a favourite walk).

Mind map: a complex diagram in which several ideas are organised via links around some central idea or theme.

Minority influence: a majority being influenced to accept the beliefs or behaviour of a minority.

Misleading information: incorrect information that may be given in good faith or deliberately (also known as misinformation).

Mnemonic techniques: artificial systems or methods that are used to enhance people's memory. The techniques all involve providing a structure so that even random material can be organised effectively at the time of learning, and they provide a retrieval structure (typically through the use of cues) that makes it easy to recall learned material.

Mode: the most frequently occurring score among participants' scores in a given condition.

Modelling: a form of learning or therapy based on observing a model and imitating that behaviour.

Monotropy hypothesis: the notion that infants have an innate tendency to form strong bonds with one caregiver, usually their mother.

Multi-store model: a model in which memory is divided into three stores; sensory, short-term, and long-term memory. This model is no longer favoured, as research has shown that memory is much more complex than this.

Mundane realism: the use of an artificial situation that closely resembles a natural situation.

Mutation: a genetic change that can then be inherited by any offspring.

Natural experiment: a type of experiment where use is made of some naturally occurring variable(s).

Natural selection: the process by which individuals are selected because they are best adapted to their environment.

Naturalistic observation: an unobtrusive observational study conducted in a natural setting.

Negative correlation: as one co-variable increases the other decreases. They still vary in a constant relationship.

Neuroanatomy: the anatomy of the nervous system, i.e. the study of its structure and function.

Neuroticism: a personality dimension proposed by H. J. Eysenck; high scorers experience more intense negative emotional states than low scorers.

Noradrenaline: one of the hormones (along with **adrenaline**) produced by the adrenal glands that increases arousal by activating the sympathetic nervous system and reducing activity in the parasympathetic system.

Normal distribution: a bell-shaped distribution in which most of the scores are close to the mean. This characteristic shape is produced when measuring many psychological and biological variables, such as IQ and height.

Normative social influence: when someone conforms in order to gain liking or respect from others.

Null hypothesis: a hypothesis which states that any findings are due to chance factors and do not reflect a true difference, effect, or relationship.

Obedience to authority: behaving as instructed, usually in response to individual rather than group pressure, often in a hierarchy where the instructor is of higher status so the individual feels unable to resist or refuse to obey, though their private opinion is unlikely to change.

Observational learning: learning through imitating or copying the behaviour of others.

Observational techniques: those research techniques that involve observing behaviour, covertly or openly or as a participant in the activity.

Oedipus complex: Freud's explanation of how a boy resolves his love for his mother and feelings of rivalry towards his father by identifying with his father.

Operant conditioning: learning through reinforcement; a behaviour becomes more likely because the outcome is reinforced. Learning that is contingent on the response.

Operationalisation: defining all variables in such a way that it is easy to measure them.

Opportunity sampling: participants are selected because they are available, not because they are representative of a population.

Parasympathetic branch: the part of the **autonomic nervous system** that monitors the relaxed state, conserving resources and promoting digestion and metabolism.

Participant observations: observations in natural situations where the observer interacts directly with the participants.

Participant reactivity: the situation in which an **independent variable** has an effect on participants merely because they know they are being observed.

Pegword method: a **mnemonic technique** in which each word on a to-be-learned list is associated with those from a previously memorised list; an interactive image is formed of each pair of words.

Peripheral nervous system: see **PNS**.

Phonological loop: a component of the working memory system concerned with speech perception and production.

Physiological: concerning the study of living organisms and their parts.

Physiological approaches to stress management: techniques that try to control the body's response to stress by reducing physiological reactivity; for example taking anti-anxiety drugs to decrease the "fight or flight" responses such as raised blood pressure.

Pilot study: a smaller, preliminary study that makes it possible to check out standardised procedures and general design before investing time and money in the major study.

Pituitary–adrenal system: the second part of the stress response, where the **hypothalamus** activates the pituitary gland which in turn activates the adrenal cortex to release corticosteroid stress hormones.

Pituitary gland: an endocrine gland located in the brain. Called the "master gland" because it directs much of the activity of the endocrine system.

Placebo effect: positive responses to a drug or form of therapy based on the patient's beliefs that the drug or therapy will be effective, rather than on the actual make-up of the drug or therapy.

Planning fallacy: the false belief that a plan will succeed even though past experience suggests it won't.

Pleasure principle: the drive to do things that produce pleasure or gratification.

PNS (peripheral nervous system): part of the nervous system that excludes the brain and spinal cord, but consists of all other nerve cells in the body. The PNS is divided into the somatic nervous system and the autonomic nervous system.

Point sampling: a technique used in an observational study. One individual is observed in order to categorise their current behaviour, after which a second individual is observed.

Population: the total number of cases about which a specific statement can be made. This in itself may be unrepresentative.

Positive correlation: when two co-variables increase at the same time.

Positive reinforcement: a reward (e.g. food; money) that serves to increase the probability of any response produced shortly before it is presented.

Practice effect: an improvement in performance as a result of having done the task before.

Presumptive consent: a substitute for voluntary informed consent, it is presumed that if one set of people regard an experimental procedure as acceptable this applies to all people, including the experimental participants whose consent has not been obtained.

Primary reinforcer: something that provides positive reinforcement because it serves to satisfy some basic drive; for example, food and drink are primary reinforcers because they satisfy our hunger and thirst drives, respectively.

Prior general consent: obtaining apparent consent from research participants by arranging for them to agree in general to taking part in certain kinds of research before enlisting their involvement in an experiment.

Privation: an absence of attachments, as opposed to the loss of attachments, due to the lack of an appropriate attachment figure. Privation is likely to lead to permanent emotional damage.

Problem-focused coping: involves the use of thoughts or actions to act directly on a stressful situation. It can involve seeking information, purposeful or direct action, decision making, planning, and so on. Generally of most use when the situation can potentially be changed for the better.

Procedural knowledge: knowledge related to "knowing how", including motor skills.

Projection: attributing one's undesirable characteristics to others, as a means of coping with emotionally threatening information and protecting the ego.

Prospective study: a study designed to follow participants forward in time to observe certain events or outcomes

(e.g. coronary heart disease) that may happen to them over time.

Protection of participants from psychological harm: an ethical guideline saying that participants should be protected from psychological harm, such as distress, ridicule, or loss of self-esteem. Any risks involved in the research should be no greater than those in the participants' own lives. Debriefing can be used to counter any concern over psychological harm.

Psychiatrist: a medically trained person who specialises in the diagnosis and treatment of mental disorders.

Psychoanalysis: the form of therapy derived from psychoanalytic theory.

Psychodynamic model: a model of abnormality that regards the origin of mental disorders as psychological rather than physical, and suggests that mental illness arises out of unresolved unconscious conflicts.

Psychodynamic theory: this is an approach to understanding human behaviour and development pioneered by Freud and then developed by others; it forms part of the basis for psychoanalysis and other forms of psychodynamic therapy.

Psychological approaches to stress management: techniques to control cognitive, social, and emotional responses to stress by attempting to address underlying causes of stress, such as faulty thinking, and inappropriate emotional responses, by changing the person's perceptions of the stressor or their own control.

Psychological therapies: forms of treatment that involve the use of various psychological techniques, e.g. psychoanalysis.

Psychoneuroimmunology (PNI): the study of the effects of both stress and other psychological factors on the immune system.

Psychosexual development: Freud's stages in personality development based on the child's changing focus on different parts of the body (e.g. the mouth and the anal region). "Sexual" is roughly equivalent to "physical pleasure".

Pygmalion effect: an effect in which individuals perform surprisingly well because others expect them to; it is a kind of self-fulfilling effect in which others' expectations turn into reality.

Qualitative data: data in the form of categories (e.g. has fun watching movies; has fun watching TV).

Quantitative data: data in the form of scores or numbers (e.g. on a scale running from 1 to 7).

Quasi-experiment: research that is similar to an experiment but certain key features are lacking, such as the direct manipulation of the independent variable by the experimenter and random allocation of participants to conditions.

Questionnaire: a survey requiring written answers.

Random allocation: placing participants in different experimental conditions using random methods to ensure no differences between the groups.

Random sampling: selecting participants on some random basis (e.g. picking numbers out of a hat). Every member of the population has an equal chance of being selected.

Randomisation: the allocation of participants to conditions on a random basis, i.e. totally unbiased distribution.

Range: the difference between the highest and lowest score in any condition.

Raw scores: the data before they have been summarised in some way.

Reading span: the largest number of sentences read for comprehension from which an individual can recall all the final words more than 50% of the time; it is used as a measure of working memory capacity.

Reality principle: the drive to accommodate to the demands of the environment.

Recency effect: better free recall of the last few items in a list, where higher performance is due to the information being in short-term store.

Reciprocal inhibition: the process of inhibiting anxiety by substituting a competing response.

Reductionist: an argument or theory that reduces complex factors to a set of simple principles.

Regression: in Freudian terms, returning to an earlier stage of development as a means of coping with anxiety.

Rehearsal: the verbal repetition of information (often words), which typically has the effect of increasing our long-term memory for the rehearsed information.

Reinforced: a behaviour is more likely to re-occur because the response was agreeable.

Reliability: the extent to which a method of measurement or test produces consistent findings.

Replication: the ability to repeat the methods used in a study and achieve the same findings.

Representative sample: the notion that the sample is representative of the whole population from which it is drawn.

Repression: a main ego defence mechanism suggested by Freud, where anxiety-causing memories are kept out of conscious memory to protect the individual. This is a type of motivated forgetting, and the repressed memories can sometimes be recalled during **psychoanalysis**.

Research: the process of gaining knowledge and understanding via either theory or empirical data collection.

Research hypothesis: a statement put forward at the beginning of a study stating what you expect to happen, generated by a theory.

Retrieval: the process of recovering information stored in long-term memory. If retrieval is successful, the individual remembers the information in question.

Right to privacy: the requirement for ethical research that no participants are observed in situations that would be considered private.

Right to withdraw: the basic right of participants in a research study to stop their involvement at any point, and to withdraw their results if they wish to do so.

Role-playing experiments: studies in which participants are asked to imagine how they would behave in certain situations.

Safety-seeking behaviours: actions taken by individuals with anxiety disorders to reduce their anxiety level and prevent feared consequences.

Sample: a part of a population selected such that it is considered to be representative of the population as a whole.

Sampling bias: some people have a greater or lesser chance of being selected than they should be, given their frequency in the population.

Scattergram/scattergraph: two-dimensional representation of all the participants' scores in a correlational study.

Schema: an "organised" packet of information about the world, events, or people that is stored in long-term memory. For example, most people have a schema containing information about the normal sequence of events when having a meal in a restaurant.

Schizophrenia: a very severe disorder characterised by hallucinations, delusions, lack of emotion, and very impaired social functioning.

Science: a branch of knowledge conducted on objective principles. It is both an activity and an organised body of knowledge.

Secondary reinforcer: a reinforcer that has no natural properties of reinforcement but, through association with a primary reinforcer, becomes a reinforcer, i.e. it is learned.

Secure attachment: the result of a strong positive bond between infant and caregiver, so that although the child shows distress at separation, he or she is easily comforted by the caregiver's return.

Selection bias: when different types of individuals are assigned to groups that are to be compared, differences in behaviour between the two groups may be due to this bias rather than to differences in the ways in which the groups are treated.

Self-actualisation: fulfilling one's potential in the broadest sense.

Self-esteem: the feelings that an individual has about himself or herself.

Self-report techniques: participants provide their own account of themselves, usually by means of questionnaires, surveys, or interviews.

Semantic coding: encoding or processing words in terms of their meaning based on information stored in long-term memory.

Sensitive: in the context of statistics, "sensitive" means more precise, able to reflect small differences or changes.

Separation: the absence of the caregiver (e.g. due to work commitments, divorce, or hospitalisation), which usually causes great distress but not necessarily permanent bond disruption. Separation has a number of effects, such as protest, despair, or detachment, and if prolonged it may result in **deprivation**.

Separation anxiety: the sense of concern felt by a child when separated from their attachment figure.

Separation protest: the infant's behaviour when separated—crying or holding out their arms. Some insecurely attached infants show no protest when left by their attachment figure, whereas securely attached children do.

Serotonin: a neurotransmitter that is associated with lower arousal, sleepiness, and reduced anxiety.

Short-term memory: a temporary place for storing information during which it receives limited processing (e.g. verbal rehearsal). Short-term memory has a very limited capacity and short duration, unless the information in it is maintained through rehearsal.

Single blind: a procedure in which the participants are not informed of the condition in which they have been placed.

Situational explanation: deciding that people's actions are caused by the situation in which they find themselves rather than by their personality.

Sociability: the tendency to seek and enjoy the company of others.

Social change: the process of changing social norms such as attitudes and beliefs.

Social development: the development of a child's social skills, such as the ability to relate to and empathise with others, which is the result of interaction between the child's genes and their environment.

Social influence: how we are influenced by others, either by a group (**majority influence**) or an individual (**minority influence** or **obedience**), to change our behaviour, thinking, and/or attitudes.

Social learning theory: the view that behaviour can be explained in terms of direct and indirect reinforcement, through imitation, identification, and modelling.

Social releasers: a social behaviour or characteristic that elicits a caregiving reaction. Bowlby suggested that these were innate and critical in the process of forming attachments.

Specific phobia: extreme fear and avoidance of specific kinds of stimuli (e.g. snakes, spiders).

Split-half technique: a technique used to establish reliability by assigning items from one test randomly to two sub-tests (split-halves). The same person does both sub-tests simultaneously and their scores are compared to see if they are similar, which would suggest that the test items are reliable.

SQ3R: five strategies for effective reading: Survey, Question, Read, Recite, Review.

S–R link: an abbreviation for stimulus–response link.

Standard deviation: a measure of the spread of the scores around the mean. It is the square root of the variance and takes account of every measurement.

Standardised tests: tests on which an individual's score can be evaluated against those of a large representative sample.

Statistical infrequency/deviation from statistical norms: behaviours that are statistically rare, or deviate from the average/statistical norm as illustrated by the normal distribution curve, are classed as abnormal.

Storage: storing a memory for a period of time so that it can be used later.

Story method: a **mnemonic technique** in which a list of words is learned by linking them together within the context of a story.

Strange Situation: an experimental procedure used to test the security of a child's attachment to a caregiver. The key features are what the child does when it is left by the caregiver, and the child's behaviour at reunion, as well as responses to a stranger.

Stranger anxiety: the distress experienced by a child when approached by a stranger.

Stress: a state of psychological and physical tension produced, according to the transactional model, when there is a mismatch between the perceived demands of a situation (the stressor[s]) and the individual's perceived ability to cope. The consequent state of tension can be adaptive (eustress) or maladaptive (distress).

Stress inoculation training: a technique to reduce stress through the use of stress-management techniques and self-statements that aim to restructure the way the client thinks.

Stress management: the attempt to cope with stress by reducing the stress response, either by psychological methods (e.g. **Cognitive Behavioural Therapy**) or physiological ones (e.g. drugs).

Stressor: any factor that can trigger the stress response. Stressors are examples of individual differences, as different people respond differently to different stressors, such as exam revision. Stressors may be major life changes or daily hassles, and may be environmental or in the workplace.

Stroop task: a task that involves naming the colours in which words are printed. Performance is slowed when the words are conflicting colour words (e.g. the word RED printed in green).

Subjective organisation: the tendency for people who are asked to learn a list of random words to impose their own organisational structure on the list.

Superego: in Freud's theory, the part of the mind that embodies one's conscience. It is formed through identification with the same-sex parent.

Sympathetic branch: the part of the autonomic nervous system that activates internal organs.

Sympatho-medullary pathway: the source of the immediate stress response, also known as fight or flight, where the hypothalamus activates the ANS, which in turn activates the adrenal medulla, producing the release of the stress hormones **adrenaline** and **noradrenaline**.

Systematic de-sensitisation: a form of behaviour therapy designed to treat **phobias**, in which relaxation training and a fear hierarchy are used.

Systematic sampling: a modified version of random sampling in which the participants are selected in a quasi-random way (e.g. every 100th name from a population list).

Tardive dyskinesia: some of the long-term effects of taking neuroleptic drugs, including involuntary sucking and chewing, jerky movements, and writhing movements of the mouth or face.

Temperament hypothesis: the view that a child's temperament is responsible for the quality of attachment between the child and its caregiver, as opposed to the view that experience is more important.

Test–retest: a technique used to establish reliability, by giving the same test to participants on two separate occasions to see if their scores remain relatively similar.

Theory: a general explanation of a set of findings. It is used to produce an experimental hypothesis.

Theory of evolution: an explanation for the diversity of living species. Darwin's theory was based on the principle of natural selection.

Time sampling: a technique used in observational studies. Observations are only made during specified time periods (e.g. the first 10 minutes of each hour).

Trait: a characteristic distinguishing a particular individual.

Transactional model: an explanation for behaviour, which focuses on the interaction between various factors. The transactional model of stress explains stress in terms of the interaction between the demands of the environment and the individual's ability to cope.

Transference: the transfer of the patient's strong feelings concerning one or both parents onto the therapist.

True experiment: research where an independent variable is manipulated to observe its effects on a dependent variable and so determine a cause-and-effect relationship.

Type A personality: in biopsychology, a personality type who is typically impatient, competitive, time pressured, and hostile.

Undisclosed observation: an observational study where the participants have not been informed that it is taking place.

Validity: the soundness of the measurement tool; the extent to which it is measuring something that is real or valid.

Variables: things that vary or change.

Variance: the extent of variation of the scores around the mean.

Vicarious conditioning: receiving reinforcement by observing someone else being rewarded.

Visuo-spatial sketchpad: a component within the working memory system designed for spatial and/or visual coding.

Volunteer bias: the systematic difference between volunteers and non-volunteers.

Volunteer sampling: choosing research participants who have volunteered, e.g. by replying to an advertisement. Volunteer samples may not be representative of the general population, which means the research may not be generalisable.

Weapon focus: the finding that eyewitnesses pay so much attention to a weapon that they ignore other details and so can't remember them.

Working memory model: the model of short-term memory proposed to replace the multi-store model. It consists of a central executive plus slave systems that deal with different sensory modalities.

Working memory system: the concept that short-term (or working) memory can be subdivided into other stores that handle different modalities (sound and visual data).

REFERENCES

Abrahamsson, K.H., Berggren, U., Hallberg, L.R-M., & Carlsson, S.G. (2002). Ambivalence in coping with dental fear and avoidance: A qualitative study. *Journal of Health Psychology, 7*, 653–664.

Abrams, D., Wetherell, M., Cochrane, S., Hogg, M.A., & Turner, J.C. (1990). Knowing what to think by knowing who you are: Self-categorisation and the nature of norm formation, conformity and group polarisation. *British Journal of Social Psychology, 29*, 97–119.

Adorno, T.W., Frenkel-Brunswik, E., Levinson, D., & Sanford, R. (1950). *The authoritarian personality.* New York: Harper.

Ainsworth, M.D.S., & Bell, S.M. (1970). Attachment, exploration and separation: Illustrated by the behaviour of one-year-olds in a strange situation. *Child Development, 41*, 49–67.

Ainsworth, M.D.S., Blehar, M.C., Waters, E., & Wall, S. (1978). *Patterns of attachment: A psychological study of the strange situation.* Hillsdale, NJ: Lawrence Erlbaum Associates Inc.

Allen, V.L., & Levine, J.M. (1971). Social support and conformity: The role of independent assessment of reality. *Journal of Experimental Social Psychology, 7*, 48–58.

Allport E.W., & Postman, L. (1947). *The psychology of rumour.* New York: Holt, Rinehart, & Winston.

Almeida, D.M. (2005). Resilience and vulnerability to daily stressors assessed via diary methods. *Current Directions in Psychological Science, 14*, 64–68.

Altemeyer, B. (1981). *Right-wing authoritarianism.* Winnipeg: University of Manitoba Press.

Amelang, M., & Schmidt-Rathjens, C. (2003). Personality, cancer and coronary heart disease: Fictions and facts in the aetiological research. *Psychologische Rundschau, 54*, 12–23.

Ancona, L., & Pareyson, R. (1968). Contribution to the study of aggression: The dynamics of destructive obedience. *Archivio di Psicologia, Neurologia, e Psichiatria, 29*, 340–372.

Anderson, J. (1972). Attachment out of doors. In N. Blurton-Jones (Ed.), *Ethological studies of child behaviour.* Cambridge, UK: Cambridge University Press.

Antoni, M.H., Cruess, D.G., Cruess, S., Lutgendorf, S., Kumar, M., et al. (2000). Cognitive-behavioural stress management interaction effects on anxiety, 24-hr urinary norepinephrine output, and T-cytotoxic/suppressors cells over time among symptomatic HIV infected gay men. *Journal of Consulting and Clinical Psychology, 68*, 31–45.

Arendt, H. (1963). *Eichmann in Jerusalem: A report on the banality of evil.* New York: Viking Press.

Arndt, J., Schimel, J., Greenberg, J., & Pyszczynski, T. (2002). The intrinsic self and defensiveness: Evidence that activating the intrinsic self reduces self-handicapping and conformity. *Personality and Social Psychology Bulletin, 28*, 671–683.

Aronson, E. (1988). *The social animal* (5th ed.). New York: Freeman.

Asch, S.E. (1951). Effects of group pressure on the modification and distortion of judgements. In H. Guetzkow (Ed.), *Groups, leadership and men.* Pittsburgh, PA: Carnegie.

Asch, S.E. (1956). Studies of independence and conformity: A minority of one against a unanimous majority. *Psychological Monographs, 70*(Whole no. 416).

Ashton, H. (1997). Benzodiazepine dependency. In A. Baum, S. Newman, J. Weinman, R. West, & C. McManus (Eds.), *Cambridge handbook of psychology, health and medicine.* Cambridge, UK: Cambridge University Press.

Atkinson, R.C., & Shiffrin, R.M. (1968). Human memory: A proposed system and its control processes. In K.W. Spence & J.T. Spence (Eds.), *The psychology of learning and motivation, Vol. 2.* London: Academic Press.

Avtgis, T.A. (1998). Locus of control and persuasion, social influence, and conformity: A meta-analytic review. *Psychological Reports, 83*, 899–903.

Awad, A.G., & Voruganti, L.N. (1999). Quality of life and new antipsychotics in schizophrenia: Are patients better off? *International Journal of Social Psychiatry, 45*, 268–275.

Bachen, E., Cohen, S., & Marsland, A.L. (1997). Psychoimmunology. In A. Baum, S. Newman, J. Weinman, R. West, & C. McManus (Eds.), *Cambridge handbook of psychology, health, and medicine.* Cambridge, UK: Cambridge University Press.

Baddeley, A.D. (1966). The influence of acoustic and semantic similarity on long-term memory for word sequences. *Quarterly Journal of Experimental Psychology, 18*, 302–309.

Baddeley, A.D., & Hitch, G.J. (1974). Working memory. In G.H. Bower (Ed.), *The psychology of learning and motivation, Vol. 8.* London: Academic Press.

Baddeley, A.D., Thomson, N., & Buchanan, M. (1975). Word length and the structure of short-term memory. *Journal of Verbal Learning and Verbal Behavior, 14*, 575–589.

Bahrick, H.P., Bahrick, P.O., & Wittinger, R.P. (1975). Fifty years of memory for names and faces: A cross-sectional approach. *Journal of Experimental Psychology: General, 104*, 54–75.

Bakermans-Kranenburg, M.J., van IJzendoorn, M.H., & Juffer, F. (2003). Less is more: Meta-analyses of sensitivity and attachment interventions in early childhood. *Psychological Bulletin, 129*, 195–215.

Bales, R.F. (1950). *Interaction process analysis: A method for the study of small groups*. Reading, MA: Addison-Wesley.

Bandura, A. (1965). Influences of models' reinforcement contingencies on the acquisition of initiative responses. *Journal of Personality and Social Psychology, 1*, 589–593.

Bandura, A. (1986). *Social foundations of thought and action: A social cognitive theory*. Englewood Cliffs, NJ: Prentice Hall.

Bandura, A., & Rosenthal, T.L. (1966). Vicarious classical conditioning as a function of arousal level. *Journal of Personality and Social Psychology, 3*, 54–62.

Bandura, A., Ross, D., & Ross, S.A. (1961). Transmission of aggression through imitation of aggressive models. *Journal of Abnormal and Social Psychology, 63*, 575–582.

Banyard, P., & Hayes, N. (1994). *Psychology: Theory and application*. London: Chapman & Hall.

Barlow, D.H., Gorman, J.M., Shear, M.K., & Woods, S.W. (2000). Cognitive-behavioural therapy, imipramine, or their combination for panic disorder: A randomised controlled trial. *Journal of the American Medical Association, 283*, 2529–2536.

Baron, R.S., VanDello, J., & Brunsman, B. (1996). The forgotten variable in conformity research: The impact of task importance on social influence. *Journal of Personality and Social Psychology, 71*, 915–927.

Barr, C.E., Mednick, S.A., & Munk-Jorgenson, P. (1990). Exposure to influenza epidemics during gestation and adult schizophrenia: A forty-year study. *Archives of General Psychiatry, 47*, 869–874.

Barrett, H. (1997). How young children cope with separation: Toward a new conceptualization. *British Journal of Medical Psychology, 70*, 339–358.

Bartlett, F.C. (1932). *Remembering: A study in experimental and social psychology*. Cambridge, UK: Cambridge University Press.

Basco, M.R., & Rush, A.J. (1996). Cognitive-behavioural therapy for bipolar disorder. New York: Guilford Press.

Bates, J.E., Marvinney, D., Kelly, T., Dodge, K.A., Bennett, D.S., & Pettit, G.S. (1994). Child-care history and kindergarten adjustment. *Developmental Psychology, 30*, 690–700.

Baumrind, D. (1975). Metaethical and normative considerations governing the treatment of human subjects in the behavioural sciences. In E.C. Kennedy (Ed.), *Human rights and psychological research: A debate on psychology and ethics*. New York: Thomas Y. Crowell.

Beck, A.T. (1976). *Cognitive therapy of the emotional disorders*. New York: New American Library.

Beck, A.T., & Clark, D.A. (1988). Anxiety and depression: An information processing perspective. *Anxiety Research, 1*, 23–36.

Bellezza, F.S. (1982). Updating memory using mnemonic devices. *Cognitive Psychology, 14*, 301–327.

Belsky, J. (1999). Modern evolutionary theory and patterns of attachment. In J. Cassidy, & P.R. Shaver (Eds.), *Handbook of attachment: Theory, research, and clinical applications*. New York: Guilford Press.

Belsky, J., & Fearon, R.M.P. (2002). Early attachment security, subsequent maternal sensitivity, and later child development: Does continuity in development depend upon continuity of caregiving? *Attachment and Human Development, 4*, 361–387.

Belsky, J., & Rovine, M. (1987). Temperament and attachment security in the Strange Situation: A rapprochement. *Child Development, 58*, 787–795.

Belsky, J., & Rovine, M.J. (1988). Nonmaternal care in the first year of life and the security of parent–infant attachment. *Child Development, 59*, 157–167.

Belsky, J., Vandell, D.L., Burchinal, M., Clarke-Stewart, K.A., McCartney, K., & Tresch Owen, M. (2007). Are there long-term effects of early child care? *Child Development, 78*, 681–701.

Berens, P.L., & Ostrosky, J.D. (1988). Use of beta-blocking agents in musical performance induced anxiety. *Drug Intelligence and Clinical Pharmacy, 22*, 148–149.

Berrettini, W.H. (2000). Susceptibility loci for bipolar disorder: Overlap with inherited vulnerability to schizophrenia. *Biological Psychiatry, 47*, 245–251.

Bickman, L. (1974). Clothes make the person. *Psychology Today, 8*(4), 48–51.

Bjork, R.A., & Bjork, E.L. (1992). A new theory of disuse and an old theory of stimulus fluctuation. In A. Healy, S. Kosslyn, & R. Shiffrin (Eds.), *From learning processes to cognitive processes: Essays in honor of William K. Estes, Vol. 2*, pp. 35–67. Hillsdale, NJ: Erlbaum.

Blass, T. (1991). Understanding behaviour in the Milgram obedience experiment: The role of personality, situations, and their interactions. *Journal of Personality and Social Psychology, 60*, 398–413.

Blass, T., & Schmitt, C. (2001). The nature of perceived authority in the Milgram paradigm: Two replications. *Current Psychology, 20*, 115–121.

Bokhorst, C.L., Bakermans-Kranenburg, M.J., Fearon, R.M.P., van IJzendoorn, M.H., & Schuengel, C. (2003). The importance of shared environment in mother–infant attachment security: A behavioural genetic study. *Child Development, 74*, 1769–1782.

Bond, R. (2005). Group size and conformity. *Group Processes and Intergroup Roles, 6*, 331–354.

Bond, R., & Smith, P.B. (1996). Culture and conformity: A meta-analysis of studies using Asch's line judgement task. *Psychological Bulletin, 119*, 111–137.

Borge, A.I.H., Rutter, M., Côté, S., & Tremblay, R.E. (2004). Early childcare and physical aggression: Differentiating social selection and social causation. *Journal of Child Psychology and Psychiatry, 45*, 367–376.

Bothwell, R.K., Brigham, J.C., & Pigott, M.A. (1987). An exploratory study of personality differences in eyewitness memory. *Journal of Social Behavior and Personality, 2*, 335–343.

Bower, G.H. (1973). How to . . . uh . . . remember. *Psychology Today, 7*, 63–70.

Bower, G.H., Black, J.B., & Turner, T.J. (1979). Scripts in memory for text. *Cognitive Psychology, 11*, 177–220.

Bower, G.H., & Clark, M.C. (1969). Narrative stories as mediators for serial learning. *Psychonomic Science, 14*, 181–182.

Bower, G.H., Clark, M.C., Lesgold, A.M., & Winzenz, D. (1969). Hierarchical retrieval schemes in recall of categorised word lists. *Journal of Verbal Learning and Verbal Behavior, 8*, 323–343.

Bowlby, J. (1944). Forty-four juvenile thieves: Their characters and home life. *International Journal of Psycho-Analysis, 25*, 19–52 and 107–127.

Bowlby, J. (1951). *Maternal care and mental health*. Geneva, Switzerland: World Health Organisation.

Bowlby, J. (1953). *Child care and the growth of love*. Harmondsworth, UK: Penguin.

Bowlby, J. (1958). The nature of the child's tie to his mother. *International Journal of Psycho-Analysis, 39*, 350–373.

Bowlby, J. (1969). *Attachment and love, Vol. 1: Attachment*. London: Hogarth.

Brady, J.V. (1958). Ulcers in executive monkeys. *Scientific American, 199*, 95–100.

Brainerd, C.J., & Reyna, V.F. (2004). Fuzzy-trace theory and memory development. *Developmental Review, 24*, 396–439.

Brantigan, C.O., Brantigan, T.A., & Joseph, N. (1982). Effect of beta blockade and beta stimulation on stage fright. *American Journal of Medicine, 72*, 88–94.

Brewer, N., Weber, N., & Semmler, C. (2005). Eyewitness identification. In N. Brewer & K.D. Williams (Eds.), *Psychology and law: An empirical perspective*. New York: Guilford Press.

British Psychological Society (2006). http://www.bps.org.uk/the-society/ethics-rules-charter-code-of-conduct/code-of-conduct/code-of-conduct_home.cfm

Bronfenbrenner, U. (1988). Interacting systems in human development. In N. Bolger, A. Caspi, G. Downey, & M. Moorehouse (Eds.), *Persons in context: Developmental processes* (pp. 25–49). New York: Cambridge University Press.

Brown, G.W., & Harris, T. (1978). *Social origins of depression*. London: Tavistock.

Brown, R. (1986). *Social psychology: The second edition*. New York: The Free Press.

Bruce, T.J., & Saeed, S.A. (1999). Social anxiety disorder: A common, under-recognised mental disorder. *American Family Physician, 60*, 2311–2322.

Bruck, M., & Melnyk, L. (2004). Individual differences in children's suggestibility: A review and synthesis. *Applied Cognitive Psychology, 18*, 947–996.

Bruner, E.M., & Kelso, J.M. (1980). Gender differences in graffiti: A semiotic perspective. *Women's Studies International Quarterly, 3*, 239–252.

Bryant, B., Harris, M., & Newton, D. (1980). *Children and minders*. London: Grant McIntyre.

Budd, J.W. (2004). Mind maps as classroom exercises. *Journal of Economic Education, 35*, 35–46.

Buehler, R., Griffin, D., & Ross, M. (1994). Exploring the "planning fallacy": Why people underestimate their task completion times. *Journal of Personality and Social Psychology, 67*, 366–381.

Bus, A.G., & van IJzendoorn, M.H. (1988). Attachment and early reading: A longitudinal study. *Journal of Genetic Psychology, 149*(2), 199–210.

Bushnell, I.W.R., Sai, F., & Mullin, J.T. (1989). Neonatal recognition of the mother's face. *British Journal of Developmental Psychology, 7*, 3–13.

Butler, A.C., Chapman, J.E., Forman, E.M., & Beck, A.T. (2006). The empirical status of cognitive-behavioural therapy: A review of meta-analyses. *Clinical Psychology Review, 26*, 17–31.

Buzan, T., & Buzan, B. (1993). *The mind map book*. London: BBC Books.

Campbell, D.T., & Stanley, J.C. (1966). *Experimental and quasi-experimental designs for research*. Chicago: Rand McNally.

Carlsmith, H., Ellsworth, P., & Aronson, E. (1976). *Methods of research in social psychology*. Reading, MA: Addison-Wesley.

Carpenter, G. (1975). Mother's face and the newborn. In R. Lewin (Ed.), *Child alive*. London: Temple Smith.

Cartwright, S., & Cooper, C. (1997). *Managing workplace stress*. London: Sage.

Caspi, A., Mofitt, T.E., Newman, D.L., & Silva, P.A. (1996). Behavioral observations at age 3 years predict adult psychiatric disorders: Longitudinal evidence from a birth cohort. *Archives of General Psychiatry, 53*, 1033–1039.

Chadda, R.K., & Ahuja, N. (1990). Dhat syndrome. A sex neurosis of the Indian subcontinent. *British Journal of Psychiatry, 156*, 577–579.

Chamberlain, E. (2003). Behavioural Assessment of the Dysexecutive Syndrome (BADS): Reviewed by Elaine Chamberlain. *Journal of Occupational Psychology, Employment, and Disability, 5*, 33–37.

Chamberlain, S.R., Muller, U., Deakin, J.B., Cortlett, P.R., Dowson, J., Cardinal, R.N., et al. (2007). Lack of deleterious effects of buspirone on cognition in healthy male volunteers. *Journal of Psychopharmacology, 21*, 210–215.

Charlton, A. (1998). TV violence has little impact on children, study finds. *The Times*, 12 January, p. 5.

Charlton, T., Panting, C., Davie, R., Coles, D., & Whitmarsh, L. (2000). Children's playground behaviour across five years of broadcast television: A naturalistic study in a remote community. *Emotional and Behavioural Difficulties, 5*, 4–12.

Choy, Y., Fyer, A.J., & Lipsitz, J.D. (2007). Treatment of specific phobia in adults. *Clinical Psychology Review, 27*, 266–286.

Clark, D.M. (1986). A cognitive approach to panic. *Behaviour Research and Therapy, 24*, 461–470.

Clark, D.M. (1996). Panic disorder: From theory to therapy. In P. Salkovskis (Ed.), *Frontiers of cognitive therapy*. New York: Guilford Press.

Clark, D.M., & Wells, A. (1995). A cognitive model of social phobia. In R.R.G. Heimberg, M. Liebowitz, D.A. Hope, & S. Scheier (Eds.), *Social phobia: Diagnosis, assessment and treatment*. New York: Guilford Press.

Clarke, A.M., & Clarke, A.D.B. (1998). Early experience and the life path. *The Psychologist, 11*(9), 433–436.

Clarke-Stewart, A. (1989). Infant day care: Maligned or malignant? *American Psychologist, 44*, 266–273.

Clarke-Stewart, K.A., Gruber, C.P., & Fitzgerald, L.M. (1994). *Children at home and in day care*. Hillsdale, NJ: Lawrence Erlbaum Associates Inc.

Claxton, G. (1980). Cognitive psychology: A suitable case for what sort of treatment? In G. Claxton (Ed.), *Cognitive psychology: New directions*. London: Routledge & Kegan Paul.

Cobb, S., & Rose, R.M. (1973). Hypertension, peptic ulcer, and diabetes in air traffic controllers. *Journal of the American Medical Association, 224*, 489–492.

Cohen, G. (1983). *The psychology of cognition* (2nd ed.). London: Academic Press.

Cohen, S., Tyrrell, D.A.J., & Smith, A.P. (1991). Psychological stress and susceptibility to the common cold. *New England Journal of Medicine, 325*, 606–612.

Cole, S.R., Kawachi, I., Sesso, H.D., Paffenbarger, R.S., & Lee, I-M. (1999). Sense of exhaustion and coronary heart disease among college alumni. *American Journal of Cardiology, 84*, 1401–1405.

Collins, D.L., Baum, A., & Singer, J.E. (1983). Coping with chronic stress at Three Mile Island: Psychological and biochemical evidence. *Health Psychology, 1,* 149–166.

Collins, D.W., & Kimura, D. (1997). A large sex difference on a two-dimensional mental rotation task. *Behavior Neuroscience, 111,* 845–849.

Colman, A.M. (2001). *A dictionary of psychology.* Oxford: Oxford University Press.

Comer, R.J. (2001). *Abnormal psychology* (4th ed.). New York: Worth.

Conway, A.R.A., Kane, M.J., & Engle, R.W. (2003). Working memory capacity and its relation to general intelligence. *Trends in Cognitive Sciences, 7,* 547–552.

Coolican, H. (1994). *Research methods and statistics in psychology* (2nd ed.). London: Hodder & Stoughton.

Coolican, H. (1996). *Introduction to research methods and statistics in psychology.* London: Hodder & Stoughton.

Coolican, H. (1998). Research methods. In M.W. Eysenck (Ed.), *Psychology: An integrated approach.* London: Addison-Wesley Longman.

Coolican, H. (2004). *Research methods and statistics in psychology* (4th edn.). London: Hodder & Stoughton.

Cooper, L.A., & Shepard, R.N. (1973). Chronometric studies of the rotation of mental images. In W.G. Chase (Ed.), *Visual information processing.* New York: Academic Press.

Cox, T. (1978). *Stress.* London: Macmillan Press.

Crowley, B.J., Hayslip, B., & Hobdy, J. (2003). Psychological hardiness and adjustment to life events in adulthood. *Journal of Adult Development, 10,* 237–248.

Cruess, D.G., Antoni, M.H., Kumar, M., et al. (1999). Cognitive-behavioural stress management buffers decreases in dehydroepiandrosterone (DHAE-S) and increases in the cortisol/DHAE-S ratio and reduces mood disturbance and perceived stress among HIV-seropositive men. *Psychoneuroendocrinology, 24,* 537–549.

Crutchfield, R.S. (1955). Conformity and character. *American Psychologist, 10,* 191–198.

Cumberbatch, G. (1990). *Television advertising and sex role stereotyping: A content analysis* [Working paper IV for the Broadcasting Standards Council]. Communications Research Group, Aston University, Birmingham, UK.

Curtiss, S. (1989). The independence and task-specificity of language. In M.H. Bornstein & J.S. Bruner (Eds.), *Interaction in human development.* Hillsdale, NJ: Lawrence Erlbaum Associates Inc.

Daneman, M., & Carpenter, P.A. (1980). Individual differences in working memory and reading. *Journal of Verbal Learning and Verbal Behavior, 19,* 450–466.

Darley, J.M., & Latané, B. (1968). Bystander intervention in emergencies: Diffusion of responsibility. *Journal of Personality and Social Psychology, 8,* 377–383.

Davidson, J.R.T., DuPont, R.L., Hedges, D., & Haskins, J.T. (1999). Efficacy, safety, and tolerability of venlafaxine extended release and buspirone in outpatients with generalised anxiety disorder. *Journal of Clinical Psychiatry, 60,* 528–535.

Davison, G.C., & Neale, J.M. (1996). *Abnormal psychology* (rev. 6th ed.). New York: Wiley.

Davison, G., Neale, J.M., & Kring, A.M. (2004). *Abnormal psychology with cases.* Hoboken, NJ: John Wiley & Sons.

Day, R., Nielsen, J.A., Korten, A., Ernberg, G., et al. (1987). Stressful life events preceding the acute onset of schizophrenia: A cross-national study from the World Health Organization. *Culture, Medicine and Psychiatry, 11,* 123–205.

De Beni, R., Moè, A., & Cornoldi, C. (1997). Learning from texts or lectures: Loci mnemonics can interfere with reading but not with listening. *European Journal of Cognitive Psychology, 9,* 401–415.

de Chateau, P., & Wiberg, B. (1977). Long-term effect on mother–infant behavior of extra contact during the first hour post-partum: I. First observation at 36 hours. *Acta Paediatrica Scandinavica, 66,* 137–144.

Deese, J. (1959). On the prediction of occurrence of certain verbal intrusions in free recall. *Journal of Experimental Psychology, 58,* 17–22.

Deffenbacher, K.A., Bornstein, B.H., Penrod, S.D., & McGorty, K. (2004). A meta-analytic review of the effects of high stress on eyewitness memory. *Law and Human Behavior, 28,* 687–706.

De Leon, C.F.M., Powell, L.H., & Kaplan, B.H. (1986). Change in coronary-prone behaviours in the recurrent coronary prevention project. *Psychosomatic Medicine, 33,* 407–419.

DeLongis, A., Coyne, J.C., Dakof, G., Folkman, S., & Lazarus, R.S. (1982). The impact of daily hassles, uplifts and major life events to health status. *Health Psychology, 1,* 119–136.

DeLongis, A., Folkman, S., & Lazarus, R.S. (1988). The impact of daily stress on health and mood: Psychological and social resources as mediators. *Journal of Personality and Social Psychology, 54,* 486–495.

De Man, A., Morrison, M., & Drumheller, A. (1993). Correlates of socially restrictive and authoritarian attitudes toward mental patients in university students. *Social Behavior and Personality: An International Journal, 21,* 333–338.

Denholz, M.S., Hall, L.A., & Mann, E. (1978). Automated treatment for flight phobia: A 3½-year follow-up. *American Journal of Psychiatry, 135,* 1340–1343.

Deutsch, M., & Gerard, H.B. (1955). A study of normative and informational influence upon individual judgement. *Journal of Abnormal and Social Psychology, 51,* 629–636.

De Vreede, I.M., Burger, H., & van Vliet, I.M. (2005). Prediction of response to ECT with routinely collected data in major depression. *Journal of Affective Disorders, 86,* 323–327.

De Woolf, M.S., & van IJzendoorn, M.H. (1997). Sensitivity and attachment: A meta-analysis on parental antecedents of infant attachment. *Child Development, 68,* 571–591.

Diener, E., & Crandall, R. (1978). *Ethics in social and behavioural research.* Chicago: The University of Chicago Press.

DiNardo, P.A., Guzy, L.T., Jenkins, J.A., Bak, R.M., Tomasi, S.F., & Copland, M. (1988). Aetiology and maintenance of dog fears. *Behaviour Research and Therapy, 26,* 241–244.

Dodson, C.S., & Krueger, L.E. (2006). I misremember it well: Why older adults are unreliable eyewitnesses. *Psychological Bulletin & Review, 13,* 770–775.

Dollard, J., & Miller, N.E. (1950). *Personality and psychotherapy.* New York: McGraw-Hill.

Durand, V.M., & Barlow, D.H. (2006). *Essentials of abnormal psychology* (4th edn.). Belmont, CA: Wadsworth.

Durkin, K. (1995). *Developmental social psychology: From infancy to old age.* Oxford, UK: Blackwell.

Durrett, M.E., Otaki, M., & Richards, P. (1984). Attachment and the mother's perception of support from the father. *International Journal of Behavioral Development, 7,* 167–176.

Dyer, C. (1995). *Beginning research in psychology.* Oxford, UK: Blackwell.

Eagly, A.H. (1978). Sex differences in influenceability. *Psychological Bulletin, 85,* 86–116.

Eagly, A.H., & Carli, L. (1981). Sex of researchers and sex-typed communications as determinants of sex differences in influenceability: A meta-analysis of social influence studies. *Psychological Bulletin, 90,* 1–20.

Eakin, D.K., Schreiber, T.A., & Sergent-Marshall, S. (2003). Misinformation effects in eyewitness memory: The presence and absence of memory impairment as a function of warning and misinformation accessibility. *Journal of Experimental Psychology: Learning, Memory, and Cognition, 29,* 813–825.

Elkin, I. (1994). The NIMH Treatment of Depression Collaborative Research Program: Where we began and where we are. In S. Garsfield & A. Bergin (Eds.), *Handbook of psychotherapy and behaviour change* (4th ed.). New York: Wiley.

Erb, H-P., Bohner, G., Rank, S., & Einwiller, S. (2002). Processing minority and majority communications: The role of conflict with prior attitudes. *Personality and Social Psychology Bulletin, 28,* 1172–1182.

Erel, O., Oberman, Y., & Yirmiya, N. (2000). Maternal versus nonmaternal care and seven domains of children's development. *Psychological Bulletin, 126,* 727–747.

Ericsson, K.A. (1988). Analysis of memory performance in terms of memory skill. In R.J. Sternberg (Ed.), *Advances in the psychology of human intelligence, Vol 4.* Hillsdale, NJ: Lawrence Erlbaum Associates Inc.

Evans, P. (1998). Stress and coping. In M. Pitts & K. Phillips (Eds.), *The psychology of health* (2nd ed.). London: Routledge.

Evans, P., Clow, A., & Hucklebridge, F. (1997). Stress and the immune system. *The Psychologist, 10*(7), 303–307.

Eysenck, H.J. (1985). *Decline and fall of the Freudian empire.* London: Viking.

Eysenck, M.W. (1990). *Happiness: Facts and myths.* Hove, UK: Psychology Press.

Eysenck, M.W. (1997). *Anxiety and cognition: A unified theory.* Hove, UK: Psychology Press.

Farrand, P., Hussain, F., & Hennessy, E. (2002). The efficacy of the 'mind map' study technique. *Medical Education, 36,* 426–431.

Festinger, L., Riecken, H.W., & Schachter, S. (1956). *When prophecy fails.* Minneapolis: University of Minnesota Press.

Finlay-Jones, R.A., & Brown, G.W. (1981). Types of stressful life events and the onset of anxiety and depressive disorders. *Psychological Medicine, 11,* 803–815.

Fischhoff, B. (1977). Perceived informativeness of facts. *Journal of Experimental Psychology: Human Perception and Performance, 3,* 349–358.

Fischhoff, B., & Beyth, R. (1975). "I knew it would happen": Remembered probabilities of once-future things. *Organizational Behaviour and Human Performance, 13,* 1–16.

Fisher, R.P., Geiselman, R.E., & Amador, M. (1990). A field test of the cognitive interview: Enhancing the recollections of actual victims and witnesses of crime. *Journal of Applied Psychology, 74,* 722–727.

Fisher, R.P., Geiselman, R.E., Raymond, D.S., Jurkevich, L.M., & Warhaftig, M.L. (1987). Enhancing enhanced eyewitness memory: Refining the cognitive interview. *Journal of Police Science and Administration, 15,* 291–297.

Foa, E.B., Dancu, C.V., Hembree, E.A., Jaycox, L.H., Meadows, E.A., & Street, G.P. (1999). A comparison of exposure therapy, stress inoculation training, and their combination for reducing posttraumatic stress disorder in female assault victims. *Journal of Consulting and Clinical Psychology, 67,* 194–200.

Folkman, S., & Lazarus, R.S. (1985). If it changes it must be a process: Study of emotion and coping during three stages of a college examination. *Journal of Personality and Social Psychology, 48,* 150–170.

Folkman, S., & Moskowitz, J.T. (2004). Coping: Pitfalls and promise. *Annual Review of Psychology, 55,* 745–774.

Folkman, S., Lazarus, R.S., Dunkel-Schetter, C., DeLongis, A., & Gruen, R.J. (1986). Dynamics of a stressful encounter: Cognitive appraisal, coping, and encounter outcomes. *Journal of Personality and Social Psychology, 50,* 992–1003.

Forsythe, C.J., & Compas, B.E. (1987). Interaction of cognitive appraisals of stressful events and coping: Testing the goodness of fit hypothesis. *Cognitive Therapy and Research, 11,* 473–485.

Fraley, R.C., & Spieker, S.J. (2003). What are the differences between dimensional and categorical models of individual differences in attachment? Reply to Cassidy (2003), Cummings (2003), Sroufe (2003), and Waters and Beauchaine (2003). *Developmental Psychology, 39,* 423–429.

Franchini, L., Gasperini, M., Perez, J., Smeraldi, E., & Zanardi, R. (1997). A double-blind study of long-term treatment with setraline or fluvoxamine for prevention of highly recurrent unipolar depression. *Journal of Clinical Psychiatry, 58,* 104–107.

Franzoi, S.L. (1996). *Social psychology.* Madison, WI: Brown & Benchmark.

Freud, A., & Dann, S. (1951). An experiment in group upbringing. *Psychoanalytic Study of the Child, 6,* 127–168.

Freud, S., & Breuer, J. (1895). Studies on hysteria. In J. Strachey (Ed.), *The complete psychological works, Vol 2.* New York: Norton.

Friedman, M., & Rosenman, R.H. (1959). Association of specific overt behaviour pattern with blood and cardiovascular findings. *Journal of the American Medical Association, 96,* 1286–1296.

Friedman, M., & Rosenman, R.H. (1974). *Type A behaviour and your heart.* New York: Knopf.

Gaab, J., Blättler, N., Menzi, T., Stoyer, S., & Ehlert, U. (2003). Randomised controlled evaluation of the effects of cognitive-behavioural stress management on cortisol responses to acute stress in healthy subjects. *Psychoneuroendocrinology, 28,* 767–779.

Gamson, W.B., Fireman, B., & Rytina, S. (1982). *Encounters with unjust authority.* Homewood, IL: Dorsey Press.

Ganster, D.C., Fox, M.L., & Dwyer, D.J. (2001). Explaining employees' health care costs: A prospective examination of stressful job demands, personal control, and physiological reactivity. *Journal of Applied Psychology, 86,* 954–964.

Ganster, D.C., Schaubroeck, J., Sime, W.E., & Mayes, B.T. (1991). The nomological validity of the Type A personality among employed adults. *Journal of Applied Psychology, 76*, 143–168.

Garfield, S. "Unhappy Anniversary", *The Observer*, 2007-02-03. See http://www.guardian.co.uk/society/2003/feb/02/mentalhealth.drugs

Gates, G.A., Saegert, J., Wilson, N., Johnson, L., Shepherd, A., & Hearne, E. (1985). Effect of beta blockade on singing performance. *Annals of Otolaryngology, Rhinology and Laryngology, 94*, 570–574.

Gathercole, S., & Baddeley, A.D. (1990). Phonological memory deficits in language-disordered children: Is there a causal connection? *Journal of Memory and Language, 29*, 336–360.

Geddes, J.R., Burgess, S., Hawton, K., Jamison, K., & Goodwin, G.M. (2004). Long-term lithium therapy for bipolar disorder: Systematic review and meta-analysis of randomised controlled trials. *American Journal of Psychiatry, 161*, 217–222.

Geiselman, R.E., & Fisher, R.P. (1997). Ten years of cognitive interviewing. In D.G. Payne & F.G. Conrad (Eds.), *Intersections in basic and applied memory research*. Mahwah, NJ: Lawrence Erlbaum Associates Inc.

Geiselman, R.E., Fisher, R.P., MacKinnon, D.P., & Holland, H.L. (1985). Eyewitness memory enhancement in police interview: Cognitive retrieval mnemonics versus hypnosis. *Journal of Applied Psychology, 70*, 401–412.

Gentry, W.D., & Kobasa, S.C. (1984). Social and psychological resources mediating stress-illness relationships in humans. In W.D. Gentry (Ed.), *Handbook of behavioural medicine*. New York: Guilford Press.

Gevirtz, R. (2000). Physiology of stress. In D. Kenney, J. Carlson, J. Sheppard, & F.J. McGuigan (Eds.), *Stress and health: Research and clinical applications*. Sydney: Harwood Academic Publishers.

Gilbert, G.N., & Mulkay, M. (1984). *Opening Pandora's box: A sociological analysis of scientists' discourse*. Cambridge, UK: Cambridge University Press.

Glanzer, M., & Cunitz, A.R. (1966). Two storage mechanisms in free recall. *Journal of Verbal Learning and Verbal Behavior, 5*, 351–360.

Gleitman, H. (1986). *Psychology* (2nd ed.). London: Norton.

Goa, K.L., & Ward, A. (1986). Buspirone: A preliminary review of its pharmacological properties and therapeutic efficacy as an anxiolytic. *Drugs, 32*, 114–129.

Goldfarb, W. (1947). Variations in adolescent adjustment of institutionally reared children. *American Journal of Orthopsychiatry, 17*, 499–557.

Goleman, D. (1991, November 26). Doctors find comfort is a potent medicine. *The New York Times*.

Gottesman, I.L. (1991). *Schizophrenia genesis: The origins of madness*. New York: W.H. Freeman.

Griffiths, M.D. (1993). Fruit machine addiction in adolescence: A case study. *Journal of Gambling Studies, 9*(4), 387–399.

Gross, J., & Hayne, H. (1999). Drawing facilitates children's verbal reports after long delays. *Journal of Experimental Psychology: Applied, 5*, 265–283.

Gross, R. (1999). *Key studies in psychology* (3rd ed.). London: Hodder & Stoughton.

Grossman, K., Grossman, K.E., Spangler, S., Suess, G., & Uzner, L. (1985). Maternal sensitivity and newborn responses as related to quality of attachment in Northern Germany. In J. Bretherton & E. Waters (Eds.), Growing

points of attachment theory. *Monographs of the Society for Research in Child Development, 50*, No. 209.

Grunhaus, L., Schreiber, S., Dolberg, O.T., Hirshman, S., & Dannon, P.N. (2002). Response to ECT in major depression: Are there differences between unipolar and bipolar depression? *Bipolar Disorders, 4*(Suppl. 1), 91–93.

Guiton, P. (1966). Early experience and sexual object choice in the brown leghorn. *Animal Behaviour, 14*, 534–538.

Gunnar, M.R., & van Dulmen, M.H.M. (2007). Behaviour problems in post-institutionalised internationally adopted children. *Development and Psychopathology, 19*, 129–148.

Haas, K. (1966). Obedience: Submission to destructive orders as related to hostility. *Psychological Reports, 19*, 32–34.

Hahn, S.E., & Smith, C.S. (1999). Daily hassles and chronic stressors: Conceptual and measurement issues. *Stress Medicine, 15*, 89–101.

Hailman, J. (1992). The necessity of a "show-me" attitude in science. In J.W. Grier & T. Burk, *Biology of animal behaviour* (2nd edn.). Dubuque, IO: W.C. Brown.

Haney, C., Banks, W.C., & Zimbardo, P.G. (1973). Interpersonal dynamics in a simulated prison. *International Journal of Criminology and Penology, 1*, 69–97.

Hardy, I., & Stadelhofer, B. (2006). Concept maps wirkungsvoll als Strukturierungshilfen einsetzen: Welche Rolle spielt die Selbstkonstruktion? [The value of concept maps as providing assistance in providing structure: What role is played by self-construction?]. *Zeitschrift für Pädagogische Psychologie, 20*, 175–187.

Harlow, H.F. (1959). Love in infant monkeys. *Scientific American, 200*, 68–74.

Harlow, H.F., & Harlow, M.K. (1962). Social deprivation in monkeys. *Scientific American, 207*(5), 136–146.

Harris, T. (1997). Life events and health. In A. Baum, S. Newman, J. Weinman, R. West, & C. McManus (Eds.), *Cambridge handbook of psychology, health, and medicine*. Cambridge, UK: Cambridge University Press.

Harrison, L.J., & Ungerer, J.A. (2002). Maternal employment and infant–mother attachment security at 12 months postpartum. *Developmental Psychology, 38*, 758–773.

Harvey, A.G., Clark, D.M., Ehlers, A., & Rapee, R.M. (2000). Social anxiety and self-impression: Cognitive preparation enhances the beneficial effects of video feedback following a stressful social task. *Behaviour Research and Therapy, 38*, 1183–1192.

Haskins, R. (1985). Public school aggression among children with varying day-care experience. *Child Development, 56*, 689–703.

Hay, D.F., & Vespo, J.E. (1988). Social learning perspectives on the development of the mother–child relationship. In B. Birns & D.F. Hay (Eds.), *The different faces of motherhood*. New York: Plenum Press.

Haynes, S.G., Feinleib, M., & Kannel, W.B. (1980). The relationship of psychosocial factors to coronary heart disease in the Framingham Study: III. Eight-year incidence of coronary heart disease. *American Journal of Epidemiology, 111*, 37–58.

Hazan, C., & Shaver, P.R. (1987). Romantic love conceptualised as an attachment process. *Journal of Personality and Social Psychology, 52*, 511–524.

Heath, W.P., & Erickson, J.R. (1998). Memory for central and peripheral actions and props after various post-event presentations. *Legal and Criminal Psychology*, 3, 321–346.

Heather, N. (1976). *Radical perspectives in psychology*. London: Methuen.

Heine, S.J., Lehman, D.R., Markus, H.R., & Kitayama, S. (1999). Is there a universal need for positive self-regard? *Psychological Review*, 106, 766–794.

Herman, D., & Green, J. (1991). *Madness: A study guide*. London: BBC Education.

Hirschfeld, R.M. (1999). Efficacy of SSRIs and newer antidepressants in severe depression: Comparison with TCAs. *Journal of Clinical Psychiatry*, 60, 326–335.

Hitch, G., & Baddeley, A.D. (1976). Verbal reasoning and working memory. *Quarterly Journal of Experimental Psychology*, 28, 603–621.

Hockey, G.R.J., Davies, S., & Gray, M.M. (1972). Forgetting as a function of sleep at different times of day. *Quarterly Journal of Experimental Psychology*, 24, 386–393.

Hodges, J., & Tizard, B. (1989). Social and family relationships of ex-institutional adolescents. *Journal of Child Psychology and Psychiatry*, 30, 77–97.

Hofling, K.C., Brotzman, E., Dalrymple, S., Graves, N., & Pierce, C.M. (1966). An experimental study in the nurse–physician relationship. *Journal of Nervous and Mental Disorders*, 143, 171–180.

Høglend, P. (2004). Analysis of transference in psychodynamic psychotherapy: A review of empirical research. *Canadian Journal of Psychoanalysis*, 12, 279–300.

Høglend, P., Amlo, S., Marble, A., Bøgwald, K.P., Sørbye, O., Sjaastad, M.C., et al. (2006). Analysis of the patient–therapist relationship in dynamic psychotherapy: An experimental study of transference interpretations. *American Journal of Psychiatry*, 163, 1739–1746.

Høglend, P., Bøgwald, K-P., Amlo, S., Heyerdahl, O., Sørbye, O., Marble, A., et al. (2000). Assessment of change in dynamic psychotherapy. *Journal of Psychotherapy Practice and Research*, 9, 190–199.

Høglend, P., Engelstad, V., Sørbye, O., et al. (1994). The role of insight in exploratory psychodynamic psychotherapy. *British Journal of Medical Psychology*, 67, 305–317.

Holland, C.D. (1967). Sources of variance in the experimental investigation of behavioural disturbance. *Dissertation Abstracts International*, 29, 2802A (University Microfilm No. 69–2146).

Holmes, T.H., & Rahe, R.H. (1967). The social readjustment rating scale. *Journal of Psychosomatic Research*, 11, 213–218.

Homan, R. (1991). *The ethics of social research*. London: Longman.

House, J.S., Landis, K.R., & Umberson, D. (1988). Social relationships and health. *Science*, 241, 540–545.

Howes, C., Galinsky, E., & Kontos, S. (1998). Caregiver sensitivity and attachment. *Social Development*, 7(1), 25–36.

Howes, C., Matheson, C.C., & Hamilton, C.E. (1994). Maternal, teacher, and child care correlates of children's relationships with peers. *Child Development*, 65(1), 264–273.

Howes, C., Smith, E., & Galinsky, E. (1995). *The Florida child care quality improvement study*. New York: Families & Work Institute.

Hsu, L., & Hsieh, S-I. (2005). Concept maps as an assessment tool in a nursing course. *Journal of Professional Nursing*, 21, 141–149.

Ihlebaek, C., Lave, T., Eilertsen, D.E., & Magnussen, S. (2003). Memory for a staged criminal event witnessed live and on video. *Memory*, 11, 319–327.

Immelmann, K. (1972). Sexual and other long-term aspects of imprinting in birds and other species. In D.S. Lehrmann, R.A. Hinde, & E. Shaw (Eds.), *Advances in the study of behaviour, Vol. 4*. New York: Academic Press.

Jacobs, J. (1887). Experiments on 'prehension'. *Mind*, 12, 75–79.

Jacobson, J.L., & Wille, D.E. (1986). The influence of attachment pattern on developmental changes in peer interaction from the toddler to the preschool period. *Child Development*, 57, 338–347.

Jacoby, L.L., Bishara, A.J., Hessels, S., & Toth, J.P. (2005). Aging, subjective experience, and cognitive control: Dramatic false remembering by older adults. *Journal of Experimental Psychology: General*, 134, 131–148.

Jahoda, M. (1958). *Current concepts of positive mental health*. New York: Basic Books.

James, O. (1997). Serotonin: A chemical feel-good factor. *Psychology Review*, 4, 34.

Janis, I. (1972). *Victims of groupthink: A psychological study of foreign-policy decisions and fiascos*. Boston: Houghton-Mifflin.

Jenkins, J.G., & Dallenbach, K.M. (1924). Oblivescence during sleep and waking. *American Journal of Psychology*, 35, 605–612.

Johansson, G., Aronson, G., & Lindstroem, B.O. (1978). Social psychological and neuroendocrine stress reactions in highly mechanised work. *Ergonomics*, 21, 583–599.

Johnson, J.G., & Sherman, M.F. (1997). Daily hassles mediate the relationship between major life events and psychiatric symptomatology: Longitudinal findings from an adolescent sample. *Journal of Social and Clinical Psychology*, 16, 389–404.

Johnson, R.D., & Downing, L.L. (1979). Deindividuation and valence of cues: Effects on prosocial and antisocial behaviour. *Journal of Personality and Social Psychology*, 39, 1532–1538.

Kagan, J. (1984). *The nature of the child*. New York: Basic Books.

Kagan, J., Kearsley, R.B., & Zelazo, P.R. (1980). *Infancy: Its place in human development*. Cambridge, MA: Harvard University Press.

Kahneman, D., & Tversky, A. (1979). Intuitive prediction: Biases and corrective procedures. *TIMS Studies in Management Science*, 12, 313–327.

Kalakoski, V., & Saariluoma, P. (2001). Taxi drivers' exceptional memory of street names. *Memory & Cognition*, 29, 634–638.

Kario, K., McEwen, B.S., & Pickering, T.G. (2003). Disasters and the heart: A review of the effects of earthquake-induced stress on cardiovascular disease. *Hypertension Research*, 26, 355–367.

Kashima, Y., & Kashima, E.S. (2003). Individualism, GNP, climate, and pronoun drop: Is individualism determined by affluence and climate, or does language use play a role? *Journal of Cross-Cultural Psychology*, 34, 125–134.

Keast, A., Brewer, N., & Wells, G.L. (2007). Children's metacognitive judgments in an eyewitness identification task. *Journal of Experimental Child Psychology*, 97(4), 286–314.

Kelman, H.C. (1958). Compliance, identification and internalisation: Three processes of attitude change. *Journal of Conflict Resolution*, 2, 51–60.

Kelman, H.C. (1972). The rights of the subject in social research: An analysis in terms of relative power and legitimacy. *American Psychologist, 27*, 989–1016.

Kelman, H., & Lawrence, L. (1972). Assignment of responsibility in the case of Lt. Calley: Preliminary report on a national survey. *Journal of Social Issues, 28*, 177–212.

Kendall, P.X., & Hammen, C. (1998). *Abnormal psychology* (2nd Edn.). Boston, MA: Houghton Mifflin.

Kendler, K.S., Karkowski, L., & Prescott, C.A. (1998). Stressful life events and major depression: Risk period, long-term contextual threat and diagnostic specificity. *Journal of Nervous and Mental Disease, 186*, 661–669.

Kendler, K.S., Kuhn, J., & Prescott, C.A. (2004). The interrelationship of neuroticism, sex, and stressful life events in the prediction of episodes of major depression. *American Journal of Psychiatry, 161*, 631–636.

Kendler, K.S., Neale, M.C., Prescott, C.A., Kessler, R.C., Heath, A.C., Corey, L.A., et al. (1996). Childhood parental loss and alcoholism in women: A causal analysis using a twin-family design. *Psychological Medicine, 26*, 79–95.

Kenny, D.T. (2006). Music performance anxiety: Origins, phenomenology, assessment and treatment. *Context: Journal of Music Research, 5*, 1–10.

Keppel, G., & Underwood, B.J. (1962). Proactive inhibition in short-term retention of single items. *Journal of Verbal Learning and Verbal Behavior, 1*, 153–161.

Khan, F., & Patel, P. (1996). A study of the impact of hassles versus life events on health outcome measures in students and the general population. *Proceedings of the British Psychological Society, 4*(1), 32.

Khoshaba, D.M., & Maddi, S.R. (2001). *HardiTraining*. Newport Beach, CA: Hardiness Institute.

Kiecolt-Glaser, J.K., Garner, W., Speicher, C.E., Penn, G.M., Holliday, J., & Glaser, R. (1984). Psychosocial modifiers of immunocompetence in medical students. *Psychosomatic Medicine, 46*, 7–14.

Kiecolt-Glaser, J.K., Marucha, P.T., Malarkey, W.B., Mercado, A.M., & Glaser, R. (1995). Slowing of wound healing by psychological stress. *Lancet, 346*, 1194–1196.

Kierein, M., & Gold, M. (2000). Pygmalion in work organizations: A meta-analysis. *Journal of Organization Behavior, 21*, 913–928.

Kim, H., & Markus, H.R. (1999). Uniqueness or deviance, harmony or conformity: A cultural analysis. *Journal of Personality and Social Psychology, 77*, 785–800.

Kivimäki, M., Leino-Arjas, P., Luukkonen, R., Riihimäki, H., Vahtera, J., & Kirjonen, J. (2002). Work stress and risk of cardiovascular mortality: Prospective cohort study of industrial employees. *British Medical Journal, 325*, 857.

Kivlighan, D.M., Multon, K.D., & Patton, M.J. (2000). Insight and symptom reduction in time-limited psychoanalytic counselling. *Journal of Counselling Psychology, 47*, 50–58.

Klag, S., & Bradley, G. (2004). The role of hardiness in stress and illness: An exploration of the effect of negative affectivity and gender. *British Journal of Health Psychology, 9*, 137–161.

Klauer, K.C., & Zhao, Z. (2004). Double dissociations in visual and spatial short-term memory. *Journal of Experimental Psychology: General, 133*, 355–381.

Klaus, M.H., & Kennell, J.H. (1976). *Parent–infant bonding*. St Louis: Mosby.

Kobasa, S.C. (1979). Stressful events, personality, and health: An inquiry into hardiness. *Journal of Personality and Social Psychology, 37*, 1–11.

Kobasa, S.C., Maddi, S.R., & Puccetti, M.C. (1982). Personality and exercise as buffers in the stress–illness relationship. *Journal of Behavioural Medicine, 5*, 391–404.

Kobasa, S.C., Maddi, S.R., Puccetti, M.C., & Zola, M.A. (1985). Effectiveness of hardiness, exercise and social support as resources against illness. *Journal of Psychosomatic Research, 29*, 525–533.

Kohnken, G., Milne, R., Memon, A., & Bull, R. (1999). The cognitive interview: A meta-analysis. *Psychology of Crime Law, 5*, 3–27.

Koluchová, J. (1976). The further development of twins after severe and prolonged deprivation: A second report. *Journal of Child Psychology and Psychiatry, 17*, 181–188.

Koluchová, J. (1991). Severely deprived twins after twenty-two years' observation. *Studia Psychologica, 33*, 23–28.

Kuper, H., Marmot, M., & Hemingway, H. (2002a). Systematic review of prospective cohort studies of psychosocial factors in the aetiology and prognosis of coronary heart disease. *Seminars in Vascular Medicine, 2*, 267–314.

Kuper, H., Singha-Manoux, A., Siegrist, J., et al. (2002b). When reciprocity fails: Effort-reward imbalance in relation to coronary heart disease and health functioning within the Whitehall II study. *Occupational and Environmental Medicine, 59*, 777–784.

Kurosawa, K. (1993). The effects of self-consciousness and self-esteem on conformity to a majority. *Japanese Journal of Psychology, 63*, 379–387.

Kutakoff, L., Levin, J., & Arluke, A., (1987). Are the times changing? An analysis of gender differences in sexual graffiti. *Sex Roles, 16*, 1–7.

Lader, M., & Scotto, J.C. (1998). A multicentre double-blind comparison of hydroxyzine, buspirone and placebo in patients with generalized anxiety disorder. *Psychopharmacology, 139*, 402–406.

Larsen, J.D., Baddeley, A.D., & Andrade, J. (2000). Phonological similarity and the irrelevant speech effect: Implications for models of short-term memory. *Memory, 8*, 145–157.

Lau, J., Antman, E.M., Jimenez-Silva, J., Kuperlnik, B., Mostpeller, F., & Chalmers, T.C. (1992). Cumulative meta-analysis of therapeutic trials for myocardial infarction. *New England Journal of Medicine, 327*, 248–254.

Lau, R., & Russell, D. (1980). Attributions in the sports pages. *Journal of Personality and Social Psychology, 39*, 29–38.

Lawrie, S.M., & Abukmeil, S.S. (1998). Brain abnormality in schizophrenia. A systematic and quantitative review of volumetric magnetic resonance imaging studies. *British Journal of Psychiatry, 172*, 110–120.

Lazarus, R.S. (1993). Coping theory and research: Past, present, and future. *Psychosomatic Medicine, 55*, 234–247.

Lazarus, R.S., & Folkman, S. (1984). *Stress, appraisal and coping*. New York: Springer.

Lee, C., Gavriel, H., Drummon, P., Richards, J., & Greenwald, R. (2002). Treatment of PTSD: Stress inoculation training with prolonged exposure compared to EMDR. *Journal of Clinical Psychology, 58*, 1071–1089.

Lee, H. (1997). *Virginia Woolf*. London: Vintage.

Lesar, T.S., Briceland, L., & Stein, D.S. (1997). Factors related to errors in medication prescribing. *Journal of the American Medical Association, 277*, 312–317.

Levin, R.B., & Gross, A.M. (1985). The role of relaxation in systematic desensitization. *Behavior Research and Therapies, 23*(2), 187–196.

Levine, J., Warrenburg, S., Kerns, R., Schwartz, G., Delaney, R., Fontana, A., et al. (1987). The role of denial in recovery from coronary heart disease. *Psychosomatic Medicine, 49*, 109–117.

Lewinsohn, P.M., Joiner, T.E. Jr., & Rohde, P. (2001). Evaluation of cognitive diathesis–stress models in predicting major depressive disorder in adolescents. *Journal of Abnormal Psychology, 110*, 203–215.

Lindsay, D.S., Allen, B.P., Chan, J.C.K., & Dahl, L.C. (2004). Eyewitness suggestibility and source similarity: Intrusions of details from one event into memory reports of another event. *Journal of Memory and Language, 50*, 96–111.

Locke, E.A. (1968). Toward a theory of task motivation and incentives. *Organizational Behavior and Human Performance, 3*, 157–189.

Lockwood, A.H. (1989). Medical problems of musicians. *New England Journal of Medicine, 320*, 221–227.

Loftus, E. (1979). *Eyewitness testimony*. Cambridge, MA: Harvard University Press.

Loftus, E.F. (1992). When a lie becomes memory's truth: Memory distortion after exposure to misinformation. *Current Directions in Psychological Science, 13*, 145–147.

Loftus, E.F. (2004). Memories of things unseen. *Current Directions in Psychological Science, 13*, 145–147.

Loftus, E.F., Loftus, G.R., & Messo, J. (1987). Some facts about "weapons focus". *Law and Human Behavior, 11*, 55–62.

Loftus, E.F., & Palmer, J.C. (1974). Reconstruction of automobile destruction: An example of the interaction between language and memory. *Journal of Verbal Learning and Verbal Behavior, 13*, 585–589.

Loftus, E.F., & Zanni, G. (1975). Eyewitness testimony: The influence of the wording of a question. *Bulletin of the Psychonomic Society, 5*, 86–88.

Logie, R.H., Baddeley, A.D., Mane, A., Donchin, E., & Sheptak, R. (1989). Working memory and the analysis of a complex skill by secondary task methodology. *Acta Psychologica, 71*, 53–87.

London, P., & Lim, H. (1964). Yielding reason to social pressure: Task complexity and expectation in conformity. *Journal of Personality, 33*, 75–98.

Lozoff, B. (1983). Birth and "bonding" in non-industrial societies. *Developmental Medicine and Child Neurology, 25*, 595–600.

Lucas, T., Alexander, S., Firestone, I.J., & Baltes, B.B. (2006). Self-efficacy and independence from social influence: Discovery of an efficacy–difficulty effect. *Social Influence, 1*, 58–80.

Lucini, D., Di Fede, G., Parati, G., & Pagani, M. (2005). Impact of chronic psychosocial stress on autonomic cardiovascular regulation in otherwise healthy subjects. *Hypertension, 46*, 1201–1206.

Maass, A., & Clark, R.D. (1983). Internalisation versus compliance: Differential processes underlying minority influence and conformity. *European Journal of Social Psychology, 13*, 197–215.

Maccoby, E.E. (1980). *Social development: Psychological growth and the parent–child relationship*. San Diego, CA: Harcourt Brace Jovanovich.

MacLeod, A. (1998). Therapeutic interventions. In M.W. Eysenck (Ed.), *Psychology: An integrated approach*. Harlow, UK: Addison Wesley Longman.

Maddi, S.R. (2007). Relevance of hardiness assessment and training to the military context. *Military Psychology, 19*, 61–70.

Maher, B.A. (1966). *Principles of psychopathology: An experimental approach*. New York: McGraw-Hill.

Main, M., & Solomon, J. (1986). Discovery of a disorganised disoriented attachment pattern. In T.B. Brazelton & M.W. Yogman (Eds.), *Affective development in infancy*. Norwood, NJ: Ablex.

Main, M., & Weston, D.R. (1981). The quality of the toddler's relationship to mother and father: Related to conflict behaviour and the readiness to establish new relationships. *Child Development, 52*, 932–940.

Mandler, G. (1967). Organisation and memory. In K.W. Spence & J.T. Spence (Eds.), *The psychology of learning and motivation: Advances in research and theory, Vol. 1*. London: Academic Press.

Manstead, A.S.R., & Semin, G.R. (1996). Methodology in social psychology: Putting ideas to the test. In M. Hewstone, W. Stroebe, & G.M. Stephenson (Eds.), *Introduction to social psychology* (2nd ed.). Oxford, UK: Blackwell.

Marcus, B., & Schutz, A. (2005). Who are the people reluctant to participate in research? Personality correlates of four different types of non-response as inferred from self- and observer ratings. *Journal of Personality, 73*, 959–984.

Marcus-Newhall, A., Pedersen, W.C., Carlson, M., & Miller, N. (2000). Displaced aggression is alive and well: A meta-analytic review. *Journal of Personality and Social Psychology, 78*, 670–689.

Marmot, M.G., Bosma, H., Hemingway, H., Brunner, E., & Stansfeld, S. (1997). Contribution of job control and other risk factors to social variations in coronary heart disease incidence. *Lancet, 350*, 235–239.

Marsh, P., Fox, K., Carnibella, G., McCann, J. & Marsh, J. (1996). *Football Violence in Europe*. The Amsterdam Group.

Marshall, N.L. (2004). The quality of early child care and children's development. *Current Directions in Psychological Science, 13*, 165–168.

Martin, R.A. (1989). Techniques for data acquisition and analysis in field investigations of stress. In R.W.J. Neufeld (Ed.), *Advances in the investigation of psychological stress*. New York: Wiley.

Martin, R., Hewstone, M., & Martin, P.Y. (2003). Resistance to persuasive messages as a function of majority and minority status. *Journal of Experimental Social Psychology, 39*, 585–593.

Marucha, P.T., Kiecolt-Glaser, J.K., & Favagehi, M. (1998). Mucosal wound healing is impaired by examination stress. *Psychosomatic Medicine, 60*, 362–365.

Maslach, C., Santee, R.T., & Wade, C. (1987). Individuation, gender role, and dissent: Personality mediators of situational forces. *Journal of Personality and Social Psychology, 53*, 1088–1093.

Maslow, A.H. (1954). *Motivation and personality*. New York: Harper.

Mason, J.W. (1975). A historical view of the stress field. *Journal of Human Stress, 1,* 22–36.

Matt, G.E., & Navarro, A.M. (1997). What meta-analyses have and have not taught us about psychotherapy effects: A review and future directions. *Clinical Psychology Review, 17,* 1–32.

Matthews, K.A. (1988). Coronary heart disease and Type A behaviour: Update on an alternative to the Booth-Kewley and Friedman (1987). Quantitative review. *Psychological Bulletin, 104,* 373–380.

Matthews, K.A., Glass, D.C., Rosenman, R.H., & Bortner, R.W. (1977). Competitive drive, Pattern A, and coronary heart disease: A further analysis of some data from the Western Collaborative Group. *Journal of Chronic Diseases, 30,* 489–498.

Mayall, B., & Petrie, P. (1983). *Childminding and day nurseries: What kind of care?* London: Heinemann Educational Books.

McDermott, K.B., & Roediger, H.L. (1998). Attempting to avoid illusory memories: Robust false recognition of associates persists under conditions of explicit warnings and immediate testing. *Journal of Memory and Language, 39,* 508–520.

McGlynn, F.D., Mealiea, W.L., & Landau, D.L (1981). The current status of systematic desensitisation. *Clinical Psychology Review, 1,* 149–179.

McGlynn, F.D., Smitherman, T.A., & Gothard, K.D. (2004). Comment on the status of systematic desensitisation. *Behavior Modification, 28,* 194–205.

McGuffin, P., Katz, R., Watkins, S., & Rutherford, J. (1996). A hospital-based twin register of the heritability of DSM-IV unipolar depression. *Archives of General Psychiatry, 53,* 129–136.

Meeus, W.H.J., & Raaijmakers, Q.A.W. (1995). Obedience in modern society: The Utrecht studies. *Journal of Social Issues, 51*(3), 155–175.

Meichenbaum, D. (1977). *Cognitive-behaviour modification: An integrative approach.* New York: Plenum Press.

Meichenbaum, D. (1985). *Stress inoculation training.* New York: Pergamon.

Melamed, S., Shirom, A., Toker, S., Berliner, S., & Shapira, I. (2006). Burnout and risk of cardiovascular disease: Evidence, possible causal paths, and promising research directions. *Psychological Bulletin, 132,* 327–353.

Menzies, R.G., & Clarke, J.C. (1993). The aetiology of childhood water phobia. *Behaviour Research and Therapy, 31,* 499–501.

Metra, M., Nodari, S., D'Aloia, A., Bontempi, L., Boldi, E., & Cas, L.D. (2000). A rationale for the use of [beta]-blockers as standard treatment for heart failure. *American Heart Journal, 139,* 511–521.

Meyers, R.A., Brashers, D.E., & Hanner, J. (2000). Majority–minority influence: Identifying argumentative patterns and predicting argument–outcome links. *Journal of Communication, 50,* 3–30.

Milgram, S. (1963). Behavioural study of obedience. *Journal of Abnormal and Social Psychology, 67,* 371–378.

Milgram, S. (1974). *Obedience to authority: An experimental view.* New York: Harper & Row.

Milgram, S. (1992). *The individual in a social world* (2nd ed.). New York: McGraw-Hill.

Miller, F.D. (1975). *An experimental study of obedience to authority of varying legitimacy.* Unpublished doctoral dissertation, Harvard University.

Miller, G.A. (1956). The magical number seven, plus or minus two: Some limits on our capacity for processing information. *Psychological Review, 63,* 81–97.

Miller, T.Q., Turner, C.W., Tindale, R.S., Posavac, E.J., & Dugoni, B.L. (1991). Reasons for the trend toward null findings in research on Type A behaviour. *Psychological Bulletin, 110,* 469–485.

Milne, R., & Bull, R. (2002). Back to basics: A componential analysis of the original cognitive interview mnemonics with three age groups. *Applied Cognitive Psychology, 16,* 743–753.

Mineka, S., Davidson, M., Cook, M., & Kuir, R. (1984). Observational conditioning of snake fear in rhesus monkeys. *Journal of Abnormal Psychology, 93,* 355–372.

Mitte, K. (2005). A meta-analysis of the efficacy of psycho- and pharmacotherapy in panic disorder with and without agoraphobia. *Journal of Affective Disorders, 88,* 27–45.

Miyake, A., Friedman, N.P., Emerson, M.J., Witzki, A.H., Howerter, A., & Wager, T. (2000). The unity and diversity of executive functions and their contributions to complex "frontal lobe" tasks: A latent variable analysis. *Cognitive Psychology, 41,* 49–100.

Modigliani, A., & Rochat, F. (1995). The role of interaction sequences and the timing of resistance in shaping obedience and defiance to authority. *Journal of Social Issues, 51,* 107–123.

Monat, A., & Lazarus, R.S. (Eds.). (1991). *Stress and coping: An anthology* (3rd ed.). New York: Columbia University Press.

Montello, D.R., Lovelace, K.L., Golledge, R.G., & Self, C.M. (1999). Sex-related differences and similarities in geographic and environmental spatial abilities. *Annals of the Association of American Geographers, 89,* 515–534.

Moore, P.J., Ebbesen, E.B., & Konecni, V.J. (1994). *What does real eyewitness testimony look like? An archival analysis of witnesses to adult felony crimes.* Technical report: University of California, San Diego, CA, Law and Psychology Program.

Morgan, H., & Raffle, C. (1999). Does reducing safety behaviours improve treatment response in patients with social phobia? *Australian and New Zealand Journal of Psychiatry, 33,* 503–510.

Morris, P.E. (1979). Strategies for learning and recall. In M.M. Gruneberg & P.E. Morris (Eds.), *Applied problems in memory.* London: Academic Press.

Morris, P.E., & Reid, R.L. (1970). The repeated use of mnemonic imagery. *Psychonomic Science, 20,* 337–338.

Moscovici, S. (1980). Toward a theory of conversion behaviour. In L. Berkowitz (Ed.), *Advances in experimental social psychology, Vol. 13.* New York: Academic Press.

Moscovici, S. (1985). Social influence and conformity. In G. Lindzey & E. Aronson (Eds.), *Handbook of social psychology* (3rd ed.). New York: Random House.

Moscovici, S., Lage, E., & Naffrenchoux, M. (1969). Influence of a consistent minority on the responses of a majority in a colour perception task. *Sociometry, 32,* 365–380.

Moscovitz, S. (1983). *Love despite hate: Child survivors of the Holocaust and their adult lives.* New York: Schocken.

Mowrer, O.H. (1947). On the dual nature of learning: A reinterpretation of "conditioning" and "problem-solving". *Harvard Educational Review, 17,* 102–148.

Mueller-Johnson, K., & Ceci, S.J. (2004). Memory and suggestibility in older adults: Live event participation and repeated interview. *Applied Cognitive Psychology*, *18*, 1109–1127.

Myrtek, M. (2001). Meta-analyses of prospective studies on coronary heart disease, Type A personality, and hostility. *International Journal of Cardiology*, *79*, 245–251.

Nemeth, C., Swedlund, M., & Kanki, G. (1974). Patterning of the minority's responses and their influence on the majority. *European Journal of Social Psychology*, *4*, 53–64.

Nesbit, J.C., & Adescope, O.O. (2006). Learning with concept and knowledge maps: A meta-analysis. *Review of Educational Research*, *76*, 413–448.

Newmark, C.S., Frerking, R.A., Cook, L., & Newmark, L. (1973). Endorsement of Ellis' irrational beliefs as a function of psychopathology. *Journal of Clinical Psychology*, *29*, 300–302.

NICHD Early Child Care Research Network (1997). The effects of infant child care on infant–mother attachment security: Results of the NICHD study of early child care. *Child Development*, *68*(5), 860–879.

NICHD Early Child Care Research Network (2002). Child-care structure → process → outcome: Direct and indirect effects of child-care quality on young children's development. *Psychological Science*, *13*, 199–206.

NICHD Early Child Care Research Network (2003a). Does quality of child care affect child outcomes at age $4\frac{1}{2}$? *Developmental Psychology*, *39*, 451–469.

NICHD Early Child Care Research Network (2003b). Does amount of time spent in child care predict socioemotional adjustment during the transition to kindergarten? *Child Development*, *74*, 976–1005.

Nisbett, R.E., & Wilson, T.D. (1977). Telling more than we can know: Verbal reports on mental processes. *Psychological Review*, *84*, 231–259.

O'Connor, T.G., Caspi, A., De Fries, J.C., & Plomin, R. (2000). Are associations between parental divorce and children's adjustment genetically mediated? An adoption study. *Developmental Psychology*, *36*, 429–437.

O'Connor, T.G., & Croft, C.M. (2001). A twin study of attachment in preschool children. *Child Development*, *72*, 1501–1511.

Orne, M.T. (1962). On the social psychology of the psychological experiment: With particular reference to demand characteristics and their implications. *American Psychologist*, *17*, 776–783.

Orne, M.T., & Holland, C.C. (1968). On the ecological validity of laboratory deceptions. *International Journal of Psychiatry*, *6*(4), 282–293.

Oyserman, D., Coon, H.M., & Kemmelmeier, M. (2002). Rethinking individualism and collectivism: Evaluation of theoretical assumptions and meta-analyses. *Psychological Bulletin*, *128*, 3–72.

Pagnin, D., de Queiroz, V., Pini, S., & Cassano, G.B. (2004). Efficacy of ECT in depression: A meta-analytic review. *Journal of ECT*, *20*, 13–20.

Papagno, C., Valentine, T., & Baddeley, A.D. (1991). Phonological short-term memory and foreign-language learning. *Journal of Memory & Language*, *30*, 331–347.

Parke, R.D. (1981). *Fathers*. Cambridge, MA: Harvard University Press.

Pauli-Pott, U., Haverkock, A., Pott, W., Beckmann, D. (2007). Negative emotionality, attachment quality, and behaviour problems in early childhood. *Infant Mental Health Journal*, *28*, 39–53.

Penley, J.A., Tomaka, J., & Wiebe, J.S. (2002). The association of coping to physical and psychological health outcomes: A meta-analytic review. *Journal of Behavioral Medicine*, *25*, 551–603.

Pennebaker, J.W., Hendler, C.S., Durrett, M.E., & Richards, P. (1981). Social factors influencing absenteeism due to illness in nursery school children. *Child Development*, *52*, 692–700.

Pepler, D.J., & Craig, W.M. (1995). A peek behind the fence: Naturalistic observations of aggressive children with remote audiovisual recording. *Developmental Psychology*, *31*, 548–553.

Perrin, S., & Spencer, C. (1980). The Asch effect: A child of its time. *Bulletin of the British Psychological Society*, *33*, 405–406.

Peters, D.P. (1988). Eyewitness memory in a natural setting. In M.M. Gruneberg, P.E. Morris, & R.N. Sykes (Eds.), *Practical aspects of memory: Current research and issues: Vol. 1. Memory in everyday life*. Chichester, UK: Wiley.

Peterson, C., Seligman, M.E., & Valliant, G.E. (1988). Pessimistic explanatory style is a risk factor for physical illness: A thirty-five year longitudinal study. *Journal of Personality and Social Psychology*, *55*, 23–27.

Peterson, L.R., & Peterson, M.J. (1959). Short-term retention of individual verbal items. *Journal of Experimental Psychology*, *58*, 193–198.

Petrides, G., Fink, M., Husain, M.M., et al. (2001). ECT remission rates in psychotic versus nonpsychotic depressed patients: A report from CORE. *Journal of ECT*, *17*, 244–253.

Phillips, D., Mekos, D., Scarr, S., McCartney, K., & Abbott-Shim, M. (2000). Within and beyond the classroom door: Assessing quality in child care centres. *Early Childhood Research Quarterly*, *15*, 475–496.

Pickel, K.L. (1999). The influence of context on the "weapon focus" effect. *Law and Human Behavior*, *23*, 299–311.

Piliavin, I.M., Rodin, J., & Piliavin, J.A. (1969). Good samaritanism: An underground phenomenon? *Journal of Personality and Social Psychology*, *13*, 289–299.

Posner, M.I. (1969). Abstraction and the process of recognition. In J.T. Spence & G.H. Bower (Eds.), *The psychology of learning and motivation: Advances in learning and motivation*, Vol. 3. New York: Academic Press.

Pozzulo, J.D., & Lindsay, R.C.L. (1998). Identification accuracy of children versus adults: A meta-analysis. *Law and Human Behavior*, *22*, 549–570.

Prien, R.F., & Potter, W.Z. (1993). Maintenance treatment for mood disorders. In D.L. Dunner (Ed.), *Current psychiatric therapy*. Philadelphia: Saunders.

Rahe, R.H., & Arthur, R.J. (1977). Life change patterns surrounding illness experience. In A. Monat & R.S. Lazarus (Eds.), *Stress and coping*. New York: Columbia University Press.

Rahe, R.H., Mahan, J., & Arthur, R. (1970). Prediction of near-future health-change from subjects' preceding life changes. *Journal of Psychosomatic Research*, *14*, 401–406.

Rank, S.G., & Jacobsen, C.K. (1977). Hospital nurses' compliance with medication overdose orders: A failure to replicate. *Journal of Health and Social Behaviour,* *18,* 188–193.

Raulin, M.L., & Graziano, A.M. (1994). Quasi-experiments and correlational studies. In A.M. Colman (Ed.), *Companion encyclopaedia of psychology, Vol. 2.* London: Routledge.

Reicher, S., & Haslam, S.A. (2006). Rethinking the psychology of tyranny: The BBC prison study. *British Journal of Social Psychology, 45,* 1–40.

Reinherz, H.Z., Giaconia, R.M., Hauf, A.M., Carmola, B.A., Wasserman, M.S., & Paradis, D. (2000). General and specific childhood risk factors for depression and drug disorders by early adulthood. *Journal of the American Academy of Child and Adolescent Psychiatry,* *39,* 223–231.

Remington, G., & Kapur, S. (2000). Atypical antipsychotics: Are some more atypical than others? *Psychopharmacology, 148,* 3–15.

Richardson, J.T. (1994). Gender differences in mental rotation. *Perceptual and Motor Skills, 78,* 435–448.

Rickels, K., DeMartinis, N., & Aufdrembrinke, B. (2000). A double-blind, placebo-controlled trial of abecarnil and diazepam in the treatment of patients with generalised anxiety disorder. *Journal of Clinical Psychopharmacology, 20,* 12–18.

Ridley, S.M., McWilliam, R.A., & Oates, C.S. (2000). Observed engagement as an indicator of child care programme quality. *Early Education and Development,* *11,* 133–146.

Riley, V. (1981). Psychoneuroendocrine influence on immuno-competence and neoplasia. *Science, 212,* 1100–1109.

Robbins, T.W., Anderson, E.J., Barker, D.R., Bradley, A.C., Fearnyhough, C., Henson, R., et al. (1996). Working memory in chess. *Memory & Cognition, 24,* 83–93.

Robertson, J., & Bowlby, J. (1952). Responses of young children to separation from their mothers. *Courier Centre International de l'Enfance, 2,* 131–142.

Robertson, J., & Robertson, J. (1971). Young children in brief separation. *Psychoanalytic Study of the Child,* *26,* 264–315.

Robles, T.F., Glaser, R., & Kiecolt-Glaser, J.K. (2005). Out of balance: A new look at chronic stress, depression, and immunity. *Current Directions in Psychological Science,* *14,* 111–115.

Roediger, H.L. III, & Karpicke, J.D. (2006). Test-enhanced learning: Taking memory tests improves long-term retention. *Psychological Science, 17,* 249–255.

Rogers, C.R. (1959). A theory of therapy, personality, and interpersonal relationships as developed in the client-centred framework. In S. Koch (Ed.), *Psychology: A study of a science.* New York: McGraw-Hill.

Roggman, L.A., Langlois, J.H., Hubbs-Tait, L., & Rieser-Danner, L.A. (1994). Infant daycare, attachment and the "file-drawer" problem. *Child Development, 65,* 1429–1443.

Rosen, G.M., Glasgow, R.E., & Barrera, M., Jr. (1976). A controlled study to assess the clinical efficacy of totally self-administered systematic desensitization. *Journal of Consulting and Clinical Psychology,* *44,* 208–217.

Rosenberg, M.J. (1965). When dissonance fails: On eliminating evaluation apprehension from attitude measurement. *Journal of Personality and Social Psychology, 1,* 28–42.

Rosenhan, D. (1969). Some origins of concern for others. In P. Mussen, J. Langer, & M. Covington (Eds.), *Trends and issues in developmental psychology.* New York: Holt, Rinehart & Winston.

Rosenhan, D.L., & Seligman, M.E.P. (1989). *Abnormal psychology* (2nd ed.). New York: Norton.

Rosenthal, A.M. (1964). *Thirty-eight witnesses.* New York: McGraw-Hill.

Rosenthal, R. (1966). *Experimenter effects in behavioural research.* New York: Appleton-Century-Crofts.

Rosenthal, R. (2003). Covert communication in laboratories, classrooms, and the truly real world. *Current Directions in Psychological Science,* *12,* 151–154.

Rosenthal, R., & Jacobson, L. (1968). *Pygmalion in the classroom.* New York: Holt, Rinehart & Winston.

Ross, L., Bierbrauer, G., & Hofman, S. (1976). The role of attribution processes in conformity and dissent. *American Psychologist, 31,* 148–157.

Ross, L., & Nisbett, R.E. (1991). *The person and the situation: Perspectives of social psychology.* Philadelphia: Temple University Press.

Ross, S., & Lawrence, K.A. (1968). Some observations on memory artifice. *Psychonomic Science, 13,* 107–108.

Roth, A., & Fonagy, P. (2005). *What works for whom?: A critical review of psychotherapy research* (2nd ed.). New York: Guilford Press.

Rothbaum, F., Pott, M., Azuma, H., & Weisz, J. (2000). The development of close relationships in Japan and the United States: Paths of symbiotic harmony and generative tension. *Child Development, 71,* 1121–1142.

Rotter, J.B. (1966). Generalised expectancies for internal versus external control of reinforcement. *Psychological Monographs, 80,* whole no. 609.

Roy, D.F. (1991). Improving recall by eyewitnesses through the cognitive interview: Practical applications and implications for the police service. *The Psychologist: Bulletin of the British Psychological Society, 4,* 398–400.

Rundus, D. (1971). Analysis of rehearsal processes in free recall. *Journal of Experimental Psychology, 89,* 63–77.

Rutter, M. (1981). *Maternal deprivation reassessed* (2nd ed.). Harmondsworth, UK: Penguin.

Rutter, M., & The ERA Study Team (1998). Developmental catch-up and deficit following adoption after severe early privation. *Journal of Child Psychology and Psychiatry,* *39,* 465–476.

Rymer, R. (1993). *Genie: Escape from a silent childhood.* London: Michael Joseph.

Sabini, J., Siepman, M., & Stein, J. (2001). The really fundamental attribution error. *Psychological Inquiry,* *12,* 1–15.

Sagi, A., & Lewkowicz, K.S. (1987). A cross-cultural evaluation of attachment research. In J.W.C. Tavecchio & M.H. van IJzendoorn (Eds.), *Attachment in social networks: Contributions to the Bowlby–Ainsworth attachment theory.* Amsterdam: Elsevier.

Sagi, A., van IJzendoorn, M.H., & Koren-Karie, N. (1991). Primary appraisal of the Strange Situation: A cross-cultural analysis of the pre-separation episodes. *Developmental Psychology, 27,* 587–596.

Salkovskis, P.M., Clark, D.M., & Gelder, M.G. (1996). Cognition–behaviour links in the persistence of panic. *Behaviour Research and Therapy, 34,* 453–458.

Salkovskis, P.M., Clark, D.M., Hackmann, A., Wells, A., & Gelder, M.G. (1999). An experimental investigation of the role of safety-seeking behaviours in the maintenance of panic disorder and agoraphobia. *Behaviour Research and Therapy, 37,* 559–574.

Santee, R.T., & Maslach (1982). To agree or not to agree: Personal dissent amid social pressure to conform. *Journal of Personality and Social Psychology, 42,* 690–700.

Schaffer, H.R., & Emerson, P.E. (1964). The development of social attachments in infancy. *Monographs of the Society for Research on Child Development* (Whole no. 29).

Schaufeli, W.B., & Enzmann, D. (1998). *The burnout companion to study and practice: A critical analysis.* Hove, UK: Psychology Press.

Schliefer, S.J., Keller, S.E., Camerino, M., Thornton, J.C., & Stein, M. (1983). Suppression of lymphocyte stimulation following bereavement. *Journal of the American Medical Association, 250,* 374–377.

Schuitemaker, G.E., Dinant, G.F., Van Der Pol, G.A., & Appels, A. (2004). Assessment of vital exhaustion and identification of subjects at increased risk of myocardial infarction in general practice. *Psychosomatics, 45,* 414–418.

Schurz, G. (1985). Experimental examination of the relationship between personality characteristics and the readiness of destructive obedience to authorities. *Zeitschrift für experimentelle und angewandte Psychologie, 32,* 160–177.

Schwartz, A.R., Gerin, W., Davidson, K.W., Pickering, T.G., Brosschot, J.F., Thayer, J.F., et al. (2003). Toward a causal model of cardiovascular responses to stress and the development of cardiovascular disease. *Psychosomatic Medicine, 65,* 22–35.

Schwarz, J.C., Strickland, R.G., & Krolick, G. (1974). Infant day care; behavioral effects at pre-school age. *Developmental Psychology, 10,* 502–506.

Segerstrom, S.C., & Miller, G.E. (2004). Psychological stress and the human immune system: A metaanalytic study of 30 years of inquiry. *Psychological Bulletin, 130,* 601–630.

Selye, H. (1936). A syndrome produced by diverse nocuous agents. *Nature, 138,* 32.

Selye, H. (1950). *Stress.* Montreal, Canada: Acta.

Shaffer, D.R. (1993). *Developmental psychology.* Pacific Grove, CA: Brooks/Cole.

Shallice, T., & Warrington, E.K. (1970). Independent functioning of verbal memory stores: A neuropsychological study. *Quarterly Journal of Experimental Psychology, 22,* 261–273.

Shaver, P.R., & Hazan, C. (1993). Adult romantic attachment: Theory and evidence. In D. Perlman & W. Jones (Eds.), *Advances in personal relationships Vol. 4* (pp. 29–70). London: Kingsley.

Shea, J.D.C. (1981). Changes in interpersonal distances and categories of play behaviour in the early weeks of preschool. *Developmental Psychology, 17,* 417–425.

Sher, L. (2004). Daily hassles, cortisol, and the pathogenesis of depression. *Medical Hypotheses, 62,* 198–202.

Sherif, M. (1935). A study of some factors in perception. *Archives of Psychology, 27,* 187.

Sherman, S.J. (1980). On the self-erasing nature of errors of prediction. *Journal of Personality and Social Psychology, 39,* 211–221.

Shotland, R.L., & Straw, M.K. (1976). Bystander response to an assault: When a man attacks a woman. *Journal of Personality and Social Psychology, 34,* 990–999.

Shuell, T.J. (1969). Clustering and organization in free recall. *Psychological Bulletin, 72,* 353–374.

Shute, R.E. (1975). The impact of peer pressure on the verbally expressed drug attitudes of male college students. *American Journal of Drug and Alcohol Abuse, 2,* 231–243.

Sigal, J.J., Rossignol, M., Perry, J.C., & Ouimet, M.C. (2003). Unwanted infants: Psychological and physical consequences of inadequate orphanage care 50 years later. *American Journal of Orthopsychiatry, 73,* 3–12.

Sigall, H., Aronson, E., & Van Hoose, T. (1970). The cooperative subject: Myth or reality? *Journal of Experimental Social Psychology, 6,* 1–10.

Silverman, I. (1977). *The human subject in the psychological laboratory.* Oxford, UK: Pergamon.

Silverman, I., Shulman, A.D., & Wiesenthal, D. (1970). Effects of deceiving and debriefing psychological subjects on performance in later experiments. *Journal of Personality and Social Psychology, 21,* 219–227.

Simon, H.A. (1974). How big is a chunk? *Science, 183,* 483–488.

Skinner, B.F. (1938). *The behaviour of organisms.* New York: Appleton-Century-Crofts.

Skinner, E.A., Edge, K., Altman, J., & Sherwood, H. (2003). Searching for the structure of coping: A review and critique of category systems for classifying ways of coping. *Psychological Bulletin, 129,* 216–269.

Smith, E.E., & Jonides, J. (1997). Working memory: A view from neuroimaging. *Cognitive Psychology, 33,* 5–42.

Smith, E.R., & Mackie, D.M. (2000). *Social psychology* (2nd ed.). New York: Psychology Press.

Smith, L.A., Roman, A., Dollard, M.F., Winefield, A.H., & Siegrist, J. (2005). Effort–reward imbalance at work: The effects of work stress on anger and cardiovascular disease symptoms in a community sample. *Stress and Health, 21,* 113–128.

Smith, P., & Bond, M.H. (1993). *Social psychology across cultures: Analysis and perspectives.* New York: Harvester Wheatsheaf.

Smith, P.B., & Bond, M.H. (1993). *Social psychology across cultures.* London: Prentice Hall.

Smyke, A.T., Koga, S.F., Johnson, D.E., Fox, N.A., Marshall, P.J., Nelson, C.A., et al. (2007). The caregiving context in institution-reared infants and toddlers in Romania. *Journal of Child Psychology and Psychiatry, 48,* 210–218.

Soderstrom, M., Dolbier, C., Leiferman, J., & Steinhardt, M. (2000). The relationship of hardiness, coping strategies, and perceived stress to symptoms of illness. *Journal of Behavioral Medicine, 23,* 311–328.

Soutter, A. (1995). Case report: Successful treatment of a case of extreme isolation. *European Child and Adolescent Psychiatry, 4,* 39–45.

Spangler, G. (1990). Mother, child, and situational correlates of toddlers' social competence. *Infant Behavior and Development, 13,* 405–419.

Spector, P.E., Dwyer, D.J., & Jex, S.M. (1988). Relation of job stressors to affective, health, and performance outcomes. A comparison of multiple data sources. *Journal of Applied Psychology, 73,* 11–19.

Spiers, H.J., Maguire, E.A., & Burgess, N. (2001). Hippocampal amnesia. *Neurocase, 7,* 357–382.

Spitz, R.A. (1945). Hospitalism: An inquiry into the genesis of psychiatric conditions in early childhood. *Psychoanalytic Study of the Child, 1,* 113–117.

Spitz, R.A., & Wolf, K.M. (1946). Anaclitic depression. *Psychoanalytic Study of the Child, 2,* 313–342.

Sroufe, L.A. (1990). An organizational perspective on the self. In D. Cicchetti & M. Beeghly (Eds.), *The self in transition: Infancy to childhood.* Chicago: University of Chicago Press.

Stams, G-J.J.M., Juffer, F., & van IJzendoorn, M.H. (2002). Maternal sensitivity, infant attachment, and temperament in early childhood predict adjustment in middle childhood: The case of adopted children and their biologically unrelated parents. *Developmental Psychology, 38,* 806–821.

Standing, L.G., Conezio, J., & Haber, N. (1970). Perception and memory for pictures: Single-trial learning of 2500 visual stimuli. *Psychonomic Science, 19,* 73–74.

Sterbin, A., & Rakow, E. (1996). *Self-esteem, locus of control, and student achievement.* Paper presented at the Annual Meeting of the Mid-South Educational Research Association, Tuscaloosa, Alabama.

Stevens, S., Hynan, M.T., & Allen, M. (2000). A meta-analysis of common factor and specific treatment effects across the outcome domains of the phase model of psychotherapy. *Clinical Psychology: Science and Practice, 7,* 273–290.

Stewart, S.A. (2005). The effects of benzodiazepines on cognition. *Journal of Clinical Psychiatry, 66*(Suppl 2), 9–13.

Stirling, J.D., & Hellewell, J.S.E. (1999). *Psychopathology.* London: Routledge.

Stone, A.A., Reed, B.R., & Neale, J.M. (1987). Changes in daily life event frequency precede episodes of physical symptoms. *Journal of Human Stress, 13,* 70–74.

Strassberg, D.S., & Lowe, K. (1995). Volunteer bias in sexuality research. *Archives Sexual Behavior, 24,* 369–382.

Stretch, D.D. (1994). Experimental design. In A.M. Colman (Ed.), *Companion encyclopedia of psychology, Vol. 2.* London: Routledge.

Strike, P., & Steptoe, A. (2004). Psychosocial factors in the development of coronary artery disease. *Progress in Cardiovascular Disease, 46,* 337–347.

Stuss, D.T., & Alexander, M.P. (2007). Is there a dysexecutive syndrome? *Philosophical Transactions of the Royal Society B, 362,* 901–915.7

Subbotsky, E.V. (1994). The formation of independent behaviour in preschoolers: An experimental analysis of conformity and independence. *International Journal of Behavioral Development, 17,* 289–310.

Sue, D., Sue, D., & Sue, S. (1994). *Understanding abnormal behaviour.* Boston, MA: Houghton Mifflin.

Sulin, R.A., & Dooling, D.J. (1974). Intrusion of a thematic idea in retention of prose. *Journal of Experimental Psychology, 103,* 255–262.

Symington, T., Currie, A.R., Curran, R.S., & Davidson, J. (1955). The reaction of the adrenal cortex in conditions of stress. *Ciba Foundations Colloquia on Endocrinology, 20,* 156–164.

Szasz, T.S. (1960). *The myth of mental illness.* London: Paladin.

Szewczyk-Sokolowski, M., Bost, K.K., & Wainwright, A.B. (2005). Attachment, temperament, and preschool children's peer acceptance. *Social Development, 14,* 379–397.

Tavris, C. (1974). The frozen world of the familiar stranger. *Psychology Today, June,* 71–80.

Tharyan, P., & Adams, C.E. (2005). Electroconvulsive therapy for schizophrenia. *Cochrane Database Systematic Review,* April 18, CD000076.

Thomas, L.K. (1998). *Multicultural aspects of attachment.* http://www.bereavement.demon.co.uk/lbn/attachment/lennox.html. [See also Thomas, L.K. (1995). Psychotherapy in the context of race and culture. In S. Fernando (Ed.), *Mental health in a multi-ethnic society.* London: Routledge.]

Thompson, R.A. (2000). The legacy of early attachments. *Child Development, 71,* 145–152.

Tilker, H.A. (1970). Socially responsible behaviour as a function of observer responsibility and video feedback. *Journal of Personality and Social Psychology, 14,* 95–100.

Tizard, B. (1979). Language at home and at school. In C.B. Cazden & D. Harvey (Eds.), *Language in early childhood education.* Washington, DC: National Association for the Education of Young Children.

Tollestrup, P.A., Turtle, J.W., & Yuille, J.C. (1994). Actual victims and witnesses to robbery and fraud: An archival analysis. In D.F. Ross, J.D. Read, & M.P. Toglia (Eds.), *Adult eyewitness testimony: Current trends and developments.* New York: Wiley.

Tronick, E.Z., Morelli, G.A., & Ivey, P.K. (1992). The Efe forager infant and toddler's pattern of social relationships: Multiple and simultaneous. *Developmental Psychology, 28,* 568–577.

Tuckey, M.R., & Brewer, N. (2003a). How schemas affect eyewitness memory over repeated retrieval attempts. *Applied Cognitive Psychology, 7,* 785–800.

Tuckey, M.R., & Brewer, N. (2003b). The influence of schemas, stimulus ambiguity, and interview schedule on eyewitness memory over time. *Journal of Experimental Psychology: Applied, 9,* 101–118.

Tulving, E. (1962). Subjective organisation in free recall of "unrelated" words. *Psychological Review, 69,* 344–354.

Tulving, E., & Pearlstone, Z. (1966). Availability versus accessibility of information in memory for words. *Journal of Verbal Learning and Verbal Behavior, 5,* 381–391.

Turner, L.H., & Solomon, R.L. (1962). Human traumatic avoidance learning: Theory and experiments on the operant–respondent distinction and failures to learn. *Psychological Monographs, 76*(40; Whole no. 559).

Twisk, J.W.R., Snel, J., Kemper, H.C.G., & van Mechelen, W. (1999). Changes in daily hassles and life events and the relationship with coronary heart disease risk factors: A 2-year longitudinal study in 27–29-year-old males and females. *Journal of Psychosomatic Research, 46,* 229–240.

Tyrell, J.B., & Baxter, J.D. (1981). Glucocorticoid therapy. In P. Felig, J.D. Baxter, A.E. Broadus, & L.A. Frohman (Eds.), *Endocrinology and metabolism.* New York: McGraw-Hill.

Valentine, T., Pickering, A., & Darling, S. (2003). Characteristics of eyewitness identification that predict the outcome of real line-ups. *Applied Cognitive Psychology, 17,* 969–993.

Van Amermaet, E. (2001). Social influence in small groups. In M. Hewstone & W. Stroebe (Eds.), *Introduction to social psychology* (3rd ed.). Oxford, UK: Blackwell.

Vandell, D.L., & Corasaniti, M.A. (1990). *Variations in early child care: Do they predict subsequent social, emotional, and cognitive differences?* Unpublished manuscript, University of Wisconsin, Madison.

[Noted in Andersson, B-E. (1992). Effects of daycare on cognitive and socioemotional competence of thirteen-year-old Swedish schoolchildren. *Child Development, 63*, 20–36.]

van IJzendoorn, M.H., & Kroonenberg, P.M. (1988). Cross-cultural patterns of attachment: A meta-analysis of the Strange Situation. *Child Development, 59*, 147–156.

Van IJzendoorn, M.H., Verfeijken, C.M.J., Bakermans-Kranenburg, M.J., & Riksen-Walraven, J.M. (2004). Assessing attachment security with the attachment Q sort: Meta-analytic evidence for the validity of the observer AQS. *Child Development, 75*, 1188–1213.

Van Os, J., Park, S., & Jones, P. (2001). Neuroticism, life events and mental health: evidence for person-environment correlation. *British Journal of Psychiatry, 178* (suppl. 40), s72–s77.

Warren, R., & Zgourides, G.D. (1991). *Anxiety disorders: A rational–emotive perspective.* New York: Pergamon Press.

Warrington, E.K., & Shallice, T. (1972). Neuropsychological evidence of visual storage in short-term memory tasks. *Quarterly Journal of Experimental Psychology, 24*, 30–40.

Wartner, U.G., Grossmann, K., Fremmer-Bombik, E., & Suess, G. (1994). Attachment patterns at age six in South Germany: Predictability from infancy and implications for preschool behaviour. *Child Development, 65*, 1014–1027.

Watson, J.B., & Rayner, R. (1920). Conditioned emotional reactions. *Journal of Experimental Psychology, 3*, 1–14.

Weiner, H., Thaler, M., Reiser, M.F., & Mirsky, I.A. (1957). Etiology of duodenal ulcer: I. Relation to specific psychological characteristics to rate of gastric secretion (serum pepsinogen). *Psychosomatic Medicine, 19*, 1–10.

Weinfield, N.S., Whaley, G.J.L., & Egeland, B. (2004). Continuity, discontinuity, and coherence in attachment from infancy to late adolescence: Sequelae of organisation and disorganisation. *Attachment and Human Development, 6*, 73–97.

Weist, R.M. (1972). The role of rehearsal: Recopy or reconstruct. *Journal of Verbal Learning and Verbal Behavior, 11*, 440–450.

Wells, G.L., Liepe, M.R., & Ostrom, T.M. (1979). Guidelines for empirically assessing the fairness of a lineup. *Law and Human Behaviour, 3*, 285–293.

Westen, D. (1996). *Psychology: Mind, brain, and culture.* New York: Wiley.

Whyte, W.F. (1943). *Street corner society: The social structure of an Italian slum.* Chicago: University of Chicago Press.

Williams, J.M., & Warchal, J. (1981). The relationship between assertiveness, internal-external locus of control, and overt conformity. *Journal of Psychology, 109*, 93–96.

Williams, T.P., & Sogon, S. (1984). Group composition and conforming behaviour in Japanese students. *Japanese Psychological Research, 26*, 231–234.

Wilson, B.A., Alderman, N., Burgess, P., Emslie, H., & Evans, J. (1996). *Behavioural assessment of the dysexecutive syndrome.* Bury St Edmunds, Suffolk: Thames Valley Test Company.

Wilson, G.T., & Davison, G.C. (1971). Processes of fear reduction in systematic desensitisation: Animal studies. *Psychological Bulletin, 76*, 1–14.

Wilson, K., Roe, B., & Wright, L. (1998). Telephone or face-to-face interviews? A decision made on the basis of a pilot study. *International Journal of Nursing Studies, 35*, 314–321.

Wilson, S., Brown, N., Mejia, C., & Lavori, P. (2002). Effects of interviewer characteristics on reported sexual behavior of California Latino couples. *Hispanic Journal of Behavioral Sciences, 24*(1), 38–62.

Windgassen, K. (1992). Treatment with neuroleptics: The patient's perspective. *Acta Psychiatrica Scandinavica, 86*, 405–410.

Wolfson, A. "Trial to start for $200 million lawsuit over strip-search hoax", *Louisville Courier-Journal,* 2007-09-09. See http://www.usatoday.com/news/nation/2007-09-09-mcdonaldslawsuit_N.htm

Wolpe, J. (1958). *Psychotherapy by reciprocal inhibition.* Stanford, CA: Stanford University Press.

Wolpe, J. (1969). *The practice of behaviour therapy.* Oxford, UK: Pergamon Press.

Wood, W., Lundgren, S., Ouellette, J.A., Busceme, S., & Blackstone, T. (1994). Minority influence: A meta-analytic review of social influence processes. *Psychological Bulletin, 115*, 323–345.

Wright, D.B. & Stroud, J.N. (2002). Age differences in lineup identification accuracy: People are better with their own age. *Law and Human Behavior, 26*, 6, 641–654.

Wu, A.W., Folkman, S., McPhee, S.J., & Lo, B. (1993). How house officers cope with their mistakes. *Western Journal of Medicine, 159*, 565–569.

Young, S.D., Adelstein, B.D., & Ellis, S.R. (2007). Demand characteristics in assessing motion sickness in a virtual environment: Or does taking a motion sickness questionnaire make you sick? *IEEE Transactions on Visualization and Computer Graphics, 13*, 422–428.

Yuille, J.C., & Cutshall, J.L. (1986). A case study of eyewitness memory of a crime. *Journal of Applied Psychology, 71*, 291–301.

Zakowski, S.G., Hall, M.H., Klein, L.C., & Baum, A. (2001). Appraised group, coping, and stress in a community sample: A test of the goodness-of-fit hypothesis. *Annals of Behavioral Medicine, 23*, 158–165.

Zegoib, L.E., Arnold, S., & Forehand, R. (1975). An examination of observer effects in parent–child interactions. *Child Development, 46*, 509–512.

Zimbardo, P. (1969). The human choice: Individuation, reason, and order versus deindividuation, impulse, and chaos. In W.J. Arnold & D. Levine (Eds.), *Nebraska Symposium on Motivation, 17.* Lincoln, NE: University of Nebraska Press.

Zimbardo, P.G. (1973). On the ethics of intervention in human psychological research: With special reference to the Stanford prison experiment. *Cognition, 2*, 243–256.

Zimbardo, P.G. (1989). *Quiet rage: The Stanford Prison Experiment video.* Stanford, CA: Stanford University.

INDEX

Page numbers in **bold** indicate glossary entries.

ILLUSTRATION CREDITS